KEYGUIDE

ARGENTINA

CONTENTS

275

246

164

76

UNDERSTANDING ARGENTINA

Understanding Argentina is an introduction to Argentina, its economy, history and its people, giving a real insight into the country. Living Argentina gets under the skin of the country today, while The Story of Argentina takes you through its past.

Argentina, at 2,780,000sq km (1,074,000sq miles), is the second-largest nation in South America and the eighth-biggest country on the planet. With barely 40 million inhabitants, a third of them squeezed into the capital city Buenos Aires, the country is extremely thinly populated, especially in Patagonia—the wild but hauntingly beautiful southern quarter. Stretching from Paraguay and Bolivia and almost reaching to the frosty Antarctic, Argentina offers an amazing range of landscapes and supports an astonishing variety of flora and fauna. Distances between sights are mind-boggling and, unless time is no object, it is best to explore a single region rather than trying to see every major sight.

SOCIETY & RELIGION

A proud people with strong beliefs, Argentines are passionate about their culture, yet hospitable to visitors. Family and friends take pride of place, especially children, and divorce rates are relatively low, with many young couples continuing to live with their parents. Eating out, looking good and dressing well take precedence over having a big house, buying a new car or possessing the latest technology.

Argentina can seem a paradox. The quality of education is high and Argentines show a keen interest in art and music, yet prime-time TV seems mostly taken up with lightweight chat shows and soaps. Although Argentine society mostly comprises a well-educated middle class, there are increasing numbers of super rich, while a sizeable underclass inhabits shanty towns on the edges of the main cities. Many of the national institutions, such as congress, the judiciary and the education system, were modelled on those of democratic Europe and North America, and yet Argentina has all too often been ruled by authoritarian regimes, not least the military junta that held power between 1976 and 1983.

For a country that celebrated its bicentenary as recently as 2010, Argentina has forged a strong identity. This is due, in part, to the universal and highly idiosyncratic use of a single language, Spanish (*castellano*), introduced by the colonial power in the 16th century. The country's countless communities—Anglo-Argentine, Irish, Italian, Croatian, Syrio-Lebanese, Greek, Armenian and Danish—have melded into one nation without losing many of their cultural attributes, including food and religion.

Roman Catholicism is the official religion and the vast majority of Argentines are nominally Catholic, but there is a rich spiritual tradition in which Christian ritual and pre-Columbian customs and symbolism have merged. Anglicanism, Judaism and Islam also have a strong presence, though most of the country's Muslims, of Syrio-Lebanese origin, are secular.

ARGENTINE PASSIONS

Fútbol (soccer) is a national passion. Even non-nationals are expected to choose between River Plate and Boca Juniors, the two biggest soccer teams. Argentina has excelled at the sport since British immigrants introduced it in the late 19th century and, today, stars like Palermo and Messi are idolized on and off the pitch.

Tango is entwined with the urban culture and to find it you will need to head to Argentina's cities—its birthplace, Buenos Aires, but also the major cities of Córdoba, Mendoza and Rosario, where tango is particularly extravagant. The North and the Litoral have their own musical folklore that is every bit as dramatic and often more authentic and reflects the spirit of the land.

LANDSCAPES

Argentina's midriff is one enormous field of grass grazed by cattle whose meat is unrivalled worldwide. Silky tassels of pampas grass (*cortaderas*) add to the natural beauty of the supremely fertile land, which is ideal for growing crops such as wheat, maize, soya, fruit and potatoes. In contrast are the bone-dry upland deserts of the altiplano or *puna* (high plains) of Salta and Catamarca, the unending steppe of Patagonia and the desolate landscape of the island of Tierra del Fuego.

A lush strip of territory stretches northeast from Buenos Aires. Pitted with lakes and marshes and striped with rivers, the Litoral is Argentina's most tropical region. Sultry summers and mild winters create the perfect conditions for tea and *mate* plantations (▷ 23), and a hospitable environment for birdlife. Above all, this enticing region is characterized by water, in the form of falls such as the mighty Iguazú, reservoirs and natural springs.

Much of Argentina has a reliable rainfall and the fertile pampas tends to be evergreen. Although a terrible drought took its toll on livestock and crops in 2008 and 2009, it was followed by compensatory wet summers. In the westerly reaches of the country, however, rainfall may be a rare event. Farmers irrigate their crops using an intricate system first introduced by the Incas, drawing on a plentiful supply of snowmelt from the Andes.

ECONOMY

Argentina built its wealth on the land. Commodities, such as cereals, beef and by-products of wool and leather, dominated the world markets from the late 19th century until the Great Depression and World War II deprived farmers of their valuable export markets. Today, soy (much of it GMO) and sorghum take up huge expanses of farmland and have dramatically changed the eco-system, the agricultural balance and possibly even the climate.

During the 1990s, parity between the peso and the US dollar made it cheaper to import goods than to produce them and Argentines flocked abroad on holiday while domestic tourism floundered. The bubble inevitably burst in 2001, with a violent and scarring economic crisis. Today, confidence and stability have returned and Argentina is once again an emerging economy and has won a place in the G20.

Although agricultural produce forms the majority of the country's exports, paper, textiles and automobiles also account for a sizeable percentage of trade. Tourism is increasingly important, with numbers of domestic and overseas visitors growing every year.

DEMOGRAPHY

The country's population stands at just over 40 million, growing by just over 1.05 per cent annually. Argentina's higher standard of living and quality of education has always attracted migrants from neighbouring countries and around four per cent of the population were born in another country, mostly Paraguay, Bolivia and Chile.

Today, the population of greater Buenos Aires stands at 13 million, one third of the national population, while several million more live in major cities such as Córdoba, Rosario, Mendoza and Tucumán. There has been a noticeable move from the countryside to urban centres in recent years—partly because agriculture has become decreasingly labour intensive. The 2010 census also indicated a slight trend of population drift towards Patagonia as many Argentines sought new back-to-nature lifestyles, often taking advantage of the tourism boom, tax breaks and other incentives.

The countryside, with its flora and fauna, strong traditions and natural beauty, is what brings people to Argentina but the towns and cities are not without their charms. Buenos Aires and Rosario, Salta and Corrientes are replete with fine architecture, some of it dating to colonial times or to the heyday of Argentina's wealth, plus the odd masterpiece of modern design—all of which make urban life in Argentina a true pleasure.

ARGENTINA'S REGIONS AT A GLANCE

Buenos Aires and Around The huge capital city of Buenos Aires is also the world capital of tango. Each of the city's *barrios* has a distinct flavour. South of the busy downtown area, San Telmo displays faded elegance while Boca is a gritty working-class neighbourhood, with a famous soccer stadium. In the north, Retiro and Recoleta are resoundingly chic, with their sumptuous palaces, expensive boutiques and opulent art galleries. Farther out, the parklands of Palermo stretch towards leafy Belgrano and the prosperous suburbs of San Isidro and sultry El Tigre. Within a day's reach are the traditional *estancias* (patrician ranches), rural idylls dotted around the pampas and the Atlantic Ocean resort of Mar del Plata.

Atlantic Patagonia and Tierra del Fuego The triangle of steppe at the far south of the Americas bears the evocative name of Patagonia and its long Atlantic coastline comprises a series of estuaries, bays and headlands, favoured by penguins, whales and elephant seals for breeding and resting. The desolate scenery and magnificent wildlife around the Península Valdés is the big draw hereabouts. Ushuaia, overlooking the beautiful Beagle Channel, the diving centre of Puerto Madryn, and quaint Gaiman, with its traditional Welsh tea rooms, are three of the region's main towns.

Andean Patagonia Inland from the Patagonian seaboard, some of the world's most breathtaking mountain and lake landscapes are strung along the Andes, preserved by mammoth national parks. The glaciers—Perito Moreno, perhaps, being the most famous—spill into magically coloured lakes and offer some truly unforgettable sights. This virgin land of sub-Antarctic woodlands and bare steppe entices crowds of trekkers and tourists from spring to autumn, yet the enormous expanses mean that you can still be alone. Bariloche, capital of the Lake District, is busy year-round, offering trekking in summer and skiing in winter. The region's other main resort, El Calafate,

the gateway to the Parque Nacional Los Glaciares, is extremely busy in summer. However, access in winter is often difficult and many places are closed.

Central Argentina The highlands near historic Córdoba and the *bodegas* (vineyards) around modern Mendoza are the region's highlights and have been favoured by domestic tourists for years for their mild climate, rugged scenery and Jesuit churches. White-water rafting near San Rafael, horse riding in the vicinity of Ischilín and mountaineering around Aconcagua are further draws. The natural wonders of Talampaya National Park and Ischigualasto Provincial Park make trips to either the provinces of La Rioja or San Juan a memorable experience.

The North Dominated by the atmospheric colonial city of Salta and its intriguing hinterland of mountains, vineyards and dramatic gorges, the North is a favourite tourist destination. Each of Salta's neighbouring provinces—Tucumán, Jujuy and Catamarca—has its own charms, too. The Tafí del Valle offers alpine scenery and endless opportunities for rambling while Andean villages punctuate Quebrada de Humahuaca. Catamarca is home to beautiful chapels, flamingo-filled lagoons and picturesque villages, such as Belén, where wool is turned into collectable ponchos. Blindingly white salt lakes and pitch-black pumice fields, misty jungle and pre-Incan ruins are just some of the many attractions of this historic region.

Iguazú Falls and the Litoral The leviathan waterfalls straddling the Brazilian border at Iguazú are one of the world's great natural wonders but Argentina's

Above Gauchos *at the Feria de Mataderos, Buenos Aires*
Left *The wetlands of the Esteros del Iberá*

BO

PY

JUJUY

CL

SALTA

FORMOSA

TUCUMÁN

CHACO

CATAMARCA

SANTIAGO
DEL ESTERO

MISIONES

CORRIENTES

BR

LA RIOJA

SANTA FÉ

SAN JUAN

CÓRDOBA

ENTRE
RÍOS

UY

SAN
LUÍS

MENDOZA

LA PAMPA

BUENOS AIRES

NEUQUÉN

RÍO NEGRO

CHUBUT

CL

SANTA CRUZ

northeastern reaches in the Litoral have plenty more to offer. At the bird-filled Esteros del Iberá marshlands spotting black caimans and furry capybaras is easy. Other marvels include a protected palm grove, El Palmar, a set of cascades, the Saltos del Moconá, and the Chaco, the country's least accessible sub-region, home to some of the county's best concentrations of flora and fauna. City lovers should not feel left out, especially in Rosario, a beguiling metropolis with some very fine architecture plus a row of river beaches nearby. Flaky Corrientes, sultry Posadas and fun-loving Colón are other towns also worth checking out. Last but not least, the Jesuit ruins at San Ignacio and the grand Palacio San José, are relics of the region's illustrious past.

BUENOS AIRES AND AROUND

Avenida de Mayo (▷ 70) A showcase of the city's architecture, this elegant avenue links the presidential palace to the national parliament.

La Bombonera (▷ 72) In a city where soccer is a religion, the Boca Juniors stadium is one of the temples to the beautiful game.

Cementerio de la Recoleta (▷ 92) Evita is just one of the illustrious patriots whose remains lie in this landmark Buenos Aires graveyard.

Magnolia Hotel Boutique (▷ 121–122) Just a short hop away from the hippest streets of Palermo Soho, this understatedly luxurious boutique hotel lives up to high expectations.

MALBA (▷ 81) Housed in a stunning contemporary building in the trendy *barrio* of Palermo, this collection of Latin-American artworks is exemplary.

Plaza Dorrego, San Telmo (▷ 98) The nerve centre of charming San Telmo, Plaza Dorrego is a great place to see and hear alfresco tango and is also home to a weekend antiques fair.

San Antonio de Areco (▷ 94–95) Surrounded by a cluster of historic *estancias* (patrician ranches), Areco is famed for its *gaucho* traditions.

Tigre (▷ 101) Sultry, subtropical and laid back, El Tigre gives access to the marshlands of the beguiling Paraná delta.

ATLANTIC PATAGONIA AND TIERRA DEL FUEGO

Estancia Harberton (▷ 129) One of the great pioneering *estancias* of the South, Harberton offers warm hospitality and an unforgettable experience.

Parque Nacional Tierra del Fuego (▷ 131) In this chunk of natural beauty, giant woodpeckers and grey foxes are among the wildlife waiting to be viewed.

Puerto Pirámides (▷ 135) The whale-watching capital of South America lies by a gorgeous bay on the marvellous Península Valdés.

Punta Tombo (▷ 136) A reserve where half a million comical Magellanic penguins waddle across your path.

Rincón Chico (▷ 151) Modern facilities notwithstanding, step back a century at this wonderful Valdés *estancia*, with its own elephant seal colony down on the beach.

Ty Nain tea house, Gaiman (▷ 144) Toast, scones and delicious Welsh cakes are all served on the best bone china at this traditional *casa de té*.

ANDEAN PATAGONIA

Bodegas Patagónicas (▷ 157) The world's most southerly vineyards produce fabulous reds and whites and one of the wineries doubles up as a top-class resort.

El Casco Art Hotel, Bariloche (▷ 190) This sybaritic hotel on the banks of the alluring Lago Nahuel Huapi is also a world-class art gallery.

Cueva de las Manos (▷ 158–159) Millennia-old rock paintings are on view in an outdoor gallery of pre-Columbian art.

Fitz Roy sector, Parque Nacional Los Glaciares (▷ 168) Trekkers of every stripe revel in this paradise of mountain trails where the reward is a stunning Andean landscape.

Glaciar Perito Moreno (▷ 166–167) This powerhouse of blue ice and white frost is one of the planet's few glaciers that is not receding.

Laguna Larga Lodge (▷ 189) In a secluded spot on a poetic lagoon, this fishing lodge combines the perfect conditions for angling with creature comforts and top-notch food and wine.

Leleque (▷ 161) One of the newest museums in Argentina and one of the best, Leleque encapsulates the story of Patagonia's against-the-odds human presence.

Volcán Lanín (▷ 163) A perfect Japanese-woodcut cone of a volcano framed by stands of *araucarias* (monkey-puzzle trees) and reflected in mirror-like finger lakes.

CENTRAL ARGENTINA

Aconcagua and the Alta Montaña (▷ 194–195) Seeing the world's tallest mountain outside the Himalayas doesn't require real stamina—climbing it does.

Córdoba (▷ 196–199) Argentina's second city owes its historic importance to the presence of the Society of Jesus (Jesuits), who left great churches, schools and a major university.

Mendoza (▷ 204–207) The Cuyo's biggest metropolis draws on delicious local produce and world-class wines to offer the best dining opportunities in Argentina outside the capital.

Parque Nacional Talampaya (▷ 208) The tall terracotta-hued cliffs lining a dramatic canyon are humbling, while overhead you may spot condors cruising as well as a plethora of other wildlife.

Parque Provincial Ischigualasto (▷ 209) Argentina's Moon Valley offers weird rock formations that glow orange red at sunset or an eerie white in the moonlight.

Tupungato (▷ 211) This is the perfect base for exploring the great *bodegas* of the Mendoza Province.

THE NORTH

Cachi (▷ 233) In this charming Andean hamlet everything, from church confessionals to street signs, is made of cactus timber.

Cafayate (▷ 234) Most of Salta's up-and-coming high-altitude *bodegas* are within reach of the capital of the Valles Calchaquíes.

Legado Mítico, Salta (▷ 264) With spacious rooms, which are tastefully decorated according to inspired themes, this hotel qualifies as one of the country's top places to stay.

Posada de Luz, Tilcara (▷ 265) The views are truly breathtaking, the rooms are utterly charming and you can watch hummingbirds from your own patio.

Purmamarca (▷ 236) Take a trek above the village to enjoy views of a wonderful 17th-century church, an age-old tree and a huddle of low houses in the shadow of a multicoloured mountain.

Salinas Grandes (▷ 244) Blindingly white salt flats where everything is a mirage, but the houses made of salt are real.

Tafí del Valle (▷ 248) Famed for its ancient standing stones, fresh cheeses and mild climate, this alpine village offers clean air and excellent hiking.

Tren a las Nubes (▷ 254–255) One of the world's great train journeys takes you up, up, up into the clouds.

IGUAZÚ FALLS AND THE LITORAL

Colón (▷ 270) The perfect place for messing around in boats, hunting for semi-precious stones and indulging in subtropical *farniente* (sweet nothing).

Esteros del Iberá (▷ 272–273) Scores of bird varieties flit, hop and swim around silvery lagoons in one of the continent's major wetlands.

Iguazú (▷ 274–277) When Eleanor Roosevelt uttered the words 'Poor Niagara!' she said it all.

Palacio San José (▷ 278) This opulent mansion offers an insight into the life of the upper classes in 19th-century Argentina.

Puerto Valle (▷ 300) On the bonny banks of the sea-like Río Paraná, this modern *estancia* offers peace and quiet and is the perfect place to soak up the views.

San Ignacio Miní (▷ 285) The magnificent site of a crumbling Jesuit mission, set among seductive tropical vegetation.

UNDERSTANDING ARGENTINA

TOP EXPERIENCES

Taste a rich malbec or a floral torrontés at the Finca Las Nubes (▷ 234) near Cafayate.

Attend a tango show in San Telmo (▷ 98) and marvel at the dazzling footwork and bewitching live music.

Learn Spanish at a professionally run school in Rosario (▷ 280–283), a mini-Buenos Aires without the tourists.

Enjoy a *dulce de leche* ice cream at Un'Altra Volta (▷ 113), a luxury *heladería* with several branches around the capital.

Go trekking in the Fitz Roy sector of the Parque Nacional Los Glaciares (▷ 166–168)—your effort is rewarded by out-of-this-world views of the Andean peaks.

Snap up bargain clothes and accessories at the boutiques of Palermo Soho (▷ 85–86).

Treat yourself to a luxurious stay on an *estancia*, perhaps La Bamba (▷ 124) near San Antonio de Areco or Santa Inés (▷ 300) high up in Misiones Province.

Watch whales in a boat off the Península Valdés (▷ 132–133) or from your hotel room at Puerto Pirámides (▷ 135).

Get close to caiman and capybara in the glittering lagoons of the Esteros del Iberá (▷ 272).

Savour delicious pasta at a restaurant in Mendoza (▷ 204–207) with wines fermented just up the road.

Take a train to the clouds from Salta (▷ 254–255), to the *fin del mundo* ('end of the world') from Ushuaia (▷ 147) or back in time to the pioneering days from Esquel (▷ 160).

Listen to live folk music at a traditional *peña* in Salta (▷ 240–243) or San Miguel de Tucumán (▷ 246).

Attend a polo match or perhaps hone your horse-riding skills and play in one.

Experience the excitement of a football (soccer) derby between local rivals Boca Juniors and River Plate at the Estadio Monumental (▷ 113) or La Bombonera (▷ 72, 113).

Ride a horse at Dos Lunas (▷ 226), an idyllic *estancia* in the moorlands of northern Córdoba.

Lap up the light of a full moon at the Valle de la Luna at the Parque Provincial Ischigualasto (▷ 209).

Relish a juicy steak at a *parrilla* (steakhouse) just about anywhere in the country.

Drive Ruta 40 through the Gaudiesque scenery on the road to Cachi (▷ 250–251).

Get wet at Iguazú on a boat ride (▷ 274–277) to the main falls where you can indulge in the world's most impressive shower.

Observe birds in the Parque Nacional Calilegua (▷ 237) by the lakes of northern Patagonia (▷ 180–181) or at the Reserva Ecológica Costanera Sur (▷ 91), a stone's throw from the heart of Buenos Aires.

Below left *Trekkers against a backdrop of Cerro Aconcagua*
Below *Tango, a quintessentially Argentine dance*

LIVING ARGENTINA

UNDERSTANDING | LIVING ARGENTINA

The landscapes make the long journey to the Southern Cone worth all the time and effort and Argentina has them all: from the massive wall of the Andean cordillera, where you can admire or climb some of the highest peaks in the world, to the crumbly cliffs and shifting dunes of the Atlantic coast, where penguins and elephant seals make their home. In the far northwestern corner, tropical latitudes combined with contrasting altitudes produce a startling microcosm: the dense vegetation of the bird-filled subtropical yungas; the bleached *salinas*, where salmon-pink flamingos graze and flocks of wispy-fleeced vicuñas roam; polychrome rocks, looming like giants above gravel-strewn riverbeds; and brick-red and asphalt-black cones of volcanos that erupted only centuries back. The relentless *estepa patagónica* (Patagonian steppe) exerts a mysterious magnetism, while the sweaty humidity of the Litoral invites a slower pace, its verdant meadows, lush jungle and ruddy earth being easy on the eye. The Lake District is, perhaps, the most picturesque part of the country, while the most stereotypical landscape of Argentina is the Pampa—pancake-flat, extremely fertile and punctuated by the occasional tree or windmill, not unlike a subtropical version of Holland.

HOME TO *MATE*

Mate, an infusion made from the crushed leaves and stems of the *Ilex paraguayensis* (*yerba mate*), is widely drunk in Argentina (▷ 23). Related to the holly, *yerba mate* grows only in the iron-rich earth of northeastern Argentina, southwestern Brazil and eastern Paraguay. It is more of a shrub than a tree, with evergreen leaves, insignificant greenish-white flowers and a tiny maroon-coloured fruit. The wide rivers of the Litoral—from the flat marshes and lagoons of the Esteros del Iberá to the lush verdant vegetation of Misiones province—create the perfect habitat for the tree. Although there are large plantations of the *yerba mate*, they rarely grow in the wild and the species is now on the International Union for Conservation of Nature's list of near-threatened plants.

Clockwise from top *Volcán Lanín, in Parque Nacional Lanín; Patagonia's arid desert landscape, home to foxes, armadillos and rheas; Lago Nahuel Huapi, in Parque Nacional Nahuel Huapi, the country's oldest national park*

LAKELAND BIOTOPES

A verdant sliver of land hugging the Andes in northern Patagonia, the Lake District is peppered with lakes of all dimensions and colours, ranging from tiny emerald ponds tucked away in deep woodland to gigantic expanses of sapphire water the size of a small European country. One of the biggest, Lago Nahuel Huapi (▷ 171), has silvery-blue fingers that poke into a magnificent national park, partly blanketed in virgin forest that is home to native animals such as the *huemul* (south Andean deer) and its shyer cousin, the *pudú* — the world's smallest deer. Native trees, such as the long-living *alerce* (Patagonian cypress) and the scaly *araucaria* (monkey-puzzle tree).lend the landscape its unique appearance. Specimens of the Patagonian cypress (known locally as *lahuán*) have been estimated at being more than 3,000 years old, making them some of the oldest living organisms on the planet. The trees have been declared national monuments.

A DESERT AT RISK

Travel writer Paul Theroux hardly had a good word to say about the desolate Patagonian landscape in his classic *The Old Patagonian Express*. Certainly this *estepa* (steppe), often known as the Patagonian Desert, is the largest desert on the American continent. The ash spewed out by a succession of volcanic eruptions has made the region even more arid and most of Patagonia is a sandy plain carpeted with prickly gorse, home to desert-loving snakes, armadillos, foxes and rheas. As human settlement increased, dams were built to provide water, otherwise a scarce commodity, and increasingly large areas have been allocated to agriculture, tree plantations and even vineyards, leading international conservation organizations to express concerns about the environment. Foreign investors have bought huge sections of Patagonia, often for commercial purposes, while ecological and conservation groups are campaigning to protect this unique landscape.

ARGENTINA'S GRANARY

Pampas is probably the landscape that everyone associates with Argentina. While much of this flat region is a patchwork of fertile fields grazed year-round by contented cattle, the green landscape turns to gold in the lead-up to the autumn harvests of wheat, maize and sunflowers, while increasingly large swathes are now sown with GMO soya, to satisfy massive export demands from Asian markets. The northern section, the *pampa seca* (dry pampa), centred on the province of Santa Fe along with parts of Córdoba and Buenos Aires, fed the country and much of the industrialized world from the late 19th century until the 1940s, when World War II deprived the country of its export markets. Crops grown here were the motor of Argentine prosperity, or at least of those aristocratic landowners who carved out the markets between them, building impressive *estancias* and French-style palaces to show off their wealth.

LIFE ON THE *PUNA*

Puna (an Incan word), also known by the Spanish name of *altiplano*, refers to the majestic, desert-like plains in the far northwest of the country that form part of the highest upland plateau outside the Himalayas. An altitude averaging 3,800m (12,460ft) above sea level results in cool to very cold temperatures throughout the year and living conditions are extremely tough here. Isolated indigenous communities eke out an existence by herding llamas and alpacas. Like their livestock, they build up extra red corpuscles in their blood to make up for the lack of oxygen. Cut off from the rest of the country, the local people maintain strong traditions, such as chewing coca leaves to stave off altitude sickness and playing the *bombo* (a large drum) and other Andean instruments. Pachamama, the Earth Mother, is still revered in colourful ceremonies and fascinating customs.

The amazingly fertile lands of Argentina yield a mouth-watering variety of produce that is both plentiful and healthy, and in a country where livestock roam the land freely and most production techniques are respectful of nature, the organic label is often not necessary. Few visitors to Argentina can bring themselves to eat beef anywhere else afterwards and what better accompaniment to a juicy tender steak than a glass or two of ruby-red wine from the sun-soaked wineries of Mendoza? Around two thirds of Argentine wine is produced in the province, where the sun shines for more than 300 days a year. But there are some fantastic wines coming out of wineries elsewhere in the country, too. These include the high-altitude *bodegas* around Cafayate, Amaicha and Fiambalá. Newcomers in northern Patagonia are already winning international prizes for their crisp chardonnays and smooth malbecs. You can even find vineyards in the pampa of Buenos Aires province, and near Colón, where wine grapes had not been exploited commercially for centuries. While much of the wine is inexpensive, often known as *vino patero* (trodden wine), some of the finest Argentine vintages regularly rank among the world's top 100.

KING MALBEC

Every autumn the purple berries of the malbec grape blaze on vines across Argentina. In its native France, malbec is found mostly in the southwestern Cahors region, although its tannin-rich juice is also used in some claret. The malbec variety was introduced in the 1870s, along with other French *cépages*, as part of President Sarmiento's drive to make the country more European. Malbec took so well to Argentina's soils and climate that it was soon adopted as the national grape variety. Tens of thousands of acres are now planted with malbec, from the prize-winning Colomé *bodega* (▷ 263) in Salta Province to the world's most southerly vineyards near Neuquén (▷ 162). The 2009 malbec produced by the Altos Las Hormigas winery in Mendoza is ruby-red with dark aromas of blackberry, cherry and chocolate, which makes it the perfect wine to accompany Argentine beef.

Clockwise from top *Smooth malbecs are produced in Argentina, with some wines ranking among the world's finest; enjoy succulent Argentine beef cooked on a* parrilla (grill); *vineyards at Catena Zapata* bodega, *in Mendoza province, the heartland of Argentine wine production*

KINDEST CUTS

Every Argentine BBQ—*asado* at home or *parrilla* in a restaurant—begins with a medley of innards, known as *achuras*. The most popular are *chinchulines* (small intestines) and *mollejas* (sweetbreads), served crispy yet succulent. Sizzling *chorizos*, meaty sausages quite unlike the spicy Spanish variety, and rich *morcillas*, black puddings, are also likely to be on the menu. Another common ingredient is *provoleta*, a melted round cheese grilled with oregano. Do not miss the delicious *asado de tira*, knuckle-like ribs cut across the bone and served well done. *Entraña* (skirt) and *vacío* (flank) are tender steak cuts, bursting with flavour. But the grand finale is always a choice between *bife de chorizo* (strip), *bife ancho* (rib-eye) and *lomo* (filet mignon), all of which are best served as *jugoso* (rare) as possible.

DULCE DE LECHE

Dulce de leche is a defining feature of Argentine life. Although similar products exist in other countries, Argentina claims *dulce de leche* as its own and to be the best. Simply made by boiling milk, sugar and vanilla together until they form a thick luscious caramel, *dulce de leche* can be eaten with a spoon, spread on toast or dolloped onto puddings. It is one of the most popular ice-cream flavours in the country and true fans will love *dulce de leche extra*, which has ripples of *dulce de leche* running through ice cream made with yet more *dulce de leche*. It is the most common filling for *alfajores*, maize-biscuits sandwiched together and coated in chocolate or meringue. You might well want to take a jar home with you as a gift, or simply to eat yourself, though it is unlikely to last long.

BEEF IS NOT THE ONLY MEAT

Although the meat of the Hereford and Aberdeen Angus dominates the counter at a traditional Argentine butcher's shop, other meats are popular, too. The typical Patagonian *asado a la cruz*—a whole carcass speared on a metal cross and grilled over an open pit—is reserved for succulent lamb *(cordero patagónico)*. In the northwest of Argentina, llama and *ñandú*, the ostrich-like rhea, are frequently consumed and are especially appreciated for being low in cholesterol. The woodlands of the Lake District teem with game, such as deer *(ciervo)* and wild boar *(jabalí)*, and their meats frequently grace local menus, often served with locally grown red fruit. The meat of the *yacaré*, or caiman, tastes like a combination of fish and chicken and is best sampled in the Litoral, where *yacaré* are bred for their meat and leather.

MAIZE— THE ANDEAN STAPLE

Many of the regional specialities of northwestern Argentina are based on the sacred ingredient of corn, or maize, known throughout Argentina by its Quechua name of *choclo*—one of the staple foods of the Incas. A number of delicious dishes are made with maize, and these are best savoured in the warmer months when it is in season. These include two popular concoctions served as starters or snacks: *Humitas* are packets of creamy maize purée mixed with mild cheese and steamed in *chalas*, or green corn husks, while *tamales* are similar, but are ball shaped and stuffed with minced beef instead of cheese. Both are served with *ají*, a spicy tomato sauce made with chilli. Another favourite is *locro*—a nourishing stew made with corn, beans and pumpkin and enriched with bits of pork—best savoured on cold nights in the *altiplano*.

Enormously fertile and rich in natural resources, Argentina was listed as the world's fifth-wealthiest country in the 1920s, but ineffective governments and failed economic policies have taken their toll on Argentina's affluence over the past century. Between 1880 and 1920, Argentina grew incredibly rich on foreign investments and sold beef, leather, wool, wheat and a whole range of other staple goods to the rest of the world. Wealth poured in and landowners built grand *estancias* in the country, opulent palaces were constructed and marble monuments embellished the streets. But a sea change in the world economic balance and above all the stock market crash of 1929 resulted in collapsed markets. Matters were made worse during World War II, when Argentina's exports were curtailed further by blockades. A series of totalitarian military regimes, such as the 1950s junta, the Dirty War (1976–83) and feeble attempts at parliamentary democracy in between eventually resulted in the economic crisis of 2001, which left many middle-class Argentines much poorer. Ten years on, Argentina is again experiencing rapid growth and recovery and is once again emerging as a leading political force in South America.

Clockwise from top *Mar del Plata's Playa Bristol, a popular summer escape for the citizens of Buenos Aires; harvesting the soybean crop near Salto; Eva Perón, affectionately known as Evita, immortalized in stone in the Barrio Norte, Buenos Aires*

PERONISM

Peronism—officially called Justicialism—is extremely difficult to define and is divided by seemingly contradictory factions. In the 1940s, its founder Juan Domingo Perón and his second wife, Eva Duarte, saw their Partido Justicialista (PJ or Social Justice Party) as a radical anti-establishment movement, aimed at improving the workers' living conditions while fighting off foreign influences, especially those of countries such as Britain and the United States. Although the Peróns openly expressed admiration for Mussolini and his brand of Italian Fascism, and Perón accepted exile in Franco's Spain, Peronism never espoused the extreme racism of Hitler's Nazi party. However, Argentina did remain neutral for most of World War II and allowed many Nazis to settle in the country when the war was over. Despite Perón's outward display of reactionary and authoritarian tendencies, one of his achievements (keenly urged by his wife, Evita) was to grant women the vote in 1947.

SOYA CRAZY

Desperate to lift the economy off its knees, Argentine governments allowed genetically modified soybeans to be planted across the country at the end of the 20th century. Some 200,000sq km (78,000sq miles) is now sown with this controversial crop and most of the seed is from a strain developed by a US-based agricultural biotechnology corporation, which is resistant to a pesticide marketed by the same company. Tempted by rocketing world market prices and a growing demand from China, Argentine farmers didn't rotate the soybeans with other crops and robbed the soil of its fertility. Smaller farmers could not afford to buy the seed, while the low labour intensity of the crop led to a rise in rural unemployment. The full ecological and climatic effects of this soya craze are still unknown but the future of GMO in Argentina depends on whether the government decides to tackle the problems it causes or allow the crop to continue to drive economic growth.

'CRISIS? WHAT CRISIS?'

In 2001, after years of apparent prosperity, falsely based on peso-dollar parity, massive privatization and IMF loans, the Argentine economic bubble burst. Many Argentines had seen the crisis coming and were sending money abroad until economics minister, Domingo Cavallo, prevented further bank withdrawals. Growing protests came to a head a few days before Christmas, when rioting left more than 20 people dead. President Fernando de la Rúa left office in shame. After weeks of confusion, a caretaker government emerged and devalued the peso. The Argentines demonstrated incredible resilience and many commentators, observing the busy restaurants and crowded shopping malls, were tempted to say: 'Crisis? What crisis?'

TOURISM SAVES THE DAY

Until the turn of the 21st century, Argentina's unrealistic exchange rate and high cost of living deterred domestic and international tourists. Argentines could afford to spend their holidays abroad and often did, mainly in Uruguay, Brazil and the Dominican Republic. But the 2001 devaluation of the peso left many Argentines with no option but to rediscover their own country, gravitating towards destinations such as Salta and Iguazú. The local tourist industry capitalized on the trend, and domestic and international tourism began to grow. Thousands of new hotels opened, many of them aimed at the top end of the market, as tour agencies mushroomed and facilities were upgraded to accommodate the growing numbers of overseas tourists.

TANGO AND MUSIC

Musical talent is found in abundance in Argentina. Excellent rock and jazz, classical and folk can be heard in venues around the country, while Buenos Aires attracts the biggest names. Home-grown rock, known as *rock nacional*, shares the airwaves with foreign artists and is played live at a number of festivals throughout the year. Naturally tango, the world-famous dance, dominates the performing arts, at least in the mind of the tourist. The accompanying hauntingly melancholic music is frequently performed without dancing, and any chance to attend a performance of a leading *orquesta típica* (tango band) should not be missed. When the Teatro Colón reopened in 2010, Buenos Aires regained its world-class opera house and concert hall, while the great Argentine tenors José Cura and Marcelo Álvarez, and pianists Daniel Barenboim and Martha Argerich are famous around the world. Among local jazz musicians, Adrián Iaies, director of the annual Buenos Aires Jazz Festival, and his quartet stand out. Based on traditional music, *música folklorica* is mostly found in the North and no visit is complete without an evening in a *peña*, a tavern where you can eat local fare, drink wine and listen to zambas and other ballads. In the northeast, the favourite genre is *chamamé* and its Guaraní name is an onomatopoeic reference to its upbeat tempo.

DANCE FROM THE DOCKS

Possibly deriving its name from an African word for slave market, tango, Argentina's gift to the world, saw its beginnings in the unsavoury docklands of Buenos Aires towards the end of the 19th century. Declared part of the world's cultural heritage in 2009 by UNESCO, tango may actually be a hybrid of European ballroom dancing, with elements from the polka, tarantella and the waltz, combined with hints of the slaves' *candombe,* but its true origins are unknown. Tango's inauspicious beginnings meant that it took several years for the art form to be accepted by Argentine society, while most military governments did their best to stamp it out. But Perón encouraged tango, as part of his nationalist politics and Argentines quickly embraced their national dance. In Buenos Aires, visitors will see and hear tango everywhere from the streets to the clubs.

Clockwise from top *Tango show in Buenos Aires; dancing the tango in the working-class Boca barrio of Buenos Aires; tango shoes for sale, Buenos Aires*

PROTESTS IN THE *PEÑAS*

Folk music, or *folklore*, is mostly played and accompanies dance in the *peñas* of the Northwest, though you can also hear excellent performances in Buenos Aires. Regarded as primitive and outmoded, this music fell out of favour in the early 20th century. Then, in the 1950s, two groups originating in Salta, Los Chalchaleros and Los Fronterizos, led a revival and played a key role in the protest movement against the military juntas of the 1970s and 1980s. Artists such as the legendary singer-songwriter Atahualpa Yupanqui (1908–92) and velvet-voiced Mercedes Sosa (1935–2009) were instrumental in its revival and used *folklore* to bridge differences between indigenous communities and the rest of Argentine society. More recently, Soledad Pastorutti, with her best-selling albums *Poncho al Viento* and *La Sole*, and Juana Molina, who is also an acclaimed actress, have helped to bring *folklore* into the 21st century, with new rhythms and electronic elements.

SIX-AND-EIGHT INNOVATORS

Astor Piazzolla (1921–92) invented *nuevo tango*, or new tango, by introducing elements of jazz and classical music plus the use of counterpoint to the traditional rhythms of tango. As a young man, he played with Aníbal Troilo (1914–75), who was the leading *bandoneón* player in the Golden Age of tango, the 1940s and 50s. The *bandoneón* is an accordion-like instrument that gives tango music its special haunting quality. Piazzolla went on to form the much-admired Octeto Buenos Aires in the 1950s and wrote the moving classic *Adiós, Nonino* following the death of his father in 1959. The other leading innovators in tango were José Libertella (1933–2004) and Luis Stazo (b.1930), who together founded the prodigious Sexteto Mayor in the 1970s. The band has undergone a number of changes to its membership over the years, but steadfastly remains a leading force in the competitive world of the *orquesta típica*, the traditional tango band.

LITORAL LAMENT

Tango may enjoy great popularity in the cities, but throughout the Litoral, *chamamé* is king. The music and dance form originated in the indigenous Guaraní communities, while the presence of Jesuits in the region, with their strong emphasis on religious music, also influenced the style by introducing instruments such as the guitar, violin and accordion. Elements of the polka and other European dances brought by the Volga Germans can also be detected in the dance movements. There are different kinds of *chamamé*, including the *orillero*, with hints of tango, the *maceta*, a jaunty version much played at rural fiestas, and the *cangüí*, a sad lament. One of the leading exponents of contemporary *chamamé* is Horatio 'Chango' Spasiuk, an accordionist and composer of Ukrainian origins; look out for his 2009 album, *Pynandí*.

KING AND HEIR

The best-known tango singer of all time has to be French-born Carlos Gardel (1887–1935). The King of Tango, or the 'Criollo Songthrush' as he was also known, put tango song on the world map, partly thanks to a number of French-made films that recorded his crooning for posterity. Gardel's death in a plane crash sent the whole of Latin America into mourning and his tomb in Chacarita cemetery, Buenos Aires, is still a place of pilgrimage: It is customary to place a burning cigarette between the fingers of his bronze statue atop the grave. Roberto 'El Polaco' Goyeneche (1926–94) started his career imitating the late Gardel in the 1940s, but soon forged his own style, and was regarded as the best tango singer of the 1950s. Nicknamed 'the Pole' for his fair hair and Slavic features, Goyeneche was actually of Basque origin.

Argentina is a country that holds its customs and traditions dear. Some were inherited from the country's early colonial days and many owe their origins to the indigenous communities that populated Argentina before the conquistadors arrived. Catholicism is practised with obvious signs of syncretism, while pre-Columbian beliefs and rituals are intermingled with the trappings of Christianity. This mingling of ideas and practices can be seen in many of the festivals and ceremonies, which are celebrated with devotion in the North. Gualeguaychú's Carnaval, for example, is a colourful affair involving feather headdresses and much banging of drums and has its origins in ancient pagan rituals. *Criollo* culture has bequeathed no end of customs that are peculiar to the region, not least the consumption of *mate*, a tea-like infusion that quells the appetite and stimulates the metabolism. In addition, Argentines even have their own games: *pato*, a relative of polo; *truco*, a trickery-based card game, imported from Europe; and *el juego del sapo*, a parlour game that is said to have been invented by the Incas. Of all the decorative art forms to be found in Argentina, *filete* or *fileteado* is the most distinctive: a stylized and often humorous adornment painted on buses and street signs.

FILETEADO

Seen on shopfronts and the sides of buses, on footwear and even as tattoos, the *fileteado* or *filete* is a distinctive art form that is peculiar to Argentina and, above all, to Buenos Aires, where it is known specifically as *filete porteño*. Swirling scrolls and extravagant flourishes are typical patterns, while the Argentine flag and colours, white and sky-blue, often feature prominently in the designs. Heavy shading is frequently added to create a *trompe l'oeil* effect. The origins of *fileteado* are unknown but the art form may have been introduced, like so much else in Argentina, from Italy. In the 1970s it was banned from public transport—possibly because it was often associated with tango and other anti-establishment activities—but it has been enjoying a major revival in recent years, along with tango itself.

Clockwise from top *A plantation of* yerba mate, *Argentina's native holly tree, whose leaves are crushed to make a popular drink; a roadside shrine to Argentine folk hero Gauchito Gil; cups of* mate *for sale in San Telmo market, Buenos Aires*

GREEN GOLD

For many Argentines *yerba mate*, an infusion made from the crushed leaves and stems of Argentina's native holly tree, is a staple product like bread or milk. A glance at any supermarket shelf will reveal row upon row of *mate*, bearing the logos of dozens of different producers. *Mate* is more than a drink, though, it is an age-old custom based on the notions of generosity and sharing. Although it is possible to indulge alone, more often than not *mate* is passed around among friends or family. Don't be surprised if a complete stranger offers you a cup of the stuff and expects you to share. Usually drunk hot, *mate* is sipped through a *bombilla* (straw), which has small perforations and strains the *yerba* out. Cold *tereré*, which is made with the same leaves, is popular in the humid Litoral.

ROADSIDE SHRINES

Roadside shrines are set up in honour of Gauchito Gil and Difunta Correa, the two leading Argentine folk saints. Those marked by tangled masses of red flags are dedicated to Antonio 'Gauchito' Gil, a deserter in the civil war. Before his execution, he predicted that the executioner's son was very ill and that only by praying for Gil's soul could he save his son's life, which according to the legend turned out to be the case. Piles of bottles of water mark the shrines to Deolinda 'Difunta' Correa. Her cult is based on the story that she left home with her baby in search of her husband, also a fighter in the civil war. She collapsed and died by the side of the road, but her baby was found miraculously alive, having suckled at her mother's breast long after her death.

ALL THE SAINTS

Argentina has a rich spiritual tradition and outward displays of religious devotion are commonplace. It is not unusual for Argentines to cross themselves when they pass a church or a cemetery, while expressions such as *'Gracias a Dios'* ('Thank God') and *'Si Dios Quiere'* ('God willing') frequently punctuate conversation. Taxi- and bus-drivers will often have a small shrine on top of their dashboard and rosaries, crosses or pictures of the Virgin Mary dangling in their windscreens, while many Argentines wear a crucifix or have an icon of their favourite saint on their mantelpiece. One of the most popular figures is San Cayetano, the patron saint of labour, to whom ordinary people pray when they want a job or are afraid of losing the one they have. There are religious festivals and parades held throughout the country, while thousands of Argentines make pilgrimages to revered sites such as Catamarca (▷ 244) and Salta cathedrals (▷ 241) to venerate the Virgin Mary.

TRUCO

Truco, a card game requiring well-honed tactical skills, is a highly popular import from the Mediterranean. The modern version, played across Argentina, uses a Spanish card deck of 40 *naipes* or *barajas*. The game is essentially based on a player tricking his or her opponents, partly by moving quickly, but also distracting the other players with conversation and joking. Out-and-out cheating is forbidden, despite the urban myth to the contrary — it is said to appeal to Argentines as they love breaking rules. Usually involving two pairs of players, *truco* is all about winning tricks, with the ace of spades scoring highest. Messages are passed between partners by an established set of *señas* (signs), while the score is kept using dry beans (*porotos*), though matchsticks are often used instead. This custom has entered Argentine slang — *'te ganaste un poroto'* ('you have won yourself a bean') means you have scored a point.

Argentina encompasses an incredible range of climates and habitats—from the moist tropics in the far north to the arid steppe of Tierra del Fuego, where nothing holds back the icy blasts blowing up from Antarctica. Not surprisingly, few other countries rival the eco-diversity of Argentina's habitats. Trees and shrubs, such as the *ombú*, a gigantic perennial, can be found in every shape and size, while myriad cactus varieties, from the minute to the mammoth, spike the highlands and plains alike. Thousands of visitors to Argentina make a special journey to spot southern right whales frolicking off the Península Valdés; or to tick dozens of birds off their checklist in the marshlands of Corrientes or the forests of Salta; or to see penguins, dolphins and cormorants at their breeding grounds along the Atlantic coast. Llamas, condors, armadillos and foxes are just four more natives that delight both naturalists and nature lovers. Well-run national parks and their dedicated *guardaparques* (park rangers) help preserve these precious environments, while an army of professional local guides and eco-tourist agencies will help you see what you are looking for and keep you properly informed.

THE NOBLE CONDOR

The most emblematic of all Argentina's rich and varied birdlife is the condor. This giant of a bird is a symbol of the grandiose Andes and has always been sacred to indigenous people. With its 3m-plus (10ft) wingspan, the Andean condor (*Vultur gryphus*) creates an unmistakeable silhouette when soaring high above the rocky crags of the cordillera, the great Andean range. The condor's magnificent wings form a solid rectangle fringed with six finger-like plumes, a shape that was often reproduced in ancient rock paintings or on pre-Columbian ceramics. Owing to its huge size and tendency to fly high, the condor was always associated with the sun god by indigenous communities, while its bones and organs were often sought for their supposed medicinal qualities.

Clockwise from top *The scarlet blooms of the* ceibo, *the Argentine national flower; llamas, the strongest of the four indigenous camelids, are still reared for meat and wool; a Magellanic penguin—colonies half-a-million strong inhabit rookeries on the Península Valdés during the breeding season*

CEIBO, THE NATIONAL TREE

Argentina's national flower, the *ceibo (Erythrina crista-galli)* is in fact a tree blossom. Its striking scarlet hue and unusual shape explains the tree's common English name, the coral tree. Native to South America, the *ceibo* can be found growing in the wild and it graces many of the avenues and parks in the country's towns and cities. There are some fine examples of *ceibos* in Buenos Aires's botanical gardens and any time between November and February you can see the blazing racemes of red flowers. The plant's rich nectar attracts all kinds of insects, including bees, and the resulting honey is fragrant and delicious. Thanks to the poor quality of its wood, which makes it unsuitable for making paper or furniture, the trees have been saved from mass destruction, though indigenous communities still use the bark for making traditional drums, known as *bombos*.

CUDDLY CAMELIDS

All along the Andean range, but especially in the highland *altiplano* or *puna*, you can spot four cousins of the camel, known collectively as camelids. Prized by the Incas as an important source of meat and wool, all four camelids were given Quecha names. The largest is the short-haired guanaco, with its cinnamon to auburn coat colour and doe-like eyes. Shy by nature, guanacos have a tendency to leap across roads in front of traffic. Rather smaller and even shier is the delicate little vicuña, whose incredibly fine wool is prized even more than cashmere. More familiar outside South America are the more woolly alpaca and llama, which have been domesticated for centuries and are still raised for their meat and wool. The two are not easy to tell apart, but the alpaca is quite a lot smaller. Far stronger than the alpaca, the llama was used by Andeans to carry surprisingly heavy loads, and is still popular with modern-day trekkers.

MARINE MAMMALS

While humans might feel that Argentina does not have the world's best beaches, many marine mammals disagree. The sheltered bays along the Patagonian shore are favoured for reproduction and repose by a number of cetaceans and members of the seal family. The whale-watching season around Península Valdés (▷ 132–133) stretches from late June until December; November is when you are likely to see mothers with their calves, a wonderful sight to behold. From March to early April, orcas may occasionally be seen acrobatically attacking sea lion pups for their lunch at Punta Norte (▷ 133), while male elephant seals, great brutes of the ocean, fight ferociously over their harems at Punta Delgada (▷ 132) every October. It isn't all blood and gore though, as dolphins and seals frolic all along the seaboard, entertaining thousands of visitors.

ENDANGERED BIRDS

Argentina's avifauna numbers over 1,000 different species and the country's diverse landscapes provide habitats for around 120 birds on the endangered list— including two members of the albatross family, and the turkey-like *yacutinga* (black-fronted piping guan). Aves Argentinas, a national non-governmental organization, works hard to protect the country's birdlife and several areas of Argentina have been awarded national and international preservation status, including Parque Nacional Iguazú (▷ 275–276) and Reserva Ecológica (▷ 91), on the doorstep of Buenos Aires's downtown and home to the city's only wild flamingos. In the remote *puna* of northwestern Argentina, the Esteros del Iberá and the cloud forests of the North, it is not difficult to see over 100 different species in a day or two, while a couple of dozen species are found only in Argentina.

Argentina can lay claim to some fabulous cities — not least the mesmerizing capital — and most Argentines live in urban areas. Yet the country's great wealth was founded on agriculture and the worldwide exports of wheat and meat, and there is a deeply entrenched rural tradition in Argentine culture. It is very easy to get out into the *campo*, even from Buenos Aires, and many city-dwellers have a second home (*quinta* or *chacra*), often with a large garden or *parque*. The Argentines' attachment to the rural idyll can be found in the large and beautiful parks that grace just about every city. Around the turn of the 20th century, the city authorities hired the Frenchman Charles Thays to landscape most of the parks and his designs tended toward the English style of garden, imitating nature rather than geometry. Wealthy landowners also commissioned Thays to embellish the parks around their patrician ranches, known as *estancias* or *fincas*, many of which are now luxury hotels or tourist attractions. Horses and horsemanship are key elements of country life, where the most emblematic figure is the cowboy or *gaucho*. *Gauchos*, with their own colourful customs and *cultura criolla*, have taken on quasi-mythical dimensions and are immortalized in some of the great classics of Argentine literature.

ESTANCIA ELEGANCE

In the 19th and early 20th century a number of Argentine landowners made a fortune selling beef, cereal and other produce to a hungry world. They became Argentina's de facto aristocracy and wanted to show off their wealth by building fabulous homes. All across Argentina, manors and palaces, French-style chateaux and mock-Tudor mansions sprang up, often with beautiful landscaped gardens to match. The Petit Chateau and Casa Normanda in Buenos Aires Province are prime examples. European architects and landscape gardeners, or Argentines trained in Europe, were assigned these costly projects. In the far north, these stately homes are often known as *fincas*, while the majority, especially those in Buenos Aires Province, are called *estancias*. *Quintas* and *chacras* are usually smaller and found in the suburbs of big cities such as Mendoza, Neuquén or the capital.

Clockwise from top *Estancia La Cinacina, San Antonio de Areco;* the gaucho *has become synonymous with Argentine rural life and traditions;* traditionally gauchos wore their knives tucked into the back of their leather belts

LUXURY IN THE STICKS

Living or staying in the country, even in remote corners of the far South, does not necessarily mean roughing it. There are a number of *estancias* around the country that offer luxury accommodation, often with a four-meals-a-day package that is guaranteed to add on a few kilos even during a short stay. One of the grandest *estancias* is El Ombú (▷ 124) near San Antonio de Areco, which was built for an army officer in the 1880s. Guests are treated to transfers to and from Buenos Aires by private plane and stay in the splendid Italianate house, which is set in 4ha (10 acres) of landscaped parkland. Among the entertainments on offer are horse rides, golf, tennis, a ride in a sulky and all manner of *gaucho* rodeo antics, especially laid on for visitors. Other outstanding *estancias* include Puesto Viejo (▷ 123) near Buenos Aires and La Bamba (▷ 124), near San Antonio de Areco. An alternative to staying at the *estancia* is to arrange a day visit or *día de campo*.

THE *CRIOLLO* HORSE

The term *criollo* refers to anyone or anything originating in Argentina (often specifically in the provinces rather than in urbane Buenos Aires) and has no greater exponent than the *gaucho* on his horse. Although primitive ancestors of the horse roamed the plains thousands of years ago, it was the Spanish conquistadors (later to become *criollos* themselves) who reintroduced equines to Argentine soil following their conquests in the 16th century. In an irony of history these *caballos ibéricos*, sturdy steeds bred for their strength and stamina rather than their finesse, played a vital role in the wars of independence from Spain only to be rejected as vulgar afterwards, with nobler breeds winning favour. A revival took place in the 20th century as the *caballos ibéricos* began to be bred once more (but known as *caballos criollos*). They are now considered the best horse for long-distance trekking, especially in Patagonia and the Andes.

LOOKING THE PART

Like all Argentines, *gauchos* take an unabashed pride in their appearance and are always impeccably turned out from head to toe. Hats are part of their uniform and might be a Basque *boina* (beret), worn at a jaunty angle, or a wide-brimmed sombrero, favoured in the sunnier northern climes. Shirts made of the best cotton are often checked and set off by a stylish neckerchief. The traditional *bombachas de campo*, comfortably baggy breeches that button at the ankle, are secured by a leather belt, at the back of which the *gaucho* tucks his *facón* (knife). Footwear is usually riding boots or shoes but many *gauchos* prefer espadrilles *(alpargatas)*, which are often gaudily hued, the *gaucho's* only concession to colour. Specialized shops across the country sell this garb and you might like to kit yourself out for the full *gaucho* experience.

GAUCHOS IN BOOKS

La literatura gauchesca is a school of Argentine writing that was most prolific from 1870 to 1920. The first major proponent was José Hernández (1834–86), whose major work, *El Gaucho Martín Fierro*, is a verse epic regarded as a classic of Argentine literature. The eponymous hero is a kind of Argentine Robin Hood and the poem, published in two parts in the 1870s, greatly romanticizes *gaucho* life while indirectly criticizing the authorities. The style is similar to the popular ballads that would have been sung around many a campfire in the mid-19th century. *Don Segundo Sombra* (1926), a late *gauchesco* novel by aristocratic writer Ricardo Güiraldes (1886–1927), takes a far less flattering look at *gaucho* life. A museum in San Antonio de Areco named after Güiraldes (▷ 95) offers a fascinating insight into *gaucho* culture, which has changed little over the centuries.

One thing that strikes visitors to Argentina is the superficial homogeneity of the population. While most citizens are of European or Levantine origin, the further north and west you head the more people display characteristics of the indigenous peoples, whose intrepid ancestors crossed the frozen straits between eastern Russia and Alaska before migrating southwards through the Americas. The handsome features and salon-perfect hair of the locals often impresses visitors, although some Argentines can seem obsessive about their appearance. Over Argentina's two centuries of nationhood, however, a number of figures have emerged as makers and shakers, with many Argentines achieving international fame, not least Eva Perón and Ernesto 'Che' Guevara, both of whose personae featured in Hollywood blockbusters. Consistently voted the 'greatest ever Argentine' in media polls, General San Martín was the hero of independence, while latter-day heroes include sports stars, such as polo champion Adolfo Cambiaso, whose rugged good looks grace many a magazine. On the feminine side of things, the phenomenon of the *vedette* plays a key role in Argentine society and the glamorous TV star Susana Giménez is one of the most enduring.

Clockwise from top *International polo star Adolfo Cambiaso in action at the 2010 Veuve Clicquot Gold Cup at Cowdray Park in England; a mural in San Telmo, Buenos Aires, of revolutionary Che Guevara; Eva Perón, a controversial figure, loved by the workers and hated by the Argentine elite*

ADOLFO CAMBIASO — THE POLO PIN-UP

Adolfo 'Dolfi' Cambiaso (b.1975) is generally regarded to be the best polo player in the world. He has won every national and international championship and broken all the goal-scoring records in the book; he scored over 600 goals in the Argentine Open alone. Off the polo field, he has built a successful business marketing his own top-end brand of men's clothing, La Dolfina — a line that naturally includes stylish polo shirts. Modelling his own clothing ranges, he is regularly pictured in the glossy gossip magazines and is married to top model María Vásquez, with whom he has two children, Mía and Adolfo Junior.

EVITA—THE LEGEND

María Eva 'Evita' Duarte de Perón (1919–52) was the second wife of Juan Perón. Immortalized in a musical film starring Madonna, Eva started out as a radio actress and met Perón at an event to raise money for the victims of an earthquake in San Juan. As First Lady (1946–52), Evita travelled around Europe on a glamorous and highly publicized diplomatic tour. In Argentina, she won the adulation of the workers, known as the *descamisados* (the 'shirtless'), for campaigning on their behalf for improved pay. In a famous speech from the Casa Rosada, she renounced her nomination for the Vice-Presidency, while barely able to stand up owing to advanced cervical cancer. The first Argentine to receive chemotherapy, Evita died aged 33, having been named the Spiritual Leader of the Nation, and was given a massive state funeral.

SUSANA GIMÉNEZ— CHAT-SHOW HOST

Blonde and beautiful, Susana Giménez (b.1944) is a frequent feature on the front covers of the glossy magazines that plaster street kiosks thoughout the country. Having begun her career as a model in the 1960s, she shot to fame when she appeared in a soap advert and went on to appear in dozens of 1960s and '70s films, often scantily clad. For years she was also a leading TV personality—a glamorous revue dancer and singer paid to act out fake feuds with other celebrities for the public's amusement. Since 1987, she has hosted her own TV chat show, *Hola Susana*, on which she receives Hollywood stars and chart-topping pop singers. Reportedly, this has made her the highest-paid TV personality in Argentine history, though nobody apart from Susana seems to know exactly how much she earns.

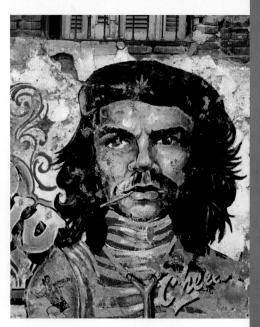

SAN MARTÍN— THE LIBERATOR

José Francisco de San Martín y Matorras (1778–1850) helped not only Argentina but also Chile and Peru to achieve their independence from Spain, and is often known simply as El Libertador. Avenues and mountains, stations and towns have all been named in his honour, while many streets and *barrios* bear the name of Boulogne-sur-Mer, the French city where he died in exile. Born in Yapeyú, northern Argentina, he was educated in Spain, where he cut his military teeth in the wars against Napoleon. Back in South America, he led courageous campaigns against the colonial power, but left again when Argentina opted to be a republic, not a monarchy. San Martín's portrait features on the five-peso note, his statue embellishes many a central plaza and the day of his death, 17 August, is a national holiday.

CHE GUEVARA— THE ICON

Ernesto 'Che' Guevara (1928–67), born in Rosario, spent much of his childhood in the mountains near Córdoba, where his parents hoped to cure his chronic asthma. While studying medicine in 1951, he embarked on a life-changing motorcycle journey across South America. He was struck by the terrible poverty and inequalities that he saw. Shortly after, he travelled through Central America where he met a number of leading radicals and took part in the Cuban Revolution. He was brutally executed by a Bolivian army officer, while trying to 'export' the revolution to the rest of Latin America. Although Che is given little official recognition in Argentina, photographer Alberto Korda's iconic portrait (showing him with a black beret, a bushy beard and a distant gaze) is recognized around the world.

Argentina's national soccer team won gold at the Athens and Beijing olympics, but hasn't won the World Cup since 1986. In fact Argentina had carried off the FIFA trophy only once before, winning at home in 1978 amid much controversy off the pitch (over the ruling dictatorship) and on it (with high tension between the hosts and their Dutch opponents). Despite having stellar players such as Messi and Higuaín and getting off to a solid first-round start, the 2010 Selección, coached by former soccer star Diego Maradona, disappointed fans when they were defeated 4–0 by Germany in the quarter finals of the World Cup in South Africa. Soccer may be the country's favourite sport, but polo and tennis are also popular. Guillermo Vilas, now a coach, put Argentine tennis on the world map in the 1970s by winning four Grand Slam titles. Since then, Gabriela Sabatini, David Nalbandian and Juan Martín del Potro, among other Argentine players, have all been ranked in the world top five. Throughout the country, Argentines take a keen interest in sports — hockey, basketball, tennis, polo, golf and Formula 1 all have their followers and Argentina does well in all of them.

Above *Lionel Messi playing in Argentina's quarter-final match against Germany in the 2010 World Cup in South Africa*

POLO ON THE PAMPAS

Played in Persia around three millennia ago, polo was adopted in Argentina soon after its modern rules were established in Britain in the 1870s. Thanks to a long tradition of horsemanship and a plentiful supply of top-class ponies, the country came to dominate the world game, winning Olympic gold medals in 1924 and 1936 (the last time it was an Olympic sport). Juan Carlos 'El Inglés' Harriott (b.1936) is generally regarded as the greatest polo player of all time. He famously appeared in a national whisky advert hitting a backhander through his horse's legs, a shot that has inspired tennis champions among others. Today, Adolfo Cambiaso (▷ 28) ranks as the world's best player. There are plenty of opportunities to watch world-class polo around Argentina and, if your horse-riding skills are up to it, you might even try your hand with a polo mallet.

GOD'S GOALS

Along with Pelé, Diego Maradona (b.1960) is generally regarded as one of the most talented footballers the world has ever seen. He began his professional career at the age of 16 and six years later, after his World Cup debut, was transferred from Boca Juniors to Barcelona for a then world-record fee of around US$8.5 million. Both his goals against England in the 1986 World Cup went down in history: one was dubbed 'the goal of the century', while the other was the controversial 'Hand of God' goal, an undoubted handball. Sadly, his later career, which included stints at Napoli, Seville and back at Boca Juniors, was marred by health problems. With these issues behind him, Maradona's biggest comeback was his selection as the national team manager in 2008 but following defeat in the 2010 World Cup quarter-final his contract was not renewed.

THE STORY OF ARGENTINA

Argentina is less known for its pre-Columbian history than Peru and Colombia, because the Inca civilization barely penetrated the country's territory and human history is younger here than elsewhere. It is believed that South America's indigenous peoples originated in eastern Asia and crossed the Bering Strait to Alaska during the Ice Age, gradually drifting south until they reached Tierra del Fuego around 4000BC. The fact that pre-European communities left fewer vestiges of their habitation than the Incas is possibly due to their nomadic lifestyles or because their sites were destroyed by natural causes or invaders. Yet there are some fabulous pre-Columbian sites in the country, such as the Cueva de las Manos in central Patagonia, where members of the Toldense culture left enigmatic polychrome frescos on an arid cliff-face around 10 millennia ago. Other important sites include the carefully restored fortified settlements in the far northwest, at Quilmes and Tastil, Tilcara and Shinkal. Some cultures produced fine ceramics and others artworks of varying degrees of sophistication. In particular, superb crafts by the Condorhuasi, Aguada and Diaguita can be seen at museums all over the North and in Buenos Aires.

THE YÁMANA— A LOST COMMUNITY

The most southerly community of indigenous people was that of the Yámana or Yaganes, who settled along the inhospitable coasts of Tierra del Fuego around 4000BC. They wore no clothes but kept warm by smearing their bodies with blubber grease and squatting around sheltered bonfires, which gave the island its name, 'Land of Fire'. The arrival of Europeans in the 16th century was catastrophic as the local population was decimated by foreign diseases or hunted down by the settlers. Some Yámanas were taken to Europe and displayed like circus animals. In one notorious incident, Jemmy Button, so named because he was taken from his family for the price of a button, was educated at an English college and presented to King William IV's court in London before being shipped back to Tierra del Fuego.

Clockwise from top *The spectacular landscapes of the high Andean cordillera; petroglyphs at Parque Nacional Talampaya in La Rioja Province; prehistoric paintings at Cueva de las Manos, in Santa Cruz Province, Patagonia*

BEFORE THE INCAS

The ninth century AD saw the emergence of two ethnic groups, the Diaguitas and the Calchaquíes, who gave their name to the valleys of western Salta. Both communities were sedentary farmers, who developed artificial channels to irrigate their crops of corn, pumpkin and beans, a system still used today. They also bred llamas for meat and wool and used them as beasts of burden. The Diaguitas, whose name literally means 'mountain people', lived in the modern-day provinces of Salta, Tucumán, Catamarca and La Rioja. Divided into clans, sometimes they confederated, especially to fight invaders such as the Incas and later the Spanish, but they also fought each other, as witnessed by the fortresses they built and the weapons they used. The separate groups communicated through a single tongue, Cacán, which was extinct by the 17th century and remains only in place names such as Amaicha and Hualfín.

CERAMICS AND PETROGLYPHS

Some of the country's most beautiful pre-Columbian ceramics are displayed at the Museo Arqueológico in Belén (▷ 233), Catamarca Province. The museum houses a superb collection of Diaguita artefacts including anthropomorphic and zoomorphic vessels plus pots and plates decorated with naive depictions of pumas, snakes and llamas. The later works, dating from AD1000 until the arrival of the Incas, include outsized urns decorated with abstract designs that have meanings that were lost with their civilizations. Similar motifs — symbolic representations of animals and geometric patterns — can be seen on open rock faces at a number of impressive sites, such as Cerro Colorado (▷ 200) in Córdoba and Talampaya (▷ 208) in La Rioja. There are probably thousands more of these mysterious petroglyphs waiting to be discovered in the remote mountains of Andean Argentina.

VESTIGES AND RUINS

Although Argentina has no pre-Columbian sites to rival Machu Picchu in Peru or Chichén Itza in Mexico, there are a number of ruined fortresses and settlements that are worth seeing, often owing to their dramatic strategic locations. One of the most intriguing sites is the Parque de los Menhires (▷ 248) just outside Tafí del Valle, a series of standing stones planted in the fields to face the sun by a pre-Incan tribe who lived in the area around the first century BC. These show some similarity to the standing stones found in Brittany and western Britain, but it is likely that the monuments, some of them over 4m (13ft) tall, were fertility symbols. Another major site is the *pukará* (fortress) at Quilmes (▷ 236) in Tucumán Province. Inhabited between AD800 and the mid-17th century, the painstakingly restored stone terraces and buildings blend beautifully into the mountainside.

THE INCAS AND QUECHUA

The Incas, whose capital was Cuzco in today's Peru, began to build an empire in earnest as late as the 15th century, and arrived in what is now northern Argentina only a few decades before the Spanish. Like the Romans, they built roads and imposed their language, Quechua, as a *lingua franca* on the local communities. In the southern reaches of *Tawantinsuyu*, the Incan realm, the main vestiges of their influence were the mummified corpses uncovered at the tops of Andean peaks, which included the touching remains of three ritually sacrificed children found atop Volcán Llullaillaco, west of Salta, and displayed in one of the city's museums (▷ 242). Despite all the Incan and European efforts to obliterate the local community, Quechua left lasting marks on the modern Argentine language in words like *puna* and llama, *palta* (avocado) and condor.

South America's first European settlers were either Spaniards or conquistadors sent by the Spanish Crown, interested above all else in finding gold. The lands now known as Argentina turned out not even to contain silver that the earliest explorers thought they had found. Subsequently they were mostly neglected. Added to that, the initial contacts with the indigenous communities were difficult, to say the least. The first colony on the Río de la Plata fell foul of the indigenous Querandí and many of the settlers killed and so it was not until the late 16th century that Buenos Aires became established. The Jesuits took advantage of the Spanish Crown's lack of interest, setting up what was effectively a parallel empire in the 18th century until the King of Spain had them expelled. Run as a Viceroyalty, the southern reaches of the empire to the east of the Andes were increasingly stifled by autocratic restrictions imposed from Madrid, but Napoleon's invasion of Iberia created a power vacuum. The British, opportunistic as ever, tried to fill it by invading Buenos Aires but were repulsed by an increasingly defiant population, who eventually declared independence from Spain in 1810.

Clockwise from top *The ruins of the Jesuit church of San Ignacio Miní, Misiones Province, northern Argentina; European influences can be seen in the architecture of many Argentine cities; the Jesuits were expelled from Argentina in 1767 and many Jesuit buildings fell into disrepair*

ABNORMAL CONQUESTS

Three famous navigators sent by the Spanish Crown explored the coasts of what is now Argentina in the early 16th century: Andalusian Juan Díaz de Solís was either killed in a mutiny or eaten by the Charrúa; Portuguese Ferdinand Magellan sailed all the way down the Patagonian seaboard to the straits that now bear his name; and Venetian sailor Sebastian Cabot (son of John) built a small fort near present-day Rosario in 1526. Pedro de Mendoza's colony, set up in 1536 in what is now San Telmo, had to be abandoned owing to strong resistance from the indigenous community, so Buenos Aires had to be founded twice. The second attempt in 1580 by Juan de Garay succeeded largely because of the large numbers of wild cattle and horses descended from animals left there by Mendoza.

MISSION IMPOSSIBLE

The Society of Jesus played a major role in colonial Argentina, setting up *estancias* in Córdoba, where they also founded one of the first universities in Latin America. Originally encouraged by the Spanish monarchy to settle and convert the pagan Indians to Catholicism, the Jesuits began building their missions in and around what is now Argentina's Misiones Province in the early 17th century. Life was tough for the Guaraní residents, but the Jesuits protected them from the region's brutal Portuguese slavers. When the Crown tried to crush the Jesuits with heavy taxation, they simply increased their production of highly valued *mate* and tobacco. With the support of disgruntled locals, the authorities began attacking the missions, and the final blow came in 1767 when King Charles III ordered the expulsion of the Society of Jesus from all his colonies.

GOOD ENOUGH FOR VICEROYALTY

The Spanish headquarters in South America was Lima, the capital of the Viceroyalty, and most early settlers reached Argentine soil from Alto Perú, taking the Inca Route known as the Camino Real (Royal Way). In the late 16th century, the cities of Salta, La Rioja and Jujuy were founded in the Northwest, the region where you can still see the finest vestiges of colonial times, in its churches, convents and municipal buildings. The other main colonial centres were San Juan, Mendoza (named after the ill-fated explorer) and Córdoba, which flourished thanks to its Jesuit University. When the British started taking an interest in Latin America in the late 18th century, following the Jesuits' expulsion, the Spanish decided to protect the empire's Atlantic flank and created the Viceroyalty of the River Plate, with Buenos Aires as its capital.

SILVER MIRAGE

When explorer Sebastian Cabot arrived in the region in the 16th century, silver gifts were presented to him by the indigenous people, and he believed he had discovered a land rich in natural resources. This turned out, much to the colonizers' dismay, not to be the case. It is believed that another Portuguese explorer, Aleixo Garcia, a member of De Solis's earlier expedition, left the silver there. Garcia may have reached the Incan empire some time before Pizarro—and possibly even have discovered the Iguazú Falls—and brought the silver from the mines of modern-day Peru.

The name Argentina (from the Latin *argentum*, meaning 'silver') was coined in a 16th-century Venetian atlas—possibly just after Cabot's arrival. Although there are several references to 'Argentina' in various 17th-century documents, the name was not adopted by the independent nation until around the middle of the 19th century.

BRITISH OPPORTUNISM

The Spanish authorities made themselves highly unpopular by throttling commerce in the new Viceroyalty, by forcing the colony to import staples such as olive oil from Spain. There were even restrictions on the production of artworks, which was confined to Alto Perú, although local artists worked in secret. Smuggling began to thrive, much of it controlled by the British, whose seafarers and pirates outmatched the Spanish and Portuguese navies. Sensing an opportunity with the rise of a moneyed merchant class in and around Buenos Aires, plus local interest in the French Revolution and American Independence, the British invaded the city in June 1806 and again in July 1807. But they were repulsed in two rebellions, La Reconquista and La Defensa, when local women helped by pouring boiling oil onto the British troops. Even so, to this day there are Argentines who will tell their theories about Argentina's fate 'If only we…'

The 19th century saw the Vice-Royalty of the River Plate gain its independence from Spain—celebrated every year on 25 May—and the gradual emergence of a new nation, which in the middle of the century finally decided to call itself Argentina. The colonies originally wanted to remain a part of the Spanish empire and many were even ardent monarchists, not least the leading hero of the liberation, General José de San Martín. But the successful defence against the British and the continuing uncertainties after Napoleon's invasion of Spain encouraged them to break away. In the first half of the century, national politics were dominated by two distinct groups: the Unitarists, who wanted power to be centralized in Buenos Aires; and their Federalist opponents, who wanted to exercise power in their provincial fiefdoms. The second half of the century was a period of earnest nation building, both in terms of the creation of a modern state with working institutions and a determined effort to settle and defend its huge territory. That meant encouraging immigrants from all over Europe and the Middle East to make Argentina their home and an unsavoury military campaign directed against the 'human obstacles' to colonization, the communities of indigenous peoples who were often hostile to the Europeanization of their ancestral lands.

THE MAY REVOLUTION

Spanish Viceroy Sobremonte fled during the 1806 British invasion of Buenos Aires but when his replacement, autocratic Viscount Balthasar de Cisneros, reintroduced trade restrictions, the citizens of Buenos Aires decided that enough was enough. On 25 May 1810, wearing blue and white ribbons (later to be the national colours), they demonstrated on what would become known as the Plaza de Mayo and the first independent government, the Primera Junta (First Council), was sworn in. The Spanish tried to stir up a counter-rebellion but a number of skilled generals, led by San Martín, overcame the resistance. On 9 July 1816—now celebrated annually as a national holiday—a congress was held in Tucumán, officially declaring the independence of the United Provinces of the River Plate.

Clockwise from top *Cerro de la Gloria monument in Parque General San Martín, Mendoza, which commemorates Argentina's struggle for independence from Spain; a bust of Domingo Sarmiento, Argentine president from 1868–74; the Argentine flag, a symbol of national unity*

RED, WHITE AND BLUE

At the Tucumán Congress, independence hero General Manuel Belgrano's suggestion for the Argentine flag — said to be inspired by the immense blue skies of the pampas and the omnipresent sun — was accepted, and the anniversary of his death, 20 June 1820, is commemorated every year as national Flag Day. The blue and white stripes may have united the nation ever since, but the first 40 years of Argentine history were marred by civil war. Both the centralists, or Unitarists, who favoured conservative blue (despite their more progressionist, pro-European leanings), and the Federalists ,or Colorados, who adopted a radical red as their symbol (even though they tended to be more reactionary), opposed the flag. For a decade following Tucumán, the different provincial bosses — known by the Spanish title *caudillo*, meaning 'little head' — battled for power and only in 1826 did Bernardino Rivadavia, a Unitarist of African slave descent, become the country's first president.

THE CALIGULA OF THE RIVER PLATE

Gaucho chief Juan Manuel de Rosas (1793–1877) began his military career when barely a teenager, taking part in the defence of Buenos Aires against the British invasions of 1806 and 1807. Rosas quickly became the leading *caudillo* in Buenos Aires, and when political and economic crises brought down Rivadavia, Rosas stepped in and declared a Confederation. Once in power, he became a ruthless dictator who oppressed and killed dozens of opponents by means of a personal militia, the Mazorca (its name, 'Maize Cob', may have referred to the tightly serried ranks of its members, like grains of corn). The Caligula of the River Plate, as he became known among his enemies, met his match in another *caudillo*, Justo José de Urquiza, who defeated him in 1853 at the Battle of Caseros. Rosas went into exile in England and lived on a Hampshire farm until his death. Notwithstanding his grisly past, Rosas is commemorated with statues and place names across the country.

THE ARCHITECTS OF ARGENTINA

Having escaped the Rosas dictatorship, Argentina enjoyed little respite under the leadership of Justo José de Urquiza (1801–70), who tried (but failed) to impose his own Federalist regime. He was finally ousted in 1861 by the governor of Buenos Aires, Unitarist Bartolomé Mitre, who set about modernizing the country and created the new Republic of Argentina, to which he was elected president the following year. He and his passionately pro-European successor, Domingo Sarmiento, set about industrializing the country, encouraging the British to trade and build railways and adopting French and Anglo-Saxon models of education. The *caudillo's* day was not over, as shown by the rise of General Roca in the 1880s, but Argentina was firmly established as an increasingly prosperous nation state with strong institutions and a modern government.

PROMISED LANDS

The extensive rail network and expanded harbours, meant that the country could start capitalizing on the natural wealth of its land and began exporting huge quantities of wool, leather and cereals to Europe. Argentina's prosperous *estancias* and *latifundios* (mega-farms) needed more workers while the government wanted to protect its territory from hostile neighbours. Promoters were sent to Europe and the Ottoman Empire to entice settlers, often with the promise of free land. A look at the list of ships that dropped anchor in Buenos Aires between 1880 and 1920 is telling: they included the *Nuremberg*, the *Britannia*, the *Garibaldi* and the *Asturias*. Many of the six million immigrants, from Wales, Galicia, Genoa and Syria, who arrived during this period found a bright new future on Argentine soil. Equally, others got no further than the tenement slums of Buenos Aires.

Argentina's heyday of wealth and confidence coincided with its centenary of independence in 1910, when President Alcorta led nationwide celebrations including a gala evening at the new Teatro Colón, in Buenos Aires, and the inauguration of huge monuments, many of which were donated by the country's different ethnic communities. The Anglo-Argentines' contribution was the tower on the Plaza San Martín that vaguely resembles Big Ben, in London. Nonetheless, the increasingly strong trade unions boycotted the ceremonies, foreshadowing some of the problems that were to dog the country later in the century. The 40 years following the Centenary were marked by a trio of rises and falls. Increased trade made Argentina one of the world's wealthiest nations, but economic decline, triggered by the Great Depression and World War II, followed. The Radical party emerged as a progressive political force to replace conservatism, but economic decline and the appearance on the political scene of one Juan Domingo Perón led to its decline. Perón formed an incredibly popular duo with his second wife, Eva Duarte, better known as Evita, and Peronism became a political force to be reckoned with. Evita's untimely death at the age of 33 and his waning popularity resulted in a military coup.

Clockwise from top *Juan and Eva Perón, along with government officials, greet the May Day crowds on Buenos Aires's Plaza de Mayo in 1951; Evita, immortalized in bronze at the Museo Evita in the barrio of Palermo, Buenos Aires; Monumento de los Españoles, Buenos Aires*

CENTENNIAL MONUMENTS

The country's different ethnic communities clubbed together to build monuments for the centennial year in 1910, most of which became icons in Buenos Aires's cityscape. The Spanish gifted the city the Monumento de los Españoles, a lavish marble and bronze sculpture that graces a busy roundabout in the *barrio* of Palermo, while the Anglo-Argentine community erected the Torre de los Ingleses, which still looms above the lower reaches of Plaza San Martín in Retiro. In general, however, the Argentine public saw the centennial festivities, such as the gala performance at the Teatro Colón, as elitist and a number of influential trade unions staged protest demonstrations.

RADICAL CHANGE

Conservative president Roque Sáenz Peña introduced universal male suffrage and secret ballots, reforms that allowed the opposition Radical party, founded in the 1890s, to gain power in 1916. Hipólito Yrigoyen entered the Casa Rosada, followed by Marcelo T. de Alvear. More progressive and less dictatorial than their predecessors, they were still decidedly patrician and the growing working classes began to express their discontent in the form of strikes and uprisings, some of which were brutally repressed. Economic decline following the 1929 stock-market crash took its toll on the Radicals and the military took control in the 1930s, installing a series of puppet coalition governments.

PERÓN'S RISE AND FALL

Appointed Labour Minister in 1943, Juan Domingo Perón made himself a hero of the trade unions by improving working conditions. His socialist tendencies rankled his bosses and he was jailed on trumped up charges in 1945. Mass demonstrations forced the government to release him and he was elected to the Presidency the following year. Perón's success has largely been attributed to his wife, Eva. Her death in 1952 marked the beginning of disillusionment with his authoritarian regime. Perón's grip began to falter, and he lost allies in the armed forces and the Catholic Church. When the press attacked him, too, he responded with restrictions on the freedom of expression. In June 1955, navy planes strafed the Plaza de Mayo, killing more than 300 of Perón's supporters. Three months later, in the Revolución Libertadora, Perón was overthrown by a military coup.

EVITA

Poor and illegitimate, Eva Duarte, dubbed Evita by her supporters, started out as a minor actress, until she met Juan Perón at a fund-raising concert. Evita's main political achievement was the introduction of female suffrage in 1947, but when she tried to stand on the same presidential ticket as her husband four years later, with the resounding support of the unions, the military blocked the move. Adored by the workers, she was hated by the upper classes and officers, who resented her anti-establishment politics and despised her humble origins. Evita divided the country—when she fell ill contradictory graffiti could be seen around the country praying for her recovery or cynically thanking God for inventing cancer. After her death in 1952, her body was smuggled to Italy and buried under a false name, although she was later buried in Recoleta Cemetery (▷ 92) in Buenos Aires.

Like most of South America, Argentina was ruled by men in uniform for much of the 20th century. Having ousted Perón, the armed forces condemned their country to a period of stagnation and economic decline that was to last until the 1980s. Aware of the Peróns' lingering popularity, they set about eradicating any mention of the couple's names and even their presidential palace was ripped down. Meanwhile Perón was exiled to Franco's Spain, having first stayed in Venezuela, where he met his third wife, María Estela Martínez, better known as Isabelita. When General Lonardi was seen as too soft on Peronists, General Aramburu replaced him and then tried to have Perón assassinated. Arturo Frondizi won the elections in 1958, legalized Peronism and paradoxically forged friendly relations with both Kennedy in the US and Castro in Cuba — even meeting Che Guevara in his palace in Olivos. When he refused to annul the 1962 elections won by the Peronists, the military seized power once more. The country switched between relatively liberal governments and vicious dictatorships before Perón was eventually allowed back, shortly before his death, and was succeeded by his wife, who relied on unorthodox advice to govern. Anarchy and chaos gave way to state terrorism, armed conflict with Britain over the Islas Malvinas (Falkland Islands) and, finally, a return to democracy in 1983.

COUPS AND GUERRILLAS

From 1958 to 1973 Argentina took one step forward and two steps back on the road to democracy. The armed forces decided to hold free presidential elections, which were won by the Union Cívica Radical Intransigente. President Frondizi's overtures to Peronism and his clandestine meeting with Che Guevara proved too much for the army officers, who sent him into exile on an island near Tigre. Another democratic president, Arturo Illia, leader of a less conservative wing of the Radicals, held power from 1963 to 1966 and pushed through some reforms such as a minimum wage. But he was ousted by General Onganía, who led the 'Revolución Argentina', a fascist dictatorship tacitly supported by the US and Europe. Left-wing militants began to organize armed guerrilla groups, such as the Montoneros, who were set on staging a revolution of their own.

Clockwise from top *The monument on Plaza San Martín, Buenos Aires, commemorating those who died in the Falklands (Las Malvinas) conflict; now the country is more stable, courts are hearing human rights cases related to the Dirty War*

THE DIRTY WAR

Argentina was run by four military juntas between 1976 and 1983 and, against the background of a spiralling Cold War, lived through two wars of its own. A civil war was unleashed by the military governors set on ridding the country of those who opposed its reactionary policies, which included intellectuals, students, ethnic and religious minorities, socialists and radicals. In the Process of National Reorganization, more aptly known as the Guerra Sucia (Dirty War), the military dictatorship used a campaign of terror to keep the civilian population in line. During this time some 30,000 people simply disappeared. In 1982, President Galtieri entered into war with Britain over sovereignty of the Islas Malvinas (Falkland Islands). Military failure brought down the dictatorship and free elections were held the following year.

PERÓN'S COMEBACK

When, on 20 June 1973, Perón, aged 77, returned to his homeland in a chartered Alitalia plane, having spent some 18 years living in exile, he was as sick as his country. Opposing militant groups fought out their battle at Ezeiza airport, turning a rapturous welcome party attended by half a million people into a bloodbath, in which at least a dozen left-wing supporters were killed. Perón was elected president in September 1973, with his third wife María Estela Martínez de Perón as his Vice-President, but was unable to control the squabbling factions within his own movement. Against a background of economic crisis and high inflation, he relied heavily on his private secretary, the openly fascist José López Rega. When Perón died of a heart attack on 1 July 1974, the reins were handed to his widow, a former dancer, who was totally uprepared for office.

ISABELITA AND HER RASPUTIN

José López Rega, the Social Welfare Minister masterminded the Ezeiza massacre of left-wing Peronists in 1973. He set up a death squad known as the Triple A (Argentine Anti-Communist Alliance), using funds siphoned from his bloated ministerial budget, to eliminate opponents. Totally unprepared for office, María Estela Martínez de Perón (nicknamed Isabelita), foolishly trusted him. She proved a disastrous president, as the country fast spiralled out of control with hyperinflation and widespread political murders. After a military coup in 1976, Rega and Isabelita went separately into exile in Spain. Rega was later extradited and died in prison in Buenos Aires awaiting trial for human rights violations in 1989, but the Spanish courts rejected calls for Isabelita's extradition in 2007.

A SHAKY START

Radical candidate Raúl Alfonsín (1927–2009) won the 1983 presidential elections by a comfortable margin over the Peronists and quickly set about trying to rebuild the country from the ashes of dictatorship and war. Having to struggle with hyperinflation and a huge deficit, he drew on his experience as a human rights lawyer to bring about national conciliation. The negotiations required difficult compromise and included controversial amnesty laws that were later revoked, once the country had become more stable. Yet, despite the introduction of a new currency and other stringent measures, inflation went into several digits and social unrest ensued. Alfonsín called early presidential elections in May 1989, which were won by the Peronists; it was the first transfer of power from one civilian government to another in six decades.

President Menem, a larger-than-life character espousing neo-liberal policies, dominated the 1990s. Argentines, overjoyed to see the back of vicious dictatorship, embraced the era of unrealistic economics and apparent prosperity with their typical gusto. The espousal of peso–dollar parity meant wealthier citizens could afford imported luxury goods and regular holidays abroad. Yet the heavy price to pay for IMF loans was the devastation of national industry and domestically owned companies, as everything, from oil fields to telecoms, was sold in unsatisfactory deals. The overvalued peso meant that exports plummeted while the national debt piled up year after year. The resulting economic bubble burst violently when Menem's Radical successor, De La Rúa, was in the Casa Rosada. Massive devaluation of the currency led Argentina to default on international loans and social unrest and political mayhem ensued. The news hit the world headlines in December 2001 as Argentines rioted in Buenos Aires. There followed an interregnum under Peronist bigwig Eduardo Duhalde, during which the treasury supremo, Lavagna, was hailed as the saviour of the Argentine economy. Néstor Kirchner, a Patagonian representing a more left-wing strand of the Peronist party, then won the 2003 presidential elections. His wife, Cristina Fernández, took over in 2007.

FLAMBOYANT *CAUDILLO*
Justicalist Party candidate Carlos Menem, the son of La Rioja wine-makers originally from Syria, trounced his UCR rival Eduardo Angeloz in the 1989 presidential elections. Forced to become a Catholic (his family were secular Muslims) to hold office, Menem took to the presidency with relish. Adopting the stance of a 19th-century *caudillo* (regional warlord), he ruthlessly implemented IMF-imposed monetarism. The historic railways and other valuable assets were sold off and the unrealistic economic policy based on one peso to the US dollar lured the middle classes into a false sense of security. Re-elected in 1994, he reluctantly stepped aside in 1999, after a second term punctuated by all manner of scandals, including an alleged attempt to fiddle with the constitution in order to stand for a third term.

Clockwise from top *President Cristina Fernández Kirchner, the first woman to be elected to the presidency; Néstor Kirchner, Argentine President from 2003 to 2007; former president, Carlos Menem*

GREY MAN IN THE PINK HOUSE

After the excitement of the Menem years, Argentines voted a self-declared bore into power at the turn of the millennium. Deliberately colourless, Fernando De La Rúa prided himself on being the opposite of his jet-setting predecessor. Unfortunately for him and his compatriots, his presidency turned out to be all too exciting. After a vain attempt to put the country's finances into order, he was forced to bring back Menem's own economics minister, Cavallo, who quickly became public enemy number one, when he introduced the so-called 'playpen' policy, which prevented Argentines from accessing their bank accounts and sending money abroad. As his coalition partners abandoned ship, De La Rúa resigned in humiliation in December 2001, leaving the Casa Rosada in an army helicopter.

ECONOMIC AND POLITICAL MELTDOWN

The last week of 2001 famously saw five presidents in office, following Argentina's financial collapse and street fighting in which dozens were killed and injured. The international community feared the worst, a military coup, but one of Menem's most positive achievements had been to ensure that the armed forces respected democracy. In a state of shock, the whole country demonstrated and protested, with whole families banging pots and pans or rattling keys to voice their outrage. The unlikely *deus ex machina* was union-backed Peronist leader Eduardo Duhalde, whose interim presidency ushered in stability and a semblance of order. Under his economics minister, Roberto Lavagna, the peso eventually stabilized at a much more realistic exchange rate of three to four pesos to the US dollar.

BACK ON TRACK

True to his word, Eduardo Duhalde, who had stepped into the political breach in 2002 following the financial crisis, called presidential elections in 2003. Menem tried to stage a comeback and scored well in the first round of voting, but it was clear that the relatively unknown Néstor Kirchner, Peronist governor of the southern province of Santa Cruz, was the front-runner. Menem withdrew to self-imposed exile in Chile. Kirchner, an unpredictable firebrand, built on the new economic stability, with soaring exports, an unprecedented industrial revival and a huge public works campaign. Increasingly criticized for his autocratic style and dubbed the 'Penguin', owing to his unfortunate physique, Kirchner decided it was time to hand over power to his wife.

THE PENGUIN DYNASTY

Cristina Fernández, Kirchner's wife, became the first woman elected to the office of president of Argentina. Riding the wave of her husband's popularity, 'CFK', as she is known, won the 2007 elections by a wide margin, but soon ran into problems, as financial and political scandals marred her early days in office. Cristina's main obstacle has been a long, drawn-out battle with the rural community. Her government's attempts to tax agricultural exports, such as meat and soybeans, were thwarted in a Senate vote in which the Vice-President, Julio Cobos, famously voted with the opposition. Her popularity is waning despite inevitable comparisons with Evita. Cristina has become increasingly known for her autocratic tendencies, her obsession with glamorous outfits and a series of political gaffes.

Argentina has just notched up two centuries of existence as an independent nation and is still experiencing growing pains. Many of the concerns facing Argentine society are the same as elsewhere — the growing gap between rich and poor; drugs and social problems; the affects of the world economic slump; the tension between hi-tech modernity and traditional ways of life. But the decade since Argentina's own major crisis has seen tangible improvements, with rocketing production and exports, new roads, houses and hospitals, and an improved human-rights record. Moreover, domestic and international tourism has unexpectedly turned into a boom industry. Ironic, given that only a few years ago the peso-dollar parity made it cheaper for Argentines to holiday in Miami than in Mendoza.

Above *The people of Buenos Aires throng the Avenida 9 de Julio during the celebrations of the bicentenary in 2010*

SAME OLD STORY

Although partly set in the 1970s, director Juan José Campanella's 2009 Oscar-winning film *El Secreto de sus Ojos (The Secret in their Eyes)* sums up the mood in contemporary Argentina. Sombre and bleak in its treatment of the country's judicial system and set against a background of political chaos and corruption, the film is highly critical of Argentine society, with its red tape and vested interests, social divisions and mistrust of authority. Yet the film has a happy ending (despite its heart-rending *denouement*) and is infused with friendship and solidarity, endless joking and ironic repartee. Equally, while Argentina could do more to harness some of its assets — high levels of literacy, the great fertility of its land, the potential for developing solar and wind power — it is a country that incites optimism.

THE BICENTENARY

Argentina celebrated its 2010 bicentenary with rather less style than its centenary, as lingering economic troubles and much political infighting marred the celebrations. It got off to a bad start when President Cristina Fernández sacked the head of the central bank for refusing to obey her order to transfer reserves to a special fund for the bicentennial events. As often, the matter was a storm in a *mate* cup, but it left a bitter taste. On a more positive note, the year kicked off with a huge rock and tango concert in Mar del Plata and a re-creation of San Martín's crossing of the Andes that liberated Argentina from Spain. On 25 May, the anniversary of Argentine independence, the Colón opera house finally re-opened its doors with a performance of *Aïda* — harking back to its first opening in 1908.

ON THE MOVE

On the Move gives you detailed advice and information about the various options for travelling to Argentina before explaining the best ways to get around the country once you are there. Handy tips help you with everything from buying tickets to renting a car.

ARRIVING BY AIR

Most international flights to Argentina arrive at Buenos Aires's Ezeiza International Airport, Aeropuerto Internacional Ministro Pistarini. There are a number of other international airports around the country, which mostly connect with neighbouring South American countries. There are daily non-stop flights to Buenos Aires from London, various cities in the US, France, Spain, Italy and South Africa but flights from all other non-Latin American destinations make a stop in Brazil, Chile or the US. All flights from Montevideo and Punta del Este in Uruguay, and the occasional flight from Chile and Brazil, arrive at Aeroparque Jorge Newbery, the capital's domestic airport in Palermo.

Most travellers continuing their journey to another destination in Argentina will need to transfer from Ezeiza to Aeroparque Jorge Newbery. A small number of Aerolíneas Argentinas flights (to destinations such as Ushuaia in Tierra del Fuego and Bariloche and El Calafate in Patagonia) also depart from Ezeiza, so check your booking carefully.

The other main domestic airline in Argentina, LAN Argentina, uses Aeroparque for all its domestic flights plus some flights from Brazil and Chile. In any case, you will need to clear your luggage through customs before continuing your journey.

Ingeniero Aeronáutico Ambrosio L.V. Taravella International Airport in Córdoba, Argentina's second-largest city, has recently expanded its timetable to include some direct flights from Brazil, Chile and Paraguay. A few other airports around Argentina also have international connections, in particular Mendoza and Ushuaia with flights to Chile, and Salta with connections to Bolivia.

EZEIZA INTERNATIONAL AIRPORT

Argentina's largest airport is officially called Ministro Pistarini International Airport but is better known as Ezeiza after the small town where it is located, 35km (22 miles) southwest of central Buenos Aires. Ezeiza is a relatively small airport by international standards, handling around seven million passengers a year. The airport

has undergone significant expansion and renovation since 2000, with a modern Departures hall at Terminal A and state-of-the-art Arrivals hall due for completion by 2012.

» It has two main terminals: A and B. Terminal A serves most of the international airlines and Terminal B accommodates Aerolíneas Argentinas, Argentina's flag-carrying airline, for its international and domestic flights (except those out of Aeroparque). It is a five-minute walk, via a covered walkway, between terminals A and B or travellers can use the free shuttle bus. There are free baggage trolleys (carts) at both terminals, while porters will help you to get around for a small charge.

» There is a vast duty-free shop just past passport control in Terminal A, before entering luggage recovery. Your maximum allowance is US$300 per adult (▷ panel, 304). No vegetable or meat products are allowed into the country and there are restrictions on the amount of currency you can bring in.

» Most non-nationals, arriving from destinations outside Argentina, do not require a visa (▷ 304), but have to go through customs and passport controls in the usual way. Nationals of Australia, Canada and the United States must fill in an extra form, enter a special channel at customs and pay a reciprocity fee—US$100, US$70 and US$140 respectively.

❯❯ Once you have recovered your luggage, it is scanned by customs officials and subject to spot checks. This can cause significant delays in reaching Arrivals and it is a good idea to allow one to two hours after landing.

❯❯ In Arrivals, Terminal A, you will find tourist information desks located immediately at the exit from customs (daily 8–8), plus fast-food outlets, cafés and restaurants around the main concourse.

❯❯ Several major car rental and *remise* (radio taxi) firms have counters by the exit from Customs. Internet access and phones can also be found on the main concourse in various *locutorios* (call and internet centres, ▷ 315). There are ATMs and a bank located by the main exit. A bureau de change is available in the luggage hall and on the main concourse, but you will get much more advantageous rates at banks in the city centre. It might be wise to change just enough to pay for your transport, although this can also be done by credit card.

❯❯ Terminal B offers basic facilities to travellers including a couple of cafés, a bureau de change and public telephones. You will need to go around to Terminal A to benefit from the services it offers.

Transport from Ezeiza to Central Buenos Aires

By taxi: The quickest and most convenient way to the city centre from Ezeiza is by *remise* (radio taxi). *Remises* are available 24 hours a day and several companies have desks in the Arrivals hall in Terminals A and B. Compare prices and availability before buying a ticket. The two main *remise* companies are Manuel Tienda León (tel 011/4315-

MAJOR AIRLINES	
AIRLINE	**WEBSITE**
Aerolíneas Argentinas	www.aerolineas.com.ar
Air France	www.airfrance.com
American Airlines	www.aa.com
Andes	www.andesonline.com
British Airways	www.britishairways.com
Continental Airlines	www.continental.com
Delta	www.delta.com
Iberia	www.iberia.com
LAN	www.lan.com
Lufthansa	www.lufthansa.com
PLUNA	www.pluna.aero
Qantas	www.qantas.com.au
South African Airways	www.flysaa.com
TAM	www.tam.com.br
United Airlines	www.united.com

5115; www.tiendaleon.com.ar) and Transfer Express (tel 011/4312-8883). Expect to pay around $170 for the trip, including your luggage and motorway tolls. You can pay by credit card, in pesos or US dollars. After paying, take your receipt and wait by the office for your driver to escort you to the vehicle. You will need to give your driver the exact address of where you want to go. The journey time to central Buenos Aires is around 50 minutes, though it can take considerably longer in adverse traffic and weather conditions.

Avoid standard cabs, queuing outside the international terminal, because you are unlikely to save any time or money. It is not unknown for unwary passengers to be conned by unscrupulous taxi drivers, although this is a rare occurrence.

Some hotels offer a transfer from the airport. This may be free but often comes at a high price: Check with the hotel before departure.

By minibus: Manuel Tienda León (MTL) also runs a 24-hour minibus service. Buses run twice an hour during the day, and every hour on the hour from midnight–6am. A one-way transfer to their main office at Terminal Madero in Retiro costs $50 but, for an additional charge, MTL will take passengers to most addresses within the city centre.

Many of the city's hostels offer a similar airport shuttle service, which

must be booked in advance online at www.hostelshuttle.com.ar.

By bus: Bus No. 60, departs every 15 minutes (7 days a week, 24 hours a day) from a stop outside the airport terminal. The journey costs $1.50 and takes around 2 hours to reach Avenida de Mayo.

By car: Driving a car in Buenos Aires is not recommended, but if you are heading off to the provinces, there are car rental firms in the Arrivals hall in Terminal A. The main firms are Hertz (tel 011/4480-0054), Avis (tel 011/4984-8142) and Localiza (tel 011/4480 9387).

Transport from Ezeiza to Aeroparque Jorge Newbery

By Minibus or taxi: Manuel Tienda León also runs a daily minibus service between Aeroparque and Ezeiza. The transfer costs $50 (a taxi costs around $150). Departures are every hour and the journey takes about 75 minutes.

AEROPARQUE JORGE NEWBERY

Aeroparque Metropolitano Jorge Newbery (usually known as Aeroparque) is 2km (1.25 miles) northeast of Buenos Aires in Palermo's Costanera Norte. It is a modern, compact and easy-to-use airport on two floors with baggage trolleys (carts) supplied at convenient locations. The check-in counters,

ON THE MOVE   ARRIVING

47

clearly marked by airline, are downstairs. The departures lounge and gates are upstairs, where you'll also find an array of shops and cafés. There are more cafés and an impressive range of duty-free shops (including luxury clothes stores) airside. ATMs, car rental and *remise* (radio taxi) counters are clustered downstairs, while *locutorios* are upstairs.

Transport from Aeroparque Jorge Newbery

By taxi: Plentiful taxis filter through a rank in front of the airport terminal by Arrivals. At peak times expect long queues. The supervisor expects a $1 tip for holding doors open. The journey time to Palermo is 15 minutes and costs around $20. To other *barrios* journeys take less than 30 minutes and cost $25–$40. Expect your journey to be longer during peak times (Mon–Fri 7.30–9, 5.30–7).

Manuel Tienda León (tel 011/4315-5115; www.tiendaleon.com.ar) has *remises* (radio cabs) and, depending on your destination in the city, these cost $20 to $50. The desks are at Arrivals on both sides of the exit from luggage delivery. You usually have to wait for your driver after pre-paying the fare (wait by the desk on the city side) but the cars are comfortable and have more room for luggage than a standard taxi. Tips are not expected on pre-paid fares.

By minibus: Manuel Tienda León runs a regular minibus service

(hourly) between Aeroparque and its Madero terminus. One-way costs $17 with a free onward service to most destinations within the city centre.

By Bus: Bus No. 33 departs every 10–15 minutes (7 days a week, 24 hours a day) from outside Arrivals and terminates on the Paseo Colón on the riverside downtown. The bus costs $1.20 and takes 40–50 minutes depending on the traffic. It is not advisable to take the bus during peak travel times, especially if you have a lot of luggage.

CÓRDOBA INTERNACIONAL AIRPORT

Córdoba's Aeropuerto Internacional Ingeniero Aeronáutico Ambrosio L.V. Taravella is located at Pajas Blancas, 9km (5.5 miles) north of the city. Modernized and expanded in the early 2000s, it is now the country's third-biggest airport and receives flights from Rio, Montevideo, Iguazú and Salta as well as Aeroparque. It is a user-friendly airport, with the check-in counters, ATMs, car rental and *remise* (radio taxi) counters on the lower level. Upstairs is the departures lounge and gates, where you'll also find shops, cafés and *locutorios* (call centres).

Transport to Central Córdoba

By taxi: Taxis and *remises* leave from a rank just outside Arrivals and cost around $50 to the city centre. The journey should take less than 30 minutes in normal traffic,

USEFUL AIRPORT CONTACTS

General Airport Information:
www.aa2000.com.ar

Ezeiza: 011/5480-6111

Aeroparque: 011/5480-3000

Córdoba: 0351/475-0874

longer during peak times.

By minibus: Transfer Express (0351/475-9201) runs a shuttle service for departures and arrivals (the timing coincides with scheduled flight times) and costs around $40. The stop is just outside Arrivals.

Car rental: Avis (0351/475-0785) and Hertz (0351/475-0581) have offices at the airport, with counters at Arrivals (daily 24 hours) but it is advisable to book your vehicle ahead of your arrival.

DEPARTURES

» When leaving Argentina, remember that pesos are worthless outside the country but you can use them to buy goods in the airport duty-free shops.

» It is advisable to have luggage safety-wrapped in heavy-duty plastic, as there have been a number of reported incidents where valuables have been stolen from checked-in luggage. This service is available at the entrance to Departures and costs $50 a bag.

» You should allow three hours for check-in and customs but, perhaps, a little less if you checked in online.

» All departure taxes are now included in the ticket price.

GETTING AROUND BUENOS AIRES

Public transport in Buenos Aires can seem chaotic and it is often easier to hop in a taxi, which despite recent fare increases is a less expensive choice here than in most comparable cities. The mostly efficient underground railway *(subte)* is useful for getting to some destinations and the antique Línea A is an experience in itself. Since the public transport system was privatized in the late 1990s, buses, trains and *subte* have been run by separate companies. There are two rival integrated transport ticket systems now available, SUBE and Monedero, which can be used on the *subte* and certain bus routes. Simply buy a plastic card and add money to it from time to time, which at least means you don't need coins for every bus ride or to queue for *subte* tickets.

BY BUS

Known as *colectivos*, or colloquially as *bondis*, the city's privately run single-decker buses are noisy and fast but there are lots of them.

» On most routes, the frequency varies from four to seven buses an hour.

» Bus stops *(paradas)* are marked by discreet dark-blue signs, atop pavement-side posts, and show the route number and terminus, plus some of the main stops on the route. Don't expect to see any shelters, route maps or timetables, although passengers do queue for the bus.

» If you can work out the route you need, hop on the bus and tell the *colectivero* (driver) where you are going. It is a good idea to name a street intersection. Don't expect drivers to speak English but they should tell you how much you need to slot in the machine for your ticket *(boleto)*—usually around $1.20. Make sure you have change for the fare, as banknotes are not accepted.

» There is no night bus service but many buses, such as No. 5 and No. 86, run 24 hours a day, seven days a week.

» Buses are the best means of reaching Boca and San Telmo, Recoleta and parts of downtown Buenos Aires.

» It is worth buying a copy of *Guía T*. This inexpensive booklet, available at all pavement newspaper kiosks, contains page-by-page maps of the city and shows all the bus routes.

» The most useful website for bus routes is www.xcolectivo.com.ar/colectivo.

BY TRAM

Apart from the touristy Tranvía Histórico in the outlying *barrio* of Caballito, there is only one tram running in Buenos Aires, the Tranvía del Este in Puerto Madero (▷ 91). Since 2007, this bright yellow tram has slid up and down the renovated tracks between the northern end of Dique 4 and the southern end of Dique 2 and there are plans to extend the route in either direction.

» The tram runs parallel to Avenida Alicia Moreau de Justo between avenidas Córdoba and Independencia and stops at the intersection of avenidas Corrientes and Belgrano.

» The tram stops are clearly marked and the fare is $1 per journey. There are ticket machines on the platform. Inspectors on the trams check that travellers have purchased a ticket.

» Trams run every 15 minutes (Mon–Sat 8–11, Sun 9–10) and it takes 10 minutes to go from one end of the track to the other.

BY *SUBTE*

Run privately by Metrovías, the *subte* was built in 1913 and is one of the oldest subways in the world. It is not the most convenient or the most comfortable metro service but it provides a relatively fast and economical means of getting to destinations such as Palermo, downtown and the Plaza San Martín.

» There are six lines: A, the oldest and most picturesque, running from

Plaza de Mayo to the western *barrios*; B from the downtown riverside to the northwestern *barrios*; C connecting Retiro railway station to another major commuter hub at Constitución; D from Plaza de Mayo to Palermo and Belgrano; E from Plaza de Mayo to the southwestern *barrios*; and the new H line, which runs from Once to the southern *barrios*.

» Linea D will get you to many destinations in Palermo (▷ 84–87). Linea A runs along Avenida de Mayo (▷ 70), while several lines converge at the Obelisco (▷ 69) and at the Plaza de Mayo (▷ 88–89).

» Each route is colour coded on *subte* maps and at stations.

» There is a regular service (daily 5am–10.30pm), though industrial action is not infrequent.

» Trains are frequent (around 5 to 10 an hour) but can get crowded at peak hours (7.30–9am and (5.30–7pm).

» Tickets cost $1.10 and you can buy several tickets at once or buy a *SubtePass* valid for several journeys.

» A *Monedero* card, which can be recharged with cash, may be worth getting if you plan to use the *subte* a lot. Check online at www. monedero.com.ar for details.

» To access the platforms, put your ticket through the slot by the barriers and hold on to it, especially if it has remaining journeys. You don't need your ticket to exit the station.

» You can download a *subte* map at www.subte.com.ar. Alternatively contact customer services (tel 011/4555-1616; Mon–Fri 8–8). For more general information on routes visit one of the tourist information offices in Buenos Aires or visit www.metrovias.com.ar.

BY TRAIN

There is an extensive network of trains covering Buenos Aires but visitors are most likely to use the relatively comfortable suburban trains that run from Retiro station to Tigre (▷ 101) via Belgrano and San Isidro.

» The service is regular and frequent, but the trains get crowded at peak times (7.30–9am and 5.30–7pm) and not all trains are air-conditioned.

» Buy tickets at the automatic machines (a single fare from Retiro to Tigre is $1.35) then check the board to find out the time and platform of the next train.

» The train service is slow but efficient and in addition to Tigre, it is worthwhile using the train (from Belgrano) to visit the Museo de Arte Español Enrique Larreta (▷ 80).

» For travel information, including timetables and fares, consult TBA's website at www.tbanet.com.ar.

FERRIES

There are fast and slow services from Buenos Aires to Montevideo and the beautiful old town of Colonia del Sacramento (▷ 73) in Uruguay.

» Buquebus/Ferrytur runs a regular ferry and catamaran service from the Dársena Norte terminal at the eastern end of Avenida Córdoba to both Colonia del Sacramento and Montevideo. You can book online, by phone or at either of the Buquebus offices in Buenos Aires (Avenida Córdoba 867 or Posadas 1452; tel 011/4316-6500; www.buquebus.com; Mon–Fri 9–7, Sat 9–2).

» The enclosed catamarans to Colonia del Sacramento take one hour and the ferries take two and a half hours. There are several crossings a day in the summer but these get booked up so it's worth making a reservation. In winter crossings are only once or twice a day. Ask at the ferry company's main offices about special deals including accommodation.

» Visa requirements for Uruguay are similar to those for Argentina (▷ 304) and both are members of Mercosur, a commercial union of South American states (www.

mercosur.int). You must fill out an immigration form and present your passport at Argentine and Uruguayan passport and customs controls.

TAXIS

Taxis in Buenos Aires are black and yellow, and are usually easy to find anywhere in the city centre, even late at night. Although taxis are generally safe it is wise to take a car with a company telephone number marked on the outside. Before installing yourself take a good look at the driver and make sure their photo ID, hanging on the back of their seat, matches their face. When in doubt ask hotel or restaurant staff to call a *remise* (radio taxi).

» Use low denomination banknotes when paying the fare, as many drivers do not carry adequate change for larger notes. This will also help to avoid any confusion over the change due—scams have been reported.

» There are taxi ranks at airports, stations and bus terminals but you can also hail a taxi anywhere in the street. If you see a red light and the word *LIBRE* lit, this means the cab is free for rental and can be hailed.

» Ensure that the driver switches the meter on when you set off. The starting fare is around $6, jumping up $0.60 every 200m (218 yards) or every minute when stationary. It is customary to round up to the nearest $0.50 or peso but tipping is not expected.

» For longer journeys, for example to Ezeiza airport or in certain *barrios*, it is better to order a *remise* (radio cab). Try Ciudad (tel 011/4923-7007), Premium (tel 011/4374-6666) or Tres Sargentos (tel 011/4312-0057).

SIGHTSEEING TOURS

There are several companies offering tours of the city by bus or minibus. Two of the most reliable companies are Buenos Aires Tur (Lavalle 1444 PB Of, 8/9/10, C.P. Buenos Aires 1048; tel 011/4371-2390; www. buenosairestur.com) and Tangol (Florida 971, Planta Baja, Local 31, Buenos Aires 1005; tel 011/4312-7276; www.tangol.com).

CAR RENTAL IN ARGENTINA

Renting a car is ideal if you want to explore Argentina properly, although driving in the big cities, especially in Buenos Aires, is best avoided. Most of the major car rental companies have agencies throughout the country, often conveniently located at airports. Car rental is relatively expensive in Argentina but the cheapest option is not always the most advisable. The more economical local companies have modern serviceable cars but they might not have the nationwide rescue-and-emergency coverage of the big international names. Some companies have four-wheel-drive (4WD) vehicles or pick-up trucks available to rent, although they are expensive. Drop-off charges, for all vehicles, are high, so avoid returning vehicles in a different location. Insurance is expensive.

RENTING YOUR CAR

›› A standard car is fine for driving around most routes in Argentina. If, however, you intend to leave main routes, for example driving along the RN-40 that has long stretches of unpaved road, a 4WD vehicle would be a good option.

›› Check your insurance cover before you leave home. When in doubt, buy extra insurance as accidents do happen. Consider paying with a credit card that offers comprehensive car rental insurance if you have one.

›› To rent a vehicle you must be aged over 21 (some companies rent to over 25s only) and have a valid driver's licence.

›› If your national driver's licence has no photo, then you'll need to obtain an international driver's permit in your home country before departure.

›› You will need a credit card to guarantee the deposit because extras will usually be deducted automatically from this card. A few local rental companies accept cash only and may require an extra cash deposit, though this is increasingly rare.

›› The car rental company should ask you to sign the contract or rental agreement and there may be a small charge for each additional driver.

›› Pay attention during the exterior and interior checks, as any extra damage to the vehicle will be charged to you. Ask whether the car takes petrol (*nafta*) or diesel (*gasoil/diesel*).

ON THE ROAD

›› Always carry photo ID (for example, your passport), as well as your driving licence and keep all your documents in a safe place. Road checks are frequent and you will need to present documents to the police when asked.

›› Even if the fuel tank is not full when you collect the car, it will usually have to be returned with the fuel gauge at the same level as when you picked it up.

›› By law, your car should be equipped with a fire extinguisher, two warning triangles, a rigid towbar and a first-aid kit. Check that your rental company has provided these items before setting out.

›› Child seats are compulsory and can be obtained when renting a car. Inform the company in advance of your requirements.

›› If you have an accident involving another driver make sure you get all their details and note down the registration plate of their vehicle. The police are mostly helpful but if you feel you are not being taken seriously or they are favouring the Argentine driver, stand your ground and remain calm.

›› Your car rental company should provide you with the telephone number of a car breakdown service in case you have a problem with the car.

›› If you are driving around Argentina, it is a good idea to carry a mobile

phone for emergencies, although you may not be able to get a signal in more rural areas.

TIPS

›› Make sure you pay any parking and road traffic fines you receive promptly and before leaving the country.

›› When renting a car, it is usually best to opt for unlimited mileage because distances are huge and charges for excess mileage are astronomical.

›› You cannot take rental cars across international borders without a special permit issued by the rental company. If you need one, ask for this in advance and make sure you are insured to drive in another country.

AUTOMATIC CARS

Most rental cars are manual, and automatic vehicles are not widely available in Argentina. If you prefer to drive gear-free then make your reservation well in advance and insist on an automatic.

CAR RENTAL COMPANIES		
COMPANY	**TELEPHONE NUMBER**	**WEBSITE**
Alamo	0810/999-25266	www.alamoargentina.com.ar
Avis	0810/999-12847	www.avis.com.ar
Budget	0810/444-2834	www.budget.com.ar
Hertz	0810/222- 43789	www.milletrentacar.com.ar
Thrifty	011/4326-0338	www.thrifty.com.ar

DRIVING AND CYCLING

Argentina has an extensive road network, although the quality of the road surfaces varies considerably from region to region. In remote areas, especially in Patagonia and the North, many roads are not paved, so drive carefully and slowly and consider renting a 4WD vehicle. One of the joys of driving in Argentina is the lack of traffic and the feeling of open space, although it is worth bearing in mind that distances are gigantic and conditions are not always as good as in other industrialized countries. As a rule of thumb allow an hour for every 80km (50 miles) maximum in normal terrain, but no more than 50km (31 miles) an hour in mountainous areas or along minor roads. Most of the road network consists of two-lane highway, with intermittent stretches that have a third lane for overtaking, while dual carriageways (*semi-autopistas* or *autovías*) and motorways (*autopistas*) account for only a small fraction of the country's roads.

DOCUMENTS

You must have your passport and your driver's licence ready for inspection by the police. If your national driver's licence is without a photo then you'll need to obtain an International Driving Permit before travelling. It is useful to have a permit in any case, as Argentine police prefer them. Permits can be obtained from post offices and motoring associations in your home country. If you are renting a car, make sure that you carry the car rental agreement, plus all the vehicle's documents, which should be given to you when you collect the car.

BASIC RULES OF THE ROAD

» Drivers must be at least 17 years of age and hold a full driver's licence.
» Your car must be equipped with a fire extinguisher, two warning triangles, a rigid towbar and a first-aid kit so check you have these items before setting out.
» Seatbelts and child seats are compulsory in both the front and back of the car.
» You must drive on the right and overtake on the left.
» Give way to traffic coming from the right, unless you are on a major highway or the road sign says otherwise.
» When you are driving in non-urban areas, you must use dipped headlights at all times, day and night, whatever the weather. Flashed headlights from an oncoming vehicle may mean get out of the way or could be a useful reminder to turn your headlights on.

» The alcohol limit is 0.05 per cent, although you can be prevented from driving and even arrested if a police officer believes you are under the influence of drink or drugs.
» You may be fined for violating the Highway Code (*código vial*) and some of the rules may differ from those in your home country. Visit http://en.ruta0.com (in English and Spanish) for information on driving and planning routes in Argentina.

SPEED LIMITS

» All distances and speeds are measured in kilometres.
» The standard speed limit in built-up areas is 40kph (24mph). This goes up to 60kph (37mph) along avenues and 110kph (68mph) when driving outside built-up areas.
» The speed limit on divided highways is 120kph (74mph) and 130kph (80mph) on expressways. The minimum speed on expressways is 40kph (24mph).
» There may be specific speed restrictions in certain areas. These are marked using the international speed-limit red-circle signs.

WARNINGS AND SAFETY

» You may witness a lot of impatient, reckless and, even, aggressive driving in Argentina and speeding and dangerous manoeuvres are commonplace. As a consequence, accidents are frequent in Argentina and the road-accident mortality rate is high by international standards. Drive defensively and don't drive if you are tired.

›› Drivers often overtake where they should not, for example on double white lines, on curves, on bridges, in poor visibility and where there is insufficient time to do so. Do not imitate them and be prepared to yield to oncoming cars overtaking another vehicle.

›› Speed traps and radar are commonly used by the police, so ensure that you know the speed limit of the road you are driving along and don't exceed it. In some areas, especially on the outskirts of towns and cities, radar-controlled traffic lights operate. These lights will change to red if you exceed the indicated speed limit.

›› Roads and traffic (especially bicycles and farm vehicles) may be poorly lit or unlit at night. It is advisable to avoid driving at dusk or at night.

›› Getting stuck behind a truck or farm vehicle is quite common in rural areas, although they will often let you pass when it is safe to do so. Slow vehicles might use their left-hand indicator to tell you that it is safe to overtake.

›› There are many dilapidated cars on Argentine roads, even in towns and cities, which are often slow, prone to sudden breakdowns and without working lights.

›› Police road checks are frequent. Officers are usually polite and will ask for your documents. It is wise to cooperate fully and patiently, but insist that they do not take your documents out of your sight. Most police officers don't speak English.

›› Poor road surfaces, potholes and no road markings are quite common in many parts of the country. If driving on a road where this is the case, err on the side of caution and drive more slowly than usual.

›› When driving on steeply banked, gravel roads keep your speed down, avoid sudden braking and take bends

very slowly because it is easy to flip the car over.

›› The low oxygen at high altitudes may affect the car engine as much as you. If the engine starts to labour, slow down and turn the air-conditioning off.

›› At some provincial borders (for example Mendoza) health officers will check to see if you are carrying fresh fruit or vegetables, which may be confiscated in some cases. You might also be charged a peso or two to have the car's undercarriage sprayed with pesticide.

TOLLS AND MOTORWAYS

›› Many roads are private concessions and some of these charge road tolls. Tolls tend to be low (often $1 to $2) but vary in frequency and often occur when you least expect them (for example, along poorly maintained single-carriageway roads). Some toll booths, especially near big cities, are for subscribers or credit cards only, so make sure you queue in the manual lane.

›› Motorways (*autopistas*) and dual-carriageways (*semi-autopistas* or *autovías*) account for only a small fraction of Argentine roads and they vary in quality. Some of these roads don't charge tolls or meet international standards.

›› Do not expect much in the way of motorway services, so keep your fuel tank topped up and always carry plenty of water and a few provisions in the car.

›› The latest editions of road maps don't always show some of the newer motorways. Look out for road signs pointing the way to the *autopista* (motorway), which are much faster than the standard national roads.

BREAKDOWNS AND ACCIDENTS

›› Punctures are common but so are *gomerías* (tyre-repair workshops), where you can have tyres mended quickly and inexpensively. A *gomería* is often indicated by a tyre hanging by the roadside and many of the larger fuel stations offer this service,

too. It is wise to insist that the car rental company provides two spare tyres, particularly if you are planning to travel along poorly surfaced roads in remote areas.

›› If you break down, move the car off the road, if possible. Turn on the hazard warning lights and position the red warning triangles 50m (55 yards) behind and in front of the vehicle. Telephone the number of the car breakdown service, usually provided by your car rental company. Although, be warned, you may not be able to get a mobile-phone signal in many rural areas. Along most national roads and some provincial roads there are well-indicated emergency satellite telephones at regular intervals.

›› Unfortunately accidents are commonplace in Argentina, owing to the poor roads and dangerous driving habits. If you are unfortunate enough to be involved in an accident, call 101 for the police and 107 for medical assistance.

›› If you are involved in an accident, avoid getting into an argument with the other driver. Stay calm, be polite and do not sign any papers that you don't understand. Make sure that you swap contact details and insurance numbers with the other driver.

PARKING

» Parking is not easy in some town centres and it is usually best to use a car park (*playa de estacionamiento* or *playa*). These are mostly small empty building lots where you make yourself known and leave the car with the keys in the ignition. The parking attendant will park your car and retrieve it for you when you return. You will be issued (or make sure you are) with a ticket with the time. Parking is usually charged by the hour (or half-day/day). Many hotels in towns and cities have their own car parks and usually don't charge extra for guests to park. Check when making your reservation.

» Street parking systems vary from place to place, but it is usually parking meters and/or uniformed wardens (make sure you get a receipt/ticket in return). Apart from downtown Buenos Aires, parking charges are reasonable.

» Towing away and clamping are rare, unless you are obstructing an important exit or entrance, but parking tickets are common. Your car rental company will charge you (by your credit card) for any parking fines that you incur.

» Never leave valuables or your documents in the car, even if it is locked and alarmed.

» At some tourist attractions and outside restaurants young boys or unemployed people offer to guard your car for a fee (at least a peso). It is a good idea to accept their offer but never give them the keys and pay them afterwards.

BUYING FUEL

» Fuel stations are usually open long hours and many operate 24 hours.

» The quality of fuel may vary slightly and you might prefer to choose one of the main companies (YPF, Shell or Petrobras).

» Most fuel stations, even large ones by highways, have attended service and you should not serve yourself. Unleaded petrol is *nafta* and diesel is *gasoil*. If you want a full tank, ask for *lleno con nafta/gasoil, por favor*.

» The attendant will probably clean your windscreen and, if asked, will check the water (*agua*) and oil (*aceite*) levels and tyre pressures (*presión de las gomas/cubiertas*). In any case, a small tip of a peso is appreciated.

» Fuel stations tend to be clustered around urban areas but may be few and far between in more rural areas, so it is wise not to let your petrol tank go below half a tank.

» At the time of writing, petrol costs $4.50 per litre ($20.45 per gallon) and diesel $4.25 per litre ($19.30 per gallon) in Buenos Aires. The cost of fuel varies from region to region and costs half this amount in Patagonia, where it is heavily subsidized.

MOTORCYCLES

It is relatively difficult to find motorcycles of any description to rent in Argentina, although buggies and similar vehicles are popular in tourist resorts. One company that rents motorcycles is GoodBike (www.goodbike.com.ar), based in the northern suburbs of Buenos Aires. The rules for renting a motorcycle are similar to those applied to renting a car (▷ 51). Although you will see many locals breaking the law, wearing a crash helmet is compulsory at all times when riding a motorcycle.

CYCLING

There are great cycling opportunities throughout the country and many cities have introduced cycle paths (*bicisendas*), albeit with varying degrees of success. It is usually easy to find somewhere to rent a mountain bike but the quality of rental operators ranges widely.

» Take the usual precautions, bearing in mind the terrain, climate and sheer distances involved.

» Wear protective clothing and a helmet. Equally, beware of motorized traffic, as drivers are not always very considerate towards cyclists.

» Wind is another major factor to take into consideration and gravel roads can be slippery, particularly after heavy rains. If you are interested in cycling in Argentina, you might want to read the excellent book by Walter Sienko, *Latin America by Bike*.

ROAD CLASSIFICATION

Ruta Nacional (RN)

RN roads are the main roads, which form a nationwide grid, but vary from gravel tracks to fast multi-lane motorways. On maps the number is shown inside a small shield.

Ruta Provincial (RP)

RP indicates major provincial roads, numbered within each province, and their quality may differ a great deal. RP roads are shown on maps with the number inside a small rectangle.

Ruta Complementaria (RC)

RC roads are mostly found in Tierra del Fuego, where these minor roads follow a special lettering system (for example RCb) that sets them apart from the numbered RN and RP roads.

LONG-DISTANCE BUSES

In a country with few train services, long-distance buses (*ómnibus* or *micros*) are vital. You can reach all but the most remote destinations by bus. Distances are huge and journeys can take a couple of days, but it is a good way to see the country. There are dozens of private long-distance bus companies in Argentina, some of them nationwide, others regionally or provincially based. There is a lot of competition on most routes and fares are very reasonable.

PRICES AND TICKETS

›› Buses are much cheaper than flying and the standards of service are generally high, although poor road surfaces in rural areas can turn the vehicles into uncomfortable boneshakers.
›› On long-distance routes, which often entail overnight journeys, you can opt for a *cama* (flat bed) or a *semi-cama* (reclining seat).
›› Ask for advice at your hotel on the best company to use locally or compare routes and prices with different buses before booking.
›› You can usually buy the ticket at the last minute but it is worth reserving ahead, especially if you want a particular seat or are heading to a popular destination in high season or at a weekend. You might be able to do this online or at a city-centre booking office (bus terminals are often located outside the town).
›› Some typical fares with a *semi-cama* are: Buenos Aires to Iguazú $300; Buenos Aires to Salta $400; and Buenos Aires to Bariloche $300.

ONBOARD SERVICES

›› Departures are usually extremely punctual, but always allow for delays en route if you have a plane to catch—roadworks are usually the main culprit.
›› On most services you check in your luggage, either at the counter or next to the bus. The hold attendants will expect a small tip in exchange for the luggage ticket (which protects you from theft). Keep both the ticket

Above *In Argentina most long-distance buses are run by private companies*

stub, to retrieve your bags, and your journey ticket, as it may be checked several times during the journey, as well as when boarding the bus.
›› On long-distance journeys, food and drink is often included in the ticket price and on luxury services it can be very good quality. There are often vendors at stops who may also come onto the bus to sell refreshments.
›› On long-distance journeys there will often be entertainment in the form of a DVD. The type of film varies from Hollywood blockbusters to violent crime movies, so take care which seat you choose and be prepared to block your ears and eyes (sometimes headphones are supplied).

NATIONAL BUS COMPANIES

There are dozens of local, regional and national bus companies, some of which also offer international routes to other South American countries. The four companies listed below offer a nationwide service

to Mendoza, central Argentina, the North and Patagonia respectively.
›› From the main Retiro bus terminal in Buenos Aires you can reach just about any destination around the country, though to get off the beaten track you will need to reach a regional hub first, for example Jujuy or Bariloche.
›› The Retiro bus station, Terminal de Omnibus (tel 011/4310-0700; www.tebasa.com.ar) is at Avenida Antártida Argentina and Calle 10. The best way to get there is by taxi and owing to its location next to a poverty-stricken shanty town you should not linger in the vicinity. Once inside the terminal, consult the main information desk to find out which section of the terminus houses the companies with bus services to your destination.
›› A useful website is www.omnilineas.com.ar, in which you can type in your destination to get comparative information about the bus companies, journey time and ticket prices.

MAJOR BUS COMPANIES

COMPANY	TELEPHONE NUMBER	WEBSITE
Andesmar	011/6385-3031	www.andesmar.com
Chevallier	011/4000-5255	www.nuevachevallier.com
La Veloz del Norte	0800/444-8356	www.lavelozcallcenter.com.ar
Vía Bariloche	0800/333-7575	www.viabariloche.com.ar

	Buenos Aires	Córdoba	Mendoza	Posadas	Puerto Madryn	Río Gallegos	Salta	San Carlos de Bariloche	Ushuaia
Buenos Aires		651	991	840	1064	2033	1281	1343	2312
Córdoba	651		457	919	1253	2231	743	1235	2554
Mendoza	991	457		1385	1136	2040	956	927	2374
Posadas	840	919	1385		1895	2881	989	2055	3143
Puerto Madryn	1064	1253	1136	1895		1009	1974	554	1321
Río Gallegos	2033	2231	2040	2881	1009		2932	1156	349
Salta	1281	743	956	989	1974	2932		1868	3260
San Carlos de Bariloche	1343	1235	927	2055	554	1156	1868		1503
Ushuaia	2312	2554	2374	3143	1321	349	3260	1503	

The above chart shows the direct distance in kilometres between major towns in Argentina

TAXIS

Although fares are more expensive than a few years ago, taxis are still a cost-effective way for visitors to get around, especially in the provinces. In Buenos Aires, the flag rate is $6 and rises by $0.60 every 200m (218 yards), but in most other cities and resorts the fare is around half this price. In the capital, the taxi livery is black and yellow but this varies from city to city.

» Taxis are usually plentiful and can be flagged down anywhere. There are also ranks at strategic points, such as airports and transport terminals. At airports, it is generally better to opt for a *remise* (radio cab), which saves queuing and, in Buenos Aires, ensures your safety. There are some dishonest taxi touts at Ezeiza and Aeroparque airports, despite the determined efforts of the police. Hotels, restaurants and other establishments may offer to call a *remise* or the doorman might hail a taxi for you.

» Taxis take a maximum of four passengers but often have limited room for luggage. Ask for a large car or van if you have several bags.

» A red light in the windscreen with the word *LIBRE* indicates that the taxi is available for rental. Once inside, make sure the meter is switched on and, especially in the capital, check that the photograph on the driver's ID is of the person driving the car. When giving the address of your destination, it helps to give the street and intersection (for example, Santa Fe and Sarmiento) rather than the street and number.

» Most taxi drivers have a good knowledge of the city and expect music and/or plenty of conversation, especially if your Spanish is up to it.

» In Buenos Aires and most other cities, the meter shows the exact fare but there are places around the country where the meter displays a figure that is converted according to an official chart.

» In rural areas or at tourist destinations, you might be able to negotiate a price for a specific excursion, including waiting time, or for a half- or full-day journey. Agree the price before setting out and don't pay the driver until you are returned to your starting place.

» Tipping taxi drivers is not customary but you are expected to round up the fare to the nearest $0.50 or peso. Drivers are required to have change but often run out, so it is always a good idea to pay with a small banknote (even $50 bills are often rejected).

» The majority of drivers are honest and friendly but if you think you are being cheated stand your ground and seek help if possible.

DOMESTIC FLIGHTS

In view of the enormous size of Argentina and the lack of other fast alternatives, you are likely to use domestic flights to fly from one place to another. Although planes will save you time, it should be said that domestic air travel is relatively expensive. There are no low-cost companies and there are few routes that do not involve Buenos Aires. Getting from A to B will usually mean a stopover in the capital, even when that route seems illogical, geographically speaking.

AIRLINES

Argentina's volatile economy means that many airlines have gone out of business and there are now just three main airlines that dominate the air-travel market: Aerolíneas Argentinas (www.aerolineas.com.ar), the flag carrier, plus its national subsidiary, Austral; LAN Argentina (www.lan.com), the Argentine offshoot of Chile's national airline; and Andes (www.andesonline.com), a private company based in Salta, offering a handful of rare and useful inter-provincial routes.

›› Aerolíneas has the widest coverage and may be the only choice for getting to many towns and cities, such as Posadas and Neuquén. Sold and resold, the renationalized veteran company is a shadow of its former self, with ageing aircraft, frequent delays, vulnerability to strike action and no-frills service, but it has a good safety record and some flights to tourist destinations leave from Ezeiza International Airport (▷ 46–47), which can prove convenient.

›› LAN invariably provides a first-class service, with brand-new planes and unrivalled punctuality, but it has a more limited network linking the major tourist sights, such as Ushuaia, Mendoza and Iguazú, to Aeroparque Jorge Newbery domestic airport (▷ 47–48).

›› LADE (Líneas Aereas del Estado, www.lade.com.ar), based in Comodoro Rivadavia, is run by the Argentine air force and has flights between several Patagonian destinations and to Buenos Aires, also. Fares are highly subsidized but the service is erratic and not always reliable.

›› Airline tickets can be bought at travel agents or online and their websites carry information about timetables and special offers, which are mostly for package holidays that include accommodation. The cheapest fares are reserved for Argentine residents. LAN is a member of oneworld and, like Aerolíneas, has its own frequent flyer programme and there are reduced fares and increased baggage allowances for travel around South America if your onward flight is with LAN or one of its partners.

AIRPORTS AND FLIGHTS

Aeroparque Jorge Newbery (▷ 47–48) is located in Palermo, is easily accessed from the capital's central *barrios* and has excellent facilities for passengers. Most other airports around the country have at least one reasonably good cafeteria, plus banks, a choice of car rental offices and shops selling local produce. Airport security is serious in Argentina but may seem relaxed to North American and European visitors. It is rare to be asked to remove shoes or your belt, or take laptops out of their case, or drink a bottle of mineral water to save binning it.

You will need an official ID to check in and at the gate, but you won't need your ticket to enter the terminal because all flights in Argentina are e-ticketed and fares include all taxes. Get to the airport an hour before departure. If you need to connect between the capital's domestic and international airports, there are regular minibuses with Manuel Tienda León (tel 011/4315-5115; www.tiendaleon.com.ar) costing around $50 or *remises* (radio cabs) for $170.

All flights are non-smoking, as are most airport buildings. Onboard catering is usually limited to snacks and drinks—even on longer flights from Buenos Aires to Patagonia and Ushuaia—so it is a good idea to stock up on provisions for the flight.

GETTING FROM THE AIRPORT

Most provincial airports are relatively close to the city or resorts they serve and there is a minibus shuttle to meet most incoming flights along with *remises*, which are cheaper in the provinces than in the captial, and reasonably priced taxis. For the latter, there is usually an information board detailing tariffs or you could ask at the information desk for the going rate. Outside the capital, few taxi drivers are dishonest. At main resorts, your hotel might arrange your transfer but these can be more expensive than a taxi, so ascertain the charge beforehand.

Social awareness and concerted efforts by the authorities have greatly improved access and facilities for people with disabilities *(discapacitados)* in recent years but there is still a long way to go. The difficult terrain in many areas of Argentina makes access for people with mobility difficulties problematic but top hotels and major tourist sights, such as the Iguazú Falls, have all improved their disabled facilities. Moreover, most Argentines are extremely helpful and there will usually be volunteers to help lift wheelchairs or give assistance.

PREPARATION AND PLANNING
It is advisable to plan ahead if you want to visit Argentina and there are a number of organizations and travel agencies that are able to give specialist information about finding accommodation and getting around for people with a disability or mobility difficulties.

Holiday Care is based in the UK (tel 0845/1249-971; www.holidaycare.org.uk) and provides holiday information for people with disabilities, including accommodation and useful travel blogs.

Mobility International is based in the USA (tel 541/343-1284; www.miusa.org) and promotes international travel and exchange schemes for people with disabilities.

Society for Accessible Travel and Hospitality (SATH) (tel 212/447-7284; www.sath.org) is a US-based organization offering travel advice for visitors with disabilities and promoting awareness of their travel requirements.

Dec Third (www.decthird.com) is an Argentine-based agency offering advice and putting together tailored tours and excursions for visitors with disabilities.

ARRIVING BY AIR
Check with your airline about the arrangements they can offer and the facilities available at Ezeiza and Córdoba airports. Both international airports have elevators to all levels and wheelchairs are available for passengers at most Argentine airports, but it is best to call ahead to let them know your needs. A taxi will take you to your hotel. The more expensive hotels and resorts usually have good facilities and are accustomed to serving guests with disabilities or mobility difficulties. Many new hotels have accommodation and bathrooms adapted for visitors with disabilities, but these may not be to the standards that you are accustomed to in your home country. Check with your hotel about their facilities beforehand.

GETTING AROUND ARGENTINA
Buenos Aires and other cities may present some difficulties for people with disabilities because of the general lack of provision. City pavements and ramps built into street corners are often in a poor state of repair. There is disabled access to most official buildings and some museums but it is always advisable to check ahead. Conventional taxis are not suitable for people with disabilities and usually cannot store wheelchairs in the trunk but you can call a *remise* company (▷ 47) and ask for a special vehicle *(para discapacitados)*. A few buses have wheelchair access although not the majority. Dogs are welcome almost everywhere in Argentina so seeing dogs for the blind are unlikely to be refused.

REGIONS

This chapter is divided into six regions of Argentina (▷ 8–9). Region names are for the purposes of this book only and places of interest are listed alphabetically in each region.

REGIONS ARGENTINA

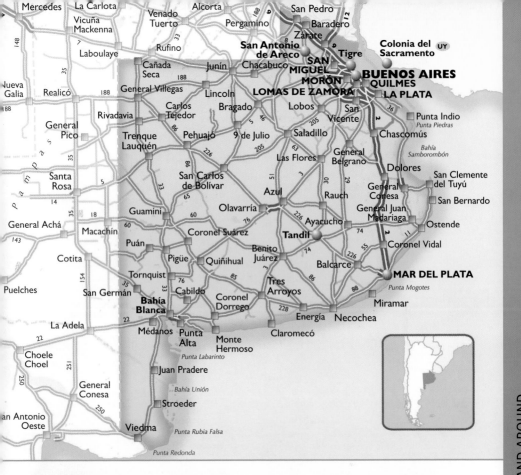

BUENOS AIRES AND AROUND

Argentina's supremely elegant capital, abutting the Río de la Plata, is home to 13 million inhabitants, one third of the country's population, making Greater Buenos Aires one of the world's biggest conurbations. Often dubbed *la París de Sudamérica* (Paris of South America), its sporting venues and shopping, café-hopping and gastronomy plus all-night partying are reminiscent of other great cities—London and Milan, Madrid and New York—and it is impossible to be indifferent to this vibrant city.

In the hectic *microcentro*, the landmark Casa Rosada, the pink presidential palace, and the imposing Teatro Colón opera house stand out among the many sights. Highlights south of the centre include the Feria San Telmo, a lively weekend antiques fair, and Caminito, a tiny street in the Boca district where the houses are painted in pastel shades. To the north, the stylish neighbourhoods of Retiro, Recoleta and Palermo offer opulent palaces, leafy parks, luxury boutique hotels, bars and restaurants. In addition to the famous Recoleta cemetery, you can visit some of the city's finest museums, such as the world-class modern art museum MALBA. The newest barrio, Puerto Madero, to the east, combines revamped docklands with a popular nature reserve, part of the Costanera Sur. The *subte* (metro), a go-everywhere bus network and keenly priced taxis will take you anywhere you want to go in this great metropolis.

Stray outside the city, into the Buenos Aires Province, and you will discover a huge expanse of pampas stretching to the Atlantic seaboard, where you can investigate beach resorts, such as Mar del Plata, reachable by car or bus. Closer to hand, the patrician suburb of San Isidro and the subtropical Tigre lie to the north of the city, a short train ride away. You can even visit another country by taking a ferry across the vast estuary to gem-like Colonia del Sacramento in Uruguay. Tradition-steeped San Antonio de Areco, to the west of BA, and sleepy Tandil, due south, are two of the most interesting rural towns in Argentina and, if you want to escape the city for a couple of days, there are a number of historic *estancias* (ranches) where you can stay overnight.

AV LEOPOLDO LUGONES
AV LEOPOLDO LUGONES

Aeroparque
Jorge Newbery

Museo
Nacional
de Aeronáutico

Jardín de
Infancia Mitre

Plaza
República del
Ecuador

Plaza
República
de Pakistán

AVENIDA

Hipódromo
Argentino
de Palermo

Velódromo
Municipal

1

Plaza
Rep de Haití

Bosques de Palermo

Avenida Belisario Roldán

AVENIDA

Corralón
Municipal
de Palermo

Campo
Argentino
de Polo

Museo de Artes
Plásticas
Eduardo Sívori

AVENIDA PRESIDENTE

Planetario
Galileo

Plaza del
Hipódromo
Argentino

AVENIDA DORREGO

Avenida Infanta Isabel

Plaza
Dr B Goudi
Monolito
Histórico

SARMIENTO

Parque
Jorge
Newbery

Campo
Hípico Militar

ESTACIÓN
3 DE FEBRERO

Freyre

Parque 3 de Febrero

Monumento
al General Urquiza

Avenida Casares

AVENIDA DEL LIBERTADOR

Av Presidente Pedro Montt

Parque
Holanda

Lago
de Palermo

Av Belisario Roldán

Club de Amigos

Dorrego

Clay

Baez

Cervido

Av F Kennedy

Av J F Kennedy

Av Iraola

AVENIDA

Lago
Victoria
Ocampo

FIGUEROA ALCORTA

Avenida Adolfo Berro

2

Arce

Arenales

Andrés Arguibel

Avenida Luis
María Campos

Juan F Seguí

Demaría

Cervido

Cervido

Maria de Oro

Juncal

Justo Santa

Colombia

Plaza
Int Seeber

Monumento
de los Españoles

Monumento
a Sarmiento

Plaza Sicilia

Jardín
Japonés

Castex

Celix

Arévalo

Museo de Arte
Español Enrique Larreta

AVENIDA INTENDENTE BULLRICH

Godoy Cruz

Fray Justo Santa

AVENIDA DEL LIBERTADOR

Plaza
Alemania

Castex

Calvo

Bonpland

AVENIDA SANTA FE

Berutti

AVENIDA SARMIENTO

República de la India

Cervino

Juan F Seguí

Castex

Charcas

Fitz Roy

Humboldt

Palermo

Berutti

Jardín
Zoológico

República de la India

Cabello

Lafinur

República Árabe Siria

Guatemala

Raúl Scalabrini Ortiz

Museo
Hernández

3

AVENIDA JUAN B JUSTO

ESTACIÓN
PALERMO

Predio la Rural

Teatro
Municipal

Museo
Evita

Gutenberg

Uriarte

PALERMO

Araoz

Plaza
Sobral

Bulnes

Ruggieri

Godoy Cruz

Santa María de Oro

Plaza
Italia

Guemes

Thames

Uriarte

Plaza Italia

Jardín Botánico
C Thays

Museo
Botánico

AVENIDA GENERAL LAS HERAS

French

Juncal

Parque
Las Heras

Darregueira

Serrano

Charcas

AVENIDA SANTA FE

República Árabe Siria

Raúl Scalabrini Ortiz

Guatemala

Guemes

Guatemala

Armenia

Malabia

Scalabrini
Ortiz

Araoz

Berutti

Arenales

Jerónimo Salguero

AVENIDA CORONEL DIAZ

Billinghurst

Nicaragua

**PALERMO
VIEJO**

Charcas

San
Mateo

Jerónimo Salguero

Sánchez de

Thames

Serrano

Gurruchaga

Cen Lucio

Plaza
Guemes

República Dominicana

Arenales

Juncal

4

**PALERMO
SOHO**

Gurruchaga

El Salvador

Costa Rica

Plaza
Camp del
Desierto

Guatemala

Julián Alvarez

Bulnes
(Alto Palermo)

Vidt

Bulnes

Berutti

Plaza Julio
Cortázar

Armenia

Costa Rica

Medrano

Av Honduras

Malabia

El Salvador

Costa Rica

Medrano

Julián Alvarez

Soler

Paraguay

Norberto Mansilla

Charcas

AVENIDA CORONEL DIAZ

Sánchez de Bustamante

Guemes

Agüero

AVENIDA SANTA

Gorriti

Jose Antonio Cabrera

Araoz

Gorriti

Julián Alvarez

El Salvador

Julián Alvarez

Jerónimo Salguero

Paraguay

Charcas

Cen
Lucio

Billinghurst

Callo

Paraguay

5

AVENIDA CORDOBA

Pringles

AV HONDURAS

Gorriti

Mario Bravo

Soler

Sánchez de Bustamante

Agüero

Laprida

Norberto

AVENIDA

Araoz

Julián Alvarez

Jose Antonio Cabrera

Lavalleja

Gascon

Bulnes

Museo
Xul Solar

Callo

Lucio

Agüero

Laprida

Mansilla

Jufre

Lambaré

Lavalleja

F A de Figueroa

AVENIDA MEDRANO

AV CORDOBA

Jerónimo Salguero

D I M de Alchorena

Jean Jaures

Plaza
M de
Andrea

A   ESTADO DE ISRAEL   **B**   AVENIDA CORDOBA   **C**

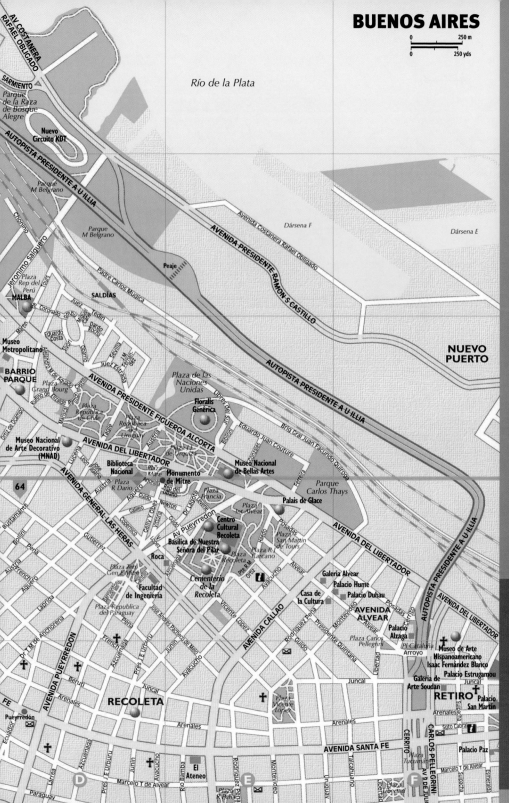

BUENOS AIRES

0   250 m
0   250 yds

AV COSTANERA RAFAEL OBLIGADO

SARMIENTO

Río de la Plata

Parque de la Raza de Bosque Alegre

Nuevo Circuito KDT

AUTOPISTA PRESIDENTE A U ILLIA

Chorroa

Parque M Belgrano

Parque M Belgrano

Dársena F

Dársena E

Peaje

Avenida Costanera Rafael Obligado

AVENIDA PRESIDENTE RAMON S CASTILLO

Jeronimo Salguero

Padre Carlos Mugica

Plaza Rep del Perú

MALBA

SALDÍAS

AUTOPISTA PRESIDENTE A U ILLIA

NUEVO PUERTO

Museo Metropolitano

BARRIO PARQUE

Plaza Grand Bourg

Plaza República de Chile

AVENIDA PRESIDENTE FIGUEROA ALCORTA

Plaza de las Naciones Unidas

Floralis Genérica

Museo Nacional de Arte Decorativo (MNAD)

Plaza República del Uruguay

AVENIDA DEL LIBERTADOR

Plaza R de Urquiza

Eduardo Juan Couture

Brig Gral Juan Facundo Quiroga

Biblioteca Nacional

Monumento de Mitre

Plaza R Dario

Museo Nacional de Bellas Artes

Parque Carlos Thays

AVENIDA GENERAL LAS HERAS

Plaza Francia

Plaza Int Alvear

Palais de Glace

AVENIDA DEL LIBERTADOR

Av Pueyrredon

Centro Cultural Recoleta

Plaza San Martin de Tours

Posadas

Basílica de Nuestra Señora del Pilar

Roca

Plaza Recoleta

Plaza R J Carcano

Plaza Gen E Mitre

Facultad de Ingeniería

Cementerio de la Recoleta

Galeria Alvear

Palacio Hume

Palacio Duhau

AVENIDA ALVEAR

Plaza Andres Pacheco de Melo

Plaza República del Paraguay

Vicente López

Casa de la Cultura

Palacio Alzaga

AVENIDA PUEYRREDON

Rodriguez Peña

Presidente Quintana

Plaza Carlos Pellegrini

Pl Cataluña

Arroyo

Museo de Arte Hispanoamericano Isaac Fernández Blanco

Palacio Estrugamou

RECOLETA

AVENIDA CALLAO

Plaza Vicente López

Galeria de Arte Soudan

RETIRO

Palacio San Martin

Arenales

Juncal

Arenales

Juncal

Palacio Paz

FE

Pueyrredon

El Ateneo

AVENIDA SANTA FE

CERRITO

CARLOS PELLEGRINI

Plaza Tucuman

AV 9 DE JULIO

Paraguay

D   **E**   **F**

64

63

REGIONS   BUENOS AIRES AND AROUND • CITY MAP

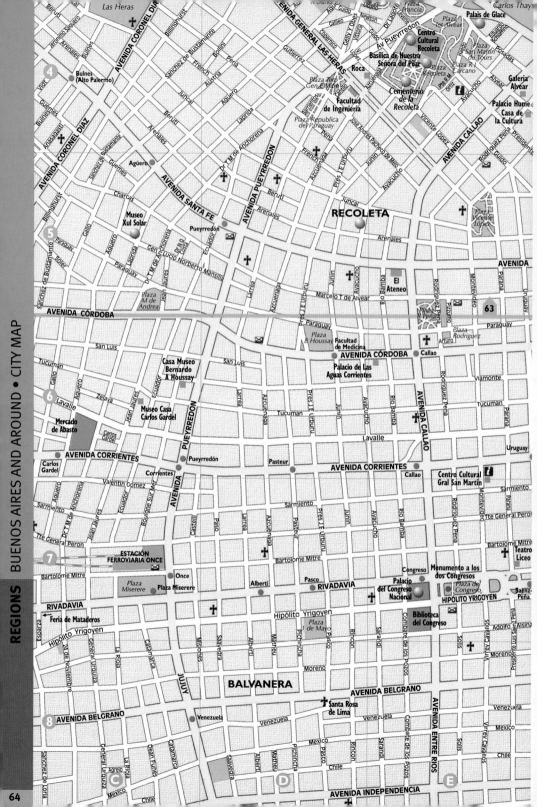

250 m
250 yds

TERMINAL DE OMNIBUS RETIRO

AVENIDA DEL LIBERTADOR

AVENIDA ANTÁRTIDA ARGENTINA

AVENIDA DEL LIBERTADOR

AUTOPISTA PRESIDENTE A. ILLIA

Padre Carlos Mugica

Av de los Inmigrantes

Av Comodoro Py

Combate de los Pozos Brava

Estado Mayor General de La Armada

Corbeta Uruguay

Avenida Ing José N Quartino

Palacio Duhau

AVENIDA ALVEAR

Palacio Alzaga

Plaza Carlos Pellegrini

Posadas

Montevideo

Quintana

Libertad

Juncal

Arenales

SANTA FE

Museo de Arte Hispanoamericano Isaac Fernández Blanco

Palacio Estrugamou

Galería de Arte Soudan

RETIRO

Palacio San Martín

CRUCERO BELGRANO

GEN BELGRANO

Sgto Cabral

Suipacha

Arenales

Santa Fe

General San Martín

Palacio Paz

Parques Nacionales

Museo de Armas de la Nación

Marcelo T de Alvear

Esmeralda

Maipú

Paraguay

ESTACIÓN FERROVIARIA RETIRO

Retiro

Torre de los Ingleses

Plaza Libertador General San Martín

AV GILARDO GILARDI

AV RAMOS MEJÍA

DR G M ZUVIRÍA

SAN MARTÍN

Dr R Rojas

L N ALEM

Basílica del Santísimo Sacramento

Tres Sargentos

Florida

Reconquista

Ing E Butt

Paraera

Antepuerto

Dársena Norte

Museo Hotel de Inmigrantes

Colonia, Montevideo, Piriapolis

Plaza Canada

Avenida Antártida Argentina

AVENIDA EDUARDO MADERO

Terminal Buquebus Ferrys y Aliscafos

Blvd Cecilia Grierson

Córdoba

Museo Fortabat

Alvear

Barra

Reserva Ecológica Costanera Sur

AVENIDA CÓRDOBA

Galerías Pacífico

Viamonte

SAN NICOLÁS

Tucuman

Lavalle

Lavalle

Florida

Esmeralda

Carlos Pellegrini

25 de Mayo

L N ALEM

Alvear Ocampo

Plaza Roma

V Ocampo

Corrientes

Luna Park

T Guevara

Buque Museo Corbeta Uruguay

Trinidad Guevara

Dique 4

Victoria Ocampo

Juana Manso

AVENIDA COST Tristán Achával Rodríguez

Avenida de los Italianos

Teatro Cervantes

Museo Nacional de Teatro

Plaza Lavalle

Plaza Santa Cruz

VIAMONTE

LIBERTAD

Tribunales

Teatro Colón

Palacio de Justicia

CERRITO

AV 9 DE JULIO

CARLOS PELLEGRINI

AV 9 DE JULIO

Talcahuano

Libertad

Cerrito

El Obelisco

Plaza de la República

9 de Julio

AVENIDA CORRIENTES

Diagonal Norte

MICRO CENTRO

ROQUE SAENZ PEÑA

Bartolome Mitre

Iglesia San Miguel Arcangel

Palacio Bencich

Catedral

Mitre

Archivo y Museo Histórico del Banco de la Provincia

Museo Banco

Tte General Perón

Policial

Secretaría de Comunicaciones

Sarmiento

25 DE MAYO

Catedral Anglicana

L N ALEM

San Martín

Reconquista

Av Rosales

Monumento a Manuel Belgrano

ESTACIÓN PUERTO MADERO

Manuela Sáenz

Plaza Madero Este

PUERTO MADERO

Buque Museo Fragata A R A Pres Sarmiento

Museo de las Telecomunicaciones

Carola Lorenzini

LA CITY

Catedral Metropolitana

Monumento a Juan de Garay

Casa de Gobierno/ Casa Rosada

Plaza de Mayo

Plaza de Mayo

RIVADAVIA

HIPÓLITO YRIGOYEN

Museo de la Ciudad

Basílica de San Francisco

MANZANA FRANCISCANA

Parque Colón

Dique 3

Olga Cossettini

Juana Manso

Aimé Paine

Juana Manuela Gorriti

Azucena

Villaflor

Azucena Villaflor

UCA

Tte General Perón

Palacio Barolo

AVENIDA DE MAYO

Rivadavia

Lima

Palacio San Miguel

Avenida de Mayo

Hipólito Yrigoyen

Iglesia San Juan Bautista

MONSERRAT

Moreno

Bolívar

Adolfo Alsina

Iglesia San Ignacio

MANZANA DE LAS LUCES

Museo Etnografico

Nacional del Grabado

AVENIDA BELGRANO

Basílica de Santo Domingo

Venezuela

Belgrano

Aduana

Belgrano

AVENIDA PASEO COLÓN

AVENIDA ING HUERGO

Azucena

Villaflor

Martha Salotti

Nuestra Señora de Montserrat

Plaza Jujuy

Mariano Moreno

Plaza Formosa

Teatro del Sur

BERNARDO DE YRIGOYEN

AV 9 DE JULIO

LIMA

Santiago del Estero

Salta

Lima

Santiago del Estero

San José

Chacabuco

Piedras

Tacuarí

Defensa

Mexico

Chile

San Lorenzo

Museo Tecnológico Ing Latzina

El Zanjón

Dique 2

Independencia

Petrona Eyle

Aimé Paine

Encarnación Ezcurra

Plaza Chaco

Museo de Traje

AVENIDA INDEPENDENCIA

Independencia

Estados Unidos

Iglesia del Nazareno

Independencia

Inmaculada Concepción

Dr J M Giuffra

La Boca, San Telmo

CANTO AL TRABAJO

Blvd Rosario Penaloza

F

G

H

REGIONS **BUENOS AIRES AND AROUND • CITY MAP**

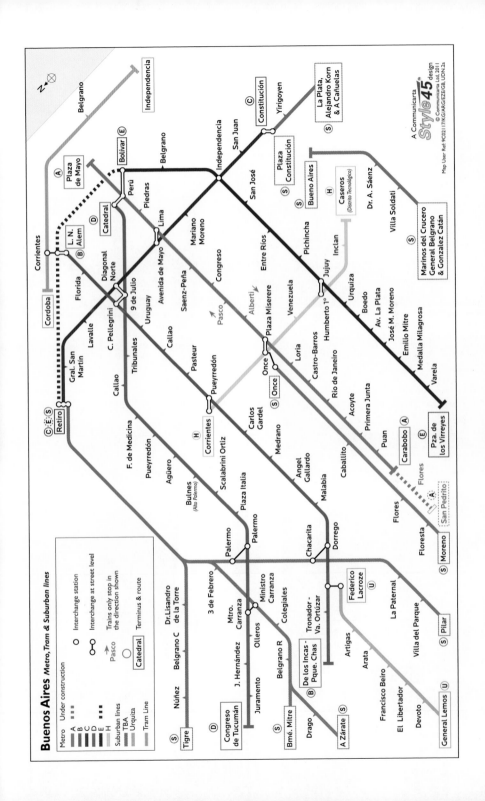

Buenos Aires *Metro, Tram & Suburban lines*

Metro   Under construction
A
B
C
D
E
H

Suburban lines
TBA
Urquiza

Tram Line

○ Interchange station
○–○ Interchange at street level

→ Trains only stop in
Pasco   the direction shown

◯ Pasco

Catedral   Terminus & route

A Communicarta
Style 45 design
© Communicarta Ltd. 2011
Map User Ref: RC02117/KGJARGEZEIGB.UDN.2a

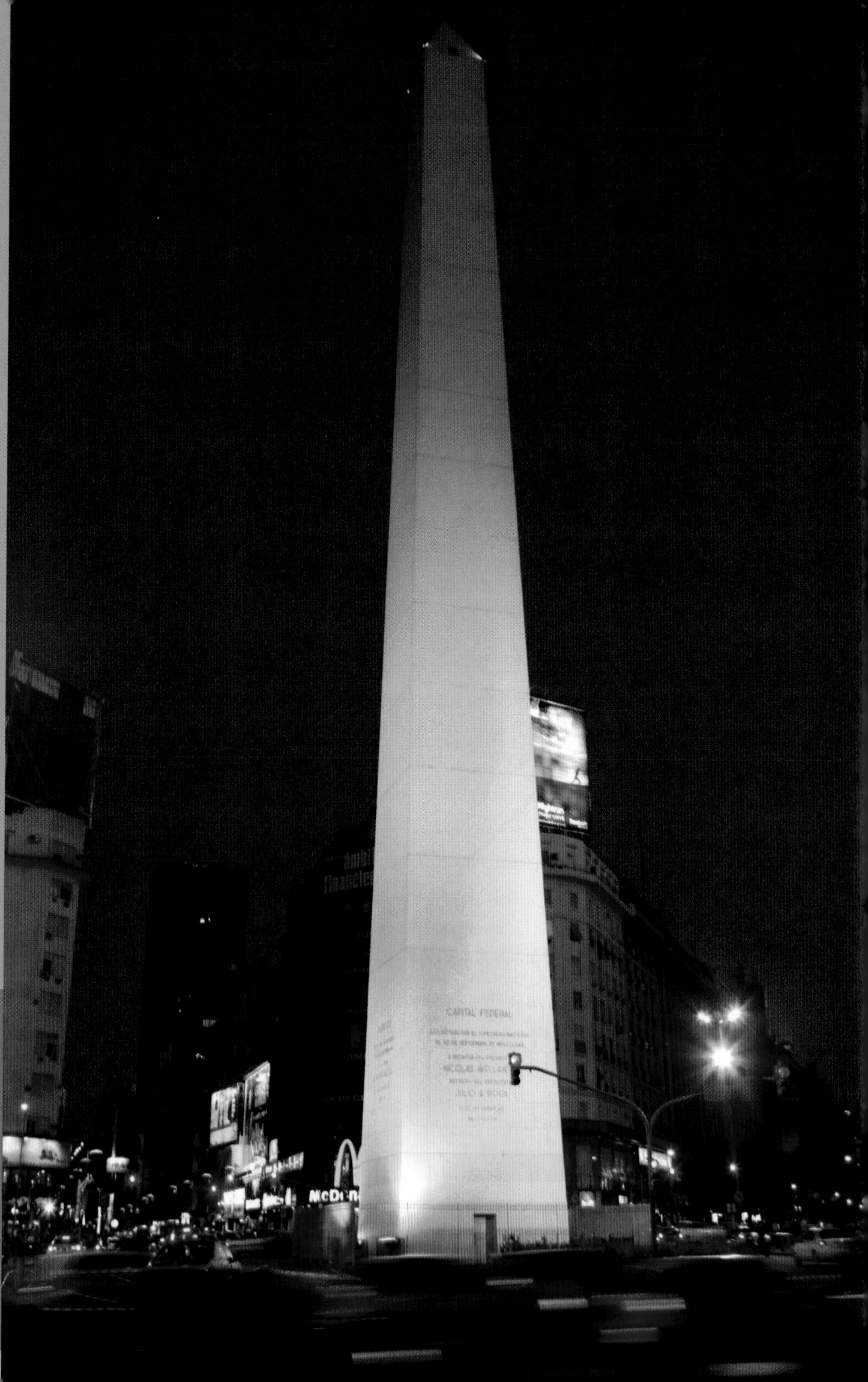
CAPITAL FEDERAL

AVENIDA 9 DE JULIO

Named after Argentina's Independence Day, 9 July 1816, the impressive Avenida 9 de Julio is a goliath of a street, 12 lanes wide and over 1km (0.5 miles) long, making it quite a challenge to negotiate. Built to alleviate city traffic in the 1960s, 9 de Julio divides downtown from the rest of the city, so you are bound to need to cross it at some point during your stay.

EL OBELISCO

The Obelisco, an off-white stake, pierces the sky where 9 de Julio intersects Avenida Corrientes. A major city landmark standing 67m (220ft) tall, this monument was erected in 1936 to commemorate the first foundation of Buenos Aires four centuries earlier. The Plaza de la República, a vast and busy plaza-style traffic island encircling the obelisk, is a favourite place for football supporters to celebrate victories. The plaza and the Obelisco have also been used for countless political demonstrations over the years.

OTHER LANDMARKS

In addition to the Teatro Colón (▷ 100), one of the most impressive buildings along 9 de Julio—mostly lined with fairly nondescript modern office blocks, topped by enormous advertising hoardings—is the neoclassical French embassy at the corner with Avenida Alvear. The building was due to be demolished to make way for the avenue itself but a petition from the French government saved it from destruction. Another landmark, on the opposite side of 9 de Julio, is the Prourban building, a distinctive postmodern white cylinder known by locals as El Rulero (Hair-curler), a skyscraper crowned by the logo of the telecoms firm Claro.

INFORMATION

✚ 65 F6 ✉ Avenida 9 de Julio
🚇 Avenida de Mayo (C), Constitución (C), Independencia (C/E), Moreno (C), San Juan (C), 9 de Julio (D), Carlos Pellegrini (B) 🚌 6, 7, 9, 10, 17, 23, 24, 26, 29, 45, 50, 70, 99, 109, 111, 142, 146, 155

TIPS

❯❯ As a pedestrian, always use the crossings with lights to cross 9 de Julio; it will take a couple of stages to get from one side to the other.
❯❯ Confusingly, the official street names change on either side of the avenue and to the north and south of Avenida Rivadavia: they are Cerrito, Carlos Pellegrini, Bernardo de Yrigoyen and Lima.
❯❯ Visit at night, when the floodlit Obelisco is a particularly impressive sight.

Above *Pedestrians crossing busy Avenida 9 de Julio*
Opposite *The Obelisco, a city landmark*

INFORMATION

www.avenidademayo.org.ar (in Spanish)
🕂 65 F7 ✉ Avenida de Mayo
🚇 Avenida de Mayo (A) 🚌 2, 4, 6, 50

TIPS

›› Demonstrators favour the Avenida because it links the presidential palace to parliament. It is best avoided during demonstrations.

›› Under the avenue runs the city's oldest *subte* line, Línea A, which opened in 1913. Some of the stations are historic monuments and Estación Perú has been refurbished to its original state. To visit the historic *subte* stations you will need to buy a ticket ($1.10), so you may as well take a ride and the old wooden trains are themselves an attraction.

›› The Palacio Barolo can only be visited by prior appointment (tel 011/5502-79035, www.pbarolo.com.ar).

›› Stop for a coffee at Café Tortoni (▷ 111), the city's best-known *confitería*, which has been serving refreshments to the famous and less famous for 150 years.

Above *The grandiose lobby of the 1923 Palacio Barolo building*

AVENIDA DE MAYO

An elegant thoroughfare linking Plaza de Mayo (▷ 88–89) to Plaza del Congreso, the broad tree-lined Avenida de Mayo is often likened to the Champs Elysées in Paris. Lined with some of the city's most emblematic edifices, its slightly faded grandeur fascinates visitors as they search for the famous Café Tortoni (▷ 111) or amble along the dozen blocks between the Casa Rosada (▷ 88–89) and the Palacio del Congreso Nacional (▷ 80). At street level, your gaze will, undoubtedly, be directed upwards, to the domes and ornate decorations that embellish the avenue's many art nouveau and art deco buildings.

LA PRENSA

Heading west along Avenida de Mayo, from Plaza de Mayo, you will at once stumble upon La Prensa. The building has a French-style neo-baroque exterior, topped by a bronze of Athena, which is visible only from across the avenue. One of the finest examples of beaux-arts architecture on the continent, it was completed in 1898 using materials and architects brought from Europe. It is the former headquarters of the once-influential *La Prensa* newspaper, founded in 1869 by José Paz, whose extravagant palace stands on Plaza San Martín (▷ 90). The building was famous for its loud siren, which sounded whenever a major event took place; it was first used when King Umberto I of Italy was assassinated in July 1900. *La Prensa* never recovered from Perón's restrictions of media expression. In 1988 the building was sold to the municipal authorities and transformed into the city's culture headquarters, Casa de la Cultura de Buenos Aires. The marvellous interior is open for visits (Mon–Fri 9–6, Sat 9–1; free) and special events, often focused on tango.

PALACIO BAROLO

West of Avenida 9 de Julio (▷ 68–69), one of the city's most curious silhouettes pokes into the sky. The exotically eclectic Palacio Barolo, a building conceived in homage to Dante's *Divine Comedy*, was completed in 1923 for Luis Barolo, a highly successful sheep farmer and woollens exporter, and used as offices. The lighthouse on the top brings the building's height to a total of 100m (328ft). There are fabulous panoramic views of the city from the top. Visits are by prior appointment (▷ Tips panel).

BASÍLICA DEL SANTÍSIMO SACRAMENTO

www.bue.gov.ar

The finest church in upmarket Retiro, the Basílica del Santísimo Sacramento, was completed in 1916. It is a monument to one lady, wealthy heiress and socialite Mercedes Castellanos de Anchorena, who lived in the nearby Palacio San Martín (▷ 90), and her melodramatic mausoleum lurks down in the crypt. Influenced by the Sacré-Coeur Basilica in Paris, Santísimo Sacramento was designed by French architects and built by master craftsmen from France, Belgium and Italy, with materials imported from Europe. The exterior is understated, despite the five svelte towers and great dome. Inside, the Italian marble, Moroccan onyx, Italian *majolica* tiles and French bronze form a grandiloquent yet harmonious mass of colour and detail. Try to attend an organ recital and enjoy the rich tone of the 1912 French instrument, which fills the basilica and demonstrates its fine acoustics.

🕇 65 G5 ✉ San Martín 1039, Retiro 🕐 Daily 9–6 👋 Free 🚇 San Martín (C) 🚌 10, 17, 60, 67, 92, 110

LA BOCA

▷ 72.

CATEDRAL ANGLICANA

www.catedralanglicana.com

The Catedral Anglicana de San Juan Bautista stands only two blocks to the north of the country's main Catholic church, the Catedral Metropolitana (▷ below). The cathedral is evidence of the important role played by the Anglo-Argentine community in national history and Sunday services (in English) have been celebrated here since the 1830s. The seat of the Anglican bishop, this 19th-century neoclassical church contains an altar decorated with wooden objects crafted by indigenous people from the Chaco, in the far north of Argentina.

🕇 65 G6 ✉ 25 de Mayo 282, downtown 🕐 Daily 9–6; Sunday service 9.30 in English, 11.15 in Spanish 👋 Free 🚇 Leandro Alem (B) 🚌 2, 4, 6, 50

CATEDRAL METROPOLITANA

The first colonial church built on the current site of Catedral Metropolitana was a humble structure of wood and mud brick. This first church, like the series of badly built successors, collapsed and following independence it was decided that Argentina should have a principal cathedral. Interrupted several times, the construction of a neoclassical cathedral, with its facade modelled

on the Palais Bourbon in Paris, was finally completed in 1863. The 12 sober columns, one for each Apostle, lend the cathedral the air of a Roman temple. In contrast, the sculpted bas-relief work in the pediments, the work of Frenchman Joseph Dubourdieu in the 1860s, portrays the reunion of Joseph with his father and eleven brothers. This Old Testament story is used as an allegory to describe national unity in the wake of civil war. The interior still contains some elements from the colonial era, most notably the Spanish rococo altarpiece dated 1785. Argentine visitors make a special pilgrimage to the mausoleum to visit the remains of independence hero General San Martín (▷ 29). French sculptor Albert Carrier-Belleuse designed the marble monument and the black sarcophagus is guarded by three female figures—allegories of Argentina, Chile and Peru, which were all liberated from the Spanish crown.

🕇 65 G7 ✉ San Martín 27, Plaza de Mayo, downtown ☎ 011/4331-2845 🕐 Mon–Fri 8–7, Sat–Sun 9–7.30; guided tours daily 👋 Free 🚇 Bolívar (E), Catedral (D), Plaza de Mayo (A) 🚌 4, 64, 130

COLONIA DEL SACRAMENTO

▷ 73.

Right *The Catedral Metropolitana*
Below *Basílica del Santísimo Sacramento*

INFORMATION

www.museoboquense.com

✚ Off map 65 F8 🛈 Pedro de Mendoza 1851 🕐 Fri–Sun 10–6 🚌 29, 53, 64, 152

TIPS

›› Be discreet, keep valuables out of sight, and do not go wandering off the main tourist trail, as this is one of the poorest parts of the city and muggings do occur.

›› Attending a soccer match here can be exhilarating but is not without danger; it is best to go with someone you can trust, such as a travel agency (▷ 113).

›› On hot days, avoid the Riachuelo because it can get very smelly.

Above *Street art at El Caminito, a once-derelict site transformed by artist Benito Quinquela Martín*

LA BOCA

Colourful little Boca, at the mouth of the Riachuelo brook, curls around the malodorous natural harbour of Vuelta de Rocha. One of the city's poorer southern *barrios*, it is synonymous with its world-famous football team, Boca Juniors. The team's home ground, Estadio Alberto J. Armando, built in 1940 and renovated 50 years later, is better known as La Bombonera (the Chocolate Box, ▷ 113). This nickname comes from its diminutive size—the capacity is a mere 49,000 seats—and its unusual steep-sided shape. A visit to the Museo de la Pasión Boquense at Brandsen 805 includes a stadium tour (tel 011/4362-1100; daily 10–6; $28–$40). Better still, attend a match but remember the fans' motto: 'La Bombonera does not tremble, it beats like a heart'.

EL CAMINITO AND MUSEO DE BELLAS ARTES DE LA BOCA

El Caminito, the Buenos Aires sight most seen on postcards, was a derelict railway siding until local artist Benito Quinquela Martín (1890–1977) turned it into a piece of open-air artwork using leftover tins of paints. Pairs of dancers regularly oblige the many visitors with displays of their talents and there are artworks for sale by local artists. Quinquela Martín's works are on permanent display in the Museo de Bellas Artes at Pedro de Mendoza 1835 (tel 011/4301-1080; Tue–Fri 10.30–5.30, Sat–Sun 11–5.30; free). His vigorous oils focus on the shipyards and factories of his home *barrio* and capture the shimmer of light on the murky waters of the Riachuelo.

FUNDACIÓN PROA

An Italianate mansion overlooking the Riachuelo houses one of the city's most vibrant creative spaces, the Fundación PROA. Always at the cutting edge of Argentine and world art, the PROA has undertaken all manner of exciting projects including illuminating the iconic transporter bridge across the Riachuelo at Pedro de Mendoza 1929 (tel 011/4104-1000; Tue–Sun 11–7; guided tours Tue–Fri, Sun 5pm, Sat 3pm; adult/child $3).

COLONIA DEL SACRAMENTO

A short boat trip away from Buenos Aires, the neighbouring country of Uruguay offers a number of possible excursions, not least to the colonial jewel of Colonia del Sacramento. Founded by the Portuguese in the late 17th century, Colonia has retained many of its original buildings, not least the imposing Iglesia Matriz, built in 1680 and the oldest church in Uruguay.

THE OLD TOWN

Barrio Histórico fills a tiny headland on the Río de la Plata. Just eight blocks long and five wide, it can be explored easily in a day. The nearby riverside beaches (the best is Playa Ferrando, within walking distance) make Colonia a great place to spend a couple of days getting away from it all, and there is some top-notch accommodation should you decide to overnight here.

One of the first Colonia sights you see, if you approach by water, is the white lighthouse El Faro, which can be climbed for fabulous views of the town (daily 12.30–6, open longer hours in Jan and Feb). The Old Town's two main squares are the Plaza de Armas, where the ruins of the Portuguese Governor's house are still visible, and the Plaza Mayor, a restful garden filled with palms and other subtropical trees.

MUSEUMS

A single ticket will get you into four of the Old Town's little museums (daily 11–4.45; UR$25) which, above all, give you a glimpse inside typical colonial houses. A stone's throw from each other, the museums collectively contain exhibits on the Portuguese colony and society in the Casa Nacarello, the mid-18th-century Spanish takeover and *azulejos* (glazed wall tiles introduced by the Portuguese).

Below Stucco houses in the Calle de los Suspiros

INFORMATION

✚ 347 L11   ℹ Flores and Rivera
☎ 598/522-6141   ◷ Mon–Fri 8–7, Sat–Sun 10–6   🎬 The main ferry company is Buquebus (tel 011/4316-6500; www.buquebus.com). Boats leave from Dársena Norte terminal at Avenida Antártida Argentina 821, in Retiro. The number of sailings varies from once to several times daily, depending on the season and day of week. Fast boats (catamarans) take just over one hour, slow boats take 2.5 hours. The return fare is around $200 but varies according to season and day of week (check with Buquebus for special offers). Book ahead, especially for sailings at weekends and in high season (Dec–Mar, Easter, weekend nearest to 9 Jul).

TIPS

➤ Although it is possible to take a day trip to Colonia from Buenos Aires, it's worth staying a night or two. There are plenty of sights to see and it is more relaxing.
➤ Remember when booking flights or ferries that Uruguay applies daylight saving from early October to mid-March, making it one hour ahead of Argentina.

Above and left *The Feria de Mataderos is a popular weekend event*

ESTACIÓN FERROVIARIA RETIRO

www.tebasa.com.ar

The city's major commuter railway station—a trio of termini—the Estación Retiro is also a national monument and regarded as one of the finest buildings of its kind in the world. Inaugurated in 1915, Retiro was designed by four British architects and engineers and its impressive steel skeleton was manufactured in Liverpool and re-assembled in situ. If you use the Mitre terminus, the one nearest Plaza San Martín, to get to Belgrano, San Isidro (▷ 97) or Tigre (▷ 101), take time to admire the French-style facade, with its harmonious colonnades and majestic cupola. The interior is opulently elegant also, with art nouveau English porcelain wall and ceiling tiles, and the station's coffeehouse, Café Retiro, has polished woodwork and gleaming chandeliers.

✚ 65 G4 ✉ Ramos Mejía 1358, Retiro
🚇 San Martín (C)

FERIA DE MATADEROS

www.feriademataderos.com.ar

Created in 1986, the lively Feria de las Artesanías y Tradiciones Populares Argentinas was intended to revive the long-neglected *criollo* culture in the capital and the market has been a resounding success. On most weekends throughout the year, a couple of streets, near one of the city's main livestock markets in the far-flung *barrio* of Mataderos, come alive with folk music and all manner of *gaucho* antics. Over 300 stalls sell everything from meat *empanadas* (pasties) and leather goods to books and *mate* paraphernalia. The *feria* is a great place to pick up a poncho or hunt for gifts to take home. The heady aroma of grilled steak invariably fills the air and the blood-curdling yodel of *chamamé* musicians incites visitors to dance. On the agenda, also, is the *chacarera*, a folk dance that involves lots of foot stamping and handkerchief waving, as well as other dances. The highlight of any visit, however, will be the displays of *gaucho* skills. These performances often include the dramatic *corrida de sortija*, in which traditionally garbed horsemen ride at full gallop towards a small ring, the size of a wedding band, hanging from a ribbon and attempt to pass a spearhead through it.

✚ Off map 64 C7 ✉ Lisandro de la Torre and Avenida de los Corrales, Mataderos ☎ 011/4687-5602 🕐 Dec–Feb Sat 11–sunset; Apr–Nov Sun 11–sunset. Closed Mar 🍴 Free 🚌 55, 80, 92, 126

JARDÍN BOTÁNICO CARLOS THAYS ▷ 75.

MANZANA FRANCISCANA

The Franciscan Order played a leading role in the city's history and was allocated this downtown *manzana* (block) when Juan de Garay laid out the city in 1580. Originally made of adobe, the buildings were replaced by stone in the 18th century. The existing complex is dominated by the eclectic Basílica de San Francisco and the neighbouring Capilla de San Roque, with its German-style neo-baroque facade. Both have been extensively remodelled and restored, mostly after anticlerical Peronists burned down the churches in 1955 to protest against military repression. The sober Convento de San Francisco, next door, has been open to the public since 2007. A number of interesting secular and religious artefacts are on display in its small museum, Museo Monseñor Bottaro, including a 'time capsule' buried in the basilica in 1908, containing newspaper clippings from that year.

✚ 65 G7 ✉ Defensa and Alsina, downtown ☎ 011/4331-0625 🕐 Basílica de San Francisco and Capilla de San Roque: Mon–Sat 9–5; Museo Monseñor Bottaro: daily 10–4 🍴 Basílica de San Francisco and Capilla de San Roque: adult/child $5; Museo Monseñor Bottaro: adult/child $7 🚇 Plaza de Mayo (A) 🚌 2, 4, 6, 50

JARDÍN BOTÁNICO CARLOS THAYS

Designed by the French botanist and landscape artist Charles Thays (1849–1934), the city's botanical garden was inaugurated at the end of the 19th century. Forming a tranquil 7ha (17-acre) triangle at the heart of busy Palermo, the garden is home to more than 5,000 species of trees and shrubs, including ceibos, tipas, oaks and ombúes. While Thays was director of the city parks, he lived with his family in the gardens in an English-style brick mansion, La Casona, which now houses administration offices and an information centre. One of the five magnificent glasshouses is a huge wrought-iron construction, which was highly acclaimed at the 1889 Exposition Universelle in Paris and shelters more than 2,000 tropical plants, many of them native to Argentina.

THEMES

A large section of the gardens are laid out by geographical theme, with areas set aside for each region of the country. Outstanding, also, are the Roman garden, with a grove of cypresses and laurels, the French garden and the Japanese garden with its gingkos and other Asian species. In addition to a vegetable garden, there is also a sensory garden (El Jardín de los Sentidos), designed for people with visual impairments.

MONUMENTS

Another highlight is the collection of sculptures, busts and other monuments, including a small bronze of Thays himself, located next to La Casona, and a statue of Mercury, overlooking the Roman garden. The centrepiece of the Italianate garden near the entrance is a circular lily pond, adorned with an enchanting statue of a nymph, *Ondina del Plata*, by Lucio Correa Morales.

INFORMATION

www.buenosaires.gov.ar/areas/med_ambiente/botanico

✚ 62 B3 ✉ Avenida Santa Fé 3951, Plaza Italia, Palermo ☎ 011/4831-4527 🕐 Sep–Apr daily 8–7; May–Aug 8–6; guided visits Fri 10.30am, Sat–Sun and hols 10.30am and 3pm. Tours in English and night tour (last Fri of month) by prior arrangement 🤚 Free Ⓜ Plaza Italia (D)

TIPS

» Ask at the information centre for a leaflet to go on a self-guided tour or consult the website for details of guided tours in English.

» Many of the trees and plants are labelled but *100 Trees of Argentina* by Eduardo Haene & Gustavo Aparicio (Albatros, 2008) is a helpful guide.

» Look out for the garden's large population of abandoned cats, tended by a dedicated group of volunteers.

Below *Sculptures and bronzes are found throughout the Jardín Botánico*

INTRODUCTION

Argentina is not known for its beaches, probably because neighbouring Brazil has whiter sands and warmer waters, but the string of ocean resorts along the coast of Buenos Aires Province offers plenty of seaside fun, including boat trips, surfing, a lively nightlife and top-rate seafood restaurants. Mar del Plata is one of the most popular Argentine seaside resorts. During January and February, Mardel (as the resort is also known), becomes almost unbearably crowded as Porteños escaping the capital and other Argentines settle down to enjoy three or four weeks' summer holiday. The capital's theatres also move down to the coast to entertain the holidaymakers, while Mirta Legrand, the legendary Argentine chat-show hostess, lunches live with her glamorous television guests in one of the city's best hotels.

The resorts along the coastline between Punta Rasa and Punta Mogotes are joined by the RP-11, known as the Interbalnearia (inter-beach road). Varied in tone and atmosphere, these include brash San Clemente del Tuyú, laidback Villa Gesell, tranquil Mar de las Pampas and cool Mar Azul. But the most exclusive resorts are Pinamar and Cariló, where stylish boutiques and expensive restaurants back the dune-fringed sandy beaches.

WHAT TO SEE

PLAYA BRISTOL AND THE RAMBLA CASINO

The sweeping bay below the centre of Mar del Plata is where you'll find the city's most popular beach, the broad sands of Playa Bristol, with its mosaic of parasols

INFORMATION

✚ 351 L14 ℹ Boulevard Marítimo P. Peralta Ramos 2270 (Edifico Casino) ☎ 0223/495-1777 ◷ Mon–Sat 8–8, Sun 10–5 🚌 Long-distance bus from Retiro 🚆 Trains from Buenos Aires

Above *Fishing boats in the popular resort of Mar del Plata*

and beach towels in the height of summer. This, together with the smaller Playa Popular, just to the north, is where the crowds gather. Looming in the backdrop are the distinctive silhouettes of the Rambla Casino's grandiose buildings, including the casino itself and the Hotel Provincial, which houses a theatre and tourist information centre, on the Avenida Colón.

At the top of the huge staircase, leading down to the strand, are two great stone sea lions, one of Mar del Plata's best-known sights. As you follow the *rambla* (seafront promenade) to the south, you reach Punta Piedras, topped by the Torreón del Monje, a Gaudiesque building built in 1904. Inside, there is a café where you can enjoy great views over the bay.

LOMA STELLA MARIS
The smart residential neighbourhood immediately south of the city centre, Loma Stella Maris lies on a *loma* (hill) at the end of the main thoroughfare, Avenida Colón. On either side of this avenue are two of the city's main museums, which are great for a rainy day. The Museo del Mar (Colón 1114; www.museodelmar. org; daily 10–9; $8) has an aquarium with Patagonian sharks and other fish. One of the highlights of the aquarium is its world-class collection of more than 30,000 shells from around the globe.

Opposite the aquarium is the Museo Municipal de Arte at Colón 1189 (Mon, Wed–Fri 2–8, Sat–Sun 1–7; $2), which is housed in the beautiful art nouveau interior of the Villa Ortiz Basualdo. The gallery is dedicated to local painter Juan Carlos Castignano (1908–72) and many of his handsome artworks of Mar del Plata are on display here, along with contemporary works by other Argentine artists.

CENTRO CULTURAL VICTORIA OCAMPO
Leafy Divino Rostro is another attractive *barrio*, a short way west of Loma Stella Maris and worth a visit to see the Centro Cultural Victoria Ocampo. Writer and socialite Victoria Ocampo, whose main residence is in San Isidro (▷ 97), inherited this English-style wooden house from her great-aunt and had it shipped to Argentina in 1911. She bequeathed it to UNESCO but the city authorities bought it in the 1980s and restored it to its former glory, giving visitors the unique opportunity to see how the monied classes lived in Mar del Plata a century ago.
✉ Matheu 1851 ☎ 0223/492-0569 🕐 Wed–Mon 12–6; guided tours regularly from 2.30pm
✋ Adult/child $3

MORE TO SEE
PINAMAR
www.pinamar.gov.ar
In the 1930s, a pine grove was planted among the sand dunes, some 350km (210 miles) southeast of Buenos Aires, and the resort of Pinamar has not stopped growing since. Favoured by the country's political elite, it has an urbane feel, enhanced by the high-rise hotels and smart villas. As the resort has grown it has swallowed up smaller ones to the south, such as Ostende and Valeria del Mar, which are quieter and more chic. Pinamar's main drag, Avenida Bunge, is where you'll find restaurants and trendy boutiques. The main activity on the beach, apart from lounging, is sandboarding on the giant dunes.
✚ 351 L13

CARILÓ
www.cariloweb.com
Immediately south of Pinamar is the chic resort of Cariló, with its pine-backed dunes. In addition to some excellent hotels and superb restaurants, you can find some top-class shopping in a variety of smart malls and arcades, including the picturesque Paseo Epuyén and the quaint Feria del Bosque.

>> To escape the summer crowds, visit Mar del Plata in the early or late summer. During the week is especially pleasant.
>> Always book accommodation ahead of time, to avoid disappointment.
>> The better beaches are to the north of the city, past the Playa La Perla.
>> If you seek peace and quiet, choose one of the more select resorts, such as Cariló.
>> Head for the fishing harbour and its colourful boats in Mar del Plata, if you want to escape the crowds and enjoy a more authentic experience.
>> Save the trio of excellent museums for bad weather, which can happen even in summer.

Below *Sea lions basking in the sun*

MUSEO DE ARTE HISPANOAMERICANO ISAAC FERNÁNDEZ BLANCO

INFORMATION

www.museofernandezblanco.
buenosaires.gob.ar

✚ 65 F4 ✉ Suipacha 1422
☎ 011/4327-0228 🌐 Tue–Fri 2–7, Sat–
Sun and public holidays 11–7 ♿ Adult/
child $1 🚇 San Martín (C) 🚌 10, 17, 45,
56, 59, 67, 70, 86, 91, 100, 105

INTRODUCTION

The Museo de Arte Hispanoamericano Isaac Fernández Blanco is one of the best museums in the city and contains a remarkable collection of Spanish-American art. Several private holdings of colonial art, including the Noel brothers' own incredible collection, were merged to form today's museum. The museum took its name from a patrician engineer, Isaac Fernández Blanco, who inherited a fortune in his thirties and started collecting artworks from all over the continent. When Fernández died in 1928, he left his remarkable art collection to the city.

Displayed in beautifully lit cases, most of the works date from the 17th and early 18th centuries and were produced in colonial Peru and Alto Peru, at a time when it was forbidden for craftsmen to work anywhere except Spanish America. The exhibition is divided by themes such as colonization, conquest of the Andes, Jesuit and indigenous cultures, and the Orient.

WHAT TO SEE

THE BUILDING

The museum is housed in the fabulous Palacio Noel, a neo-colonial house on the edge of Retiro, built in the 1920s by architect Martín Noel, who donated it to the city in 1936. Noel wanted to break away from imitation Parisian palaces, such as Palacio San Martín and Palacio Paz (▷ 90), and based his designs on the 18th-century baroque architecture of the Peruvian capital, Lima. The simple white walls, sombre bow windows with intricate window grilles and typically Peruvian balconies make it the ideal home for the artefacts on display inside.

The building suffered damage when a terrorist bomb destroyed the nearby Israeli embassy in 1992 but, following years of careful restoration, the building now appears almost unscathed.

Above *The neo-colonial Palacio Noel, built in the 1920s but inspired by 18th-century baroque architecture in Lima, Peru*

GROUND FLOOR GALLERIES

On your right, as you enter the museum, is an amazingly ornate 18th-century silver sacrarium or tabernacle adorned with a portrait of Christ on a copper plaque, plus its matching *arco* (a silver arch that would have been placed over it). Master silversmiths in La Paz crafted both items in the early 18th century. Look out, too, for a colonial Brazilian silver votive lamp, polychrome furniture made by Bolivian craftsmen and, on the walls, a fine set of Guaraní statues, carved from native wood at the Jesuit missions in the northeast of Argentina. There are also a number of paintings from the famous Escuela Cusqueña (Cusco School) based in the Peruvian city of Cusco. Mainly dating from the 18th century, these handsome oil paintings depict religious subjects by combining traditional Catholic imagery with indigenous motifs. Two noteworthy examples are the anonymous *Virgin of Mercy Crowned by the Holy Trinity* and *Mary Magdalene* by Antonio Bermejo.

UPSTAIRS GALLERIES

Upstairs, you are presented with a case piled high with dozens of beautiful dolls collected from all over Latin America. The theme switches from the dominance of Peru and Alto Peru to the newfound confidence of Buenos Aires, as a major imperial port. A series of rooms illustrates these themes with informative panels, sound effects and well-lit displays of furniture, paintings and silverwork. One of the displays shows how the silversmiths of Potosí (in present-day Bolivia) continued to dominate the trade, even when porcelain and tortoiseshell items from Asia became fashionable. Other themes are the craftsmen of Quito (now the capital of Ecuador) and the cult of the Virgin Mary and its impact on cultural life. A large exhibition of clothing and paintings depicts how Buenos Aires rivalled Lima following the creation of the Vice-Royalty of the River Plate in 1776.

TIPS

» Don't miss the basement, with its interesting exhibits of silverware, clothing and a reconstructed colonial kitchen. There is also a space used for temporary exhibitions.

» The garden, with its palm fronds and bushy shrubs, is a wonderfully relaxing place to enjoy a few moments of peace and quiet.

» Find out about the occasional classical concerts held inside the house; these are usually advertised at the museum entrance.

Below right *Head to the museum's relaxing garden to enjoy some peaceful solitude*
Below *The museum's collection includes ornate 17th- and 18th-century colonial silverware*

Above *The 17th-century Jesuit church of San Ignacio, Manzana de las Luces*

MANZANA DE LAS LUCES

www.manzanadelasluces.gov.ar
The historic Manzana de las Luces (Block of Enlightenment) began life in the 17th century as the Jesuit headquarters, but the Society of Jesus was expelled from the Spanish colonies by regal order in 1767. The block, which is bounded by calles Alsina, Bolívar, Moreno and Perú, can be visited on guided tours in Spanish (some English commentary), and is worth seeing for a glimpse of early colonial Buenos Aires. The Manzana's patios and chamber, which used to host the provincial parliament, are now used for regular concerts and other performances.

Within the Manzana lie a number of educational institutions, including the Colegio Nacional (CNBA), Argentina's most prestigious college (tel 011/4331-1290; www.cnba.uba.ar; guided visits only, book at least one week in advance). The school's current building, begun in 1910 but not inaugurated until 1938, was built in a sober French academic style, with a distinctive mansard roof. The pièce de résistance, the Aula Magna, was inspired by the Opéra Garnier in Paris and is where students receive their graduation diplomas, customarily from the Argentine President.

At the corner of Alsina and Bolívar, San Ignacio, built by the Jesuits in 1675, is the city's oldest church. The interior is unassuming, with the exception of a baroque altar and icon, both contemporary to the church's original construction.
🚇 65 G7 ✉ Perú 272, downtown ☎ 011/4343-3260 🕐 Manzana de las Luces: guided tours Mon–Fri 3, Sat–Sun 3, 4.30 and 6. Check beforehand.
💵 Adult/child $5 🚇 Bolívar (E), Catedral (D), Perú (A)

MUSEO DE ARTE ESPAÑOL ENRIQUE LARRETA

www.museolarreta.buenosaires.gob.ar
Sedate Belgrano is a residential *barrio* immediately to the north of Palermo, with a handful of excellent hotels and restaurants. Near Plaza Belgrano, the main square, you can visit a superb Andalucian mansion built at the beginning of the 20th century for effete Uruguayan aristocrat Enrique Larreta and his wife, Josefina Anchorena. When Larreta died in 1961, the *hacienda* and its opulent contents were bequeathed to the city, which turned it into a museum of Spanish Art. While living in Spain from 1900 to 1916, Larreta amassed sumptuous paintings and furniture, plus a shipload of silverware and porcelain, and most of his collection is on display in these fantastically ornate surroundings. The Andalucian-style garden, which can be visited separately, is a marvellous retreat. A huge ombú growing here provides welcome shade under its leafy branches, and blue-flowered agapanthus and shiny leaved magnolia proliferate.
🚇 Off map 62 A2 ✉ Juramento 2291, Belgrano ☎ 011/4784-4040 🕐 Mon, Wed–Fri 3–8, Sat–Sun 10–1, 3–8; guided visits Sun 4 and 6 💵 Museum: $3 (free on Thu); garden: free 🚇 Juramento (D)

MUSEO DE ARTE HISPANOAMERICANO ISAAC FERNÁNDEZ BLANCO
▷ 78–79.

MUSEO DE ARTE LATINOAMERICANO DE BUENOS AIRES (MALBA)
▷ 81.

MUSEO DE LA CIUDAD

www.museodelaciudad.buenosaires.gob.ar
Wedged between the Manzana Franciscana (▷ 74) and the Manzana de las Luces (▷ left), the city museum occupies a wonderful double town house, known as the Casa de los Querubines (House of the Cherubim). The house was built in 1894 for the owner of Farmacia de la Estrella at Defensa 201 — one of the oldest buildings in the city and also worth a visit for its gorgeous interior (Mon–Fri 8–8, Sat 8–1). The museum stages regular exhibitions about the city, while its eclectic collection includes a wide range of objects, ranging from old postcards and photographs to examples of *fileteado* (a colourful form of stylized decoration), vintage toys and items of furniture.
🚇 65 G7 ✉ Defensa 219, downtown ☎ 011/4331-9855 🕐 Daily 11–7 💵 Adult/child $1. Free Mon and Wed 🚇 Plaza de Mayo (A) 🚌 2, 4, 6, 50

PALACIO DEL CONGRESO NACIONAL

www.congreso.gov.ar
Argentina's national parliament building, the Palacio del Congreso Nacional, looms over the Plaza del Congreso at the western extremity of the Avenida de Mayo (▷ 70). Palatial in name and stature, the edifice is topped by a distinctive Greco-Roman cupola, 80m (262ft) in height. The architect, Italian engineer Vittorio Meano, began building in 1897 but was murdered in 1904, two years before completion. The interior can be visited on guided tours when Congress is in recess. One of the highlights is a two-tonne chandelier, with figures representing the Argentine nation and all its provinces.
🚇 64 E7 ✉ Hipólito Yrigoyen 1846, downtown ☎ 011/6310-7222 🕐 Mon–Fri 8–7, Sat–Sun 9–7.30; guided tours (in English) Mon, Tue, Thu and Fri 11 and 4 💵 Free 🚇 Congreso (A) 🚌 2, 4, 6, 50

MUSEO DE ARTE LATINOAMERICANO DE BUENOS AIRES (MALBA)

Ensconced in its showpiece building in the *barrio* of Palermo, the stunning Museum of Latin American Art (MALBA) has consistently attracted crowds to its refined permanent collection and excellent temporary exhibitions since it opened its doors in 2001. MALBA's core exhibition is the world-class Costantini Collection, representing nearly 80 modern and contemporary artists from across the continent. Multi-millionaire businessman and art collector Eduardo Costantini donated his private collection of artworks to the museum as part of a non-profit foundation intended to promote Latin American art and give the city the public modern art gallery it deserved.

PERMANENT COLLECTION

Every modern artistic movement and just about every Latin American country from Argentina to Venezuela are represented in the 200-piece permanent collection. Highlights from the 1930s and '40s are Joaquín Torres-García's monochrome *Composition symétrique universelle en blanc et noir (Universal symmetric composition in black and white*, 1931), Emiliano di Cavalcanti's colourful *Mulheres com frutas (Women with fruits*, 1932), Frida Kahlo's *Autorretrato con chango y loro (Self-portrait with monkey and parrot*, 1942) and Wilfredo Lam's *La mañana verde (The green morning*, 1943). Works by contemporary creators, such as Guillermo Kuitca's *Siete últimas canciones (Seven last songs*, 1987) and José Bedia's *Recuerdos de aquel viaje (Memories of that journey*, 1996), bring the collection up to date.

TEMPORARY SHOWS

Temporary shows are dedicated to individual artists and over the years have included non-Latin American artists, such as Andy Warhol (1928–87) and Roy Lichtenstein (1923–97), plus Argentines such as Xul Solar (1887–1963) and León Ferrari (b.1920). Other exhibitions are thematic and range from video-sculpture to contemporary fashion.

THE BUILDING

Three brilliant architects from Córdoba—Gastón Atelman, Martín Fourcade and Alfredo Tapia—won the competition to build the MALBA and their masterpiece is regarded as one of the best modern buildings in the city. Clean lines, huge plate-glass windows and efficient use of space are just three of the features of this architectural gem. An integral part of the MALBA is an outstanding shop called Tienda Malba, which sells art books, catalogues and designer objects, including fabulous jewellery. There is a dynamic cinema also, malba.cine, which screens arthouse films and films related to modern art.

INFORMATION

www.malba.org.ar

✚ 63 D2 ✉ Avenida Presidente Figueroa Alcorta 3415 ☎ 011/4808-6500 ⏲ Thu–Mon 12–8, Wed 12–9; guided tours Wed and Sun 4pm (in Spanish; call ahead for an English-speaking guide) ✋ Adult \$20, child (under 5) free, reduced-price entry Wed \$8 🚌 67, 102, 130 ♿ ☕

TIPS

» The museum is open later and the admission price is much lower on Wednesdays.

» Check the website for news of exhibitions and films being shown at the on-site cinema.

» Stop for refreshments at the gallery's French-style Café des Arts (tel 011/4808-0754; daily 9–midnight), which has indoor seating and a fine terrace.

Below *MALBA's galleries are light, airy and spacious*

INFORMATION

www.mnba.org.ar

✚ 62 E3 ✉ Avenida del Libertador 1473, Recoleta ☎ 011/5288-9900 🕐 Tue–Fri 12.30–7.30, Sat–Sun 9.30–7.30 👤 Free 🚌 17, 62, 93, 130

INTRODUCTION

The Museo Nacional de Bellas Artes is Argentina's most important fine art museum, with an impressive array of Argentine, Latin American and international paintings and sculptures. Housed in a rust-red neoclassical building along the Avenida del Libertador, its permanent collection comprises mostly 19th- and 20th-century artworks, many by European artists or by Argentines whose Old World influences are plain to see. The museum's collection includes 12,000 items, but only a tenth or so is on display at any given time. As a result, the collection always feels fresh, while major artworks are nearly always on view.

WHAT TO SEE

GROUND-FLOOR GALLERIES

The ground floor is mostly European artworks, including the Hirsch bequest, left to the state by wealthy landowners and art collectors, which includes a fabulous anonymous retable from Spain and portraits by Hals and Rembrandt. You can admire paintings by El Greco, Zurbarán and Rubens while the French Impressionists—Degas, Monet, Toulouse-Lautrec and Renoir—are all well represented. As you would expect in a city where French art is so highly prized, there is an impressive collection of Rodin sculptures; one of them, *Study of Hands for the Secret* is back in the museum having disappeared a few years ago, only to be found by a refuse collector. One curiosity is the inclusion of work by Argentine-born Lucio Fontana in the international room. Originally from Rosario, Fontana settled in Italy, which may explain why his paintings are not upstairs with his compatriots.

Above *Behind the museum's neoclassical facade lies a collection of 19th- and 20th-century artworks*

FIRST FLOOR

As you climb the staircase to the upper floor, you can see three works by contrasting Argentine artists: a classical bronze torso by Rogelio Yrurtia, Antonio Berni's moving *Juanito Laguna aprende a leer* (*Juanito Laguna learns to read*, 1961) and Antonio Seguí's *Autorretrato de las vocaciones frustradas* (*Self-portrait of frustrated vocations*, 1963).

In the first room, there is a wonderful collection of fine pre-Columbian objects including terracotta, textiles and a fabulous bronze disc carved with a stylized face and snakes. This is followed by a set of Mexican wooden panels inlaid with mother-of-pearl, showing scenes of the Spanish conquest of the Americas.

Early Argentine art is displayed in the next two rooms, with paintings by Scot Richard Adams and the great master Prilidiano Pueyrredón representing the embryonic Argentine school from 1851. The following three rooms are divided into sections by panels and include paintings of *gaucho* life and typical Buenos Aires scenes, by Cesáreo Bernaldo de Quirós and Ernesto de la Cárcova, as well as a number of European-style artworks by Eduardo Sívori (▷ 86).

MODERN ARGENTINE WORKS

Two great Argentine artists that made their mark in the first half of the 20th century, Fernando Fader and Benito Quinquela Martín (▷ 72), both have artworks on display here, too. Fernando Fader was born in Bordeaux but managed to forge a truly *criollo* style with his paintings of idyllic scenes of the Argentine countryside. Benito Quinquela Martín's paintings show the shimmering light on the Riachuelo, with backdrops of industry and harbour life.

The last and largest room in the museum traces the history of Argentine art from the early 20th century to the present day. Outstanding names are Xul Solar (▷ 93), Raquel Forner, Libero Badii and Nicolás García Uriburu, each of whom represents a different period and have wildly varying styles. Don't miss Fermín Eguía's intriguing surreal work *Pintura* (*Painting*, 1974), which shows a hen with a woman's head and a fork stuck in its back standing on a table laid for a meal. For something more peaceful, have a look at Raúl Soldi's *La hamaca* (*The rocking chair*, 1933) in which a young woman rests in a chair as horses gallop across the pampas in the background.

TIPS

▷▷ The museum is free of charge, so you could plan more than one visit—perhaps one to see the European art on the ground floor and another to see the Argentine works upstairs.

▷▷ Don't bother with the audioguide, which is available in Spanish and English; it whizzes you round in an hour but isn't very informative.

▷▷ The second floor is used for temporary exhibitions, often of photography, as are rooms 16 and 17 and the extension at the back. These collections are often worth seeing and are free.

Below Puerto de Buenos Aires in 1834 *by Richard Adams*

INFORMATION

www.palermonline.com.ar/turismo
⊞ 62 B4 🚇 Bulnes (D), Ministro Carranza (D), Plaza Italia (D), Palermo (D), Scalabrini Ortiz (D)

INTRODUCTION

A reminder of the city's strong Italian heritage, Palermo, the biggest and greenest of the city's *barrios*, is named after a Franciscan monastery dedicated to San Benito, the patron saint of Palermo in Italy. According to local myth, however, the *barrio* is named after a 16th-century Sicilian settler, Giovanni Domenico Palermo, who founded a farm on drained marshes to the north of Buenos Aires. Like Recoleta immediately to its south, Palermo became fashionable when the middle classes settled here from San Telmo, following an epidemic of yellow fever in the 1870s. Immigrants from across Europe made it their home in the early 20th century—the Polish and Armenian communities are still among the biggest. Once the vast parklands had been laid out by landscape architect Charles Thays, the *barrio* became even more desirable, although the neighbourhood's central section, Palermo Viejo (Old Palermo), retained a less savoury reputation until the late 20th century, when gentrification began in earnest. Palermo is inextricably linked to one of the country's greatest writers, Jorge Luis Borges (1899–1986), who spent much of his childhood in the *barrio*, while Julio Cortázar (1914–84), another great man of letters, is honoured with a plaza named after him.

Palermo makes a great base for visiting the city sights, many of which lie within its boundaries, and you can choose from a host of trendy hotels occupying carefully renovated houses in mostly low-rise Palermo Viejo. A chequerboard of cobbled streets and airy plazas, this heartland is also home to myriad boutiques, a raft of bars and some of the city's best restaurants. The *barrio's* huge park to the east, the Parque 3 de Febrero, is part of the green belt known as the Bosques de Palermo, where you can visit the city's planetarium or rent rowing boats. In addition to seeing modern Latin American art at MALBA (▷ 81), you might like to investigate more traditional Argentine painting at the Museo Sívori, traditional crafts at the Museo de Arte Decorativo or intriguing memorabilia at the Museo Evita, dedicated to the legendary First Lady.

Moreover, the city's zoo, botanical gardens and Japanese garden are the perfect places to while away a few hours. Alternatively, you could wander around Barrio Parque, a compact knot of elegant streets and exclusive residences. Shopping opportunities are plentiful throughout the *barrio*, whether in the quirky shops of Palermo Viejo or in the more conventional stores along busy Avenida Santa Fé, which leads to Alto Palermo, with its shiny shopping mall.

Above *Plaza Serrano in picturesque Palermo Viejo*

WHAT TO SEE
BOSQUES DE PALERMO
The Bosques de Palermo stretch towards the Río de la Plata and Aeroparque Jorge Newbery and take up the whole of the northeastern third of Palermo. The Hipódromo Argentino (the national racecourse), polo fields, tennis courts and a beautiful rose garden are all located within this enormous expanse of green. At its core, and covering almost 5sq km (2sq miles), is the landscaped Parque 3 de Febrero, with its lawns and sweeping paths, which throng with footballers, joggers and inline skaters, especially on weekends. The lakeside is a great place for a picnic and popular with families on Sundays and public holidays. At the eastern edge of the park is the futuristic hemisphere of Planetario Galileo Galilei (▷ 114), a fun place for astronomy fans of all ages. At the entrance, is a disturbingly gigantic meteorite found in the Chaco in the 1960s.

✚ 62 B1 ✉ Avenida del Libertador Ⓜ Plaza Italia

MUSEO NACIONAL DE ARTE DECORATIVO (MNAD)
www.mnad.org.ar
When a member of the highly influential Errázuriz family from Chile married the daughter of the breathtakingly rich Alvears, the result could only be impressive. Matías Errázuriz Ortúzar and his wife spent the early years of their marriage in Paris, where he was a diplomat, and amassed a magnificent collection of European furniture and artworks. On their return to Buenos Aires in 1916, the couple needed a house large enough and stylish enough to show off their spoils. French architect René Sergent (1865–1927), who designed many patrician homes in the Argentine capital, obliged with a fabulous mansion, the Palacio Errázuriz. The house was built using European materials and was inaugurated in 1918 with a society ball. Pianist Arthur Rubinstein and ballerina Anna Pavlova are just two of the great artists who once performed in the Grand Hall, the venue of some of the most exclusive events ever held in the city, before or since. Later the family fell on hard times and sold their mansion to the state and it was turned into the Museo Nacional de Arte Decorativo (MNAD). The occasional classical concert and an annual carol service are held here, but the real reason for any visit is to see the museum's varied collection of European cabinets and oils, silverware and tapestries. El Greco and Fragonard are just two of the great painters whose works are on display in these sumptuous surroundings.

✚ 63 D3 ✉ Avenida del Libertador 1902 ☎ 011/4801-8248 🕐 Mar–Dec Tue–Sun 2–7; Jan–Feb Tue–Sat 2–7; guided visits in English Tue–Sat 2.30, in Spanish Tue, Thu, Sat 4.30, Sun 2.30, 4.30, in French Tue 2.30 ✋ Adult/child $5; free Tue; guided visits $15 🚌 10, 59, 60, 67, 130 🍴 ☕

MUSEO EVITA
http://museoevita.org
Whether you want to find out more about Argentina's most famous First Lady, Eva Perón, complete your pilgrimage tour of the city or, perhaps, are already an ardent fan, don't miss the excellent Museo Evita. The museum is housed in an early 20th-century town house, with a facade inspired by the Spanish Renaissance, and was home to Evita's own Social Aid Foundation in the 1940s. Inside, historic footage of her political rallies, photographs, and clothes and shoes from her chic wardrobe tell Evita's rags-to-riches story in intriguing detail.

✚ 62 B3 ✉ Lafinur 2988 ☎ 011/4807-0306 🕐 Tue–Sun 11–7 (last admission 6.30); guided tours (in Spanish, English, Portuguese and French) Tue–Sun can be booked by telephone or e-mail 🖐 Adult/child $15; tours extra $10 Ⓜ Plaza Italia/Scalabrini Ortiz (D) 🍴 ☕

PALERMO VIEJO
The enticingly picturesque epicentre of Palermo, known as Palermo Viejo, is subdivided into Palermo Soho, to the southeast of the main railway track, and Palermo Hollywood, to the northwest. Both areas are packed with boutique

TIPS
➤➤ The Museo Evita, the MNAD and the Jardín Japonés each have an excellent tea room and restaurant, with Argentine, French and Japanese cuisines available, respectively.
➤➤ Contrasting social conditions and Palermo's popularity with tourists mean that petty theft and even muggings are not unknown, so stay within sight of passers-by, especially in the big parks, at dusk and at night.
➤➤ Parts of the *barrio*, especially near the junction of Avenida Santa Fé and Humboldt, are prone to flooding after heavy rain.
➤➤ At the main gates of the zoo, drivers of traditional *mateos* (horse carriages) untiringly vie for custom. Agree on a price before setting out on a ride.

Below *Joggers at Parque 3 de Febrero, at the heart of the Bosques de Palermo*

hotels and fashion boutiques, cafés and bars, glamorous restaurants and neighbourhood *parrillas*, where you can stop to sample freshly grilled Argentine beef. The subtle difference is that Palermo Soho (named after the New York neighbourhood) is a little more bohemian, more traditional and more discreet, while Palermo Hollywood, named for its TV and cinema connections, is more glitzy and trendy. Its northernmost tip, near Avenida Dorrego, has accumulated so many hip salad bars it is now known as Palermo Rúcula (rocket or arugula).

➕ 62 A4 🚇 Palermo/Plaza Italia (D) 🚌 39, 55, 60, 64, 67, 93, 152

MORE TO SEE
BARRIO PARQUE
Laid out by Charles Thays in 1912, this microcosm of Palermo high life is a maze of curvaceous streets. A stroll through this miniature *barrio*, with Calle Ombú at its hub, lets you ogle at some of the most original and unashamedly opulent houses in the city.

➕ 63 D3 ✉ Avenida del Libertador and Ortiz de Ocampo, Palermo 🚌 10, 59, 60, 67, 130

JARDÍN JAPONÉS
www.jardinjapones.org.ar

A cameo of Japan in the midst of Palermo, the peaceful Jardín Japonés is beautifully landscaped with gnarled bonsais and colourful azaleas growing around a lake filled with coy carp and crossed by a red footbridge. There is an active cultural centre with a fine restaurant attached.

➕ 62 C2 ✉ Avenida Figueroa Alcorta and Avenida Casares ☎ 011/4804-4922 🕐 Daily 10–6 ✋ Adult/child Mon, Wed–Fri $3; Sat–Sun and national holidays $4; free on Tue; free guided tours daily at 3pm (call ahead) 🚇 Scalabrini Ortiz (D) 🚌 10, 15, 37, 59, 60, 67, 93, 95, 102, 108, 118, 128, 130, 141, 160, 188 🍴 ▣

JARDÍN ZOOLÓGICO
www.zoobuenosaires.com.ar

Alpacas from northern Argentina, zebras from Africa and all kinds of creatures from around the world live in the city's historic zoo. There are architectural wonders to admire, too, including ornate temples, a pagoda and a state-of-the-art aquarium.

➕ 62 B3 ✉ Plaza Italia, Palermo ☎ 011/4011-9900 🕐 Daily 10–6 ✋ Adult $18, child (under 13) free; passport to all the zoo's attractions, including aquarium $27, otherwise each attraction $7.50 🚇 Plaza Italia (D) 🚌 10, 12, 15, 21, 29, 34, 39, 41, 57, 59, 60, 64, 67, 68, 93, 95, 111, 118, 128, 141, 152, 160, 161, 188, 194

MONUMENTO DE LOS ESPAÑOLES
Gifted by Spain to mark Argentina's centenary in 1910 (but not inaugurated until 1927), this dazzling confection of marble and bronze dominates one of the *barrio*'s busiest intersections.

➕ 62 B2 ✉ Avenida Sarmiento and Avenida del Libertador 🚇 Plaza Italia (D) 🚌 10, 15, 37, 59, 60, 67, 93, 95, 102, 108, 118, 128, 130, 141, 160, 188

MUSEO DE ARTES PLÁSTICAS EDUARDO SÍVORI
www.museosivori.org.ar

Near the rose garden in the Parque 3 de Febrero, the Museo de Artes Plásticas Eduardo Sívori displays only a fraction of its huge treasure of Argentine paintings and sculptures at any given time, including the handsome landscape *Pampa* (1902), by Sívori (1847–1918).

➕ 62 B1 ✉ Avenida Infanta Isabel 555 ☎ 011/4778-3899 🕐 Tue–Fri 12–8, Sat–Sun 10–8 ✋ Adult/child $3; free on Wed 🚇 Plaza Italia (D)

Left *Jardín Japonés in Parque 3 de Febrero, a peaceful place to escape the bustle of city life*
Opposite *The buildings in Barrio Parque are some of the most opulent in the city*

INFORMATION

✚ 65 G7 ✉ Plaza de Mayo, downtown
Ⓜ Bolívar (E), Catedral (D), Perú (A),
Plaza de Mayo (A) 🚌 2, 4, 6, 50, 93, 99

INTRODUCTION

A busy square at the far eastern end of the Avenida de Mayo, the Plaza de Mayo was named after the 1810 May Revolution, which ushered in Argentine independence. With a few isolated palms, the dusky-pink Casa Rosada, the presidential palace, overlooks this large open oblong on its eastern flank. Built on the site of Juan de Garay's colonial Plaza de Armas, the plaza took its present shape in the early 20th century, when city mayor Torcuato de Alvear demolished the neoclassical colonnade that surrounded it. The whitewashed facade of the Cabildo, the colonial government house opposite Casa Rosada, is all that remains today.

Over the decades, the plaza has been the scene of political demonstrations and protests, some of them violent and bloody. One of the worst was on 16 June 1955, when the armed forces bombed an anti-church protest by Peronists, demonstrating against moves by the Catholic hierarchy to stop Evita from being canonized. In April 1982, huge crowds gathered to support the Argentine invasion of Las Malvinas (Falklands Islands), and from 1977 to 2006 the Mothers of the Plaza de Mayo regularly marched around the square, wearing their trademark white headscarves, to draw attention to the thousands of people who disappeared during the Dirty War of the mid-1970s and early 1980s (▷ 40). The women ended their resistance marches in recognition of the more progressive policies of the Kirchner administration, but continue to gather here every Thursday to publicize other social causes.

WHAT TO SEE

CASA ROSADA

www.casarosada.gov.ar

The Casa Rosada is officially called the Casa de Gobierno (Government House), but everyone refers to it by its colour, which is the most interesting feature of its physical appearance. The building itself, the result of much reworking in the late 19th century, is Italianate neoclassical in style, complete with loggias. The distinctive hue, the result of adding ox blood to whitewash, was extremely

Above *The Casa Rosada, the presidential palace, on Plaza de Mayo*

popular in colonial Argentina. President Menem had it painted shocking pink but, since restoration work in 2007, it has become a more subdued pinkish-beige colour. Its balcony was used by Evita to address massive crowds in her famous 1951 speech, when she announced her decision not to run for the Vice-Presidency, and by President Galtieri, during the South Atlantic conflict. Menem, controversially, allowed Madonna to sing *Don't Cry for Me, Argentina* from the balcony for the 1996 Alan Parker film *Evita*.

✉ Hipólito Yrigoyen 219 ☎ 011/4344-3804 🕐 Mon–Fri 10–6, Sun 2–6 👋 Free

CABILDO

Cabildo was the name given to the seats of Spanish colonial councils. The Cabildo of Buenos Aires was built sporadically during the 18th century but much of it was demolished in the 19th century to make way for wider streets, including Avenida de Mayo. Architect Mario Buschiazzo remodelled the exterior in the 1940s, in an attempt to make it look as it had in colonial times, with red roof tiles and whitewashed walls. Dwarfed by surrounding buildings and discreet compared with the Casa Rosada and Catedral Metropolitana (▷ 71), the Cabildo is often overlooked. It is, however, worth a look inside for its beautifully preserved interior and handsome patio. The Museo Nacional del Cabildo y de la Revolución de Mayo contains a small collection of art and artefacts, including some delightful watercolours by Carlos Enrique Pellegrini (1800–75).

✉ Bolívar 65, Plaza de Mayo ☎ 011/4334-1782 🕐 Tue–Fri 11.30–6, Sat 2–6, Sun 1–6 👋 Adult/child $2; free Fri

MORE TO SEE

PARQUE COLÓN

The semicircular garden that buffers the eastern facade of the Casa Rosada from the busy riverside traffic is the Parque Colón. The garden is dominated by a white marble statue of Christopher Columbus (Colón in Spanish) looking in the direction of his native Europe. The city's Italian community donated the garden to mark Argentina's centenary in 1910.

PIRÁMIDE DE MAYO

More of an obelisk than a pyramid, this modest white monument, topped by a statue of liberty since 1850, was erected in 1811, the first anniversary of the May Revolution. The Pirámide de Mayo acts as the centre point for all demonstrations and other events that take place on the Plaza de Mayo.

✉ Plaza de Mayo, downtown

TIPS

›› Like the Avenida de Mayo, the square regularly witnesses political and other demonstrations. The best advice is to stay away if you see lots of police and protesters, and come back another day.

›› Make sure you have photo ID with you if you want to see inside the Casa Rosada.

Above *The Pirámide de Mayo, erected on the first anniversary of Argentine independence*
Left *The whitewashed, colonial-style Cabildo building*

INFORMATION
⊞ 65 G5 ⊠ Plaza San Martín, Retiro
⊙ San Martín (C)

TIPS

›› At the Palacio Paz and the Palacio San Martín you can go on guided visits in Spanish or English; check the timetable posted at the main gates.

›› The Torre de los Ingleses is occasionally used for small exhibitions. Visitors can also climb the tower and enjoy great views of the city.

›› The plaza is a wonderful place for a picnic, you can stock up at the Disco supermarket at Esmeralda 1365.

PLAZA LIBERTADOR GENERAL SAN MARTÍN

Created by landscape architect Charles Thays, the majestic Plaza San Martín (as it is more commonly known) is a showpiece for the patrician *barrio* of Retiro. The grassy lawns and shaded benches are a welcome retreat for thousands of commuters, while the indigo-blossomed jacarandas and a venerable *gomero* (rubber tree), plus *ceibos*, palms and other trees form a handsome backdrop for a fine bronze of General San Martín (▷ 29), hero of independence, himself.

TOWERS AND MEMORIALS

To the east, concealing the Basílica del Santísimo Sacramento (▷ 71), the austerely rationalist Edificio Kavanagh was the tallest building in South America when it was inaugurated in 1936. The unusual wedge-shaped building is still one of the most prestigious addresses in town. At the lower, northern end of the plaza stands the Torre de los Ingleses, a 1910 centenary gift to the nation from the Anglo-Argentine community which is vaguely reminiscent of London landmark Big Ben. Nearby, Argentinian servicemen solemnly guard the simple monument dedicated to their fellow countrymen who lost their lives during the 1982 Las Malvinas (Falkland Islands) conflict.

PARISIAN-STYLE PALACES

Both Palacio Paz and Palacio San Martín, on the southwest and northwest sides of the plaza respectively, were built in the first decade of the 20th century for aristocratic families. Media mogul José Paz and wealthy heiress and socialite Mercedes Castellanos de Anchorena each wanted their homes to look like a Parisian *palais*. Paz opted for a combination of the Louvre and Versailles for his palace, while the Palacio San Martín is modelled partly on the elegant Hôtel de Condé. The striking French exteriors of these buildings help to explain the reason why Buenos Aires, in its heyday, was known as the Paris of the South.

The Palacio Paz (Avenida Santa Fé; tel 011/4311-1071; guided visits in English, Wed and Thu 3.30pm; $35) is now an officers' club and also houses the Museo de Armas de la Nación, a moderately interesting military museum. Palacio San Martín (Arenales 761; tel 011/4819-9092; guided visits in Spanish or English, Mon and Wed at 2.30pm) is the official home of the Foreign Ministry.

Below *Palacio San Martín, modelled on a Parisian palace*

PUERTO MADERO

Named after moneyed local merchant Eduardo Madero (1823–94), Puerto Madero was originally built to British designs in the 1880s. Within two decades, with Argentina's exports booming far beyond expectations, the small harbour became redundant. After a century of dereliction, the city fathers saw its potential as a new *barrio*, based on London's docklands and Barcelona's renovated harbourfront. The handsome red-brick wharves and remarkably intact warehouses were transformed into trendy bars and condos, while the docks attracted luxury yachts galore.

RESERVA ECOLÓGICA COSTANERA SUR

As contractors competed to build the country's highest skyscraper—a battle that still rages in Argentina—the city authorities declared the polders to the east an ecological reserve. The Reserva Ecológica Costanera Sur now serves as a wonderful green lung of pampas and lagoons that delights city-dwellers and visitors alike (tel 011/4315-4129; Nov–Mar Tue–Sun 8–7; Apr–Oct 8–6; rangers' walks Sat–Sun 10.30am and 3.30pm, times vary for night guided walks during full moon; free). In addition to joggers and ramblers, the reserve also attracts myriad birds, such as great egrets and black-necked swans, which thrive in this astonishing habitat of willows and acacias beside a series of shallow lagoons along the banks of the Río de la Plata. Coypus, a type of water rat, and lizards also inhabit the reserve.

DIQUES

Four rectangular *diques* (docks), numbered 1 to 4 heading from south to north, form a watery chain along the eastern limit of the city's downtown. This is where some of the city's most expensive real estate is to be found in converted Madero warehouses, along with some deluxe restaurants.

Spanning Dique 3 is a streamlined white footbridge, El Puente de la Mujer (Women's Bridge), designed by the internationally acclaimed Spanish architect Santiago Calatrava. Two beautifully preserved British-built 19th-century sailing ships, *Fragata Presidente Sarmiento* (daily 9–8; adult/child $2) and *Corbeta Uruguay* (daily 10–9; $1) are usually moored in Diques 3 and 4, respectively, and are worth a visit to see their handsome interiors.

At the top of Dique 4, a purpose-built edifice with a distinctive curved roof houses one of the finest private art collections in the country, the Museo Fortabat (Olga Cossettini 141; tel 011/4310-6600; Tue–Sun 12–9, guided tours 3pm and 5pm; adult $15, child under 12 free). In addition to outstanding works by Argentine artists and Egyptian artefacts, the collection includes paintings and sculptures by two of the Brueghels, plus Dali, Chagall, Rodin and Turner, to name but a few great international names.

INFORMATION

www.puertomadero.com
www.coleccionfortabat.org.ar
✚ 65 H7 ✉ Puerto Madero
🚇 Alem (B) 🚌 2, 6, 20, 61, 130, 140;
Tram Córdoba

TIPS

» Twice a day (and once at night when there is a full moon) *guardaparques* (rangers) give guided walks around the Reserva Ecológica and explain the flora and fauna.

» Take plenty of water, use sunscreen and wear a sunhat if you visit the reserve during the day. Apply insect repellent liberally during the evening.

» The Costanera Sur, which runs along the eastern edge of the *barrio*, is a great place for jogging or having a picnic.

Above *Santiago Calatrava's stunning footbridge, El Puente de la Mujer, spanning the docks at Puerto Madero*

REGIONS BUENOS AIRES AND AROUND • SIGHTS

Above *The Cementerio de la Recoleta, a showcase of 19th-century grandeur*

INFORMATION

www.info-recoleta.com

✚ 64 D5 ✉ Recoleta Ⓜ Callao (D)
🚌 10, 17, 60, 67, 92, 110

INTRODUCTION

Recoleta has been one of the smartest *barrios* in Buenos Aires since the city's gentry settled here to escape plague-ridden San Telmo in the 1870s. Many of the refined residences still stand, although some have been converted into elegant hotels, sophisticated restaurants or tea rooms. The neighbourhood's most visited sight has to be the exclusive cemetery, the Cementerio de la Recoleta, which is a melancholy showcase of late 19th-century grandeur. Nearby are other gems, including the beautiful Basílica Nuestra Señora del Pilar and a vibrant arts centre. A museum devoted to 20th-century genius Xul Solar, a landmark exhibition space and a unique floral sculpture will help to fill a day's sightseeing in this charming district.

WHAT TO SEE
CEMENTERIO DE LA RECOLETA

www.cementeriorecoleta.com.ar

One of the most exclusive and photogenic graveyards in the world, the Cementerio de la Recoleta began life as a humble burial ground in the early 19th century. But as Recoleta became the place to live in the 1870s, its denizens needed an appropriately grand cemetery to honour their deceased. You can easily spend an hour or so in the cemetery looking at the ornate graves, although most visitors make a beeline for the (rather plain) Duarte family vault, where Evita was put to rest in the 1970s, albeit after lengthy negotiations with the authorities.

✚ 64 E4 ✉ Avenida Quintana and Junín 🕐 Daily 7–6; guided tours Mar–Nov last Sun in the month 2.30 ✋ Free

MORE TO SEE

BASÍLICA DE NUESTRA SEÑORA DEL PILAR

Next to the cemetery entrance stands the city's most appealing colonial church. Plain white on the outside, the basilica, consecrated in 1732, is finely decorated inside and contains an ornate baroque silver altarpiece from Peru. You can also visit the cloisters, where the main attraction is a collection of striking colonial silverware.

✠ 64 E4 ✉ Recoleta ⏰ Mon–Sat 10.30–6.15, Sun 2.30–6.15; guided visits (in Spanish) most Sun at 3pm ✋ Free

CENTRO CULTURAL RECOLETA

http://centroculturalrecoleta.org
Close to the Basílica de Nuestra Señora del Pilar is the Centro Cultural Recoleta (CCR), which is housed in part of a Franciscan monastery. The building was restored and remodelled in the 1980s to make way for this avant-garde centre, and its various spaces are used to promote contemporary painting, sculpture, photography, theatre, dance and other performance arts.

✠ 64 E4 ✉ Junín 1930, Recoleta ☎ 011/4803-1040 ⏰ Mon–Fri 2–9, Sat–Sun 10–9 ✋ Adult/child $1

FLORALIS GENÉRICA

Installed in 2002, the Floralis Genérica sculpture is one of Buenos Aires's most recognizable icons. It was a gift to the city from one of its famous sons, the architect and designer Eduardo Catalano (1917–2010), and was intended to boost morale as the country emerged from deep economic crisis. Constructed using 18 tons of aluminium and stainless steel, it is 20m (65.5ft) high when closed and spans 40m (131ft) when opened. Each one of its 13m-high (42.5ft) petals is reflected in a giant pool at the centre of the Plaza de las Naciones Unidas, and they open and close every morning and evening just like a real flower using hydraulic mechanics. On the evenings of 25 May (National Day), 21 September, Christmas Day and New Year's Eve, the flower's petals remain open for the night, and seeing the open flower lit up is a special experience.

✠ 63 E3 ✉ Plaza de las Naciones Unidas, Recoleta 🚌 17, 124, 130

MUSEO XUL SOLAR

www.xulsolar.org.ar
Oscar Agustín Alejandro Schulz Solari (1887–1963), better known as Xul Solar, was one of Argentina's most original artists and one of the few to have a museum in the capital dedicated exclusively to his work. A fascinating polymath, Solar was prolific in producing distinctive paintings, in a style often likened to that of Paul Klee, the Swiss Expressionist painter. Many of Solar's paintings can be seen at the Fundación Pan Klub, where he had his studio.

✠ 64 C5 ✉ Laprida 1212, Recoleta ☎ 011/4824-3302 ⏰ Feb–Dec Tue–Fri 12–8, Sat 12–7 ✋ Adult/child $10 🚇 Agüero (D)

PALAIS DE GLACE

www.palaisdeglace.gob.ar
Officially known as the Palacio Nacional de las Artes, this exhibition hall is usually referred to as the Palais de Glace (Ice Palace) because it started life as an ice-skating rink. The unusual round, belle-époque edifice is often cited as the place where, in the 1920s, tango finally gained its acceptance as a respectable dance form. Today, it is an avant-garde space used for photographic and other exhibitions, and the projection of videos and documentaries as part of the Kino Palais project.

✠ 64 E4 ✉ Posadas 1725, Recoleta ☎ 011/4804-1163 ⏰ Tue–Fri 12–8, Sat–Sun 10–8; guided tours (in Spanish) Sat–Sun 4pm and 6pm ✋ Adult/child $2; guided tours free 🚌 10, 17, 60, 67, 92, 110

TIPS

›› La Biela is a famous *confitería* (brasserie-cum-café) opposite the main gates of the cemetery. Its smart salons and shady terrace are pleasant places to take a break from sightseeing but the prices, especially on the terrace, are inflated.

›› If you have time, try to include a visit to the national fine art museum, the MNBA (▷ 82–83).

Below *Eduardo Catalano's Floralis Genérica sculpture, gifted to the city in 2002 as Argentina emerged from economic crisis*

BUENOS AIRES AND AROUND • SIGHTS

REGIONS

Above *The town's bars and* pulperías *give a real flavour of* criollo *culture*

INFORMATION

www.sanantoniodeareco.com/turismo/
347 K11 Arellano and Zerboni
02326/453165 Daily 8–8 Two
bus companies, Nueva Chevallier and
Pullman General Belgrano, run regular
services to San Antonio de Areco; both
take 2 hours from Buenos Aires's Retiro
terminal 90 mins from Buenos Aires;
head northwest along Panamericana
towards Rosario and then take RN8 at
Pilar Panamericana towards Rosario and
then take RN8 at Pilar

INTRODUCTION

San Antonio de Areco, a charming little *gaucho* town sitting on the banks of the Río Areco just 113km (70 miles) northwest of the capital, gives a taste of rural Argentina at its best. Despite years of tourism, Areco, as it is popularly known, has maintained a remarkably authentic atmosphere, with its cobbled streets and fine neo-colonial architecture. In addition to attractive single-storey houses, flaking colonial facades and intricate iron grilles, you can visit a host of craftsmen's workshops (*talleres*) turning out fabulous textiles and metalwork. One of the city's main attractions is a museum dedicated to *gaucho* tradition, but the real reason for coming is to soak up the laidback rustic ambience, discover its many *criollo* bars and restored *pulperías* (a cross between a grocer's shop and a spaghetti-western saloon). The town becomes especially animated during the week-long Día de la Tradición celebrations in November (▷ 115).

WHAT TO SEE

THE TOWN CENTRE

Plaza Ruiz de Arellano is Areco's main square and the site of the Italianate Iglesia Parroquial San Antonio de Padua, which has a simple but elegant facade with a statue of the saint in a niche decorated with blue and white tiles. More impressive is the pink *municipalidad*, a neo-colonial building built in the early 20th century, while the highlight of the town centre is opposite the church, the Centro Cultural y Talller Draghi (Lavalle 387; tel 02326/454219; Mon–Sat 9–1, 3.30–7.30, Sun 10–1, guided visits 11, 5, 6; $10). Here, you can see (and buy) some magnificent vintage and modern specimens of *platería criolla* (traditional silverware), which dates back to the 18th century, when silversmiths began creating a distinctively Argentine style in their work. One block north of the main square, the Centro Cultural Usina Vieja (Alsina 66; tel 02326/454722; Tue–Sun 11–7; free) has an interesting display of local exhibits, plus a fine set of *gaucho* cartoons by Buenos Aires-born artist Florencio Molina Campos (1891–1959).

MUSEO GAUCHESCO RICARDO GÜIRALDES

www.museoguiraldes.com.ar

If you take the Puente Viejo across the Río Areco to the northwest of the town centre, you'll reach the open landscape of the Parque Criollo, used for *gaucho* displays during traditional festivals. Along the road, named after the great novelist Ricardo Güiraldes (▷ 27), you can find the museum of the same name, dedicated to *gaucho* lore and history. The entrance of the museum features a restored *pulpería* (rural inn-cum-store), which was used as the setting for an opening scene in Güiraldes's 1926 *gauchesco* novel, *Don Segundo Sombra*. Inside, you can see traditional *mate* cups and *boleadoras* (balls on lassos, used by *gauchos* to catch animals), plus some impressive silverware. Some of the highlights include a set of early black-and-white photos of *gauchos* and a collection of beautiful paintings of the pampas by Uruguayan master Pedro Figari (1861–1938).

✉ Camino Ricardo Güiraldes s/n, San Antonio de Areco ☎ 02326/455839 🕐 Wed–Mon 11–5 💰 Adult/child $4

THE *ESTANCIAS*

The tourist *estancias* offer the perfect place to base yourself for a truly memorable rural experience, while enjoying the luxury of the facilities. La Bamba (▷ 124) and El Ombú (▷ 124), both of which are within easy reach of Areco, are fabulous examples. La Bamba is so atmospheric that it was used as the setting for María Luisa Bemberg's award-winning 1984 romantic film *Camila*. If an overnight stay is prohibitively expensive, each *estanica* offers the opportunity to see their fine architecture and beautifully landscaped gardens on a *día de campo* (a day in the country)—a wonderful alternative. This package usually includes a barbecue lunch, high tea and some physical activity to work off all those calories, such as horseback riding or swimming in the pool. Usually you will also be treated to an impressive display of *gaucho* rodeo skills. Another *estancia*, La Cinacina (▷ 124), is conveniently located in the town itself, half a dozen blocks west of the main plaza.

TIPS

❯❯ Although you can see San Antonio de Areco as a day trip, it is far more enjoyable to stay overnight either at one of the town's boutique hotels or at one of the nearby tourist *estancias* (▷ 124), which are among the best in the country.

❯❯ Terrible floods devastated Areco in December 2009, the first in living memory, and they have left indelible damage.

Below *A gaucho at work rounding up horses*

SAN ISIDRO

The prosperous municipality of San Isidro lies in Buenos Aires's leafy, affluent northern suburbs, an area known generically as the Zona Norte. The three fine mansions open to the public here are rich reward for the trek beyond the city limits. San Isidro's historic heart is dominated by its lofty neo-Gothic Cathedral, built by French architects at the end of the 19th century and famed for its stained glass. At weekends, a colourful arts-and-crafts fair takes place on the nearby Plaza de San Isidro.

VILLA OCAMPO

The eclectic Villa Ocampo, about ten blocks north of the plaza and cathedral, is where the virulently anti-Peronist intellectual Victoria Ocampo kept a literary salon. Ocampo entertained famous guests from the world over, including Argentine writer Jorge Luis Borges, English author Graham Greene and architect Le Corbusier. UNESCO has owned Villa Ocampo, with its fabulous antique and art-filled rooms and landscaped gardens, since the 1970s and the house is now a cultural centre. There are guided tours at weekends (Elortondo 1837; tel 011/4732-4988, www.villaocampo.org; Thu–Sun 12.30–6; guided tours from 2pm; adult $10 Thu–Fri, $15 Sat–Sun, child under 12 free).

QUINTA LOS OMBÚES

Just behind the cathedral, the 18th-century Quinta Los Ombúes is one of the oldest houses in the city and is where Mariquita Sánchez de Thompson famously entertained General San Martín and General Belgrano. Donated to the city in 2005, the mansion now houses San Isidro's library and archive, but the house itself and the family collection of fabulous, Federalist-themed artworks and furniture are the main attractions. The charming garden affords fine views of the Río de la Plata (774 Beccar Varela; tel 011/4575-4038, www.quintalosombues. com.ar; Apr–Oct Tue, Thu 10–6, Sat–Sun 2–6; Nov–Mar Tue, Thu 10–6, Sat–Sun 3–7; free).

CASA PUEYRREDÓN

The late 18th-century Casa del General Pueyrredón houses the Museo Histórico Municipal, San Isidro's history museum (Rivera Indarte 48; tel 011/4512-3131; Tue, Thu 2–6, Sat–Sun 3–7; free). The museum displays memorabilia relating to General Pueyrredón, famous for playing a leading part in Argentina's independence. In the garden is an ancient algarrobo tree under which Pueyrredón is said to have discussed politics with General San Martín.

INFORMATION

www.sanisidro.gov.ar
⊞ 347 K11 ⓘ Ituzaingo 608, on the corner of Avenida del Libertador, near Plaza Mitre ☎ 011/4512-3209 ⓒ Daily 9–5 🚌 60, 168 🚉 Retiro to Estación San Isidro; Tren de la Costa

TIPS

➤➤ You can reach San Isidro either by taking an efficient suburban train from the Estación Retiro (▷ 50) or the special tourist locomotive, the Tren de la Costa (▷ 106–107), which makes frequent stops and has its own station (also called Estación San Isidro) next to Plaza Mitre.

➤➤ San Isidro makes an excellent day trip from the capital but you could also visit it en route to Tigre (▷ 101).

➤➤ Zona Norte is not just about leafy, villa-lined avenues. Head southwest of Plaza Mitre and there are some outstanding restaurants and interesting shops along the main street, Belgrano.

Above and opposite *Villa Ocampo, set amid beautiful landscaped gardens*

INFORMATION

www.feriadesantelmo.com

🚇 65 G8 ✉ San Telmo

🚊 Independencia (C/E) 🚌 29, 64, 86

TIPS

➤➤ Keep a firm grip on your valuables in San Telmo, especially when threading your way through the crowds at the weekly *feria* (market) on Sundays.

➤➤ Feria de San Pedro Telmo is a good place to buy traditional *fileteado* artwork (▷ 80).

➤➤ The covered Mercado Municipal de San Telmo (Calle Defensa; Mon–Sat 7–2, 4.30–9, Sun 7–2) is one of the most colourful markets in the city, where you'll find antiques and curios alongside fruit, vegetable and meat stalls. The street itself is lined with antique shops, though be warned that bargains are few and far between.

➤➤ If you are shopping for genuine antiques, avoid the markets and find a reputable antiques dealer. Make sure you are given an authenticated certificate and receipt, to avoid any problems when taking your purchase out of the country.

Above *Dancing the tango on Plaza Dorrego in the heart of San Telmo*

SAN TELMO

Faded grandeur sums up the enchanting *barrio* of San Telmo. Following Argentine independence, it was *the* place to live, but an outbreak of yellow fever in the 1870s saw the *barrio's* popularity plummet and it never quite recovered. Since 2000, however, the area has seen a revival, with many of its crumbling town houses transformed into luxury apartments and boutique hotels.

The *barrio* retains its close links with tango, which can be seen and heard on the streets around Plaza Dorrego, especially on Sundays, when the Feria de San Pedro Telmo takes over. The market is a collectors' paradise, with all manner of items, from vintage vinyl records to art deco glassware, for sale.

PARQUE LEZAMA

In 1857, wealthy Porteño José Gregorio Lezama bought a parcel of land in southern San Telmo where he built a beautiful mansion and planted some fine trees. When he died, his widow donated the land to the city with the proviso that it become a park named after her husband. The bombastic monument at the northwestern corner of this leafy rhombus commemorates the spot where Pedro de Mendoza founded the city in 1536. Opposite is the Monumento a la Cordialidad Internacional, a gift from Uruguay, decorated with the constellations on the day that Buenos Aires was founded.

On the park's western edge, at Defensa 1600, is Lezama's attractive Italianate mansion. The house became the Museo Histórico National (tel 011/4307-1182; Tue–Sun 11–6; $3) at the end of the 19th century, when the park became state property. Exhibits detail Argentina's 19th-century history and include a collection of portraits. The highlight is the fabulous Tarja de Potosí (currently undergoing restoration), a gold and silver shield given to General Belgrano by the women of the Bolivian city of Potosí for his part in freeing their country from Spanish rule.

PASAJE SAN LORENZO AND ZANJÓN

www.elzanjon.com.ar

Visits to El Zanjón de Granados, at Defensa 755, give an insight into the city's 18th-century foundations (tel 011/4361-3002; Zanjón one-hour tours Mon–Fri 11–4, Sun 1–6; Casa Mínima 30-minute tours Mon–Fri 10.30–4; $25). Guided tours take you through a maze of underground passages and waterpipes. At ground level, Pasaje San Lorenzo is a well-preserved alleyway of typical San Telmo houses, including Casa Mínima at No. 380, barely 2m (6.5ft) wide.

TANDIL

Set among the lush fields of the wet pampa, 330km (205 miles) south of Buenos Aires, Tandil is a traditional *gaucho* town. The town's main attraction is the surrounding moorland of the sierras, where some of the peaks rise to more than 500m (1,640ft) above sea level. These rugged hills are perfect for easy rambling, horseback riding and mountain biking, while the more adventurous might like to investigate the many opportunities for canoeing and abseiling. The town has a good selection of hotels and restaurants, making an overnight stay a good option. Try to avoid coming in January, when the town is at its most crowded.

THE TOWN

Cobbled with granite from the nearby Sistema de Tandilia hills, Tandil's streets form a colonial-style chequerboard, with the Plaza Independencia as its hub. On the square, the neo-Romanesque Iglesia del Santísimo Sacramento, like its grander namesake in Buenos Aires, is modelled on the Sacré-Coeur in Paris. The square and its immediate vicinity are a great place to soak up the rural atmosphere at a café terrace or take part in the traditional *paseo* (evening stroll). A beautiful old building at 4 de Abril 845, to the north of the town centre, houses the modest Museo Tradicionalista (tel 02293/435573; Tue–Sun 4–8; $3), where the main curiosity is the collection of old photos of the original Piedra Movediza.

PIEDRA MOVEDIZA

On 29 February 1912, Tandil lost its best-known sight, the Piedra Movediza (Moving Stone), a 350-ton lump of granite finely balanced, as if by magic, on the top of a striped cliff. People came from far and wide to marvel at this natural wonder, sometimes standing precariously atop the boulder or setting off fireworks to make it wobble. When the great rock finally toppled over and smashed to pieces—possibly as the result of human action—its memory lived on into the 21st century. Finally, in 2007, in the presence of President Kirchner and other dignitaries, a convincing cement replica was unveiled at the same spot. The rock is now the centrepiece of the Parque Lítico La Movediza, immediately to the north of the town and within walking distance.

INFORMATION

www.tandil.gov.ar

✈ 351 K13 ✉ Tandil, Provincia de Buenos Aires 🛈 Avenida Espora 1120 ☎ 02293/432073 🕓 Mon–Sat 8–8, Sun 9–1 🚌 Long-distance buses from Retiro bus station 🚍 Take the Ezeiza and Cañuelas direction from Buenos Aires, then the RN3 to Las Flores. Turn left onto RP-30 via Rauch to Tandil

TIPS

▶▶ The best way to explore the hills around Tandil is with a guide (ask at the tourist information office), as the best trekking land is privately owned and you need a permit to explore.

▶▶ If you want to visit the sierras under your own steam, head to the Cerro El Centinela, 5km (3 miles) from the town centre, along a well-signposted path. The highlight of this walk is the 7m-high (23ft) Centinela stone, delicately balanced on a pointed rock.

▶▶ To see some native fauna, including *guanacos*, head to the Reserva Natural Sierra del Tigre, just south of the town.

Below *Tandil is a typical gaucho town and is popular with Argentine holidaymakers*

INFORMATION

www.teatrocolon.org.ar

✚ 65 F6 ✉ Cerrito 618, downtown
☎ 011/4378-7100/7344 ⏰ Ticket office:
Tue–Sat 10–8; guided tours Mon–Fri 11
and 5, Sat 9, 10, 11 and 12 ✋ Guided
tours: Adult $10, child (5–12) $5, child
under 5 free Ⓜ Tribunales (D)

TIPS

›› Even if you don't make it to a
performance, you can go on a guided tour
of this fabulous theatre, with a visit to the
costume and set workshops thrown in if
you are lucky.
›› Don't be surprised to see that non-
residents are charged more for tickets
than residents.

TEATRO COLÓN

One of the world's truly great opera houses, the imposing Teatro Colón
(Columbus Theatre) is the pride and joy of Buenos Aires and the most prestigious
building on the Avenida 9 de Julio (▷ 69). The second opera house on this site,
the current building was inaugurated in 1908 on the country's national holiday,
25 May, with a highly acclaimed performance of Verdi's *Aida*. After prolonged
modernization, it reopened on 25 May 2010, as part of Argentina's bicentenary
celebrations. *Swan Lake* and *La Bohème* were part of the reopening gala, while
cellist Yo-Yo Ma and local girl Paloma Herrera of the American Ballet Theatre
were on the theatre's programme later in the year.

ILL-FATED HISTORY

Reading the theatre's history, you might think the Colón was jinxed—in fact, it
sounds not unlike the plot of the most far-fetched opera. Neapolitan architect
Francesco Tamburini, also the architect of the Casa Rosada, laid the cornerstone
of the building in 1889 but construction was delayed, due to various squabbles,
economic crises and deaths, and wasn't completed for another 20 years. Belgian
architect Jules Dormal, who also designed the Hipódromo Argentino racecourse
in Palermo (▷ 85) and the Parque 3 de Febrero (▷ 85), oversaw the completion
of the theatre and it finally opened in 1908. Dormal is responsible for the more
sober French-style elements in the theatre's Italianate exterior.

A CENTURY OF MUSIC AND DANCE

Despite its inauspicious start, the Teatro Colón is one of the world's most
illustrious opera and ballet houses. The long list of names of opera singers,
dancers, composers and conductors that have featured on the Colón's
programme over the past century reads like a history of international classical
music. Igor Stravinsky and Richard Strauss, José van Dam and Jessye Norman,
Joan Sutherland and Plácido Domingo have all performed here, as have
homegrown stars, such as Daniel Barenboim and Julio Bocca, José Cura and
Martha Argerich.

Regarded as among the world's top five opera houses in terms of acoustics,
the theatre is also one of the biggest, with a total capacity of more than 3,500.
The interior, including a magnificent Carrara marble staircase, is pure Italian
Renaissance, while the opulent Salón Dorado (Golden Hall), where countless
bottles of champagne have been quaffed over the decades, is said to have been
inspired by the Palace of Versailles, in France. The auditorium's rich decor of gold
and scarlet velvet is set off by the delicate 1960s frescos in the huge dome, the
work of influential Argentine artist Raúl Soldi.

Below *Teatro Colón, the city's prestigious
opera house on Avenida 9 de Julio*

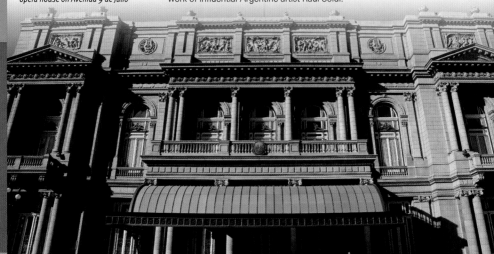

TIGRE

A mere 28km (17 miles) north of Buenos Aires, Tigre is an alluring destination on the delta of the mighty Río Paraná, where it spills into the vast Río de la Plata estuary. The river drags silt and branches from its tropical upper reaches in Brazil and deposits them near Tigre, forming new islets and planting new forests as it goes. The result is a relaxingly verdant landscape of wooded islands separated by a labyrinth of waterways, plied by picturesque wooden launches — a kind of suptropical Venice.

The town takes its name from the *tigres* (jaguars) that were hunted in the thick forest when the first settlers arrived. Tigre's heyday was the turn of the 20th century, when its famous casino and hotel was a playground for wealthy holidaymakers, but competition from foreign resorts and government restrictions on gambling saw its decline in the 1940s.

MUSEO DE ARTE TIGRE (MAT)

www.mat.gov.ar

If you want to see a remnant of Tigre's heyday, make for the fabulous art museum, the MAT, at the Paseo Victorica s/n (tel 011/4512-4528; Wed–Fri 9–7, Sat–Sun 12–7, guided tours every hour; adult/child $5). Housed in the immaculately renovated Tigre Club, at the end of the picturesque Paseo Victorica, the museum is reached by crossing the bridge over the Río Tigre near the Estación Fluvial. Built in 1912 on the banks of the Río Luján, the MAT is a magnificent building designed by French architects and decorated with ornate European fittings. It was the first casino in Argentina but closed in 1933, when the government decided it was too close to the capital for the good of society. It was derelict for decades, until the municipality took it over and turned it into a marvellous art museum, dedicated to the country's great masters, including late 19th- and early 20th-century works by realist painter Eduardo Sívori. The old ballroom now serves as a gallery of paintings about ports, including works by Boca artist Quinquela Martín (▷ 72).

PARQUE DE LA COSTA

The sprawling Parque de la Costa (▷ 114) is one of the largest theme parks in Latin America. It is aimed at families, with man-made mountains and lighthouses for the adventurous to climb, sound-and-light shows to watch and some exciting rides to keep children entertained, including some hair-raising roller coasters.

INFORMATION

www.tigre.gov.ar

✚ 347 K11 ℹ Mitre 305, Estación Fluvial ◷ Daily 9–5 ☎ 011/4512-4498 🚌 Bus 60 (marked 'Panamericana') from Constitución and Central Buenos Aires 🚆 Trains from Retiro to Estación Delta or Tren de la Costa from Olivos

TIPS

›› It's easy to visit Tigre by train, either on the suburban line from Retiro's Mitre or on the tourist Tren de la Costa (▷ 106–107) from Olivos. Both services arrive at Tigre's port, or Estación Fluvial, where you can catch public launches run by three companies: Delta (tel 011/4749-0537; www.lineasdelta.com. ar), Interisleña (tel 011/4749-0900) and Jilgüero (tel 011/4749-0987).
›› Take the four-hour round trip to the Paraná de las Palmas or get off at one of the stops such as Tres Bocas and walk along the canals and channels.
›› In summer, people bathe in Tigre's waterways and, despite the busy traffic and the muddy brown colour, the water is surprisingly clean and refreshingly cool.
›› Mosquitoes are rampant on summer evenings, so insect repellent is essential.
›› There are many opportunities to practise water sports, such as rowing, kayaking and wakeboarding.

Above *Boats cruise Tigre's labyrinthine network of waterways*

PLAZA DE MAYO TO PLAZA PELLEGRINI

Starting at the monumental Plaza de Mayo, this varied walk takes you along the pedestrian-only Calle Florida, one of the city's main shopping streets, through La City, the financial district with its imposing bank buildings and grand churches, to the exclusive *barrio* of Retiro. Cross the colossal Avenida 9 de Julio for a glimpse of the city's patrician heartland over the border in Recoleta.

THE WALK

Distance: 2.2km (1.25 miles)
Time: 2–3 hours
Start at: Plaza de Mayo
End at: Plaza Carlos Pellegrini

★ Start at the Plaza de Mayo—the city's nerve centre. You can get there by *subte*, bus or you may prefer to take a taxi. To the east of the plaza is the unmissable pink Casa Rosada (▷ 88–89), the official residence of the Argentine government.

Head west from the Plaza de Mayo along Avenida de Mayo and, almost at once, you'll stumble across the stunning La Prensa building (▷ 70). Turn right into Calle Perú, which shortly becomes Calle Florida.

❶ Florida is a ten-block-long street lined with a huge assortment of stores selling everything from CDs to leather jackets and fast food. It may

not be the classiest street in the city, but the crowds, street vendors and pavement tango dancers make it a vibrant place.

Continue to the intersection with Bartolome Mitre. On the corner, to your right, is the former Banco de Boston, a masterpiece of ornate Hispanic architecture. Another block north, at the corner with Perón, is the fabulous 14-storey Galería Güemes.

❷ Even if you aren't interested in shopping, it is worth popping inside art nouveau Galería Güemes to admire the beautiful stained-glass cupolas, marble pillars and brass statues (www.galeriaguemes.com.ar; Mon–Fri 8–8 Sat 9–3). The building also houses a renovated art nouveau theatre, home of the Piazolla tango show, and there are guided visits to the observation deck on the 14th floor (Thu 4pm; free).

Make a detour from Florida by turning right and heading two blocks east along Perón, then turn left up Reconquista, to the Basílica de Nuestra Señora de la Merced (La Merced) and the Convento San Ramón, on the corner with Perón.

❸ La Merced dates from the late 18th-century, with a 1905 facade. Note the tympanum depicting General Belgrano's defeat of the Spanish at Tucumán in 1812. Adjoining the basilica, the Convento San Ramón has a restaurant where you could stop for lunch. Backing on to the convent, on 25 de Mayo, is the mid-19th century neoclassical Catedral Anglicana (▷ 71).

Turn left along Sarmiento to Calle Florida. Turn right to continue northwards, passing Galería Mitre at No. 343, home to the department store Falabella.

Opposite *Galerías Pacífico shopping mall*

Cross Avenida Corrientes—look left to see the Obelisco (▷ 69) in the distance—and continue along Florida. Half way along the next block, on your left, is Café Richmond, a great place to have a coffee. Continue for three more blocks to reach Galerías Pacífico, at the intersection with Avenida Córdoba, one of the city's great shopping centres.

❹ Built in the late 19th century, Galerías Pacífico (▷ 109) is a haven of upmarket boutiques and cafés. Its interior is decorated with frescos, painted by famous Argentine artists.

Continue for two more blocks to Plaza Libertador General San Martín (▷ 90). At the end of Florida, skirt around the plaza in a clockwise direction to pass in front of the Palacio Paz (▷ 90) at the corner of Santa Fé and Esmeralda. Cross Santa Fé and head along Esmeralda past the Palacio San Martín, another Parisian-styled building, as far as the corner with Arroyo. To the right stands the opulent Palacio Estrugamou.

❺ Built in 1905 for the Estrugamou family, the *palacio* is one of the finest examples of the city's residential architecture.

Turn left along Arroyo and swing past a series of art galleries, as the street meanders towards the Avenida 9 de Julio. A short detour along Suipacha leads to the Museo de Arte Hispanoamericano Isaac Fernández Blanco (▷ 78–79), with the Plaza Embajada de Israel, at the corner of Arroyo and Suipacha.

❻ A plaque in Hebrew and Spanish marks the spot in Plaza Embajada de Israel where the Israeli embassy stood until it was torn apart by a terrorist bomb in 1992. The attack left 29 people dead and dozens injured.

One more block brings you to the Avenida 9 de Julio. Cross over, using

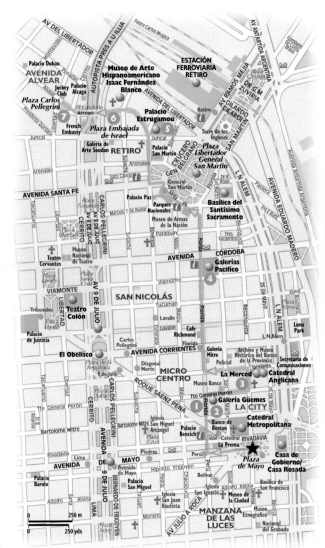

the traffic lights, admiring the French embassy (▷ 69) on the opposite side as you do. Behind the embassy is the ritzy Plaza Carlos Pellegrini.

❼ The plaza was named after the late 19th-century president, Carlos Pellegrini, and at its heart there is a statue of him, sculpted in Carrara marble with bronze allegories of Progress and Justice on either side.

WHERE TO EAT
CAFÉ RICHMOND
This historic café on Calle Florida

is a great place to soak up the atmosphere.
✉ Florida 468 ☎ 011/4322-134
🕐 Mon–Sat 7am–10pm

GRANIX
▷ 117.

EL PATIO DE SAN RAMÓN
Set in a cloister of the Convento San Ramón and overlooking a tranquil grassed area, this is a great spot for lunch.
✉ Reconquista 269
🕐 Mon–Fri 12–2.30

REGIONS BUENOS AIRES AND AROUND • WALK

103

SAN TELMO AND MONSERRAT

For many people San Telmo, where the city was first founded in the 16th century, is the most quintessential of its *barrios*. It became *the* place to live soon after Independence and is becoming fashionable once more. Immediately to the north, the downtown parish of Monserrat looks very similar and even locals are not sure where the boundary lies. This walk along Calle Defensa takes you through the historic heart of the city.

THE WALK

Distance: 1.7km (1 mile)
Time: 2–3 hours
Start at: Parque Lezama
End at: Plaza de Mayo

★ Start at Parque Lezama (▷ 98) in the heart of San Telmo. The best way to get there is by taxi. In addition to seeing the Museo Histórico Nacional (▷ 98), housed in a fabulous red-and-white Italianate mansion, and various monuments to the founding of the city, you might like to take a look inside the Catedral Ortodoxa Rusa, the city's main Russian church.

❶ Many members of Argentina's sizeable Russian Orthodox community live in Buenos Aires and this beautiful church is their centre of worship. Admire the blue onion domes and Venetian mosaic above the door from Parque Lezama's northern side, before entering to see the fine interior, including precious icons given by Tsar Nicolas II.

After leaving the church, turn right up Defensa and keep walking for three blocks, pass under Autopista 25 de Mayo (motorway), and as far as busy Avenida San Juan. Turn right and you will find two minor museums.

❷ The Museo de Arte Moderno, housed in a disused tobacco factory, has a small but representative collection of contemporary Argentine art, while next door is the Museo del Cine, with massive archives about Argentine film. The two museums are currently being combined and converted into a major cultural centre.

Follow your steps back to Calle Defensa, cross Avenida San Juan, and continue for half a block to the attractive Pasaje de la Defensa.

❸ Pasaje de la Defensa, a small arcade at Defensa 1179 full of stores selling bric-a-brac, is typical of a late 19th-century San Telmo house. There is a good café in the handsome patio. Another half block north along Defensa brings you to Plaza Dorrego, surrounded by interesting shops and places to eat. The Sunday Feria de San Pedro Telmo (▷ 98) is held here.

Keep along Defensa for another three and a half blocks to pass the colourful Mercado Municipal (▷ 98). Take a peek inside to see the tempting displays of fruit and vegetables then continue to reach the entrance to El Zanjón, where you can visit more historic buildings, including the narrowest house in the city, the Casa Mínima (▷ 98), along Pasaje San Lorenzo.

You have now entered Monserrat where you should keep going

Opposite *Goods for sale at the Sunday Feria de San Pedro Telmo*

along Defensa, although a couple of excellent shops might draw your attention: Materia Urbana, at Defensa 707, showcases Argentine designers while Laguanacazul, at 677, sells beautiful contemporary textiles based on traditional motifs and has a basement art gallery. Continue for another two blocks to reach the Basílica de Santo Domingo, on the corner with Avenida Belgrano.

❹ The Basílica de Santo Domingo is a rather sombre late 18th-century church, which was captured for a short time by the British during their invasion in 1806. In the courtyard, at the front, is a mausoleum to General Belgrano, a hero of the War of Independence, comprising an Italian marble base and a number of bronze allegorical statues and topped by a symbolic sarcophagus, surmounted by an eagle and palm fronds.

Walk another block along Defensa and turn right along Moreno to the next corner, where you will find the Museo Etnográfico.

❺ The Museo Etnográfico Juan Bautista Ambrosetti contains some fine exhibits on the country's indigenous cultures, such as the Mapuche and the Yámana, and is worth a look if time permits. Otherwise you might want to forge on to the nearby Manzana Franciscana (▷ 74), the Museo de la Ciudad (▷ 80) and the Manzana de las Luces (▷ 80), three of the downtown's major sights, which lie along Calle Defensa or, in the case of the Manzana de las Luces, a block over to the west.

One block along Defensa to the north of the Museo de la Ciudad, the street opens out into the iconic Plaza de Mayo (▷ 88–89). Here you can take the *subte* to another part of the city, after taking a good look at the Casa Rosada, which dominates the square to the east.

WHEN TO GO

From midday onwards is best, when most of the sights will be open for visits. Avoid ambling along this route early in the morning or after dark.

WHERE TO EAT
LA VINERÍA DE GUALTERIO BOLÍVAR

www.lavineriadegualteriobolivar.com
Enjoy memorable cuisine at this inventive tapas bar, between Estados Unidos and Independencia. The 33-ingredient salad is a good option.
✉ Bolívar 865 ☎ 011/4361-4709
🕐 Tue–Sun 1–4, 9–12

PLACES TO VISIT
MUSEO DE ARTE MODERNO

www.museodeartemoderno.buenosaires.gov.ar
✉ Avenida Córdoba 946 ☎ 011/4342-3001 🕐 Mon–Fri 10–6 💲 Free

MUSEO DEL CINE

www.museodelcine.buenosaires.gov.ar
✉ Avenida Córdoba ☎ 011/4303-2882
🕐 Mon–Fri 10–6 💲 Free

MUSEO ETNOGRÁFICO

✉ Moreno 350 ☎ 011/4331-7788
🕐 Feb–Dec Tue– Fri 1–7, Sat–Sun 3–7
💲 Free

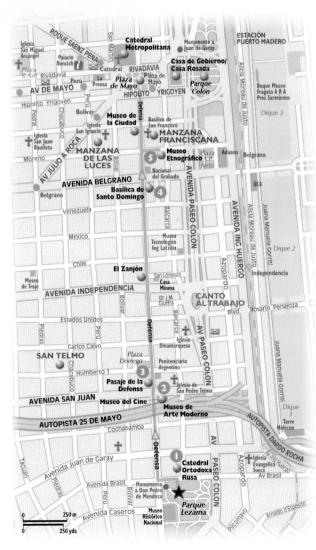

TOUR

TREN DE LA COSTA

This tourist train is one of the most pleasant ways of getting to Tigre, running smoothly along specially converted electrified tracks by the riverside, through some of the city's most attractive suburbs. You will first need to get to Olivos, just outside the city limits, but that poses no problems.

THE TRAIN RIDE

Distance: 15.5km (10 miles)
Time: 3–4 hours
Start at: Estación Maipú, Olivos
End at: Estación Delta, Tigre

The journey time from Olivos to Tigre is 25 minutes, but there are plenty of interesting stops along the way and, once you have your ticket, you can hop on and off whenever you want. The shiny green train is made up of two luxurious mock-Victorian coaches and holds up to 200 passengers. There is a departure three times an hour on average. For more information about the train service and a timetable visit www.trendelacosta.com.ar.

★ Start at the southern terminus of Estación Maipú in Olivos, a suburb to the north of the city. To get there, take a train from the Retiro station (▷ 74) heading for Estación Bartolomé Mitre. There is

a pedestrian bridge across Avenida Maipú to get you from the Mitre line station (also called Maipú) to the terminal.

❶ Olivos is where the Argentine president has an out-of-town residence. At the end of the day, the president retreats from the machinations of government to the 19th-century Quinta de Olivos, built by Prilidiano Pueyrredón, who also constructed the Casa Pueyrredón in San Isidro (▷ 96–97). The house is not open to the public and is surrounded by a large garden protected by high brick walls. It is only one block away from the station so you could try to catch a glimpse, time permitting.

Hop on the train at Estación Maipú in Olivos. You can buy tickets on board ($12 single, $24 return), so there is no need to get one before you get on.

❷ Just a couple of minutes into the journey, you'll pass Estación Borges, named after the great 20th-century Argentine poet and fiction writer, Jorge Luis Borges—the station is also known as Estación de las Artes. If you get off here you can have a coffee at a literary-themed café, Luna Cornea (daily 9–7). The vine-draped pergolas add to the picturesqueness of it all while a short wander will take you deeper into the peaceful little squares of residential Olivos.

Back on the train, the next station, Estación Libertador, is another two minutes down the line.

❸ A small shopping centre at Estación Libertador sells some upmarket clothes, including a big local name, Paula Cahen d'Anvers, while there is an entertainment area for children with food, drink and electronic games.

After a further two minutes, the train reaches Estación Anchorena, which has a tango theme.

❹ Here, you could stop for lunch on the deck terrace of El Andén on the station platform (daily 11–11). The restaurant is just a short hop from the station and offers marvellous views of Río de la Plata and back towards the city.

The next stop, British-style Estación Barrancas, is a further three minutes along the track.

❺ This is the only station along the line built entirely of wood. You can rent roller skates or bicycles at the Bike 'n' Coffee stall to head up and down the trackside path or, for something more tranquil, tour the local antique market (open weekends).

Back on the train, you'll notice that the rails run close by the riverfront along this section of track. The shores here are protected as a nature reserve, a little like the Costanera Sur (▷ 91).

Another three minutes and you arrive at the main stop along the way, the Estación San Isidro.

❻ At San Isidro, you'll find an outdoor commercial centre, the four-screen Atlas cinema, a couple of excellent restaurants and a pub or two. The sights of San Isidro's historic centre (▷ 96–97) are within easy reach, too.

The next stop is Punta Chica station, four minutes after San Isidro, and is also a worthwhile lunchtime stop, with La Avelina restaurant, famed all around for its excellent *parrilla*. Stay on the train to reach Marina Nueva.

❼ This is the newest station on the line and serves the yachting

marina. The marina is a relaxing place for a stroll and there is a Dutch-style café, serving delicious coffee and pastries.

The two following stops—two and four minutes later, respectively—are San Fernando and Canal de San Fernando. San Fernando is next to the Sailing Club, where you might enquire about yacht trips out into the estuary, while the second stop is for train maintenance. Back on the train, your final destination is Estación Delta, in Tigre (▷ 101), a subtropical Venice.

❽ The station is situated right next to the Parque de la Costa theme park (▷ 114), a casino and a handicraft market. Spend the rest of the day in

Tigre, strolling, kayaking or taking a boat trip through the delta. Either return on the Tren de la Costa or take the normal suburban train from the nearby Tigre station.

WHEN TO GO
It is probably best to try to do this ride in the morning, to leave plenty of time for the visits along the way, and perhaps make the most of a trip to Tigre.

WHERE TO EAT
LA AVELINA
Famed for its excellent *parrilla*, La Avelina is a great place to stop for lunch.
✉ General Arias 3698 ☎ 011/4732-0774
🕐 Daily 12.30pm–1am

IL NOVO MARÍA LUJÁN DEL TIGRE
▷ 119.

SHOPPING

ALTO PALERMO

www.altopalermo.com.ar

In the part of town known as Alto Palermo, this large shiny mall positively bursts with tempting stores, including reliable national clothing chains, such as Ayres, Chocolate, Kevingston and Bensimon. There is also a branch of Yenny's, the bookshop chain, where you can find some excellent coffee-table editions to take home or sample some Argentine literature. Have a restorative espresso or buy some *alfajores* (cookies) at Havanna. ⊠ Santa Fé 3253 ☎ 011/5777-8000 🕓 Daily 10–10 🚇 Bulnes (D) 🚌 12, 15, 39, 64, 152 🍴 🖥

ARANDÚ

www.arandu.com.ar

Arandú has branches in Retiro and Recoleta, and the stores are perfect examples of a great Argentine institution, the *talabartería*. The shops will fit you out in true *gaucho* style, with traditional belts, stylish hats, gaudy espadrilles, shirts and, of course, *bombachas del campo* (baggy trousers with button-down cuffs). *Mate*-making paraphernalia and beautiful knives with bone or wooden handles are also sold here. ⊠ Paraguay 1259, Retiro ☎ 011/4816-3689 🕓 Mon–Fri 9.30–8.30, Sat 9.30–1.30 🚌 10, 59, 111

ATENEO GRAND SPLENDID

The Ateneo Grand Splendid was built as a theatre in 1919 and iconic tango singer Carlos Gardel once sang here, but it was converted into a cinema a decade later and is now one of the world's most beautiful bookshops. There is a good café at the back, where great Argentine actors and singers once trod the boards, but the real attraction, apart from the books, is the magnificent interior, topped by a beautiful ceiling painted by Italian artist Nazareno Orlandi. ⊠ Avenida Santa Fé 1860, Recoleta ☎ 011/4811-6104 🕓 Mon–Thu 9am–10pm, Fri–Sat 9–midnight, Sun 12–10 🚇 Callao (D) 🚌 12, 39, 152 📅

BAILARÍN PORTENO

Should you want to kit yourself out from head to toe for a night out at the *milonga*, this unassuming shop in downtown San Nicolás is the place. Felt hats, sharp suits and swanky jackets for him; slinky dresses, giddy high heels and costume jewellery for her. There are also books, CDs and DVDs about tango. ⊠ Suipacha 251, downtown ☎ 011/4390-4067 🕓 Mon–Fri 9.30–8.30, Sat 9.30–1.30 🚇 Avenida de Mayo (C)

BALTHAZAR

www.balthazarshop.com

This modern menswear store has handsome branches in San Telmo and Palermo, in addition to a keenly priced factory outlet in San Telmo. Treat yourself to an alpaca wool scarf in fetching stripes or a stylish silk tie. Italian-style shirts are made to match the elegant clubbish blazers, while unusual cufflinks will put a finishing touch to any outfit. ⊠ Defensa 887, San Telmo ☎ 011/4300-6926 🕓 Mon–Sat 11–8, Sun 11–5 🚌 10, 29, 195

CASA LÓPEZ

www.casalopez.com.ar

With branches in the Galerías Pacífico and Patio Bullrich malls, this venerable house of leather has its HQ on the upper-class Plaza San Martín. Jackets and trenchcoats, for both sexes, come with matching bags, luggage, wallets and purses, many of which are made of native skins such as yacaré (caiman or crocodile) and capybara (carpincho, a huge amphibious rodent native to northeast Argentina). ⊠ Marcelo T. de Alvear 640, Retiro ☎ 011/4311-3044 🕓 Mon–Fri 9–8, Sat 9.30–7, Sun 10–6 🚇 General San Martín (C) 🚌 10, 17, 59, 70, 101

EL CID

www.el-cid.com.ar

El Cid is renowned for its superb tailoring and clean-cut clothes for men by local designer Nestor Goldberg. Whether you prefer a classic, formal style or more casual clothes, El Cid has something for you, and there is an impressive line of stylish accessories, bags and shoes, too. The leather jackets are particularly well made.

✉ Gurruchaga 1732, Palermo
☎ 011/4832-3339 🕐 Mon–Sat 11–8, Sun 3–7 🚌 34, 39, 55, 166

CHICCO RUIZ

www.lourdeschiccoruiz.com.ar
The Imelda Marcos in you might get some satisfaction at this fabulous shoe shop in Palermo Soho. Lourdes Chicco Ruiz makes her footwear for fashion-conscious women in the old-fashioned way, using the finest leather and beautiful wooden trees. Colourful and playful, sober and stylish, there is something for every taste, but handmade shoes of this quality do not come cheap.

✉ Thames 1780, Palermo
☎ 011/4831-1264 🕐 Mon–Sat 12–8, Sun 2–8 🚌 34, 55, 166

COMME IL FAUT

www.commeilfaut.com.ar
One of many well concealed secrets along the oh-so-French Rue des Artisans, this Recoleta shoe shop just off smart Calle Arenales prides itself on purveying the best tango footwear money can buy. Alicia Muñiz is the queen of the tango slingback and she prides herself on creating heels that are works of art. A good shoe is vital for good dancing and this shop makes shoes 'as they should be'. Alicia's other slogan is 'So many shoes, so little time'.

✉ Rue des Artisans M, Arenales 1239, Retiro ☎ 011/4815-5690 🕐 Mon–Fri 11–7, Sat 11–3 🚌 39, 101, 111, 152

LA DOLFINA

www.ladolfina.com
Polo heart throb Adolfo Cambiaso has his own line of menswear that combines rural practicality with urban chic—ranging from well-cut bermuda shorts and best-cotton dress shirts to polo shirts and elegantly cut jeans. The clothes in this shop are

smart casual at its very best, as you'd expect at the lower end of the aristocratic Avenida Alvear.

✉ Avenida Alvear 1315, Retiro
☎ 011/4815-2698 🕐 Mon–Fri 10–8, Sat 10–6 🚌 17, 59, 67, 102

ETIQUETA NEGRA

www.etiquetanegra.us
This classy menswear chain has branches in the Galerías Pacífico, Patio Bullrich and Unicenter shopping malls, as well as farther afield in Las Cañitas and San Isidro. Shopping here is an experience—the vintage cars and Harley Davidsons displayed in the stores are museum pieces in their own right. The slim-fit suits, whiter-than-white cotton shirts and sleek leather shoes do not come cheap but they are made to last. There is a women's range, too, but choices are more limited.

✉ Galerías Pacífico 316, Florida 737, downtown ☎ 011/5555-5316 🕐 Mon–Sat 10–9, Sun 12–9 🚇 Florida (B) 🚌 6, 93, 130, 152

GALERÍAS PACÍFICO

www.progaleriaspacifico.com.ar
Once a Parisian-style department store, Pacífico has blossomed into one of the city's most refined shopping malls, with striking frescoes by leading Argentine artists looking down on three storeys of boutiques and chain shops, including some big international names. The food hall on the lower floor offers a range of places to eat, from smart cafés to handy fast-food outlets, elegantly encircling a soothing fountain. There is also a small cinema complex and an arts centre.

✉ Florida 737, downtown
☎ 011/5555-5100 🕐 Mon–Sat 10–9, Sun 12–9 🚇 Florida (B) 🚌 6, 93, 130, 152
🍴 🛍

HUMAWACA

www.humawaca.com
The ladies of Palermo and Recoleta like their handbags so Humawaca has branches in both *barrios*, where the best Argentine leather is reborn as unusual clutches and purses. Two of the shop's exclusives are a

shoulder bag with an iPod feature and a briefcase with a removable solar panel that allows you to recharge small appliances, such as mobile phones.

✉ El Salvador 4692, Palermo
☎ 011/4832-2662 🕐 Mon–Sat 11–8, Sun 3–8 🚌 39, 55, 151, 168

INFINIT

www.infinitnet.com
Glasses and sunglasses are very good value in Buenos Aires and you can find some fun designs you cannot get elsewhere, so bring your prescription with you. This alluring corner shop in Palermo Soho specializes in retro frames including a range decorated with sports cars. Infinit will do their best to make your glasses within a few days.

✉ Thames 1602, Palermo
☎ 011/4831-7070 🕐 Mon–Sat 11–8, Sun 3–7 🚌 39, 55

JUANA DE ARCO

www.juanadearco.net
Mariana Cortés is the driving force behind this fabulous Palermo boutique, with a basement art gallery. Her beautiful, brightly coloured fabrics combine traditional South American techniques, such as *ñandutí* (Paraguayan lace), with contemporary designs to create eye-catching garments. Mariana even turns her hand to some avant-garde menswear, too.

✉ El Salvador 4762, Palermo
☎ 011/4833-1621 🕐 Mon–Sat 10–8, Sun 1–8 🚌 15, 34, 39

LO DE JOAQUÍN ALBERDI

www.lodejoaquinalberdi.com.ar
This Palermo *vinoteca* (wine store) gives tastings of the outstanding wines on sale here. Otherwise, just ask a member of the extremely helpful staff for some guidance through the labyrinth of bottles that line the walls. The shop stocks red, white and sparkling wines from the country's leading *bodegas*, plus one or two off-the-beaten track wineries.

✉ Borges 1772, Palermo
☎ 011/4832-5329 🕐 Mon–Sat 10–9.30, Sun 12.30–9.30 🚌 34, 55, 93

MANU LIZARRALDE
www.manulizarralde.com
For rings and pendants, bracelets and necklaces, look no further than this Palermo gem shop. Aquamarines, emeralds and amethysts are harmoniously combined with exotic stones like star rutilos, lodolites and Paraiba tourmalines by master craftsman Manu Lizarralde. The designs, such as the rutilated quartz earrings set in Argentine silver, are timeless creations with a contemporary spark.

✉ Gorriti 5078, Palermo
☎ 011/4832-6252 ⊙ Mon–Sat 11–8, Sun 2–8 🚌 55, 151, 168

PATIO BULLRICH
www.shoppingbullrich.com.ar
Buenos Aires has no shortage of beautiful shopping malls that will make even the most ardent mall-hater change their mind. This historic building used to be a livestock market but was given a new lease of life as a glossy shopping centre. As at many of the city's malls, the idea is to spend a whole afternoon checking out the latest fashion, people-watching at a smart café,

sipping Bellinis at the bar and maybe segueing into an evening at the movies.

✉ Avenida del Libertador 750, Recoleta
☎ 011/4814-7400 ⊙ Daily 10–9
🚌 67, 92, 130 🍴 🛒

PESQUEIRA
www.pesqueiratm.com
Not far from Palermo's lively Plaza Cortázar hub, this delightful little boutique showcases designer Valeria Pesqueira's pretty women's clothes. Polka-dot prints and florals dominate the fresh, naive dresses and smocks, while the matching laptop bags are part of the apparel of any self-respecting Palermitana. The prices are refreshing, too.

✉ Armenia 1493, Palermo ☎ 011/4833-7218 ⊙ Mon–Sat 11–8 🚌 15, 55, 151, 168

SABATER HERMANOS
www.shnos.com.ar
This Palermo landmark is run by the third generation of soap makers and it is worth stopping by their shop, even if you decide not to take any scented golf balls or marijuana leaf soaps home with you as an ephemeral souvenir. In fact, most of

the amusing and appealing designs look too good to use but the shop smells great and aromatic scents such as green tea and cedar are big favourites.

✉ Gurruchaga 1821, Palermo
☎ 011/4833-3004 ⊙ Mon–Sat 10–8, Sun 1–7 🚌 39, 55, 151

ENTERTAINMENT AND NIGHTLIFE

ALSINA
www.palacioalsina.com
This downtown clubbing venue has an impressive post-industrial decor and pulsates into the early hours to the sounds of artists such as John Digweed and M.A.N.D.Y. on Saturday State and Friday night gay nights. Early birds might prefer the Sunday Club One, where the dancing starts mid-afternoon and finishes well before midnight. The dance floor has a capacity of 3,000 plus, but there is a balcony where you can people-watch and get away from the hustle and bustle for a while.

✉ Alsina 940, downtown ☎ 011/4331-1277 ⊙ Wed 7pm–1am, Fri–Sat 1am–5am, Sun 3pm–10pm. Closed Jan 🚇 Moreno (C) 🚌 10, 17, 59, 64, 86

ASIA DE CUBA
www.asiadecuba.com.ar
Throughout the week this fashionable yet relaxed restaurant-nightclub overlooking Puerto Madero docks lures a trendy crowd with different events and varied musical styles. The food revolves around fresh sushi but the drinks list is long and the hours of fun seem to be never-ending. Dress up or you'll feel conspicuous.

✉ Pierina Dialessi 750, Puerto Madero
☎ 011/4671-9310 ⊙ Tue–Sat 9pm–6am
✋ $60 cover charge 🚌 2, 130, 152

BELUSHI MARTINI BAR
www.belushi.com.ar
Perfectly mixed negronis and margaritas and, of course, classic Martinis accompany the appetizing *tablas* (snack boards) covered with

Left *Long-established Café Tortoni, once the favoured haunt of the city's literati*

cheese, olives and all manner of goodies at this stylish cocktail bar in ever-trendy Palermo. This is the type of place where celebs hold their birthday parties in the hope of being in a glossy mag the next day.

✉ Honduras 5333, Palermo
☎ 011/4831-8665 ⏰ Thu–Sat 8pm–2am
🚌 34, 55, 166

CAFÉ RETIRO

Located within the Retiro train station, this handsome art nouveau *confitería* has been restored to its former glory, with solid columns and soaring cupolas, polished tiled floors and burnished wooden panelling. It is a great place to have a leisurely breakfast before taking the train to Tigre or San Isidro. At lunchtime there is a *menú del día*, usually with a steak or pasta—perfect with an ice-cold beer or a glass of wine—and followed by a traditional *flan* or *budín de pan* (bread pudding).

✉ Retiro station, Ramos Mejía 1358, Retiro
☎ 011/4516-0902 ⏰ Daily 6.30am–10pm
🚇 Retiro (C)

CAFÉ TORTONI

www.cafetortoni.com.ar

The Tortoni moved to its current location in 1880 but hardly anything has changed since. Every Argentine writer and artist worth his or her salt has chewed the fat at its basement *peña* or club—sadly closed in the 1940s—while countless politicians have sipped champagne or drunk espresso in its opulent salons, famed for their stained-glass windows. These days, foreigners outnumber the locals, but, coach-loads of photo-snapping tourists notwithstanding, it is still a great place to listen to tango, play billiards or people-watch over a *café con leche con medialunas* (milky coffee with croissants).

✉ Avenida de Mayo 829, downtown
☎ 011/4342-4328 ⏰ Daily 8am–1am
🚇 Piedras (A), Avenida de Mayo (C)

CENTRO CULTURAL TORQUATO TASSO

www.torquatotasso.com.ar

This old-fashioned café-concert bar in the heart of San Telmo, overlooking

Above *Dancing the tango at the upstairs ballroom of the Confitería Ideal*

the historic Parque Lezama, is the place to hear tango music played to perfection. The cultural centre, named after an Italian poet, serves food and drink but its raison d'être is preserving tango as an art form rather than a tourist attraction. Regularly performing the classics here is the remarkable Selección Nacional de Tango, an 18-member band, plus resident singers Susana Rinaldi and Osvaldo Piro, two veterans of the art. This is a place not to be missed.

✉ Defensa 1575, San Telmo
☎ 011/4307-6506 ⏰ Fri–Sun from 10pm (occasionally Wed and Thu also)
🚇 Independencia (C) 🚌 10, 17, 24, 29, 39, 64, 152

CONFITERÍA IDEAL

www.confiteriaideal.com

Nobody cares that this place is musty and dusty, with net curtains in the windows. Inside, the faded grandeur of the belle-époque dining room and the upstairs ballroom delight locals and visitors alike, while the tango shows are of the highest quality, sometimes featuring the city's top-ranking musicians, singers and dancers vying for the crowd's acclaim and applause. Prepare for an evening with plenty of nostalgia and rip-roaring entertainment.

✉ Suipacha 380, downtown
☎ 011/5265-8069 ⏰ Daily 10.30pm–4am;

milongas Wed–Mon 2–8.30pm 🎫 $50 cover charge during shows 🚇 Diagonal Norte (C)
🚌 10, 24, 70, 100

CONGO

The leather interior of this leading Palermo bar is extremely comfortable, while crowds queue to get into its spotlit garden after midnight. The other big attraction here is the fabulous selection of cocktails at the stunning backlit bar. Try the Bossa Nova, the house special, a near-lethal but delicious blend of rum, brandy, Galliano, passion fruit and a dash of honey.

✉ Honduras 5329, Palermo ☎ 011/4833-5857 ⏰ Wed, Thu 8pm–4am, Fri, Sat 8pm–6am 🚌 31, 34, 39, 166

ESQUINA HOMERO MANZI

www.esquinahomeromanzi.com.ar

Named for one of the great tango composers and musicians, this venerable institution offers private and group tango classes in the early evening before putting on one of the best dinner-shows in the city. The fabulous quintet, three couples of dancers and two top-rate singers give their all to make it an evening to remember. In the elegant restaurant you can choose from three different menus.

✉ San Juan 3601, Boedo
☎ 011/4957-8488 ⏰ Daily dinner 9pm; show 10pm 🎫 Show: $200 🚇 Boedo (E)

HOYTS ABASTO

www.hoyts.com.ar

The multiplex cinema in the Abasto shopping centre is one of the best in the city and the main venue for the internationally acclaimed BAFICI indie film festival in April (▷ 115). The rest of the year, the program is subtitled Hollywood hits mostly.

✉ Avenida Corrientes 3247, Balvanera
☎ 0810/4000-2923 🕓 Daily 12–12
Ⓜ Carlos Gardel (B) 🚌 24, 26, 41, 62, 146, 188

LUNA PARK

www.lunapark.com.ar

The 8,000-seater Stadium Luna Park is an art deco relic that has survived to host some of the biggest national and international names from the world of music, plus boxing matches, cycling championships and volleyball competitions. Frank Sinatra, mega-bands Oasis and Deep Purple, and the Harlem Globetrotters have all been on the arena's programme, while Pope John Paul II addressed a huge adoring crowd during one of his visits to the city. It is famous for being where Perón spotted Evita and asked her out on a date.

✉ Avenida Madero 420, downtown
☎ 011/5279-5279 Ⓜ Leandro Alem (B)
🚌 4, 20, 28, 130, 140

MILIÓN

www.milion.com.ar

This glorious bar in ritzy Recoleta, housed in an early 20th-century Gallic town house, serves tapas and cocktails in its delightful garden and has a refined upstairs restaurant serving excellent Argentine dishes. The house is used as a venue for regular photography and other arts shows.

✉ Paraná 1048, Recoleta
☎ 011/4815-9925 🕓 Mon–Sat noon–3am, Sun 8pm–2pm 🚌 29, 39, 152

ND/ATENEO

www.ndateneo.com.ar

One of the best music venues in a music-loving city, the classic ND/Ateneo attracts some of the country's leading rock, jazz, folk and tango artists to perform at its regular Friday and Saturday evening concerts. On a good week, there might be an event on Thursday and Sunday, too, while the arts centre's schedules may include poetry recitals, film screenings, drama performances or special evenings of techno-tango.

✉ Paraguay 918, Retiro ☎ 011/4328-2888
🕓 Thu–Sun from 10pm 💰 From $50
Ⓜ Tribunales (D)

PACHÁ

www.pachabuenosaires.com

Pachá is one of the top dancing venues in the city, so expect salons thronging with designer-dressed revellers, VIP lounges, free-flowing champagne, starlit dance patios and terraces with wonderful views of the Río de la Plata. Leading national and international DJs make sure the strutting and bopping go on well into the dawn zone.

✉ Avenida Costanera Rafael Obligado and La Pampa, Palermo ☎ 011/4788-4280
🕓 Sat 1am–dawn. Closed Jan 💰 $50 cover charge 🚌 37, 160

PEÑA DEL COLORADO

www.lapeniadelcolorado.com.ar

While this legendary *peña*, one of the few in the capital, occasionally hosts tango, jazz and light rock acts, its mainstay is traditional Argentine folk music. The restaurant menu is firmly rooted in northwestern cuisine and serves *empanadas* (pasties), *tamales* (filled dumplings made with corn) and *locro* (a maize-based stew). To complete the *criollo* cultural experience, there is a *mate* bar, serving up freshly brewed *yerba* with traditional snacks.

✉ Güemes 3657, Palermo
☎ 011/4822-1038 🕓 Daily noon–3am (sometimes closed Mon for private events); concerts 10pm 💰 $25–$30 🚌 55, 60, 64, 152

EL QUERANDÍ

www.querandi.com.ar

This historic neo-colonial building had an art deco facelift in the 1920s and was impeccably restored in the 1990s, when it became one of the city's leading tango venues. Its chessboard dancefloor, handsome cedar panelling and Viennese-style chairs make it a fine setting for a series of tango tableaux. Despite being unashamedly aimed at tourists, the quality of the dancers, live musicians and choreography leave nothing to be desired. The food is fine but it may be better to opt for the show-only option.

✉ Perú 302, San Telmo
☎ 011/5199-1771 🕓 Daily, dinner 9pm; show 10.30pm 💰 Show: $200
Ⓜ Independencia (C) 🚌 10, 17, 24, 29, 39, 64, 152

SEÑOR TANGO

www.senortango.com.ar

Although its claim to deliver the most amazing tango show in the history of the art form is hype, this is certainly the place for tango at its most spectacular. Tonnes of juicy steaks and litres of Argentine wine are consumed every night in this cavernous hall in the traditional *barrio* of Barracas. Expect to see *gauchos* on horses at the entrance and to hear some over-the-top crooning by showy singers, including a rendering of *Don't Cry for Me* as a grand finale, but the atmosphere is electric. Take a taxi to get there.

✉ Vieytes 1655, Barracas ☎ 011/4303-0231 🕐 Daily dinner 8.30; show 9.30 ✋ Show $125; dinner and show $400

THELONIOUS CLUB
www.thelonious.com.ar
Sip a dry Martini or a cosmopolitan at the city's top jazz venue, where you can hear home-grown sounds and, occasionally, big names from abroad. Modelled on the best New York jazz clubs, Thelonious has a mellow atmosphere and a lively schedule, with regular appearances by one of the best Argentine jazz groups, Escalandrum, which features percussionist Pipi Piazzolla, grandson of the tango giant, Astor.

✉ Salguero 1884, Palermo ☎ 011/4829-1562 🕐 Daily 9.30pm ✋ $10–$25 🚇 Bulnes (D)

UN'ALTRA VOLTA
www.unaltravolta.com.ar
Luscious brownies, apple crumble and frothy capuccinos are all good reasons to visit one of the smart branches of this stylish chain. But most people keep coming back because they want to try one more of the fabulous ice cream flavours: a dozen different chocolate varieties, including the house special with Piemontese hazelnuts, tangy lemon or tangerine, but best of all, seven heavenly kinds of *dulce de leche*.

✉ Libertador 3060, Palermo ☎ 011/4783-4048 🕐 Sun–Thu 8am–2am, Fri 8am–3am, Sat 8am–4am ✋ From $10 🚇 Scalabrini Ortiz (D)

SPORTS AND ACTIVITIES
CAMPO ARGENTINO DE POLO
www.aapolo.com
The national polo pitch, like many of the city's major sporting venues, is in Palermo, while the neighbouring mini-*barrio* of Las Cañitas is traditionally a hangout for polo players. It hosts the Argentine open

championship from November to December. Tickets for tournaments are easily obtained on Ticketek (www.ticketek.com.ar). The venue is also used for rock concerts, hosting well-known artists, such as Oasis and Shakira.

✉ Avenida del Libertador 4300, Palermo ☎ 011/4777-6444 🕐 Nov–Dec 🚇 Palermo/Carranza (D)

CAMPO DE GOLF DE LA CIUDAD DE BUENOS AIRES
The city's best links are situated in Palermo and this 18-hole course is notorious for featuring some tricky bunkers. Fees and hire costs are low by international standards.

✉ Avenida Tornquist 6397 ☎ 011/4772-7261 🕐 Tue–Sun 7.30–5 ✋ Day pass: $30 🚇 Palermo (D)

ESTADIO ALBERTO J. ARMANDO
www.bocajuniors.com.ar
www.tangol.com
Better known by its nickname of La Bombonera (The Chocolate Box), this iconic football stadium is home to the legendary Boca Juniors, where Maradona shot to fame. It is best to pay a little extra for a seat in the *platea baja* (lower section) of the stadium. Leave your valuables at home and it is advisable to arrange your ticket through a tour operator, such as Tangol (Florida 971; tel 011/4312-7276, www.tangol.com). Tour prices vary but usually include transfers to the stadium, a tour guide and a ticket to your chosen game.

✉ Brandsen 805, Boca ☎ 011/4309-4700 🚌 10, 29, 53, 64, 152

ESTADIO MONUMENTAL
www.cariverplate.com.ar
www.tangol.com
The monumental stadium, the home turf for Boca's rivals River Plate, is located in the middle-income *barrio* of Núñez, just north of Palermo. Bigger and more comfortable than La Bombonera, it can get just as boisterous and, again, it is best to book your ticket via a reputable tour operator, such as Tangol. The stadium also stages frequent concerts by

internationally renowned artists. There are also guided tours of the 60,000-seat stadium.

✉ Avenida Figueroa Alcorta 7597, Núñez ☎ 011/4789-1200 🕐 Guided tours daily 11–5, hourly on the hour ✋ Guided tours: $45 🚌 29, 42, 107, 130

HIPÓDROMO ARGENTINO
www.palermo.com.ar
Horse racing is less important than you might think for such an equestrian-loving nation but it is worth attending the races to admire the marvellous early 20th-century grandstand, a belle-époque masterpiece.

✉ Avenida del Libertador 4101, Palermo ☎ 011/4778-2800 🕐 Sat–Mon, Fri ✋ Free (main stand only) 🚌 10, 34, 130, 160, 166

PARQUE NORTE
www.parquenorte.com
This outdoor complex in Núñez, a well-heeled northern *barrio*, has three large swimming pools with waterslides plus tennis, basketball, football and beach volleyball courts. Poolside space and sunloungers are at a premium in good weather.

✉ Avenida Cantilo and Güiraldes, Palermo ☎ 011/4787-1382 🕐 Pools: 9am–8pm; sports: 8am–midnight ✋ $10–$35 🚌 28, 33, 37, 42, 45, 107, 160

PERÚ BEACH
www.peru-beach.com.ar
This riverside complex in Acasusso, near San Isidro, focuses on windsurfing and kitesurfing, with a reputed school for all levels, but also offers kayaking, a climbing wall, roller hockey, skateboarding, pilates and spinning classes in a well-equipped gym. There is a lifeguard service and the on-site Toien beach bar (www.toien.com.ar) is a great place to relax.

✉ Elcano 794 and Perú, Acassuso ☎ 011/4793-5986 🕐 Oct–Mar daily 9–8; Apr–Sep 10–6 ✋ Gym day pass: $100 🚌 168 🚉 Tren de la Costa: Barrancas station

SALGUERO TENIS
Many tennis clubs in the city require membership but this Palermo club

offers tennis (on clay) and squash at very reasonable day rates.

✉ Salguero 3350, Palermo
☎ 011/4802-2930 🕓 Daily 8am–midnight
✋ $100 per day

TAZZ SALGUERO
www.tazzbars.com
This popular after-hours office bar on Palermo's riverside Costanera Norte is one of the best places in the city to go for bowling. There are half a dozen computerized lanes, plus darts, table football and pool.

✉ Avenida Rafael Obligado and Salguero, Palermo ☎ 011/4807-8299 🕓 Tue–Sun 6pm–3am

URBAN BIKING
en.urbanbiking.com
Buenos Aires is finally catching on to the ecological benefits of cycling and cycle paths are being developed around the city. The highly professional crew at Urban Biking can arrange a variety of interesting tours, either in a group or individually, with options including a night ride to check out the nightlife, plus conventional sightseeing and cycle tours to the Tigre Delta. Bikes, helmets and refreshments, including *mate*, are included. Call or email for details of start points.

✉ Moliere 2801 ☎ 011/4568-4321
✋ US$40–US$80

HEALTH AND BEAUTY
MEGATLÓN
www.megatlon.com
You can buy a day pass at this top-rate gym chain, which has branches at several locations in the city including downtown and Recoleta. The quality of machines and variety of classes are generally good.

✉ Arenales 1930, Recoleta
☎ 011/4811-2565 🕓 Mon–Fri 7am–11pm, Sat 9–8 ✋ Day pass $75 🚇 Callao (D)
🚌 37, 39, 111, 152

SER SPA
www.aguaclubspa.com
Indulge in some pampering at this smart Palermo spa, located in a

beautiful Parisian-style town house. Relax in the Jacuzzi or saunas or choose from a range of expert massages and beauty treatments.

✉ Cerviño 3626, Palermo
☎ 011/4807-4688 🕓 Mon–Fri 7.30am–10.30pm, Sat 11–9, Sun 12–8 ✋ Massages from $120 🚇 Scalabrini Ortiz (D)

CHILDREN
MUSEO DE LOS NIÑOS
www.museoabasto.org.ar
The motto of this fun museum for children in the Abasto shopping centre is 'playing at being grown-ups without stopping being kids'. Designed as a small-scale town, it allows children to find out about the workings of shops, banks and factories by means of hands-on exhibits and installations, while also learning about ecology and technology. Occasional special events, such as circuses and competitions, are popular, too.

✉ Avenida Corrientes 3247, Balvanera
☎ 011/4861-2325 🕓 Tue–Sun, national holidays 1–8 ✋ Adult $10–$15, child $18–$30, half-price between 7–8pm 🚇 Carlos Gardel (B) 🚌 24, 26, 41, 62, 146, 188

PARQUE DE LA COSTA
www.parquedelacosta.com.ar
Parque de la Costa is the biggest theme park of its kind in South America. The park includes a huge variety of fun rides and roller coasters, with names such as Vertigo Xtremo and Boomerang, and the new spin ride Torbellino, plus dancing fountains and dodgems. You can go up a lighthouse for great views of the delta or have a go at mountaineering

on the climbing-wall, known as Aconcagua.

✉ Vivanco 1509, Tigre ☎ 011/4002-6000
🕓 May–Sep Sat–Sun 11–7; Oct–Apr daily 11am–8pm (last entry 7pm) ✋ Adult/child $60 🚉 Estación Delta (Tren de la Costa)

PLANETARIO GALILEO GALILEI
www.planetario.gov.ar
The city's planetarium is handily located in the great parkland of Palermo's Bosques. The 1960s building is showing its age, but some of the exhibits are fascinating. Look out for the colossal meteorites that fell on northern Argentina 4,000 years ago. Special effects and hands-on displays explain the workings of the universe to visitors of all ages. There are shows at weekends and on public holidays, too.

✉ Avenida Sarmiento and Belisario Roldán
☎ 011/4771-9393 🕓 Mon–Thu 9–5, Fri–Sun 1–7 ✋ Adult $10, child (under 12) free

TEMAIKÈN
www.temaiken.com.ar
This wildlife park 50km (31 miles) north of the city, near Escobar, is easily reached and makes a good day trip. Temaikèn is a wonderful place to see native fauna, such as pumas and tapirs, and the park's aquarium, with its penguins and sharks, is a definite highlight. Save some time to explore the bat house.

✉ RN25 km1, Escobar, Provincia de Buenos Aires ☎ 03488-436900
🕓 Dec–Feb Tue–Sun 10–7; Mar–Nov Tue–Sun 10–6 ✋ Adult $65, child (3–10) $50, under 3 free; half price Tue, excluding hols 🚌 60 (marked 'Ramal Escobar')

Right Gauchos *at the Feria de Mataderos*

FEBRUARY

BUENOS AIRES FASHION WEEK

www.bafweek.com

Every fashion-conscious city has to have its fashion week and Buenos Aires—one of Latin America's design hubs—is no exception. Being the southern hemisphere means that February is the time for a sneak preview of the forthcoming autumn and winter collections.

COPA CLARO

www.copatelmex.com

The city closes down and moves to the coast or across to Uruguay in January, but February sees some action in the shape of one of the country's major tennis championships, held at the city's Lawn Tennis Club in Palermo. Local heroes fight it out on clay with mainly Hispanic rivals.

☎ 011/4117-7110

APRIL

BUENOS AIRES FESTIVAL INTERNACIONAL DE CINE INDEPENDIENTE

www.bafici.gov.ar

The Hoyts Abasto cinema (▷ 112) is the principal venue for the city's exciting indie film festival, which attracts some international names in the film industry and is a chance to mingle with lots of arty types while checking out some excellent movies.

GALLERY NIGHTS

www.artealdia.com

The last Friday of April is the start of eight months of late-night art gallery viewings, repeated on the last Friday of every month until November, when the galleries close down until the following year.

FERIA INTERNACIONAL DEL LIBRO DE BUENOS AIRES

The three-week Feria Internacional del Libro de Buenos Aires, held every year at the end of April, is the biggest Spanish-language book fair in the world. In 2011 guest speaker Mario Vargas Llosa, Nobel Laureate, caused a stir by outspokenly criticizing the Argentine government. Buenos Aires was chosen to be World Book Capital in 2011.

MAY

CARRERA DE MOZOS Y CAMARERAS

www.apthgra.com

Buenos Aires sets out to emulate Paris in mid-May with a much loved race for waiters of both genders. Competitors run up and down the Avenida de Mayo doing their utmost to prevent a glass of water and two bottles toppling off their trays.

JUNE

ARTEBA

www.arteba.com

Buenos Aires takes its art seriously and this annual contemporary art fair gathers avant-garde painting and sculpture from worldwide art dealers, although the focus is on local and Latin American artists. In 2010, there was a fabulous turnout as representatives from Chile, Venezuela, Colombia, Mexico and Spain came to celebrate Argentina's 200 years of independence. The venue changes annually.

JULY

EXPOSICIÓN DE GANADERÍA

www.exposicionrural.com.ar

Late winter is the time to bring the countryside into the city, with a huge exhibition of livestock and *gauchos* at the magnificent Predio La Rural in Palermo.

AUGUST

FESTIVAL Y MUNDIAL DEL TANGO

www.festivaldetango.gob.ar

www.mundialdetango.gob.ar

Festival y Mundial del Tango is just one of many tango events held in Buenos Aires throughout the year, but the world championships brings tango dancers from around the world to compete for a glittering crown and the prestige of winning on tango's home turf. The festival takes place in various venues around the city—check online for more detailed information.

SEPTEMBER

VINOS Y BODEGAS

www.expovinosybodegas.com.ar

Another great not-to-miss extravaganza held in the marvellous surroundings of the Predio La Rural is the Vinos y Bodegas. This time, barrels and bottles take over from beef and cowboy boots, as wine-producers, oenologists, vintners and sommeliers show off about wine.

OCTOBER

MARATÓN INTERNACIONAL DE BUENOS AIRES

www.maratondebuenosaires.com

BA's marathon has only been going a few years but is already a popular event and on many a runner's calendar.

NOVEMBER

DÍA DE LA TRADICIÓN

On 10 November each year, the whole country celebrates *criollo* culture and traditions, but in San Antonio de Areco the event lasts a week. Expect lots of grilled meat and rodeo antics.

DECEMBER

BUENOS AIRES JAZZ FESTIVAL INTERNACIONAL

www.buenosairesjazz.gov.ar

Tango and rock often seem to dominate the local music scene but there is a lot of inventive jazz going on in the city, too, and the international jazz festival is usually held during the first week of December. Check the website for dates and venue.

EATING

PRICES AND SYMBOLS

The restaurants are listed alphabetically (excluding El, La and Los). The prices given are the average for a two-course lunch (L) and a three-course dinner (D) for one person, without drinks. The wine price is for the least expensive bottle. All the restaurants listed accept credit cards unless otherwise stated. Prices are given in Argentine pesos ($) unless otherwise noted.

For a key to the symbols, ▷ 2.

BUENOS AIRES

LA BIELA
www.labiela.com
This classic *confitería*, a haunt of Formula One hero Fangio in the 1950s, occupies an unassuming building opposite the entrance to La Recoleta cemetery. Although more expensive, it is worth sitting outside on the terrace. The house speciality is *lomo Biela*, grilled beef in a crusty sandwich served with French fries.
✉ Avenida Presidente Manuel Quintana 600, Recoleta ☎ 011/4804-0449 ⊕ Daily 8am–1am ✋ L $30, D $50, Wine $20
🚌 60, 64, 92, 110, 152, 188

CABAÑA LAS LILAS
www.laslilas.com.ar
Expensive and touristy, Cabaña las Lilas remains the classic Puerto

Madero haunt. The tender slabs of *bife de chorizo* and *ojo de bife* are grilled perfectly. Start your meal with a tasty carpaccio of Portobello mushrooms and finish with the mouth-watering *tarte tatin*, served with cinnamon ice cream. Service is impeccable and the wine list is unimpeachable, while the elegant ambience is smart without being stuffy. Weather permitting, you can sit on the terrace and enjoy fabulous views of the docks.
✉ Alicia Moreau de Justo 516, Puerto Madero ☎ 011/4313-1336 ⊕ Daily noon–1am ✋ L $70, D $120, Wine $50
🚇 Leandro Alem (B)

LA CABRERA
www.parrillalacabrera.com.ar
It is not easy to make a reservation at this excellent corner-house *parrilla* (grill) in a leafy part of Palermo Viejo (or at its younger sister, La Cabrera Norte, a few doors up), so you might have to wait on the pavement outside and sip champagne until a table becomes available. The quality and size of the succulent *bife de chorizo* is overwhelming and while you wait for your steaks to sizzle you can sample a delicious variety of tapas, including butter bean and aubergine (eggplant) salad, tiny potatoes and

sweet cherry tomatoes, served in elegant little china pots.
✉ Cabrera 5099, Palermo ☎ 011/4831-7002 ⊕ Mon 12.30–4, Tue–Sun 12.30–4, 8pm–1am ✋ L $60, D $80, Wine $23 🚌 55

CASA FÉLIX
www.colectivofelix.com
It is worth the short trek out to Chacarita for this *puertas cerradas* (closed doors) establishment for its exciting meat-free fare concocted by Diego Félix. He and his wife, Sanra, travel around the Americas in search of new ingredients and novel ideas, before transposing them to their intimate suburban kitchen. In their tiny dining room a lucky few can taste unusual inventions, such as rocket (arugula) and spinach salad with *chañar* (native fruit) dressing and grilled *surubí* (catfish) with *manioc* (root vegetable) and *aguaribay* (native herb), perhaps rounded off with coconut rice pudding with lavender ice cream. Make sure you inform the proprietors of any dietary requirements at the time of booking.
ℹ Reservations by email (diego@diegofelix. com) only. When your reservation is confirmed, Casa Felix will email their address in the Chacarita *barrio* ☎ 011/4555-1882 ⊕ Thu–Sat 9.30 ✋ D $150, Wine $35

Opposite Cabaña las Lilas, a Puerto Madero institution serving superb steaks

CASEROS

www.caserosrestaurante.com.ar

Tucked away near San Telmo's Parque Lezama, this unpretentious bistro serves French-influenced cuisine using seasonal fresh ingredients from the market. Huge windows, overlooking the handsome avenue outside, enhance the restaurant's all-white interior. A typical *menú del día* might include a couscous salad followed by steak with carrots and fennel. Save room for the creamy *arroz con leche* (rice pudding). You can eat at pavement-side tables during fine weather.

✉ Caseros 486, San Telmo
☎ 011/4307-4729 🕐 Tue–Sat 12–12. Closed Mon evening 🖐 L $36, D $60, Wine $25 🚌 33, 39, 62, 64, 143

COMO EN CASA

www.tortascomoencasa.com

For some of the best fruit tarts and chocolate cakes in town, try this elegant tea room, where you can also feast on savoury quiches, freshly made sandwiches and delicious cheesecakes. There is a wide variety of teas and infusions and a choice of perfectly brewed coffees. Alternatively, try a *licuado* (milkshake) blended with fresh fruit. There are several branches in BA but this one, in Recoleta, is housed in an elegant Parisian-style palace.

✉ Laprida 1782, Recoleta
☎ 011/4829-0624 🕐 Daily 9–9 🖐 From $20 🚇 Agüero (D) 🚌 12, 39, 64, 152

EL CUARTITO

www.galeriaelcuartito.com.ar

Head to this Retiro pizzeria to enjoy generously topped pizzas, from classic margaritas to *fuggazza* (savory onion) with mozzarella, or juicy *empanadas* straight from the wood-fired oven. There is a lively atmosphere, brisk service and a rough-and-ready ambience of blaring soccer on the TV, glaring neons and Formica tables, for which you might have to wait. Order one of the thirst-

quenching litre bottles of ice-cold beer to accompany your pizza.

✉ Talcahuano 937, downtown
☎ 011/4816-4331 🕐 Daily noon–1am 🖐 L $25, D $35, Wine $18 🚇 Tribunales (D)

DON JULIO

Leather tablecloths and walls lined with empty wine bottles are the setting for this unmissable Palermo *parrilla*. This is the kind of place where you might consider not sharing the *bife de chorizo*, even though it covers the plate. Pumpkin and spinach soufflé is just one of the vegetarian specials. The expert waiters can help you choose from the extensive wine list from the California Bodegas Aguirre Winery & Vineyards.

✉ Guatemala 4691, Palermo
☎ 011/4832-6058 🕐 Daily 12–4, 7.30–1 🖐 L $55, D $75, Wine $21 🚇 Palermo 🚌 35, 55, 93, 111, 161

EXPERIENCIA DEL FIN DEL MUNDO

www.bodegadelfindelmundo.com/Experiencia

Check out some groundbreaking Patagonian wines at this sumptuous Palermo Hollywood restaurant. Kick off with a kir royal with a difference: Patagonian sparkling wine with a tot of malbec reduction. Then marry a surprisingly rich Pinot Noir with succulent lamb from the wilds of the south. The food is innovative without being pretentious, and the cellars are bursting with exciting wines.

✉ Honduras 5663, Palermo ☎ 011/4852-6661 🕐 Tue–Sun 12–4, 8–12 🖐 L $70, D $90, Wine $30 🚌 39, 93, 111, 161

GRANIX

www.granix.com.ar

On the first floor of one of the city's most magnificent shopping arcades, Granix serves a variety of fresh salads and vegetarian dishes. The food is excellent at this fixed-price, self-service restaurant, and extremely good value for money. Buy a ticket at the entrance, on the first floor, take a tray and choose from a range of dishes that might include asparagus quiche, sweetcorn au gratin and

carrot soufflé, plus fruit-based drinks and healthy desserts, such as home-made *flan*. No wine available.

✉ Florida 165, downtown ☎ 011/4343-4020 🕐 Mon–Fri 11–3 🖐 L $25 🚇 Florida (B)

MARK'S DELI

www.markspalermo.com

This New York-style deli on one of the hippest corners of Palermo Soho serves smoked salmon bagels and home-made lemonade that approach Manhattan levels of authenticity. The jumbo cookies and frothy lattes are certainly up to scratch. No credit cards are accepted.

✉ El Salvador 4701, Palermo ☎ 011/4832-6244 🕐 Daily 9–9 🖐 L $20 🚌 15, 39, 55

ØLSEN

The Scandinavian theme goes all the way, from the pine-grove and minimalist sculptures in the front garden to the vodka shots that accompany the food. A fabulous place for Sunday brunch, ultra-trendy Ølsen specializes in cured and smoked meats and fish, such as Patagonian trout with blinis, while the bar mixes some of the best cocktails in the city. This is a place to be seen, but the food is first-rate, too.

✉ Gorriti 5870, Palermo
☎ 011/4776-7677 🕐 Tue–Sat 12.30pm–2am, Sun 10.30am–1am 🖐 L $60, D $85, Wine $25 🚌 39, 93, 111, 161

OVIEDO

www.oviedoresto.com.ar

Highly sophisticated Spanish gastronomy is what Oviedo does best. This stylish restaurant has a handsome mosaic floor, immaculate starched tablecloths and extremely polite waiters. The superb fish and seafood are brought fresh from Mar del Plata—ask for the catch of the day. Starters include steamed clams, scallop carpaccio or lightly grilled baby squid, while the wine list includes some outstanding Chardonnays served by the glass.

✉ Beruti 2602, Recoleta ☎ 011/4822-5415 🕐 Mon–Sat 12–3.30, 8pm–1am 🖐 L $70, D $100, Wine $28 🚇 Pueyrredón (D) 🚌 12, 64, 152

PARRILLA PEÑA

This traditional neighbourhood *parrilla* in the downtown *barrio* of San Nicolás is a treat. Expect white tablecloths and old-fashioned waiters, who can recommend the perfect wine to accompany your succulent *bife de chorizo* or crispy *tira de asado* (ribs). Start with a bubbling grilled *provoleta* (provolone) with oregano and a simple salad, mixed at the table. Even though Peña is firmly on the tourist radar, it is true to itself.

✉ Rodríguez Peña 682 ☎ 011/4371-5643 🕐 Mon–Sat 12.30–4, 8–1, Sun 12.30–4 ✋ L $30, D $45, Wine $19 🚇 Callao (B)

IL PICCOLO VAPORE

www.ilpiccolovapore.com

Don't be put off by the kitsch exterior or the equally garish interior, Il Piccolo Vapore is one of the last of Boca's traditional Italian *cantinas* and attracts locals as well as curious tourists. This is a great place to savour fried squid and roast chicken, perfectly cooked pasta and delicious ice cream, and the house wine flows in rivers. Earthy musical cabaret and dance shows often accompany the four-course set dinner.

✉ Necochea 1190, Boca ☎ 011/4301–4455 🕐 Daily 11am–1am ✋ L $30, D $50, Wine $21 🚌 20, 25, 29, 53, 64

POZO SANTO

www.pozosanto.com.ar

This restaurant is the best of the many upmarket Peruvian restaurants in the city. Pozo Santo effortlessly combines a luxurious decor of fine colonial artwork and rustic handicrafts with exciting Andean cuisine. Located in Palermo Soho, it is twinned with one of Lima's classic restaurants, La Carreta. Chef Rafael Rivera prepares tantalizing *ceviches* (marinated fish with chilli), a fabulous *ají de gallina* (spicy chicken stew) and simple grilled tuna with stir-fried vegetables. You should certainly taste Peru's national cocktail, the *pisco sour* (grappa shaken with lemon juice).

✉ El Salvador 4968, Palermo ☎ 011/4833-1611 🕐 Mon–Sat 12.30–3, 8–1 ✋ L $75, D $100, Wine $23 🚌 15, 55, 57, 110

PURATIERRA

www.puratierra.com.ar

Defining itself as a bastion of South American cooking, this handsome Belgrano restaurant doubles as one of the city's best cake shops, Puro Cacao. Dishes are created using simple rustic ingredients, such as rabbit and sweet potatoes, quail and squash, sea bass and fennel, though not necessarily on the same plate. There are a couple of tables outside but the interior is also enticing. The wine list is so overwhelming you might want some help choosing.

✉ 3 de Febrero 1167, Belgrano ☎ 011/4899-2007 🕐 Mon–Sat 8pm–1am ✋ D $90, Wine $25 🚇 Olleros (D) 🚌 41, 42, 59, 63, 67, 68, 152, 161

SUCRE

www.sucrerestaurant.com.ar

Chef Gonzalo Sacot and his pastry chef Pamela Villar continue to wow guests at this modern bar-restaurant in Belgrano Chico. The clean-lines and open kitchen create a sophisticated ambience that is matched by some of the city's most adventurous cuisine. A typical dinner might start with a carpaccio of beef with white truffle salt, followed by linguini with langoustines and fresh coriander (cilantro), and finish with lemon and almond cake with strawberry sorbet.

✉ Sucre 676, Belgrano ☎ 011/4782-9082 🕐 Daily 12–4, 7.30–1 ✋ L $70, D $95, Wine $28 🚌 37, 130

SUDESTADA

www.sudestadabuenosaires.com

At this tiny Palermo Soho cornerhouse you can start with a cocktail blended with a Korean rice wine to get your tastebuds ready for some of the spiciest food in the city. Starters might include Singaporean steamed dumplings and mains could feature curries, wok stir-fries or noodles. The star dish is *nem cua*, perfectly crisp pork and shrimp spring rolls. Reservations advised.

✉ Guatemala 5602, Palermo ☎ 011/4776-3777 🕐 Mon–Sat 12–3.30, 8–1 ✋ L $40, D $75, Wine $21 🚇 Palermo (D) 🚌 15, 55, 111

TANCAT

Tancat is a little bit of Barcelona in downtown Retiro, as mellow lighting, Hispanic decor and guitar music set the scene for some delicious Iberian tapas. Sangria and draught beer in small glasses, succulent baby squid and perfectly grilled fish transport you to the Costa Brava. The place gets very busy with local office workers at lunchtime but is quieter and more romantic in the evening. Make sure you taste the melt-in-the mouth *crema catalana*, a Catalan crème brûlée.

✉ Paraguay 645, Retiro ☎ 011/4312-5442 🕐 Mon–Sat noon–1am ✋ L $45, D $60, Wine $22 🚇 San Martín (C)

TANDOOR

www.tandoor.com.ar

Winning the Indian embassy's seal of approval is never easy, but this smart Recoleta restaurant has done so with its delicious curries and perfect naan breads. Try the mild spicy fish curry with tomatoes and yoghurt fresh from the tandoor or an aromatic curry of succulent Patagonian lamb. There are plenty of vegetarian dishes to choose from, too. Either iced lemonade with fresh mint or salty *lassi* is the perfect match for the piquant food.

✉ Laprida 1293, Recoleta ☎ 011/4821-3676 🕐 Daily 12–4, 8pm–1am ✋ L $60, D $80, Wine $19 🚇 Agüero (D) 🚌 12, 39, 64, 152

TEGUI

www.tegui.com.ar

You need to ring the bell to get into chef supremo Germán Martitegui's latest venture—a sure sign you are in the city's trendiest restaurant. The wine cellar takes up a whole wall, while the open kitchen lets you see the gastronomic wizards at work as they produce delicate nouvelle cuisine extravaganzas. Voted one of the world's best new restaurants by the design and lifestyle magazine *Wallpaper**.

✉ Costa Rica 5852, Palermo ☎ 011/5291-3333 🕐 Tue–Sat 12–3, 8–midnight ✋ L $80, D $150, Wine $60 🚌 34, 55, 108

TOMO 1

www.tomo1.com.ar

Tomo 1, in the classic downtown Panamericano hotel, is one of the city's landmark restaurants and the ideal place for a special-occasion meal. Refurbished in 2008, the restaurant remains as traditional as ever, with unrivalled service. Try the pear, watercress and Brie salad to start, followed with *ñandú* (ostrich) ravioli in mango sauce or Patagonian lamb with braised artichoke hearts and broad bean purée.

✉ Carlos Pellegrini 521, downtown
☎ 011/4326-6698 🕐 Mon–Fri 12–3, 7.30–midnight, Sat 7.30–midnight
🍽 L $180, D $250, Wine $65 🚇 Carlos Pellegrini (B) 🚌 10, 17, 29

LAS VIOLETAS

www.lasvioletas.com

Since 1884 this fabulous Almagro café-restaurant with art nouveau stained glass and beautifully restored panelling has served elegant lunches, high teas and dinners with great panache. The cheese-, salmon- or pumpkin-filled ravioli come with flavour-packed sauces such as *Caruso* (tomatoes, walnuts and mushrooms) or *scarparo* (basil, cream and tomato). Try to make a detour here, if only for a coffee and a treat from the *mesa dulce* (cake buffet).

✉ Avenida Rivadavia 3899, Almagro
☎ 011/4958-7387 🕐 Daily 8am–1am
🍽 L $35, D $55, Wine $18 🚇 Castro Barros (A)

MAR DEL PLATA
LA CABANA DEL BOSQUE

www.lacabaniadelbosque.com.ar

This famous *salon de té* in the Bosque Peralta Ramos, 10km (6 miles) from the centre, is set in an enchanting English-style cottage garden, and filled with stuffed animals, wooden sculptures and fossils discovered on the beach. The piece de résistance here is the array of calorific gateaux and cheesecakes.

✉ Bosque Peralta Ramos, Mar del Plata
☎ 0223/4673007 🕐 Daily 2–9 🍽 From $25

Right *Sucre restaurant, in Belgrano Chico*

SAN ANTONIO DE ARECO
LA ARCADÍA

Arcadian pleasures really do await the palate at this beautiful Areco restaurant, renowned for its delicious steaks, pasta and other lovingly prepared dishes. A mixed salad might start your meal, followed by, perhaps, chicken breast stuffed with chestnuts and almonds or a full *parrilla* (mixed grill). The high-ceilinged dining room, with elegant columns and impressive chandeliers, has fabulous views of the Río Areco, at a handy location just off the RN-8 trunk road.

✉ Alsina 6, San Antonio de Areco
☎ 02326/454271 🕐 Daily 12.30–4, 8–midnight 🍽 L $40, D $60, Wine $18

SAN ISIDRO
O'FARRELL

www.ofarrellrestaurant.com

At one of the classiest restaurants in the affluent Zona Norte, you can taste award-winning food based on seasonal ingredients, grilled or smoked using native woods. Hubert O'Farrell has Irish roots but the food is resolutely Latin with the likes of saffron risotto with jumbo shrimp and octopus or baby squid served with smoked corn tapenade and crispy bacon. Opened in 2001, this superb restaurant has weathered the economic crises with barely a bruise.

✉ Avenida del Libertador 15274, San Isidro
☎ 011/4742-4869 🕐 Mar–Dec Mon–Fri 12.30–4, 7.30–1, Sat 7.30pm–2am; Jan–Feb Mon–Fri 7.30–1, Sat 7.30pm–2am 🍽 L $75, D $100, Wine $35 🚊 San Isidro

TANDIL
EL CLUB

www.comercialtandil.com.ar/empresas/el_club

The gleaming chequerboard floor, fine paintings and elegant tables with wooden chairs all contribute to the club-like feel at this sophisticated restaurant serving safe, unpretentious food. The quality and quantity of the *parrillada* (mixed grill) of beef offal and prime cuts will astound you, while the excellent wine list will make you forget you are out in the sticks.

✉ General Pinto 636, Tandil
☎ 02293/435878 🕐 Daily 12.30–3.30, 8–midnight 🍽 L $40, D $65, Wine $20

TIGRE
IL NOVO MARÍA LUJÁN DEL TIGRE

www.ilnovomariadellujan.com

Occupying pride of place on the banks of the Río Luján, with an airy terrace to take in the riverside views, Il Novo María Luján del Tigre is a gem. The elegant peach walls, white tablecloths and handsome wooden chairs create the perfect setting in which to enjoy fine Italian cuisine. Try the crab ravioli in squid ink or veal escalopes in Marsala sauce, with tempting charlottes, ice creams and zabaglione for dessert. The service is faultless, too.

✉ Paseo Victorica 611, Tigre
☎ 011/4731-9613 🕐 Daily 8.30am–1am
🍽 L $40, D $60, Wine $21 🚊 Tigre station

PRICES AND SYMBOLS

Prices are the lowest and highest for a double room for one night. Breakfast is included unless noted otherwise. All the hotels listed accept credit cards unless otherwise stated. Note that rates vary widely throughout the year. Prices are given in US dollars (US$) unless otherwise stated.

For a key to the symbols, ▷ 2.

BUENOS AIRES

ALGODÓN MANSION

www.algodonmansion.com
This stunningly luxurious hotel is housed in a 1912 French-style neoclassical mansion in the heart of Recoleta. The conversion work completed in 2010 resulted in a refined establishment where every room is spacious and elegant. There is a small spa and rooftop pool, but the star attraction is the Chez Nous restaurant (open to the public). Have a cocktail in the bar first.
✉ Montevideo 1467, Recoleta
☎ 011/3530-7777 🖐 US$400–US$1,500
🚌 60, 102, 110 🛈 10 🏊 Outdoor

ALVEAR PALACE

www.alvearpalace.com
This venerable Recoleta establishment, on one of the city's most exclusive avenues, is one of the most elegant hotels in the country— even more so since its tasteful renovation. The spacious salons and airy bedrooms are decorated in Louis XVI and Empire styles, reinforcing the notion that Buenos Aires is the Paris of the South. Personal butler service, Hermès toiletries and mobile telephones on loan are just some of the little extras provided by this marvellous palace. The indoor swimming pool, La Bourgogne restaurant and high teas are all Buenos Aires institutions.
✉ Avenida Alvear 1891, Recoleta
☎ 011/4808-2100 🖐 US$380–US$450
🚌 67, 93, 130 🛈 197 🏊 Indoor

AXEL

www.axelhotels.com/buenosaires/
With two other hotels in Barcelona and Berlin, the Axel group runs this hetero-friendly gay boutique hotel in downtown Buenos Aires. Famed for its glass-bottomed swimming pool, the venue for regular Buenos Aires Bleu VIP Pool Parties, the Axel also has the Cosmo Bar, for daytime rendezvous, and Sky Bar, when the pool is the centrepiece of evening cocktails. There is a wellness centre on the premises while the three categories of room all come with sexy prism-glass shower cubicles.
✉ Venezuela 649, downtown
☎ 011/4136-9393 🖐 US$105–US$120
🚌 Belgrano (E) 🚇 2, 10, 26, 29 🛈 48
🏊 Outdoor

CASA CALMA

www.casacalma.com.ar
There could scarcely be a sharper contrast between the hectic downtown rush outside and the relaxed calm inside this oasis of environmentally conscious well-being. Claiming to be Argentina's first hotel dedicated to an organic lifestyle, it certainly conveys a sense that you are here to be pampered. The rooms are fresh, modern and comfortable and each has an iPod dock, a Jacuzzi and complimentary natural toiletries. Energy-saving lights and cooling wall-gardens are all part of the eco-friendly ethos.
✉ Suipacha 1015, downtown
☎ 011/5199-2800 🖐 US$240 🚇 San Martín (C) 🚌 17, 59, 61, 62, 75, 92, 100, 130, 152 🛈

CASA ESMERALDA

www.casaesmeralda.com.ar
The skyblue exterior doesn't seem to match the name, but this small

French-run Palermo hostel is a real gem. There are four simply furnished but comfortable private rooms with adjoining bathrooms and two small dormitories. The best thing about the place is the relaxing garden, with hammocks hanging from the trees. The staff can arrange Spanish lessons, bicycle rentals and often have barbecues on the roof terrace.
✉ Honduras 5765, Palermo ☎ 011/4772-2446 👐 US$40 (excluding breakfast) 🚌 39, 93, 111 🛏 4 (plus 2 dorms)

CRAFT HIP

www.crafthotel.com
Craft Hip overlooks Plaza Armenia, one of Palermo Viejo's few green spaces, and the park-side rooms have a view of its lush greenery, letting in the city's bright lights through big windows. All the rooms have iPod docks, DVD players and one of the rooms, 'Song', even has an old-fashioned gramophone player which the front desk will loan records to play on it. On the rooftop deck billowing gauze curtains flutter over comfortable four-poster sunloungers.
✉ Nicaragua 4583, Palermo ☎ 011/4833-0060 👐 US$135–US$150 🚌 34, 36, 55, 93, 161 🛏 10 ♿

DESIGN SUITES

www.designsuites.com
Billed as an oasis in the heart of the city, this smart Recoleta hotel lives up to its name. The slick suites, decorated in soothing pale greys and sage greens, are paragons of cutting-edge design and equipped with the latest technology, including DVD players and plasma-screen TVs. You have access to the nearby Club Privado Megatlón, one of the city's most exclusive gyms, where you can use the swimming pool as well as the fitness machines and saunas. There are sister hotels in Bariloche, Salta (▷ 264) and El Calafate.
✉ Marcelo T. de Alvear 1683, Recoleta ☎ 011/4814-8700 👐 US$180–US$220 🚇 Callao (D) 🛏 40 ♿ 🏊 Nearby 🦽 Nearby

FAENA HOTEL AND UNIVERSE

www.faenahotelanduniverse.com
This slick establishment in squeaky new Puerto Madero is housed in a disused cereals silo, but the joint efforts of flamboyant owner Alan Faena and French designer Philippe Starck have produced a dramatically impressive complex that includes an array of luxurious rooms, a fabulous spa and gym, a swimming pool with a poolside bar and a choice of places to eat. El Mercado serves homely fare in an eclectically decorated inn, with rustic seating around an outdoor patio, while the white interior of El Bistro sets the place apart.
✉ Martha Salotti 445 ☎ 011/4010-9000 👐 US$350–US$420 🚇 Leandro Alem 🚌 2, 130, 152 🛏 50 ♿ 🏊 Outdoor 🦽

FIVE COOL ROOMS

www.fivehotelbuenosaires.com
Five Cool Rooms is just that, though you can choose between small, medium, large and extra large. All the rooms are stylish and comfortable but the extra-large room comes with a spacious private terrace and its own salon. The panoramic roof deck with bamboo canes and gravel is a great place to bronze in the daytime, while in the evening it becomes the venue of impromptu barbecues—you could even try being *asador* (barbecue chef) for the night. If the rooms are not big enough for you, ask about the owners' furnished apartments for short-term rent in the vicinity.
✉ Honduras 4742, Palermo ☎ 011/5235-5555 👐 US$150–US$180 🚌 39, 93 🛏 5 ♿ 🏊 Outdoor Jacuzzi

FOUR SEASONS

www.fourseasons.com/buenosaires
True to the standards of this luxury chain, the Buenos Aires Four Seasons, in Recoleta, offers comfort and reliable professional service. You can choose between the well-appointed rooms with all the usual facilities in a modern tower block and the much more expensive La Mansión, a beautiful 1916 belle-époque mansion that is reminiscent of a French château. There are seven exclusive suites of varying sizes

and degrees of luxury, all displaying restored stained glass and gilded mouldings. There is a very attractive pool and, of course, a spa.
✉ Posadas 1086, Recoleta ☎ 011/4321-1200 👐 US$400–US$600 🚌 67, 93, 130 🛏 138 (plus 27 suites) ♿ 🏊 Outdoor 🦽

LEGADO MÍTICO

www.legadomitico.com
Lacking some of the wow factor of its sister hotel in Salta (▷ 264), Legado Mítico nonetheless is a themed hotel with panache. Calling itself a small emblematic hotel, it is stylish and eminently comfortable, with spacious themed rooms, and each one decorated with Argentine motifs. In 'El Gaucho' a fine painting of cattle looms over the bed, while 'El Tanguero' tips a wink to the great tango crooner Gardel. The bathrooms are stunning, while the service is eminently professional. It's hard to find a more elegant and unusual hotel in the city.
✉ Gurruchaga 1848, Palermo ☎ 011/4833-1300 👐 US$300–US$350 🚌 39, 55, 93, 152 🛏 11 ♿

MADERO

www.hotelmadero.com
This excellent contemporary hotel belonging to the Sofitel chain is in the heart of Puerto Madero. It has 197 spacious rooms that are both stylish and comfortable, plus a top-class spa, a state-of-the-art gym, a heated pool, saunas and a solarium. Rëd, the stylish hotel restaurant, offers a creative menu with more than 600 different Argentine vintages on its wine list.
✉ Rosario Vera Peñaloza 360, Puerto Madero ☎ 011/5776-7777 👐 US$250–US$300 🚇 Leandro N. Alem (B) 🚌 2, 130, 152 🛏 197 ♿ 🏊 Indoor 🦽

MAGNOLIA HOTEL BOUTIQUE

www.magnoliahotel.com.ar
Everything from the stunning art nouveau house with its remarkable stained-glass windows to the delicious breakfasts and attentive service makes this hotel a true winner. You are offered a glass

of wine to welcome you and the helpful staff give useful advice. There is a laptop for guests to use on the premises during their stay, too. Each of the eight rooms is individually decorated and furnished with antiques or top-notch repro wardrobes and chests. Slightly away from the well-trodden parts of Palermo Soho, it is conveniently located nonetheless, in a quiet residential part of Palermo.

✉ Julián Álvarez 1746, Palermo Soho ☎ 011/4867-4900 ✋ US$200–US$240 🚌 15, 57, 110, 160 🛏 8 💲

MANSÍON VITRAUX
www.mansionvitraux.com
Mansión Vitraux, just up the road from San Telmo's Plaza Dorrego, announces itself as a boutique hotel, wine lounge and spa. The wine lounge is the lower-level tasting room that doubles up as an unusual breakfast bar, serving omelettes and freshly squeezed orange juice in the morning and, later on, opt to taste the premium malbecs and chardonnays that tantalizingly line the walls of the see-through cellar. Rooms are modern and bright and there is a roof deck with views of an 18th-century Jesuit church.

✉ Carlos Calvo 369, San Telmo ☎ 011/4300-6886 ✋ US$250–US$290 🚌 10, 22, 29, 126 🛏 12 💲 🏊 Outdoor heated plunge pool 🛎

MINE
www.minehotel.com
Contemporary design pervades this Palermo Soho boutique hotel, from the minimalist facade to the Zen patio-style garden with its ribbon plunge pool. The standard rooms are a little cramped so it is worth splashing out on one of the eight superior category rooms, which have queen-size beds, laptop-size safes and DVD players. Decor is bright and vitalizing, with top-quality textiles. Breakfast is served in the stylish bistro and includes eggs cooked to order.

✉ Gorriti 4770, Palermo ☎ 011/4832-1100 ✋ US$190–US$230 🚌 15, 55, 168 🛏 20 💲 🏊 Outdoor plunge pool

MORENO
www.morenobuenosaires.com
This fabulous art deco building in deepest San Telmo hits you with its style as soon as you walk into the green-tiled lobby and take the antique service lift to reception. Accommodation ranges from very large rooms to lofts, the size of a city apartment, each with a giant Jacuzzi. With its own theatre and tango lounge and a restaurant serving techno-emotional food inspired by Spain's El Bulli, you can tell this is no ordinary hotel—it is unashamedly trendy.

✉ Moreno 376, San Telmo ☎ 011/6091-2000 ✋ US$100–US$120 🚇 Bolívar 🚌 29, 56 🛏 39 💲

NH JOUSTEN
www.nh-hotels.com
The reliable, no-nonsense Spanish chain has a number of hotels across Argentina and of the cluster in the capital this four-star establishment stands out for its fabulous early 19th-century building in downtown Buenos Aires, its 84 spacious and invitingly sober rooms, and the quality of the service. The original entrance, emblazoned with the old and new hotel's name, is a work of art in itself. Check the NH website for the other Buenos Aires hotels in the chain.

✉ Avenida Corrientes 280, downtown ☎ 011/4321-6750 ✋ US$120–US$135 🚇 Leandro Alem (B) 🛏 84 💲 🛎

NUSS
www.nusshotel.com
Part of an old Spanish convent, this luxurious corner-house hotel in chic Palermo Soho is not monastic in the least, although the 20 rooms and two suites are arranged around a cloister-like patio. Each of the rooms is tastefully decorated with fabulous repro furniture, including a chaise longue you'll never want to leave and stylish reading lamps you'd like to take home. The rooftop deck and pool are great places to relax. The hotel has a small spa and the deli lobby lounge is the perfect place for a snack. Enquire about the 'four nights pay for three' packages available.

✉ El Salvador 4916, Palermo ☎ 011/4833-8100 ✋ US$300–US$350 🚌 34, 55, 166 🛏 20 rooms, 2 suites 💲 🏊 Outdoor plunge

OHO DE SAN TELMO
www.ohodesantelmo.com.ar
Part of a citywide chain of hostels, the San Telmo branch provides WiFi, in addition to safe boxes and lockers, a good breakfast and friendly service. The lodgings range from six-bed dorms to single, double, triple and quadruple rooms with or without a private bathroom. There is 24-hour security available. Loan of towels and bed linen are further extras.

✉ Tacuari 595, San Telmo ☎ 011/4116-2908 ✋ US$90–$110 (excluding breakfast) 🚇 Independencia (C) 🛏 10

PALACIO DUHAU
www.buenosaires.park.hyatt.com
The Park Hyatt chain runs this monumental palace in Recoleta with professional ease and spoils its guests with butler service and designer toiletries. The decor is a little bland but there is an air of understated luxury about the place. To luxuriate in grandeur, request a room in the old palace buildings.

✉ Avenida Alvear 1661, Recoleta ☎ 011/5171-1234 ✋ US$400–US$850 🚌 67, 93, 130 🛏 75 💲 🏊 Indoor 🛎

PALERMITANO
www.palermitano.biz
The eight standard and six superior rooms plus two suites in this handsome Palermo hotel have luxurious marble bathrooms, flat-screen TVs, iPod docks and Slavonian oak floors. A roof deck with a small pool, baby-sitting service and organic toiletries are just some of the services offered at this charming newcomer.

✉ Uriarte 1648, Palermo ☎ 011/4897-2100 ✋ US$270–US$370 🚇 Plaza Italia 🛏 14 💲 🏊 Outdoor

PUROBAIRES
www.purobaires.com.ar
Each of the 11 rooms in this Palermo Soho boutique hotel has panoramic

views and a balcony—some of which overlook a minimalist garden—in keeping with the avant-garde design of the whole hotel. The elegant rooms are furnished with white leather bedheads and smooth Scandinavian pine furniture and flooring. There is a spa offering hot stone and mud therapies along with more conventional massages, facials and body treatments.

✉ Niceto Vega 4788, Palermo
☎ 011/4139-0100 🖐 US$140—US$280
🚇 Malabia (B) 🛈 11 🔧 🏊 Outdoor

RACÓ DE BUENOS AIRES

www.racodebuenosaires.com.ar
This beautiful hotel in a 19th-century town house is decorated with a tasteful mix of rattan and pale woods, white leather and dark purple cushions. The location is far from central but public transport will get you to the city centre in a few minutes.

✉ Yapeyu 271, Almagro ☎ 011/3530-6075
🖐 US$100—US$200 🚇 Castro Barros (A)
🛈 8 🔧

RIBERA SUR

www.riberasurhotel.com.ar
This San Telmo hotel has an unlikely location; hidden away on the Paseo Colón, off the Plaza Dorrego tourist beat. There are only 16 rooms but they are all ultra-comfortable and decorated in appealing pastel shades with extra touches such as colourful Mapuche carpets.

✉ Paseo Colón 1145, San Telmo
☎ 011/4361-7398 🖐 US$100—US$120
🚌 93, 152 🛈 32 🔧 🏊 Outdoor

ROONEY'S

www.rooneysboutiquehotel.com
Once the residence of Leopoldo Lugones, an eccentric Argentine writer who took his own life in 1938, this beautiful boutique hotel really can claim to be close to the Obelisco (▷ 69). The 14 suites are spacious, ranging from deluxe to apartments with two rooms and kitchenettes. Furnishing and decor throughout the hotel are a stunning blend of classical and contemporary. There are even free tango lessons, should

Above *The luxurious Nuss hotel, in the exclusive Palermo* barrio

you decide you want to learn.
✉ Sarmiento 1775, downtown
☎ 011/5252-5060 🖐 US$170—US$220
🚌 12, 37, 124 🛈 14 🔧

CARILÓ

HOSTERÍA CARILÓ

www.hosteriacarilo.com.ar
Equipped with a relaxing spa and two swimming pools, this appealing four-star hotel offers four types of rooms, from spacious double rooms to mini-apartments for self-catering. The hotel's excellent restaurant offers delicious Mediterranean cuisine, with a possibility of dining on the outdoor deck. On the beach, the hotel provides deckchairs and parasols for the exclusive use of patrons.

✉ Avutarda and Jacarandá, Cariló
☎ 02254/570704 🖐 US$120—US$140
🛈 33 🔧 🏊 Outdoor and indoor 🍴

EZEIZA

PUESTO VIEJO

www.puestoviejopoloclub.com.ar
Just 15 minutes from Ezeiza international airport and 45 minutes from downtown Buenos Aires, this *estancia*-like polo club is set amid delightful woodland and has several polo fields. The comfortable rooms are situated in a ranch-style building. Delicious meals are served outside or in the rustic dining room. Relax by the swimming pool overlooking the practice pitch, go horseback riding, try your hand at polo or simply just enjoy the relaxing atmosphere. Thanks to the location this is a great place to unwind at the beginning or, better still, the end of your trip.

✉ RN-6 s/n Cañuelas ☎ 011/5597-6644 🖐 US$250—US$300 🛈 8
🏊 Outdoor

COLONIA DEL SACRAMENTO
POSADA PLAZA MAYOR
www.posadaplazamayor.com

This classic *posada* in the heart of the city's *casco histórico* (historic centre) is housed in a mid-19th-century building and a beautifully restored 18th-century Portuguese mansion, with bare stone walls. It has a dozen handsome rooms set around a wisteria-scented patio and three more on the upper floor. The decor is fresh and floral, without being too fussy, while the service is tip-top.

✉ Calle del Comercio 111, Colonia del Sacramento ☎ 598 52 23193 🖐 US$180–US$230 🛈 15 ⊡

JUNÍN
ESTANCIA LA ORIENTAL
www.estancia-laoriental.com

Near the rural town of Junín, 200km (124 miles) west of Buenos Aires, this working ranch is set in the middle of bucolic farmlands with its own lagoon, and a stay here is a fabulous way of seeing how *criollo* life has remained unchanged in decades. The museum-like house is reminiscent of a small French manor, and framed by an avenue of plane trees. Sheltered by palms and glossy leaved magnolias, this sumptuous little palace has exquisitely decorated rooms and every comfort. The owners are delightfully hospitable and the food is down-to-earth rustic Argentine fare with lots of beef. Make sure you get precise directions for getting here.

✉ Junín ☎ 02362/15-640866; 011/15-51465210 🖐 US$200–US$240 🛈 9 🏊 Outdoor

MAR DEL PLATA
SAINTE JEANNE
www.hotelsaintejeanne.com

A truly gorgeous new hotel, Sainte Jeanne is in the fashionable Los Troncos district of the resort, only a few blocks from the beach. Rooms are decorated with soothing pastel colours, while the top-floor spa has a fabulous swimming pool, with built-in Jacuzzis, jets and showers. The ground floor restaurant serves

up delicious fare, too. Every room is equipped with an iPod dock and a Nespresso machine.

✉ Güemes 2850, Mar del Plata ☎ 0223/4209200 🖐 $750–$1,200 🛈 20 🏊 Indoor

PINAMAR
POSADA PECOS
www.posadapecos.com.ar

This family-oriented *posada* in the heart of the resort has 32 plain but comfortable rooms. You will want to spend most of your time down at the dunes, but there is a grassy garden with loungers, where you can relax in the shade of tropical palms. A full buffet breakfast is served outside, weather permitting.

✉ Del Odiseo 448, Esquina de los Silenios, Pinamar ☎ 02254/484386 🖐 US$110–US$130 🛈 32

SAN ANTONIO DE ARECO
ESTANCIA LA BAMBA
www.la-bamba.com.ar

Reopened in 2008, after extensive refurbishments, this famous *estancia* has retained its rustic charm and age-old varnish. Shaded by a grove of centennial trees, the terracotta-hued facade and graceful gallery of the great *casco* (historic house) is a monument in itself. The 11 rooms, with four-poster beds and polished parquet floors, exude luxury, while the garden, designed by renowned 19th-century landscape architect Charles Thays, invites guests to indulge in lingering promenades. There is an excellent spa, too, so it is just the place for some self-indulgence.

☎ 011/4444-6560 🖐 US$180–US$200 full board 🛈 11 🏊 Outdoor

ESTANCIA LA CINACINA
www.lacinacina.com.ar

The great advantage of La Cinacina over the other Areco *estancias* is that you don't need your own transport to get here because it is located right in the middle of town. The emphasis here is on simplicity and warm fireside hospitality. The 12 rooms and two suites have air-conditioning and central heating, gleaming wooden

floors and beamed ceilings and are furnished with pristine white linens, offering a true taste of *gaucho* homeliness.

✉ Lavalle 1, San Antonio de Areco ☎ 011/5252-1414 🖐 US$160–$200 🛈 14

ESTANCIA EL OMBÚ
www.estanciaelombu.com

The current owner's grandfather acquired El Ombú in the 1930s, but the *estancia* was built in the late 19th century by General Richieri, who received the land as a reward for his leading part in the Conquest of the Desert in the 1870s. The magnificent *casco* has nine rooms with private bathrooms and offers unassuming comfort in typical pampas style. There is a small pool by the house and a larger one with a deck, while you can explore the 300ha (740 acres) of park on horseback. The ranch's 500-strong herd of pedigree Hereford and Aberdeen Angus makes sure there's always plenty of beef for the barbecue.

✉ Ruta 31, Cuartel VI, Villa Lía, San Antonio de Areco ☎ 02326/492080 🖐 US$320–US$400 🛈 9 🏊 Outdoor

PATIO DE MORENO
www.patiodemoreno.com

The 11 handsome rooms in this well-situated boutique hotel in the historic centre of Areco either overlook the lush garden and swimming pool or the picturesque street. There is a glazed central patio, perfect for sunny but cool winter days. The foyer's chequerboard floor and floral armchairs set the tone for a comfortable stay in the *gaucho* tradition of hospitality. The hotel wine bar has vintages from the cellar to accompany the delicious quiches and sandwiches served in the restaurant.

✉ Moreno and San Martín, San Antonio de Areco ☎ 02326/455197 🖐 US$120–US$140 🛈 11 ⊡ 🏊 Outdoor

SAN ISIDRO
VILLA ISIDRO
www.villaisidro.com.ar

In the historic quarter of San Isidro, this wonderful boutique hotel combines traditional touches with contemporary design. Each of the 10 rooms is different in style, decor and size, for example room 8 has a reproduction Louis XV bed and a large balcony overlooking the garden and swimming pool. The Roble spa offers saunas and ultra-relaxing massage treatments. Ask about guided tours of San Isidro and Tigre.

✉ Avenida del Libertador 15935, San Isidro ☎ 011/4742-3366 ✋ US$125–US$140 🚉 San Isidro train station 🛈 10 ♿ 🏊 Outdoor

TANDIL
HOSTERÍA AVE MARÍA
www.avemariatandil.com.ar
Looking more like a gingerbread house than a hotel, Ave María is run as a labour of love by owner Asunción Pereyra Iraola de Zubiaurre, who grows asparagus and rhubarb in her well-tended kitchen garden. Set in a lush park of magnolia, walnut and eucalyptus trees, the house and its swimming pool are havens of peace and quiet, providing the perfect place to recharge your batteries. The rates include horseback riding and either lunch or dinner cooked exquisitely at the lodge.

✉ Circuito Turístico Paraje La Porteña, Tandil ☎ 02293/422843 ✋ $1,000–$1,300

half board 🚌 From Tandil, continue on RP-30 towards Benito Juárez and 10km (6 miles) later follow sign to Circuito Turístico; 700m (215ft) to the right is the entrance to Ave María 🛈 14 🏊 Outdoor

POSADA DE LOS PÁJAROS
www.posadapajaros-spa.com
This fine spa hotel has a fabulous restaurant where the produce is organic—fruit, vegetables and herbs are all grown on the premises. Natural oils are used in the range of massages and beauty treatments on offer. The location is convenient too, just 6km (4 miles) outside the town, with admirable views of the Serranías hills and moorland. Laze by the pool or, for something more energetic, take the hotel's mountain bikes and explore the surrounding countryside.

☎ 02293/432013 ✋ $380–$480 🛈 16 🏊 Outdoor

TIGRE
BONANZA DELTAVENTURA
www.deltaventura.com
This late 19th-century mansion, now run as a stylish lodge, is highly recommended. Bountiful and adventure-oriented, this marvellous resting place on the delta is the ideal place for getting away from it all. Sit back and relax in hammocks and

deckchairs by the water's edge or, if you are feeling more energetic, burn off some calories on the bicycles or kayaks, or on the football pitch. You can then put the calories back on by indulging in the delicious home-made food, created using locally grown produce. The excellent birdwatching and interpretative tours of the delta run from the lodge are options not to be missed.

✉ Río Carpachay km 13, Tigre ☎ 011/4728-1674 ✋ $440–$500 including all meals 🛈 8

VILLA VICTORIA
www.hotelvillavictoria.com.ar
This stunning small hotel is run by a Swedish-Argentine family and lives up to the Nordic reputation for discreet hospitality, comfort and style. The three rooms and two suites have Swedish names, such as Linné and Nobel, while best of all is the Victoria Suite. The grand villa is set among an idyllic park and facilities include a swimming pool and clay tennis courts.

✉ Avenida Liniers 566, Tigre ☎ 011/4731-2281 ✋ $300–$700 🚉 Tigre 🛈 5 ♿ 🏊 Outdoor

Below *The Nuss hotel in Palermo Soho, a masterclass in understated luxury*

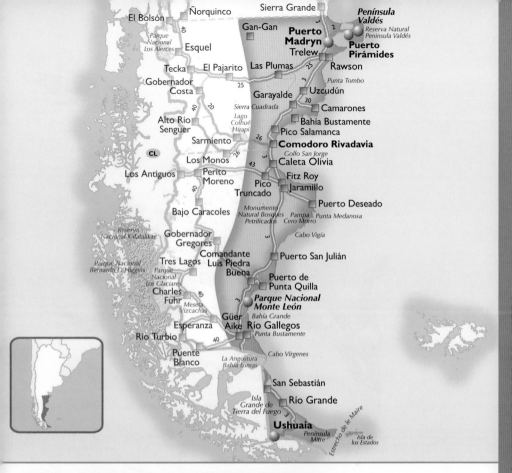

Map labels:

El Bolsón · Norquinco · Sierra Grande · **Península Valdés**
Parque Nacional Los Alerces · Esquel · Gan-Gan · **Puerto Madryn** · Trelew · Reserva Natural Península Valdés · **Puerto Pirámides**
Tecka · El Pajarito · Las Plumas · Rawson
Gobernador Costa · Garayalde · Uzcudún · Punta Tombo
Sierra Cuadrada · Camarones
Alto Río Senguer · Lago Colhué Huapi · Bahía Bustamente
Sarmiento · Pico Salamanca · **Comodoro Rivadavia**
CL · Los Monos · Golfo San Jorge · Caleta Olivia
Los Antiguos · Perito Moreno · Fitz Roy
Pico Truncado · Jaramillo
Bajo Caracoles · Monumento Natural Bosques Petrificados · Pampa Cero Morro · Punta Medanosa · **Puerto Deseado**
Reserva Nacional Kidalalikac · Gobernador Gregores · Cabo Vigía
Parque Nacional Bernardo O'Higgins · Tres Lagos · Comandante Luis Piedra Buena · Puerto San Julián
Parque Nacional Los Glaciares · Puerto de Punta Quilla
Charles Fuhr · Meseta Vizcachas · **Parque Nacional Monte León**
Güer Aike · Bahía Grande · Río Gallegos
Esperanza · Punta Bustamente
Río Turbio · Puente Blanco · La Angostura Bahía Lomas · Cabo Vírgenes
San Sebastián
Isla Grande de Tierra del Fuego · Río Grande
Ushuaia · Península Mitre · Estrecho de le Maire · Isla de los Estados

ATLANTIC PATAGONIA AND TIERRA DEL FUEGO

Beyond the fertile pampas, the seemingly boundless Patagonian steppe stretches down towards the southernmost tip of the South American continent, almost touching Antarctica. The Atlantic coast of this legendary land, more than 2,000km (1,240 miles) long, is mostly barren cliffs and empty beaches. The chilly waters and blustery climate suit penguins and dolphins better than humans. It's not the place for a sun-and-sand holiday, but a world-class location for seeing wildlife: dark rocks topped by great colonies of sea lions and golden sands where giant elephant seals come to rest and breed. The place not to miss is the Península Valdés, a headland aptly shaped like a whale's tail where you can watch southern right whales swimming and diving in the clear Atlantic waters off its shores. Black-and-white orcas are another attraction, especially in March when they patrol the waters on the hunt for seals. The unique flooded estuary at Puerto Deseado and the turquoise bay at Puerto San Julián are perfect places for seeing dolphins and a wonderful variety of seabirds.

As far as towns and cities are concerned, Puerto Madryn, renowned for its scuba diving, is a handy base for Valdés, though it is more rewarding to stay on the peninsula itself. A way south, in the picturesque lower Chubut valley, Welsh influences are evident, with a large community descended from Welsh immigrants. Beyond the Monte León National Park—home to more penguins and other wildlife—Río Gallegos is a pioneering town with a reputation for trout fishing. Far and away the most alluring town is Ushuaia, capital of Argentine Tierra del Fuego, the biggest island in South America, shared with Chile. Backed by the snowy peaks of the Andean tail, Ushuaia is a relaxing resort, with some top hotels and the Parque Nacional Tierra del Fuego on its doorstep. The great RN-3 arterial road links the mainland's key urban centres, while five regional airports will help you cross those gigantic distances.

BAHÍA BUSTAMANTE
www.bahiabustamante.com

Eking a living out of its prolific kelp harvest, where even the streets are named for different types of seaweed, tiny Bahía Bustamante is a delightful little harbour village that is permanently inhabited by 10 men, one woman and 50,000 Magellanic penguins. Founded in 1953, Bustamante sits on the sweeping Golfo San Jorge close by the reddish rocks of the Gravina headland that enclose a cove of crystalline waters known as Caleta Malaspina. Near by, the deeply indented coastline and sandy beaches form a perfect habitat for sea lions, penguins and dozens of birds, including the endangered Olrog's gull. This rare seagull, with its striking jet-black and white plumage and golden yellow beak, feeds off the area's plentiful crabs. You can even stay in beautifully decorated kelper (seaweed cropper) cottages; ask in the village for details.

✚ 353 E19 ✉ Bahía Bustamante, Provincia de Chubut ☎ 011/5032-8677 🚗 Take RN-3 from Trelew and turn left (eastwards) at km1674 towards Bahía Bustamante

CABO VÍRGENES
www.patagonia-argentina.com/i/atlantica/gallegos/virgenes.php
www.seabirds.org/study-argentina.htm

Portuguese explorer Ferdinand Magellan reached the Strait that now bears his name on 15 October 1520, the feast day of Saint Ursula and the Eleven Thousand Virgins, and named this cape, the southernmost point of the Argentine mainland, after Ursula's companions. This windswept headland's history has been a sad one; it was settled in 1584 but all but one of the 300 Spaniards that landed here died of disease, starvation or attacks by the indigenous Tehuelche. Today, the only inhabitants are the Argentine navy, who operate a landmark lighthouse here, and a 90,000-strong colony of Magellanic penguins—one of the largest in

Argentina. Both the lighthouse and the Reserva Faunística Provincial can be visited on day tours from Río Gallegos (▷ 136).

✚ 357 D25 ✉ Cabo Vírgenes, Provincia de Santa Cruz 🚗 RN-40 km0, 133km (82 miles) south of Río Gallegos 🚌 Tours from Río Gallegos and Ushuaia

ESTANCIA HARBERTON
www.estanciaharberton.com
www.acatushun.com

Often visited as part of a boat trip or overland excursion from Ushuaia (▷ 138–139), the historic Estancia Harberton, on Tierra del Fuego, was founded in 1886 by missionary Reverend Thomas Bridges, who named it after his wife's home village in Devon. Bridges compiled a dictionary of the indigenous Yámana language and his son Lucas published his memoirs, *The Uttermost Part of the Earth* (▷ 317). Guided visits take in the sturdy outbuildings and pretty botanical garden. Marine biologist Rae Natalie Prosser, wife of Tommy Goodall, Thomas Bridges's great-grandson, runs the fascinating Museo Acatushún (Oct–Apr daily 10–7; adult $15, child under 15 free), dedicated to the local marine fauna within the *estancia* grounds. You can have lunch or afternoon tea in the tea room (▷ 149) and even stay overnight.

✚ 357 E27 ✉ Estancia Harberton, Canal de Beagle, Tierra del Fuego ③ Daily 10–7 🚗 RN-3 east of Ushuaia for 40km (25 miles) to Rancho Hambre, then RN-33 (formerly the RCj) for 45km (28 miles) to Estancia Harberton (no fuel stations locally, so a full tank is recommended) 🚢 Regular catamaran services from Ushuaia 🚌 Coach and boat tours from Ushuaia

GAIMAN
www.argentinaturismo.com.ar/gaiman/
www.trelew.com/espectaculos/desafio/index.html

It was an American, David Roberts from Pennsylvania, who founded Gaiman, the most Welsh of all the villages along the lower Chubut valley. Yet this village really is a little piece of Wales transplanted to northern Patagonia, with its austere

chapels, melodious eisteddfod (music festival) and welcoming guest houses. Above all, Gaiman is celebrated for its *casas de té* (tea rooms) serving well-brewed Earl Grey tea in china cups, with scones, toast and delicious *torta negra* (dark fruit cake), a local speciality that is made to a jealously guarded recipe.

The intriguing Parque El Desafío (▷ 144), on the banks of the Chubut River in Gaiman, was created out of recycled junk by the late Joaquín Alonso, who combined ingenuity with a wicked sense of humour.

✚ 353 F18 ✉ Gaiman, Provincia de Chubut ℹ Casa de Cultura, Rivadavia and Belgrano ☎ 02965/491571 ③ Mon–Sat 9–8, Sun 1–8 🚌 Buses from Trelew and Puerto Madryn 🚗 16km (10 miles) west of Trelew via RN-25 🚌 Tours from Puerto Madryn

MONUMENTO NATURAL BOSQUES PETRIFICADOS
www.parquesnacionales.gov.ar

Were it not for these petrified tree-trunks, and those littering the plains near Sarmiento, it would be hard to believe that the empty wastes of northern Patagonia were once carpeted with forest. The Monumento Natural Bosques Petrificados was created to protect these geological wonders from pillaging. Some of the logs, buried in ash from a Cretacean-era volcanic eruption, measure more than 30m (98ft) in length and 3m (10ft) in diameter. Set among an eerie landscape of basalt, the stony araucaria logs are best seen in the evening, when they glow like embers in the setting sun. The remote location of the forest means it's advisable to take supplies of food and water with you and make sure your car has a full tank of fuel before setting off.

✚ 355 D21 ✉ Northeast of Santa Cruz ☎ 02974/851000 ③ Nov–Mar daily 9–8; Apr–Oct 10–5 💲 Free 🚗 50km (31 miles) along RP-49 from RN-3; 256km (159 miles) from Puerto Deseado; and 50km (31 miles) south of Jaramillo 🚌 Tours from Puerto Deseado

INFORMATION

www.pnmonteleon.com.ar

355 D24 Rangers' office at RN-3 at km2385 02962/489184 Nov–Mar daily 9–8; Apr–Oct 10–6 Adult $20, child (under 16) free Nearest airport Río Gallegos RN-3 northwards from Río Gallegos or southwards from Puerto San Julián

TIPS

>> Don't expect to see the natural rock arch that used to be the park's symbol and featured in lots of publicity; it collapsed in 2006.

>> Bring water, food, warm clothing and binoculars with you.

>> To benefit to the full, stay at the Hostería Monte León *estancia* (▷ 150–151). This will enable you to be at the park at the best times, dawn and dusk.

PARQUE NACIONAL MONTE LEÓN

A 400m (122ft) puma-shaped promontory of beige rock rising from the ultramarine waters of the South Atlantic gives its name to Argentina's only coastal national park, the Parque Nacional Monte León. Stretching along almost 40km (25 miles) of seaboard in the most desolate reaches of Atlantic Patagonia, this remote park was created in 2004 to protect the area's amazing biodiversity, including the country's fourth-biggest colony of Magellanic penguins. It covers a total of 62,000ha (153,140 acres) sandwiched between the RN-3 and the seafront, and its undulating plains of thick gorse and scrubby grass are the ideal habitat for foxes, pumas and dozens of birds, plus large herds of guanaco.

SHEEP, GUANO AND AN *ESTANCIA*

The British-owned Southern Patagonia Sheep Farming Company Ltd built an *estancia* here at the beginning of the 20th century. In 1920, the *estancia* was bought by the Braun family and they continued herding and shearing sheep until well into the 21st century. The family house now operates as a luxurious tourist *estancia* (▷ 150–151), a private concession within the national park. The extraction of guano (seabird excrement) from the cliffs for use as a fertilizer was also big business until the 1930s, when the invention of chemical alternatives led to a sharp drop in demand.

EXPLORING THE PARK

The park's main entrance is easy to spot from the main road, in particular the crimson roofs of the former shearing-shed. You must register with the helpful *guardaparques* (rangers), who will advise you on how to visit the park, explain what there is to see, tell you when high and low tides are due, as well as recommend knowledgeable guides. The road leading into the park and as far as the ocean edge is a 24km (15-mile) meander of gravel, which may be closed to traffic after heavy rains, although this is a rare occurrence. The entrance gate, 7km (4 miles) south of the rangers' office along the RN-3, is well marked.

Down at the beach, there is a pleasant café serving snacks. From here, you can admire the rugged views of the sandy cliffs, flat-topped islands and jagged rocks, including the Isla Monte León, where three cormorant varieties cohabit. You can walk out to this steep-sided, guano-streaked block at low tide, for a closer look at the birds.

Below *Flat-topped Isla Monte León*

PARQUE NACIONAL TIERRA DEL FUEGO

www.tierradelfuego.org.ar/pntf/

Not only is the Parque Nacional Tierra del Fuego pleasing on the eye, it is also easy on the foot. With several short and relatively easy trails, its terrain is within the grasp of even the least adventurous hiker. Tougher trekkers might take up the challenge of the ascent to Cerro Guanaco from the shores of Lago Roca, where views of the park and the Beagle Channel are breathtaking. These 630sq km (246sq miles) of sub-polar forest, dotted with lakes of all shapes and sizes, are home to noisy austral parakeets and green-backed firecrown hummingbirds, striking Magellanic woodpeckers and white or brown kelp geese, buff-furred guanacos and both red and grey foxes.

✚ 357 D27 ✉ San Martin 1395, Ushuaia ☎ 02901/421315 ⏱ Nov–Feb daily 9–8; Mar–Oct 10–5 💵 Adult $50, child (under 16) free 🚌 Regular buses from Ushuaia 🚆 Tren del Fin del Mundo (▷ 147) from Estación del Fin del Mundo, 8km (5 miles) west of Ushuaia 🚢 Boats from Ushuaia, ask at Muelle or Ushuaia's tourist information office (▷ 138) for details 🚗 12km (7 miles) west of Ushuaia 🚩 Tours from Ushuaia

PENÍNSULA VALDÉS

▷ 132–133.

PUERTO DESEADO

www.turismo.deseado.gov.ar

Adventurer Thomas Cavendish circumnavigated the globe in his ship *Desire* and, in 1586, sailed up the sunken estuary that now bears its name, the Ría Deseado, along with the fishing and military port that overlooks it, Puerto Deseado. Unique in South America, the *ría* is a wide river valley that has been invaded by the sea, despite being more than 40km (25 miles) inland. Its craggy cliffs and sandbanks are home to colonies of penguins and cormorants, oystercatchers and sea lions plus the snowy sheathbill, a handsome bird whose plumage fits the description. Another visitor is the Commerson's dolphin (*tonina overa*), which plays

Above *Lapataia River in Parque Nacional Tierra del Fuego*

to the crowds near the tour boats that ply the *ría* (▷ 144). Weather permitting the boats sail to the Isla Pingüino, for close-up views of the bright-tufted rockhopper penguins. The only other nesting colonies are on the Falklands (Las Malvinas) and on a small island off Tierra del Fuego.

✚ 355 F21 ✉ Puerto Deseado, Provincia de Santa Cruz 🛈 San Martín 1525 ☎ 02974/870220 ⏱ Nov–Mar daily 8am–9pm; Apr–Oct Mon–Fri 8–5 🚌 Buses from Trelew, Comodoro Rivadavia and Río Gallegos

PUERTO MADRYN

▷ 134.

PUERTO PIRÁMIDES

▷ 135.

PUERTO SAN JULIÁN

www.argentinaturismo.com.ar/puertosanjulian

Visit the historic little port of Puerto San Julián and follow in the footsteps of Darwin, Magellan and many

Magellanic penguins. The town is no beauty—according to urban legend, when Magellan arrived here in 1520, he named it Patagonia when he saw the locals' enormous feet (*patagón* in Spanish)—but the bayside location is the real pull. You can easily spot the penguins (sometimes they stagger into town), plus Commerson's dolphins and four types of cormorant by taking a boat tour (▷ 145) around the turquoise waters. Back on dry land, you might take a look at the true-size replica of Magellan's famed *carrack*, the *Nao Victoria*, the first ship known to have sailed around the world and returned to its homeport.

✚ 355 E23 ✉ Puerto San Julián, Provincia de Santa Cruz 🛈 San Martín and Rivadavia ☎ 02962/452009 ⏱ Mon–Fri 7–9, Sat–Sun 9–9 (restricted times in winter) 🚌 Buses from Río Gallegos (nearest airport) and from Buenos Aires 🚗 352km (218 miles) from Río Gallegos on RN-3

INFORMATION

www.enpeninsulavaldes.com

http://whc.unesco.org/en/list/937

✚ 353 G17 ℹ RN-3, El Desempeño, near the reserve entrance

☎ 02965/485271 🕐 Apr–Oct daily 10–6; Nov–Mar 9–8 💲 US$17 🚌 Buses from Madryn 🚗 RN-3 north of Madryn to Pirámides, then RP-2 to Punta Delgada ✈ Tours from Puerto Deseado, Puerto Madryn, Trelew and Ushuaia

INTRODUCTION

Declared a World Heritage Site in 1999, the awe-inspiring Península Valdés is a cornucopia of marine wildlife. Whales and orcas, sea lions and sea elephants, petrels and penguins, cormorants and terns all cohabit this fin-shaped promontory jutting into the beryl-hued waters of the Atlantic. A network of unpaved roads and cliff-top trails takes you round this sandy flipper of land, whose scrub-covered plains teem with rheas (ostrich), *maras* (Patagonian hares) and skunks. The landscape is typically bleak Patagonian steppe, but the peninsula offers such a fantastic range of fauna and such spectacular natural wonders that you'll soon forget the humdrum flatness of it all.

The peninsula is joined to the mainland by the threadlike Istmo Carlos Ameghino, along whose backbone runs a metalled road from the RN-3 junction just to the north of Madryn all the way to Puerto Pirámides (▷ 135). Halfway along this road at El Desempeño is the reserve entrance and tollbooth where you pay your fee. Beyond Pirámides, the gravel RP-2 leads to Punta Delgada, from where the RP-47 runs along the east coast to Punta Norte, passing Punta Cantor and Caleta Valdés. Punta Norte can be joined directly from Pirámides by taking the inland RP-3.

WHAT TO SEE

PUNTA DELGADA

www.puntadelgada.com

The southeastern cape, Punta Delgada, hosts two fine places to stay, one in a lighthouse (▷ 151) and the other in a handsome ranch (▷ 151). At the foot of fossil-encrusted cliffs, long sandy beaches are home for much of the year to communities of blubbery elephant seals, which come to fight, breed, mature and rest before returning to the ocean. The beaches are private property—in order to descend to the ocean edge you must either stay at the on-site hotels or pay for a guided visit at El Faro Hotel de Campo (tel 02965/458444). The peninsula is the only continental breeding ground for the elephant seals, so seeing them this close is a unique experience.

✚ 353 G17

Above *Coastline views at Punta Delgada, the southeastern cape of Península Valdés*
Opposite *Magellanic penguins at Caleta Valdés*

PUNTA CANTOR

Halfway along the coastal RP-3, the headland of Punta Cantor is home to another large colony of sea elephants. You cannot go down to the beach and have to make do with a vantage point on a ridge below the cliff-top. Even so, with good binoculars you can get a good view of the churlish bulls duelling over a bevy of cows during the mating season (between October and November). Some of the males, with their trunk-like noses, weigh over 2,500kg (1,136lbs), more than five times heavier than the females.

CALETA VALDÉS

The road north to Caleta Valdés is where you are likeliest to spot armadillos, skunks and ostrich-like *ñandúes* (rheas). It is best not to get too close to the skunks as you might get sprayed, while the rheas, especially parents with their chicks, will probably scuttle into the gorse as soon as you get out of your vehicle. The Caleta is an elongated, shallow inlet formed by a gravel spit, the perfect habitat for sea lions, elephant seal and Magellanic penguins. In March and April, black and white orcas torpedo into the Caleta and then launch themselves onto the beach hoping to gulp down a sea lion or sea elephant pup for lunch.

MORE TO SEE
ISLA DE LOS PÁJAROS

Just beyond the reserve entrance a sign points to the Isla de los Pájaros (Bird Island). More than 520 species of bird are known to exist on the island and many of those birds are in danger of extinction, so landing is forbidden, but from the isthmus you can train a telescope on a huge colony of gulls, cormorants, herons and other birds.

It's worthwhile stopping off at the Centro de Interpretaciones, near the Isla de los Pájaros turnoff, to get information about the local wildlife and see the skeleton of a beached whale.

PUNTA NORTE

The northernmost tip of the peninsula is another scene of rare orca attacks on sea lion pups between late March and early April but you'll be unlikely to witness them.

✚ 353 G17

TIPS

➤➤ There are plenty of tour operators in Puerto Madryn (▷ 134) and a daily bus will get you there and back, but for more freedom you might prefer to drive yourself and base yourself on the peninsula itself. Alternatively, hire a private driver or guide for the day.

➤➤ If you choose to drive around the peninsula, drive carefully and slowly, never above 50kph (31mph), as the steeply banked gravel roads can be treacherous.

➤➤ Nature lovers can opt to stay at one of the *estancias* (▷ 151) dotted along the peninsula's cliff-fringed coastline, which offer exclusive opportunities to get up close to the local wildlife.

➤➤ The prime location for whale-watching is Puerto Pirámides (▷ 135), from where the boat trips leave.

➤➤ The whale-watching season runs from late June to December, but towards the end of this period only mothers and calves remain and to see them you must go out further into the gulf.

INFORMATION

www.madryn.gov.ar/turismo

353 F17 ✉ Puerto Madryn, Provincia de Chubut 🛈 Julio Roca 223 ☎ 02965/453504 ⊙ Dec–Mar Mon–Fri 7–11, Sat–Sun 8–11; Apr–Nov Mon–Fri 7–9, Sat–Sun 8–9 🚌 Long-distance buses from Buenos Aires and Río Gallegos ✈ Puerto Madryn airport (limited connections); Trelew airport is 65km (40 miles) to the south 🚗 RN-3 from Buenos Aires 1,450km (899 miles)

TIPS

›› Puerto Madryn has its own airport but Trelew airport is better served and there is a convenient shuttle bus to the town
›› It is forbidden by law to dive with the whales but some operators offer *excursiones especiales* where you get very close.

PUERTO MADRYN

Succulent seafood is served along the beautiful beachfront with views of the cerulean Golfo Nuevo, where whales swim in clear waters—these are just some of the attractions of Puerto Madryn, Argentina's diving capital par excellence and the gateway to Península Valdés (▷ 132–133). Thanks to its fine hotels, excellent restaurants and great tour operators, Madryn is a good base for visiting the Península Valdés. The main attraction is scuba diving, with several companies offering underwater explorations of shipwrecks and up-close marine life. If diving is not your thing, however, there is still plenty to do, including discovering the area's amazing marine fauna at the Ecocentro or oceanography museum.

ECOCENTRO

www.ecocentro.org.ar

The Ecocentro on Julio Verne 3784 (tel 02965/457470; Oct to late Dec Wed–Mon 3–8; late Dec–Feb Wed–Mon 10–1 when cruise ships in port, 5–9; Jan–Feb 10am–1pm when cruise ships in port; Apr–Jun Tue–Sun 3–7; adult $38, child under 6 free) occupies a clean-lined purpose-built edifice, topped by a panoramic tower that offers staggering views of the Golfo Nuevo. Between June and December, you might even spot southern right whales from its huge windows. Complete with a charming café and top-quality souvenir shop, this didactic centre focuses on marine fauna. In addition to plentiful information and expert guides, it offers all manner of permanent exhibits, ranging from a touch pool filled with inter-tide invertebrates to the whole skeleton of a whale. Temporary exhibitions illustrate specific aspects of ocean life, with the emphasis on ecology.

MUSEO PROVINCIAL DE CIENCIAS NATURALES Y OCEANOGRÁFICO

A Catalan entrepreneur and trader, who made his fortune in the fledgling town at the end of the 19th century, built the neoclassical Chalet Pujol, known locally as El Castillo de Madryn, in 1917. On García and Menéndez, it now houses the Museo Provincial de Ciencias Naturales y Oceanográfico, an interesting visit for a rainy day (tel 02965/451139; Mon–Fri 9–12, 3–7, Sat–Sun 3–7; $10). Beautifully restored, the splendid villa, with its superb spiral stone staircase, enjoys wonderful views of the bay, in particular from the top of its tower. It displays a collection of memorabilia from the early pioneering days of the Welsh settlements along with fascinating exhibits of regional fauna and flora. One of the highlights is a spectacular whale baleen that hangs from the ceiling in one of the impeccably renovated rooms.

Above *The skeleton of a southern right whale on display outside the Ecocentro*

PUERTO PIRÁMIDES

At the end of the 19th century the bustling little port of Puerto Pirámides earned its livelihood from wool; nowadays its revenue comes from tourism, as whale-watching has become big business. On the Península Valdés (▷ 132–133), on the opposite side of the horseshoe-shaped Golfo Nuevo from Puerto Madryn, Puerto Pirámides is an excellent base from which to see the southern right whales that come to the sheltered waters of the gulf to breed and feed every winter, around June, and remain until early summer. Mothers and their calves are the last to leave, in December, often steering clear of the shores, which means you need to sail out into the middle of the gulf to see them. But in late winter and spring you can effortlessly spy them from the comfort of your own bedroom. In fact, the whales come so close to Puerto Pirámides that they often run the risk of beaching.

WHALE-WATCHING TOURS

The town sits just beyond the entrance to the Península Valdés reserve. From its unpaved main drag, aptly named Avenida de la Ballenas (Whales Avenue), two side roads descend to the beach. Along with a variety of lodgings, restaurants and other services, half a dozen professional whale-safari companies have their offices within walking distance of one another, along these three streets. Outfits vary in age and experience but all are highly professional so you might just like to do a quick tour of the options and get a feeling for the different guides and operations. Services and prices vary little but certain times might suit you better than others. You should also find out what kind of boat you'll be going out in. The aim of the boat trips into the gulf is to get close to the whales, which plunge playfully beneath the boats, somersault powerfully out of the water and then disappear into the depths with a flick of their gigantic tails. You, too, can dive in the bay's clear but chilly waters, or take a kayak tour (▷ 145), or rent a mountain bike to explore the local area. You can obtain details of rental companies from the helpful tourist office.

INFORMATION

www.puertopiramides.gov.ar/turismo/en/
✚ 353 F17 🛈 Municipalidad, Avenida de las Ballenas s/n ☎ 02965/495048
🚌 Buses from Madryn twice daily
✈ Nearest airports Puerto Madryn and Trelew 🚗 85km (53 miles) from Puerto Madryn via RP-2

TIPS

» All the whale-watching tour companies keep a respectful distance from the whales but it is worth checking the type of boat being used for a given sailing. The semi-rigid inflatable zodiacs allow you to get much closer to the whales but they tend to rollercoaster more in rough waves than the solid timber boats.

» Most of the time the sheltered Golfo Nuevo is smooth but in high winds boat trips can be bumpy, so take anti-seasickness medication, if necessary, before setting off.

» Avoid Pirámides in January and February when instead of whales there are just hordes of noisy holidaymakers.

» For more information about whales and other fauna, consult the excellent municipal website.

Below *Southern right whales come to breed and feed in the sheltered waters of the Golfo Nuevo close to Puerto Pirámides during the winter months*

PUNTA TOMBO

www.puntatombo.com

Seemingly inhabited by countless small waiters, the Punta Tombo rookery is home to half a million Magellanic penguins every summer, from October to February (or maybe a little longer), making it the largest penguin colony in South America. Magellanic penguins keep the same mates for life and come ashore to the same nesting site year after year. These comical and curious birds nest and breed along this beautiful sweep of littoral, 100km (62 miles) south of Trelew, where you can get up surprisingly close to them as they huddle beneath bushes, scuttle across the sand and swim in the blue-green ocean.

The reserve is extremely well organized, with a café and shop at the entrance, an information centre and a series of well-marked trails. Obey all instructions not to disturb the penguins because, although they are accustomed to human presence, they do not appreciate having the paths to their burrows blocked and may become disoriented. Punta Tombo can be reached down the unpaved RP-1, a turnoff from the main RN-3, but the best way to reach the rookery is on an organized excursion from Trelew (▷ 146).

🕂 353 F18 ✉ Punta Tombo, Provincia de Chubut 🕐 Sep–Mar daily 9–7 👆 $30 🚌 Bus from Trelew or excursions from Trelew 🚗 RN-3 for 100km (62 miles), signposted to Punta Tombo 🚶 Tours from Trelew

RÍO GALLEGOS

www.turismo.riogallegos.gov.ar

The hardy provincial capital of Santa Cruz, Río Gallegos sits on the estuary of its namesake river, renowned for its record-breaking brown trout. Shopping for all kinds of outdoor gear along the main commercial street can be especially worthwhile as prices are lower than in the Patagonian resorts. Tourist facilities are a bit thin on the ground, although it's worth asking the tourist information office about local tour operators that can take you to Cabo Vírgenes (▷ 129),

Above *Skeleton on display in Trelew's Museo Paleontológico Egidio Feruglio*
Opposite *Well-marked trails at Punta Tombo allow visitors to see Magellanic penguins up close*

with its monumental lighthouse and penguin colony.

The Museo de los Pioneros on El Cano and Alberdi (tel 02966/437763; daily 10–7; free), in the town's oldest house, has a small collection of memorabilia from pioneering days, which is worth visiting. You might also like to check out the Salesian Catedral de Nuestra Señora de Luján (a Catholic missionary order). This prefabricated church (Mon–Fri 10–5, Sat–Sun 2–6; free), on the leafy Plaza San Martín, the town's main square, was erected at the end of the 19th century using forced indigenous labour.

🕂 356 D25 ✉ Río Gallegos, Provincia de Santa Cruz ℹ Roca 863 ☎ 02966/438725 🕐 Mon–Fri 9–6, Sat 10–1.30, 5–8 🚌 Buses from Buenos Aires ✈ Airport 7km (4.5 miles) west of the city; taxi is the only connecting transport 🚗 RN-3 for 2,680km (1,662 miles) from Buenos Aires

TRELEW

Trelew, the main city in the Welsh-dominated lower Chubut valley, got its name from Lewis Jones, one of the early settlers in northern Patagonia and builder of the area's first railway. The centre is built around

the park-like Plaza de Independencia, but the two main sights are closer to the bigger Plaza Centenario. The first is the small Museo Regional Pueblo de Luis, in the disused train station (Avenida Fontana and Avenida Lewis Jones; tel 02965/424062; Mon–Fri 8–8, Sat–Sun, national holidays 2–8; $5). It illustrates the difficult arrival of the Welsh and how they cohabited with the indigenous Tehuelche.

Nearby is the first-rate Museo Paleontológico Egidio Feruglio (Avenida Fontana 140; tel 02965/432100; Mon–Fri 10–6, Sat–Sun and public hols 9–8; $33). The fascinating displays of dinosaur skeletons and eggs, and impressive special effects, make this museum a memorable experience. Trelew has some good hotels and restaurants but you might prefer to stay in the rural idyll of nearby Gaiman (▷ 129) famed for its tea rooms, which serve Welsh-style high tea complete with scones and fruitcake.

🕂 353 F18 ✉ Trelew, Provincia de Chubut ℹ Mitre 387 ☎ 02965/420139 🕐 Mon–Fri 8–8, Sat–Sun 9–9 🚌 Buses from Buenos Aires and Puerto Madryn ✈ Airport 5km (3 miles) northeast of town

Ceda el paso al pingüino
Respetar zona demarcada
Give way to penguins
Keep within the trails
GRACIAS
thank you

INFORMATION

www.turismoushuaia.com
www.ushuaia.gov.ar/turismo.php
www.allpatagonia.com

🚩 357 E27 ✉ Ushuaia, Provincia
de Tierra del Fuego ℹ San Martín
674 ☎ 02901/424550 🕐 Mon–Fri
8–10, Sat–Sun 9–8 ✈ Ushuaia airport
(Malvinas Argentinas) 4km (2.5 miles)
southwest; frequent flights from Buenos
Aires and El Calafate; transfer by taxi
🚌 Long-distance buses from Buenos
Aires via Puerto Madryn, Río Gallegos and
Río Grande 🚗 RN-3 from Buenos Aires

INTRODUCTION

Although there are small settlements on the Isla Navarino and research centres on Antarctica itself, Ushuaia can safely claim to be the most southerly town in the world at 54° 48°S. The label '*fin del mundo*' (world's end) is attached to a museum and a train, and to just about everything else, and there certainly is a feeling of remoteness about the place. Its proximity to the Antarctic—cruise ships depart for the great white continent from its harbour—means that its climate is chilly, even in the summer, but the long luminous days from November to February, the fabulous setting on the Beagle Channel with the Martial mountain range looming behind, and the high quality of its tourist facilities make Ushuaia one of Argentina's great destinations.

A great sprawl of a place, tilted on a slope all the way down to the waterfront, Ushuaia is by far the biggest town on the huge island of Tierra del Fuego, half of which belongs to Chile—with which Argentina has disputed certain Beagle Channel islets (Picton, Lennox and Nueva) in the past. Officially it is the capital of Argentina's biggest province, Tierra del Fuego, Antártida e Islas del Atlántico Sur, which also takes in some island territories, and a gigantic chunk of Antarctica, not recognized as Argentine territory under international law.

WHAT TO SEE
THE TOWN

Modern but randomly built, Ushuaia won't win any prizes for town planning or architectural beauty, but it has a pioneering atmosphere and some of the finest hotels and restaurants in the region. It is a major fishing port and the delicious flesh of the huge king crab finds its way on to many local menus, while hot chocolate is served in many bars and cafés, most welcome on days when the bitter southerly wind blows.

Above *Sprawling Ushuaia, backed by the Martial mountains*

You can easily spend a few action-packed days in the town and its hinterland, or taking adventurous boat trips out into the Channel. With more time, you could explore deeper into the Tierra del Fuego archipelago, although the northern two thirds are even flatter and bleaker than the Patagonian mainland.

Near the town you can enjoy the unspoilt beauties of the Parque Nacional Tierra del Fuego (▷ 131), the centennial hospitality of the very English Estancia Harberton (▷ 129), and the world-end ski resorts of Glaciar Martial and Sierra Alvear. Within the city itself, there are three interesting museums, covering the town's recent history as a western settlement (the first Caucasian to live here was Anglican missionary Reverend Stirling in 1869), its pre-European populations (most of which were decimated as a result of the European presence) and the town's role as a remote penal colony during the first half of the 20th century.

From the *muelle turístico* (tourist pier), you can take a variety of boat trips into the legendary Beagle Channel, named after Darwin's ship, in which he explored these icy waters in the 1830s.

MUSEO DEL FIN DEL MUNDO

www.museodelfindelmundo.org.ar
The museum is an interesting introduction to life down in the Fuegian archipelago. The first of its six main rooms houses an exhibit that narrates the story of the local indigenous peoples, the Mannekenk and Selk'nam (Ona) tribes and the canoe-faring Yámana (Yaghans), and their first contact with European settlers, which was not always happy. A figurehead from the *Duchess of Albany*, a ship that ran aground near Ushuaia in 1893, dominates the section on navigation. The second room focuses on Ushuaia's post-colonization development, with a reproduction of a typical *almacén* or store. In the third, you can learn about the town's role as a prison colony, with some fascinating documents relating to some of the larger-than-life inmates, while the fourth is dedicated to Fuegian birds, including the imposing albatross, plus dozens of other species. The fifth is used for temporary exhibits, and the sixth preserves the gleaming wood and brass installations of the Banco de la Nación (national bank), which had its headquarters here until the 1970s.
✚ 140 E2 ✉ Avenida Maipú 173 ☎ 02901/421863 🕐 Oct–Apr daily 9–8; May–Sep Mon–Sat 12–7 ✋ $20

Below right *The Museo Marítimo y Presidio testifies to Ushuaia's time as a penal colony*
Below *Views on the road towards the Parque Nacional Tierra del Fuego*

TIPS
❯❯ Unless you are here for the skiing, avoid Tierra del Fuego in the winter as the days are short and it is very difficult to get around, but autumn is fabulous, with mild days and blazing tree foliage. Expect high winds at all times of the year.
❯❯ A good way to get a glimpse of the prison at the pricey Museo Marítimo is to have a coffee in the *confitería*.
❯❯ Some of the most rewarding experiences are to be had by staying at one of the atmospheric tourist *estancias* on Tierra del Fuego.
❯❯ The museums are worth saving for inclement weather, which is not infrequent in these parts.

MUSEO MARÍTIMO Y PRESIDIO

www.museomaritimo.com

To find out more about Ushuaia's fascinating, if sombre, past as a penal colony you can visit the Museo Marítimo y Presidio, just a hop away from the Museo del Fin del Mundo. The main attraction is the unusual jail building itself, on which construction began in 1902. The jail is organized like the spokes of half a wheel radiating in wings from a central hub, or Rotunda. You can visit the cells to get some idea of what prison life was like, but to see the reconstruction of the lighthouse that inspired Jules Verne's visionary novel *Lighthouse at the End of the World* (1905), which once stood on a nearby island, you must go on a free guided tour (daily 10.30am).

The maritime museum has some marvellous scale models of ships that loomed large in Fuegian history, including the *Fragata Sarmiento*, the original of which is now in Puerto Madero (▷ 91) in Buenos Aires, plus a reconstruction of a Yámana bark canoe. In addition, there is an art gallery with paintings by local artists and a small museum about the Antarctic, the Museo Antártico.

✚ 140 E1 ✉ Yaganes and Gobernador Paz ☎ 02901/437481 ◷ Daily 9–8 ✋ $60

CANAL DE BEAGLE (BEAGLE CHANNEL)

The best way to get a feel for the city and its dramatic mountainous backdrop is to get in a boat and explore the Canal de Beagle (named after Darwin's ship, *The Beagle*). The conventional trips in catamarans and sailboats leave from the *muelle turístico* (tourist pier) and take in three islands (Bridges, Pájaros and Los Lobos), sailing round the Les Eclaireurs lighthouse, before heading back to Ushuaia.

Some trips include a short trek on Isla H—so called because of its shape—where you can see Yámana *conchales* (shell middens or dumps), plus plenty of birds, including petrels, skuas, terns and albatrosses. A chance to glimpse fabulous birds, sea lions, Peale's dolphins and, if you are lucky, minke whales is the aim of the trips and they don't disappoint. Longer trips take in Estancia Harberton (▷ 129) and the penguin rookeries on Isla Martillo.

✚ 357 D27

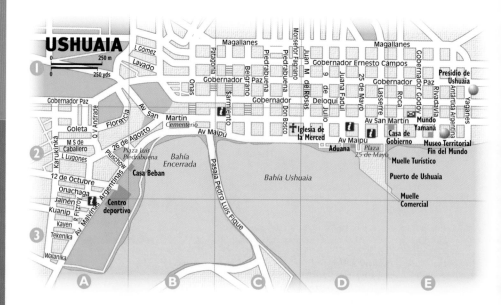

MORE TO SEE
REST OF TIERRA DEL FUEGO

If you have time and like these faraway climes, it might be worth spending a few days exploring the rest of Argentine Tierra del Fuego, in particular the national park (▷ 131). You can rent a car in Ushuaia and go exploring or take one of the organized excursions of the Argentine half of the island.

Near to Ushuaia, beyond the 430m (1,410ft) Garibaldi mountain pass, with its amazing views, are some fabulously rugged and unpopulated landscapes, mostly around the beautiful but largely inaccessible Lago Fagnano. The village of Tolhuin, at the lake's head, makes a reasonable base.

The northernmost swathes of Tierra del Fuego are pretty bleak, as is the workaday town of Río Grande, and unless you are keen on sports fishing, this area is best left alone.

✚ 357 D26

MUSEO YÁMANA

This delightful interpretation centre in Ushuaia uses evocative dioramas to illustrate the extinct cultures of the indigenous Yámana people who settled Tierra del Fuego around 4000BC (▷ 32).

✉ Rivadavia 56, Ushuaia ✉ 029/0142-2874 🕓 Daily 10–8 ✋ $10

SKI RESORTS

www.cerrocastor.com

The only reason to come to Ushuaia in the winter months is to take advantage of the world's most southerly snow sports resorts. Downhill and cross-country skiing, snowmobiles, sledding and snowboarding are all practised at Cerro Castor (▷ 146) in the Sierra Alvear, a modern ski centre 26km (16 miles) out of town.

Above *Remote Les Eclaireurs lighthouse in the Beagle Channel*

EXPLORING TIERRA DEL FUEGO

If the atmosphere of the planet's most southerly inhabited archipelago has you hooked, why not base yourself in Ushuaia, rent a vehicle and drive out into the wilds of Tierra del Fuego. This route heaves you up over the Garibaldi mountain pass and on to the great plains in the central and northern parts of the island. It is not worth going all the way to the rather dull Río Grande, so stop short and stay overnight at one of the island's most hospitable *estancias*, rather than trying to complete the return trip in one day (though it is possible).

THE DRIVE

Distance: 450km (270 miles)
Time: 7 hours without detours
Start/End at: Ushuaia

★ Always take provisions for a journey of this kind and consider having a picnic, although sub-Antarctic winds might put paid to this plan. From the centre of Ushuaia head eastwards, following signs to Río Grande. The RN-3 road clambers northeastwards through beautiful southern beech forest and into the mountains, where the island's winter sports centres are located. You can enjoy fabulous vistas of the Fuegian dales and the tooth-edged mountain ranges, including the dramatic peak of Monte Olivia (1,490m/454ft), which isolate the south of the island from its northern plains.

Nearly 40km (25 miles) from Ushuaia on the RN-3, the RN-33 (formerly the RCj) turn-off to the right takes you through fabulous woods. Here, you will see the windswept flag trees, featured on postcards throughout Argentina, on the way to the historic Estancia Harberton, which is 45km (28 miles) from the turn-off.

❶ You can take one of the excellent guided visits at Estancia Harberton (▷ 129) and find about about the local marine fauna at the Museo Acatushún. The *estancia* is also a good place for lunch (or afternoon tea) or you could extend your tour and stay overnight here.

Return to the RN-33 (RCj) turn-off with the RN-3, then continue on the RN-3 for 10km (6 miles) to the lofty Paso Garibaldi at 430m (1,376ft)

before dipping towards little Lago Escondido and touching the southern bank of the much larger Lago Fagnano.

❷ A great finger lake, over 100km (62 miles) long, Lago Fagnano is also signposted 'Kami' (the indigenous Selk'nam name). It cuts the main island of Tierra del Fuego almost into two and, like the whole Fuegian archipelago, it is shared with Chile. Occupying a narrow valley formed by gentle hills, most of it is accessible only by boat and its fish-rich waters are popular with anglers.

For a short distance, the RN-3 skirts the lake before splitting in two: The left fork is a causeway across the lake, affording wonderful westward views of the turquoise water, while the faster right branch takes you directly to Tolhuin. Some 7km (4 miles) before Tolhuin, the pleasant Hostería Kaikén has a handsome bar and an excellent restaurant, both with views of the lake. Alternatively, continue to Tolhuin.

❸ With all the basic amenities and a couple of good places to eat, the town of Tolhuin mainly serves as a stopover before continuing along the RN-3 towards the north of the island and the mainland. A popular stop for refreshments is the Panadería La Unión, famed for its *facturas* (sticky pastries). There is also a pizzeria called Capricho, a decent restaurant called Amistad and a *parrilla* renowned for its lamb, all within walking distance of the *panadería*.

By taking a detour along the RCh, branching to the left off the main road 22km (14 miles) north of Tolhuin (signposted Estancia Carmen), and heading northwards along the RCf, you will rejoin the RN-3 a short distance south of Río Grande. From here, it is 60km (37 miles) south back along the RN-3, in the direction of Ushuaia, to reach Estancia Viamonte.

This 180km (112-mile) diversion will take you through beautiful copses of beech and *lenga* and across fertile sheep meadows. There are views of volcanic peaks to the south beyond the twin lakes, Lago Yehuin and Lago Chepelmut, and you might spot condors nesting on the crags between the two lakes.

Otherwise, keep going until you reach the junction with the RCa, another 18km (11 miles) north of the RCh turnoff.

❹ The scenic RCa takes you eastwards, then southeastwards over brownish plains and past enchanting woodlands towards the Atlantic coast. You can enjoy stunning views of the coast south of Cabo San Pablo and at low tide (get local advice

about the tides) you can walk out to the *Desdémona*, which was wrecked in the 1980s.

The road continues for 17km (10.5 miles) through coastal wetlands to the Estancia La Fueguina and after that a difficult track peters out at Estancia María Luisa, another 20km (12 miles) further on. Neither *estancia* can be visited but the views along this isolated road are marvellous. Beyond, stretches the mysterious Península Mitre, the southeast tip of Tierra del Fuego, so here you'll need to backtrack to the RCa turn-off and rejoin the RN-3. A little less than 40km (25 miles) north from the RCa turn-off you will reach Estancia Viamonte.

❺ Estancia Viamonte was built in 1902 by Lucas Bridges, assisted by the locals, and is still run by his descendants, the Goodalls, whose sheep number more than 20,000. One of the island's most historic farms is given pride of place in Bridges' wonderful memoirs, *The Uttermost Part of the Earth*. Consider staying here a night or two before returning to Ushuaia on the RN-3.

WHEN TO GO
Tierra del Fuego is usually inaccessible from June to August, windy from September to November, busy but fine from December to early February and beautifully autumnal from mid-February until after Easter. Leave early in the morning and make the most of the long austral days.

TOURIST INFORMATION
✉ San Martín 674, Ushuaia
☎ 02901/424550
🕐 Mon–Fri 8–10, Sat–Sun 9–8

WHERE TO EAT
PANADERÍA LA UNIÓN
▷ 145.

HOSTERÍA KAIKÉN
▷ 152–153.

WHERE TO STAY
ESTANCIA VIAMONTE
▷ 152–153.

TIP
» It is worth renting a 4WD, especially if you want to get off the main route and on to the gravel side roads. If you plan to drive around Tierra del Fuego, book your vehicle well ahead.

CABO VÍRGENES
EL FIN Y EL CABO
El Fin y El Cabo literally means 'the end and the cape', which accurately describes the location of the most southerly shop-cum-café on the South American continent. This delightful little place belongs to the Monte Dinero *estancia*, and the menu is an antidote to the blustery gales that blow around Cabo Vírgenes. The friendly staff dish out hot chocolate with cakes or tea and toast with home-made jams and marmalades.
✉ RN-40 km0 ☎ 02966/428922 ⏰ Call ahead for times ✋ From $20 🚌 RN-3 to Río Gallegos and RN-40 to Cabo Vírgenes

GAIMAN
PARQUE EL DESAFÍO
Joaquín Alonso, known as the Dalí of Gaiman for his eccentric personality and prodigious creativity, took decades to create this park in his garden. He recycled thousands of cans and plastic bottles, turning them into weird and wonderful constructions, such as a tower 'in homage to himself' and many different installations, hung with witty signs and comments on the wastefulness of modern society. Since his death, the park has been run by his daughter.
✉ Avenida Brown 52 ⏰ Mon–Fri 3–7, Sat–Sun 9–7 ✋ Adult $10, child free

TY NAIN
www.cpatagonia.com/gaiman/ty-nain
In a late 19th-century ivy-clad house, descendants of the original Welsh settlers serve local specialities *torta negra* (dark fruitcake), originally reserved for weddings, and custard pie with tea in proper teapots. When you have had your fill, you might stagger into the adjoining little museum, which is crammed with objects relating to the life of the Welsh in Gaiman.
✉ Hipólito Yrigoyen 283 ☎ 02965/491126 ⏰ Daily 11–6 ✋ From $20

PUERTO DESEADO
DARWIN EXPEDITIONS
www.darwin-expeditions.com
Based next to the docks you pass on the way into the town, Darwin runs first-rate boat trips around the Ría Deseado and up the Cañadon Torcida, a narrow cliff-lined channel. You can spot dolphins on the way to Isla de los Pájaros or, weather permitting, sail out to the Isla Pingüino, home to the Antarctic rockhopper penguin. There are longer trips up the estuary to the Miradores de Darwin bluffs or land excursions to the Monumento Natural Bosques Petrificados (▷ 129), too.
✉ España 2551 ☎ 0297 156 247 554 (cell phone) ✋ From $70

PUERTO MADRYN
BERNARDINO CLUB DE MAR
This is the best place to rent mountain bikes and there are a couple of excursions to try. One tour heads northwards along the coast by the old Puerto Pirámides road to Playa Doradilla, 17km/10.5 miles from Puerto Madryn, where you spot whales in the early evening between June and September. The other trip heads to the sea-lion colony at Punta Loma, some 20km (12 miles) to the south of the city centre, by a more scenic route.
✉ Brown and Perlotti ☎ 02965/452083 ⏰ Daily 9–6 ✋ Tours start from $80

HUELLAS Y COSTAS
www.huellasycostas.com
In addition to hiking and bicycle tours, this tour company can arrange one- or multi-day camping and sea-kayaking outings that allow you to get closer to the wildlife than in the bigger excursion boats. Kayak trips are limited to eight people and include all the necessary equipment, an energy pack and a lunchbox.
✉ Morgan 1995 ☎ 02965/470143 ✋ Day trips start from $160

MADRYN BUCEO
www.madrynbuceo.com
This excellent outfit offers a range of diving activities for novices and more experienced divers. Many of the guides are English-speaking (check before you set out) and safety is of the highest order. They are all PADI-affiliated operators and will sell or rent out equipment to visitors. Lessons, night dives and excursions farther afield are all possible, so ask for the full range of services and compare prices with similar companies before signing up.
✉ Boulevard Brown, 3a Rotonda ☎ 02961/556-4422 ✋ Baptism: $250

MANOS DEL SUR
www.manosdelsur.com.ar
This creative shop stocks Patagonian crafts, including wooden trays decorated with sea fossils and dried flowers, hand-painted ceramic mugs and *mate* holders, leather handbags and rucksacks, beautifully fashioned knives with horn handles and some rather kitsch metal statuettes of penguins and whale flukes.
✉ Avenida Roca 516 ☎ 02965/472539 ⏰ Mon–Sat 9–7

TOWANDA
This enticing coffee shop by the pier serves an array of delicious home-made pastries and sandwiches, Italian-style coffee and several types of tea. There are usually paintings by local artists on the walls.
✉ Roque Saenz Peña 41 ☎ 02965/473806 ⏰ Daily 9–8 ✋ From $25

TURISMO PUMA
www.turismopuma.com
If you base yourself in Madryn and don't feel up to driving to the various sights in the region (distances are long and roads can be trying) then fix yourself up with Turismo Puma. The tours feature well-organized excursions to Península Valdés (▷ 132–133), the penguin colony at Punta Tombo (▷ 136) or urban tours to Trelew (▷ 136) and Gaiman (▷ 129).
✉ 28 de Julio 46 ☎ 02965/451063 ⏰ Daily 9–7 ✋ Day trip to Punta Tombo $30

PUERTO PIRÁMIDES
LA ESTACIÓN
This slightly ramshackle hut along the main drag sells an array of bric-a-brac, posters, exotic furnishings and amusing objects. The main theme is national and international rock music but the sounds you hear will tend to be Latin pop. A great place for a drink in the evening, La Estación also cooks excellent fresh pasta dishes, and in good weather you can sit on the airy veranda.
✉ Avenida de las Ballenas s/n ☎ 02965/495047 ⏰ Nov–Feb daily 10am–1am; Mar–Oct noon–11pm

PATAGONIA EXPLORERS
www.patagoniaexplorers.com
Patagonia Explorers offers excellent guided, small-group kayak trips in the Golfo Nuevo and Golfo San José, on either side of the Península Valdés (▷ 132–133), from half-day paddles to full nine-day expeditions. During the whale season, there are special whale-watching expeditions, and in the summer there are trips to see sea lions and marine birds, making the most of the long hours of daylight.
✉ Avenida de las Ballenas s/n ☎ 02965/15-340619 ⏰ Long trips Oct–May; day trips all year ✋ 3-hour outing US$50; 8-day kayak trip US$1,750

SOUTHERN SPIRIT CRUISES
www.southernspirit.com.ar
There are several respected operators taking boats out into the Gulf to see southern right whales in action, but Southern Spirit has the edge in terms of service. All tours are accompanied by a bilingual guide. Like all operators, the skippers observe strict regulations about keeping a respectful distance from the whales, although the calves will often get very close and dive beneath the boat—a memorable experience.
✉ Avenida de las Ballenas and Primera Bajada ☎ 02965/473043 ⏰ 1 Jun to 15 Dec ✋ $180 ($300 for sunset trip)

PUERTO SAN JULIÁN
EXCURSIONES PINOCHO
www.pinochoexcursiones.com.ar
Excursiones Pinocho offers excellent outings in the bay with English commentaries by volunteer biologists. The best time for seeing dolphins and cormorants is from early December to Easter, and Señor Pinocho will always give a scrupulously honest appraisal of your chances of spotting them.
✉ San Martín s/n ☎ 02962/454600 ✋ $60

RÍO GALLEGOS
RINCÓN GAUCHO
Río Gallegos is a good place for shopping. You can find most things you might need for outdoor activities without paying the inflated prices of El Calafate or Ushuaia. This wonderful leather shop on Avenida Roca can fit you out with hats and belts, beautifully embossed with the logo, or you might opt for a knife with a leather sheath or a pair of chaps.
✉ Avenida Roca 619 ☎ 02966/420669 ⏰ Mon–Fri 10–6, Sat 10–1

TOLHUIN
PANADERÍA LA UNIÓN
www.panaderialaunion.com
This bakery is a Tierra del Fuego institution. Stop for a coffee and a pastry, or stock up with provisions before leaving on an excursion. Day-trippers make use of the clean toilets and internet connection. Don't leave without trying the delicious *facturas* (sweet pastries).
✉ Jeujepen 450 ☎ 02901/492202 ⏰ Daily 7am–midnight ✋ From $15

TRELEW

CALON HUILLI

www.calonhuilli.com.ar

This wonderfully helpful company has a range of tours, including seeing the penguins at their rookeries or a day trip to the Península Valdés (▷ 132–133). Agrotourism is also popular and Calon Huilli can arrange visits to *estancias* to see farm activities such as sheep shearing.

✉ Belgrano 693 ☎ 02965/426632
✋ Penguin rookery: $140; day trips $190

MARGARITA BAR

This popular bar specializes in cocktails, though the food is good, too, especially the salads. There is often live music, mostly jazz, on nights during the week, while this is where the young people of Trelew hang out and dance at the weekends.

✉ Avenida Roca and Roque Sáenz Peña ☎ 02965/432126 🕐 Evenings until late

USHUAIA

ALL PATAGONIA

www.allpatagonia.com

This excellent all-round tour operator can arrange safaris and excursions, including birdwatching tours and nature expeditions. The outfit also specializes in trips to the Antarctic, to which Ushuaia is a major gateway.

✉ Juana Fadul 60, Ushuaia
☎ 02901/433622 ✋ Day trips start from $160

Below *Chocolate-covered* alfajores *(cookies)*

ANTIGUA CASA BEBÁN

This quaint house with decorative gables was prefabricated in Sweden and reconstructed in the outskirts of Ushuaia in 1913. It hosts interesting photography and art exhibitions, as well as movie screenings; it was designated Ushuaia's Bicentenary House in 2010.

✉ Maipú and Plüschow ☎ 02901/431386
🕐 Variable, check ahead ✋ Free

CANAL FUN

www.canalfun.com

This imaginative company has a range of interesting trips to Tierra del Fuego, including a 10-hour day trip to Estancia Harberton (▷ 129) and on to Gable Island in the Beagle Channel (▷ 140–141) or one- to three-day kayak adventures. Emphasis is on activity rather than sitting in a bus.

✉ 9 de Julio 118 ☎ 02901/437395
✋ 1-day kayak US$100; day trip to Estancia Harberton $170

CERRO CASTOR

www.cerrocastor.com

This modern ski centre, 26km (16 miles) out of the town, offers 30km (18 miles) of pistes, including some black runs up to 2km (1.25 miles) long. Facing south, the centre gets the best powder and, being on the same latitude as Moscow, cold winters. There are snow machines for those pesky dry seasons.

✉ San Martín 740, Ushuaia/RN-3 km26
☎ 02901/422244 🕐 Daily Jun–Sep
✋ Day pass $200

GOTAMA EXPEDICIONES

www.gotama-expediciones.com

This professional outfit offers guided backcountry skiing for advanced skiers and rents equipment at reasonable prices. Expeditions take you to the downhill (*esqui alpino*) pistes close to Ushuaia, the Club Andino, 3km (2 miles) from town, and the more impressive one by Glaciar Martial, 7km (4 miles) away. There is an excellent ski school, too, for those who want to learn or improve their skills on the slopes.

☎ 02901/15-550807 🕐 Daily 10–3.30
✋ Classes $500 per day

KÜAR

▷ 149.

LAGUNA NEGRA

www.lagunanegra.com.ar

Southern Argentina is famed for its chocolate and Laguna Negra—with a branch in El Calafate, too—is renowned for the quality of its bars and flakes (*ramas*), its *alfajores* (chocolate-covered cookies sandwiched with jam or *dulce de leche*) and its chocolate raisins. You can take your goodies away for those energy-consuming walks or sit down inside with coffee or hot chocolate.

✉ San Martín 513 ☎ 02901/431144
🕐 Mon–Fri 10–7, Sat 10–2

NUNATAK ADVENTURE

www.nunatakadventure.com

Nunatak's special treats are sea kayaking and canoeing, following in the wake of the indigenous Yámana, who spent most of their life at sea. The company also do land-based tours, including tough treks up into the mountains above Ushuaia. One of their unique trips is the demanding day trek to the Ojo del Albino (Albino Eye) glacier, which includes ice trekking using crampons.

✉ 25 de Mayo 296 ☎ 02901/430329
🕐 All year ✋ Day trek $180

RENATA RAFALAK

Renata Rafalak makes some of the best crafts in southern Patagonia and is acclaimed for her charming reproductions of the *lenga* bark masks worn by the Selk'nam and Yámana in their Hain and Kina initiation ceremonies. The masks, painted in black, white and ochre, make unusual wall decorations.

✉ Piedrabuena 51 ☎ 02901/435386
🕐 Call ahead for opening times

RUMBO SUR

www.rumbosur.com.ar

This is a specialist company with tours that range from short boat trips out to sea to cruises in the South Atlantic and Antarctica that you will want to prepare for well ahead. The 2.5-hour catamaran trip to see seals out in the Beagle Channel is their most popular excursion.

✉ San Martín 350 ☎ 02901/422275

✋ Half-day trips $70

TANTE SARA

www.cafebartantesara.com.ar

Tante Sara is a café-bar that is
extremely popular for its excellent
chocolate and cakes. The house
speciality is the *torta fueguina* (rich
fruitcake laced with brandy) that is
sold in a smart tin. This is also an
excellent place to buy sandwiches
and other goodies for a picnic.

✉ San Martín 701 ☎ 02901/433710

🕒 Dec–Feb daily 9–10; Mar–Nov Mon–
Sat 10–6

TIERRA DE HUMOS

www.tierradehumos.com

Attached to the excellent Bodegón
Fueguino restaurant, this shop is a
great place to pick up postcards,
souvenirs, T-shirts or warm woollen
clothing. There are excellent arts and
crafts, too.

✉ San Martín 861 ☎ 02901/433050

🕒 Daily 10–7

TOLKEYEN

www.tolkeyenpatagonia.com

This outstanding travel company,
which also has a branch in El
Calafate, offers land and sea tours,
plus all kinds of winter sport activities
in and out of Ushuaia. This can be a
great way of getting to and around
the Parque Nacional Tierra del Fuego
(▷ 131) or to Lago Fagnano in
the middle of the island. Another
excellent option is their boat trip to
Estancia Harberton (▷ 129).

✉ San Martín 1267 ☎ 02901/424504

✋ Half-day trips $70

TREN DEL FIN DEL MUNDO

www.trendelfindelmundo.com.ar

Using a line built by convicts to
transport timber from the forests,
the Fin del Mundo train journey
is popular with tourists. Leaving
three to four times a day in season
from the special Estación del Fin
del Mundo, 8km (5 miles) west of
Ushuaia, this steam locomotive
chugs along a narrow gauge through
the Río Pipo valley to the Parque

Nacional Tierra del Fuego, 2km
(1.25 miles) short of the main gate.
Commentators provide passengers
with historical background in English
and Spanish. Most people take the
train one way and a bus back.

✉ RN-3 km3402 ☎ 02901/431600

🕒 3 to 5 times daily ✋ $110 one-way,
under 5 free

TRES MARÍAS EXCURSIONES

www.tresmariasweb.com

This well-established company offers
exclusive fishing-boat trips for groups
of up to 10 people to Isla-H and
other sites along the Beagle Channel
(▷ 140–141). The intrepid seafarer
can charter trips along the Fuegian
channels or even an expedition
round Cape Horn. Héctor Monsalve
has some 30 years' experience as a

fisherman and deep-sea diver, so you
are in good hands.

✉ Antonio Romero 515 ☎ 02901/436416

✋ Boat trips $80–$180

USHUAIA DIVERS

www.ushuaiadivers.com.ar

As the name so succinctly suggests,
this is a diving outfit, offering
beginners' courses, as well as trips
into the Beagle Channel to look for
centolla (king crab) and sea lions.
Trips usually start off at the Les
Eclaireurs lighthouse in the Beagle
Channel (▷ 140–141) and head
for the Isla de los Lobos for the first
submersion. Isla Bridge and the Isla
de los Pájaros (▷ 140) are other
favoured sites.

✉ L.N. Alem 4509 ☎ 02901/444701

✋ Half-day $160

MARCH

ORCA ATTACKS

www.puertopiramides.gov.ar/turismo/
en/index.htm

Every year between the middle of
March and early April huge orcas
can be seen speeding along the
coast at Punta Norte and launching
themselves on the beaches to catch
sea lion pups—it is a bit gory but
certainly spectacular.

MAY

WHALE VIGIL

www.puertopiramides.gov.ar/turismo/
en/index.htm

It is very exciting to be in Puerto
Pirámides for *Vigilia* at the end of
May, when prizes go to whoever
spots the first southern right whale
arriving in the Golfo Nuevo.

JUNE

JAZZ AL FIN

www.jazzalfin.com.ar

This annual jazz festival in Ushuaia
takes place over five days, usually at
the beginning of the month,
and showcases the best in
Argentine jazz.

FIESTA NACIONAL DE LA NOCHE MÁS LARGA

www.ushuaia-info.com.ar

Midwinter's day, when there is only
seven hours of daylight, is marked
by a torch-lit ski descent at Cerro
Martial, the snow sport resort just
behind Ushuaia.

AUGUST

FESTIVAL INTERNACIONAL DE CINE DE MONTAÑA

www.shhfestival.com

Ushuaia's respected International
Mountain Film Festival focuses on
movies about the uplands, with
special emphasis on the Andes and
their culture.

SEPTEMBER

TRELEW EISTEDDFOD

www.eisteddfod.org.ar

During the Chubut valley's main
festival of Welsh culture, Trelew's
main plaza hosts poetry, music and
other arts, when the Sillón del Bardo
(Bard's Chair) is awarded for the best
poetry in Welsh and the Corona del
Bardo (Bard's Crown) for the best
in Spanish.

PRICES AND SYMBOLS

The restaurants are listed alphabetically (excluding El, La and Los). The prices given are the average for a two-course lunch (L) and a three-course dinner (D) for one person, without drinks. The wine price is for the least expensive bottle. All the restaurants listed accept credit cards unless otherwise stated. Prices are given in Argentine pesos ($) unless otherwise noted.

For a key to the symbols, ▷ 2.

GAIMAN

PLAS Y COED

www.plasycoed.com.ar
One of the oldest and most traditional of the Welsh guest houses in Gaiman, this is a great place for sandwiches and cakes. Sunday lunches are popular too, with roast meat with roast potatoes and Yorkshire pudding. If you are around for Christmas, expect mulled wine, roast turkey and traditional British Christmas pudding and mince pies.
✉ Irigoyen 320 ☎ 02965/491133
🕐 Daily 11–4, 7–11 ✋ L $25, D $40, Wine $20

PUERTO DESEADO

PUERTO CRISTAL

The town's most upmarket restaurant overlooks a small lagoon near the sea and its huge picture windows offer commanding views of the busy harbour. This is a popular place with tourists and locals, who flock here for delicious grilled meat and fresh seafood from the day's haul.
✉ Avenida España 1698 ☎ 02974/870378
🕐 Thu–Tue 12–3.30, 7.30–12, Wed 7.30–12
✋ L $30, D $60 ,Wine $17

PUERTO DARWIN

www.darwin-expeditions.com
The Darwin outfit not only offers memorable excursions by sea and land (▷ 144), it also has this beautiful wooden cabin overlooking the harbour and the *ría*. Enjoy a hot drink and a snack or lunch while you are waiting to embark, or warm up after the trip when the weather is nippy. Expect excellent home-cooked food and superb views across the bird-filled estuary.
✉ España 2551 ☎ 02971/5624-7554
🕐 Daily 10–7 ✋ L $35

PUERTO MADRYN

CACCAROS

In this laid-back little bistro on the waterfront you can enjoy mellow music and perfectly cooked fish. The meat dishes, mostly created using lamb and veal, are equally delicious. In good weather, you can sit on the terrace, which is set back a little from the seafront esplanade. If you just want a snack, the sandwiches are beautifully fresh, too.
✉ Avenida Roca 385 ☎ 02965/453767
🕐 Daily 12.30–3, 7.30–11 ✋ L $35, D $50, Wine $17

NATIVO SUR

Wonderfully atmospheric with its indigenous-style decor, this beach restaurant enjoys remarkable ocean views. The seafood specials are highly recommended and you might like to try the catch of the day with a wok of vegetables. Everything about this place is upmarket, from the welcoming staff to the delicious, well-presented desserts.
✉ Boulevard Brown 1900
☎ 02965/457403 🕐 Tue–Sun 12–4, 8–12
✋ L $35, D $50, Wine $19

EL NAÚTICO

www.cantinaelnautico.com.ar
This outstanding bistro opened in the 1960s and has built an excellent reputation locally for its superb food. The impressive menu includes dishes such as scallops with Roquefort cheese and Basque-style sole with an onion and green pepper sauce. Finish with an ice cream or banana pancakes.
✉ Avenida Roca 790 ☎ 02965/471404
🕐 Daily 12.30–2.30, 7–11 ✋ L $35, D $50, Wine $15

TASKA BELTZA

Ricardo Chaves helms the kitchen and turns out a mean plate of seafood pasta. Choose between smoked salmon *gnocchis* or black ravioli stuffed with king crab. Fish of the day is cooked to perfection *en papillote* or grilled. Try the red tuna or black hake with red pepper sauce. If you want a change from fish, then the succulent lamb kebab is highly recommended. The restaurant serves the best Patagonian wines from the cellar to accompany your meal.

✉ 9 de Julio 461 ☎ 02965/474003
🕐 Tue–Sun 8pm–1am ✋ D $58, Wine $21

TERRAZA

Right on the ocean, Terraza enjoys marvellous views. The restaurant is renowned for its well-stocked cellar and sophisticated ingredients, which might include board of smoked venison, wild boar, trout or local cheeses. Main courses are mostly based on seafood, lamb, beef or fresh pasta while the desserts, made with Patagonian fruit, are spectacular.

✉ Boulevard Brown 759 ☎ 02965/473250
🕐 Tue–Sun 12.30–4.30, 7.30–12 ✋ L $45, D $68, Wine $21

PUERTO PIRÁMIDES
LAS RESTINGAS

www.lasrestingas.com

Las Restingas is one of the best hotels in the region and its restaurant is of the highest standard. The bar serves imaginative cocktails and the service is brisk. The fish and seafood dishes are truly exceptional and matched by the very best wines. The restaurant occupies the very best vantage point in Pirámides, so the views are fabulous, too.

✉ Hotel Las Restingas ☎ 02965/495101
🕐 Daily 12.30–12 ✋ L $40, D $65, Wine $25

PUERTO SAN JULIÁN
LA RURAL

Although the quality varies, La Rural pleases locals and occasional visitors with perfectly grilled shark and elephant fish. A meal here may be no great gastronomic experience but it exudes authenticity.

✉ Ameghino 811 ☎ 02962/454066
🕐 Daily 12.30–2.30, 7–11 ✋ L $24, D $35, Wine $16

RÍO GALLEGOS
LAGUANACAZUL

www.laguanacazul.com

Riverside Laguanacazul is so popular with locals and so well established on the tourist trail a reservation is advisable. Start with the hearty onion and potato soup, then choose one of the fabulous fish dishes and end with a volcano of the chocolate variety. The service is friendly and wines are expertly served.

✉ Lista and Sarmiento ☎ 02966/444114
🕐 Tue–Sun 12.30–3, 7.30–12 ✋ L $55, D $80, Wine $24

TIERRA DEL FUEGO
ESTANCIA HARBERTON

www.estanciaharberton.com

At historic Estancia Harberton, you have a choice of two restaurants. The little Mánacatush tea room, in the original Bridges's house, serves hot beverages, home-made cakes and pies all day, and hearty, simple dishes at lunchtime. The purpose-built Parrilla Acawaia, on a hill overlooking the farm, enjoys fabulous views. Grilled meats, served with fresh salads, dominate the menu. Reserve online, there is no telephone.

✉ Estancia Harberton 🕐 Daily 10–7 (lunch 12–3.30) ✋ Tea room: L $40; *parrilla*: L $70, Wine $25 🚗 RN-3 east of Ushuaia for 40km (25 miles) to Rancho Hambre, then RN-33 (formerly the RCj) for 45km (28 miles) to Canal de Beagle (no fuel stations locally, so a full fuel tank is recommended)

TRELEW
NOUVEAU CHATEAU VIEUX

Trelew is not overflowing with good restaurants but this determinedly Gallic establishment is a leading contender for the title of best. It serves up beautifully cooked main courses of lamb, rabbit and fish and has the best wine cellar in the valley.

✉ 25 de Mayo and Bell ☎ 02965/424408
🕐 Daily 12.30–4, 7–12 ✋ L $50, D $70, Wine $21

USHUAIA
BODEGÓN FUEGUINO

www.tierradehumos.com

One of the more rustic restaurants in the Fuegian capital, Bodegón Fueguino has an inviting dining room with timber beams. Wooden benches with comfy sheepskin cushions and yellow walls hung with local artwork complete the picture. The food is good, honest fare, with the emphasis on fresh pasta and huge *picadas* (platters of cheese and cold cuts), including the renowned Patagonian smoked hams. Grilled lamb is another speciailty, while the draught beer is a deliciously hoppy homebrew.

✉ San Martín 859 ☎ 02901/431972
🕐 Daily 12.30–4, 7–12 ✋ L $20, D $40, Wine $18

KAUPÉ

www.kaupe.com.ar

Not only are you invited into a typical Ushuaian home but you can enjoy a gastronomic experience like none other, with dishes such as king crab and spinach chowder, crab dressed with wedges of lemon and crab pancakes in a saffron sauce. There are meat dishes, succulent fish and some excellent vegetarian alternatives, too. Fine food, attentive service and breathtaking views are all part of the package. Ask for a glass of Argentine Champagne to accompany your dessert.

✉ Roca 470 ☎ 02901/422704 🕐 Mon–Sat 7.30pm–1am ✋ D $85, Wine $30

KÜAR

www.kuar.com.ar

This trendy bar and restaurant ticks all the boxes with style, beauty and, above all, location. Küar's unrivalled situation, overlooking the Beagle Channel, makes it the perfect place to drink home-brewed ale, nibble on tapas or tacos and just watch the changing sea views. It goes without saying that it gets packed at sunset and if you manage to grab a seat or a beanbag, you'll see why.

✉ Avenida Perito Moreno 2232
☎ 02901/437396 🕐 Mon–Fri 12–3, 6–2, Sat–Sun 6pm–2am ✋ L $45, D $75, Wine $25

PRICES AND SYMBOLS

Prices are the lowest and highest for a double room for one night. Breakfast is included unless noted otherwise. All the hotels listed accept credit cards unless otherwise stated. Note that rates vary widely throughout the year. Prices are given in US dollars (US$) unless otherwise stated.

For a key to the symbols, ▷ 2.

GAIMAN
HOSTERÍA GWESTY TYWI

www.hosteria-gwestytywi.com.ar
The flowery bedspreads and fussy curtains at this pretty guest house in the Chubut valley are not to everyone's taste, but the comfortable rooms offer a colourful respite from the bleak Patagonian landscape outside. The welcome is warm and the breakfasts and teas are legendary.
✉ Chacra 202 ☎ 02965/491292
✋ $180 ⓘ 6 🏊

PLAS Y COED

www.plasycoed.com.ar
This gorgeous tea room (▷ 148) also offers simple accommodation. The three plain but functional rooms (with shared bathroom) are given Welsh names—Gaeaf (winter), Gwanwyn (spring) and Hydref (autumn)—and are decorated in white, green and orange colour schemes respectively. The beautiful rose garden is a lovely place to relax.
✉ Irigoyen 320 ☎ 02965/491133
✋ $120 ⓘ 3

POSADA LOS MIMBRES

www.posadalosmimbres.com.ar
On the banks of the Río Chubut, this wonderful *posada* has two buildings. The old house has three bedrooms with private bathrooms, a comfortable reading room and a dining room. The brighter and more modern, purpose-built bungalow has three spacious rooms and a living room with an open fire. There's usually rabbit for lunch and lamb for dinner, while salads and fruit come from the kitchen garden and orchard.
✉ Chacra 211 ☎ 02965/491299 ✋ $270
ⓘ 6 🚗 From centre of Gaiman, follow signs to Capilla Salem and turn right at signpost to the *posada*

YR HEN FFORDD

www.yrhenffordd.com.ar
This centennial home has been smartly modernized. Its handful of rooms, all with private bathrooms, are simply decorated with white walls and scarlet bed throws. Close to the centre of the town, it is an excellent budget option.
✉ Michael Jones 342 ☎ 02965/491394
✋ $110 ⓘ 4

PARQUE NACIONAL MONTE LEÓN
HOSTERÍA MONTE LEÓN

www.monteleon-patagonia.com
Run as a private concession within the grounds of the Parque Monte León national park, this wonderful *hostería* is housed in the early 20th-century ranch manager's lodge, which was built in Britain and shipped here in sections. The kitchen, with its old-fashioned range, produces mouth-watering dishes at breakfast and dinner. The four rooms, which share two bathrooms, are large, with soaring ceilings. The comfortable beds have

sheep's wool mattresses and soft, warm feather quilts.

✉ RN-3 km2399 ☎ 011/4621-4780
✋ $310–$350 ▯ 4

PENÍNSULA VALDÉS

ESTANCIA LA ERNESTINA

www.laernestina.com.ar

Estancia La Ernestina has an enviable location at Punta Norte, overlooking the sea and some of the peninsula's wildlife. The six rooms are unpretentious, with minimalist decor and sloping roofs. The *asado* room is frequently put to good use roasting Patagonian lamb or barbecuing fish, and one of the house specialities is the succulent paella. Credit cards are not accepted.

✉ Near Punta Norte ☎ 02965/15-661079
🕐 1 Mar to 24 Apr; 20 Sep to 1 Dec
✋ US$420–US$500, including all meals
▯ 6 🚗 The *estancia* lies on the coast just south of Punta Norte via the RP-47, which heads towards Caleta Valdés; Punta Norte can be reached from Puerto Pirámides via the RP-3

FARO PUNTA DELGADA

www.puntadelgada.com

This cliff-edge complex, dominated by the eponymous raspberry-pink lighthouse (*faro*) dating to 1905, has 27 very comfortable rooms and a delightful restaurant. The location, at Punta Delgada, is superb. After enjoying an excellent breakfast, you can descend to the beach and observe the bumper colony of elephant seals.

✉ Península Valdés ☎ 02965/458444
✋ US$110–US$220 ▯ 27 🚗 Follow signs to Faro when you reach Punta Delgada coming from Puerto Pirámides

RINCÓN CHICO

www.rinconchico.com.ar

Eight cosy rooms are strung along a fabulous galleried longhouse, each with stripped pine floors and high-tog duvets to keep you warm. Hospitality and seclusion is the key to the Rincón Chico's success. Unlike many other lodgings in the region,

day visits are not allowed, giving guests the place to themselves. In the traditional dining room dishes such as lamb stew and fruit fritters are served, while the homely living area is decorated with fine art with a maritime theme. The main reasons for staying here, however, are the cliff-top hikes, horseback rides, bicycle trips and unforgettable visits to the *estancia's* private beach, with its impressive colony of gigantic elephant seals. Credit cards are not accepted.

✉ Punta Delgada ☎ 02965/471733
✋ US$560, including all meals ▯ 8
🚗 Follow signs to Rincón Chico just before reaching Punta Delgada from Puerto Pirámides

PUERTO DESEADO

HOTEL LOS ACANTILADOS

Puerto Deseado offers fabulous opportunities to see Patagonia's marine wildlife but its hotels can be disappointing. Rooms at Hotel Los Acantilados are on the small, rather plain side but there are picture windows and a *confitería*. The accommodation may not be exciting, but its location means that you'll probably spend more time watching dolphins in the *ría* than lounging around in the hotel.

✉ Pueyrredón and España
☎ 02974/872167 ✋ $220–$250 ▯ 20

PUERTO MADRYN

EL GUALICHO

elgualicho.com.ar

If you are looking for budget lodgings on the Península Valdés this is the place for you. Hip and fun sum up this well-run hostel. Smart double rooms are decorated in peach and lemon tones, while the dorms go more for zingy lime hues.

✉ Marcos A. Zar 480 ☎ 02965/454163
✋ $170–$250 double, $48–$60 per person in dorm ▯ 10

HOTEL PIRÉN

www.hotelpiren.com.ar

This very pleasant modern hotel is right on the Golfo Nuevo and, rightly, boasts that you can see whales playing in the sea from your balcony.

The rooms are smartly functional and the bathrooms are decorated with beautiful tiles. Ask for a room with a view of the ocean.

✉ Avenida Roca 439 ☎ 02965/272456
✋ $240–$270 ▯ 15

POSADA DEL MADRYN

www.la-posada.com.ar

This professionally run *posada* is located in the leafy outskirts of Madryn but a short taxi ride will get you into town. Rooms have mint green soft furnishings and white walls, giving this charming, modern *posada* a very cool appearance, while the vast lawns outside provide plenty of space to relax.

✉ Abraham Matthews 2951
☎ 02965/474087 ✋ $300–$350 ▯ 24

PUERTO PIRÁMIDES

DEL NÓMADE HOSTERÍA ECOLÓGICA

www.ecohosteria.com.ar

This purpose-built *hostería* in Puerto Pirámides has environmentally friendly accommodation and uses water recycling and solar energy. The sleek rooms are well maintained and have small patios. The owners and staff are extremely helpful and can organize whale-watching tours. Breakfast is scrumptious home-made breads and cakes. Everything is as near perfect as possible.

✉ Avenida de las Ballenas s/n
☎ 02965/495044 ✋ US$170–US$200
▯ 8

THE PARADISE

www.hosteriaparadise.com.ar

The external appearance of this rather bland red-brick *hostería* belies its comfortable interior. Some rooms have en suite Jacuzzis, but all are comfortable and decorated in bright colours. The hotel's restaurant, The Paradise, has an excellent reputation and serves tasty seafood dishes.

✉ Segunda Bajada ☎ 02965/495030
✋ US$218–US$250 ▯ 12

LAS RESTINGAS

www.lasrestingas.com

Las Restingas's main advantage is its location, set right on the bay front. The dozen rooms are smart but simple, with bare brick walls and tiled floors. Rooms have balconies on the first floor and terraces on the ground floor and all enjoy the hotel's superb views of the ocean. There is a small fitness centre and spa. The restaurant is one of the best in town (▷ 149).

✉ Playa s/n ☎ 02965/495101
🛏 US$150–US$300 🛈 12 🍴

RÍO GALLEGOS
ESTANCIA MONTE DINERO
www.montedinero.com.ar

Named for the hill overlooking the Magellan Strait, where tiny amounts of gold were found in the late 19th century, this wonderful *estancia* right next to Cabo Vírgenes (▷ 129) is a great place to learn about life on a Patagonian farm. You can visit the lighthouse, see the nearby penguin rookery, observe sheep shearing and drink tea at the *confitería*. There are six surprisingly comfortable rooms in the fabulous Casa Grande, the main residential building on the ranch.

✉ RN-40 km0 ☎ 02966/428922
🛏 US$130–US$150 per person, including all meals 🛈 6

HOTEL PATAGONIA
www.hotel-patagonia.com

Gallegos is not packed with great places to stay but this business-style hotel has 85 smartly decorated and comfortable rooms, suites and roomy penthouses. The hotel also has a garden, health club and restaurant. Parking is available.

✉ Fagnano 64 ☎ 02966/444969
🛏 $485–$540 🛈 85 🍴

RÍO GRANDE
POSADA DE LOS SAUCES
Don't go out of your way to stay in Río Grande unless you are into fly-fishing (the town is renowned for its massive brown trout) but if you are in town and need a bed for the night, try this angler-oriented motel. Rooms are attractive, very comfortable, and some have Jacuzzis. Although this is definitely a fisherman's haunt, the staff can also organize trekking and horseback riding on the nearby steppe. The hotel restaurant is

excellent, with plenty of grilled lamb and stuffed salmon on the menu.

✉ El Cano 839 ☎ 02964/430868
🛏 $250–$310 🛈 20

TIERRA DEL FUEGO
ESTANCIA HARBERTON
www.estanciaharberton.com

Although the historic Harberton *estancia* (▷ 129) mainly caters for day visits, there are two small guest houses, the charming Old Shepherd's House, with two triple rooms with private bath, and the more rustic Old Cookhouse, one of the original buildings, with a double room, a bunk dorm, and shared bath. For both guest houses, the deal includes tea on arrival (before 6pm), bed and breakfast, and a number of guided tours around the grounds. Note, there is no telephone, so reservations should be made online and you must arrive by 7pm.

✉ Estancia Harberton, Canal de Beagle, Tierra del Fuego 🕐 Oct–Apr 🛏 US$90–US$120 per person 🛈 2 triples, 1 double, 1 dorm 🚗 RN-3 east of Ushuaia for 40km (25 miles) to Rancho Hambre, then RN-33 (formerly the RCj) for 45km (28 miles) to Canal de Beagle (no fuel stations locally, so a full fuel tank is recommended)

ESTANCIA MARÍA BEHETY
www.maribety.com.ar

Notorious wool magnate José Menéndez ruled the roost of Tierra del Fuego at the beginning of the 20th century and his *segunda Argentina estancia* covers a massive 150,000ha (370,500 acres). Mainly aimed at anglers, the two lodges in the *estancia*'s grounds offer smart luxury accommodation. Lodge María Behety is plainer but closer to the Río Grande while the villa is older and more attractive, with brass bedsteads and classic decor.

✉ RCc, km16.5, Río Grande, 9420 Tierra del Fuego ☎ 02964/430345 🛏 US$100–US$135 per person 🛈 8 rooms in lodge, 6 rooms in villa 🚗 From Río Grande, take the RCc; *estancia* is 16.5km (10 miles) away

ESTANCIA RIVADAVIA
Myrna Antunovic, the granddaughter of the Croatian pioneer who founded

the place in 1925, runs this gorgeous working *estancia* in the heart of Tierra del Fuego as a tourist lodge. There are five comfortable rooms, with plenty of attention to detail, and an alluring living room with an open fire. The 10,000ha (24,700-acre) grounds include a chunk of mountain and two sizeable lakes, so there are plenty of activities and hiking trails for guests to enjoy here.

✉ Cerro Jeujupen s/n ☎ 02901/492186
🛏 US$230–US$250 per person, including breakfast and either lunch or dinner 🛈 2 doubles, two twin rooms and one single 🚗 From Tolhuin head northwards on RN-3, direction Río Grande, and turn left after 20km (12.5 miles) onto RCh; *estancia* is signposted off to right after around 18km (11 miles) of gravel road

ESTANCIA ROLITO
www.tierradelfuego.org.ar/rolito

Rolito, like many *estancias* in these parts, was started in the 1920s. The supremely hospitable Annie Luna, whose father founded the *estancia*, knows how to make guests feel at home. The accommodation is rustic but comfortable and the food is delicious, while the extensive grounds invite exploration on horseback or on foot. The warmth of the interiors and the lupin-filled gardens soften the austerity of the wooden, tin-roofed huts.

✉ RCa, 14km (8.5 miles) from junction with RN-3 ☎ 02901/437351 🛏 US$210–US$250 per person, including breakfast and either lunch or dinner 🛈 4 double rooms

ESTANCIA VIAMONTE
www.estanciaviamonte.com

This *estancia* is the original home of Lucas Bridges, one of the English pioneers in the archipelago, who also founded the marvellous Estancia Harberton. The *estancia* lives up to its name, with fabulous sea vistas from its generous bow windows. The food is excellent and plentiful, mostly based on organic produce from the farm and sheep ranch, while activities include fly-fishing in the nearby Río Ewan and rides on horseback into the unspoiled steppe.

✉ Estancia Viamonte C.C.8, 9420 Rio

Grande, Tierra del Fuego ☎ 02964/430861 ⏱ Nov–March ⚲ US$160–US$180 per person, including breakfast and either lunch or dinner ⚏ 3 doubles 🚗 Take RN-3 from Río Grande (and the airport) southwards for 20km (12.5 miles); *estancia* is near the main road and clearly signposted

TOLHUIN
HOSTERÍA KAIKÉN
www.hosteriakaiken.com
Built in the 1960s, this welcoming *hostería* is strategically located on the beautiful Lago Fagnano. It underwent renovation a few years ago and each of the 20 rooms is supremely comfortable, some of them with Jacuzzis in the modern bathrooms. Enjoy a drink by the fireside in the Oikén bar or sample some typical Fuegian specialities, such as lake salmon, in the *hostería's* excellent restaurant.
✉ RN 3 km2958 ☎ 02901/492372 ⚲ US$150–US$170 ⚏ 20

TRELEW
LA CASONA DEL RÍO
www.lacasonadelrio.com.ar
Trelew lacks good accommodation, but this fabulous English-style guest house in the city's southeastern outskirts is an excellent place to stay. The fairy-tale house has a roof shaped like a witch's hat and a beautiful riverside location among lush vegetation where the sound of bird song is almost overpowering. Inside, the comfortable rooms are decorated in restful whites, while the kitchen produces hearty meals, in addition to delicious breakfasts.
✉ Chacra 105 ☎ 02965/438343 ⚲ US$120–US$140 ⚏ 3 🚗 5km (3 miles) from Trelew

USHUAIA
LA CASA
www.silviacasalaga.com.ar
This wonderful eco-friendly wooden guest house is such a pioneering establishment—one of the first of its kind in the city—that it is simply known as 'The House'. The owner, an architect from Buenos Aires, designed the house herself. The six bedrooms share three bathrooms.

The friendly host speaks excellent English.
✉ Gobernador Paz 1380 ☎ 02901/423202 ⚲ $225–$250 ⚏ 6

CUMBRES DEL MARTIAL
www.cumbresdelmartial.com.ar
Everything about this luxurious hotel, up high by the chairlift to the glacier, is wonderful. The cottage-like villa has six comfortable and attractive rooms, each bearing the name of a fruit or delicacy. Enjoy delicious cakes in the tea room or dine on tender lamb goulash or an array of fondues in the Cabana restaurant. In El Club spa, serious pampering is the order of the day.
✉ Luis Martial 3560 ☎ 02901/424779 ⚲ US$235–US$270 ⚏ 6

FREESTYLE
www.ushuaiafreestyle.com
This beautiful hotel offers two styles of accommodation under one roof. Freestyle is a stylish hostel, with wooden bunks in spotless dorms and a living area with soft leather chairs. Next door is the Alto Andino urban lodge, with gorgeous double rooms and suites plus a superb bar on the top floor with all-round panoramas of Ushuaia.
✉ Gobernador Paz 868 ☎ 02901/430920 or 02901/432874 ⚲ $400–$450 ⚏ 18

LAS HAYAS
www.lashayashotel.com
At Las Hayas the linen is Portuguese, the towels Peruvian and windows German but the views are pure Argentine. This large hotel is perched on the mountainside, 3km (2 miles) out of the city, and has clean, comfortable rooms. There is also an excellent spa and an indoor swimming pool. A regular shuttle service takes guests to the harbour.
✉ Avenida Los Ñires 3040 ☎ 02901/430710 ⚲ US$180–US$270 ⚏ 93 🏊 Indoor

HOTEL DEL GLACIAR
www.hoteldelglaciar.com
This large hotel right next to the chairlift up to the Glaciar Martial, the glacier that hangs above the city,

has 124 rooms. Rooms range from doubles to quintuples and suites, and all have wonderful views, either of the mountains behind or, in the more expensive rooms, of the bay. The decor is cosy rather than stylish but is pleasing and there is a homely comfort about the place.
✉ Avenida Luis Fernando Martial 2355 ☎ 02901/430640 ⚲ US$170–US$260 ⚏ 124

MACONDO
www.macondohouse.com
This beautifully appointed city-centre hotel is stylishly decorated in sleek whites and attractive slate. It has a wonderful communal area offering breathtaking views of the bay, while the capacious rooms are flooded with natural light. All of the rooms feature contemporary bathrooms with high-specification stone fittings.
✉ Gobernador Paz 1410 ☎ 02901/437576 ⚲ US$125–US$140 ⚏ 12

MIL 810
www.hotel1810.com
This smart boutique hotel has a fourth-floor breakfast room enjoying great views of the Beagle Channel, and the boat pier is only two blocks away. The 30 rooms all have flat-screen TVs, central heating and disabled access. The hotel is modern and well designed throughout, from the smart decor in the bedrooms to the pebble retention wall in the stylish lounge.
✉ 25 de Mayo 245 ☎ 02901/437710 ⚲ US$150–US$170 ⚏ 30

YAKUSH
www.hostelyakush.com.ar
Definitely the best youth hostel in Tierra del Fuego, Yakush is bright and cheery, with fun artwork on the walls, impeccably clean dorms and double rooms with bathrooms. Beds are comfortable and linens crisp. The large lounge in the attic has futons for lazy afternoons and the back garden has fabulous views.
✉ Piedrabuena 118, Ushuaia ☎ 02901/435807 ⚲ $220–$250 with bath ⚏ 6

ANDEAN PATAGONIA

Many visitors to Argentina yearn only for Patagonia, the country's southern triangle whose name feeds the imagination. The Patagonia they most want to see is a stunningly beautiful land of volcanic peaks and shining lakes, dense highland forests and blue-white glaciers—a paradise for trekkers and nature lovers of every stripe. In the northern segment, known as the Lake District, finger-like lakes and lagoons of every shade of blue nestle among some of the least spoiled terrains on the planet. A trio of comfortable resorts—alternative El Bolsón, busy Bariloche and chic Villa La Angostura—offer all manner of amenities, from cosy bungalows to luxury hotels, and from rustic breweries to superb restaurants.

It is certainly worth getting off the beaten path and exploring, which is easy to do in a region where the main road, the legendary RN-40, is still being tarmacked along much of its length. The dinosaur park and the petrified forests of Sarmiento, the world's southernmost wineries near Neuquén and an exemplary ethnographic museum at Leleque are just some of the lesser-known sights in the region. Better publicized, but not easy to access, the prehistoric cave paintings at the Cueva de las Manos Pintados are worth the effort. More lakes and peaks are on display at two national parks in the middle of the region: Lanín and Los Alerces, close to Esquel and San Martín de los Andes, respectively.

But the prize destinations in Andean Patagonia are the glaciers and mountains of the supremely beautiful Parque Nacional Los Glaciares, in the south. Served by a busy airport, bustling El Calafate overflows with top-rate accommodation and restaurants. The Glaciar Perito Moreno is the heavyweight hereabouts, a juggernaut of ice spilling into a jade-green lake. A short distance to the north, El Chaltén is the ideal base for some of the most memorable trekking on Earth, in the shadow of the defiant peaks of the Fitz Roy range.

Opposite View over Lake Nahuel Huapi, in the heart of the Argentine lake district

ALUMINÉ
www.alumine.gov.ar

Slow-paced little Aluminé, sitting high on the banks of its namesake river, shifts up a gear every March to celebrate the native pine-nut harvest, with the Fiesta del Pehuén. Regarded as a catch-and-release fishing paradise, Aluminé also offers some of the region's best white-water rafting. There are grade three and four runs along the Río Aluminé, where the national championships are held every October, when the spring snowmelt swells the river flow. The trout served in the laid-back town's restaurants easily rival the fish found in the town of Junín (▷ 160).

✚ 348 B15 ✉ Aluminé, Provincia de Neuquén ℹ Cristian Joubert 326 ☎ 02942/496001 ⏰ Daily 8am–9pm 🚌 Buses from Zapala and Neuquén 🚗 RP-23 northwards from Junín de los Andes 🚩 Tour companies in Aluminé organize white-water rafting and kayaking; boat trips from Villa Pehuenia

BODEGAS PATAGÓNICAS
www.valleperdido.com.ar
www.bodeganqn.com.ar
www.familiaschroeder.com
www.bodegadelfindelmundo.com

Just outside the minuscule oasis town of San Patricio del Chañar, 41km (25.5 miles) northwest of Neuquén, there are four excellent Patagonian wineries, the *bodegas patagónicas*, which form the region's fledgling Ruta del Vino (wine route). All the wineries offer tours of the vineyards and cellars, tastings and the opportunity to buy bottles of wine to take home.

At the Schroeder family *bodega*, (tel 0299/489-9600; Mon–Fri hourly 9am–5pm, Sat–Sun by prior arrangement only; $15) tours include a visit to the 'dinosaur cellar', where dinosaur bones were excavated, and there is an excellent restaurant and bar, open daily for lunch. Bodega NQN also offers tours (tel 0299/489-7500; Mon–Fri 9–12, 2–4; Sat–Sun and national holidays 10.30–4.30;

free) and has an excellent restaurant on the premises, too. Bodega Valle Perdido doubles as a luxury hotel (▷ 190), set among a sea of vines. Even if you don't stay the night, you can tour this fabulous winery, relax in the pool and wine spa, or sample top-notch food in the restaurant (tel 0299/507-2176; Mon, Wed and Fri, 11am and 7pm; US$40 includes a bottle of wine). Lastly, visitors to Bodega del Fin del Mundo (tel 0299/485-5004; Tue–Fri 10–4, Sat–Sun and national holidays 10–5; free) tour the fermenting rooms, barrels and cellars by means of an aerial walkway. The name of this last winery, 'winery at the end of the world' recalls the fact that these are among the world's most southerly vineyards, possibly only outstripped by wineries on New Zealand's South Island.

✚ 348 D14 ☎ San Patricio del Chañar, 41km (25.5 miles) northwest of Neuquén via the RP-7

EL BOLSÓN
www.elbolson.gov.ar

Nuclear-free and determinedly alternative in character, El Bolsón provides the perfect antidote to both the furious tourism of Bariloche (▷ 174–175) and the urbane luxury of Villa la Angostura (▷ 172). Nestling in a verdant valley and surrounded by mountains that invite visitors to hike for days, El Bolsón has attracted nature lovers and hippy types ever since UFOs were, allegedly, spotted near Cerro Piltriquitrón in the 1960s.

The fertile market gardens surrounding the town produce luscious raspberries and blackcurrants plus a generous crop of beer hops, celebrated in the form of real-ale festival at the Fiesta del Lúpulo (▷ 185) at the end of February. The soft fruit are also turned into ice cream. The town's main *heladería* (ice-cream shop), Jauja (▷ 182), proved so successful that it opened another branch in Bariloche, 125km (77.5 miles) to the north. The beer is also tip-top, particularly at the town's namesake brewery, where some of the production is flavoured, Belgian-style, with local fruits.

Apart from hiking and indulging in beer and ice cream, you can listen to jazz at one of the country's top jazz festivals in early December (▷ 185), shop at the town's fun crafts market (Tue, Thu and Sat 10–8), or visit the Bosque Tallado (www.elbosquetallado.com; daily 9–7; $1), 39 artistically carved tree stumps on the slopes of Mount Piltriquitrón, which looms over the town to the east—the mount is best reached by car (or taxi) as it is 13km (8 miles) from the town and then a steep 1.2km (0.75-mile) walk.

✚ 352 B17 ✉ El Bolsón, Provincia de Río Negro ℹ San Martín and Roca ☎ 02944/492604 ⏰ Mon–Sat 8–11, Sun 9–11 🚌 Buses from Bariloche

Below *The fermentation tanks in the massive vat hall of Bodega del Fin del Mundo, Neuquén*

INFORMATION

www.welcomeargentina.com/paseos/
cuevamanospintadas/

🏠 354 C21 ✉ 50km (31 miles) north
of Bajo Caracoles, Provincia de Santa Cruz
🕐 Daily 9–7 ✋ Adult $30
☎ The access road to the cavern is
along a 50km (31-mile) gravel track
leading north from Bajo Caracoles, a tiny
settlement 130km (80.5 miles) south of
Perito Moreno village. The parking area at
the end of this track is 600m (654 yards)
from the cavern's entrance 🚌 Tours from
Perito Moreno

TIPS

» One of the easiest ways of getting to
the cavern is to take a tour from Perito
Moreno (▷ 172).

» It is best to visit in the morning or late
afternoon, when there are large numbers
of birds along the canyon.

» Take plenty of water and food, plus the
usual protection from the sun.

» There is direct access to the site from
the Estancia de las Manos Pintadas, via
a scenic road, then a steep vertiginous
climb down the cliff side to the river and
up again to the cave itself, so it is not
for everyone.

CUEVA DE LAS MANOS

Cueva de las Manos, an alfresco collage dating back thousands of years,
testifies to the fact that there has been a human presence here for millennia.
Nobody knows why the Toldense and Tehuelche artists painted this fresco or
why they stopped adding to it 1,300 years ago. The techniques used, the local
microclimate and the fact that the paintings run along a groove in the cliff,
protected from the elements by overhanging rock, explain how they survived to
this day.

The cavern is in a bone-dry spot along a cliff face above the Canón del Río
Pinturas, just off the RN-40 south of Perito Moreno (▷ 172). The sheer wonder
of this priceless age-old art was internationally acknowledged in 1999, when the
remote cavern was awarded UNESCO World Heritage Site status.

NATURAL ART

The paintings were created between 7500BC and AD700, by indigenous artists
using hollow reeds to blow natural pigments around their hands, and then sealed
for posterity using an effective natural varnish made of guanaco grease mixed
with urine. Calafate berry juice and ground charcoal, plant sap and crushed
rock gave the stencils their many colours—white and black, golden yellow and
blood red, bright green and dark purple, plus every shade of ochre. In addition to
the 829 hands, there are human figures, rhea trails, puma paws, guanacos and
scorpions, and all kinds of abstract and geometrical shapes.

The prehistoric artwork, which has suffered some vandalism and graffiti in the
past, is now jealously guarded and you must be accompanied by a *guardaparque*
(ranger) to see the paintings. The rangers usually speak Spanish only but they do
point out some of the main motifs.

Opposite *Indigenous artists painted animals such as guanacos on the cavern's walls*
Below *The cavern lies in a remote location south of Perito Moreno*

EL CALAFATE

www.elcalafate.com

El Calafate is where visitors come in search of the natural wonders of the Parque Nacional Los Glaciares (▷ 166–168). This fast-growing resort is Argentina's self-styled Capital of the Glaciers. It is a tight-knit modern community strung along Avenida San Martín, the main street, which is crammed full of souvenir shops, travel agencies, bars and cafés, plus an outstanding restaurant or two. There is no shortage of accommodation either, with places in town, in panoramic locations on the nearby foothills or overlooking Lago Argentino. There are countless excursions to keep you busy but the star attraction is the Glaciar Perito Moreno (▷ 166–167), on the town's doorstep.

The *calafate* plant, the indigenous word for the box-leaved barberry (*Berberis buxifolia*), gives the town its name. The bushes are covered in thorns and its wood contains *berberina*, used for medicines and as a traditional dye. The purplish fruit, not unlike blueberries, is used to make ice creams, jams and a filling for *alfajores* (chocolate-covered biscuits). Locals like to remind you that '*Él que come el calafate, volverá*' ('Whoever eats the *calafate* berries will come back').

♦ 354 B24 ✉ El Calafate, Provincia de Santa Cruz 🛈 Coronel Rosales and Avenida San Martín ☎ 02902/491090 🕐 Daily 8–8 🚌 Buses from Río Gallegos and other major destinations ✈ Airport is 15km (9 miles) east of El Calafate; regular flights daily from Buenos Aires (mostly Aeroparque) and Ushuaia

EL CHALTÉN

www.elchalten.com

Whereas El Calafate is the gateway to the southern section of the Parque Nacional Los Glaciares (▷ 166–168), smaller El Chaltén gives access to the northern Fitz Roy section and its fabulous network of mountain trails. El Chaltén is a bit straggly and its facilities and accommodation options are slightly more limited than El Calafate's, but it is in a

remarkable setting and is the first port of call if you want to explore the beautiful upland area around the thrusting peaks of Monte Fitz Roy (3,405m/11,168ft) and Cerro Torre (3,102m/10,175ft). As well as the town's tourist information centre, there are a number of outstanding tour operators (▷ 183) and guides that can arrange tours, give advice about the area or accompany you on walks and climbs.

♦ 354 B23 ✉ El Chaltén, Provincia de Santa Cruz 🛈 Güemes 21 ☎ 02962/493011 🕐 Dec–Feb daily 8–8; Mar–Nov Mon–Fri 9–6 🚌 Buses from El Calafate 🚗 From El Calafate (and airport), head east to junction with RN-40, then head northwards to El Chaltén turn-off; continue for 90km (56 miles) on paved road to El Chaltén

CUEVA DE LAS MANOS

▷ 158.

ESQUEL

www.argentinaturismo.com.ar/esquel

Short of staying in the park itself, the Lake District settlement of Esquel is the place to base yourself if you want to be close to the Parque Nacional Los Alerces (▷ 164–165). This friendly market town doubles as a ski centre in the winter for the resort of La Hoya, 12km (7.5 miles) from the town centre and popular with families, on the slopes of the barren Cerro Torres.

The other main attraction is the narrow-gauge steam railway that once transported wool from the *estancias*. Built in the 1920s and '30s, the line stretched over 400km (248 miles) to Ingeniero Jacobacci but the service was closed in 1993. These days, La Trochita (▷ 184), also known as the Old Patagonian Express, runs a limited service as a tourist railway from Esquel to Nahuel Pan, 22km (13.5 miles) away.

♦ 352 B18 ✉ Esquel, Provincia de Chubut 🛈 Alvear and Sarmiento ☎ 02945/451927 🕐 Jan, Feb daily 7–11; Mar–Dec 8–8 🚌 Buses from Bariloche and other major destinations ✈ Airport is 21km (13 miles) east of town 🚗 Take the RN-258 from Bariloche via El Bolsón

JUNÍN DE LOS ANDES

www.junindelosandes.gov.ar

Junín de los Andes is a gateway to the Parque Nacional Lanín, another of the great Lake District parks. A less sophisticated town than neighbouring San Martín de los Andes (▷ 172), Junín is more central than Aluminé (▷ 157) and Villa Pehuenia (▷ 172). The fish-rich rivers in the town's backyard attract anglers and trout takes pride of place on the restaurants' menus.

During the Fiesta del Puestero in the middle of February Junín comes alive with folk music and *gaucho* events, arts and crafts displays and barbecues.

On the main square, the Plaza San Martín, an unusual Alpine-style church, the Santuario de la Beata Laura Vicuña, is dedicated to a Chilean girl brought up in Junín by Salesian nuns who was regarded as a demi-saint for her devotion to her faith. Inside, you can see beautiful textile panels woven by the indigenous Mapuche.

♦ 348 B15 ✉ Junín de los Andes, Provincia de Neuquén 🛈 Padre Milanesio and Coronel Suárez (Plaza San Martín) ☎ 02972/491160 🕐 Daily 7–9 🚌 Buses from Bariloche and other major destinations 🚗 From San Martín de los Andes take RN-234 eastwards and northwards for approximately 50km (31 miles)

Below *View of town with flamingos*

LELEQUE

The fabulous Museo Leleque, which opened in 2000, is housed in a beautifully restored outbuilding of an *estancia* of the same name in northern Patagonia, 80km (49.5 miles) south of El Bolsón (▷ 157). In turn, Estancia Leleque is part of a huge sheep-farming estate owned by Benetton textiles and clothing group, an international brand and one of the biggest landowners in Argentina. The museum is reached via a short gravel track off the RN-40, at a point where the road and La Trochita railway (▷ 184) almost touch. The attractively presented exhibits trace the history of the region's indigenous peoples, its pioneers and the relations between them, by means of an impressive collection of memorabilia collected and lovingly restored by the late Pablo Korscheneweski, a settler born in Odessa in 1925.

HIGHLIGHTS

The first room is dedicated to the original inhabitants of the region, who arrived 13,000 years ago, and there are displays of stone implements and fragments of early ceramics together with flint arrowheads and animal remains. Next is an exhibit entitled 'El Contacto', explaining how the earliest European settlers in the 16th century interacted with the indigenous peoples. Room Three details the influx of immigrants from Europe and North America, Chile and Lebanon, and the pioneering spirit that kept communities alive in harsh conditions. The last room illustrates Patagonian society by displays of photographs and documents about the region's railways and communications, politics and education.

BOLICHE

The highlight, though, is the painstakingly restored *boliche* (a general store that doubled up as a meeting place, pub and restaurant). Here, you can have a snack or something to drink, surrounded by a collection of preserved old bric-a-brac, including the working old cash register.

INFORMATION

www.interpatagonia.com/paseos/leleque

✚ 352 B17 ✉ RN-40 km1440

☎ 02945/455151 🕐 Jan–Feb Thu–Tue 11–7; Mar–Apr, Jul–Dec Thu–Tue 11–5

✋ $15 🚌 RN-40 from El Bolsón, turn left (east) at km1440 signpost and continue for 2.5km (1.5 miles) to museum

TIPS

›› The museum is difficult to get to by public transport. Buses stop at the gate on the RN-40 but it is another 2.5km (1.5 miles) to the museum.

›› Opening times can be erratic, so telephone ahead to check that it is open before setting out.

›› It is worth buying the excellent museum catalogue.

Above *The Museo Leleque, housed in a restored outbuilding on a huge sheep-farming estate*

INFORMATION

www.neuquentur.gob.ar
www.mnbaneuquen.com.ar
www.villaelchocon.org.ar

➕ 348 D14 ✉ Neuquén, Provincia de Neuquén 🛈 Félix San Martín 182 ☎ 0299/442-4089 🕐 Daily 7–11 🚌 Buses from major destinations ✈ Airport 5km (3 miles) west of city; regular flights from Buenos Aires 🚗 RN-22 from Bahía Blanca in Provincia de Buenos Aires

TIPS

>> Before setting out for the *bodegas* (▷ 157) get detailed directions from the tourist centre, or from the *bodega* itself, as it is not obvious.

>> The MNBA has a fine bookshop and an excellent café, both open the same hours as the museum.

>> There are other dinosaur-related sites within reach of the city, including clutches of dinosaur eggs and dinosaur footprints imprinted in rocks. Ask for details at the tourist information office.

Above The Giganotosaurus carolinii skeleton at the Museo Municipal Ernesto Bachmann in Villa El Chocón

NEUQUÉN

The thriving capital of the northernmost Patagonian province, Neuquén lies at the confluence of the Neuquén and Limay rivers and in the summer, the sandy beaches along the banks are crowded with locals. Modern Neuquén built its wealth on the oil in the surrounding steppe and the apple and pear orchards, which are irrigated by enormous dams along the rivers. Its appeal stems from its proximity to Chañar and the Patagonian wine routes to the north and the Valle de los Dinosaurios, in which some of the biggest dinosaurs have been unearthed.

MUSEO NATIONAL DE BELLAS ARTES DE NEUQUÉN

Opened in 2004, the MNBA is the best fine arts museum in Patagonia (Mitre and Santa Cruz; tel 0299/443-6268; Tue–Sat 8am–9pm, Sun and hols 4–8; free). The spacious, luminous galleries in this prize-winning edifice, designed by renowned Argentine architect Mario Roberto Álvarez, house an enviable collection of Argentine and international art, ranging from the Dutch Golden Age (Hals and Rembrandt) to French Impressionism (Manet) and from the precursors of Latin American painting (Pueyrredón and Pellegrini) to contemporary national artists (Pablo Suárez and Liliana Porter). The themes of the world-class temporary exhibitions have included Picasso and modern Spanish sculpture.

MUSEO MUNICIPAL ERNESTO BACHMANN

Forget Tyrannosaurus rex, the dinosaurs discovered in the valleys around Neuquén in the 1990s dwarf the giants of the previously known dinosaur world. Next to the biggest reservoir in Argentina, the Embalse Ezequiel Ramos Mexía, the modest village of Villa El Chocón is home to a wonderful museum dedicated to the great prehistoric beasts (tel 0299/490-1230; Dec–Feb daily 7–9, Mar–Nov 8–7). The museum is named after Ernesto Bachmann (1894–1970), a self-taught palaeontologist of Swiss origin, who unearthed many of the dinosaur skeletons. Among other fascinating exhibits, the museum contains the skeleton of *Giganotosaurus carolinii*, which measured 13m (43ft) in length, stood nearly 5m (16ft) tall and probably weighed 8 tonnes. There is an alarmingly lifelike replica of the dinosaur that almost fills the room.

PARQUE NACIONAL LANÍN

Created to protect 3,790sq km (1,463sq miles) of virgin Andean rainforest and its wildlife, and lying in the shadow of the eponymous Volcán Lanín, Parque Nacional Lanín is Argentina's third-biggest national park and one of its most beautiful. To the north and east, the park is accessed from a raft of resorts, including Aluminé (▷ 157), San Martín de los Andes (▷ 172), Villa Pehuenia (▷ 172) and Junín de los Andes (▷ 160). To the south, the park adjoins the magnificent Parque Nacional Nahuel Huapi (▷ 169–171), linked by the stunning Ruta de los Siete Lagos (▷ 180–181). Beyond the northern limits, the Pehuenia circuit, starting in Aluminé, skirts the highly photogenic Lagos Aluminé, Moquehue and Ñorquinco. Parallel to the park's eastern border, the RN-234 and RP-23 link the peripheral resorts to Bariloche (▷ 174–175), the region's main tourist hub.

HIGHLIGHTS OF THE PARK

The snowy sugarloaf of the Volcán Lanín (3,776m/12,385ft) dominates most of the views within the huge park, but is best seen reflected in the mirror-like waters of the park's many blue and green lakes. The biggest lake, Lago Huechulafquen, is within easy reach of Junín de los Andes via the RP-61. The views of the volcano are just as spectacular from the RP-62, which passes several finger lakes on its giddy way to the Chilean border. It takes two or three days to climb to the top of the Volcán Lanín but you will need plenty of stamina and good equipment. Register with the Lago Tromen rangers' office before setting out and preferably go with a guide.

The park is also known for its stands of the native araucaria tree (or *pehuén*). These scaly-branched trees can be spotted along the RP-62, near the Argentine customs post, and also by the RP-60, north of Junín, where they form a striking foreground for views of the volcano itself.

The main activity within the park is trekking through the unspoilt habitat, along fairly well marked trails. Some of the best trekking is in the northern section of the park, around Quillén and its lake, one of the most beautiful within the park. Ask at the tourist information office for local guides that can accompany you.

INFORMATION

www.parquenacionallanin.gov.ar
tresparques.com.ar/lanin

🪧 348 B15 ✉ Provincia de Neuquén
ℹ Perito Moreno and Elordi, San Martín de los Andes ☎ 02972/427233 🕐 Daily 8–1 🎟 Adult $30, child (under 16) free
🚌 Buses from Bariloche and Buenos Aires to San Martín de los Andes, Junín de los Andes, Aluminé and Villa Pehuenia
✈ Flights to Bariloche (nearest airport)
🚗 Take the RP-23 between Junín de los Andes and Aluminé; from here, several roads lead westwards into the park, heading towards the Chilean border
🚩 Tour companies in Aluminé and Junín de los Andes organize trekking and guided tours up Volcan Lanín

TIPS

›› The most convenient bases for visiting the park are San Martín de los Andes, Junín de los Andes, Aluminé and Villa Pehuenia.
›› You can visit a number of the Mapuche communities living in or near the park and buy locally produced artworks.
›› There is hardly any public transport in the park so you'll either need a car or to go on a tour.
›› You can camp within the park or ask at the tourist office for a list of accommodation close to the park.

Below Beautiful snow-capped Volcán Lanín, rising 3,776m (12,385ft), dominates views of the park

REGIONS | ANDEAN PATAGONIA • SIGHTS

163

INFORMATION

www.parquesnacionales.gov.ar

✚ 352 B18 ✉ Parque Nacional Los Alerces, Provincia de Chubut ℹ Centro de Informes, Villa Futalaufquén, Chubut ☎ 02945/471020 ⏰ Daily 8–9 ✋ Jan–Feb adult $30, child (under 16) free; Mar–Dec free 🚌 Buses to Esquel and Trevelín from all major destinations ✈ Flights to Esquel from Buenos Aires 🚉 The nearest main towns are Esquel and Trevelín, both lying on RN-258 off the RN-40, south from El Bolsón. From Esquel take RN-258 southwards towards Trevelín and branch westwards after 10km (6 miles) towards Villa Futalaufquén (main entrance). Alternatively, can be approached north via Cholila (northern gate, Portada Norte) 🚐 Tour operators in Bariloche and Esquel

Above *Lago Cisne from El Alerzal Milenario trail*

INTRODUCTION

Parque Nacional Los Alerces was created in the 1930s to protect the remaining specimens of *Fitzroya cupressoides,* a tree commonly known as *alerce* or *lahuán,* its Mapuche name. This Patagonian cypress, so-called because it resembles the true cypress, is one of the oldest species of tree still growing. Its incredible longevity means that many of the surviving examples are estimated to be more than 4,000 years old. Apart from the *alerce,* the park's dense rainforest is made up mainly of the *coihue,* an elegant evergreen, along with a whole gamut of native trees and plants, including the golden-flowered, lily-like *amancay.*

The park covers 2,630sq km (1,015sq miles) and lies at the southern tip of the Argentine Lake District, sandwiched between the RN-40 and the Chilean border. Geographically, it is centred on the three-legged Lago Futalaufquén's sapphire waters. Most of the park's accommodation is along the banks, most of it rustic and over-priced, although camping in the park is also an option. If you want comfortable accommodation, gourmet food and perhaps to try angling, stay at a luxury fishing lodge on the banks of the Laguna Larga (▷ 189), immediately to the east of Villa Futalaufquén.

Apart from fishing, the other main activity in the park is trekking and there are more than 130km (80.5 miles) of public paths to enjoy. The westernmost section of the park, hard up against the Andean summits along the Chilean border, is out of bounds and home to the endangered *huemul* and *pudú,* two species of native deer, both of which are extremely difficult to spot. Dozens of bird species flit around the dense vegetation, including the giant hummingbird and its diminutive cousin, the green-backed firecrown, the Magellanic woodpecker and Des Mur's wiretail, as well as the condor.

WHAT TO SEE

VILLA FUTALAUFQUÉN AND LAGO FUTALAUFQUÉN

Villa Futalaufquén, the main settlement within the park, is little more than a small arboretum and information centre where you can get advice about camping, trekking and fishing in the park.

After Villa Futalaufquén, the road skirts around the eastern shore of the misshapen Lago Futalaufquén, climbing Punta Matos, where you can admire fabulous views of all three branches of the lake and its forested slopes. If you want to go trekking then one of the best trails in the park is the El Dedal circuit, which takes around seven hours to complete and offers some memorable views of the lake.

EL ABUELO

If you want to see the lakes, Safari Lacustre to the northern end of Lago Menéndez is an excellent tour. Boats leave at noon from Puerto Chucao, at the southern end of the lake, which is reached by a footbridge (*pasarela*) over the Río Arrayanes near Lago Verde, north of Lago Futalaufquén. Crossing Lago Menéndez you'll catch a glimpse of the Cerro Torrecillas glacier, which is receding fast and is expected to melt by the end of the century. After landing, a 3km (1.85-mile) path through dense rainforest, fuchsia bushes and *arrayanes* (native myrtles) leads to the spot near the banks of Lago Cisne where the great grandfather tree, El Abuelo, stands—an immense *alerce* over 2m (6ft) in diameter and 57m (187ft) tall and estimated to be 2,600 years old.

MORE TO SEE

BUTCH CASSIDY'S CABIN

From 1901 to 1905, Butch Cassidy and the Sundance Kid, the American bandits, lived in exile in the small Patagonian town of Cholila to the north of the park. The dilapidated old wooden hut they made their home has been restored as a minor tourist attraction. Ask in Cholila or Esquel (▷ 160) for details.

TIPS

>> The main entrance to the park is the Portada Centro, just over 30km (18.5 miles) from Esquel. The other entrance is the Portada Norte, on the way to Cholila and Butch Cassidy's Cabin.

>> The best base for visiting the park is Esquel (▷ 160), a short distance to the east, or Trevelín (▷ 172), though its facilities are rather more limited.

>> Apart from some accommodation and restaurants, there are no services inside the park, so make sure you get fuel and other provisions before you leave Esquel.

>> Visit the information office at Futalaufquén to get information about the park, including its flora and fauna and the trails that zigzag up and down the mountainsides.

>> Camping in the park is an option but bear in mind that this is one of the wettest places in Argentina, with more than 800mm (31in) of rainfall annually.

>> The RP-71 is the main road through the park and is paved between the park limits and the Intendencia (park ranger's office) but a dirt track leads north from here, so a 4WD might be useful.

>> To be sure of experiencing the Safari Lacustre, call ahead (tel 02945/15-465941; www.brazosur.com.ar) or book a tour with one of the tour operators in Esquel. Boats fill up fast in high season but they don't sail if there are too few people.

>> To the north of the park, beyond the Portada Norte gate and Lago Rivadavia along the road towards Cholila, a number of cabins and a fishing lodge are strung along the Río Carrileufú, one of the best spots for fishing in the region.

>> If you are fishing, salmon and trout are considered fair game but you are expected to release any native fish you catch, such as the *perca criolla* and *puyén grande*. Ask for details at the information office when you buy your permit.

Left *El Abuelo (the 'grandfather') alerce, a massive 57m (187ft) tall and some 2,600 years old*

INFORMATION

www.losglaciares.com

www.fernandezcampbell.com

🞤 354 B23 ✉ Parque Nacional Los Glaciares, Provincia de Santa Cruz ℹ Información, Libertador 1302, El Calafate ☎ 02902/491090 🕐 Daily 8am–10pm 🖐 Adult $70, child (under 16) free 🚌 Two main park entrances reached via El Calafate (Perito Moreno glacier) and El Chaltén (Fitz Roy sector) 🚢 Various tour operators in El Calafate and El Chaltén ❓ The best trekking map available is the 1:50,000 *Monte Fitz Roy & Cerro Torre* published by Zagier & Urruty, on sale in El Chaltén, which includes a 1:100,000 scale map of the Lago del Desierto area. *Trekking in Chaltén and Lago del Desierto* by Miguel A. Alonso is also an informative guide

INTRODUCTION

Thanks to its stunning scenery of jewel-like lakes and gigantic glaciers, Parque National Los Glaciares is a world-class attraction. The park covers a massive 4,459sq km (1,721sq miles), though much of it is inaccessible. It is within reach of the tourist-friendly settlements of El Calafate (▷ 160) and El Chaltén (▷ 160) and most of the main sites huddle around the gorgeous Lago Argentino, the third-biggest lake in South America, with a surface area of 1,600sq km (618sq miles). Fed by ice-melt, its waters are uninvitingly chilly but on a sunny day this mini-sea can look like a bay in the Mediterranean or Caribbean.

To the east of the lake is mostly windswept plain, with little more than sparse scrub to break the monotony, but the farther west you head, the more fantastic the landscape. Carpets of gnarled southern beech, which blaze red and orange in the autumn, spill down to the lake's shores, while snowy mountain peaks, many exceeding 2,000m (6,560ft) above sea level, can be glimpsed on the horizon.

In the southern sector of the park, grandiose glaciers, including the world-famous Perito Moreno, creak their way down from the Hielo Continental Sur, one of the biggest ice caps outside the polar regions. The glaciers form skyscrapers of ice along the water's edge and the frequent calving of icebergs is an unforgettable sight. Equally memorable are the jagged peaks of the northern Fitz Roy sector, hard by El Chaltén, the country's self-styled trekking capital. A number of trails lift you closer to these out-of-this-world Andean vistas, and you can let llamas take some of the strain by carrying your luggage.

WHAT TO SEE

GLACIAR PERITO MORENO

The legendary Glaciar Perito Moreno sweeps down from a huge expanse of Andean snow and ice, ending in a serrated wall of bluish icicles with barely a streak of dirt to spoil its pristine beauty. When it touches the iceberg channel, Canal de los Témpanos, great chunks of ice splash noisily into the turquoise waters, up to 60m (197ft) below, forming shoals of icebergs.

Above *The spectacular Glaciar Perito Moreno, in the southern sector of the park*

Still advancing at around 5–10cm/2–4in every day in winter, Perito Moreno is famed for its ability to form a natural dam that floods the surrounding area, until the ice-bridge eventually bursts under pressure. Over the years this has happened at irregular intervals but the dams failed to burst between 1988 and 2004, since when there have been a couple of dramatic explosions, detonating huge quantities of crushed ice into the lake. Especially during warmer weather, you are treated to the chalk-on-slate sound of glacial creeping. The glacier looks at its best in the early morning and late afternoon light.

You could drive, take a bus or taxi to the glacier or go on an organized trip (▷ 183) but, however you get there, you will need to enter the national park at its main entrance on the Península de Magallanes, to the west of El Calafate. The fee is valid all day so it is worth getting there early to make the most of it. A number of boardwalks take you along the far end of the peninsula for vistas of the glacier. Frequent boat trips from Puerto Bajo de las Sombras get up close to the mesmerizing ice cliff, and you can even go ice-trekking on the glacier itself. There are cafés and you could treat yourself to lunch at the luxurious Los Notros hotel (▷ 189).

✉ Access from El Calafate 🚌 Twice-daily bus service ($50) from El Calafate 🚗 Take the RP-11 (direct route) or the more picturesque RP-15 (signposted Estancia Anita) immediately to the west of El Calafate. After Estancia Alta Vista, turn right and then left after 12km (7.5 miles) to reach the park entrance, where the entrance fee must be paid 🛥 Tours from El Calafate

BRAZO NORTE BOAT TRIP

Leaving from Puerto Bandera, 40km (25 miles) west of El Calafate, you can also sail in a modern catamaran or launch up the Brazo Norte to see more glaciers. One of the best tour operators is René Fernández Campbell in El Calafate (▷ 183). Among the glaciers you may see are the mighty Upsala, the 100m-high (328ft) Spegazzini and the bijou Onelli. Although you should be warned that icebergs block some of the channels, especially Brazo Upsala. At 60km (37 miles) long, the Upsala glacier is the second longest in South America (after the Pío X Glacier in Chile), but is receding fast, which is why the channel is getting choked with ice. Even when the Brazo Upsala is out of bounds, the logjam of icebergs at its entrance is worth seeing, as the bergs are often weird and wonderful shapes. If you can't get to see some of the glaciers, most tours will chug along Canal de los Témpanos instead to see the Perito Moreno from the water.

TIPS

» The best times to visit are spring and autumn (Nov to mid-Dec and Mar–Apr); in summer it can get a bit overcrowded and in winter access can be difficult and many places are closed.

» It is a good idea to book every stage of your trip well in advance and to leave plenty of extra time in case weather conditions are against you.

» With the wind coming off the ice, the temperature at the glaciers can be a lot colder than in the centre of El Calafate or down in El Chaltén. Always take extra clothes, as sudden weather changes are frequent.

» At the Perito Moreno glacier stick to the boardwalks as there have been many deaths owing to ice blocks or waves hitting people who stray off the path.

» If you suffer from motion sickness, take anti-emetic medicine before heading out on any boat trips because the water can be rough. Be sure to dress in warm, water- and windproof clothing and take your own food and drink because prices are high on-board.

Below left *Newly created icebergs in the Canal de los Témpanos below the Glaciar Perito Moreno*
Below *A detail of the glacier's beautiful ice caverns*

>> The national park visitors' centre for the Fitz Roy sector (tel 02962/493004; 8am–6pm), 800m (0.5 miles) south of El Chaltén, should be your first port of call. Volunteers tell visitors about the regulations in the park. There are informative wildlife exhibits and a useful message board, too. All climbers must register here and fishing licences can be purchased at the desk (or in El Chaltén).
>> Lighting campfires in the whole park and riding horses in the Fitz Roy sector are banned but llamas are used as pack animals for treks.

FITZ ROY SECTOR

The northern extremity of the park, the Fitz Roy sector, is home to incredible mountain scenery, including the spike of Monte Fitz Roy (3,405m/11,168ft), Cerro Poincenot, Aguja Saint-Exupéry and Cerro Torre, a 3,102m (10,174ft) rock tower. These magnificent peaks form the shape of a thumbless hand, which is reflected in a series of upland lakes and lagoons.

Access to this section of the park is via El Chaltén (▷ 160) and there are a number of trails into the mountains that give views of the surreal scenery of the Fitz Roy range, while the intrepid can attempt to climb the peaks. It is worth going on an accompanied tour (▷ 183), even though most of the trails are well marked. To see the landscape at its most beautiful, consider camping overnight, to see the sun rise and set over the mountains.

The shortest walk leads to the Chorrillo del Salto, a dramatic waterfall set among mossy rocks and dead *lenga* trees, a 10-minute ramble off the RP-23, 30 minutes beyond the Madsen campsite to the north of El Chaltén. If you have time and like camping, the three-day Fitz Roy–Cerro Torre loop through the middle of the park is one of the best options. Other routes take you up to the Lagunas Madre and Hija, a pair of small lakes favoured by upland geese *(cauquenes)*, to Campamento De Agostini and then on to the opaque Laguna Torre or up into the areas beyond the national park, where yet more glaciers and eye-catching Andean peaks await.
✉ Access from El Chaltén

MORE TO SEE
LAGO ROCA

Little Lago Roca is strictly speaking the southern leg of Lago Argentino, just over 50km (31 miles) southwest of El Calafate. Its southern shores are carpeted with beautiful woodland that lends itself to horseback riding and trekking, especially in the hills of the Cordón de los Cristales. Here, you can see indigenous rock art dating back three millennia (take the signposted trail to the left of the main road just before Lago Roca campsite). You can also do the four-hour hike to the top of Cerro Cristales, where there are fabulous views of the Torres del Paine range over the border in Chile.

Below *Monte Fitz Roy, in the northern sector of the park*

INTRODUCTION

Parque Nacional Nahuel Huapi, the oldest Argentine national park, is a glorious chunk of the Andean cordillera with an adjoining swathe of steppe where a peacock-tail of lakes fans out. Dominating the park is the Monte Tronador, an extinct volcano, bedecked with fast-receding glaciers and topped by three peaks—the Argentino (3,410m/11,184ft), Internacional (3,554m/11,657ft) and Chileno (3,478m/11,408ft). Other magnificent mountains around the park are reflected in the myriad lagoons. To access this wonderful landscape, with its fascinating flora and fauna, you have a choice of the luxury resort of Villa La Angostura (▷ 172), with its lakeside lodges, laid-back and bohemian El Bolsón (▷ 157) or the mega-resort of Bariloche (▷ 174–175).

Dr Francisco P. Moreno, reverently known as 'Perito' (meaning 'expert'), donated the land to the state in 1903 to safeguard it for future generations and a national park was created in 1934. The park now covers 7,100sq km (2,741sq miles), mostly within the watershed of the gigantic Lago Nahuel Huapi. This glacial lake covers 557sq km (215sq miles) and is formed of countless islands and spindly peninsulas with its finger-like fjords and probing inlets.

Birdlife is a major attraction in the park, in particular the Magellanic woodpecker, the green-backed firecrown hummingbird, the creeping chucao tapaculo and the austral parakeet, but you are more likely to hear than see them. In addition to the native guanaco, rhea and fox, the woodland and steppe are also inhabited by large numbers of red deer and wild boar, introduced for hunting. Roast boar *(jabalí)* and venison carpaccio feature on many local menus.

Heavy rainfall in the western reaches of the park irrigates the rainforest, which becomes a riot of autumn colours in March and April. Most of the sights lie within the central zone, but also within easy reach of Bariloche is Lago Nahuel Huapi and Parque Nacional Los Arrayanes on the Península Quetrihué. More off the beaten track are the southern reaches, beyond Lago Gutierrez, with more challenging outings to the majestic Monte Tronador. To the far north, best explored by taking the Circuito Grande and Siete Lagos itineraries, lies the equally sumptuous expanse of the Parque Nacional Lanín (▷ 163).

INFORMATION

www.nahuelhuapi.gov.ar
www.welcomeargentina.com/parques/losarrayanes.html

✚ 348 B16 ✉ Parque Nacional Nahuel Huapi, Provincia de Santa Cruz ⊙ All year daily 24hrs. Access may be difficult in winter due to heavy snowfalls 🛈 Intendencia del Parque Nacional Nahuel Huapi ✉ Avenida San Martín 24, Bariloche ☎ 02944/423111 ⊙ Dec–Feb Mon–Fri 8–8, Sat–Sun 9–8; Mar–Nov daily 9–3 🚌 Main access from Bariloche and Villa La Angostura, which are located inside the park: RN-258 heads southwards from Bariloche to Villa Mascardi and on to El Bolsón; RN-237 heads east and north from Bariloche towards Junín de los Andes, at the eastern end of the Lago Nahuel Huapi; the RN-231 heads westwards towards Villa La Angostura and then on to the Seven Lakes route 🚗 Tour operators in Bariloche and Villa La Angostura offer a range of tours, including bicycle rental, trekking, horse trekking, paragliding and rafting

Above View across Lago Nahuel Huapi

TIPS

>> Summers in the park are warm while winters can be bitter and snowy. Gales blow in spring, which is otherwise a good time to visit, as is autumn, when there is less wind and the deciduous trees are ablaze with colour.

>> Snow can fall as late as December and as early as March at higher altitudes and trekking is not advisable outside high season.

>> The *Guía Sendas y Bosques de Lanín y Nahuel Huapi* is a very useful trail guide but is in Spanish only.

>> Start your visit to Parque Nacional Los Arrayanes early (the park opens at 8am), when the park is quieter and you can enjoy the wildlife.

Below right *Lago Nahuel Huapi*
Below *The native myrtle tree* (arrayán), *in Parque Nacional Los Arrayanes*

WHAT TO SEE

THE SOUTHERN REACHES

The RN-258 road southwards towards El Bolsón (▷ 157) leads past the gorgeous Lago Gutiérrez and southern shores that can be explored from the fabulous Peuma Hue *estancia* (▷ 191). The main road continues along the southern shores of V-shaped Lago Mascardi, where a track (toll fee) takes you westwards (right) around the western lakeshore and on towards Monte Tronador (3,554m/11,657ft). At the Los Rápidos campground, take either the left fork in a westerly direction to Lago Hess and the Cascada de los Alerces waterfall or the right branch northwards to Pampa Linda, where there are fabulous views of the glaciers hanging off Monte Tronador. Both roads are single track and there is a timetable for travel in either direction.

Enquire in Bariloche about tours beyond Pampa Linda to the Ventisquero Negro (Black Glacier) lookout, an offshoot of the Glaciar Río Manso on the higher slopes of Monte Tronador. There are short trails to the colossal Saltillo de las Nalcas, a waterfall surrounded by wild rhubarb, and lots of paths to explore around Pampa Linda.

ISLA VICTORIA AND PUERTO BLEST

www.patagonia.com.ar
www.islavictoriayarrayanes.com
If a boat trip onto the lake is on your agenda, you might consider the classic trip from Puerto Pañuelo to Isla Victoria, where you can see rock paintings, laze on lakeside beaches and take the chairlift to Cerro Bella Vista before continuing on to the Parque Nacional Los Arrayanes (▷ right). Another outing reaches Puerto Blest near the Chilean border. The itinerary starts with a 75-minute boat trip from Puerto Pañuelo and then a minibus to Lago Frías, where condors roost on nearby crags. The trip also includes a short walk to see the Cascada Los Cántaros waterfall, which drops like a staircase from the mountain cliffs.

CIRCUITO GRANDE

The 245km (152-mile) Circuito Grande leads out of Bariloche eastwards along the busy RN-237, past the airport, to Junín de los Andes. The first attraction on the route is the Valle Encantado, where pine forests lining the steep Limay valley are spiked with huge stone needles forming a bizarre Gaudiesque landscape. At Confluencia, just over 70km (43.5 miles) from Bariloche, the RP-65 branches off to the left towards Villa Traful. A few minutes beyond Lago Traful (▷ opposite), at the dramatic El Portezuela pass, the Circuito Grande joins up with the Ruta de los Siete Lagos (▷ 180–181) at the northern end of Lagos Correntoso before returning to Bariloche, via Villa La Angostura along the RN-231.

PARQUE NACIONAL LOS ARRAYANES

Like a Russian doll, the Parque Nacional Los Arrayanes is wrapped delicately inside the Nahuel Huapi National Park and was created to give some tender loving care to a grove of precious *arrayanes* or native myrtles. The *arrayán* has a flaky, tawny bark and spiral-shaped trunk. Often reaching a height of 15m (49ft), the tree can live for hundreds of years, provided it grows next to cool water. In late summer, its tiny white flowers give way to edible bluish-black berries.

The beautiful Bosque de los Arrayanes stands at the extremity of the Península Quetrihué, which juts into Lago Nahuel Huapi near Villa La Angostura (▷ 172). Most of the headland is densely forested with *coihue*, *radal* and other endangered trees. A 600m (654-yard) boardwalk takes you under a canopy of shiny foliage and reddish trunks. You can reach the *bosque* from the nearby resort of Villa La Angostura on foot (allow five or six hours to get there and back) or take a boat trip from either Angostura or Bariloche. After a steep climb to the lookout point *(mirador)*, the route is fairly flat and not too tough. Catamaran excursions are available all year but get booked up in advance in the summer.
✚ 348 B16 ⊕ Dec–Feb daily 8–9; Mar–Nov 8–6 💵 $50 🛈 Intendencia (park rangers' office) at Bahía Mansa, near neck of peninsula ☎ 02944/494152 ⊕ Daily 8–8 🚢 Tours from Angostura and Bariloche; catamaran excursions (www.bosquelosarrayanes.com.ar; $98 each way, $178 round trip)

MORE TO SEE

LAGO TRAFUL

Intensely blue Lago Traful, popular with fishermen, can be accessed along the RP-65, which skirts the southern shore, or from the Ruta de los Siete Lagos (▷ 180–181), crossing El Portezuelo pass and heading through the Valle de los Machis with its *coihue* trees, beneath Pico Traful (2,040m/6,691ft). A further 5km (3 miles) east along the RP-65 is a lookout point, Mirador Pared del Viento, above a precipitous rock face that plunges into the lake.
✚ 348 B16

Above *Catamaran excursions are a popular way to see Parque Nacional Los Arrayanes*

Above *The attractive town of San Martín de los Andes on the shores of Lago Lacár*

PERITO MORENO

www.interpatagonia.com/peritomoreno
It says a lot about the northwestern reaches of Santa Cruz Province that, despite a population of a mere 5,000 residents, Perito Moreno—not to be confused with the Perito Moreno glacier or the national park to the south—is regarded as the big city hereabouts. For the visitor, the town's strategic position, on the legendary RN-40, makes it a handy stopover, with a few hotels, restaurants and amenities. It is also a base for visiting the prehistoric rock paintings at the Cueva de las Manos (▷ 158–159).
➕ 354 C21 ✉ Perito Moreno, Provincia de Santa Cruz ℹ️ San Martín and Gendarmería Nacional ☎ 02963/432732 🕐 Daily 7–11 🚌 Buses from Bariloche and El Chaltén ✈ Flights to El Calafate 🚌 From El Calafate, take the RN-40 northwards; Perito Moreno is approximately 630km (390 miles) away (allow a minimum of 14 hours/2 days driving)

SAN CARLOS DE BARILOCHE
▷ 174–175.

SAN MARTÍN DE LOS ANDES

www.sanmartindelosandes.gov.ar
Lapped by the choppy waters of Lago Lácar, the handsome Lake District resort of San Martín de los Andes is one of the main gateways to the pristine landscapes of the Parque Nacional Lanín (▷ 163). It is also the destination, or starting point, of the famed Seven Lakes Route (Ruta de los Siete Lagos, ▷ 180–181), which, in fact, winds its way past a dozen or so lakes and lagoons.

San Martín's well-kept streets and appealing central square, the Plaza San Martín, are lined with a wide range of accommodation, restaurants, chocolate shops and other utilities. For compelling views of the lake and surrounding mountains, it is worth climbing to Mirador Arrayán, to the southwest, and Mirador Bandurrias, among dense oak woods to the northeast.
➕ 348 B16 ✉ San Martín de los Andes, Provincia de Neuquén ℹ️ Plaza San Martín ☎ 02972/427347 🕐 Daily 8am–10pm 🚌 Buses from all major destinations ✈ Flights to Bariloche 🚌 From Bariloche, take the RN-234 northwards

SARMIENTO
▷ 173.

TREVELÍN

www.trevelin.gob.ar
The main attraction of the rather straggling village of Trevelín is a lovingly restored flour mill. Built in 1918, this sturdy brick edifice now houses the Museo Histórico Regional Viejo Molino (Molino Viejo 488; tel 02945/480545; daily 11–6; $5), which displays an eclectic array of clothing, farm equipment and photographs, tracing local history from the arrival of the first Welsh settlers in these parts in the 1880s.
➕ 352 B18 ✉ Trevelín, Provincia de Chubut ℹ️ Plaza Coronel Fontana ☎ 02945/480120 🕐 Daily 8–8 🚌 Buses from Esquel ✈ Flights to Esquel; Trevelín is 35km (22 miles) from the airport 🚌 From Esquel, take the RN-258 southwest for 20km (12.5 miles)

VILLA LA ANGOSTURA

www.laangostura.com
Villa La Angostura, the most luxurious resort in the Lake District, spills along the grassy northernmost shores of the beautiful Lago Nahuel Huapi, where a maze of woodland tracks, concealed behind lush pine groves, leads to some of the plushest hotels and lodges in the country.

The town centre, with stone buildings designed by architect Alejandro Bustillo, is immaculately manicured. The main thoroughfare, Avenida Arrayanes, is lined with shops and restaurants. Angostura is the ideal base for exploring the northern sector of the Parque Nacional Nahuel Huapi (▷ 169–171) and, in particular, the Parque Nacional Los Arrayanes (▷ 171), an idyllic peninsula that terminates in a magical wild myrtle grove.
➕ 348 B16 ✉ Villa La Angostura, Provincia de Neuquén ℹ️ Avenida Siete Lagos 93 ☎ 02944/494124 🕐 Dec–Feb daily 8–10; Mar–Nov 9–8.30 🚌 Buses from Bariloche ✈ Flights to Bariloche 🚌 80km (50 miles) from Bariloche; take the RN-237 northeast, then RN-231 west and follow lakeside to Villa La Angostura

VILLA PEHUENIA

www.villapehuenia.org
www.villapehuenia.gov.ar
Parque Nacional Lanín's answer to Angostura, Villa Pehuenia, enjoys a remarkable location on the shimmering Lago Aluminé, quietly isolated from the town of Aluminé. *Posadas* and cabins offer every comfort and, despite being a rapidly expanding holiday resort, the town revels in its remoteness and lack of modern amenities. Although Villa Pehuenia lies outside the national park itself, the surrounding landscapes are every bit as stunning.

The main activities are fly-fishing and trekking around the lake. More hiking is possible around Moquehue, 25km (16 miles) further west, near where the forested slopes of Volcán Batea Mahuida drop abruptly to the shores of Lago Moquehue.
➕ 348 B14 ✉ Villa Pehuenia, Provincia de Neuquén ℹ️ km11, road to Aluminé ☎ 02942/498044 🕐 Dec–Feb daily 9–9; Mar–Nov 10–6 🚌 Buses from Aluminé 🚌 60km (37 miles) from Aluminé; take the RP-23 northwards, then turn left to Villa Pehuenia

SARMIENTO

Since the early 20th century, a close-knit community of enterprising Welsh, Lithuanian and Boer settlers and their descendants have squeezed a living out of the hostile lands surrounding tough little Sarmiento, despite the arid ground and inhospitable climate. Just outside the town, two indigo lakes, Lago Musters and Lago Colhué Huapi, peppered pink by flocks of hardy flamingos, are the only relief in the otherwise arid steppe. Irrigation from the lakes supports cherry farms and market gardens, which combined with resistant livestock and a large barracks, maintain the town's economy. Sarmiento is conveniently situated at a crossroads between Atlantic Patagonia and the Lake District, and it is worth a visit for a trio of attractions: a museum, a dinosaur park and a petrified forest.

PARQUE PALEONTOLÓGICO AND MUSEO REGIONAL

In the rather austere town centre you can visit the outdoor Parque Paleontológico (a staff member must accompany all visitors; ask at the tourist office for details), a local Jurassic park with convincing life-size replicas of dinosaurs whose remains were uncovered in northern Patagonia. The town's pioneering spirit is encapsulated in an outstanding ethnographic museum, the Museo Regional Desiderio Torres (20 de Junio 114; Mon–Fri 9–5, Sat–Sun 11–5; $3), housed in the nearby former train station, where you can also see fine textiles produced by the indigenous Mapuche and Tehuelche communities, plus dinosaur bones and a gallery of old photographs.

BOSQUE PETRIFICADO SARMIENTO

Some 40km (25 miles) to the south of Sarmiento, via a gravel track, is the Bosque Petrificado Sarmiento (Oct–Mar daily 9–9; Apr–Sep 9–6; $10), where well-preserved 65-million-year-old araucaria trunks are scattered across a rocky steppe against colourful cliffs. Even if you have already seen the Monumento Nacional Bosques Petrificados (▷ 129), in northeastern Santa Cruz Province, the dramatic landscape makes the trek worthwhile. The Petrified Forest was formed by mineral-rich water trickling over the fallen trees over hundreds of thousands of years. The highlight is a hollow trunk, reminiscent of a giant prehistoric Yule log. One of the easiest ways to get to the *bosque* is by *remise* (radio taxi): Ask at the tourist office for details.

INFORMATION

www.coloniasarmiento.gov.ar/turismo/index.php

✚ 352 D20 ✉ Sarmiento, Provincia de Chubut 🛈 Pietrobelli 388 ☎ 02974/898220 🕐 Dec–Mar daily 8am–11pm; Apr–Nov 9–8 🚌 Buses from Esquel and Comodoro Rivadavia ✈ Frequent flights to Comodoro Rivadavia (nearest airport) and Trelew from Buenos Aires 🚗 Take RN-3 south from Trelew for 375km (232.5 miles) to Comodoro Rivadavia and then the RN-26 due west for 155km (96 miles) to Sarmiento

TIPS

»» In early February, horse-riding displays and folk music dominates the two-day Festival de Doma y Folklore, held at the Club Deportivo on the RN-26.
»» The best way to see the petrified forests is to ask about guides at the tourist office.

Below *Petrified araucaria trees at the Bosque Petrificado Sarmiento, 45km (25 miles) south of Sarmiento*

INFORMATION

www.barilochepatagonia.info
www.bariloche.gov.ar
 348 B16 San Carlos de Bariloche, Provincia de Río Negro Centro Cívico
 02944/429850 9–9 Buses from all major destinations Regular flights (up to four a day in high season) from Buenos Aires (mostly Aeroparque)
 Airport is 14km (9 miles) east of the city

INTRODUCTION

Known simply as Bariloche, this is the Lake District's main resort, beautifully situated on the banks of Lago Nahuel Huapi and backed by jagged Andean peaks. Nearly a million visitors, from across Argentina and the globe, flock here each year to visit the huge Parque Nacional Nahuel Huapi (169–171), with its jigsaw of lakes and forests, mountains and waterfalls, and the town is overflowing with excellent hotels and hostels catering to all budgets, cabin complexes, chocolate shops, bars and pubs, souvenir stores and travel agencies. Bariloche has its own airport and is well served by intercity buses, so getting there is easy. Myriad tour operators lay on excursions and tours, such as the popular half-day Circuito Chico (right), but you might like the freedom of your own transport.

The city itself is a sprawling mass of houses and tourist facilities, stretching westwards along the lakeshore and up the lower slopes of the mountains behind, including Cerro Catedral, where there is a ski resort. The handsome Centro Cívico is an exception, displaying noble architecture, as does the city's soaring cathedral. Nearby, the Museo de la Patagonia is wonderfully old fashioned, with a huge collection of exhibits relating to Patagonia and the history of the region.

WHAT TO SEE
CENTRO CÍVICO

Downtown clusters around the architecturally impressive Centro Cívico, an austere but harmonious set of stone-and-timber buildings that wouldn't look out of place in Scotland or Scandinavia. Built in 1939, they are the work of Ernesto de Estrada, who worked closely with Alejandro Bustillo (1889–1982), the prolific architect who designed the famous Llao Llao hotel (191) and the centre of Villa La Angostura (172).

In addition to the municipality, which also houses the tourist information centre, you can find the city's main museum, the Museo de la Patagonia, built in the same Nordic style, using the local greenish-grey granite. In the middle of the plaza, there is an equestrian statue of General Roca with his back to the lake. Local dog owners often bring their St. Bernards here—complete with brandy casks—for tourist photo opportunities.

Above *A bay just outside Bariloche*

MUSEO DE LA PATAGONIA

www.bariloche.com.ar/museo

Officially named after the great explorer and naturalist Francisco Moreno (1852–1919), the Patagonian museum covers a range of regional themes: from the indigenous people and traditions to the War of the Desert (1879–80) in which thousands of Argentines were massacred. Documents, maps and artwork illustrate this fascinating and, at times, gruesome history and the story of Bariloche more generally. One of the highlights is a cartoon depicting Perito Moreno as a wet nurse to Theodore Roosevelt during the latter's visit in 1913. Natural history is also well represented, with rooms full of slightly musty but informative displays of stuffed animals and birds from the region.

✉ Centro Cívico ☎ 02944/422309 🕓 Tue–Fri 10–12.30, 2–7, Sat 10–5 ✋ $5

CIRCUITO CHICO

The Circuito Chico (small circuit) is a tour from Bariloche that takes about four hours. The route heads along the lake, past cabins and tourist complexes, and then on to Estrada's Capilla San Eduardo, a beautiful church constructed of cypress wood. Across the water, you can catch sight of one of Alejandro Bustillo's most celebrated buildings, the luxury hotel Llao Llao (▷ 191), an Alpine structure that appears in many travel brochures. Farther west, before the end of the itinerary, is Colonia Suiza. This remarkable village was founded in 1895 by three Swiss brothers and is now famed for its Swiss food. From here, there are several walks, including one to Mirador López (a viewpoint), for tremendous lake views.

MORE TO SEE

CATEDRAL NUESTRA SENORA DEL NAHUEL HUAPI

Alejandro Bustillo designed Bariloche's cathedral, which lies at the intersection of O'Connor and Beschtedt Admiral. The cathedral is surrounded by tranquil gardens and its fine stained-glass windows illustrate events in Patagonian history, such as the first Mass on Argentine soil, held by Ferdinand Magellan in 1521.

CERRO CATEDRAL

Cerro Catedral, 19km (12 miles) from Bariloche, gets its name from its summits (2,405m/7,888ft) that are shaped like Gothic spires. Trekkers favour the slopes, though there is a cable car and chairlift if you want to enjoy the views without the legwork. In winter, the village at its foot, Villa Catedral, is a popular ski resort, with nearly 70km (43.5 miles) of runs.

TIPS

›› Bariloche is at its busiest in January and February, when the weather is usually at its best. If you prefer to have a bit of breathing space, visit in spring or autumn, when it is quieter. Alternatively, you might prefer to stay in the relative tranquillity of Villa La Angostura (▷ 172) or El Bolsón (▷ 157), or at one of the quieter lakeside hotels and *estancias* nearer the city.

›› A number of beaches are strung along the lakeshores but the water is very cold, so you might prefer to check out the outdoor swimming pool at the Complejo Deportivo Municipal (Mon–Sat 11–8, Sun noon–8; $3).

›› Parking in Bariloche is a complicated affair. Ask at the tourist office for details of the ticket scheme for street parking.

›› You can get useful information about trekking and mountain climbing from the Club Andino Bariloche at 20 de Febrero 30 (www.clubandino.org).

›› The road leading westwards out of the city is Avenida Rosas and, shortly, becomes Avenida Bustillo. Addresses are usually given in terms of kilometres, counted from zero.

Below *The spectacular view from Cerro Campanario over Lago Nahuel Huapi*

LAGUNA DE LOS TRES

If you go on only one trek in the Fitz Roy sector of the Parque Nacional Los Glaciares, then it should be up to the Laguna de los Tres for incredible close-up views of the Fitz Roy range. The route is well signposted but take a map and consider being accompanied by a guide. Although the trek is perfectly safe, adverse climatic conditions and the surrounding terrain can make it very unpleasant if you get lost. The overall ascent is 900m (2,952ft) and there are some steep sections, but the vistas of this stellar section of the Andes are truly unforgettable.

THE WALK

Distance: 26km (16 miles)
Time: 8 hours without stops; 2 days with an overnight stop
Start at: El Chaltén
End at: El Chaltén

★ Start in the centre of El Chaltén on Avenida Güemes, turn right along Lago del Desierto and then left on to Avenida San Martín, which gently slopes upwards to the beginning of the trail.

The hike starts at the house above the Camping Madsen campsite, at the northern end of the avenue, about 1km (0.5 miles) from the junction with Lago del Desierto. The signs are clear and you immediately start gently ascending the wooded slopes of Cerro Rosado and Cerro León, quickly gaining views of the

Fitz Roy range again. Continue for 4km (2.5 miles) alongside a ravine, gouged out by the Chorillo del Salto brook, to reach a path leading to the left. After 1km (0.5 miles), you reach the campsite next to Laguna Capri.

❶ Stop for a while at Laguna Capri and admire the fabulous views. You can camp overnight here, but the site is exposed to strong winds and you should not drink the water in the lake.

Return to the main path and, a little beyond the side turning, signposted to Laguna Madre, cross a bubbling stream and then the Chorrillo del Salto. The path then continues to reach the Campamento Poincenot campsite. At this point, you will have been walking for about two to three hours (about 10km/6 miles).

❷ The Campamento Poincenot is a convenient place to spend the night. The site gets its name from Jacques Poincenot, one of the team of French climbers who made the first recorded ascent of Monte Fitz Roy in the early 1950s. Unlike his colleagues, he never saw the summit because he drowned on the way to the top. The large, dispersed campsite nestles in beautiful *lenga* and *ñire* woods on the eastern bank of the Río Blanco. There are views of the Fitz Roy range from various vantage points, worth bearing in mind when pitching your tent. This is a far more sheltered spot than the campsite by Laguna Capri and you are closer to the mountains, so the views are better. The campsite is rudimentary, however, and takes no reservations, so you will need to bring all your own equipment or hire a guide in El Chaltén.

❸ From Poincenot, there are a couple of complementary trails to explore, if time and weather permit. The first is a 10km (6-mile) trail along the west bank of the Río Blanco towards the Piedra del Fraile, a vast boulder. The second trail heads along the Chorrillo del Salto to Laguna Madre and Laguna Hija for 10km (6 miles), and passes a pretty pair of lakes favoured by upland geese.

Back on the main route, cross the principal stream of the Río Blanco using the wooden bridge. (There is another ramshackle bridge from where a path climbs through the trees to the, signposted, Río Blanco campsite, which is suitable for mountain-climbers.) Catch your breath as the path starts to climb abruptly to the top of a ridge. This steep section is fairly short and there are no paths off the route, so you cannot get lost.

Levelling off and still on the path, you cross a muddy meadow and then another ridge beyond where you'll enjoy super views of your destination, the Laguna de los Tres.

❹ Three to five hours (15km/ 9 miles) from El Chaltén, you will reach the stunningly beautiful aquamarine lake, Laguna de los Tres. In addition to Monte Fitz Roy you can see a gamut of peaks, including Cerro Poincenot and Aguja Saint-Exupéry, named after the French writer, who was also an early aviator in South America.

Continue past the outcrop to your left for more stunning views taking in the dark Laguna Sucia, 200m (656ft) below the Laguna de los Tres and separated by a sharp ridge. Above Lago Sucia (literally 'Dirty Lake', due to its relative murkiness) dangles the impressive Glaciar Río Blanco, which regularly calves little bergs into the lake, making huge explosions. You might like to stay up here as late as is safe and then retrace your steps to the Poincenot campsite, where you can stay overnight and return to El Chaltén in the morning. If you see that the weather is changing, then head back into town.

TOURIST INFORMATION
EL CHALTÉN
🛈 Güemes 21 ☎ 02962/493011
🕐 Dec–Feb daily 8–8; Mar–Nov Mon–Fri 9–6

WHEN TO GO
In the southern parks, March is the optimum time for walking. Spring (October and November) can be blustery and summer (December to February) can be busy. Between Easter and September, forget it. Set out early, after taking a weather check and consider camping overnight, if you want to see the mountains at their best, sunset and sunrise.

WHERE TO EAT
Take your own provisions with you. If you are going on a guided tour, food will probably be provided but check in advance with your tour operator.

TIPS
›› This trail can be done as part of the rewarding three-day loop (50km/31 miles) around the whole southern sector of Parque Nacional Los Glaciares.
›› Take plenty of warm clothing, food, drink and waterproofs with you.
›› Check the weather forecast before setting out because a bright morning can give way to a nasty storm within an hour or two.

Opposite *Beautiful Laguna Capri*
Below *The jagged peaks of Monte Fitz Roy, an unforgettable sight*

SOUTHERN SANTA CRUZ PROVINCE

Part of the mindblowing experience of southern Patagonia is witnessing at first-hand its desolate emptiness. The distances in this classic but challenging drive across the Santa Cruz steppe are huge and it should not be attempted in one day. Choose between the delightful Hostería Monte León and a hotel in the regional capital, Río Gallegos, for the overnight stop. Provided you have a sense of adventure—you will need one to contemplate driving around this part of the world—you will get an unforgettable taste of the vastness and remoteness of the region. Don't try any shortcuts—what looks quicker on the map might turn out to be a virtually impassable gravel track.

THE DRIVE

Distance: 700km (420 miles) round trip
Time: At least 10 hours–stay overnight in Río Gallegos or Parque Nacional Monte León
Start at: El Calafate
End at: El Calafate

★ From the centre of El Calafate head eastwards on RP-11, following signs to Río Gallegos, past the airport. After 30km (18.5 miles), at a junction with the RN-40, turn left heading north. After crossing the Río Santa Cruz, soon after it flows out of Lago Argentino, the paved RN-40 runs alongside the rapid Río La Leona. Along this stretch of road you will pass beneath rows of rocky crags and glimpse views of the distant Fitz Roy range. By the huge new bridge over the river stands one of RN-40's best-known inns, the Hotel La Leona.

❶ Stop at Hotel La Leona for refreshments and perhaps a piece of delicious pie or cake. You could also try your hand at an old *gaucho* game, *juego de la argolla*, which involves hooking a suspended string from the ceiling on to the wall. The winner gets a free drink.

The road now offers fabulous vistas to the left (northwest) across the giant sea-green bulge of the Lago Viedma, to the spikes of the Fitz Roy range. After 25km (15.5 miles), turn left, signposted to El Chaltén (RP-21). This is a detour you might well wish to make—the road is paved all the way to El Chaltén and follows the northern shore of the lake for most of the journey.

❷ El Chaltén is the self-styled trekking capital of Argentina. The town makes an excellent base for exploring the northern Fitz Roy section and its network of mountain trails. There are a number of useful tour operators in the town that can arrange trekking tours. Alternatively, visit the local tourist information office for details of local guides.

Otherwise continue for 50km (31 miles) to reach Tres Lagos.

❸ Tres Lagos is a hamlet where you will find some basic services, including a fuel station, a shop or two and a campsite, but it is really little more than a gravely crossroads, with dirt tracks heading west into the cordillera and east towards the coast. Take the latter route, the RN-288—a well-maintained gravel road that winds across an empty expanse to reach the Atlantic coast. Drive slowly

Opposite Desolate Patagonian landscape surrounding Lago Argentino
Below Cinnamon-coloured guanaco are among the wildlife found in the area

and carefully, watching out for guanacos and rheas that occasionally leap across the road. You reach the RN-3, the main coastal highway, at Comandante Luís Piedra Buena, a two-horse town inland from Puerto Santa Cruz, the former provincial capital.

At the junction with the RN-3, turn right—in a southerly direction—and a few kilometres south of the turn-off to Puerto Santa Cruz you will reach the reception for the Parque Nacional Monte León, the country's only coastal national park.

4 Monte León National Park (▷ 130) is worth visiting for its great scenic beauty and its abundant terrestrial and marine wildlife. It also offers accommodation, making this an ideal spot for breaking the journey.

To continue the drive, travel another 160km (96 miles) south by the RN-3 to the present provincial capital, Río Gallegos.

5 Río Gallegos (▷ 136) offers little in the way of visitor attractions in itself but is a good base for visiting the most southerly point of the mainland, at Cabo Vírgenes (some 133km/80 miles to the southeast), and one of the region's biggest penguin rookeries (▷ 129).

From Río Gallegos, take the RN-40 (still referred to on most maps as the RP-5) northwest through sheep-farming country and enjoy the increasingly beguiling views of the Torres del Paine peaks across the border in Chile. At a junction 112km (67 miles) away, a road leads westwards to the international border. This spot, optimistically named Esperanza (Hope), is little more than a staging post, with a popular *confitería*. You can then forge on another 150km (90 miles) back to your starting-point at El Calafate—with dramatic views of Lago Argentino shortly before arriving.

WHERE TO EAT/STAY

There are plenty of places to stay in El Chaltén if you break the journey there, while the best bet in Monte León is the wonderful *hostería* there (▷ 150). The only hotel worth considering in Río Gallegos is the Hotel Patagonia (▷ 152). The *confiterías* at the hotel La Leona and at Esperanza are great places to stop and refuel both yourselves and your vehicle.

WHEN TO GO

Spring or summer is probably the best time and certainly avoid this drive in winter. It is worth setting out early (certainly by 8am), even if you break the journey, to avoid travelling after nightfall.

TIPS

» It is worth renting a 4WD, especially if you want to get off the main route and on to the gravel side roads. If you plan to do this drive, book your vehicle well ahead.
» Although there are a few refreshment places along the way, most are rudimentary and the best option is to stock up with provisions in El Calafate and picnic along the route.

RUTA DE LOS SIETE LAGOS

The popular Ruta de los Siete Lagos is a beautiful scenic route from Bariloche to San Martín de los Andes, through enticing wooded valleys and past seven or more beautiful lakes. The 'official' seven lakes from south to north are Nahuel Huapi, Espejo, Correntoso, Escondido, Villarino, Falkner and Machónico. The winding road offers plenty of stops along the way and places to stay, too, not least the chic Villa La Angostura, where the route officially begins and ends.

THE DRIVE

Distance: 190km (118 miles) without detours
Time: 7 hours
Start at: Bariloche
End at: San Martín de los Andes

★ From the centre of Bariloche (▷ 174–175) head eastwards, taking the first section of the Circuito Grande (▷ 170) route along the RN-237 towards Junín de los Andes. An alternative approach to the Ruta de los Siete Lagos would be to start with the Circuito Grande, via Confluencia, joining the route near El Portezuelo.

On the main route, turn left. Just across the provincial border into Neuquén Province, there is a checkpoint (where you may need to show ID and driving papers). From here, take the RN-231 signposted to Villa La Angostura. Beyond the bleak Península Huemul, the road skirts the shores of the Lago Nahuel

Huapi (▷ 169), offering fabulous views of the Brazo Huemuel inlet and the northeastern shores of Isla Victoria. After 80km (49.5 miles) from Bariloche, you will reach the resort of Villa La Angostura.

❶ Villa La Angostura (▷ 172), the most luxurious resort in the Argentine Lake District, is a popular base for exploring Parque Nacional Nahuel Huapi.

In the centre of Villa La Angostura, turn right at the crossroads, near the tourist office and the main service station (you might like to fill your tank here). Next, take the RN-231 road, signposted to San Martín de los Andes and the Paso Cardenal Samoré. This is the mountain pass that crosses into Chile. The road runs along the northernmost reaches of Lago Nahuel Huapi before crossing the Río Correntoso (3km/2 miles from Villa La Angostura)—actually a

channel linking Lago Nahuel Huapi to Lago Correntoso. Leave Lago Nahuel Huapi and after 8km (5 miles), you reach a T-junction. Turn left on to a paved road, then take the right fork on to the unpaved RN-234, signposted to San Martín de los Andes. Right by this fork in the road is lakeside Hostería Lago Espejo, a wonderful place to stop and rest.

❷ Lago Espejo is said to be the warmest, as well as the smoothest, lake in the region, although its temperature is not exactly Caribbean. Opposite the *guardaparque's* (park ranger's) house is a short 30-minute trail through the woods to a remote stretch of the western shore of Lago Correntoso, where you might like to stretch your legs and have a swim.

❸ Lago Correntoso is a beautiful elongated lake and you clipped its southern tip earlier when you crossed the Río Correntoso bridge.

Opposite Lago Machónico in Parque Nacional Lanín—one of the 'official' seven lakes

The road turns sharply to the east to skirt the lake's northern shores, with cut-away views down to the waters. Continue until you reach the Hostería Siete Lagos where there are rooms, delicious food and sites to pitch a tent. The road then makes a tight turn to the left (north) and you shortly arrive at the junction with the RP-65 near the Portezuelo. Here, you join the Ruta de los Siete Lagos, if you opted to start with the Circuito Grande. In either case, you could make a short detour along the RP-65, to admire the gem-like Lago Traful.

❹ For spectacular views of Lago Traful (▷ 171), head along the RP-65 to the Mirador Pared del Viento.

The RN-234 (still a dirt track) now carves its way through a deep gorge. Take the 2km (1.25-mile) track signposted to Cascadas Ñivinco to see five waterfalls set among beautiful forest, via a small river crossing. A short way north of these trails, you will glimpse little Lago Escondido through the trees.

❺ Lago Escondido's handsome woodland setting and intense green waters are a great place for a picnic.

From here, the road meanders over the Río Pichi Traful. Time permitting, you could stop at the well-marked Seccional Villarino. The *guardaparques* will point you in the right direction for the four-hour trek up the slopes of Cerro Falkner (2,350m/7,708ft), where you can get views of Volcán Lanín (▷ 163).

On the main route, a poor track, to the right, leads to the tip of Brazo Norte, the 'northern arm' of Lago Traful.

❻ Near the point where the tarmac resumes, stands Hostería Lago Villarino, a good place to stop for lunch or tea and maybe go horseback riding, rent a bike or go fishing.

Otherwise, continue to reach the shores of Lago Villarino.

❼ Lago Villarino, one of the smaller lakes, reflects the mighty peak of Cerro Crespo. From here, the road runs between the mountain and the penultimate lake on this route, Lago Falkner.

As you forge northwards you pass Cascada Vulliñanco, a waterfall on the left, to enter Parque Nacional Lanín (▷ 163). The park is home to Lago Machónico, and you skirt its beautiful eastern shore to reach the Mirador de Pil Pil lookout.

At Pil Pil you can catch the first glimpse of Lago Lácar. San Martín de los Andes (▷ 172), the route's final destination, lurks out of sight below, at the eastern end of the large blue lake, whose waters are regularly chopped up by winds blowing down from the Andes.

TOURIST INFORMATION
BARILOCHE
✉ Centro Cívico ☎ 02944/429850
🕐 Daily 9–9

WHEN TO GO
Avoid this tour in spring or winter when the weather conditions are unfavourable.

WHERE TO EAT/STAY
LAS BALSAS
▷ 191.

LA ESCONDIDA
▷ 191.

HOSTERÍA LAGO VILLARINO
www.hosteriavillarino.com.ar
This classy *hostería* has cosy rooms with fireplaces and bungalows.
✉ Lago Villarino ☎ 02972/427483
✋ $200–$240

TIPS
▶▶ Leave early in the morning, if you want to reach San Martín in time for lunch.
▶▶ There are plenty of places to fish along this route, but you will need to buy a permit before setting off (from tourist offices, YPF stations or campsites).
▶▶ Much of the road is paved but the unsealed section between Lago Espejo and Lago Villarino can get very dusty at times.
▶▶ Fill the tank before setting out because there are no services along the route.

ALUMINÉ

ALUMINÉ RAFTING

www.interpatagonia.com/aluminerafting/
In addition to fun and more
challenging rafting trips on the world-
class Río Aluminé, this water-sports
company can arrange kayaking, river
floating, Canadian canoeing and
'ducky' (inflatable sport catamaran)
plus a range of well-organized treks
into the Parque Nacional Lanín.
There are two- to three-day treks
into the Cordón del Chachil at over
2,800m (9,184ft).
✉ Villegas 610 ☎ 02942/496322
✋ Trips from $90

EL BOLSÓN

AVENIDA SAN MARTÍN

Both the Centro Artesanal Cumey
Antú and the Centro Artesanal
Brillante Sol, next to one another
along Avenida San Martín, sell
fabulous Mapuche weavings made
on the looms in the workshops at
the back. There is a more general
Feria Artesanal at the southern end of
Plaza Pagano on Tuesdays, Thursdays
and Saturdays, with dozens of artists
and artisans selling wares such as
musical instruments and wooden
kitchen implements. Monte Viejo has
yet more crafts, such as ceramics
and wooden crafts, plus some fine
silver jewellery.
✉ El Bolsón ☺ Varies

CENTRO CULTURAL EDUARDO GALEANO

This wonderful little arts centre stages
music and dance performances
plus some plays (mostly Spanish,
although international companies
also stage productions here).
✉ Dorrego and Onelli ☎ 02944/491503
✋ Varies

GRADO 42

www.grado42.com
There is an amazing gamut of
outdoor activities in El Bolsón
and Grado 42 can arrange rafting,
paragliding, lake diving, horse
trekking along the beautiful valleys
as well as boat tours and guides for
mountain climbing. In the winter,
the company organizes treks and ski
routes across the snow.
✉ Avenida Belgrano 406 ☎ 02944/493124
☺ Mon–Sat 8.30–9, Sun 10–1, 3–8
✋ 5-hour trek or tour $160

HELADOS JAUJA

www.heladosjauja.com
Made with the freshest ingredients,
including vitamin-packed fruit from
El Bolsón orchards and market
gardens, Jauja's ice cream is
legendary and so popular that they
recently opened two branches in
Bariloche, one in Villa La Angostura
and another in Palermo, Buenos
Aires. The only problem is which
flavour to choose—the choice is
bewildering but you might like to try
the blackcurrant or blueberry.
✉ San Martín 2867 ☎ 02944/492448
☺ 10am–11pm ✋ From $8

EL CALAFATE

AVENIDA SAN MARTÍN

There are plenty of shopping
opportunities in El Calafate, mainly
along the main drag, or in the Paseo

de los Artesanos, where you can see local craftsmen's ware on show at a row of stalls selling jewellery and leatherware, *mate* paraphernalia and slate painted with indigenous designs. You can also find beautiful woollen goods such as blankets and pullovers at Telares Andinos.

✉ Avenida San Martín 🕐 Mon–Fri 10–7, Sat–Sun 10–4

EL BODEGÓN

For lovers of dark bock and pale pilsner beers, El Bodegón is a must. Its cosy interior and friendly bar staff assure a good night out. You can have some tasty bar food, including piping hot *empanadas* (meat pasties), fresh from the oven, or hearty *locro* (maize stew). The main purpose for coming here, however, is to have a pint or two of delicious creamy ale.

✉ Avenida San Martín 522
☎ 02902/491426 🕐 6pm–midnight

CHALTÉN TRAVEL

www.chaltentravel.com

Chaltén Travel is a highly experienced travel operator with branches across the country, mainly in the far south. The Calafate branches can arrange a range of excursions to suit every taste. These include the classic trip to see the Perito Moreno glacier, a more adventurous ice trek on to the glacier, a visit to a farm to see sheep shearing, or a sailing trip to the luxurious Estancia Cristina.

✉ Avenida San Martín 1174
☎ 02902/492212 🕐 Mon–Fri 10–6, Sat–Sun 10–5 ✋ Half-day trek $230

LIBROBAR BORGES Y ÁLVAREZ

In this bookshop-cum-bar, you can sit and browse through an impressive collection of books that are scattered around tables and shelves. On the first floor, the bar is squeezed into a balcony that overlooks the main street. This is the perfect place to enjoy a cappuccino or a glass of beer, while leafing through glossy literature or people-watching. There is also an extensive menu of snacks, cakes

and pasta and it is a good place for a relaxed lunch or dinner.

✉ Avenida San Martín 1015
☎ 02902/491464 🕐 Daily 9am–11pm

RENÉ FERNÁNDEZ CAMPBELL

www.fernandezcampbell.com

With years of experience navigating the icy channels of the Parque Nacional Los Glaciares, René Fernández Campbell's reputation is rock solid and their modern catamarans are comfortable. On the way to see the glaciers, which are only visible from the water or air, you can have your picture taken by a professional photographer and indulge in drinks made with pristine ice fished from the waters.

✉ Avenida San Martín 867
☎ 02902/491155 🕐 Daily 9–6 ✋ 45-min catamaran ride to the glaciers $50; Brazo Norte boat trip $295

EL CHALTÉN
CAMINO ABIERTO

www.caminoabierto.com

Camino Abierto (Open Way), a group of travel and tour operators, provides a wide range of options, such as discovery and adventure tours in the region's national parks. One of the best tours is the 14-day Patagonia adventure—running from October to April, weather permitting—that includes the Parque Nacional Los Glaciares, Parque Nacional Torres del Paine, across the border in Chile, and the Tierra del Fuego.

✉ Calle San Martín s/n ☎ 02962/493043 ✋ Varies

CASA DE GUIAS

www.casadeguias.com.ar

The Casa de Guias is a fabulous institution that can supply details of mountain guides affiliated to the Argentine Mountain Guide Association. Contact them in advance of your visit to work out a customized tour with a guide of your choice. Alternatively, book to join one of their regular trekking tours to places such as Laguna de los Tres (▷ 176–177).

✉ Avenida San Martín s/n
☎ 02962/493118 ✋ Trek to Laguna de los Tres $140

FITZROY EXPEDICIONES

www.fitzroyexpediciones.com.ar

Pioneers in expeditions in the Fitz Roy sector of the Parque Nacional Los Glaciares, this company specializes in guided ascents of the various peaks in the Fitz Roy range and nearby. The company also offers highly acclaimed mountain-climbing courses. Another classic tour is their ice trek across the glaciers, although this requires a high level of fitness and some experience.

✉ San Martín 56 ☎ 02962/493178 ✋ 1-day expedition $400

JOSH AIKE

www.elchalten.com/lachoco/index.php

What looks like a ramshackle cabin is in fact one of southern Patagonia's real gems, renowned for making the best handmade chocolate in this part of the world. Part of El Chaltén lore, the establishment is also vaunted for serving delicious fondues (cheese as well as chocolate), crusty pizzas and fabulous tarts.

✉ Lago Desierto 104 ☎ 02962/493008 🕐 Daily 12.30–7 ✋ From $15

PATAGONIA AVENTURA

www.patagonia-aventura.com.ar

If you are based in El Chaltén and want to get close up to glaciers and sail on a turquoise lake, then Patagonia Aventura is an excellent option. The Viedma Light navigation on Lago Viedma takes around two to three hours and gets right up close to the glacier.

☎ 02962/493110 ✋ Viedma Ice Trek $390

ESQUEL
PATAGONIA VERDE

www.patagonia-verde.com.ar

This is one of the best tour operators in Esquel, with a policy of organizing environmentally friendly tours. The company runs trips to the nearby Parque Nacional Los Alerces, plus treks into the local mountains. In the winter, snow sports are on the agenda and Esquel can rent out clothing and equipment or fix you up with lessons at the La Hoya resort.

✉ 9 de Julio 926 ☎ 02945/454396 🕐 Daily 9–6 ✋ Day trip $300

LA TROCHITA

La Trochita, also known as the Old Patagonian Express, still runs along a short section of its original route. The narrow-gauge train departs for Nahuel Pan up to three times a week in high season and occasionally runs longer journeys into the Patagonian steppe.

✉ Estación de Ferrocarril at Brun and Ruggero ☎ 02945/451403 ⏰ Check at the tourist office for the timetable 🖑 $150

JUNÍN DE LOS ANDES

TROMEN TURISMO

This is one of the best operators for guided or organized excursions into the Parque Nacional Lanín. You can also rent mountain bikes, as well as camping and climbing gear. Tromen Turismo also organizes ascents of the Volcán Lanín (you are advised not to go it alone).

✉ Lonquimay 195 ☎ 02972/491498 ⏰ Mon–Fri 10–6, Sat–Sun 10–4 🖑 Day trip $310; bicycle rental $90 a day

PERITO MORENO

GUANACONDOR TOURS

This experienced tour operator can take you to the Cueva de las Manos (▷ 158–159) archaeological site. In addition, it runs a variety of trips into the remote and uninhabited mountains of northern Patagonia.

✉ Perito Moreno 1087 ☎ 02963/432303 🖑 Trip to Cueva de las Manos $180 per person

SAN CARLOS DE BARILOCHE

ARBOL

All sorts of beautifully made woollen goods, including hats and fleeces, jackets and pullovers, gloves and scarves, can be picked up at this veteran clothing shop. It also sells an appealing range of ceramics, many with indigenous designs, and various traditional ornaments.

✉ Mitre 263 ☎ 02944/423032 ⏰ Mon–Fri 10–8, Sat–Sun 11–4

BIKEWAY

www.bikeway.com.ar

This responsible outfit is highly recommended for its short bicycle

tours and longer biking expeditions into the Parque Nacional Nahuel Huapi. One of the excellent tours on offer is a nine-day mountain-bike trip for the fit and adventurous, which includes some rafting and paragliding.

✉ Moreno 237 ☎ 02944/456571 🖑 Prices vary

CABALGATAS CAROL JONES

www.caroljones.com.ar

Carol Jones is the granddaughter of Jarred Jones, a pioneer who arrived in Nahuel Huapi in the late 19th century from Texas. Carol is an expert on the national park and, in the summer, organizes top-rate horse treks into the park and its fabulous scenery. These vary is length from half a day to 10 days. During the winter, she creates her distinctive *gaucho* figures in painted ceramic. You will need a sleeping bag for the longer treks.

✉ Modesta Victoria 5600 ☎ 02944/426508 🖑 Half day $200

CERVECERÍA BLEST

Patagonia, and the Lake District in particular, have a reputation for excellent real ales and Cervecería Blest is an excellent place to try some of the local varieties. Nestling back a little from the lakeshore, this German-style establishment pours thirst-quenching pale ales and stouts by the pint, and you can also try the Belgian-style fruit flavours (raspberry and blackcurrant). Platters of cold meats and cheeses make perfect accompaniments.

✉ Avenida Bustillo km11.6 ☎ 02944/461026 ⏰ Daily 12–12

EXTREMO SUR

www.extremosur.com

Two decades of experience come into play at this impressive company that focuses on adventurous water sports such as rafting and kayaking. You must be at least six years old to take part in white-water rafting on the lower Río Manso. Equipment and waterproofs are included.

✉ Morales 765 ☎ 02944/427301 🖑 Half day $210

LIMAY TRAVEL

www.limaytravel.com.ar

One of the best general tour operators in Bariloche, Limay Travel can organize lake trips, including tours to Puerto Blest and the Isla Victoria, Circuito Chico and Circuito Grande, as well as fly-fishing excursions by boat, with an angling expert, and all the equipment.

✉ O'Connor 710 ☎ 02944/420268 ⏰ Mon–Fri 9–8, Sat–Sun 9–6 🖑 Half-day tour $175

MAMUSCHKA

www.mamuschka.com

Bariloche is sometimes dubbed Argentina's chocolate capital and the city's Swiss connection has a lot to do with it. This shop and café sells a mouth-watering array of chocolate bars and liqueur-filled chocolates, as well as delicious marzipans and nougats. It is also a great place to have breakfast and the *medialunas* (cakes) are particularly tasty.

✉ Mitre 298 ☎ 02944/423294 ⏰ Daily 8–9

PURA VIDA PATAGONIA

www.puravidapatagonia.com.ar

Although Pura Vida offers some trips to the Parque Nacional Los Alerces, it mostly makes the most of the beautiful crystalline waters of the lakes within the Parque Nacional Nahuel Huapi and can organize kayak tours that range from a half-day on Lago Gutiérrez to a 12-day trip from Lago Correntoso to Alicurá. It also runs a 14-day kayak trip from Neuquén to the ocean at Viedma.

☎ 02944/15-414053 ⏰ Call for details 🖑 Half-day tour $240

TREN A VAPOR

www.trenhistoricoavapor.com.ar

The engine and five carriages of this century-old relic from the steam age have been lovingly restored and hold up to 250 passengers. The full-day excursion starts from Bariloche and ends at the Perito Moreno station on Laguna Los Juncos. The lagoon is home to flamingos and swans, and there is an optional walk to the volcanic rock known locally as Cerro

Elefante. Also optional is the roast lamb dinner, while tango dancers entertain passengers along the way.

✉ Avenida 12 de Octubre 2400
☎ 02944/423858 ◔ Times vary, check at Bariloche tourist office ✋ $350

SAN MARTÍN DE LOS ANDES
ANDESTRACK
www.andestrack.com.ar
Trekking, horseback riding, climbing and even dog-sleighing can be arranged by this enthusiastic outfit. The lake may beckon instead, in which case Andestrack can organize kayaks, canoes and rafting.

✉ Roca 869 ☎ 02972/420588 ◔ Daily 9–6 ✋ Day trip $320

EL CLARO TURISMO
www.elclaroturismo.com.ar
This excellent dynamic venture can arrange a variety of different tours, including vehicle rental and organized excursions in the Lake District. One of the thrilling half-day trips on offer takes in the lookouts at the far end of Lago Lácar, close to the Chilean border.

✉ Coronel Díaz 751 ☎ 02972/428876 ◔ Daily 9–7 ✋ Half-day trips $180, one-day skiing $315

VILLA LA ANGOSTURA
CABALGATAS CORRENTOSO
www.cabalgatacorrentoso.com.ar
Providing tents, backpacks and utensils, but not sleeping bags, this professional company will get you kitted out and ready to explore the magnificent national parks on horseback. Trips range from a short two-hour canter along the lakeside to four-day expeditions exploring the valleys.

✉ Mirador Belvedere ☎ 02944/15-510559 ✋ One-day trek $290

GREENLEAF
www.bosquelosarrayanes.com.ar
This company can arrange a catamaran trip from Villa La Angostura to the Parque Nacional Los Arrayanes, which enables you to avoid the long walk to the tip of the Quetrihué peninsula.

FESTIVALS AND EVENTS

JANUARY
FIESTA DE MÚSICA DE VERANO
www.bariloche.org
Bariloche is a musical town and home to a highly reputed chamber music group, the Camerata Bariloche. The summer music festival lasts into February and is a collection of smaller festivals dedicated to chamber, brass and ancient music.

FEBRUARY
FIESTA NACIONAL DEL TREN A VAPOR
www.bolsonweb.com/trencito.html
El Maitén, 70km (43.5 miles) southeast of El Bolsón, is home to the main workshop of La Trochita and has an annual national steam train festival. In addition to train engines, the festival includes rodeos, folk music and food specialities.

FIESTA DEL PUESTERO
www.fiestadelpuestero.org.ar
For the past 25 years, Junín de los Andes has come alive with this traditional celebration of indigenous Huiliche culture, mingled with *criollo* customs relating to horses and music.

FIESTA DEL LÚPULO
www.bolsonweb.com/ociolupulo.htm
El Bolsón is known for its environmentally friendly ethos and also for its fabulous organic products, not least its real ales, and the annual festival is dedicated to the humble hop (▷ 157).

✉ Avenida Siete Lagos 118
☎ 02944/494004 ✋ Villa La Angostura to Parque Nacional Los Arrayanes $178 round trip

VILLA PEHUENIA
BRISAS DEL SUR
brisasdelsur.8m.com
Using modern craft, holding up to

AUGUST
FIESTA DE LA NIEVE
www.bariloche.org
Bariloche's annual winter festival brightens up the dark nights with brilliant firework displays and a torchlit descent of the snowy slopes. Expect lots of music and wintertime revelry.

OCTOBER
EISTEDDFOD
www.rhysinpatagonia.com
Trevelín's eisteddfodau are not as well known as those held in Gaiman (▷ 129) and Trelew (▷ 147), but they are part of the Welsh cultural revival, including singing and poetry recitals in Welsh and Spanish, taking place in this far-flung outcrop of Cymru.

DECEMBER
EL TRABÚN
www.sanmartindelosandes.gov.ar
Art and music combine at San Martín de los Andes in this indigenous festival—the Encounter—that attracts performers, artists, craftsmen and revellers from far and wide. Expect ceramics, indigenous instruments and delicious *asados*.

EL BOLSÓN JAZZ FESTIVAL
www.elbolsonjazz.com.ar
Held at the beginning of the month, this is one of the country's top jazz festivals and sees a host of jam sessions and open-air gigs, with jazz-related art shows at the Centro Cultural Eduardo Galeano and other venues around town.

a dozen passengers, this reliable company runs delightful lake trips on the shimmering waters of Lago Aluminé lasting approximately an hour and a half. Boats leave from the little headland by the Laguna El Manzano.

✉ Laguna El Manzano, Villa Pehuenia
☎ 02942/15-692737 ✋ $150

Above *Ku de los Andes restaurant in San Martín de los Andes*

PRICES AND SYMBOLS

The restaurants are listed alphabetically (excluding El, La and Los). The prices given are the average for a two-course lunch (L) and a three-course dinner (D) for one person, without drinks. The wine price is for the least expensive bottle. All the restaurants listed accept credit cards unless otherwise stated. Prices are given in Argentine pesos ($) unless otherwise noted.

For a key to the symbols, ▷ 2.

ALUMINÉ
SAUCO

Not surprisingly given that Aluminé is one of the country's trout-fishing centres, Sauco's house special is trout, though they also serve excellent pizza and grilled meats. The atmosphere is mellow, the service is friendly and the wines are good.

✉ Avenida RIM 26 and Candelaria ☎ 02942/496357 🕐 Daily 12.30–3.30, 7.30–11 ✋ L $32, D $47, Wine $17

EL BOLSÓN
CERRO LINDO

Named after a beautiful Andean peak overlooking the town, this popular restaurant complements its range of trout and venison dishes with more down-to-earth fare and also an excellent wine list.

✉ Avenida San Martín 2524 ☎ 02944/492899 🕐 Daily 12.30–4, 6.30pm–1am ✋ L $35, D $65, Wine $25

EL CALAFATE
CASIMIRO BIGUÁ

www.casimirobigua.com

Exclusive Casimiro Biguá is the kind of place where the President goes for a candlelit supper. It is well appointed with professional, attentive waiting staff. The wine list is remarkable, as is the menu, which includes dishes such as roast lamb in an almond crust or duo of veal and lamb fillets with a morel sauce. For simpler grilled lamb and other meats, there is the *Parrilla* a door or two along the main street (No. 993), while the *Trattoria*, four blocks away (No. 1359), serves excellent Italian fare.

✉ Avenida San Martín 963 ☎ 02902/492590 🕐 Daily 12.30–4, 6.30pm–1am ✋ L $60, D $105, Wine $30

PURA VIDA

Pura Vida is a ten-minute stroll from the centre of town but you'll want to build up an appetite for this superb wholefood restaurant, housed in a rustic building reminiscent of a Dutch barn. The restaurant specializes in natural foods and with plenty of vegetarian options on offer. One of the house favourites is a scooped-out pumpkin filled with vegetables and pumpkin chunks in a savoury sauce.

✉ Avenida San Martín 1876 ☎ 02902/493356 🕐 Thu–Tue 7.30pm–1am ✋ D $55, Wine $18

LA TABLITA

www.interpatagonia.com/latablita

This smart roadside inn has a classy stone-coloured facade and a quaint timber tower that is a landmark in El Calafate. The restaurant is always filled to the rafters with happy tourists and reserving a table is essential. La Tablita specializes in down-to-earth *parrillas* and there is lamb sizzling away on the cross spits at any given time. The wine list is huge and includes some interesting Patagonia wines.

✉ Coronel Rosales 28 ☎ 02902/491065 🕐 Sep–May Thu–Tue 12.30–4, 7–12, Wed 7–12 ✋ L $55, D $80, Wine $28

EL CHALTÉN
EL MURO

Named for the climbing wall on the outside, this charming little place serves wonderful food. The large menu includes lamb chops in a red fruit sauce, beef stew or the house special, fillet steak with a red pepper and bacon sauce. The oven-baked pizzas are huge.

✉ San Martín 912 ☎ 02962/493248 🕐 Daily 12.30–2, 7–12 🖐 L $45, D $65, Wine $25

LA TAPERA

Home cooking is the big attraction at this attractive timber lodge. The lentil soup is particularly tasty, while you can also try a range of dishes based on beef, lamb and fish and there is a good wine list. Make sure you save some room for the unusual fresh mint pancakes served with *dulce de leche*.

✉ Rojo s/n ☎ 02962/493138 🕐 Daily 7–midnight 🖐 D $45, Wine $21

ESQUEL
LA TOUR D'ARGENT

www.latourdargent.com.ar
This restaurant might not entirely bear comparison with its Parisian namesake, but it serves up great pasta and other dishes. Savour the ricotta and walnut ravioli or the fillets of trout in a mushroom sauce. The restaurant is famed for its cold-table buffet, which includes tasty concoctions such as pickled rabbit and smoked venison with Waldorf salad.

✉ San Martín 1063 ☎ 02945/454612 🕐 Daily 12.30–2.30, 7.30–midnight 🖐 L $45, D $60, Wine $21

JUNÍN DE LOS ANDES
RUCA HUENEY

www.ruca-hueney.com.ar
Overlooking the square in an imposing cornerhouse, Junín de los Andes serves simply fabulous trout. You can choose to have your fish served with black butter, Roquefort, tomato sauce, garnished with mushrooms, *à la provençale*, *à la romana* or drizzled with cream, although they are superb when simply lightly grilled and finished with a squeeze of fresh lemon.

✉ Padre Milanesia and Coronel Suárez ☎ 02972/491113 🕐 Daily 12.30–3, 7.30–12 🖐 L $45, D $62, Wine $23

Right *Enjoying a convivial meal*

SAN CARLOS DE BARILOCHE
POSADA PIEDRA DEL CÓNDOR

www.piedradelcondor.com
Perched on a bluff overlooking Lago Gutiérrez by the RN-40, this *posada* is a great place to enjoy a leisurely lunch or romantic dinner. You can choose from a range of delicious local specialities, such as boar and trout, or Patagonian lamb chops, cooked to perfection. Lighter snacks, such as sandwiches and cakes, are available at lunchtime, too.

✉ RN-40 km2022 ☎ 02944/1541-2349 🕐 Daily 12.30–3.30, 7.30–11 🖐 L $45, D $62, Wine $18

SANTOS

www.santosresto.com.ar
Intimate little Santos has only 10 tables and enjoys rave reviews, thanks to the imaginative chef and his enthusiastic crew. Kick off with a *pisco sour* (a cocktail made with lemon juice and grape brandy), then try the signature antipasti, trout and mozzarella in filo pastry, and finish with one of the fabulous desserts, such as a tiramisu, which is as good as any served in Italy. Dinner only.

✉ España and French ☎ 02944/425942 🕐 Daily 7.30pm–1am 🖐 D $65, Wine $27

SAN MARTÍN DE LOS ANDES
KU DE LOS ANDES

www.kudelosandes.com.ar
Ku de los Andes has two locations: one on San Martín's leafy central

square, a rustic *parrilla de Montaña* (mountain grill), and another on the road towards Junín de los Andes, known as a *parrilla gourmet* for its fancier menu (RN-243 and Callejón de Bello; tel 02972/425953; daily 12–4, 8–12; L $50, D $80, Wine $30). Both are fabulous and are great places to taste Patagonian specialities such as lamb lasagne, marinated trout, sweet-and-sour venison or buffalo in a three-pepper sauce. The wine list is faultless as is the service, while there are a number of dishes for celiac sufferers.

✉ Avenida San Martín 1053 ☎ 02972/427039 🕐 Daily 12–4, 8–12 🖐 L $40, D $67, Wine $24

VILLA LA ANGOSTURA
LA PORFIADA

www.parrillalaporfiada.com.ar
La Porfiada has a sister restaurant in San Martín de los Andes, as well as this branch in charming Villa La Angostura. The restaurants are renowned for their top-notch Patagonian lamb, roasted on the traditional *gaucho* cross spit. The wine bar serves some outstanding Patagonian wines, along with well-kept vintages from the rest of Argentina and farther afield. Most of the hotels in La Angostura have their own restaurants but if you are going to venture out, this is definitely the place to go.

✉ Avenida Arrayanes 8 ☎ 02944/15-571673 🕐 Daily 8am–midnight 🖐 L $55, D $80, Wine $24

Above *El Casco Art Hotel on the shores of Lago Nahuel Huapi*

PRICES AND SYMBOLS

Prices are the lowest and highest for a double room for one night. Breakfast is included unless noted otherwise. All the hotels listed accept credit cards unless otherwise stated. Note that rates vary widely throughout the year. Prices are given in US dollars (US$) unless otherwise stated.

For a key to the symbols, ▷ 2.

ALUMINÉ
LA ALDEA

www.hoteldelaldea.com.ar

The three-star Aldea hotel enjoys dream-like views of the Río Aluminé and its green valley. The well-appointed rooms are compact with comfortable beds and modern bathrooms. The restaurant comes well recommended, serving organic products from local farms.

✉ RP-23 km82, Aluminé
☎ 02942/496340 ✋ $260–$290
ⓘ 25

CUEVA DE LAS MANOS
ESTANCIA CUEVA DE LAS MANOS

www.cuevadelasmanos.net

The friendly *hostería* on the former Estancia Los Toldos is the best place to stay within reach of Cueva de las Manos (▷ 158–159). In a secluded spot, off the main RN-40, the *estancia* offers simple but comfortable rooms in a purpose-built edifice. The *corral* nearby stables horses that you can ride in the grounds and the food is simple but delicious. It's the perfect place to get away from it all.

✉ RN-40 ☎ 011/5237-4043
✋ US$150–US$170, including breakfast and either lunch or dinner ⓘ 6 🚗 RN-40, 60km (37 miles) south of Perito Moreno, clearly signposted off the main road; continue for a further 7km (4 miles) off main road to the *estancia*

EL CALAFATE
EDENIA

www.hoteledenia.com

Run like clockwork by Pascale, the energetic Belgian manager, the Edenia has a lot to recommend it. The hotel's location on a hill, to the west of El Calafate, gives great views of the lake. The hotel is closer to the glacier than the town, which means that you will be picked up last and dropped off first on organized excursions, an advantage in itself. The pleasingly decorated rooms are spacious and comfortable while the service oozes professionalism. A regular shuttle service will get you to the town centre.

✉ Manzana 642 ☎ 02902/497021
✋ US$120–US$140 ⓘ 52 🔄 🍽

MIRADOR DEL LAGO

www.miradordellago.com.ar

If you are looking for a moderately priced hotel to rest your weary limbs, the Mirador del Lago is an excellent option. The rooms are smart and comfortable while the setting is in a large poplar-lined park on the main avenue leading out of town towards the glacier. The restaurant serves wonderful fondues plus a selection of trout and lamb mains. It is worth getting up early for the plentiful buffet breakfast.

✉ Avenida Libertador San Martín 2047 ☎ 02902/493176 🖐 US$95–US$140 🛈 42

LOS NOTROS

www.losnotros.com
Los Notros, opposite to the Glaciar Perito Moreno, possibly enjoys the best location of any hotel in Patagonia. From here, you can watch the light play on the ice without leaving your room. The 32 rooms are faultless, with timber rafters, traditional carpets and incredible views. Fine cuisine in the hotel restaurant includes the house special, a delicious mushroom soup. Minimum stay of two nights; three in high season.

✉ Parque Nacional Los Glaciares, opposite glacier ☎ 02902/499510 🖐 US$550–US$900, including all meals 🛈 32

POSADA LOS ALAMOS

www.posadalosalamos.com
A true five-star hotel in the heart of El Calafate, Los Alamos combines excellent customer service with cutting-edge modernity. The 144 rooms are bright and cheerful, with armchairs and big feather beds. The Humus spa has a large indoor swimming pool, which is the perfect antidote to a hard day's trekking. The

extensive grounds have tennis courts and the Pinar golf course.

✉ Ing. Héctor Mario Guatti 1350 ☎ 02902/491144 🖐 US$170–US$200 🛈 144 🏊 Indoor 🍴

EL CHALTÉN
KAULEM

www.kaulem.com.ar
Kaulem lodge is one of several good hotels in El Chaltén and offers excellent value. The hotel's handsome timber and stone architecture blends well with the natural setting and its giant windows offer some of the finest views in town. All four double rooms enjoy views of the mountains, and the inviting living room, with its tree-trunk columns and comfy furnishings, is a great place to sit back and relax over a glass of wine.

✉ Avenida Antonio Rojo and Comandante Arrua ☎ 02962/493251 🖐 US$140–US$65 🛈 4

PUDU LODGE

www.pudulodge.com
This bijou lodge has sleek minimalist rooms and an environmentally conscious policy. The owners are El Chaltén pioneers and can arrange conventional or customized tours of the national park. Expect excellent service and a comfortable stay.

✉ Las Loicas 97 ☎ 02962/493365 🖐 US$145–US$160 🛈 12

ESQUEL
CANELA

www.canelaesquel.com.ar
Jorge Miglioli is a published photographer while Veronica belongs to a family of Patagonian pioneers and her parents run the wonderful Labrador in Sarmiento (▷ 191). Their family home, Canela, is a comfortable English-style house in the leafy suburb of Villa Ayelén, just outside the town. The five double bedrooms are well appointed and with private bathrooms. Breakfasts are filling and delicious and the owners can offer plenty of useful tips on what to do and where to eat.

✉ Los Notros, Villa Ayelén ☎ 02945/453890 🖐 US$120–US$140 🛈 5 🚗 Take the road to Trevelín from Esquel, 800m (0.5 miles) from the roundabout (traffic circle) turn right into Los Notros, and continue for two-and-a-half blocks to Canela

LAGUNA LARGA LODGE

www.lagunalargalodge.com
This beautiful fishing lodge sits on the bonny banks of the Laguna Larga, on the edge of the Parque Nacional Los Alerces. The lodge is geared towards accommodating anglers but the affable owners, Andres Stewart and his wife Gisela, are happy to host anyone who simply wants to get away from it all. Inventive cuisine is matched by an impressive wine cellar. You will need to request precise directions for getting to the lodge and you must have a prior booking.

✉ Parque Nacional Los Alerces, Esquel (call ahead for directions) ☎ 02322/402231 🖐 US$250–US$280, including all meals 🛈 6

JUNÍN DE LOS ANDES
CALEUFÚ TRAVEL LODGE

www.caleufutravellodge.com.ar
Imitating a North American-style roadside motel, this lodge is conveniently located on the main road in Junín. Accommodation is functional. Choose from small rooms with *lenga*-wood beds and modern bathrooms or *cabañas* with kitchenettes. The friendly owners lived in California and speak excellent

Below *Windswept views from the Parque Nacional Los Glaciares*

Above *Llao Llao hotel in Bariloche, designed by architect Alejandro Bustillo in the 1930s*

English. They also know the true meaning of a good breakfast. They can arrange fishing expeditions, too. ✉ Julio Roca 1323 ☎ 02972/492757 ✋ US$50–US$70 🛈 14

NEUQUÉN
BODEGA VALLE PERDIDO
www.valleperdido.com.ar
With its 18 luxury rooms and suites set among a sea of vineyards, Valle Perdido is one of the leading hotels in northern Patagonia. Wine is the leitmotiv and you can tour the vineyards to see how the wine is made and stored; the barrel vaults and tasting table are a work of art. You can also drink a glass or two of house chardonnay or malbec at the stylish wine bar or over a cordon bleu dinner and sample wine treatments in the spa. The rooms are truly luxurious and each has a mini cellar. The service is superb, too. ✉ RP-7, Picada 6, San Patricio del Chañar ☎ 011/4343-3350 ✋ US$250–US$300 🛈 18 ⬡ ⬡

PARQUE NACIONAL PERITO MORENO
ESTANCIA MENELIK
www.cielospatagonicos.com
This is a true-grit working *estancia*, a short distance outside the Parque Nacional Perito Moreno. Menelik is a great place to break your journey if you are travelling to the Cueva de

las Manos or, alternatively, to use as a base for visiting the parks, lakes and mountains in the vicinity. There are two twin rooms, a double and an apartment comprising two twins. The *estancia* arranges well-organized treks and horse rides out into the Patagonian wilderness. ✉ Take RP-37 from crossroads at Las Horquetas on RN-40 ☎ 011/4765-8085 ✋ US$125–US$140 per person, including all meals 🛈 4

SAN CARLOS DE BARILOCHE
ALDEBARÁN
www.aldebaranpatagonia.com
This charming hotel has 10 ample-size rooms with panoramic windows and balconies, giving views of the lake and mountains. Each room has a private balcony, a CD player and gleaming wooden floors. The suites are particularly impressive, with large bathrooms and living rooms. This secluded hotel is 23km (14 miles) from Bariloche on the San Pedro peninsula. The hotel also has a spa and the Sirius Restaurant is excellent. ✉ Avenida Bustillo km20.4 ☎ 02944/448678 ✋ US$200–US$260 🛈 10 ⬡ Heated indoor and outdoor

AUCA
www.aucabariloche.com.ar
This is a homely guesthouse on the slopes of Cerro Otto, 7km (4.5 miles)

west of Bariloche. Auca offers a handful of comfortable and stylishly decorated suites in a fabulous mock-Tudor house that also affords marvellous views of the lake and mountains. The owners are friendly and helpful in providing information about the local area. ✉ Soldi 231 ☎ 02944/461291 ✋ $300–$340 🛈 3

CABAÑAS DEL ARROYO
www.delarroyo.com.ar
Next to an *arroyo* (brook) that babbles past the *cabañas*, these self-catering holiday homes are some of the best in Bariloche. The rooms are decorated in functional timber and fabric and kitchens are fully equipped. The owner is very helpful and will even lend you a GPS for your car, so you won't get lost when you go off on excursions. ✉ Avenida Bustillo km4.050 ☎ 02944/442082 ✋ $360–$400 (excluding breakfast) 🛈 6

EL CASCO ART HOTEL
www.hotelelcasco.com
A stunning lakeside location 11km (7 miles) west of Bariloche, set amid lush gardens with azaleas and native trees, makes El Casco Art Hotel a very desirable place to stay. Guests are pampered and the rooms are stylish and comfortable. The highlight of this hotel, however, is that each room is dedicated to a different painter and contains works of art. Even the cocktail bar features an installation by a leading Argentine artist. ✉ Avenida Bustillo km11.500 ☎ 02944/463131 ✋ US$300–US$600 🛈 33 ⬡ ⬡ Indoor and outdoor ⬡

CHARMING LUXURY LODGE AND SPA
www.charming-bariloche.com
The understated luxury of this lodge is that rooms have individual spa facilities. The lodge-style rooms are comfortable and each has a Jacuzzi and sauna. The hotel's superb location on the lakeside means that you can admire the fabulous lake views while soaking in a soothing

bath after a hard day's trekking. Massages, colour- and aromatherapy treatments are also available.

✉ Avenida Bustillo km7.500
☎ 02944/462889 🖐 US$360–US$605
ℹ 4 suites 🏊 Outdoor 🍸

LLAO LLAO
www.llaollao.com
A landmark on the landscape around Bariloche, the historic Llao Llao (▷ 174) has moved with the times and offers stylish, contemporary accommodation. The 205 luminous rooms, many of which have lake views, range from economy doubles to a presidential suite. The fabulous Lake Moreno wing houses sumptuous suites with open fires, walk-in closets and double Jacuzzis. There is a top-rate spa, an 18-hole golf course and six restaurants offering filling teas and gourmet dinners.

✉ Avenida Bustillo km25.000
☎ 02944/448530 🖐 US$250–US$460
ℹ 205 🔄 🏊 🍸

PEUMA HUE
www.peuma-hue.com
Peuma Hue means 'place of dreams' and this *estancia* certainly occupies a dream-like location at the southern end of Lake Gutiérrez. Beautifully designed lodges are scattered discreetly around the wooded park, and guests can enjoy horseback riding, walking and birdwatching. The comfortable wooden lodges are well appointed and have huge windows giving fabulous views of the craggy peaks looming above the *estancia*. The food and service are both memorably good.

✉ Cabecera Sur, Lago Gutiérrez, RN-40 km 2014, Bariloche ☎ 02944/15-351031
🖐 US$150–US$210 ℹ 8

SAN MARTÍN DE LOS ANDES
PATAGONIA PLAZA
www.hotelpatagoniaplaza.com.ar
The Patagonia Plaza is an excellent four-star establishment with a heated swimming pool. There is also a spa, where guests can relax with one of the invigorating massages. There

are 89 rooms, ascending in size, comfort and price to a presidential suite, but even the standard rooms are perfectly comfortable. As an added luxury, all bathrooms have a hydromassage.

✉ Avenida San Martín and Rivadavia
☎ 02972/422280 🖐 US$135–US$145
ℹ 89 🔄 🏊 Heated

SARMIENTO
LABRADOR
www.hosterialabrador.com.ar
The owners of this delightful cherry farm a short way from Sarmiento are of Dutch, Boer and British origin. Nicolás and Annelies are the perfect hosts with many a tale to tell of their families' pioneering lives in this remote part of the world. Bed and breakfast can be supplemented by delicious trout or lamb-based dinners. The owners can arrange for you to visit the petrified forests and other attractions, too. The best time to visit is during the cherry harvest in early December.

☎ 0297/489-3329 🖐 US$90–US$110
ℹ 4 🚗 From Esquel on the RN-26 watch for a new bridge (alongside the old bridge) over Río Senguerr, 11km (7 miles) before Sarmiento; turn right 1km (0.5 miles) after the bridge

VILLA LA ANGOSTURA
BAJO CERO
www.bajocerohostel.com
In a place where upmarket accommodation dominates, it is good to know that excellent budget lodgings are available. Bajo Cero is a fairy-tale wooden chalet surrounded by lupin-filled gardens. Inside, there is a range of different rooms (and dorms) to choose from, each with its own bathroom. There is a very well equipped kitchen plus a barbecue grill.

✉ Avenida 7 Lagos 1200 ☎ 02944/495454
🖐 US$25–US$30, excluding breakfast
ℹ 12

LAS BALSAS
www.lasbalsas.com
The supremely elegant 15 rooms are light and combine rustic details, such as wooden floors and timber

pillars, with contemporary artwork and eco-friendly complimentary bath products. The hotel's convenient lakeside location is a huge plus, while the restaurant, helmed by chef Pablo Campoy, offers exquisite cuisine based on local produce, such as lake fish and forest game.

✉ Calle Las Balsas, Villa La Angostura
☎ 02944/494308 ⊘ Closed early May to mid-Jun 🖐 US$250–US$550 ℹ 15
🏊

LA ESCONDIDA
www.hosterialaescondida.com.ar
Standing by a peaceful and photogenic inlet of Lago Nahuel Huapi, La Escondida is a truly beautiful place to stay. The hotel's heated swimming pool is built on the banks of the river and is surrounded by impeccably mown lawns, which slope gently down to the water's edge. The sumptuous rooms offer luxuriously comfortable accommodation with plenty of attention to detail.

✉ Avenida Arrayanes 7014, Puerto Manzano ☎ 02944/475313 🖐 US$145–US$160 ℹ 14 🏊 Outdoor heated

VILLA PEHUENIA
LA BALCONADA
www.hosterialabalconada.com.ar
The name Balconada refers to the balcony-like location of this charming *hostería*, which is perched on a bluff overlooking the shimmering waters of Lago Aluminé, with breathtaking views across to Batea Mahuida volcano. These vistas can be taken in from the rooms, from the rustic *confitería* (café-bistro) and from a deck terrace where you can have lunch. Enjoy the views with a *picada patagónica* (platter of cheese and smoked meats) or a coffee. Down by the lake, there is a small beach where you can swim in crystal-clear waters.

✉ Manzana K, Lote K, Pehuenia III, Villa Pehuenia ☎ 02942/15-473843
🖐 US$110–US$130 ℹ 14 🚗 Leave Villa Pehuenia on RP-13 westwards and turn left at YPF service station; continue, turning left and right, following signs to the *hostería*.

CENTRAL ARGENTINA

The central provinces of Argentina are by no means a bland midriff. The historic city of Córdoba and its Arcadian sierras plus the world-class vineyards and dramatic Andean landscapes of the Cuyo make for some of the country's most alluring sights. Cities such as San Juan and La Rioja, capitals of their respective provinces, are best known for their sizzling summers and unhurried lifestyles, but both offer access to some of the most startling scenery in Argentina. The salmon-pink cliffs of the Parque Nacional Talampaya and the gnarled moonscapes of Ischigualasto are just two of the treats in store for visitors.

Mendoza is synonymous with wine. More than three-quarters of the country's vast production comes from its sun-soaked valleys, where the highest summits of the Andean cordillera act as a fabulous backdrop. Mendoza Province has built an entire tourist industry around its 1,000 or more *bodegas* (wineries), dozens of which are open for tours. The more adventurous will want to go white-water rafting in the Cañón del Atuel and mountaineering in the Alta Montaña. Stamina and proper training, though, are requisites for anyone tempted to climb Cerro Aconcagua, the highest mountain outside the Himalayas at just under 7,000m (22,960ft).

Córdoba is Argentina's second-largest city and in colonial times was one of the leading academic centres in the continent. Its attractions include a cluster of venerable buildings, including the prestigious Jesuit University, the eclectic cathedral with its great cupola and the 18th-century Iglesia Santa Teresa, along with a noteworthy art collection, a slew of excellent restaurants and a lively nightlife. Ever since domestic tourism began in the early 20th century, the Sierras of Córdoba Province have been a major destination. Resorts like ultra-Germanic Villa General Belgrano, bucolic Nono and Jesús María, famed for its Jesuit *estancia*, continue to attract hordes of tourists every summer and during Holy Week.

ACONCAGUA AND THE ALTA MONTAÑA

The tallest section of the Andean cordillera lies a short way west of Mendoza. Determined mountaineers may wish to climb the king of them all, Cerro Aconcagua. Others may prefer to take in the fabulous highland scenery, go for a trek in the uplands or make use of the ski resorts up in the Andean foothills. The RN-7 to Santiago de Chile doubles up as the Alta Montaña Route, signposted out of Mendoza to the south of the city, first winding past the spa town of Cacheuta and then passing through Potrerillos, a water-sports centre by a huge new reservoir.

USPALLATA AND THE ROAD UP

The multi-hued Sierra de Uspallata forms a dramatic backdrop for the poplar trees and fruit orchards of Uspallata, a village 54km (33.5 miles) north of Potrerillos on the RN-7. The main attraction is the mild climate and many people from Mendoza come here in the summer months to escape the heat. You might like to visit the Bóvedas de Uspallata (tel 0261/155570755; Tue–Sun 10–7; $2), an 18th-century iron smelting works, 1km (0.5 miles) to the north of the village.

The RN-7 heads westwards following the Río Mendoza and an ancient Inca trail, squeezing through tunnels and canyons stained red, green and yellow by iron, copper and sulphur. A little over 60km (37 miles) from Uspallata is the ski resort of Villa Los Penitentes, a series of rocky pinnacles said to resemble hooded monks. There are 26 ski pistes, ranging from nursery slopes to the black 'Las Paredes'. The chairlifts also run in the summer (weekends) to the summit of Cerro San Antonio (3,200m/10,496ft), where you can enjoy sweeping views.

A little farther on is the Puente del Inca, a natural stone arch over the Río de las Cuevas that crosses a bone-dry valley. Beneath the bridge are the ruins of a thermal resort built in the 1940s but swept away by a flood. You are no longer allowed to cross the archway or enter the old spa buildings as both are dangerously unstable, but you can still get close. Visit the tourist office in Uspallata for more information (Las Heras s/n; tel 0264/420002; daily 8–10) about all these sights.

CERRO ACONCAGUA

The ice-topped mass of Cerro Aconcagua (6,959m/22,825ft) is the world's tallest mountain outside the Himalayas. The summit is iced with five glaciers and surrounded by more than a dozen peaks over 5,000m (16,400ft). The mountain is a sacred place for the indigenous Huarpes, Mapuches and the Incas, who made human sacrifices on its summit.

Aconcagua is a popular challenge for team expeditions and go-it-alone climbers alike. Two or three thousand people, with varying levels of experience, make it to the top every year but many more turn back either because they have not properly acclimatized to the altitude or because of sudden bad weather.

INFORMATION

www.aconcagua.com
www.aconcagua.com.ar
www.aconcagua.mendoza.gov.ar
⊞ 344 B9 ⊠ Aconcagua, Provincia de Mendoza 🛈 Dirección de Atención Visitantes Parque Provincial Aconcagua, San Martín 1143, Mendoza; tel 0261/425-8751; Mon–Fri 8–6, Sat–Sun 9–1
✈ Flights to Mendoza airport
🚍 From Mendoza airport, drive south along RN-40, turn in westerly direction on RN-7 (direction Chile) and keep going past Uspallata ✈ Contact one of the four main walking operators in Aconcagua to find a guide (▷ 220)

TIPS

❯❯ If you intend to climb Aconcagua, you'll need to visit in the summer. Give yourself a couple of weeks to acclimatize and pace yourself.
❯❯ Aconcagua can be approached from the south, west or east. The western Ruta Normal from the Plaza de Mulas (4,230m/13,874ft) is the preferred route for less experienced mountaineers. Experts take the Glaciar de los Polacos route, from a base camp at Plaza Argentina, reached via a long track that starts near Punta de Vacas. The truly adventurous opt for the south face. To reach the base camp at Plaza Francia, branch off from the Plaza de Mulas trail at a spot called Confluencia (3,368m/11,047ft).

Opposite *Spectacular Cerro Aconcagua*
Below *Puente del Inca, a natural stone bridge, with the ruins of a 1940s spa*

CÓRDOBA

INFORMATION

www.cordobaturismo.gov.ar

🕂 341 F8 ✉ Córdoba, Provincia de Córdoba 🔢 Cabildo, Independencia, Plaza San Martín ☎ 0351/434-1200 🕔 Daily 8–8 🚌 Buses from all major destinations ✈ Daily flights from Buenos Aires and other major cities (less frequent) including Salta 🚐 Ingeniero Aeronáutico Ambrosio L.V. Taravella International Airport at Pajas Blancas is 9km (5.5 miles) north of city; transfer by minibus (Transfer Express) or remise

INTRODUCTION

Busy and boisterous, historic Córdoba is Argentina's second-biggest city and has an illustrious past stretching back to colonial times, when it had the continent's second most important university after Lima, in Peru, and a number of reputed Jesuit colleges that earned it the nickname of Córdoba La Docta (the Learned). The university and colleges have held on to their reputation and the city remains a powerhouse of industry and commerce. Unfortunately, it has shed some of its importance as a domestic tourist destination and in recent years has lost some of its charisma.

Nevertheless it is still an interesting city to visit, with its colonial and neo-colonial architecture, fine art collections and lively nightlife. The Cordobeses are perhaps the city's greatest assets, known for their cheerful hospitality, their sense of humour and their elegance, as well as their distinctive accent.

Jerónimo Luis de Cabrera, governor of Tucumán, founded the city on 6 July 1573 and named it after his city of origin in Spain's Andalusia. The Jesuits quickly took over a block of the city in the 1580s and founded a university in 1621. Córdoba's prosperity was inextricably linked to the Jesuits, who had a number of *estancias* dotted strategically around the city—these were vital for supplying the city with water and food. The decision by Spain to expel the Jesuits in 1767 and the creation of the Viceroyalty of the River Plate, with its capital in Buenos Aires, meant Córdoba slipped into decline and became a backwater for a decade or two until a new governor, Rafael de Sobremonte, expanded the city and secured its water supplies.

In the early 19th century, the city was on the front line of the Argentine War of Independence (1810–18), in which local hero Deán Funes played a leading part. The opening of a railway line from the capital in the 1870s began Córdoba's boom years, reflected in the city's handsome turn-of-the-century architecture, as buildings went up to house banks, theatres and aristocratic families. The city then expanded in a southerly direction as urban planning included the Parque Sarmiento, laid out by landscape architect Charles Thays. Large numbers of immigrants flooded in from Europe and the Middle East, making Córdoba a microcosm of the country in ethnic terms.

Above *The floodlit Cabildo and cathedral, on the western flank of Plaza San Martín*

The city's 20th-century history also echoes that of the rest of the country, with a series of booms and busts, interspersed by periods of political turmoil, not least the Cordobazo protests against military dictatorship in the late 1960s. The city has found it harder than others to get over the 2001 crisis but the signs of recovery are visible.

WHAT TO SEE

PLAZA SAN MARTÍN
Pedestrian-only and immaculately kept, Córdoba's main square, Plaza San Martín, has an equestrian statue of General San Martín, hero of Argentine independence (▷ 29), placed here in 1916 to commemorate 100 years of full independence from Spain. The western flank comprises two of the city's major landmarks, the monumental cathedral, inspired by the cathedral in the Spanish city of Salamanca, and the elegant two-storey Cabildo, the former city headquarters dating to colonial times.
✚ 199 B2

THE CATHEDRAL
The cathedral, the oldest in the country, is a rather ponderous mass on the outside with its decorated baroque mouldings and topped by Romanesque domes and towers. The finer details are provided by heraldic cherubim wearing feather skirts, crafted by indigenous Guaraní sculptors who worked on the cathedral's earliest construction in the late 16th century. The entrance is admirable, though, past a pair of intricately wrought iron gates and an imposing mausoleum to Deán Funes (on your left). The beautiful wooden doors originally belonged to the Jesuit temple and were moved here after the cathedral was completed in the late 18th century. Inside, the decoration is an eclectic melange of extreme baroque and neoclassical, with beautiful Valencian floor tiles, a richly embellished rococo pulpit and wall and ceiling frescoes influenced by Tiepolo and painted by local artist Emilio Caraffa.
✚ 199 B2 ✉ Plaza San Martín 🕐 Daily 9–6 ✋ Free

CABILDO
To the north of the cathedral and complementing it with its harmonious arches along the Recova, or gallery, is Córdoba's Cabildo. It was built in the 16th century, like the cathedral, but the facade was added at the end of the 18th century, under governor Sobremonte. The building is used for official ceremonies but its charming inner courtyard has frequent concerts and alfresco tango.
✚ 199 B2 ✉ Plaza San Martín ☎ 0351/434-1202 🕐 Varies ✋ Free

MONASTERIO Y IGLESIA DE SANTA TERESA
Across from the cathedral, to the south, is another historic set of religious buildings dedicated to St. Teresa of Ávila. The Iglesia Santa Teresa and adjoining Monasterio de las Carmelitas Decalzadas de Santa Teresa de Jesús date from the early 18th century and their sumptuous pink and cream facades, set off by fine wrought-iron work, belie their rather sober interiors. For more lavish artwork, visit the Museo de Arte Religioso Juan de Tejeda (Wed–Sat 9.30–12.30; $5), named after a local aristocrat who claimed to be related to the saint. There are several outstanding paintings from the Cusco in Peru and some beautiful statuary. Any visit is rewarded by access to the charming courtyards filled with jasmine and orange.
✚ 199 B2 ✉ Independencia 122 🕐 Wed–Sat 9.30–12.30 ✋ $5

MANZANA JESUÍTICA
Also known as the Manzana de los Jesuitas or the Manzana de las Luces, this complex lies a few blocks southwest of the Plaza San Martín and is palpable evidence of the Jesuits' influence on the early development of the city.

TIPS
» Córdoba has found it harder than other cities to recover from the recession and there are serious social problems sometimes manifesting themselves in petty crime. Make sure you stay on the beaten track, take taxis after dark and do not linger in areas where there are few passers-by.
» The city is lacking when it comes to really good accommodation so book well ahead to avoid disappointment. Alternatively, stay in the sierras and visit the city as a day trip.
» Avoid the city in the height of summer, when little goes on and the temperatures are high, and in mid-winter, when the continental climate can be bitingly cold.
» Walking around the city is the best way to see the major sights and you can hop in a taxi if necessary (they are cheaper here than in Buenos Aires). Buses are not convenient, especially in the central area.

Below *The 17th-century Iglesia de la Compañia de Jesús, part of the Manzana Jesuítica complex*

The main church, the Iglesia (or Templo) de la Compañía de Jesús, was inaugurated in 1671, making it the oldest Jesuit church still surviving in Argentina. Designed by the Antwerp naval architect Philippe Lemaire, it has a fabulous Paraguayan cedar-wood roof built in the shape of a ship's hull. Its rough-hewn facade, pitted with niches favoured by pigeons, is severe but inside the austerity is broken with a series of 50 painted panels depicting the history of the Jesuits. There is also a stunning baroque altarpiece attributed to the great Cusco school in Peru.

To the south of the church is the main building of the Jesuit University, now the Universidad Nacional de Córdoba. It is Argentina's oldest university, dating from 1613, and still one of the most prestigious in the country. You can visit the great library, with its valuable collection of religious artefacts, maps and incunabula; the Salón de Grados, with its sumptuous ceiling fresco; the Museo Histórico; plus the beautiful interior patios draped with pink bougainvilleas. Next door, the Colegio Nacional de Nuestra Señora de Montserrat dates from the late 18th century, though the all-male school was founded a century earlier and women were not accepted as students until 1998. The neo-colonial facade, painted pink with finely wrought window grilles, was remodelled in the 1920s but inside you can see the original Jesuit cloisters.

✚ 199 A2 ✉ Obispo Trejo 242 ☎ 0351/433-2080 🕐 Tue–Sun 9–1, 4–8. Guided tours 10, 11, 5 and 6 ✋ $5

MORE TO SEE

MUSEO DE BELLAS ARTES DR. GENARO PÉREZ

www.agora.com.ar/museogp

The city's main art museum is two blocks west and half a block north of the Cabildo. The house was built in 1905, in the style of a French mansion, for a local collector who bequeathed his collection to the city in the 1940s. The building, including its Louis XVI facade and sumptuous art nouveau lift, were lovingly restored in the 1990s. The collection focuses on local artists, such as the eponymous Genaro Pérez, along with Emilio Caraffa and more modern Argentine masters like Berni, Segui and Soldi. The temporary collections are often well worth seeing, too.

✚ 199 B1 ✉ Avenida General Paz 33 ☎ 0351/428-5905 🕐 Tue–Sat 10–8 ✋ Free

MUSEO HISTÓRICO MARQUÉS DE SOBREMONTE

www.cba.gov.ar

To find out more about the city's history, you might like to visit the provincial history museum, a block to the east of Plaza San Martín. The former residence of

Below Exhibits in the Museo de Bellas Artes Dr. Genaro Pérez, the city's principal art gallery

CORDOBA

0   250 m
0   250 yds

governor Sobremonte in the late 18th century, this is the only surviving colonial house in the city. The building is constructed of whitewashed brick, set off only by a delicate iron balcony and a pair of stone lions guarding the entrance. The interior is a reconstruction of 18th- and 19th-century domestic life in Córdoba, complemented by a collection of mainly 18th-century art, including some masterpieces from the Cusco school.

➕ 199 C2 ✉ Rosario de Santa 218 ☎ 0351/433-1661 ⏰ Tue–Fri 10–3, Sat 9–2 ✋ Adult/child $5

NUEVA CÓRDOBA AND PARQUE SARMIENTO

The Parque Sarmiento, designed by Charles Thays, is planted with thousands of trees and forms the city's lung. It is home also to sports facilities and a small zoo (www.zoo-cordoba.com.ar; daily 10–6.30; $20). The residential area created around the park is still known as Nueva Córdoba (New Córdoba) and is a mass of handsome villas and high-rise brick apartment blocks favoured by students at the massive university.

➕ Off map 199 C3

MUSEO SUPERIOR DE BELLAS ARTES EVITA

On the Plaza España is the fabulous Palacio Ferreyra, built in 1916 by the French Beaux Arts architect Paul Ernest Sanson (1836–1918). Set off by beautiful gardens, it has fine art nouveau details, such as stained-glass windows. Reopened in 2007 as the Museo Superior de Bellas Artes Evita, after years as a rather inactive art gallery, its sumptuous rooms are used to great effect to display local and national art works and occasional top-rate temporary exhibitions. One of the gallery's newest additions is a number of Picassos, donated by a museum in Madrid in 2010.

➕ Off map 199 A3 ✉ Avenida Hipólito Yrigoyen 511 ☎ 0351/434-3636 ⏰ Tue–Sun 10–8 ✋ Adult $5, child (under 12) free; free on Wed

Below *Works at the Museo de Bellas Artes Dr. Genaro Pérez, displayed in an elegant room in the 1905 French-style mansion*

CAÑÓN DEL ATUEL

www.argentinaturismo.com.ar/
sanrafael/atuel.php

One of the main attractions in the southern Mendoza Province is the Cañón del Atuel, a dramatic ravine formed by the river as it flows between two reservoirs, a short distance southwest of San Rafael (▷ 211). In addition to the stunning mountain-and-valley scenery, you can enjoy windsurfing, kayaking or, more popularly, rafting trips on the water.

Start at the Embalse El Nihuil, by taking the RP-144 towards Malargüe and then ascending the Cuesta de los Terneros to its 1,300m (4,264ft) summit for views of the valley before heading south along the RP-180. Windsurfers can rent boards at the Club de Pescadores (tel 02627/426087; www.clubdepescadoressr.com.ar; daily 9–6; $15), on the northeastern shores of the reservoir. The RP-173 (mostly unpaved) takes you northeast through a tight gorge formed by brightly coloured striped cliffs. Erosion has resulted in strange rock formations, many with amusing anthropomorphic shapes earning

Below *Paragliding is one of the adventure sports on offer at the resort of La Cumbre*

them names such as La Monja (the Nun) and El Sapo (the Toad).

Beyond a pair of dams, used for hydroelectric power as well as providing the region's water, you catch sight of the second reservoir, turquoise Embalse Valle Grande. Look out for its highly photogenic rock island, known as El Submarino (the Submarine). A high cliff-side road affords breathtaking vistas of the waters, which contrast vividly with the ochre mountainside beyond. At the northern end of the reservoir is the stretch of the Río Atuel where you can go white-water rafting (▷ 220). Although the most challenging features on the river are some mild rapids, these well-organized trips give you a chance to see the fine bucolic scenery along the Atuel valley, as you travel down river towards San Rafael.

🚩 344 C11 ✉ Cañón del Atuel, Mendoza 🚹 San Rafael (▷ 211) 🚌 From San Rafael take RP-144 in the direction of Malargüe and then the RP-180 to Embalse El Nihuil, where the route begins ◀ Tours from San Juan and San Rafael

CERRO COLORADO

www.turismocordoba.com.ar/cerrocolorado

The Reserva Cultural Natural Cerro Colorado, named for the reddish hue of its rocks, covers 300sq km (115sq miles) in the north of Córdoba Province. The reserve is protected for the beauty of its scenery and the important pre-Columbian rock paintings that decorate the mountainside. After you turn off the RN-9, a dirt track twists and turns into the reserve and, just before the village of Cerro Colorado, you must cross a ford. The village itself is a collection of a few houses in a deep valley, dominated by three peaks around 800m (2,624ft) each.

To explore the reserve, you'll need to take one of the guided tours that leave from the *guardería* (rangers' office) at the entrance to the village. The guides point out the native flora plus the fascinating petroglyphs. These ancient drawings depict llamas and condors and abstract geometric figures and were scraped

onto the pinkish sandstone rock face sometime between AD1000–1600. Minerals and plant pigments were used for this intriguing wall art, some of which has sadly been vandalized over the years. One of the drawings, of a sun god, is now in the British Museum.

✉ Cerro Colorado, Provincia de Córdoba ⏰ Daily 7–1, 2–8 ✋ $8, guided tours free 🚌 Bus from Córdoba to Santa Elena, then remise to Cerro Colorado 🚗 Take RN-9 northwards from Córdoba, via Jesús María, then take right-hand fork before Villa del Totoral and follow signs to Cerro Colorado after San José de la Dormida

CÓRDOBA

▷ 196–199.

LA CUMBRE

www.alacumbre.com

The RN-38, leading to La Rioja from Córdoba, threads along the touristy Punilla Valley, through a number of famed but rather faded resorts, such as Cosquín and La Falda, to the north of the sprawling Villa Carlos Paz, once the pearl of Córdoba's resorts. Of all these towns and villages, the one that has been saved from over-development is La Cumbre. This sedate little village has a refined air and still offers many of the attractions of the neighbouring resorts, such as paragliding, skydiving and mountain-biking, as well as superb rambling and horseback riding.

Although, many people visit La Cumbre simply to relax and enjoy the beautiful mountain scenery in the lee of the mighty Cerro Uritorco (1,950m/6,396ft), a sacred mountain and the site of frequent alleged UFO spottings. At 1,100m (3,608ft) above sea level and full of trees, the village enjoys a wonderfully temperate climate, though snow is not unheard of in the middle of winter.

🚩 341 F8 ✉ La Cumbre, Provincia de Córdoba 🚹 Avenida San Martín and Avenida Caraffa ☎ 03548/452966 ⏰ Daily 8–10 🚌 Buses from Córdoba 🚗 50km (31 miles) north of Córdoba city, along the RN-9 in the direction Santiago del Estero and then take clearly signposted turn-off to left

ISCHILÍN

www.turismocordoba.com.ar/ischilin

Between Jesús María (▷ below) and the resorts along the Punilla Valley, such as La Cumbre (▷ 200), is the less-explored area of the Sierras Chicas (Small Mountains), characterized by craggy moorland and pockets of meadowland that have been farmed for centuries, notably by the Jesuits who settled here in the 18th century. Take the scenic road leading northwest from Jesús María, past the beautiful Jesuit church at the Estancia Santa Catalina, and continue on towards Ongamira, where the well-signposted Grutas (daily 9–6; $5), caves scooped out of the sandstone rocks by erosion, are a minor attraction.

A dirt road leads north to one of the most picturesque villages in the province, tiny Ischilín, where the bright yellow facade of an early-18th-century Jesuit church, Nuestra Señora del Rosario, overlooks the sleepy green plaza. Influential painter Fernando Fader (1882–1935) came here for the climate in the hope of curing his terminal tuberculosis and his brick house now holds the Museo Casa de Fernando Fader (Tue 9–3, Wed–Sat 9–7, Sun 1–7; free). In addition to one of the Master's fine oil paintings depicting the village church, there is also a beautiful garden. You can stay overnight in the village at the delightful Hostería La Rosada (▷ 227), run by Fader's proud descendents.

➕ 341 F8 ✉ Ischilín, Provincia de Córdoba ✈ Daily flights to Córdoba from Buenos Aires and other major destinations 🚌 From Córdoba, head northwards along the RN-9 to Jesús María and turn westwards to Santa Catalina and follow signposts to Ischilín

JESÚS MARÍA

www.turismocordoba.com.ar/jesusmaria

The village of Jesús María is worth visiting for one of the Jesuit *estancias* that, together with the Jesuit buildings (▷ 197–198) in Córdoba, became a UNESCO World Cultural Heritage Site in 2000. The otherwise tranquil village stirs to life once a year for the Festival Nacional de la Doma y el Folklore, held in early January in an open-air theatre a short distance to the north. The village's 18th-century *estancia* now houses the Museo Jesuítico Nacional (Oct–Mar Mon–Fri 8–7, Sat–Sun 3–7; Apr–Sep Mon–Fri 8–7, Sat–Sun 2–6; $5, free Mon). The U-shaped main building is used for temporary exhibitions plus permanent displays dating from the *estancia's* heyday. Whereas the exterior, with its rough-hewn walls, looks like a fortress, the pristine whitewashed courtyard, with its two-tiered arched galleries, suggests monastic calm.

➕ 341 F8 ✉ Jesus María, Provincia de Córdoba 🚌 Buses from Córdoba 🚗 From Córdoba, take the RN-20 motorway (toll-road) to Villa Carlos Paz and then RN-38 northwards via Cosquín and La Falda in the direction of Cruz del Eje

LAS LEÑAS

www.laslenas.com

Backed by Cerro Las Leñas, the region's highest peak (4,351m/14,271ft) and the distinctively serrated Cerro Torrecillas (3,771m/12,368ft), Las Leñas, in southern Mendoza Province, is Argentina's top winter sports resort. The national, Brazilian and South American skiing championships are held here in August, while snow-polo, snow-rugby and snow-volleyball fixtures and skiwear fashion shows also take place here. Otherwise excellent skiing and snowboarding are to be had every June to August, although there have been a few disappointingly dry winters over the years. The extensive resort covers a total area of 350sq km (135sq miles), with 28 pistes, ranging from gentle nursery slopes to a couple of sheer black runs, while cross-country skiing and off-piste are also possible. With its breathtaking highland setting and pleasant daytime temperatures, Las Leñas is also developing into summer resort, with horse riding, hiking and rock climbing all on offer.

➕ 344 B11 ✉ Las Leñas, Provincia de Mendoza ℹ Malargüe (▷ opposite) ✈ Flights to Malargüe or San Rafael airports from Buenos Aires 🚗 Head due west from Mendoza to the Malargüe section of the RN-40, and 30km (18.5 miles) south of El Sosneado turn in a westerly direction (signposted Los Molles and Las Leñas). The resort is 50km (31 miles) from RN-40 and nearly 200km (124 miles) southwest of San Rafael

Above *Estancia Santa Catalina*

MALARGÜE

www.malargue.gov.ar

Unassuming Malargüe, the biggest town in the southernmost reaches of Mendoza Province, lies within easy reach of some of the country's most spectacular landscapes; the black and tan plains of La Payunia (▷ 202), the Caverna de la Brujas cave and the Reserva Faunística Laguna de Llancanelo, a shining lagoon crammed with aquatic birdlife. There is little to see in the town apart from a rather quirky museum and a scientific research centre, but it has a couple of good hotels and basic amenities.

Spring is the best time to see the Reserva Faunística Laguna de Llancanelo (daily 9–6; free), but throughout the year the shallow lagoon's mirror-still waters are home to large flocks of flamingos, at times so numerous that from a distance the lake's surface appears to be pink. Other birds you might spot are black-necked swans, ducks, grebes and teals. It is best to go on an organized tour from Malargüe (▷ 221) with someone who knows the terrain and the fauna, to get the most out of visiting the lagoon.

The Caverna de las Brujas (visits only with a guide from the tourist office in Malargüe; children under 7 not allowed) lies at an altitude of 1,900m (6,232ft), southwest of Malargüe. The road leading there clambers over the Cuesta del Chihuido pass, offering fabulous views of the Sierra de Palauco to the east. The whole area is covered by a thick layer of marine sedimentary rock, through which water has seeped, creating karstic cave systems, including the Caverna, which was possibly used by pre-Columbian shamans as a meeting place. Inside, there are some amazing rock formations, including impressive stalactites and stalagmites.

➕ 344 C12 ✉ Malargüe, Provincia de Mendoza ℹ RN-40 norte s/n
☎ 02627/471659 🕐 Daily 8am–9.30pm
🚌 Buses from Mendoza and San Rafael
🚌 Drive due south from Mendoza via RN-40 or in a southwesterly direction from San Rafael 🚗 Tours from Malargüe

MENDOZA
▷ 204–207.

NONO
www.turismocordoba.com.ar/nono
www.minaclavero.gov.ar
Over in western Córdoba Province, little Nono lies 175km (108.5 miles) southwest of Córdoba, beyond the great crags of the Sierra de Achala, and 5km (3 miles) from the popular resort of Mina Clavero. The village is little more than a small collection of brick buildings around a picturesque plaza and the real reason for coming here is to visit one of the country's most original museums, the Museo Rocsen (tel 03544/498218; daily 9–6; $5), 5km (3 miles) from the centre of town along a good dirt road.

Juan Santiago Bouchon, a former French diplomat whose anthropological interests, compulsive collecting and eclectic tastes are reflected in the museum's massive collection, founded the museum in the late 1960s. There are nearly 12,000 exhibits, ranging from

Incan mummies to butterflies and seashells, so it's a good idea to collect a floor plan when you enter the museum. The museum is housed in an impressive building with a red sandstone facade decorated with 49 statues of major historical figures, including Che Guevara.

➕ 345 F9 ✉ Nono, Provincia de Córdoba
ℹ Mina Clavero (10km/6 miles north via RN-20) ✉ Avenida Mitre and Avenida San Martín ☎ 03544/470171 🕐 Daily 8–10
🚌 10km (6 miles) south of Mina Clavero, junction with RP-15; RN-20 west from Córdoba, via Villa Carlos Paz

PARQUE NACIONAL TALAMPAYA
▷ 208.

PARQUE PROVINCIAL ISCHIGUALASTO
▷ 209.

RESERVA PROVINCIAL LA PAYUNIA
www.recursosnaturales.mendoza.gov.ar/payunia.html
www.karentravel.com.ar
In southern Mendoza Province, the Reserva Provincial La Payunia is a wild area of amazing beauty, sometimes referred to as the Patagonia Mendocina as it marks the transition into Patagonia proper. The mighty Volcán Payún Matrú (3,690m/12,103ft) and its neighbour Volcán Payún Liso (both inactive) loom over the landscape and the surrounding barren plain is home to large flocks of guanacos, which stand out against the dark volcanic backdrop of the Pampa Negra. This huge expanse of chocolate-coloured lava was caused by relatively recent volcanic eruptions, dating back hundreds rather than thousands of years, and 'fresh' lava flows can be seen throughout the park along with huge boulders of igneous rock spewed out by the volcanos. By contrast, oxides in the lava of the neighbouring Pampa Roja lend it a pink hue. To visit, you will need to be accompanied by a guide or approved tour operator such as the excellent Karen Travel (▷ 221).

➕ 344 C12 ✉ Reserva Provincial La Payunia, Provincia de Mendoza 🚌 From Malargüe, continue past the Caverna de las Brujas, cross the Río Grande at Bardas Blancas and continue for approximately100km (62 miles), following the river valley. Cross the river at a narrow gorge, La Pasarela. Access to the park is via a road heading east, at El Zampal 🚗 Daily tours from Malargüe

LA RIOJA
www.turismolarioja.gov.ar
The best time to visit the laid-back provincial capital of La Rioja is when the orange blossoms are out and the jacarandas ablaze, from October to November. Avoid midsummer (December), when temperatures have been known to exceed 40°C (104°F).

On the west side of Plaza 25 de Mayo is the dazzling white Casa de Gobierno, built in a neo-colonial style with pronounced Andalusian influences. On the southern edge is the cathedral, an early 20th-century building with a huge Italianate cupola, neo-gothic campaniles and Byzantine elements in the facade. Inside you can see the 17th-century image of St. Nicholas of Bari, which was carved in Peru. Save some time to visit the Museo Folklórico (tel 03822/428500; Tue–Fri 9–1, 5–8, Sat–Sun 9–1; $2), where you can admire a reconstruction of a 19th-century Riojano house complete with wine cellar, *gaucho* paraphernalia and a fully equipped kitchen. The fascinating section on local mythology features a set of beautiful terracotta statuettes representing the pantheon of South American deities, including Pachamama, Mother Earth, and Zapam-Zucum, the goddess of children, with her stylized breasts in the shape of *algarrobo*-pods.

➕ 340 D7 ✉ La Rioja, Provincia de La Rioja
ℹ Pelago B. Luna 345 ☎ 03822/426345
🕐 Daily 8–1, 5–8 🚌 Buses from all major destinations ✈ Regular flights from Buenos Aires (at least once daily). Vicente Almandos Almonacid airport is 7km (4 miles) east of the city

Opposite *The ornate interior of La Rioja's early 20th-century cathedral*

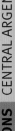

INFORMATION

www.turismo.mendoza.gov.ar

✚ 344 C10 **✉** Mendoza, Provincia de Mendoza **ℹ** Avenida San Martín 1143 **☎** 0261/420-2800 **🕐** Daily 8–2, 5–9 **🚌** Buses from all major destinations **✈** Ing. Francisco J. Gabrielli International Airport at Plumerillos, 7km (4 miles) north of the city **✈** Regular flights from Buenos Aires and Santiago de Chile

INTRODUCTION

The modern, vibrant city of Mendoza came into being after a massive earthquake struck on 20 March 1861, which reduced the old city to ruins and killed more than a third of its population. The French urban architect Ballofet swiftly rebuilt the city, with anti-seismic buildings, broad streets lined with plane trees, large squares and reassuringly low buildings. One of the largest cities in Argentina, Mendoza now sprawls along the valley of the Río Mendoza, around 100km (62 miles) east of the highest section of the Andean cordillera and their snowy summits can be seen from the city centre.

García Hurtado de Mendoza, head of the Spanish colony, first settled Mendoza in 1561 when he sent an expedition over the Andes led by Pedro del Castillo. Isolated from the rest of Chile by the great barrier of the Andes, the city soon created its own wealth, using the extensive grid of pre-Hispanic irrigation canals to plant vines and supply the rest of the country with communion wine. When the Viceroyalty of the River Plate was created in 1777, Mendoza was ruled from Córdoba and later San Martín trained his liberation Army of the Andes here before defeating the royalist troops at the Battle of Maipú in 1818. Taking a while to recover after the 1861 earthquake, Mendoza began to flourish again after the arrival of the railway in the 1880s.

At the centre of the city is the huge Plaza Independencia, formed by four smaller squares, each with a distinct character (▷ 205). The vast Parque General San Martín tilts up a hill just to the west of downtown and commands great vistas of the city and the valley. The city's economy relies heavily on its giant wine industry and, in addition to leading adventure excursions into the nearby mountains, the city's tour operators focus on ferrying tourists to the many *bodegas* that open their doors to the public. Most of the wineries are found in the fertile vineyard country to the south of the city, but the historic Bodega Escorihuela is situated in Godoy Cruz, a southern suburb.

A short way to the south of the city are the small municipalities of Luján de Cuyo and Maipú, where there are more wineries, plus a couple of museums, one dedicated to wine and the other to the leading 19th-century Argentine painter Fernando Fader.

Above *One of Argentina's largest cities, Mendoza lies in the valley of the Río Mendoza, with views of the Andean cordillera*

WHAT TO SEE
PLAZA INDEPENDENCIA

Two blocks by two, Plaza Independencia is the heart of modern Mendoza, and the meeting place of the city's two main thoroughfares—Avenida Sarmiento (east to west) and Avenida Mitre (north to south). Shaded by acacias, magnolias and sycamores, it is constantly buzzing with people and vendors selling wares. The plaza also hosts events throughout the year, including rock, folk and jazz concerts and outdoor movie screenings. The centrepiece is a monumental fountain and a mosaic mural depicting the story of independence. Here, you will also find the Museo Municipal de Arte Moderno (tel 0261/425-7279; Tue–Sat 9–1, 4–8, Sun–Mon 4–8; free), which has temporary exhibitions of contemporary art. The eastern end of the plaza hosts a crafts fair (10–6) at weekends while the western end is dominated by a huge steel structure, dating from 1942, with coloured lights that form a massive national coat of arms at night.

Along Calle Chile, on the square's western edge, you can see the Colégio Nacional Agustín Alvarez, an art nouveau school built of reinforced concrete, and the neoclassical facade of the Teatro Independencia. Look out, also, for the Park Hyatt hotel, which kept the art-deco facade of the former Plaza Hotel and is famous because Eva and Juan Perón stayed there soon after meeting.

✚ 207 C2

PARQUE GENERAL SAN MARTÍN

www.parques.mendoza.gov.ar

About ten blocks west of Plaza Independencia along the gently sloping Avenida Sarmiento, the glorious Parque General San Martín overlooks the city and is criss-crossed by avenues of planes. Its 400ha (988 acres) were landscaped in 1897 by Charles Thays and updated in the 1940s by local architect Daniel Ramos Correas. It contains the city's football stadium, an open-air theatre that hosts the annual wine festival, Fiesta de la Vendimia, every March, an anthropological museum, a majestic monument to the Army of the Andes, a rowing lake, a tennis club, the university campus, an equestrian riding club and several restaurants. There are more than 50,000 trees of 750 varieties, but among the most imposing features are the Avenida de los Plátanos and Avenida de las Palmeras, curving avenues of tall plane trees and Canary Island palms, and the fabulous Rose Garden with 500 varieties plus ancient wisterias.

TIPS

›› Mendoza is a large city but attractions inside the urban limits are thin on the ground. To get to the wineries more easily, base yourself in one of the leafy suburbs, such as Chacras de Coria.

›› Just before and during the famous wine festival in March, the Fiesta de la Vendimia, the city fills up with visitors and hotel beds are at a premium.

›› While walking around the city, watch out for treacherously deep drainage ditches along many of its thoroughfares.

›› The street naming system is complicated, with many of the avenues changing name several times. Signposting is poor too, so get a map of the city and be prepared to ask for directions.

›› To get around the huge Parque General San Martín it is best to rent a bike, take a horse and cart, or catch a bus.

Below left *Tree-shaded Plaza Independencia, in the heart of the city*
Below *Detail of the Fuente de los Continentes in Parque General San Martín*

Above *A café on Avenida Sarmiento*

The park's principal entrance is through a pair of bronze and wrought-iron gates, topped with a condor, at the far western end of Avenida Emilio Civit. A road along the northern edge of the park reaches a roundabout featuring the Caballitos de Marly, a replica in Carrara marble of the monumental horses on the Place de la Concorde in Paris. Southwest of the entrance, by the rowing lake, is the impressive Fuente de los Continentes, a dramatic set of sculptures representing humankind.

✚ Off map 207 A1

MUSEO DE CIENCIAS NATURALES Y ANTROPOLÓGICAS

South of the lake in the Parque General San Martín is the Museo de Ciencias Naturales y Antropológicas, housed in a 1930s building with a maritime design. Among the collections of stuffed animals, ancient fossils, native crafts and mummies from the Andean sacrifices, you can see shrunken heads from Ecuador and remains of dinosaurs found in southern Mendoza. There are often interesting temporary exhibitions, too.

✚ Off map 207 A1 ✉ Parque General San Martín ☎ 0261/428-7666 🕐 Tue–Fri 8–1, 2–7 Sat–Sun 3–7 ✋ $5

CITY ZOO

www.zoo.mendoza.gov.ar

Within Parque General San Martín, a 20-minute walk from the entrance, is the city's excellent zoo, on the flanks of Cerro de la Gloria. Apart from the monkeys, lions, elephants and hippos, of which there are plenty, there are lush gardens, tropical birds and interactive displays to entertain wildlife lovers of all ages.

If you decide not to visit the zoo, it is worth heading up to the top of Cerro de la Gloria, the park's highest point, to enjoy the fabulous city views. From this vantage point, you can see the imposing 1914 Monumento al Ejército Libertador, comprising a winged allegory in bronze of *Liberty* guiding General San Martín across the Andes, plus a plinth decorated with bronze friezes commemorating the local war effort.

✚ Off map 207 A2 ✉ Avenida Emilio Civit s/n ☎ 0261/428-1700 🕐 Tue–Sun 9–5 ✋ Adult/child $15, under 4 free

LUJÁN DE CUYO

Luján de Cuyo sits west of the RN-40 and is home to the city's Andes brewery (daily 10–12, 4–8) and many of the major wineries. Its main feature is the central Iglesia de Nuestra Señora de la Carrodilla (daily 10–12, 4–8; free), a 1778 church that survived the earthquake and contains a fine display of 17th- and 18th-century religious art plus some primitive frescoes depicting scenes of the grape harvest. Its main relic is an oak statue of the Virgin and Child, carried through the streets during the religious processions in the lead up to Mendoza's Fiesta de la Vendimia in early March. More impressive though is the hard-wood *Cristo de los Huarpes* dating from 1670. To the west is Chacras de Coria, an upmarket suburb crammed with patrician villas, *bodegas* and a number of excellent hotels, with plenty of *parrillas*, bars and nightclubs to keep locals and tourists busy.

✚ Off map 207 C3

CASA DE FADER

www.amigosdelfader.org.ar

In the Mayor Drummond district, on San Martín 3651 and Mayor Drummond, is Mendoza's Museo Provincial de Bellas Artes Emiliano Guiñazú, better known as the Casa de Fader, housed in a late-19th-century red sandstone mansion. Its art nouveau interior was decorated with Impressionist murals of tropical vegetation by the great Argentine artist Fernando Fader, some of whose paintings are also on display among other examples of 19th- and early 20th-century Argentine art. Outside in the exquisite garden, succulents, cypresses,

MENDOZA

0 — 250 m
0 — 250 yds

Avellaneda Nicolas
Aquirre J
AV PERÚ
AV GODOY CRUZ
MITRE
Área Fundacional
AV ESPAÑA
de Mayo
Gral Paz
Patricias
MendocinasGral
Paz
9 de Julio
AV GENERAL LAS HERAS
Moyano F
PERÚ
Chile
AV BARTOLOMÉ
AV GENERAL LAS HERAS
AV
Parque General San Martín
Necochea
Plaza Chile
Gutiérrez
AV BELGRANO
AV
Espejo
Basílica de San Francisco
Plaza San Martín
Julio de Argentino
Álvarez A
Chel
AV EMILIO CIVIT
Benegas
Teatro Independencia
Gutiérrez
Espacio Contemporáneo de Arte
Espejo
AV MARTIN
Rosas
Roca
Rodríguez
AV SARMIENTO
Plaza Independencia
AV
MARTIN ZAPATA
Martínez
Burcio
Rivadavia
CHILE
PATRICIAS
de Julio
Ruffino Ortega
Museo del Pasado Cuyano
Museo Municipal de Arte Moderno
MENDOCINAS
Rivadavia
9
AV VILLANUEVA ARISTIDES
MONTEVIDEO
Plaza Italia
Chile
MONTEVIDEO
AV SAN
Cabral
Sgto
PERÚ
San Lorenzo
Mendocinas
Plaza España
Lorenzo
AV BELGRANO
AV COLÓN
ESPAÑA
San
AV COLÓN
Olascoaga
Clark
Rodríguez Cnel
25 de Mayo
AV BARTOLOMÉ MITRE
Chile
Patricias
9 de Julio
AV ZAPATA
Maipú, Luján de Cuyo
SOBREMONTE
AV PEDRO MOLINA
AV PEDRO MOLINA
RONDEAU

A   B   C

---

magnolias and roses grow in abundance, and you can also see a number of neoclassical marble statues.

✚ Off map 207 A3 ✉ San Martín 3651 ☎ 0261/496-0224 🕐 Tue–Fri 8.30–7, Sat–Sun 3–8; guided tours Tue–Thu 2pm ✋ Adult $5, child (under 12) free

MORE TO SEE

ÁREA FUNDACIONAL

Containing domestic and artistic objects retrieved after the 1861 earthquake, the Museo del Área Fundacional (tel 0261/425-6927; Tue–Sat 8–7, Sun 3–8; $5) is on Alberdi y Videla Castillo, the site of the central square of the original city of Mendoza, 1km (0.5 miles) northeast of Plaza Independencia. You can see some of the colonial city foundations through a glass floor and there is an exhibition explaining the history of Mendoza.

Across the landscaped Plaza Pedro del Castillo, you can see the ruins of the colonial Jesuit temple, known as the Ruinas de San Francisco. In the Parque Bernardo O'Higgins is a children's playground plus an interesting, albeit musty, aquarium and serpentarium (tel 0261/425-3824; 9–1, 3–7.30; $5) containing amphibians and spiders as well as an impressive collection of live snakes.

✚ Off map 207 C1

MAIPÚ

www.maipu.gov.ar

An agreeable satellite town to the south of Mendoza, Maipú was founded in the late 19th century. Known locally as the Cuna de la Viña (Birthplace of the Vine), Maipú has always been at the heart of winemaking in the region and is home to a large number of *bodegas* plus a number of farms growing olives. At La Rural, one of the most traditional *bodegas*, is the Museo del Vino (Montecaseros 2625; tel 0261/497-2013; Mon–Sat 9–5, Sun 1–2; free), a compact exhibition about Mendoza's wine history in a sumptuous art nouveau villa.

✚ 344 C10 🚶 Pablo Pescara 190 ☎ 0261/497-2448 🚌 150, 151, 170, 172, 173, 180 from central Mendoza 🚗 Via RN-7 15km (9 miles) southeast of Mendoza; follow signs first to Luján de Cuyo via RN-40 southwards from Mendoza

Below *Vineyards at Catena Zapata bodega, Mendoza province*

INFORMATION

www.talampaya.com

✚ 340 D7 ✉ RN-150 km144, Cañon de Talampaya, Provincia de la Rioja ☎ 03825/470356 ⏱ Daily 8–6 💰 $30; excursions cost extra 🚌 Bus from Villa Unión or inter-urban bus 🅿 Halfway between San Juan and La Rioja, off the RN-76, 55km (34 miles) south of Villa Unión

TIPS

›› Visits are by guided tour only, so you must leave your car at the entrance.

›› Get to the park early to avoid the crowds and because the ochre cliffs look best in the morning light.

›› There is no regular public transport to the park although there is a bus from Villa Unión to Pagancillo, 27km (17 miles) to the north, or get an inter-urban bus to drop you at the gates, but find out how you will get back first.

›› If you have time, you can arrange to go on extra tours, one of which heads to a separate formation within the park called Ciudad Perdida (Lost City).

Above *Talampaya's spectacular 180m-high (590ft) cliffs*

PARQUE NACIONAL TALAMPAYA

A trip to Talampaya National Park is the highlight of any visit to La Rioja Province. The park's main sights are soaring terracotta-hued cliffs complete with nesting condors, surreal geological formations resembling the spires of a Gothic church, mysterious pre-Columbian rock paintings and a grove of native trees and shrubs. Declared a national park in 1997, Talampaya has been a UNESCO World Heritage Site since 2000. Located in a wide arid valley, the park covers 2,150sq km (830sq miles).

SANDSTONE CANYON

The heart of Talampaya is formed by a long, narrow canyon of sandstone, tinted a pinkish-ochre by oxidized iron. Since it was formed in the Triassic Age, some 250 million years ago, rain and wind have sliced away at the soft stone, creating 180m-high (590ft) cliffs. At the mouth of the canyon, a heap of boulders is inscribed with red, white and black drawings, made by the Aguada and Ciénaga tribes who lived here around AD1000. You can see the mortar-like depressions in the horizontal rock where they ground earth and mixed pigments to paint spirals, condors, llamas and guanacos on to the walls of rock. There is plenty of wildlife, too: foxes, hares and armadillos are frequently spotted in the valley bottom.

NATIVE FLORA AND GEOLOGIAL FORMATIONS

A little further along, the *jardín botánico* (botanical garden) is a grove of native *algarrobos*, *jarillas* and other trees and shrubs, nestling beneath the semi-cylindrical Chimenea del Eco, a smooth vertical groove in the cliffs, where guides like to show off the echoing acoustics. As the canyon widens, stop to admire the incredible geological formations. At the end of the main tour are the Tablero de Ajedrez (the chessboard), a 53m (174ft) tower of anthropomorphic rock known as El Fraile (the Monk), and a black sheet of dark stone etched with pumas and guanacos. An extension to the conventional tour takes you further on to Los Cajones, another set of angular rocks where you can climb past eagle and condor nests to take in breathtaking views.

PARQUE PROVINCIAL ISCHIGUALASTO

Better known as Valle de la Luna (Moon Valley), for its out-of-this-world scenery of ashen rocks and unearthly formations, Ischigualasto is the major attraction in San Juan Province, some 300km (186 miles) northeast of the provincial capital. Geologically unique, Ischigualasto is the only place in the world to include finds from the whole Triassic period, between 200 and 250 million years ago, making the provincial park a paradise for palaeontologists. Covering a total of 620sq km (239sq miles), Ischigualasto is a treasure-trove of prehistoric remains, including the bones of some mysterious early dinosaurs, displayed at the Museo de Ciencias Naturales in San Juan city (▷ 210). Time your visit for late afternoon, to see the park at its best, when the soft light enhances the beauty of the rocks and the mountains.

ROCK FORMATIONS

The park lies in an arid depression between two majestic ranges of pre-Andean mountains. The great hulk of the ruddy-hued Cerro El Morrado (1,700m/5,576ft), which resembles an Indian chief lying on his back, dominates the entrance of the park. Marine fossils discovered in the cliffs and rocks are evidence that the area was once submerged by the ocean, and the layers of volcanic rock have gradually been eroded by wind and water, forming undulating canyons and blocks, ranging in colour from floury white to charcoal grey, often in stripy bands. Turrets and chimneys of rock make parts of the park look like the work of Catalan architect Antoni Gaudí, and are often compared with the landscapes of Brice Canyon or Cappadocia in Turkey.

As you tour the park, you'll see various distinctive rock formations, which over the years have been given names by the locals. A set of horizontal boulders with a funnel-shaped turret is labelled El Submarino (the Submarine), while a long row of segmented rocks is called El Gusano (the Worm). A desert-like plain peppered with perfect spheres of compacted sand, which are still a mystery to geologists, has been dubbed La Cancha de Bolas (the Ball Court or Bowls Pitch). The final stretches of the park peter out into a desolate plateau backed by brick-red cliffs that glow scarlet at sunset—a fitting finale to any tour.

INFORMATION

www.ischigualasto.org

✚ 340 D7 ✉ Parque Provincial Ischigualasto, Provincia de San Juan ☎ 0264/422-7372 ◷ Daily 8–4 (gate closes at dusk) 🎟 Adult $70, child (under 6) free 🚗 Well signposted off the RP-150, about 100km (62 miles) north of San Agustín de Valle Fertil and close to the junction with RN-150 to Patquia; and just over 60km (37 miles) south of the entrance to Talampaya (▷ 208). If you do not have your own transport it is best to come on an organized bus tour from San Juan (▷ 222) 🚌 Tours from San Juan

TIPS

» Keep a lookout for the wildlife, including foxes and *vizcachas* (large rodents), *ñandúes* (ostriches) and guanacos, and the occasional condor, plus lots of small birds. Take your binoculars.
» Rare summer storms might render all or part of the park inaccessible. In the past, heavy rain destroyed some of the famous rock formations, including El Hongo (the Mushroom), still seen on postcards.

Below *El Submarino (the Submarine), one of Ischigualasto's famed rock formations*

INFORMATION

www.turismo.sanjuan.gov.ar
www.graffignawines.com/v2/arg/
museo.php
www.visitedifuntacorrea.com.ar
➕ 340 C9 ✉ San Juan,
Provincia de San Juan 🏢 Sarmiento
24 ☎ 0264/421-0004 ⏰ Daily 9–9
🚌 Buses from all major destinations
✈ Regular flights from Buenos Aires to
Las Chacritas airport, 12km (7.5 miles)
east of the city

TIPS

›› San Juan gets blisteringly hot in the
summer and the siesta here is sacrosanct.
›› A great place to cool off is the Dique de
Ullum, a reservoir to the west of the city,
where you can swim, fish and windsurf.
›› Ask at the tourist office about tours
to Ischigualasto (▷ 209), possibly
combined with Talampaya (▷ 208).

Above *The original Difunta Correa shrine,*
65km (40 miles) east of San Juan

SAN JUAN

San Juan lies in the dry, sunny valley of the Río San Juan, which roars down from
the Andes, and is the second-biggest wine-producing province, after Mendoza,
in Argentina. The birthplace of President Sarmiento, a prominent figure in the
mid-19th century, the city is better known for a terrible earthquake that killed
more than 10,000 people on 15 January 1944—the worst natural disaster in
Argentine history. Rebuilt to rigorous anti-seismic standards, the modern city is
pleasant, with a number of good hotels and restaurants. There are also a couple
of worthwhile museums, one focused on dinosaurs and the other on wine. To
the east of the city is the main pilgrimage site for the cult figure Difunta Correa.

THE MUSEUMS

The city's former train station, a noble brick edifice on España and Maipú,
houses the Museo de Ciencias Naturales (Mon–Fri 9–1; free). The museum's
main highlight is the skeleton of an early Triassic dinosaur *(Herrerasaurus
ischigualastensis)* unearthed at Ischigualasto (▷ 209), together with models of
the dinosaur and a collection of minerals taken from the province's mountains.

MUSEO SANTIAGO GRAFFIGNA

San Juan's other museum is the Museo Santiago Graffigna (Colón 1342 norte;
tel 0264/421-4227; Mon–Sat 9–5.30, Sun 10–4; free), which is housed in one of
the city's most prestigious *bodegas*, run since the 1870s by the Graffigna family.
The museum shows the history of wine and the winemaking process by means
of an audio-visual guided tour (in Spanish and English only). The tour ends in a
beautiful wine bar where you can taste and buy Graffigna wines. On Fridays and
Saturdays the bar is open until late.

SANTUARIO DE LA DIFUNTA CORREA

About 65km (40 miles) east of San Juan, the main shrine to the folk saint Difunta
Correa (▷ 23) lurks just off the RN-141 in Vallecito. In addition to the traditional
bottles of water, pilgrims and devotees leave all manner of objects, from their
driver's licence to pictures of loved ones killed in road accidents. The eclectic
offerings and guttering candles make the shrine a very moving and atmospheric
place to visit (www.visitedifuntacorrea.com.ar).

SAN RAFAEL

www.sanrafaelturismo.gov.ar
San Rafael, around 230km
(142.5 miles) south of Mendoza city,
was populated by mostly French
immigrants in the 19th century,
and has built its prosperity from
vineyards, olives and fruit trees. The
Museo de Historia Natural (Avenida
Balloffet s/n, opposite Parque
Mariano Moreno; Tue–Fri 8–1, 3–8,
Sat–Sun 8–8; free) contains some
very fine pre-Columbian ceramics
and a mummified child dating from
AD40.

Most of the 80 *bodegas* in the
area are tiny, family-run businesses
and several of them open their doors
to visitors; tours tend to be more
informal than in Mendoza and you
can usually just turn up during the
listed opening hours. Among the
best to visit are Jean Rivier (Hipólito
Yrigoyen 2385; tel 02627/432675,
www.jeanrivier.com; Mon–Fri 8–11,
3–6.30; free), founded by Swiss
winemakers and located within
the city limits; the prize-winning
Simonassi Lyon (tel 02627/430963,
www.bodegasimonassi.com;
Mon–Fri 8–5; free), housed in an
attractive farmhouse, 5km (3 miles)
south of town on the RN-143 at
Rama Caida; and the more traditional
Suter (Hipólito Yrigoyen 2850;
tel 02627/421076, www.sutersa.com.
ar; Mon–Sat 9–5; free) where you
receive a half-bottle of wine as a gift.
🚩 344 D11 ✉ San Rafael, Provincia de
Mendoza 🚹 Hipólito Yrigoyen and Balloffet
☎ 02627/424217 🕐 Daily 8–9 🚌 Buses
from Mendoza and major destinations
✈ Regular flights from Buenos Aires;
airport is 5km (3 miles) west of city
🚗 From Mendoza, take the RN-40
southwards then the RN-143 in a
southeasterly direction to San Rafael

TUPUNGATO AND LAGUNA DIAMANTE

www.tupungato.gov.ar
Within sight of a grandiose volcano,
Tupungato is a thriving little town
of late 19th-century Italian-style
houses in the fertile Valle de Uco
south of Mendoza. Some of Mendoza
Province's newest and finest *bodegas*
have made their home in the valley
and the town has been given a new
lease of life as a tourist centre.

Tupungato is also a good base
for visiting the stunning Laguna
Diamante, a highland lake set
amid guanaco pastures and green
valleys. The lagoon gets its name
from its crystalline waters in which
you can see reflections of the Cerro
Maipo (5,323m/17,459ft), a majestic
snowcapped volcano on the border
with Chile. Note that the Laguna
Diamante reserve (free) is accessible
only from mid-December to the end
of March.
🚩 344 C10 ✉ Tupungato, Provincia
de Mendoza 🚹 Belgrano 1066
☎ 02622/488007 🚗 Head south from
Mendoza along the RN-40 and follow signs
westwards to Tupungato from Tunuyán. For
Laguna Diamante, keep going along the
RN-40 southwards, fork right onto the RP-101
and then turn right after another 45km
(28 miles). The dirt track is signposted to
Laguna Diamante 🚌 Tours from Mendoza

VILLA GENERAL BELGRANO

www.elsitiodelavilla.com
Villa General Belgrano gives access to
some of the finest mountain scenery
in the province, in the nearby Sierra
de Comechingones. The town also
hosts a number of festivals through
the year, including a chocolate
festival in July and a cake fair during
Holy Week, known as the Fiesta de
la Masa Vienesa. The main festivities
are saved for the springtime
(October), when Villa General
Belgrano demonstrates its traditional
roots—many of the town's residents
are of German, Austrian and Swiss
descent—with a smaller version of
Munich's Oktoberfest in October. The
affair is rather more sedate than its
Munich counterpart, though large
amounts of beer are consumed along
with sausages, hams and tempting
Mitteleuropa-style pastries.
🚩 345 F9 ✉ Villa General Belgrano,
Provincia de Córdoba 🚹 Avenida Roca
136 ☎ 03546/461215 🕐 Daily 8.30–8.30
🚌 Buses from Córdoba and Buenos Aires
🚗 From Córdoba, head southwards from
the city on the RP-5 via Alta Gracia in the
direction of Santa Rosa de Calamuchita

VILLA UNIÓN

www.turismovillaunion.gov.ar
Nondescript Villa Unión, in La
Rioja Province, was named in the
19th century, when its people
demonstrated solidarity with
labourers thrown off a nearby
estancia by its landowners. It serves
as a good base for visiting Parque
Nacional Talampaya (▷ 208), 70km
(43.5 miles) away. The town is also
a useful base if you want to visit
the remote Reserva Provincial Las
Vicuñas (open daily; free) and Laguna
Brava, some 150km (93 miles) to the
northwest. Mostly above 4,000m
(13,120ft), this remote reserve is well
worth seeing for its altiplano scenery
and gets its name from the flocks of
vicuñas grazing on its *bofedales*, the
spongy marshes that are typical at
these heights. The best time to visit is
in spring and autumn, since summer
storms and winter blizzards make the
roads impassable. The road is best
negotiated in a 4WD or better still as
part of an organized tour.
🚩 341 G7 ✉ Villa Unión, Provincia
de la Rioja 🚹 Joaquín González s/n
☎ 03825/470543 🕐 Mon–Fri 9–7
🚌 Buses from La Rioja 🚗 From La Rioja,
head southwards to Patquia along the RN-
38, continue westwards along the RN-150
in the direction of San Agustín de Valle
Fértil and then northwards along the RP-26
🚌 Tours from San Juan (▷ 222) or La Rioja

Below *A sign in Villa General Belgrano*

CÓRDOBA'S CITY STREETS

The metropolitan area of Córdoba is huge but the historic centre lends itself to an easy promenade taking in all the main sights, principally the religious and academic buildings that gave the city its importance in colonial times. Many of the central streets are pedestrian-only, making the walk even more pleasant.

THE WALK
Distance: 1.5km (1 mile)
Time: 4 hours
Start at: Plaza San Martín
End at: Museo Histórico

★ Start at the Plaza San Martín, the historic heart of Córdoba and the site of two of its most iconic buildings, the cathedral and Cabildo.

❶ In addition to visiting the great cathedral (▷ 197) and the Cabildo (▷ 197), take time to admire the equestrian statue of General San Martín at the heart of the sqaure, the fine palms, acacias and *palo borracho* trees, easily recognizable for their swollen trunks covered with fierce-looking thorns. In season, the jacarandas and *lapachos* add splashes of colour with their indigo and rose-pink blossom.

A minor sight on the northern side of the square, but interesting nonetheless, is the minute Oratorio del Obispo Mercadillo (Rosario de Santa Fe 39), once part of the bishop's residence built in the early 18th century. In 1699, Bishop Manuel Juan Mercadillo made Córdoba the head of the great Tucumán diocese (instead of Santiago del Estero) and became the city's first bishop.

The white chapel built of *calicanto* (a mixture of lime, sand and stone) is sandwiched between rather nondescript modern edifices. Outstanding features are the elegant wrought-iron balcony and the *algarrobo*-wood door decorated with iron nails. Inside, the Museo Gregorio Funes (tel 0351/433-1542; Mon–Fri 9–1; free) displays small exhibitions of mainly religious artwork.

Head westwards along Calle Deán Funes for one-and-a-half blocks to the corner of Calle Rivera Indarte, where you will see the austere form of the neoclassical Legislatura Provincial.

❷ The monumental Legislatura Provincial (Funes 94; tel 0351/420-3559; Mon–Fri 9.30–noon; free) was built in the early 20th century to house the provincial parliament. Guided tours (every 30 mins, ask at entrance; free) offer the chance to see the sumptuous belle époque interior, with a pictorial history of the city.

Turn right along the pedestrian-only Rivera Indarte and continue for two blocks, north, to reach the ruined Cripta Jesuítica, where the street crosses Avenida Colón.

❸ The Cripta Jesuítica (daily 9–1, 3–8.30; open some evenings for tango and other events; free) is one of the city's most unusual sights. Reached by stairs from either side of the Avenida Colón, it is all that remains of an early 18th-century Jesuit noviciate that was abandoned a few decades later and demolished in 1829, when the great avenues were being built as part of the urban plan. It was rediscovered in the late 1980s when telephone cables were being laid. Its rough stone and brick walls are very atmospheric and the three harmonious naves are often used for classic concerts and tango shows.

Return to the hustle and bustle of street level and head straight back down Rivera Indarte, crossing Calle 27 de Abril, where the street name changes to Obispo Trejo, still pedestrian-only. You will reach Mandarina, a classic popular restaurant and watering hole. In another block, you will reach the famous Manzana Jesuítica complex (▷ 197–198), the pride and joy of the city's historic buildings, which was declared a World Heritage Site by UNESCO in 2000.

❹ The main buildings of the Manzana Jesuítica are worth visiting but reserve a moment to contemplate the majestic form of the neoclassical Facultad de Derecho on the opposite side of the street. Inside is a fascinating museum, with exhibits and documents outlining the history of law studies in South America.

Backtrack a short distance to Calle Caseros, turn right and then left at the next corner, heading northwards along Calle Independencia. Before reaching the Plaza San Martín once again, you pass in front of the Iglesia de Santa Teresa and the adjoining monastery. Cross the Plaza San Martín diagonally

and walk a block eastwards along Calle Rosario de Santa Fe. At the corner with Calle Alvear you reach your final destination, the Museo Histórico Marqués de Sobremonte (▷ 198–199).

❺ Before venturing inside the museum to feast your eyes on an impressive collection of colonial artwork, take time to look at the exterior of the last surviving example of a private residence from colonial times in the city. Modest and functional, its only embellishment is a lacy iron balcony held up by finely carved timber brackets. Over the otherwise unadorned archway of the main entrance is a notable example of fan vaulting. It is also worth lingering on the patio where there is a pomegranate tree believed to have been planted in the late 18th century.

TOURIST INFORMATION
✉ Cabildo, Independencia, Plaza San Martín ☎ 0351/434-1200 🕐 Daily 8–8

WHEN TO GO
This walk is best done in the morning, especially in the summer when the

afternoon heat can be blisteringly hot. Some of the sights cannot be visited in the late afternoon.

WHERE TO EAT
MANDARINA
▷ 224.

VERDE SEMPRE VERDE
Just one block from the Mandarina is Verde Sempre Verde, which serves excellent vegetarian fare.
✉ 9 de Julio 36 ☎ 0351/421-8820
🕐 Mon–Sat 11.30–3, 8–11

PLACES TO VISIT
CABILDO
▷ 197.

CATHEDRAL
▷ 197.

MANZANA JESUÍTICA
▷ 197–198.

MUSEO HISTÓRICO MARQUÉS DE SOBREMONTE
▷ 198–199.

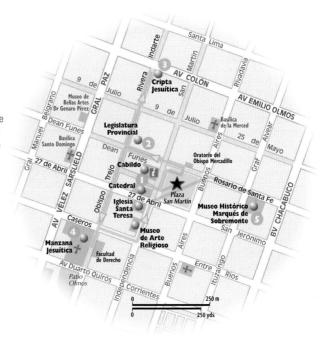

MENDOZA'S CENTRAL PLAZAS

Mendoza is an easy city to walk around. There is no world-class architecture to admire but there is a great sense of space, particularly around the Plaza Independencia and the four orbital squares, which radiate from its corners.

THE WALK

Distance: 2km (1.2 miles)
Time: 3–4 hours
Start at: Plaza Independencia
End at: Basílica de San Francisco

★ It is worth strolling around the Plaza Independencia (▷ 205) before setting out on this tour. There is a grove of beautiful trees, including feather-leafed acacias, huge-trunked sycamores and several beautiful specimens of the shiny-foliaged magnolia grandiflora, with its huge white blooms that linger through the summer.

Head one block east along Rivadavia until you reach Avenida España, then turn right and walk in a southerly direction for another block to reach Plaza España.

❶ Called Plaza Montevideo until 1949, this beautiful leafy square has since been known as Plaza España, in

honour of the rich patrician families of Hispanic origin who paid for it to be decorated. It is the most attractive of the city's plazas, with benches decorated with dazzling Andalusian ceramic tiles and paths lined with exuberant native and exotic trees and shrubs. The earth-toned terracotta flagstones alternate with smaller blue and white tiles while fountains and lily ponds complement the monument to the discovery of South America, at the southern end of the plaza. Folk music concerts are held on the plaza on 12 October each year, the Día de la Raza, in a joyful celebration of *mestizo* culture.

Head four blocks west, from the northwestern corner of the plaza, along Calle Montevideo. This is a handsome avenue of plane trees lined with appealing neo-colonial villas, many of which have brightly coloured facades, to reach Plaza Italia.

❷ Plaza Italia changed its name at the beginning of the 20th century when the city's sizeable Italian community built two monuments. The principal Italian monument, built of stone and bronze, stands at the western end of the square. It is an allegory of the *La Patria* (the Fatherland). The frieze encircling the whole monument depicts scenes of workers ploughing fields, harvesting crops and constructing buildings, in a tribute to the Italian immigrants. The central fountain is covered with more than 1,400 *majolica* tiles created by local artist Marta Moyano Graffagna, inspired by the floor of San Petronio Cathedral in Bologna. The other monument is a bronze statue of the she-wolf feeding Romulus and Remus, mythical founders of Rome, next to a marble mock-Roman pillar.

In November, the plaza is a blaze of colour thanks to the bright red flowers of its *tipa* trees. Every

Opposite Plaza España, *adorned with Andalusian ceramic tiles*

March, during the week preceding the Fiesta de la Vendimia, the park hosts the Festa in Piazza, with stalls representing all the regions of Italy. Here, you can try a range of culinary specialities and there is a fashion parade, too.

Continue four blocks to the north, via the Calle 25 de Mayo, to reach Plaza Chile.

❸ Plaza Chile got its name in recognition of the help given to the residents of Mendoza by their Chilean neighbours after the devastating 1861 earthquake. The centrepiece is a monument, built in 1947, to both heroes of Chilean and Argentine independence, General José de San Martín and Bernardo O'Higgins. There are a few other sculptures by the Chilean sculptor Lorenzo Domínguez. The other main feature of the plaza is a huge and ancient *aguaribay* tree, along with fine specimens of *tipa* and eucalyptus.

Having rested a while in the shade of these trees, head eastwards to the final of the four orbital squares, Plaza San Martín, which is four blocks away along Calle Gutiérrez.

❹ Plaza San Martín is home to the inevitable equestrian statue of General San Martín (the Liberator), facing the Andes, which he crossed with his army to defeat the Spanish after training for several weeks in Mendoza. This monument was placed here in 1904, when the square was given its current name, and is a replica of the work by French sculptor Louis Joseph Daumas in the Plaza San Martín in Buenos Aires.

Around the Plaza San Martín is Mendoza's financial district. Here, banks and insurance companies are housed in formal English-style buildings which count among the most impressive examples of architecture in Mendoza. The former

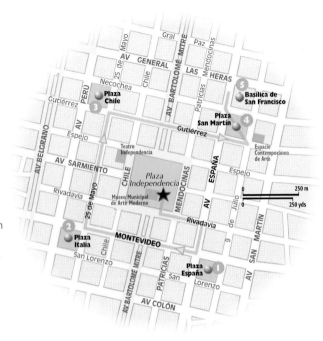

Banco de Mendoza, on the eastern side of Plaza San Martín, now hosts the Espacio Contemporáneo de Arte. Pop inside to see the octagonal entrance with its huge stained-glass cupola and find out if there is an interesting modern art show.

Finally, walk 50m (54 yards) along Avenida España to the city's most noteworthy church, the Basílica de San Francisco.

❺ Constructed between 1879 and 1893, the Basílica de San Francisco was one of the first buildings to be realized following the 1861 earthquake. The Belgian architect, Urbain Barbier, modelled his design on the neoclassical Église de la Trinité in Paris, but the pink and cream painted stucco exterior gives it a decidedly neo-colonial appearance. San Martín's daughter, son-in-law and granddaughter are buried inside and a major relic is a finely crafted rosewood staff belonging to the Liberator.

TOURIST INFORMATION
✉ Cabildo, Independencia, Plaza San Martín ☎ 0351/434-1200 🕐 Daily 8–8

WHEN TO GO
This walk can be done all year round and thanks to the shade afforded by the many trees lining the city's streets and plazas it could even be done in the afternoon.

WHERE TO EAT
LA TASCA DE PLAZA ESPAÑA
▷ 225.

PLACES TO VISIT
BASÍLICA DE SAN FRANCISCO
✉ España and Necochea, Plaza San Martín ☎ 0261/449-5100 🕐 Daily 8–12.30, 5–8.30 ✋ Free

ESPACIO CONTEMPORÁNEO DE ARTE
✉ 9 de Julio and Gutiérrez ☎ 0261/429-0117 🕐 Mon–Sat 9–1, 4–9, Sun 4–9 ✋ Free

SAN JUAN TO TALAMPAYA

San Juan often takes the back seat to Mendoza, but it is undoubtedly one of the country's most beautiful provinces. This memorable drive takes you up the RN-40 to two of Argentina's most scenic preserved parks—Talampaya and Ischigualasto. It is intended to be spread over three days, with two nights in Villa Unión. This allows time to visit Talampaya (in La Rioja Province) first thing in the morning on the second day and Ischigualasto in the late afternoon, before driving back to San Juan to return the car on the third day.

THE DRIVE

Distance: 300km (180 miles) from San Juan to Villa Unión, 600km (360 miles) round trip
Time: Three days with stops
Start at: San Juan
End at: San Juan

★ From San Juan drive northwards following signs to San José de Jáchal, via the RN-40. You travel along one of the major valleys in the pre-Cordillera, the mountains which run parallel to the main peaks of the Andes, to the west. Take the RN-150 for the final 10km (6 miles).

❶ San José, one of the most traditional *gaucho* settlements in the region, is an appealing town 160km (96 miles) north of San Juan. The main sight is the Museo Arqueológico Prieto, with some outstanding pre-Columbian artefacts.

Instead of taking the winding, roundabout RN-40 you could head for Huaco more directly via the scenic RP-456, which takes you through wonderful fertile farmland—this is the region's productive wheat basket.

The road takes you through a green valley crisscrossed by irrigation channels and dotted with handsome flour mills built of ochre mud bricks that would not look out of place in North Africa. At least four of them, El Molino, Molino de los Reyes, Molino de Sardiña and Molino de Pérez, are usually open to the public (daylight hours; free). You just need to try to find someone to let you in and show you round—a trip back in time.

The Cuesta de Huaco then leads down to the RN-40, where you reach the little hamlet of Huaco.

❷ Huaco is made up of adobe houses around a little plaza. Just outside the village is another magnificent flour mill (closed to the public), which was built at the beginning of the 19th century by the Irish Docherty family.

The final stretch of the RN-40, 110km (66 miles) from Huaco to Villa Unión, takes you through a dramatic plain, sided by crinkly desert mountain ranges, which glow deep copper-red in the evening sun—making this the best time to arrive.

❸ The otherwise nondescript town of Villa Unión (▷ 211) is the best base for visiting Parque Nacional Talampaya and Parque Provincial Ischigualasto. It makes sense to reach Talampaya as soon as it opens, to see the cliffs at their best in the early morning light.

Opposite *Lake Huaco on RN-40 en route to Parque Provincial Ischigualasto*

Below right *The distant Cerros Pintados*

❹ The entrance to Talampaya National Park (▷ 208) lies on the RN-76 to the south of Villa Unión.

❺ Another 62km (37 miles) and you reach the turn-off to Parque Provincial Ischigualasto (▷ 209), back in San Juan Province and better known by its popular name of Valle de la Luna, or Moon Valley.

As an alternative route back you could keep south via San Agustín del Valle Fertil and return to San Juan in a westerly direction along RN-141, a journey of 360km (216 miles).

WHEN TO GO

This trip can be done at any time of year. Occasionally heavy summer storms can cause problems and these tend to occur in late afternoon—just be prepared.

WHERE TO EAT

Your best bet is to stock up with food before you set out and picnic along the way. There are plenty of great places with fabulous views and you should always take provisions with you in any case.

WHERE TO STAY

CAÑÓN DE TALAMPAYA

▷ 229.

PLACES TO VISIT

MUSEO ARQUEOLÓGICO PRIETO

✉ 25 de Mayo 788, San José
☎ 02647/420298 🕐 Call ahead for opening times 🎟 Free

TIPS

» Like many road trips in the more remote parts of Argentina, this one requires some precautions, as part of it is along unpaved surfaces. It might well be worth investing in a 4WD vehicle but in any case drive slowly, be prepared for a burst tyre and take supplies in case you get stranded overnight.

» Try to reserve accommodation at Villa Unión in advance and be ready for a day's sightseeing at the two national parks.

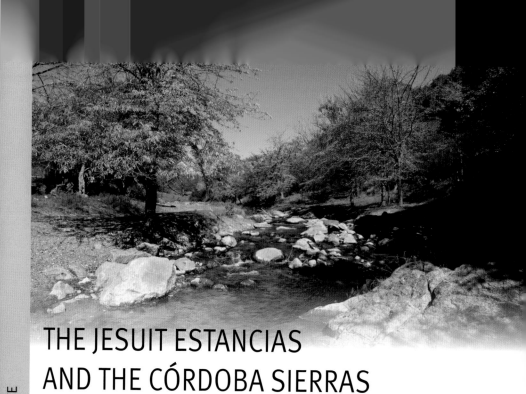

THE JESUIT ESTANCIAS AND THE CÓRDOBA SIERRAS

This exploration of Córdoba's great sierras—the oldest mountains in the country—takes you past some of the finest scenery in the region and allows you to visit Alta Gracia and Jesús María, two of the great Jesuit *estancias* that made the province the hub of colonial life in the region.

THE DRIVE

Distance: 225km (135 miles)
Time: 4 hours
Start at: Córdoba
End at: Córdoba

★From the centre of Córdoba head southwestwards along the RP-5 to Alta Gracia.

❶ Alta Gracia, 38km (23.5 miles) from Córdoba, is a pleasant little town, dominated by its 17th-century Jesuit *estancia*, which is well preserved, despite the fact that the Jesuits left more than 240 years ago, and has been restored to its former glory. The *estancia* is open to the public and includes an interesting museum dedicated to Viceroy Liniers, the representative of the Spanish Crown who lived here for a short time during the wars of Independence.

Music concerts (mostly classical) are given throughout the year.

Another of the town's highlights is the small museum devoted to the Rosario-born revolutionary Che Guevara. It is housed in the Villa Beatriz, where Ernesto, to give him his real name, spent some of his childhood on doctor's orders—the climate in the sierras was thought to be good for his chronic asthma.

Manuel de Falla, the Spanish composer, also came here for the climate and spent the final years of his life in exile from Fascist Spain, in a vain attempt to cure his tuberculosis. His villa, Los Espinillos, also functions as a museum and contains some of his belongings, including his piano, on which concerts are given from time to time.

After leaving Alta Gracia follow the signs northwards to Villa Carlos Paz. After 24km (14.5 miles) you reach the RN-38, which skirts around the eastern banks of the Lago San Roque reservoir, enabling you to avoid Villa Carlos Paz itself, once the province's pride and joy but now a rather ugly, noisy resort. Another 25km (15 miles) will bring you to the busy resort of Cosquín.

❷ Cosquín marks the start of the Punilla Valley, one of the most scenic routes in the province. One of the most popular resorts is La Cumbre (▷ 200), 35km (21 miles) north of Cosquín—domestic tourists have favoured its fine climate and genteel atmosphere for over a century.

Head eastwards along the E-66 country road, which winds over the hills of the Sierra Grande, via Ascochinga, to Jesús María, 56km (33.5 miles) away.

❸ Jesús María is a sleepy rural town that comes alive once a year for a folk festival, the Festival Nacional de la Doma y el Folklore, held in the first half of January. The main reason to visit is to witness another major Jesuit *estancia*, now housing the Museo Jesuítico Nacional (▷ 201).

To return to Córdoba drive 47km (28 miles) straight down the RN-9 in a southerly direction.

WHEN TO GO
The drive is suitable year round.

WHERE TO EAT
There are plenty of places to stop for something to eat along the way, not least the fabulous roadside *parrilla* in Jesús María. Otherwise, a great solution is to picnic: The RN-38 road bristles with places selling produce such as home-made bread, cheese, honey, hams and preserves.

WHERE TO STAY
This trip can be done in a day but you might like to break up the journey. You could stay at the fabulous Dos Lunas *estancia* (▷ 226), not far from Capilla del Monte, which involves a small detour, or in La Cumbre.

PLACES TO VISIT
ESTANCIA DE ALTA GRACIA
www.altagracia.gov.ar
✉ Avenida Padre Domingo Viera 41
☎ 03547/421303 🕐 Nov–Apr daily 9–8; May–Oct Tue–Fri 9–1, 3–7, Sat–Sun and national holidays 9.30–12.30, 3.30–6.30; guided visit (Spanish only) held four times daily 👋 $5

LOS ESPINILLOS
✉ Alta Gracia ☎ 03547/429292
🕐 Nov–Apr daily 9–8; May–Oct Tue–Sun 9–7, Mon 2–7 👋 $2, free on Wed

MUSEO CHE GUEVARA
✉ Avellaneda 501, Barrio Carlos Pellegrini
☎ 03547/428579 🕐 Nov–Apr daily 9–8; May–Oct Mon 2–7, Tue–Sun 9–7; call ahead for guided visits 👋 $5 (free on Wed)

LA CUMBRE
▷ 200.

ESTANCIA DE JESÚS MARÍA
▷ 201.

ACONCAGUA
MOUNTAINEERING OPERATORS
www.aconcagua.mendoza.gov.ar
If your heart is set on scaling Aconcagua, the highest peak outside the Himalayas, contact one of the four major local outfits: Daniel Alessio (www.alessio.com.ar), Fernando Grajales (www.grajales.net), Inka Expediciones (www.inka.com.ar) and Rudy Parra (www.rudyparra.com). You can also contact these operators through the official directorate based in Mendoza, which should always be your first port of call.

✉ Dirección de Atención Visitantes Parque Provincial Aconcagua, San Martín 1143, Mendoza ☎ 0261/425-8751 ⏰ Mon–Fri 8–6, Sat–Sun 9–1

CAÑÓN DEL ATUEL
RAFFEISH
www.vallegrande.com.ar/
raffeish_rafting.asp
This major tour operator can arrange rafting along the canyon. Trips range from one to two hours in length. It can also organize kayaking and catamaran trips around the reservoir.

✉ RP-173 km35, Valle Grande, Provincia de Mendoza ☎ 02627/436996 ⏰ Daily 9–7
✋ One hour water-rafting $120

CÓRDOBA
CALLE BELGRANO, BARRIO GÜEMES
This is the main hunting ground in the city for antiques and bric-a-brac—the main drag in this bohemian neighbourhood is full of small shops selling items, ranging from junk to real bargains.

✉ Calle Belgrano, Barrio Güemes
⏰ Mon–Sat 10–6

NATIVO VIAJES
www.cordobanativoviajes.com.ar
One of the best known tour operators in Córdoba, Nativo provides a panoply of excellent excursions to all parts of the province plus unusual outings such as the musical evening at the Alta Gracia *estancia* in July.

✉ 27 de Abril 11 ☎ 0351/424-5341
⏰ Mon–Sat 9–6 ✋ Three-hour city tour in English $95

PASEO DE LAS ARTES
Housed in the Recova, the gallery of the Cabildo on Plaza San Martín, this is a great place to pick up a souvenir. All kinds of traditional artwork is sold here, from *mate* cups to finely woven ponchos. A similar art fair is also held in the evenings at the corner of Belgrano and Achaval Rodríguez, in Nueva Córdoba.

✉ Plaza San Martín ☎ 0351/428-5600
⏰ Mon–Sat 9–2, 4–9.30

PATIO DE TANGO
Although tango is less established in Córdoba than in Buenos Aires or Rosario, there has recently been a revival, mainly driven by tourist interest. Summer tango evenings are held in the Cabildo and in cooler weather the show moves to the Cripta Jesuítica (Avenida Colón and Rivera Indarte).

✉ Plaza San Martín ☎ 0351/428-5600
⏰ Lesson Fri 9pm; show midnight
✋ Varies

TALABARTERÍA CRESPO
www.talabarteriacrespo.com.ar
Founded in the middle of the 19th century, this venerable establishment purveying leather and *gaucho*-wear specializes in garments made of the prized *carpincho* (capybara) skin—a warmly hued speckled leather that is supple and waterproof. You can also find handbags, boots, wallets, knives and *mate* paraphernalia here, too.

✉ Rivadavia 467 ☎ 0351/421-5447
⏰ Mon–Fri 10–6, Sat 9–1

TEATRO DEL LIBERTADOR GENERAL MARTÍN

teatrodellibertador.blogspot.com
Inaugurated in 1891, this is one of the most prestigious theatres in the country. It has world-class acoustics and the wooden floor can be removed to turn the auditorium into a dance hall. Performances range from tango and pop to opera and ballet.
✉ Avenida Vélez Sarsfield 365
☎ 0351/433-2332 or 0351/433-2312
◷ Box office: Mon–Sat 10–6

MALARGÜE
KAREN TRAVEL

www.karentravel.com.ar
Karen Travel runs memorable trips to the Payunia region, including Caverna de las Brujas (▷ 202) and Laguna de Llancanelo but also can arrange skiing trips at Las Leñas resort (▷ 227), which include transport, accommodation and equipment.
✉ Avenida San Martín 1056
☎ 02627/470342 ◷ Daily 9–6
✋ Half-day excursion $120

MENDOZA
ALQUIMIA

www.alquimiapub.com.ar
This bar is one of the trendiest places to hang out in Gran Mendoza. It is the kind of place where local celebs hold their birthday parties while there are frequent special nights dedicated to specific drinks.
✉ Ruta Panamericana and Cerro Aconcagua, Chacras de Coria
☎ 0261/15-515-1197 ◷ 7.30pm–3am

ARGENTINA RAFTING EXPEDICIONES

www.argentinarafting.com
Argentina Rafting Expediciones are based in Potrerillos, at the start of the Alta Montana route, but have an office in Mendoza, too. The company can arrange rafting on Río Mendoza, but also trekking, mountain-biking, kayaking, horse rides, mountaineering and more.
✉ Amigorena 86 ☎ 0261/429-6325
◷ Daily 10–6 ✋ Half day $120 plus transport from Mendoza ($40)

CATENA ZAPATA

www.catenawines.com
This opulent modern *bodega*, housed in a building that is reminiscent of a Mayan temple, is in Luján de Cuyo, south of Mendoza (▷ 206). Tours are conducted in several languages, in addition to Spanish.
✉ J Cobos s/n, Agrelo, Luján de Cuyo
☎ 0261/413-1100 ◷ Reserve ahead
✋ Free

ESCORIHUELA

www.escorihuela.com
You don't have to stray too far from the city centre to visit this traditional winery in the southern suburb of Godoy Cruz. Founded in the 1880s, it is one of the oldest in the country. There is also an art gallery and the much lauded 1884 Francis Mallmann restaurant (▷ 224–225), one of the best in the country.
✉ Belgrano 1188, Mendoza
☎ 0261/424-2744 ◷ Mon–Fri 9.30, 10.30, 11.30, 12.30, 2.30 and 3.30 ✋ Free

ESTACIÓN MIRÓ

This is the city's only gay nightclub. It holds its alternative Fiesta de la Vendimia in March, complete with the election of a drag queen of the harvest. The rest of the year can be equally outrageous but the cocktails are good and the crowd is lively.
✉ Ejército de los Andes 656, Dorrego, Mendoza ☎ 0261/431-6990 ◷ Wed, Fri–Sun 1–6am

LUIGI BOSCA

www.luigibosca.com.ar
Luigi Bosca undeniably produces some of the very best Mendocino wines so wine lovers should not miss an opportunity to include a visit to this *bodega* on any tour of the region.
✉ San Martín 2044, Luján de Cuyo
☎ 0261/498-1974 ◷ Mon–Fri 10.30, 3.30, Sat noon ✋ Tours $25

MENDOZA WINE AND BIKE TOURS

www.mendozawinebiketour.com
Excellently run mountain-bike tours around the Mendocino vineyards.
✉ Espejo 65, Mendoza ☎ 0261/15-418-4958 ✋ $130 half-day tour

SALENTEIN

www.bodegasalentein.com
The fabulous winery near Tupungato not only produces unrivalled wines but is also an architectural masterpiece. The main cellar is designed to be a veritable temple to wine and is known as the cathedral of the Mendocino wineries. Another asset is the Killka art gallery, where you can see an outstanding collection of contemporary Argentine art and regular temporary exhibitions that are always worth a glance.
✉ RP-89 and Videla, Tunuyán
☎ 02622/423556 ◷ Daily 11, 1, 3 ✋ $20

SOPPELSA

www.soppelsahelados.com
The Italian influence is evident at this popular *heladería* (ice cream shop), which has numerous branches around the city and its suburbs. Güerino Soppelsa founded the chain in the 1920s and it is now one of the city's gourmet attractions. The *sambayón* (zabaglione or Marsala custard) flavour is exceptional, while the cakes and ice cream desserts are outstanding—you might be tempted to indulge in an iced *alfajor* (chocolate-covered cookie sandwich).
✉ Espejo 299 ◷ Daily 10am–2am
✋ From $10

SOUL CAFÉ

This atmospheric little bar stages live music gigs—including jazz, rock and, occasionally, tango—most nights after 10pm.
✉ Cañon del Atuel ☎ 0261/420-1336
◷ Daily 8pm–2am

TROUT AND WINE

www.troutandwine.com
Wine lovers will find their every whim catered to by this ultra-professional outfit that takes you to all the best wineries in the region and arranges excellent accommodation, too. The company also arranges angling tours to various fish-rich lakes and rivers within reach of Mendoza, including the fabulous Laguna del Diamante.
✉ Espejo 266 ☎ 0261/425-5613
◷ Mon–Fri 10–6 ✋ Full-day wine tour, including lunch $600

VINES OF MENDOZA

www.vinesofmendoza.com

This sophisticated wine-tasting room allows you to sample the best Mendocino wines without leaving the city. The knowledgeable staff can recommend wines to try and *bodegas* to visit, and make the necessary reservations, so it is a great port of call before setting off on the *bodega* trail. You can taste a flight of five selected wines, often from lesser-known wineries, or attend a 'meet the winemaker' night every Wednesday. There is also the opportunity to invest in a parcel of vineyard.

✉ Espejo 567 ☎ 0261/438-1031
🕐 Mon–Sat 11–8 ✋ $30

WEINERT

www.bodegaweinert.com

One of the best wineries in Luján de Cuyo opens its doors to the public for tastings and tours of the premises. Founded in the 1970s, Weinert has already joined the ranks of the most acclaimed *bodegas* in the region. The malbecs and merlots are particularly popular.

✉ San Martín 5923, Chacras de Coria
☎ 0261/496-0409 🕐 Mon–Sat 10–4.40
✋ Free

LA RIOJA

MERCADO DE ARTESANÍA

Opposite the city's excellent Museo Folklórico is an equally excellent shop selling local artwork, mostly indigenous crafts such as beautifully

Below *Viñas de Segisa winery*

carved gourds, some of which are *mate* cups or sugar bowls. Native woods such as *algarrobo* and *quebracho* are fashioned into beautiful bowls and you can also find an enticing range of woollen goods, such as sweaters, gloves and ponchos. The items come with signed labels indicating the person who made it.

✉ Pelagio B Luna and Catamarca
🕐 Tue–Fri 8–12, 4–8, Sat–Sun 9–12

SAN JUAN

CAVAS DE ZONDA

www.cavasdezonda.com

To taste some really good Argentine sparkling wine, made according to the Champagne method, you might like to make the scenic trek west to Cavas de Zonda. In addition to some very good red wines, they specialize in delicious fizz and the cavas are refreshingly cool—one of the features of the cellar is that it is built into the mountainside.

✉ RP-12, km15 ☎ 0264/494-5144
🕐 Mon–Fri 10–5, Sat Sun 11–5 ✋ Free

LAS MARIANAS

www.bodegalasmarianas.com.ar

This family-run winery is one of the best along the local wine route. Founded in the 1920s and housed in a beautiful adobe building, it was bought by the enterprising Battistella family in the late 1990s and restored to its former glory. The excellent tastings pilot you through their cabernet, merlot, syrah and tempranillo wines, all of which are first rate.

✉ Calle Nueva s/n, Rinconada, Pocito,
San Juan ☎ 0264/423-1191 🕐 Mon–Sat
10–12.30, 4–8 ✋ Free

MERCADO ARTESANAL TRADICIONAL

Part of the dynamic Centro de Difusión Cultural Eva Perón—the city's leading arts centre—this excellent handicrafts market is the ideal place to find a poncho or a brightly coloured *manta* (shawl) from San José de Jáchal. In fact, it is probably easier to find authentic *criollo* goods here than in Jáchal itself.

✉ San Luis and España ☎ 0264/421-8530
🕐 Sun–Fri 9–1, 4–7, Sat 9–7

MOON VALLEY TURISMO

www.moonvalley.tur.ar

As the name suggests, this enterprise specializes in trips to Ischigualasto (▷ 209), more commonly known as Valle de la Luna or Moon Valley. Other tours include the wineries and the Parque Nacional San Guillermo, a seldom-visited reserve renowned for frequent sightings of the native puma.

✉ Rivadavia oeste 414 ☎ 0264/421-4868
🕐 Mon–Sat 9–7 ✋ Day trip $240

SAITUR SAUL SAIDEL

www.saulsaidel.com

One of the best tour operators in San Juan, Saitur Saul Saidel offers a wide range of excursions to Talampaya and Ischigualasto parks, as well as city tours. Other tours on offer include Jáchal, Rodeo and Pismanta, the shrine to folk-saint Difunta Correa in Vallecito and the wineries of San Juan.

✉ Avenida José Ignacio de la Roza
112 este ☎ 0264/422-2700 🕐 Mon–Sat
10–6 ✋ Day trip $210

TRIÁSICO VALLE DE LA LUNA

www.triasico.com.ar

Another excellent tour company, based in San Juan, which offers reliable tours that include the national park, Calingasta and its valley and the shrine to Difunta Correa.

✉ Sarmiento 40 sur ☎ 0264/422-8566
🕐 Mon–Sat 9–7 ✋ Day trip $250

VINAS DE SEGISA

www.saxsegisa.com.ar
Billing itself as San Juan's first boutique winery, Segisa is a real treat. The old cellars have been restored and host intelligent tastings that will leave you wanting to buy several cases.

✉ Aberastain and Calle 15, Rinconada, Pocito ☎ 0264/492-2000 🕐 Mon–Fri 11–6 ✋ Free

SAN RAFAEL
ATUEL TRAVEL

www.atueltravel.com.ar
This reliable outfit is worth contacting for excursions in southern Mendoza. In addition to all the conventional tours, such as the Cañón del Atuel (▷ 200) or visits to wineries, it organizes more demanding excursions, such as horse treks into the Andes or rappels in the valleys.

✉ San Juan 445 ☎ 0261/420-1336 🕐 Mon–Sat 9–6 ✋ Day trip to Caverna de las Brujas $170

RISCO VIAJES

www.riscoviajes.com
One of the best operators in the southern Mendoza Province, Risco Viajes arranges tours to Cañón del Atuel (▷ 200), with a rafting trip thrown in for good measure. Kayaking in the reservoir and adventure safaris into the Andes are other options. Farther afield, it also organizes trips to the Payunia region and Caverna de las Brujas (▷ 202).

✉ Avenida Hipólito Yrigoyen 284 ☎ 02627/436439 🕐 Mon–Sat 9–6 ✋ Kayaking in Lago Valle Grande $155

VILLA GENERAL BELGRANO
CAFÉ RISSEN

Don't miss out on a trip to the Rissen, which is popular with locals and visitors alike and located along the main drag. The coffee and cakes are the main attraction, though the sandwiches are equally delicious. Try to find room for the excellent apple strudel, which is regarded by many as the best this side of Vienna.

✉ Roca 36 ☎ 03546/462043 🕐 Daily 11–8 ✋ From $20

FESTIVALS AND EVENTS

JANUARY
FESTIVAL NACIONAL E INTERNACIONAL DE LA DOMA Y FOLKLORE

www.festival.org.ar
Tranquil Jesús María in Córdoba Province comes alive with rock and folk music during the first fortnight of January. This prestigious festival features *gaucho* skills and traditional music with major stars such as Jairo and Cuti and Roberto Carabajal, plus some artists from Brazil and other neighbouring countries.

FESTIVAL NACIONAL DE FOLKLORE

www.aquicosquin.org
Cosquín, a small town to the northwest of Córdoba, hosts an annual major folk music festival in the latter half of January. Although generally believed to have passed its heyday, the 50th festival, in 2010, starred many important national and international artists.

MARCH
FIESTA NACIONAL DE LA VENDIMIA

www.vendimia.mendoza.gov.ar
Festivities marking Mendoza's grape harvest are held annually on the first weekend of March. Carnival queens from each department in the province compete for the title of Queen of the Grape Harvest in the Acto Central, held in the Anfiteatro Frank Romero Day in the Parque General San Martín and culminating in a fireworks display. There is a parade on the Saturday morning through the centre of Mendoza, when the carnival queens and their supporters hand out local produce to the crowds. Note that hotels get booked up well in advance.

MARCH–APRIL
FIESTA DE LA MASA VIENESA

Holy Week is a big holiday time throughout the country and most resorts get booked up in advance.

In Villa General Belgrano, the week turns into a glorification of cake and pastry making during the Festa de la Masa Vienesa, with a traditional Easter-egg hunt thrown in for good measure.

JULY
FIESTA DEL CHOCOLATE ALPINO

During July, Villa General Belgrano is given over to the making and tasting of chocolate in every possible form.

OCTOBER
OKTOBERFEST

During the second week of October, usually quiet Villa General Belgrano surrenders to the power of ale during the National Beer Festival. Large quantities of lager are consumed along with sauerkraut and Frankfurter sausages. It is all good fun, though, and rarely a drunken scene.

NOVEMBER
FIESTA PROVINCIAL DE LA TRADICIÓN

Displays of horsemanship, folk music and local crafts are shown off at the national celebrations in early November, in San José de Jáchal, one of the most traditional *gaucho* settlements in the region.

DECEMBER
FERIA NAVIDEÑA

True to its *Mitteleuropa* traditions, Villa Belgrano celebrates Yuletide with gusto, so expect Father Christmas, reindeers and all. The three kings make an appearance for Epiphany and, in the meantime, *stollens* and other German goodies can be bought at the resort's shops.

TINKUNAKU

Held annually in La Rioja on 31 December, Tinkunaku, meaning 'informal meeting' in Quichoa, focuses on a procession of images of St. Nicholas of Bari, the city's patron saint, and the Christ Child.

PRICES AND SYMBOLS

The restaurants are listed alphabetically (excluding El, La and Los). The prices given are the average for a two-course lunch (L) and a three-course dinner (D) for one person, without drinks. The wine price is for the least expensive bottle. All the restaurants listed accept credit cards unless otherwise stated. Prices are given in Argentine pesos ($) unless otherwise noted.

For a key to the symbols, ▷ 2.

CÓRDOBA

MANDARINA

This excellent hideout, on one of downtown Córdoba's main pedestrian streets, is popular with students. The kitchen serves up excellent Asian fare, crusty pizzas and great pasta, along with some vegetarian dishes. It is a great place for a leisurely breakfast and even brunch at the weekends, or you can take food away if you prefer.
✉ Obispo Trejo 171 ☎ 0351/426-4909 🕓 Daily noon–2am 🖐 L $25, D $40, Wine $15

SAN HONORATO

www.sanhonorato.com.ar
San Honorato is in the smart General Paz district, a short taxi ride from the city centre. Start the evening

with a glass of wine or champagne in the brick-lined cellar, as you try specialities such as Moroccan-style preserved lemons, strong cheeses and sliced ham off the bone. Upstairs, the impeccable service is teamed with an ambitious menu. Starters might include a trout roll with caramelized banana and ginger butter while one of the delicious mains is linguini with strips of goat and oyster mushrooms. It's a popular place, so reservations are essential.
✉ Pringles and 25 de Mayo, Barrio General Paz ☎ 0351/453-5252 🕓 Tue–Fri 12.30–4, 7.30–12, Mon, Sat 7.30pm–midnight 🖐 L $65, D $82, Wine $24

LA ZETE

This Syrio-Lebanese restaurant proves how eclectic food can be in this cosmopolitan city. The *mezze* are well executed and the house special is the *shishbarak*, a type of meat ravioli served in a sharp yogurt-like sauce. Finish with a mint tea.
✉ Obispo Salguero 306 ☎ 0351/421-6352 🕓 Mon–Fri 12.30–4, 7.30–12, Sat 7.30–1 🖐 L $40, D $65, Wine $28

LA CUMBRE

GAPASAI

This inventive restaurant, enjoying fabulous valley vistas, has built up a

reputation for its adventurous food with Mediterranean flavours—the salmon carpaccio is exquisite. Try the 10-course tasting menu featuring a cocktail and appetizers, two hors d'oeuvres, two starters, two main courses, a savoury, two puddings and coffee or tea with *petit fours*.
✉ Calle 12 de Octubre s/n, Altos del Pungo, La Cumbre ☎ 03548/451694 🕓 Mon–Sat 12.30–3, 8–midnight 🖐 L $55, D $95, Wine $32

JESÚS MARÍA

EL FARO

Officially located in Caroya, this roadside *parrilla* is a real north Córdoba institution, serving sizzling hunks of prime Argentine beef side in the Brazilian *churras* style. People flock here from far and wide for a taste of the succulent goat and kid, roast on the spit. There are no vegetarian options.
✉ Juan Bautista Alberdi 245 (RN-9) ☎ 03525/466258 🕓 Daily 12–4, 7.30–midnight 🖐 L $35, D $50, Wine $18

MENDOZA

1884 FRANCIS MALLMANN

www.1884restaurante.com.ar
Flamboyant *bon vivant* and gastronome, Francis Mallmann is a celebrity chef in Argentina, and this

Opposite *Azafrán restaurant in Mendoza*

sumptuous restaurant is regarded by many as the best in the Mendoza area. The date refers to the year when the stunning Escorihuela *bodega* was built in the southern suburb of Godoy Cruz. The restaurant, housed in the winery, is an outstanding example of patrician architecture with strong Italian influences and some exquisite touches, such as the Italian *opaline* lamps. Diego Irrera, who continues Mallmann's approach of Patagonian ingredients with French finesse, now helms the kitchen. Try the local specialities of suckling pig or goat.
✉ Belgrano 1188, Godoy Cruz ☎ 0261/424-2698 ◷ Daily 8.30–midnight ✋ D $240, Wine $56

AZAFRÁN
The rustic appearance belies the highly sophisticated dining at this popular and professionally run restaurant. The pavement tables outside get snapped up quickly, so make sure you book. The marvellous dishes, such as rabbit ravioli in champagne sauce, are married with top-rate Mendocino wines with the help of the expert *sommelier*. Ask to see the cellar, where an Arthurian-style round table sits amid row upon row of handpicked vintages. Vegetarians are well catered for, too.
✉ Sarmiento 765 ☎ 0261/429-4200 ◷ Mon–Sat 12.30–4, 7.30–1 ✋ L $65, D $100, Wine $30

LA MARCHIGIANA
www.marchigiana.com.ar
The Italian influence on Argentine life, on Mendoza and on food, in particular, is enormous and this immensely popular restaurant is part of that vibrant tradition. Head for La Marchigiana to sample black pasta with seafood sauce or a memorable four-cheese lasagne. The wine list is faultless, as is the lip-smacking apple strudel, just one of the many delicious desserts. There is another branch in a suburban shopping mall.
✉ Patricias Mendocinas 1550 ☎ 0261/423-0751 ◷ Daily 12–4, 7–1 ✋ L $40, D $60, Wine $17

EL PATIO DE JESÚS MARÍA
For a first-rate *parrilla*, hop in a taxi and head for El Patio de Jesús María in the up-and-coming suburb of Chacras de Coria. The house speciality is the *diente libre* (all you can eat), comprising an *empanada* (savoury pasty) and a salad, plus all you can manage to eat from the list of beef cuts and offal, which include crispy sweetbreads, luscious *morcilla* (blood sausage) and large hunks of grilled goat and pork. Build up an appetite before you come.
✉ Viamonte 4961, Chacras de Coria ☎ 0261/496-1260 ◷ Thu–Sun 8pm–3am, Sat–Sun 12.30pm–4pm ✋ L and D $55, Wine $21

LA TASCA DE PLAZA ESPAÑA
If the city's many sophisticated temples of haute cuisine don't appeal or you want a simple meal for a change, this lively and friendly tapas bar on the charming Plaza España might be the perfect option. The decor is strikingly gaudy, with crimson walls and unusual artwork, while the food is fresh and tasty. The excellent menu includes a variety of seafood and meat dishes, and there is a much-revered veal and artichoke casserole, while one of the vegetarian options is a spicy ratatouille with cheese.
✉ Montevideo 117 ☎ 0261/423-3466 ◷ Mon–Sat 11.30–3, 7–midnight ✋ L $25, D $38, Wine $15

LA RIOJA
LA VIEJA CASONA
www.lacasonalunch.com.ar
This is an excellent place in the provincial capital for a no-nonsense *parrilla*. La Vieja Casona's homely atmosphere, old-fashioned style of service and perfectly grilled meat make for an authentic dining experience. The appealing yellow walls and impeccable tablecloths form an attractive decor, while the local wines are perfect accompaniments to the barbecued beef and goat.
✉ Rivadavia 457 ☎ 03822/425996 ◷ Daily 12.30–4, 8–midnight ✋ L $38, D $54, Wine $21

SAN JUAN
SOYCHÚ
This great vegetarian restaurant doubles up as a macrobiotic grocery store. There is a *tenedor libre* (all you can eat) buffet and it is worth getting here early as locals form lines at lunchtime to eat on the premises or to fill their lunch boxes.
✉ Avenida José Ignacio de la Roza oeste 223 ☎ 0264/422-1939 ◷ Mon–Sat 11–4, 8.30–midnight, Sun 12–3 ✋ L and D $24, Wine $15

SAN RAFAEL
LA FUSTA
This fabulous *parrilla*, in central San Rafael, is the place to sample the local speciality of grilled goat and there is chicken, beef, pork and sausages on the barbecue, too. The food is unpretentious but delicious and the house wine is good value.
✉ Hipólito Yrigoyen 538 and Beato Marcelino Champagnat ☎ 02627/428776 ◷ Daily 12.30–4, 7.30–12 ✋ L $32, D $44, Wine $18

EL RESTAURO
In a beautifully restored building on the main square, chef Ana Paula Gutiérrez runs a great *cocina de autor*—Argentina's answer to the boutique eatery. One of her signature dishes is ravioli stuffed with dried tomatoes and Mendocino olives. The wine list, as you would expect, is a marvel of balanced bouquets and *cepages*.
✉ Comandante Salas 199 and Day ☎ 02627/445482 ◷ Daily 12–4, 7–midnight ✋ L $42, D $67, Wine $22

VILLA GENERAL BELGRANO
CIERVO ROJO
www.elsitiodelavilla.com/ciervorojo
Ciervo Rojo is a *confitería* with a beer garden and live German music every Saturday night. Try a glass of the foaming *chopp* (draught beer) and sauerkraut with frankfurters or enjoy mouth-watering cooked meat platters and home-made ice cream to finish.
✉ Roca 210 ☎ 03546/461345 ◷ Daily 12–3, 8–12 ✋ L $38, D $53, Wine $18

PRICES AND SYMBOLS

The prices are the lowest and highest for a double room for one night including breakfast, unless otherwise stated. All the hotels listed accept credit cards unless otherwise stated. Note that rates can vary widely throughout the year. Prices are given in US dollars (US$) unless otherwise stated.

For a key to the symbols, ▷ 2.

CÓRDOBA

AZUR REAL

www.azurrealhotel.com

This 1915 building has been a shop and student lodgings—they claim Che Guevara stayed here when he studied medicine—but is now the city's most luxurious hotel. It has 14 rooms, ranging from simple but comfortable to large deluxe rooms. There is a fabulous deck terrace and the stylish Papagayo restaurant serves local cuisine fused with southeast Asian and Peruvian flavours.

✉ San Jerónimo 243 ☎ 0351/424-7133 👋 US$100–US$130 ❶ 14
🅢 ⛰ Outdoor

WINDSOR

www.windsortower.com

This large reputable four-star palace offers reliable, but not luxurious,

accommodation and is a good option for a night or two—long enough to see the city sights. Request a room in the superior Senior section, where the decor is more appealing and the rooms are more modern. The hotel's members of staff are very helpful and there is free off-site parking.

✉ Buenos Aires 214 ☎ 0351/422-4012 👋 US$110–US$130 ❶ 81
🅢 ⛰ Outdoor 🔲

ZOOM

www.zoomapartments.com

The Zoom apartment complex occupies an excellent downtown location and the studio lofts are extremely well equipped, with smart modern bathrooms and kitchenettes. The decor is contemporary and colourful, and the rooms have DVD players. There is an express laundry service and American-style buffet breakfast.

✉ Sucre 327 ☎ 0351/428-4665
👋 US$100–US$180 ❶ 17 apartments 🅢

LA CUMBRE

POSADA SAN ANDRÉS

www.posadasanandres.com

This gorgeous stone villa, reminiscent of an Alpine castle, is set among 7ha (17 acres) of grounds, with manicured lawns and handsome

shady trees. Built in the 1930s, the *posada* is a great place for relaxing, with an inviting swimming pool and spacious rooms. A much newer building on the site, the Casa de las Flores, has rooms complete with all the mod cons that you might expect in a luxury hotel.

✉ Avenida Benítez and Monteagudo
☎ 03548/452547 👋 US$120–US$140
❶ 6 ⛰ Outdoor

ISCHILÍN

DOS LUNAS

www.doslunas.com.ar

If you want to get away from it all and enjoy wonderful scenery, great service and experience a traditional Argentine lifestyle, book a stay at the Dos Lunas *estancia*, near the locality of Alto Ongamira, not far from the hamlet of Ischilín. The rooms are in the gorgeous neo-colonial main house and the rustic but charming galleried long house. Rooms are comfortable and well appointed with views of the mountains of northern Córdoba. The cuisine is first rate, the horse rides (including full-moon outings) are unforgettable and the swimming pool must have one of the best views in the country.

✉ Alto Ongamira ☎ 011/5032-3410
👋 US$250–US$300 per person full board

🔆 5 🏖 Outdoor 🚗 From Córdoba, take the RN-9 northwards in the direction of Jesús María. After 20km (12.5 miles), to the north of Jesús María, take the left fork, RN-60, in the direction of Deán Funes and Catamarca. Continue for 3km (2 miles) along the road then, at the turn-off to Sarmiento, turn left and cross the rail tracks, turn right and continue along 11km (7 miles) of unmade road (good state) to Cañada de Río Pinto. Turn right then left after 1,400m (1,526 yards); after 9km (5.5 miles) you reach Todos los Santos. Another 11km (7 miles) leads to the turn-off to the *hostería*, 2km (1.25 miles) off the main road

HOSTERÍA LA ROSADA

www.ischilinposada.com.ar
The family home of Fernando Fader, one of the country's greatest painters, is now a fine *posada*. La Rosada offers utterly charming accommodation, with six pleasing rooms and some delightfully rustic cabanas. The real attraction is the incredibly warm welcome reserved by the hosts, relatives of Fernando Fader, that make a stay at the *posada* an unforgettable experience.

✉ Plaza Principal, Ischilín
☎ 03521/423057 🕐 Oct–Apr daily; May–Sep Fri–Mon ✋ $180–$200 🛏 6
🚗 From Córdoba, take the RN-9 northwards in the direction of Jesús María. 20km (12.5 miles) to the north of Jesús María take the left fork, RN-60, direction Deán Funes and Catamarca. In Avellaneda turn left and take the road to Ischilín (125km/77.5 miles from Córdoba)

MALARGÜE

LAS LEÑAS COMPLEX

www.maxisol.com.ar
The hotel complex at Argentina's top ski resort offers a range of accommodation in the self-catering Delphos and Géminis aparthotels. The latter is slightly more upmarket and expensive. Swimming pools, saunas, Jacuzzis and excellent restaurants are among the facilities.

✉ Las Leñas, Mendoza ☎ 011/4393-8031
✋ $2,800–$3,300 per week 🛏 110
🏊 Indoor

RÍO GRANDE

The Río Grande won't win any prizes for decor or architecture but it is a welcoming family hotel, with pleasant rooms, conveniently located on the main street. One of the hotel's trump cards is the excellent restaurant where you can try the famed local trout as well as a range of hearty Argentine dishes.

✉ Avenida San Martín ☎ 02627/471589
✋ $250–$310 🛏 34

MENDOZA

BOHEMIA

www.bohemiahotelboutique.com
One of the few truly stylish downtown hotels in the city, the Bohemia is in a wonderful location in a leafy *barrio*, close to the glorious 400ha (988-acre) Parque General San Martín. The jazzy, comfortable rooms are spread over two floors in an elegant family townhouse, and furnished with comfy leather armchairs and eye-catching paintings. In addition to a swimming pool and wine bar, amenities include a bistro restaurant and bike rental.

✉ Granaderos 954 ☎ 0261/423-0575
✋ $310–$400 🛏 11 🔆 🏊

CASA MARGOT

www.casamargot.com.ar
A highly commendable boutique hotel in Chacras de Coria, a charming southern suburb of Mendoza, Casa Margot has only two rooms, featuring enticing brick-vaulted ceilings. The decor is bold and unusual, and the Celodonio suite has a spiral staircase leading to a cosy study. Wine spa treatments are just one of the many luxury extras provided.

✉ Italia s/n, Chacras de Coria, Luján de Cuyo ☎ 0261/496-1877 ✋ US$250–US$350 🛏 2

CAVAS WINE LODGE

www.cavaswinelodge.com
Part of the Relais et Chateaux group, this sumptuous lodge in Luján de Cuyo, to the south of Mendoza, is a genuine A-list hotel. The main building is an elegant neo-colonial mansion, where you can enjoy superb food and top-rate wines, as

befits a hotel set among 35ha (86 acres) of world-class vineyards. The cellar is definitely worth a visit, while wine-related artworks embellish every room. The luxurious bedrooms are scattered around the grounds in individual units built in a simple Moorish style, complete with mini rooftop terraces, where you can admire the stunning views of the surrounding countryside.

✉ Costa Flore s/n, Alto Agrelo, Luján de Cuyo, Mendoza ☎ 0261/410-6297
🕐 Closed Jun ✋ US$290–US$400
🛏 14 🔆 🏖 Outdoor

CAVIERES

www.caviereswines.com
The marvellous Cavieres *posada* has three rooms, housed in a modernized adobe house, with a rustic gallery and old-fashioned mosquito nets. The extensive grounds include olive groves and vineyards. Don't miss a chance to try the home-pressed oil as well as delicious jams made with fruit from the orchard. Breakfasts are delicious.

✉ Espejo 3705, Maipú, Mendoza
☎ 0261/15-6074303 ✋ $300–$320
🛏 3 🚗 Take Acceso Sur (RN-40) southwards from Mendoza city centre and turn left onto RP-60 (Maipú). In the locality of Russell turn left into Canal Pescara (after about 2km/1.25 miles) and the hotel is located at the first crossroads

CLUB TAPIZ

www.club-tapiz.com.ar
The seven sober and tasteful rooms (plus four equally plush rooms in the exclusive Casa Zolo) make staying at Club Tapiz a truly luxurious experience. This wonderful hotel in Maipú was built in the 1980s and is set among 10ha (24 acres) of premium vineyards. There is a beautiful spa, swimming pool and wine-tasting room and you can rent bicycles and helmets.

✉ Pedro Molina s/n, Maipú
☎ 0261/496-3433 ✋ US$300–US$330
🛏 11 🏖 Outdoor 🚗 Take Acceso Sur (RN-40) southwards from Mendoza city centre and turn left onto RP-60 (Maipú). Casa Tapiz is located at km2.5 in the locality of Russell

FINCA ADALGISA

www.fincaadalgisa.com.ar

Gabriela Furlotti, the third-generation owner, lovingly converted this century-old wine mansion, in the heart of Mendoza's viniculture region, into a boutique hotel. The 11 sumptuous rooms are all different, thanks to the judicious use of traditional fabrics and handpicked furnishings. One of the highlights of staying here is the dining room, which overlooks the vineyards.

✉ Pueyrredón 2222, Chacras de Coria
☎ 0261/496-0713 💧 US$240–US$290
🛏 11 🏊 Outdoor

HUENTALA

www.huentala.com

Sharing some of the facilities with the neighbouring Sheraton hotel, this boutique hotel is a prime choice and offers excellent value. The 65 rooms are comfortable and range from smart classic to roomy suites. The Kitak Cava Lounge in the basement is a great place to sample local wines.

✉ Primitivo de la Reta 1007
☎ 0261/420-0766 💧 $500–$620 🛏 65
🔁 🏊 Indoor 🍴

PARK HYATT

www.mendoza.park.hyatt.com

All that remains of the landmark Plaza Hotel is the restored 19th-century neoclassical facade with its fine Hispanic detailing. The rest of the building is a spacious modern structure, part of which is taken up by a glossy casino. The rooms are smart and comfortable but the hotel's main assets are the location, right on the Plaza de la Independencia, the excellent Bistro M, with its open-plan kitchen, and the Grill Q Argentine *parrilla*, the perfect place to sample juicy meat with top-rate Mendoza wines. The Kaua Spa specializes in wine and grape-based treatments.

✉ Chile 1124 ☎ 0261/441-1234
💧 $700–$1,100 🛏 186 🔁 🏊 Outdoor
🍴

POSADA OLIVAR

www.posadaolivar.com

The up-and-coming Chacras de Coria suburb is an ideal place to stay as it provides easy access to the main vineyards and also the city. Guests can relax in the comfortable house or in the beautiful gardens, which are planted with fruit trees, centennial olives and vines that shade the rambling grounds. There are only four spacious rooms, with en suite bathrooms, adding to the intimate feel of staying at someone's proudly kept home.

✉ Besares 978, Chacras de Coria
☎ 0261/496-0061 💧 US$110–US$130
🛏 4 🏊 Outdoor

NONO

ESTANCIA LA LEJANÍA

www.lalejania.com

An alpine *estancia* in the charming Valle de Traslasierra, one of the most idyllic regions of Córdoba Province, this excellent accommodation is run by a dedicated French couple, whose passions are Gallic hospitality and exploring the most remote sections of the Andes. The rustic wooden and stone house offers comfort and, of course, you will be treated to some great cuisine along with the local *criollo* dishes.

✉ La Lejanía, Nono ☎ 03544/498960
💧 US$180–US$210 🛏 10 🏊 Outdoor
🏠 Signposted from the village of Nono

LA RIOJA

FINCA HUAYRAPUCA (FAMATINA)

www.nueceshuayrapuca.com.ar

Huayrapuca is a fantastic *estancia* famed for its walnut groves. Located at 1,700m (5,576ft) above sea level in the Riojan village of Famatina, it is worth staying in this *estancia* just to see its beautiful adobe buildings. The rooms are deliberately rustic with exquisite textiles for bed covers and guests enjoy peace and quiet in abundance. Don't miss a visit to the nut-cracking sheds, the famous *quebraderos*.

✉ Camino a Carrizal, Barrio Galli, Famatina, La Rioja ☎ 03822/15-677488
💧 $290–$320 🛏 8 🚌 From La Rioja, take the RN-38 south, then RN-74 northwest from Patquia to Chilecito. Continue 32km (20 miles) northwards via the RN-40 to Famatina and then take the road to Carrizal

SAN JUAN

DEL BONO PARK

www.hoteldelbono.com.ar

San Juan's casino hotel is housed in a superb modern building, painted in pale ochre hues that reflect the surrounding desert. The beautiful brick-vaulted Cava restaurant is one of the best in the city, while the 1878 wine bar has an enviable selection of local and national vintages to suit every taste and budget. As for the rooms, they are smart and appealingly decorated, with contemporary fabrics and sleek wooden surfaces.

✉ Avenida José Ignacio de la Roza 1946 (oeste) ☎ 0264/426-2300 💧 $500–$620
🛏 135 🔁 🏊 Outdoor 🍴

SAN RAFAEL

LA CARMELITA

www.fincalacarmelita.com

The 20ha (49 acres) of land where this *finca* (estate) is located is an oasis in the desert of the southern Mendoza province, planted with olive and plum trees, a kitchen garden and extensive vineyards where cabernet sauvignon dominates. The hotel building is a smart brick-built edifice, with an enticing open fire in the cosy living room and comfortable modern rooms. In addition to taking part in the farm tasks, such as grape picking or tree pruning, you can also go on a trek, have a massage or take a bike ride.

✉ Carmona 2500 ☎ 02627/15-642695
💧 US$110–US$130 🛏 8 🔁 🏊 Outdoor
🚌 Take RP-143 from San Rafael (and its airport); the *finca* is 5km (3 miles) from the airport and lies 2km (1.25 miles) off the main road (clearly signposted)

HOSTEL PUESTA DEL SOL

www.complejopuestadelsol.com

Conveniently situated on the outskirts of town, this excellent hostel offers a range of budget accommodation, verdant gardens and a wonderful pool. There are standard rooms, ranging from dorms to doubles with shared bathrooms plus 20 superior doubles, with private bathrooms. There is an on-site bar, restaurant and small shop.

✉ Deán Funes 998 ☎ 02627/434881
✋ $150–$300 🛈 68 ⛲ Outdoor

TIERRA MORA
www.tierramora.com
Tierra Mora is a three-star boutique hotel and apartments and the accommodation is a combination of understated luxury and rustic charm, with raised wooden deck galleries and decorated in sandy yellow and tangerine. A swimming pool rounds off the package.
✉ Ameghino 350 ☎ 02627/447222
✋ $320–$350 🛈 36 ⛲ Outdoor

TOWER INN
www.towersanrafael.com
The four-star Tower Inn and Suites is not particularly intimate but it is perhaps the most practical place to stay in the region and this functional business oriented establishment does not lack style. Accommodation ranges from singles to comfortable doubles and deluxe suites, there is a good restaurant, a spa and a swimming pool.
✉ Avenida Hipólito Yrigoyen 774
☎ 02627/427190 ✋ $450–$600 🛈 87
⛲ Outdoor

TUPUNGATO
BODEGAS SALENTEIN
www.bodegasalentein.com/bodega/posada
Dutch-owned Salentein is one of the great names of Mendocino wine and a visit to the winery is a highlight of any trip. If you want to linger over the experience, you can opt to stay at the fabulous *posada*, a fair distance away from the main buildings within the estate. The 16 rooms are strung around gardens and patios, in a traditional-style galleried building with newer two-storey houses. The rooms are huge and impeccably well equipped, assuring a luxurious stay amid the grapes.
✉ Bodega Salentein, Tupungato
☎ 02622/429090 ✋ US$250–US$280
🛈 16 ⛲ Outdoor

TUPUNGATO DIVINO
www.tupungatodivino.com.ar
Two young professional families from Buenos Aires upped sticks

and created a little paradise of their own. In the main building, the enticing restaurant, with wine-tasting facilities, has views of Tupungato's peak and trellised vines and overlooks a superb swimming pool and long irrigation canal. Guests have easy access to some of the best wineries in the region and a mini-cellar in every room is kept well stocked. No credit cards.
✉ Ruta 89 and Calle Los Europeos
☎ 02622/15-448948 ✋ US$100–US$130
🛈 4 ⛲ Outdoor

VILLA GENERAL BELGRANO
CHAMONIX SPA
www.chamonixposada.com.ar
The exterior of the Chamonix, with its wood and stone chalet appearance, is the image of a mountain *posada*, but inside all is sleek luxury with spacious, bright rooms, waxed wooden floors and top-grade fabrics. The spa comprises a beautiful indoor pool with comfortable loungers, a sauna, gym and an impressive menu of different massages to soothe away any aches and pains.
✉ Avenida San Martín 1068
☎ 03546/464230 ✋ $530–$640 🛈 20
⛲ Indoor

POSADA LA SOÑADA
www.posadalasoniada.com.ar
The modern Swiss-chalet style architecture blends well with the local landscape and Belgrano's *Mitteleuropa* ambience. Located a short way to the south of the town, La Soñada has capacious, airy bedrooms with tiled floors and appealing high pinewood roofs. There is a handsome swimming pool in the grassy grounds and air-conditioning throughout.
✉ Ruta 5 km 84 ☎ 03546/464707
✋ $220–$370 🛈 16 ⛲ Outdoor

VILLA UNIÓN
CAÑÓN DE TALAMPAYA
www.hotelcanontalampaya.com
This is one of the best places to stay in the whole region. The smart rooms are modern, well equipped and stylishly decorated, with fabulous views of the mountains that line the valley. There is an excellent restaurant serving local wines with well-prepared local fare, a spacious lounge and patio, plus a swimming pool.
✉ Ruta 76 km202 ☎ 03825/470753
✋ $250–$340 🛈 28 ⛲ Outdoor

Below *Salentein bodega, Tupungato*

THE NORTH

Argentina's colonial heartland in the far north of the country has more in common with Bolivia and Peru than with Patagonia or Buenos Aires and a strong Andean flavour pervades every aspect of the region. Visitors come here for the arid highland landscapes, the pre-Columbian ruins, and unique culture. As you rise from the tobacco fields and sugar plantations of Salta and Tucumán, lush tropical jungle quickly gives way to bone-dry ravines, tinted with a rainbow of elements and oxides. In the upland plateaux of the altiplano, flamingos and rheas, llamas and vicuñas graze around crystalline lagoons, ringed by snow-white salt flats and the ochre peaks of extinct volcanoes.

Salta is the regional hub for tourism. Its handsome hotels and traditional *peñas* (folklore clubs), beautifully restored colonial and neo-colonial architecture, and unrivalled mountain setting make it one of the most appealing cities in the country. Of its many museums the prizewinner has to be the controversial MAAM, created to display the naturally mummified corpses of three Inca children. Although other provincial capitals—including the beguiling market town of Jujuy, the vibrant industrial powerhouse of Tucumán and the sleepy backwater of San Fernando del Valle de Catamarca—are overshadowed by Salta, they each act as gateways to their own beautiful hinterlands.

Quebrada de Humahuaca, a dramatic highland gorge, is extremely popular with visitors, and its once-traditional Andean towns—Tilcara, with its pre-Incan fort, and Purmamarca, famed for its seven-coloured hillside—have grown used to the modernity that goes with cutting-edge tourism. The lofty valleys around the contrasting villages of Cafayate and Cachi are carpeted with vineyards, yielding some of the country's finest wines. The RN-40 highway wends its way through these gorges, heading north to the Bolivian border, and south through Tucumán. Travel along this route and you'll pass the reconstructed Inca ruins at Quilmes and the enticing village of Belén, famed for its ponchos, and on to the old hamlet of Londres, the second-oldest settlement in Argentina.

AMAICHA DEL VALLE

www.norteargentino.travel

www.museopachamama.com

Amaicha is a placid hamlet in a sunny valley, located at a strategic junction where Salta, Catamarca and Tucumán provinces meet. Just outside is the Museo Pachamama (tel 03892/421-0041; daily 8.30–1, 2–6; $15). Created by local artist Héctor Cruz, the collection is housed in a grandiloquent complex of iron and stone built around cacti gardens and decorated with striking mosaics, depicting condors and llamas. Inside, you will find an impressive array of local archaeological finds and the reconstruction of a mine. Exhibits also include semi-precious stones and mineral ores, including some rhodochrosite, mined near Belén. There is also a fine collection of paintings, tapestries and ceramics from Cruz's prolific workshops and his modern designs inspired by pre-Columbian traditions, some of which are on sale at the large shop.

➕ 336 E4 ✉ Amaicha, Provincia de Tucumán 🛈 Tafí del Valle (▷ 248) 🚌 Buses from Tucumán and Cafayate 🚗 Take the RN-38 southwards, direction Catamarca, then RP-317 to Tafí del Valle and on towards Quilmes and Cafayate; from Cafayate (and Salta) take RN-40 south (direction Santa María), then turn eastwards along RP-317 direction Tafí

ANTOFAGASTA DE LA SIERRA

www.catamarcaguia.com.ar/Turismo/Tur_Antofagasta.php

Remote Antofagasta de la Sierra, 3,440m (11,283ft) above sea level, heads a huge, parched expanse of pampa ringed by jet-black volcanos and soaring Andean peaks. An oasis of feathery tamarinds and emerald alfalfa crops with traditional adobe houses, it is set among extraordinary landscapes and it is worth climbing Cerro Amarillo and Cerro de la Cruz that overlook the village for panoramic views. The local tourist office can provide a list of guides to show you the amazing sights, including flamingo-speckled lagoons. You can also buy ponchos made of beautiful alpaca and llama wool.

Don't miss the Museo Arqueológico (tel 0835/71001; Mon–Fri 8–6; $2) on the main street, where you can see a naturally mummified baby, found in the nearby mountains and believed to be nearly 2,000 years old. The display includes a set of jewels and other items that were found with the child, indicating that he or she was possibly of royal lineage.

➕ 336 D4 ✉ Antofagasta de la Sierra, Provincia de Catamarca 🛈 Municipalidad de Antofagasta de la Sierra, Avenida Belgrano s/n ☎ 03835/471001 🚌 Bus from Catamarca 🚗 Antofagasta is 260km (161 miles) due north from Belén, at the junction of the Ríos Punilla and Las Paitas, next to El Torreón; take the turning 5km (3 miles) south of Hualfín (RN-40) signposted Antofagasta de la Sierra; the road is paved almost all the way and you cannot get lost ☞ Tours available locally

BELÉN

www.turismocatamarca.gov.ar

Argentina's self-styled 'Poncho Capital' lies in a beautiful valley carpeted with olive groves and fields of paprika peppers, between the mighty Sierra de Belén and the Río Belén. Not only does Belén offer excellent accommodation and 1900 (▷ 260), one of the best restaurants in the area, it also serves as a useful base for highland treks and horse riding. In town, a number of weavers produce beautiful natural-hued blankets and clothing made of llama and sheep's wool.

Near the lively central Plaza Olmos y Aguilera, shaded by orange trees and encircled by cafés and ice-cream parlours, is the Museo Arqueológico Condor Huasi (Tue–Sat 8–1, 3–7; $2). The museum, on the first floor of the shopping arcade on San Martín and Belgrano, houses one of the country's major collections of pre-Columbian artefacts. Its impressive ceramic, bronze and silver items trace the history of the Diaguita culture from 300BC to the Inca invasions.

One of the museum's finest objects is a beautiful ceramic jaguar.

➕ 340 D5 ✉ Belén, Provincia de Catamarca 🛈 Municipalidad 🕐 Mon–Fri 9–6 🚌 Buses from Catamarca and Salta 🚗 Driving, approach Belén via the RN-40, southwards from Cafayate and Quilmes, northwards from Tinogasta in Catamarca Province

CACHI

www.cachi.todowebsalta.com.ar

The main sights in picturesque little Cachi, situated at 2,280m (7,478ft) above sea level, are clustered around the Plaza Mayor. On the north side of the plaza, shaded by palms and orange trees, stands the much-restored Iglesia San José, with its plain creamy-white facade, fine wooden floor and unusual cactus-wood altar, pews and confessionals. On the east side, in a neo-colonial house around a whitewashed patio, is the Museo de Arqueológica de San José de Cachi 'Pío Pablo Díaz' (Juan Calchaquí s/n; tel 03868/491080; Mon–Fri 9–6, Sat 10–2, Sun 10–1; $5), which displays a collection of locally excavated pre-Columbian items.

Cachi is a great place to buy local crafts, including ponchos and ceramics, or you can clamber up to the elegant colonnaded cemetery for wonderful mountain views and a panorama of the patchwork of vines and capsicum plantations in the valley. The scenic tracks to Cachi Adentro and La Aguada, a short distance out of the village, lead from the end of Calle Benjamín Zorrilla through fertile fields that blaze crimson with drying paprika peppers between March and May.

➕ 336 E3 ✉ Cachi, Provincia de Salta 🛈 Gral Güemes s/n ☎ 03868/491902 🕐 Mon–Fri 8–9, Sat–Sun 9–3, 5–9 🚌 Buses from Salta 🚗 170km (105 miles) from Salta; take the RN-68 southwards in the direction of Cafayate and turn in a westerly direction via Chicoana (direction Cachi), before driving up the steep and winding Cuesta del Obispo and past the Parque Nacional Los Cardones. In the summer (Dec–Mar) set out early to avoid storms, which can cut off roads

INFORMATION

www.cafayate.todowebsalta.com.ar
✚ 336 E4 ✉ Cafayate, Provincia de
Salta ℹ Nuestra Señora del Rosario
9 ☎ 03868/422442 🕐 Daily 8–9
🚌 Buses from Salta 🅿 Cafayate sits
at the junction of the RN-68 and RN-40,
about 190km (118 miles) south of Salta,
via Quebrada de Cafayate. From Salta
(nearest airport) follow RN-68 (signposted
Cafayate) 🚶 Tours of the *bodegas*
available locally (▷ 256)

TIPS

›› During the Serenata Cafayateña folklore
festival (▷ 259), held at the beginning
of Lent, accommodation gets booked up
in advance.

›› On the north side of the plaza there is
a crafts fair (daily 9am–11pm), which is a
good place to buy locally made souvenirs.

›› If you haven't got your own transport,
there are three small *bodegas* in Cafayate
itself: Domingo Hermanos (Nuestra
Senora del Rosario and 25 de Mayo, tel
03868/421225, www.domingohermanos.
com; Mon–Fri 8–12, 3–6, Sat 9–1.30,
Sun and national holidays 10–1); Nanni
(Chavarría 151; tel 03868/421527,
www.bodegananni.com; Mon–Sat 9–1,
2–6); and, at the entrance to the village
when coming from Salta, Vasija Secreta
(RN-40 s/n; tel 03868/421850,
www.vasijasecreta.com; Mon–Sat 9–1,
2–6), all of which offer free tours.

Above *Bodega El Esteco winery on the
outskirts of town*

CAFAYATE

Salta Province's wine capital, Cafayate, is the main town in the sunny Valles
Calchaquíes, at the foot of majestic hills and surrounded by vineyards. The
town is reached via a gorge, the magnificent Quebrada de Cafayate, which is
part of a triangular circuit (▷ 250–251) linking the town to Salta (▷ 240–243)
and Cachi (▷ 233). The town's strategic position, thriving wine industry and
excellent hotels and restaurants make it stand out as one of the most attractive
destinations in the north. A fine cathedral, a couple of minor museums and its
proximity to a slew of *bodegas* confirm its status as a major tourist resort. At
1,660m (5,444ft) above sea level, Cafayate has a mild climate, with over 350 days
of sunshine a year, bright winters and temperate summers, except on rare days
when the hot *zonda* blows from the Andes.

THE PLAZA

The town's heart is the central plaza, where the handsome Catedral de Nuestra
Señora del Rosario dominates a lively scene. One block southwest at Colón 191
is the interesting Museo Arqueológico Rodolfo Bravo (tel 03868/421054; Mon–Fri
11–9; $2), where you can see a fine collection of pre-Columbian funerary urns
and Incan artefacts. Two blocks south at Colón and Avenida Guemes s/n is the
Museo de la Vid y del Vino (tel 03868/421125; Mon–Sat 8.30–7; $2), which
is housed in a former *bodega* and contains various exhibits on winemaking,
intriguing implements and old photographs.

BODEGAS

Cafayate is renowned for the flowery, citrus-nosed whites made with the unique
torrontés grape but there are lots of good reds, too, mainly cabernet sauvignon.
Several *bodegas* open their doors to the public for tours, tastings and a chance
to buy bottles of wine. In a dramatic location 5km (3 miles) away, high on the
Camino al Divisadero, the Finca Las Nubes (tel 03868/422129; Jan–Feb daily
9–1, 3–7; Mar–Dec Mon–Sat 9.30–5, Sun 10–1; free with the purchase of a bottle
of wine) is a small *bodega* run by the Mounier family. El Esteco, at the junction
of the RN-68 and RN-40, is popular with visitors and offers regular tours (tel
03868/421139, www.elesteco.com.ar; Mon–Fri (tours hourly) 10–12, 2.30–6.30,
Sat–Sun and national holidays 10, 11 and 12). Etchart, 2km (1.25 miles) south of
the village along the RN-40, (km1047; tel 03868/421310; tours Mon–Fri hourly
9.15–3.15; Sat morning only; free; call ahead for English-speaking guide) has an
outstanding reputation, although Arnaldo Etchart, one of the doyens of Cafayate
winemaking, sold it several years ago. Etchart now has a more exclusive
boutique winery at nearby San Pedro de Yacochuya, producing exceptional
wines (tel 03868/421233, www.sanpedrodeyacochuya.com.ar; call 24 hours
ahead for free visit and wine tasting).

FIAMBALÁ

www.argentinaturismo.com.ar/fiambala
www.fiambala.gov.ar

Fiambalá is a quiet oasis town of crumbling adobe houses, set among the vineyards and olive groves of the Abaucán Valley. You can buy excellent textiles and ceramics at various workshops around the village. Just north of the Plaza Mayor at Abaucán s/n is the little Museo del Hombre (tel 03837/496250; daily 9–1, 4–8; $2), with two well-preserved pre-Columbian mummies the highlight of its collection.

Just 2km (1.25 miles) to the south, alongside the RN-60 from Tinogasta, stands the well-restored Iglesia San Pedro, a colonial chapel built in 1770. The neighbours have the key to the church, which has a handsomely plain interior, decorated with paintings of the Peruvian Cusco school. Next door, a restored mid-18th-century building houses the Museo Histórico Colonial and the Museo del Sitio (both daily 9–1, 4–8; free), while nearby on the main road towards Tinogasta is Finca Don Diego (www.fincadondiego.com; Mon–Fri 9–1 3–6.30), a state-of-the-art winery where you can taste some of the region's best wines.

Fiambalá's other claim to fame is its thermal baths (tel 03837/496250; 9am–10pm; $5), in a beautiful mountain setting 15km (9 miles) to the east. The mineral spring gushes out at over 70°C (158°F) but, by the time the water trickles to the attractive stone pools, it cools to 30°C (86°F).

✚ 340 D5 ✉ Fiambalá, Provincia de Catamarca ℹ Municipalidad ☎ 03837/496250 ◴ Daily 9–12.30, 5–9 🚌 Buses from Catamarca 🚗 From Catamarca, take RN-38 southwest and turn west at RN-60 (after 70km/43.5 miles); continue for another 250km (155 miles), via Tinogasta, to reach Fiambalá

HUMAHUACA

www.quebradadehumahuaca.com/hospedaje/humahuaca.php

Humahuaca is situated in a dramatic mountain setting at 3,000m (9,840ft) above sea level on either side of the Río Grande. The centre, on the west bank, is a grid of attractive cobbled streets, lined with neo-colonial houses and rustic adobe buildings, stretching along the steep river banks from the leafy main square. On the western side of the square is the much restored 17th-century Iglesia de Nuestra Señora de la Candelaria y San Antonio, with its austerely beautiful facade. Inside are two fine retables, one from the 17th and the other from the 18th century, depicting the Crucifixion.

Of all the sights in Humahuaca, don't miss the Monumento a la Independencia, designed by local artist Ernesto Soto Avendaño in the 1940s. This impressive group of sculptures honours the North Argentine Army that fought a total of 14 battles in Humahuaca during the War for Independence. A triumphal stairway leads from the plaza to the monument, a 20m (66ft) bronze of the indigenous Chasqui Pedro Socompa bearing the news of freedom.

✚ 336 E2 ✉ Humahuaca, Provincia de Jujuy ℹ Municipalidad ☎ 03887/421154 ◴ Daily 9–7 🚌 Buses from Jujuy and Salta 🚗 125km (77.5 miles) north from Jujuy along the RN-9 🔲 Tours from Salta (▷ 240–243) and Jujuy (▷ 247)

IRUYA

www.iruya.todowebsalta.com.ar

An enticing Andean hamlet nestling in the valley of the Río Iruya, in the far northern corner of Salta Province, Iruya has fortified walls, steep cobbled streets and whitewashed houses. At an altitude of 2,780m (9,118ft), you feel a long way from the hectic streets of Jujuy or Salta. Due north of Humahuaca along the RN-9, the RP-13 forks off to the northeast, crossing a couple of stony riverbeds before winding up a beautiful narrow valley, and then down again to Iruya via a dramatic and incredibly narrow corniche road. The point where you cross the border into Salta Province is the Abra del Cóndor pass, at a giddying and often gale-blown 3,900m (12,792ft).

✚ 336 F1 ✉ Iruya, Provincia de Salta ℹ General Güemes s/n ◴ Daily 9–6 🚌 Buses from Humahuaca 🚗 North of Humahuaca along the RN-9 then fork northeast on the RP-13; the turning is 25km (15.5 miles) north of Humahuaca 🔲 Tours from Jujay

Above *Sheep herders near Iruya*
Left *Cerro de los Siete Colores, Purmamarca*

LONDRES

Humble little Londres was founded in 1558 and is Argentina's second-oldest city. Known locally as the Cuna de la Nuez (Walnut Heartland), the town celebrates a walnut festival (▷ 259), with folk music and crafts displays, in early February.

Londres de Abajo (the lower town) centres on Plaza José Eusebio Colombres and the walnut festival is held here, in front of the lime-washed 18th-century Iglesia de San Juan Bautista. Londres de Arriba (the upper town) centres on the Plaza Hipólito Yrigoyen. The Iglesia de la Inmaculada Concepción, with its pleasing colonnade and Argentina's oldest bells, dominates the square.

A fresco on one of the outside walls of the *municipalidad* depicts the marriage between Philip of Spain and Mary Tudor of England in 1554 — an event that inspired the town's name. The nearby Museo Arqueológico (Mon–Fri 8–1; $2) contains ceramics and other finds from the Shinkal ruins, 5km (3 miles) west of the town. The sympathetically restored Shinkal ruins (Mon–Fri 8–1, 3–6; $2) offer an insight into the Diaguitas's Maya-like architecture with ceremonial steps ascending fortified mounds from where you can enjoy views of the noble Sierra de Zapata.
✚ 340 D5 ℹ Belén (▷ 233) ✉ Londres, Provincia de Catamarca 🚌 Buses from Catamarca 🚗 From Cafayate, take the RN-40 south for 280km (173.5 miles)

MOLINOS

www.molinos.todowebsalta.com.ar
Molinos makes a perfect stopover, as you make your way along the winding RN-40 between Cachi and Cafayate. The village lies about 2km (1.25 miles) to the west of the main road and is dominated by the 18th-century Iglesia de San Pedro Nolasco. Immediately opposite is the 18th-century residence of the last royalist governor of Salta, Nicolás Severo de Isasmendi, which now functions as an exquisite hotel, the Hacienda de Molinos (▷ 263). The hotel has a gorgeous main patio, where you can have a drink or a snack.

Estancia Colomé (▷ 263), 20km (12.5 miles) outside Molinos, is one the country's finest hotels. An interesting museum here is dedicated to the artist James Turrell, whose intriguing works play with light and the perception of space. The museum contains nine installations, plus a number of prints and drawings.
✚ 336 E3 ✉ Molinos, Provincia de Salta ℹ Cachi (▷ 233) or Cafayate (▷ 234) 🚌 Buses from Salta and Cachi 🚗 50km (31 miles) south of Cachi by the RN-40 and over 100km (62 miles) north of Cafayate

PARQUE NACIONAL CALILEGUA
▷ 237.

PURMAMARCA

www.argentinaturismo.com.ar/purmamarca
Picturesque Purmamarca sits at the base of a gorge, its busy main square flanked by the 17th-century Iglesia Santa Rosa de Lima. The church was built to the simple, single-towered local design and is shaded by an ancient *algarrobo* tree. At the northeast corner of the plaza, the four elegant arches of the Cabildo (the former municipal headquarters) adorn a minimalist whitewashed facade. There is a daily craft market by the Cabildo (9–6), but better quality crafts and souvenirs are sold in a number of excellent shops around the village.

Apart from its tranquil ambience, Purmamarca's main attraction is the Cerro de los Siete Colores, a crinkly cliff behind the village with rainbow stripes that range from sandy beige to deep purple. A 3km (1.8-mile) signed trail marked 'Los Colorados'

Left *Multi-coloured Cerro de los Siete Colores rising behind Purmamarca*

(Red Rocks) leads round the back of the village, where you can enjoy a panorama of this polychrome bluff. With its excellent range of accommodation and other services, Purmamarca is a great base for visiting the whole region.
✚ 336 E2 ✉ Purmamarca, Provincia de Jujuy ℹ Municipalidad 🕐 Daily 8–8 🚌 Buses from Jujuy 🚗 From Jujuy, head northwards along the RN-9 and after 60km (37 miles) turn westwards along the RN-52 (direction Chile); Purmamarca is 4km (2.5 miles) along the road

QUEBRADA DEL TORO
▷ 239.

QUILMES

www.turismoentucuman.com
First built in the ninth century AD, the indigenous Quilmes had a population of more than 3,000 in its 17th-century heyday and fiercely resisted attempts by the Spanish conquistadors at colonization. The Quilmes were finally defeated after 130 years and brutally punished with a 1,500km (930-mile) forced march to Buenos Aires with barely any food or water: Most did not survive.

The magnificent walls, houses and communal buildings in the terraced *pukará* (fortress) have been excavated and reconstructed by archaeologists. The overall effect is impressive, especially just after dawn, when the mountains behind are illuminated from the east. The entrance fee also gets you into the Quilmes museum, which contains some fascinating items found on the site, such as ceramics and stone tools. In addition, there are some expensive modern crafts by Héctor Cruz, who created the museum in Amaicha (▷ 233) 15km (9 miles) to the south.
✚ 336 E4 ✉ Quilmes, Tucumán 🕐 Daily 8–6 ☎ 03892/421075 💲 Adult $10, child (under 12) free 🚌 Buses from Cafayate stop at the junction along the RN-40; it is a 5km (3-mile) trek on a track to Quilmes 🚗 From Cafayate, take the RN-40 southwards for 48km (30 miles) to reach turnoff to Quilmes, then continue 5km (3 miles) along a track 🎫 Tours from Salta (▷ 257), Cafayate (▷ 256) and Tucumán (▷ 249)

PARQUE NACIONAL CALILEGUA

The best of the three cloud forest parks, the Parque Nacional Calilegua covers 760sq km (296sq miles) of high terrain. The land belonged to the Leach brothers, local sugar magnates of British origin, but was donated to the state for use as a national park in the 1970s to protect the clean water supplies needed for their sugar plantations in the valleys below.

Today, the park is important in protecting the rich ecosystems of the Yungas or *nuboselvas* (cloud jungles). The precipitation, altitude and latitude favour subtropical vegetation, such as *lapacho* and *palo amarillo* trees, which form a dense canopy in the summer. Although, it is easier to spot wildlife lurking in the forest in the winter, when the trees have lost their leaves. At all times the dank trunks are carpeted with moss and ferns that bristle with a bewildering mass of epiphytes and lianas.

SEEING THE PARK

The fauna is dominated by 230 bird species, which vary from huge condors and eagles to toco toucans and torrent ducks. Tiny hummingbirds are legion, while rufus-throated dippers are a perennial favourite with visitors. There are also a large number of native mammals such as crab-eating raccoons, southern river otters, Brazilian tapirs, collared peccaries and, albeit seldom spotted, pumas and jaguars.

Within the park, ordinary cars can make it along the main road as far as the Mesada de la Colmenas, where the rangers have a secondary headquarters. Beyond this point, a 4WD vehicle is required if you want to climb to the park's highest point, marked by the Abra de las Cañas monolith, at 1,700m (5,576ft).

Seven trails of varying length and difficulty have been hacked through the dense vegetation, but it is essential to seek the rangers' guidance before you set off because there aren't any maps of the park. The best way to see the park is on an organized tour (▷ Tips panel).

Below right *The giant anteater, one of the park's indigenous mammals*
Below *A toco toucan, among the 230 species of bird found at the Parque Nacional Calilegua*

INFORMATION

www.argentinaturismo.com.ar/jujuy/pncalilegua.php

🗺 337 F2 ✉ Parque Nacional Calilegua, Provincia de Jujuy

ℹ Information centre at park entrance

🕐 Daily 9–6 ☎ 03886/422046 💲 Free

🚗 The park entrance is at Aguas Negras, 120km (74.5 miles) north from Jujuy on the RN-34. At Libertador General San Martín take the RP-83, which climbs to Valle Colorado but is paved only as far as Aguas Negras 🚌 Tours from Jujuy and Salta

TIPS

» The best time to visit the park is during the spring or autumn, when temperatures and rainfall levels are moderate.

» You should protect yourself from mosquitoes with liberal applications of insect repellent during the day and night.

» If you want to see the wildlife, it is advisable to walk off the beaten track and away from the noisy trucks that trundle along the main road.

» Trekking around Calilegua takes time and it's a good idea to spend a night or two camping in the park. Morning and late afternoon are the best times to see animals and birds by streams and rivers.

» The best way to visit the park is on an organized tour. Clark Expediciones in Salta (tel 0387/497-1024) runs expert birdwatching safaris to the park.

QUEBRADA DEL TORO

Quebrada del Toro (Bull Gorge) is named for the bullish torrent that tumbles down its valley. On the ascent to its top, there is some breathtakingly varied mountain scenery of polychrome rocks and arid desert, culminating in the low-oxygen *puna*, when you eventually reach the top.

In the winter you can chug up (and down) on the legendary Tren a las Nubes (▷ 254–255). Alternatively, take an organized tour or rent a vehicle and try the suggested itinerary in this guide (▷ 252–253). There are even horseback treks to the top, which is a wonderfully leisurely way of seeing the gorge.

SANTA ROSA DE TASTIL AND TASTIL

The first settlement of note is the tiny Santa Rosa de Tastil, which is worth a quick stop (if you are travelling by road) for its diminutive Museo del Sitio, (Tue–Sat 10–6, Sun 10–2; $2), huddling beneath cactus-spiked rocks. The museum contains an impressive pre-Inca mummy and finds from nearby excavations. A short distance away is the newer Museo Regional Moisés Zerpa, (Tue–Sat 10–6, Sun 10–2; $2), which is furnished and decorated like a traditional local house, complete with cooking utensils, ceramics and textiles.

If you're lucky, the curator of the museums will show you around the pre-Inca site, signed 3km (2 miles) west, at Tastil. The well-restored remains are one of the region's largest pre-Inca towns inhabited by some 3,000 people in the 14th century AD. The vantage point stands on previously fortified heights and commands stunning valley and mountain views, overlooking the terraced farmland where the people of Tastil once eked out a living.

ABRA DE MUÑANO

The final stretch of the Quebrada del Toro lies around 35km (22 miles) beyond Tastil. Here, the parched landscape seems to haul you over the final mountain pass to the magnificent Abra de Muñano at 4,180m (13,710ft). Many people stop here and leave an offering to Pachamama.

INFORMATION

✚ 336 E3 ✉ Quebrada del Toro, Provincia de Salta 🚆 Tren a las Nubes (▷ 254–255) from Salta or the Balcarce district 🚌 From Salta, take the RN-51 signposted San Antonio de los Cobres and follow signs all the way (170km/105.5 miles), passing Campo Quijano and Chorrillos, to Tastil 🚐 Tours from Salta

TIPS

➤➤ Try to set out early, especially in the summer when it may cloud over later in the day.
➤➤ There are few opportunities for eating and drinking before you arrive in San Antonio, so it's a good idea to take some supplies with you.
➤➤ Visit Quebrada del Toro in the summer or autumn; in the dry winter season the waterfall is reduced to a trickle that barely foams above the gravel and boulders of the riverbed.

Opposite and below *Arid desert scenery at Quebrada del Toro*

REGIONS THE NORTH • SIGHTS

INFORMATION

www.turismosalta.gov.ar

336 E3 ✉ Salta, Provincia de Salta
ℹ Buenos Aires 93 ☎ 0387/431-0950
🕐 Mon–Fri 8–9, Sat–Sun 9–8 🚌 Buses
from all major destinations ✈ Martin
Miguel de Güemes airport, El Aybal, is
10km (6 miles) southwest of city. There
are several flights daily from Buenos Aires,
some stopping in Jujuy, plus less frequent
connections to Córdoba

INTRODUCTION

Salta 'La Linda' (Salta 'the Fair') is an enchanting treasure-trove of culture and tradition and the capital of one of Argentina's biggest and most prosperous provinces. No matter how often you visit Salta, there is always some new architectural gem, artistic wonder or top-rate attraction to explore. The city's dramatic highland setting at one end of the fertile Valle de Lerma, known for its tobacco plantations, perches at 1,190m (3,903ft) above sea level and enjoys a balmy climate even in the height of summer.

Salta is the northwest's unrivalled tourist headquarters and its top-quality services include excellent tour operators, handsome hotels and good restaurants. In addition to a cable car and a scenic railway, the sights include the beautiful Iglesia San Francisco and an array of museums themed on pre-Columbian culture, anthropology, local history and modern art. Some exemplary specimens of well-preserved or well-restored colonial architecture give Salta a pleasing harmony of traditional and modern.

Governor Lerma of Tucumán founded Salta on 16 April 1582, choosing the site for its strategic mountainside location and plentiful water supply. In 1776, it became the capital of a huge *intendencia* that took in most of northwestern Argentina plus the southern reaches of modern Bolivia, becoming one of the major centres in the Viceroyalty. During the War of Independence, Salta served as the headquarters of the Ejércitos del Norte and General Güemes's anti-royalist forces, when the general designed the emblematic red-and-black-poncho uniform for his *gaucho* militia.

When Buenos Aires became the capital of Argentina, the city entered a period of steady decline until the railway arrived at the end of the 19th century. Urban growth in the 1920s and 1930s explains the predominance of art nouveau and art deco influenced neo-colonial architecture. Since the turn of the 21st century, Salta has joined the ranks of Argentina's fastest growing and most dynamic cities, and its increased wealth can be seen in the remarkable self-confidence of its inhabitants and the sophistication of the services they share with visitors.

Above *The panoramic view of the city from the summit of Cerro San Bernardo*

WHAT TO SEE

PLAZA 9 DE JULIO

Salta's central square, Plaza 9 de Julio, is one of the country's most graceful spaces. Surrounded on all sides by elegant arcades, under which rows of café terraces lend themselves to idle people-watching, the plaza is a great place to while away some time, especially for a sundowner. Be prepared, though, for street vendors trying to sell you wares or clean your shoes. The well-manicured central part of the square is a collection of palms, native and exotic trees, plus iron fountains and wooden benches. In addition, there is a quaint late 19th-century bandstand, where music sometimes adds to the genial atmosphere.

THE CATHEDRAL

Looming over the northern flank of Plaza 9 de Julio, the cathedral dates from 1882. It is an Italianate neoclassical hulk of a church, with some splendid interior frescoes (the one of the Four Apostles around the cupola rewards careful scrutiny). Just inside, immediately to the left of the entrance, is the grandiose Panteón de los Héroes del Norte, where General Güemes and other local heroes are buried. In the Capilla del Señor del Milagro and Capilla de la Vírgen del Milagro, at the far end of the left and right aisles respectively, you can see holy images used during the annual Milagro celebrations (▷ 259).

✉ Espana 537 ☎ 0387/431-8206 🕐 Daily 7.30–1, 4–7 💰 Free

MUSEO HISTÓRICO DEL NORTE

www.museonor.gov.ar

Opposite the cathedral, on the southern side of the plaza, stands the white Cabildo, originally built in the early 17th century but given a facelift 200 years later, when the city became capital of the *intendencia*. The two rows of graceful arches still don't quite match. Inside is the highly eclectic Museo Histórico del Norte, with a range of exhibits from coins to baroque paintings and wooden saints. There is a fascinating collection of horse-drawn carriages in the courtyards, including a 19th-century hearse. There are superb views across the plaza from the upper-storey balcony.

✉ Caseros 549 ☎ 0387/421-5340 🕐 Tue–Fri 9–6, Sat–Sun 9–1.30 💰 Adult $5, child (under 12) free 9am–10am

TIPS

➤➤ The liveliest and trendiest neighbourhood of Salta is known as Balcarce, especially the stretch north of Avenida Entre Ríos, near the Estación Belgrano. It is lined with arts and crafts stalls in the evenings and on weekends, and there are countless restaurants, bars, discos and folk-music venues.

➤➤ San Lorenzo, a self-contained suburb of Salta only 11km (7 miles) west, enjoys a slightly cooler mountain climate and is awash with lush vegetation. Here, there are some excellent accommodation options, making it popular with visitors and locals wanting to escape the big city, especially in the summer.

➤➤ If you have an opportunity, take the guided tour of the Iglesia San Francisco, which includes the Museo de Arte Sacro. The highlight of the archaeological section is a terracotta Etruscan head from the fourth century BC.

➤➤ For superb views of the city, take the cable car to the top of the Cerro San Bernardo and then, perhaps, walk down for some exercise.

➤➤ The temperature and humidity are kept artificially low in the Museo de Arqueología de Alta Montaña (▷ 242), so bring something warm to wear.

Above and left *The exuberant Iglesia San Francisco, a city landmark*

MUSEO DE ARQUEOLOGÍA DE ALTA MONTAÑA (MAAM)

Housed in an attractive neo-Gothic building on the western side of the plaza is the Museo de Arqueología de Alta Montaña (MAAM). In one of the most significant archaeological discoveries ever made in Argentina, three naturally mummified Inca children, known as the Llullaillaco Children, were found in 1999 atop Volcán Llullaillaco (west of Salta on the Chilean frontier at 6,740m/22,107ft above sea level) by an expedition of mountaineers and scientists. The children were a six-year-old girl, struck by lightning some time after her burial, her hair plaited in two small braids with a metal plaque as an adornment; a teenage girl whose face was painted with a red pigment and who was found with fragments of coca leaf above her upper lip; and a seven-year-old boy wearing a white feather headdress.

All three children died at the end of the 15th century and their corpses are impeccably well preserved. The children are displayed, one at a time, in special refrigerated cases to startling effect (the fainthearted can skip the room where they are shown). The children were sacrificed to the Inca deities, possibly in a fertility ceremony or as an offering to the gods. They were probably concussed by means of a blunt weapon first and then left to suffocate in the extreme cold.

Dozens of exquisite artefacts, part of the treasure trove buried with the children, are on display in the museum. The exhibit is both scientific and didactic, including a film about the expedition and displays of textiles. The ground-floor bookshop is prime hunting ground for high-quality souvenirs, while there is a marvellous café offering local specialities, which is open all day.

✉ Mitre 77 ☎ 0387/437-0499 ◉ Tue–Sun and public hols 11–7.30 🖐 Adult $30, child (under 12) free 🏛 📷

IGLESIA SAN FRANCISCO

One of Salta's most photographed landmarks is the fantastic Iglesia San Francisco, built between 1750 and 1850. Designed by Luigi Giorgi, the church is an outstanding example of Italianate neo-colonial exuberance and is remarkable for its vibrant colour. Admire the ivory-white columns, the contrasting deep ox-blood walls and the profusion of Latin inscriptions, symbols and neoclassical patterns stencilled onto the walls in golden yellow hieroglyphs. The church's other imposing feature is the campanile that rises to a slender spire. The highly elaborate facade is decorated with balusters and scrolls, curlicues and pinnacles, Franciscan inscriptions plus the order's shield. The most original feature, however, is the organza-like stucco curtains that billow from the three archways, almost touching the elegant wrought-iron gates below. Inside, the decoration is plain in comparison apart from the trio of 18th-century Portuguese-style jacaranda armchairs behind the altar. In the convent cloisters there are occasional exhibitions of local arts and crafts.

✉ Caseros and Córdoba ◉ Museum: Mon–Sat 9.30–1, 3–7; guided tours Mon–Sat 9–1, 3–7 🖐 Guided tours $5

MORE TO SEE

MUSEO DE ARTE CONTEMPORÁNEO

Housed on the first floor of a beautifully renovated neo-colonial building at the northeast corner of Plaza 9 de Julio, the Museo de Arte Contemporáneo has a sleek white interior and dark parquet floors. The gallery houses a range of temporary exhibitions from local artists—from up-and-coming artists to more established local names.

✉ Zuviría 90, Plaza 9 de Julio ☎ 0387/437-0498 ◉ Tue–Fri 9–1, 4.30–8.30, Sat–Sun 10.30–1, 5–8.30 🖐 Adult/child $2

MUSEO CASA DE ARÍAS RENGEL

To the west of the Cabildo, the Museo Casa de Arías Rengel is housed in the finest vice-regal building left in the city. The main reason for a visit is to see

Below Pedestrians on the streets of Salta

Above *Statue of Hernando de Lerma by Angel Ibarra in Plaza General Güemes*
Above left *The Cabildo, home to the Museo Histórico del Norte, fronting Plaza 9 de Julio, Salta's central square*

the permanent art collection, ranging from colonial paintings to 20th-century sculpture. Look out for *St. Matthew* of the Cusco School, a large painting of *The City of Salta* (1854) by Giorgio Penutti, and some fine engravings by 20th-century Argentine artists Basaldúa, Spilimbergo and Quinquela Martín.

✉ La Florida 20 ☎ 0387/421-4714 🕐 Mon–Sat 9–1, 4–8.30 ✋ $2

CERRO SAN BERNARDO

A steep path zigzags up the overgrown flanks of Cerro San Bernardo but at 1,458m (4,782ft), you might prefer to take the *teleférico* (cable car) from the eastern end of Parque San Martín, which whizzes you up to the summit in around eight minutes (tel 0387/431-0641; daily 10–7.45; $15). At the top, there is a small garden, where you can admire panoramic views of the city and the majestic mountain range to the west. A café with a terrace serves a range of drinks and snacks.

MUSEO PROVINCIAL DE BELLAS ARTES DE SALTA

Inaugurated in December 2008, this museum is housed in the landmark Casona Usandivaras, an art nouveau mansion standing majestically at the corner of Belgrano and Sarmiento. The eleven beautifully restored rooms house a rich patrimony, which ranges from pre-Hispanic to contemporary.

✉ Avenida Belgrano and Avenida Sarmiento ☎ 0387/421-4714 🕐 Mon–Sat 9–1, 4–8.30 ✋ Adult/child $2

MUSEO DE ARTE ÉTNICO AMERICANO PAJCHA

www.museodearteetnico.com.ar

Situated in the trendy Balcarce district, the Museo de Arte Étnico Americano Pajcha is one of the best museums of American ethnic art in Argentina. The collection was the lifelong work of Liliana Madrid de Zito Fontán, a local ethnologist, and is arranged thematically and geographically around seven rooms, each with its own mood music. Although indigenous Argentine art and handicrafts dominate the exhibition, there are paintings, textiles, religious objects (Christian and pre-Columbian) and wooden articles from all over the continent, plus some beautiful photographs. The collection represents every ethnic group but the silver Mapuche jewellery and the array of Andean ceramics are the highlights.

✉ 20 de Febrero 831 ☎ 0387/422-9417 🕐 Oct–Jun Mon–Sat 9–7; Jul and Sep Tue–Sun 9–7; Holy Week and August Mon–Sat 9–7 🎫 Adult $10, child (under 12) free

SALINAS GRANDES

One of the largest and most beautiful salt flats in South America, the Salinas Grandes are set among the majestic Andean peaks high up in the altiplano of Salta and Jujuy provinces. The huge expanse of salt glistens in the sunlight, and from a distance looks deceptively like snow. The great white spaces create mirages and, after heavy summer rains, large swathes of the Salinas flood to form huge mirror-like lagoons. At all times, there are pools of brine, which attract flocks of flamingos and other waterfowl. Often groups of vicuñas graze on the golden *tola* (grass). The main gathering place for visitors or motorists is a large building made of salt bricks—a café/snack bar with toilets. You can buy little statues of *vicuñas* carved out of small blocks of salt locally, but be aware that these disintegrate over time and can seriously damage surfaces.

➕ 336 E2 ✉ Salinas Grandes, Provincias de Jujuy and Salta 🎧 Tours from Jujuy and Salta 🚌 Take the RN-52 (direction of Chile) from Purmamarca and climb the Cuesta Lipán to the Salinas

SALTA

▷ 240–243.

SAN ANTONIO DE LOS COBRES

www.sanantoniodeloscobres.todowebsalta.com.ar

A major regional crossroads at a dizzying height of 3,775m (12,382ft) above sea level, San Antonio de los Cobres is the small, windswept capital of an immense but mostly empty portion of the altiplano. The surrounding territory is remote and uninhabited but rich in minerals and with some breathtaking scenery. Most people only ever see San Antonio de los Cobres from the train station when the Tren a las Nubes (▷ 254–255) makes a short stop here on its way back down to the plains.

➕ 336 E3 ✉ San Antonio de los Cobres, Provincia de Salta 🚌 Bus from Salta 🚆 Tren a las Nubes from Salta 🚌 From Salta take the RN-51, direction San Antonio de los Cobres

SAN FERNANDO DEL VALLE DE CATAMARCA

San Fernando del Valle de Catamarca, the capital of Catamarca Province, has always been something of a backwater but it is redeemed by its wonderful setting in a deep valley, hemmed in by the emerald Sierra de Graciana and the ochre-hued Sierra de Ambato. The town's tradition of making handicrafts, especially textiles, is reflected in one of the country's major festivals, the Fiesta Nacional del Poncho (▷ 259).

The late 19th-century cathedral on the central Plaza 25 de Mayo houses a statue of the Virgin Mary which attracts huge numbers of pilgrims every year on 16 December.

Of the handful of museums, the best is the Museo Arqueológico Adán Quiroga (Sarmiento 450; tel 03833/437413; Mon–Fri 8.30–12.30, 2.30–8.30, Sat 9–1, 3.30–6.30; $4), where the main collection focuses on pre-Columbian ceramics.

➕ 341 E6 ✉ San Fernando del Valle de Catamarca, Provincia de Catamarca ℹ República 446 ☎ 03833/437791 🕐 Daily 8–9 🚌 Buses from all major destinations ✈ Felipe Varela airport is 22km (13.5 miles) south 🚌 From Tucumán, head southwards along the RN-38

SAN LORENZO

www.sanlorenzo.todowebsalta.com.ar

Alluring San Lorenzo is a leafy suburb of Salta with tree-lined avenues leading past patrician villas. Although there are no major sights here, it is close to the Andean foothills and only a ten-minute bus ride from the city centre, making it the perfect base for visiting the Salta region. The hills and ravines form outstanding walking and riding country, while the town also offers some good restaurants and other services.

Overlooking the neat village and Salta, the excellent Reserva del Huaico protects a large chunk of the verdant native forest and its varied wildlife, including wild felines and a gamut of birds. Throughout the reserve are well-maintained paths, one of which leads to a panoramic lookout affording fabulous views of

the valley and the mountains beyond. Contact the owners of the reserve to arrange a tour (▷ 258).

➕ 336 E3 ✉ San Lorenzo, Provincia de Salta 🚌 Bus from Salta 🚌 From Salta, take the road signposted San Lorenzo 🎧 Tours of the reserve available locally

SAN MIGUEL DE TUCUMÁN

▷ 246.

SAN SALVADOR DE JUJUY

▷ 247.

TAFÍ DEL VALLE

▷ 248.

TILCARA

▷ 249.

YAVI

Across the Siete Hermanos (Seven Brothers) range is the historic village of Yavi, set in a fertile valley with sloping cobbled streets and cocoa-hued adobe houses. The highlights of this high-altitude gem are found on the irregular Plaza Mayor. On one side of the plaza is the 18th-century Casa del Marqués de Tojo (daily 9–1, 2–6; $5), once the home of the region's ruling Marquis, the only holder of that rank in colonial Argentina. Inside, you'll find a small museum with a collection of artefacts and furniture. In the centre of the museum is a spacious, tree-shaded patio.

Opposite is the 17th-century Iglesia de Nuestra Señora del Rosario y San Francisco (Mon–Fri 9–1, 3–6, Sat–Sun 9–12; free). Highly unusual onyx-paned windows light the fabulous colonial interior, with its simple whitewashed nave. Some of the treasures in the collection include a fine baroque pulpit, three retables decorated with painted wooden saints and a 16th-century Flemish oil painting brought here by early colonizers.

➕ 336 E1 ✉ Yavi, Provincia de Jujuy 🚌 Bus from La Quiaca 🚌 RP-5 heading eastwards from the border town of La Quiaca

Opposite Salinas Grandes salt flats, *a vast expanse between Jujuy and Salta provinces*

REGIONS | THE NORTH • SIGHTS

INFORMATION

www.tucumanturismo.gov.ar

✚ 336 F5 ✉ San Miguel de Tucumán, Provincia de Tucumán ℹ 24 de Septiembre 484 (Plaza Independencia) ☎ 0381/430-3644 🕐 Mon–Fri 7–1, 5–9, Sat–Sun, 9–1, 5–9 ✈ Teniente Benjamin Matienzo airport is 12km (7.5 miles) east of the city. There are regular flights from Buenos Aires 🚌 1,190km (738 miles) northwest of Buenos Aires; approximately 300km (186 miles) south of Salta on the RN-9

TIPS

» There is not a great choice of accommodation in the town, so you might want to stay in the leafy suburb of Yerba Buena, which is closer to the mountains. This is also a fertile hunting ground for good places to eat and drink, too.

» Don't miss the Museo Folklórico's eclectic collection of *mate* paraphernalia, textiles and traditional musical instruments (24 de Septiembre s/n, Plaza Independencia; tel 0381/421-8250; daily 9–12.30, 5.30–8.30; $2).

SAN MIGUEL DE TUCUMÁN

In the valley of the Río Salí, in the eastern lee of the high Sierra de Aconquija, Tucumán is Argentina's fourth-largest city. The capital of a tiny but heavily populated sugar-rich province, Tucumán, as the city is more commonly known, is the biggest metropolis in the northwest and a lively urban centre, with a thriving business centre, bustling downtown area and a youthful population.

Tucumán is famous for being the place where Argentina's independence from Spain was declared on 9 July 1816. This historic event was followed by years of prosperity, as British investment and climate conditions favoured Tucumán's sugar industry. More recently, a slump in sugar prices has meant that Tucumán's farmers have had to diversify and the area is now the world's biggest lemon-producing area, as well as growing mandarins, grapefruit and kumquats. The humid climate has proved ideal for growing blueberries and strawberries, too.

PLAZA INDEPENDENCIA

The elegant Plaza Independencia is the city's focal point, with its grove of native and orange trees, large fountain, statue to Liberty and a monolith. In the southeast corner is the mid-19th-century neo-classical cathedral, its slender towers topped with blue-and-white tiled domes. On the western side of the square is the early 20th-century Casa de Gobierno.

CASA HISTÓRICA DE LA INDEPENDENCIA

www.museocasadetucuman.com.ar

Two blocks south at Congreso 151 is the Casa Histórica de la Independencia (tel 0381/431-0826; Mon–Fri 10–6, Sat–Sun 1–6; sound-and-light show Fri–Wed 9.30pm; $5, show $5). Behind the white facade, mock-Baroque columns and mighty doors there are a series of large patios, draped with bougainvillea, jasmine and tropical creepers. This is where Argentina declared its independence from Spain and its first Congress was held. Most of the patrician house was demolished in the late 19th century (this replica was completed in the 1940s). Now a national monument, the house contains a collection of armour, furniture, paintings, silverware and porcelain, while an interesting sound-and-light show (in Spanish) re-enacts the story of how the country gained its independence.

Above *Casa de Gobierno*
Right *The cathedral*

SAN SALVADOR DE JUJUY

About 100km (62 miles) to the north of Salta, San Salvador de Jujuy (Jujuy for short) lies in a fertile natural bowl, with the fabulous Quebrada de Humahuaca, a dramatic highland gorge, immediately to its north. Jujuy hosts one of Argentina's finest pieces of sacred art in its cathedral, while the interior of Iglesia San Francisco is also worth the trip. But Jujuy is essentially a springboard for visiting its rich hinterland of mountains and altiplano villages, plus the most accessible of Argentina's three cloud-forest national parks, Calilegua (▷ 237). There are some good hotels and one or two excellent restaurants in the city, which is served by an airport and good road links with Salta.

THE CATHEDRAL AND IGLESIA SAN FRANCISCO

On the west side of the Plaza General Belgrano is the cathedral (Mon–Fri 7.30–1, 5–9, Sat–Sun 8–12, 5–9; free), where the main attraction is the magnificent pulpit. Decorated in the 18th century by local artists, its harmonious compositions, elegant floral and vegetable motifs and the finesse of its carvings were inspired by pulpits in Cusco. The various tableaux in gilded, carved wood depict biblical stories.

The 1930s Iglesia San Francisco on Belgrano and Lavalle, two blocks west of the plaza, is also worth a visit. Inside the church, you'll find a delicately gilded baroque pulpit carved by craftsmen in 18th-century Bolivia. The pulpit is decorated with a profusion of little Franciscan monks staring out from endless tiers of little columns (Mon–Fri 7.30–1, 5–9, Sat–Sun 8–12, 5–9; free).

Above *The beautiful gilded and carved pulpit is one of the highlights of Jujuy's cathedral*

INFORMATION

www.turismo.jujuy.gov.ar

➕ 336 E3 ✉ San Salvador de Jujuy, Provincia de Jujuy ℹ C Ignacio Gorriti 295 ☎ 0388/4221325 ◷ Mon–Fri 7–10, Sat–Sun 9–9 🚌 Buses from Salta ✈ Regular flights from Buenos Aires, some via Salta. Dr Horacio Guzmán airport is 32km (20 miles) southeast of the city near Perico 🚗 Jujuy is about 115km (71 miles) to the north of Salta via the RN-9

TIP

▸▸ When you are in the cathedral, have a look for the curious mistake in the symbols of the four apostles decorating the pulpit; Matthew and John are correctly represented by a human figure and an eagle respectively, but Mark, symbolized by a bull, and Luke, by a lion, are the wrong way round.

INFORMATION

tafidelvalle.com/arg/turismo.php

✚ 336 E5 ✉ Tafí del Valle, Provincia de Tucumán ⓘ Avenida Gob. Critto, main plaza ☎ 03867/421880 ⏰ Daily 8–1, 6–9 🚌 Buses from Tucumán and Cafayate 🚗 From Tucumán, take the RN-38 southwards and then the RP-308 to Tafí ✋ Tours available locally

TIPS

» Tafí is the perfect base for exploring the region as Amaicha (▷ 233), Quilmes (▷ 236) and the city of Tucumán (▷ 246) are all within easy reach.

» The popular Fiesta Nacional del Queso takes place in early February and accommodation gets booked up well ahead.

» Tafí and the mountain pass to Amaicha are prone to fog, so check local weather reports before setting off.

» In addition to the official tourist office, visit the travel operator Yungas (▷ 258) at Avenida Presidente Perón 120 to get information about excursions and trekking in the area.

TAFÍ DEL VALLE

Separated from the low-lying Tucumán city by dense jungle, the highland village of Tafí del Valle sits among grassy slopes, encircled by mountain peaks criss-crossed by paths. Dry and sunny, it revels in a fresh climate, making it the perfect getaway in summer from the stifling city heat. A field of mysterious pre-Columbian standing stones, a Jesuit chapel, good accommodation and a wide choice of rural activities, make Tafí a popular tourist destination. Every February there is the Fiesta Nacional del Queso (national cheese festival). As well as celebrating the town's delicious cheeses, it attracts rock and folk musicians from all over the North and farther afield.

THE ROAD TO TAFÍ

There is plenty to see along the RP-307 from Tucumán to Tafí, as the road follows a mountain brook up through the dense and subtropical Selva Tucumana. At 2,000m (6,560ft) the road levels off into a parched valley, where the mirror-like Dique La Angostura reservoir reflects the extinct volcano, Cerro Pelao (2,680m/8,790ft). A signpost directs you to the Parque de los Menhires to a set of 2,000-year-old stones carved with patterns that are believed to have been fertility symbols (open all year; free).

Tafí is a haphazard muddle of buildings. One of the oldest is a late 18th-century Jesuit chapel, the Capilla Jesuítica de la Banda (Mon–Sat 9–7, Sun 9–4; $1), located across the Río Tafí. Inside, there are some pre-Columbian ceramics as well as paintings and furniture from the colonial period. You can also visit the traditional colonial Estancia Los Cuartos (Miguel Critto s/n; tel 0381/15-587-4230, www.estancialoscuartos.com) in the centre of town. Here, you can opt for a *día de campo*, which includes lunch and a ride on horseback, or stay overnight in one of the seven simple rooms ($190–$250 for a double room).

TREKKING

Trekking is the main activity around Tafí, but it is not advisable to attempt the trails on your own, as they are not always well marked and the weather is notoriously unpredictable here. Ask at the tourist office for a list of recommended guides. The three principal treks, which range from a few hours to all day, go up to the enticing peaks overlooking the village: Cerro El Matadero (3,050m/10,004ft), Mala-Mala (3,500m/11,480ft) and Cerro Muñoz (4,437m/14,553ft). Although, it's worth remembering that Tafí is already at 2,000m (6,560ft) above sea level.

Below *The late 18th-century Capilla Jesuítica de la Banda*

TILCARA

Authentic and traditional, Tilcara has a wonderfully joyous atmosphere and rings to the sound of Andean music. At just under 3,000m (9,840ft) above sea level, the village is encircled by giant peaks. Tilcara, one of the biggest settlements along the Quebrada de Humahuaca and the only one on the east bank, lies just off the main road, where the Río Huasomayo runs into the Río Grande. The village offers some of the best accommodation in the region and makes a convenient base if you want to explore the province.

MUSEO ARQUEOLÓGICO

Tilcara's Museo Arqueológico is housed in a beautiful colonial building on the south side of the main plaza on Belgrano s/n (tel 0388/495-5006; daily 9–12.30, 2–6; $5, free on Tue). The collection includes local finds as well as exhibits from other South American countries. There is a mummified human body from San Pedro de Atacama in Chile, a set of anthropomorphic Mochica vases, a bronze disc from Belén, and a jumble of metal and ceramic items. In the stark patio are three *menhirs* (pre-Columbian standing stones) depicting stylized figures, which were excavated from the *pukará* of Rinconada in the north of Jujuy Province.

PUKARÁ AND JARDÍN BOTÁNICO DE ALTURA

The *pukará*, 1km (0.5 miles) to the south of the village across an iron bridge, is a pre-Columbian fortress that explains Tilcara's strategic importance in the valley (tel 0388/495-5006; Mon–Sat 8.30–12.30, 4–8; Sun 9.30–12, 6–9; $5, free on Tue). Built between 1000 and 1500AD, the fortress comprises serried rows of houses built within high ramparts. Over several decades, archaeologists have convincingly reconstructed many of the dwellings. One of the most fascinating buildings is La Iglesia (church), which was a ceremonial edifice and possibly used for sacrifices (sometimes human). Set against a backdrop of imposing mountains, the fortress enjoys panoramic views in all directions.

The Jardín Botánico de Altura (daily 9–6; $5, free on Tue), shaded by the *pukará*, is a delightfully landscaped garden of local and regional flora, mostly cacti. As you wander around its stone paths you get incredible views of the *pukará* above (daily 9–6; $5, free on Tue).

Above *Tilcara is popular with visitors and makes a good base from which to explore the region*

INFORMATION

www.tilcara.com.ar

⊞ 336 E2 ✉ Tilcara, Provincia de Jujuy
ℹ Belgrano 590 ☎ 0388/495-5671
◷ Daily 7.30–9 🚌 Buses from Jujuy and Salta 🚐 82km (51 miles) north of Jujuy on the RN-9

TIPS

» Tilcara gets very busy and even a little rowdy in midsummer, particularly during El Enero Tilcareño in January, Holy Week and around 9 July. The Pachamama festival, in August, sees more festivities, wild games, music, raucous processions and much revelry. Book your accommodation well ahead.

» If you visit the archaeological museum, the *pukará* (fortress) or the botanical garden keep your ticket from the first place you visit because it is valid for the other two sights, too.

» The town's imposing colonial church, Nuestra Señora del Rosario, one block back from Plaza C. Alvarez Prado, is a good hunting ground for souvenirs or a place to eat.

» The Museo José Antonio Terry (Rivadavia 459; tel 0388/495-5005; Tue–Fri 8–12.30, 4–8.30, Sat–Sun 9–12, 2–6; $2) on the east side of the plaza, contains a collection of paintings of the local landscapes and people by the Buenos Aires painter, who settled in Tilcara.

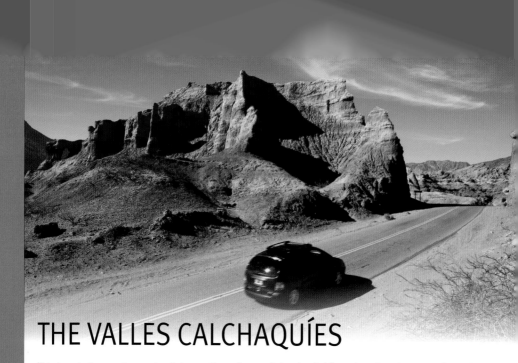

THE VALLES CALCHAQUÍES

This long but rewarding route pilots you through one of the classic itineraries of northwestern Argentina. Starting from Salta, the drive heads up through the Cuesta del Obispo to the Andean village of Cachi. You could stay here and backtrack to Salta or, time permitting, complete the circuit, taking time to enjoy the stunning scenery. The second leg of the drive winds along the scenic RN-40 to the wine capital of Cafayate. Overnight here before making the stunning descent through the Quebrada de Cafayate, back to Salta.

THE DRIVE

Distance: 515km (319 miles)
Time: At least 7 hours, exluding stops
Start at: Salta
End at: Salta

★ From the centre of Salta follow the signs to Cafayate via the RN-68 and continue south until you reach El Carril, where a sign will indicate the RP-33 road to Cachi. This scenic road strikes westwards across attractive fertile farmland and then crosses a series of fords, as you squeeze your way through the damp Quebrada de Escoipe.

The landscape becomes more dramatic at this point as you enter a steep mountain pass, winding upwards through the terraces of the Cuesta del Obispo. Drive carefully at all times: There are plenty of places to stop and admire the views.

❶ There is a sign at the top of the Cuesta pass giving the altitude as 3,347m (10,978ft), no less, as the road levels out. This spot is known as the Abra Piedra del Molino (Millstone Pass) because of a mysterious circular stone by the roadside. This is an excellent vantage point for contemplating the incredible zigzags of the road you have just climbed.

Continue on the RP-33 and, after about 20km (12.5 miles), you reach a fork in the road. Do not take the left turn to Seclantas but keep ahead to enter Parque Nacional Los Cardones.

❷ The beautiful Parque Nacional Los Cardones, one of the smallest in the country, preserves a veritable forest of *cardón* cacti, many of which reach heights of 5m (16ft). The next 10km (6 miles) are along the Recta Tin-Tin (signposted), a straight section of

road that appears to descend when it rises and vice versa owing to an optical illusion.

At Payogasta, the RP-33 merges with the RN-40, which is your route for the next 180km (111.5 miles). After 10km (6 miles), you reach Cachi (▷ 233).

❸ Cachi is a beguiling Andean hamlet. It is a good place to pick up arts and crafts souvenirs and there are a number of places for refreshments. You can choose to backtrack to Salta from here or continue with the drive.

From Cachi head southwards along the RN-40, which passes through some stunning mountain scenery as you follow the Río Calchaquí along its course. Some 60km (37 miles) south of Cachi, the silhouette of Molinos church appears on the horizon.

❹ Molinos (▷ 236) is worth a detour to visit the church and the colonial centre. Alternatively, head for the marvellous *estancia* at Colomé (▷ 263) for wine tasting, a visit to the James Turrell museum (advance booking needed) or an overnight stay.

Otherwise follow the RN-40 south, through painterly landscapes, which become markedly more startling after the hamlet of Angastaco.

A 10km (6-mile) stretch of road takes you through a series of gorges and ravines: some painted red by oxides, others ghostly white. The different rock formations have won names such as Quebrada de las Flechas (Arrow Gorge), El Canón (Canyon) and El Ventisquero (Wind Tunnel).

As you leave the mountains for the wider river valley, the terrain gradually flattens out and is planted with vineyards. You quickly reach the historic settlement of San Carlos.

❺ San Carlos is the oldest village in the valley, dating from 1551, and has an authentic colonial feel. It is worth a stop to explore its main square, dominated by a majestic 19th-century church. There are also a couple of *bodegas* to visit and a few crafts workshops selling ceramics.

From here it is only 24km (15 miles) to Cafayate (▷ 234).

❻ There are a number of excellent hotels and restaurants in Cafayate and you will probably want to stay overnight and explore the *bodegas*.

From Cafayate, backtrack 2km (1.25 miles) up the RN-40 and turn right onto the RN-68 to Salta. This part of the journey is best undertaken in the late afternoon, when the softer light and shadows enhance the beauty of the Quebrada de Cafayate.

❼ After the sand dunes, Los Médanos, created by the dry winds

and light soil of this part of the valley, your descent into the gorge begins almost at once. The tarmacked road snakes towards the valley, where the surrounding rock walls have been eroded into magical shapes. From here you will see signs to La Garganta del Diablo and El Anfiteatro.

❽ Both features are the result of geological fissures and wind erosion in the cliffs; park your car just off the main road and then take a short walk (50m/54 yards in both cases). La Garganta del Diablo is a deeper, tighter groove in the cliff, while El Anfiteatro, a natural theatre of rock, is sometimes used for outdoor concerts in good weather.

The RN-68 continues its steady descent into the fertile Valle de Lerma plains, which are full of tobacco fields and picturesque colonial villages, and brings you back to Salta.

WHEN TO GO

This route is suitable for any time of year. The main hazard is low cloud or fog on the Cuesta del Obispo, which can make driving hazardous. This is best avoided by making an early start, especially in the summer

months when the road up to Cachi is often cut off by heavy afternoon rains. If you complete the first leg only, it is best to stay in Cachi and make the descent in the morning, before the tropical storms brew.

WHERE TO EAT
POSTA DE LAS CABRAS

Halfway between Cafayate and Salta, this pretty restaurant serves an excellent selection of sandwiches, pies and cakes.

✉ Quebrada de Cafayate

WHERE TO STAY
CACHI
▷ 262.

CAFAYATE
▷ 263.

ESTANCIA COLOMÉ
▷ 263.

HACIENDA DE MOLINOS
▷ 263.

TIP

➤➤ Many organized tours squeeze this trip into one day, but it really makes sense to stop over at least one night and preferably two, for example in Cachi and/or Cafayate.

THE QUEBRADA DEL TORO
AND SALINAS GRANDES

This demanding drive takes you up the Quebrada del Toro, plying the same route taken by the famed Tren a las Nubes (▷ 254–255), and then runs across the Salinas Grandes, icy white salt flats. From here, the road zigzags down through the extraordinary Cuesta de Lipán and into enchanting Purmamarca, from where you can make your way back to Salta. Bearing in mind this classic drive will take longer than it looks on the map—you will be climbing steadily into the Andean highlands—you should make an early start and factor in an overnight stay in Purmamarca.

THE DRIVE
Distance: 600km (372 miles)
Time: At least 8 hours, excluding stops
Start at: Salta
End at: Salta

★ From the centre of Salta follow signs to San Antonio de los Cobres via the RN-51 to pass the city's airport, where you might collect your rental car. At Campo Quijano you will see one of the stations used by the famous Tren a las Nubes (▷ 254–255).

After Campo Quijano the RN-51 road begins to climb up the Quebrada del Toro (▷ 238–239).

❶ Multicoloured rocks adorn the cliffs along this section of the gorge

but there are few signs of human life, except the occasional diminutive cemetery or humble farmstead. The only village of note, as you ascend the gorge, is Santa Rosa de Tastil, with its interesting museum, and Tastil, one of the finest pre-Columbian sites in the country.

About 30km (18.5 miles) further on, the road clambers over the dramatic Abra de Muñano, the road's highest point at 4,703m (15,426ft). Just under 30km (18.5 miles) further on, you'll reach San Antonio de los Cobres (▷ 244), a desolate mining town. Continue past the town and turn off right at the main crossroads, heading in a northerly direction along the legendary RN-40 towards Salinas Grandes.

For a shorter, less challenging drive, head back down the Quebrada del Toro to Salta. But to experience the landscape in all its glory, continue for about 20km (12.5 miles) along the RN-40 and then take the right-hand turn off to El Mojón, which is about 3km (2 miles) off the main road.

❷ In the hamlet of El Mojón you will find a rudimentary *comedor* (diner), Sandro's (daily 11–7). Here, you can enjoy fabulous traditional fare and local wines.

From here, it is 80km (50 miles) to your next destination, Tres Morros. The scenery is desert-like and, apart from the occasional goatherd and his animals, you are unlikely to see another person for miles.

Opposite *General street scene*

The RN-40 cuts across the desolate altiplano of the great Andean high plains. In this barren landscape you may have the sense of being in nature's utmost wilderness.

As you head towards Tres Morros, you will catch glimpses ahead of the sparkling white expanses of the Salinas Grandes. To the southeast is the grandiose Nevado de Chani (6,200m/20,336ft), a snow-capped volcano, behind a row of honey-coloured hillocks.

❸ Tres Morros, meaning three mounds, is an accurate description of this little village. Two of the three hills form part of the village. One hill shelters the little adobe houses and church, while another is the local cemetery and is surrounded by a wall. You could climb the third for views of the village and the surrounding countryside.

Shortly after leaving Tres Morros, you reach the great wastes of the Salinas Grandes (▷ 244), by turning left along the RN-52 for 10km (6 miles).

❹ Take time to admire the otherworldly landscapes of the salt flats at Salinas Grandes, which turn into great mirrors of water when the floodwaters overspill the great Laguna de Guaylayoc to the north.

From here, backtrack 10km (6 miles) to the crossroads with the RN-40 but, this time, keep straight ahead. The RN-52 will take you down one of the most dramatic roads in the country, the zigzagging Cuesta de Lipán, which requires nerves of steel and good brakes. Slow down and enjoy.

❺ After what seems like an endless number of switchbacks and tight hairpin bends, you finally reach the valley of Purmamarca (about 40km/25 miles from the RN-40 crossroads). Here, you can start dreaming of a good meal and a glass of Cabernet Sauvignon. You'll

probably want to stay the night in Purmamarca (▷ 236)—in fact you are urged to do so. There are plenty of places to stay: Try the Amauta or La Comarca and enjoy that gourmet dinner at Los Morteros.

Leave Purmamarca the following morning and continue for 4km (2.5 miles) to reach the junction with the RN-9. Turn right and enjoy the 60km (37-mile) scenic journey down to San Salvador de Jujuy (▷ 247).

❻ If you have time, you might want to spend the day exploring the provincial capital of Jujuy. There are plenty of excellent restaurants, and the beautiful cathedral and Iglesia San Francisco are both worth visiting.

If you are in a relative hurry to get back to Salta, skirt around the city and follow the RN-9 (highway) signs for 150km (93 miles) to Salta. Otherwise, about 5km (3 miles) south of Jujuy on the RN-9, you can opt to take the slower, but more direct, road down to Salta via La Caldera. This will take you through stunning *yunga* (cloud forest), and eventually lead to Salta, 90km (56 miles) from Jujuy.

WHEN TO GO
This drive has no open or closed season. Winter offers fabulous clear skies whereas in the summer you do run the risk of the occasional storm.

WHERE TO EAT
LOS MORTEROS
▷ 260.

WHERE TO STAY
AMAUTA
▷ 263.

LA COMARCA
▷ 263.

TIPS
❯❯ Most of this route is along unpaved roads so it might be a good idea to rent a 4WD. You should also carry a basic tool kit, in case of a burst tyre.
❯❯ Always take supplies of food and water with you on these trips, and ensure that you have a full tank of fuel, especially as you will be crossing remote desert-like terrain.
❯❯ Even if you're planning an overnight stay in Purmamarca, make an early start to enjoy the best conditions and allow for delays.
❯❯ The drive is at high altitude, so people susceptible to altitude sickness may need to think carefully before undertaking it.

TREN A LAS NUBES

The Tren a las Nubes (the Train to the Clouds) is the best-known train journey in the whole of Argentina. Winding and climbing up into the Andes from Salta, its climax comes as it crosses the iconic Viaducto de la Polvorilla, which looks like something straight out of a model railway.

THE TRAIN RIDE
Distance: 434km (269 miles) round trip
Time: 16 hours
Start at: Salta train station
End at: Salta train station

★ You will need to reserve tickets at least a couple of days in advance (tel 0387/422-3033; www.trenalasnubes. com.ar). Tickets cost US$158 (with seasonal discounts available for Argentines). Start at the Estación de Salta (1,187m/3,893ft) in the Balcarce district and be ready to board well before the 7.05am scheduled departure time. You are advised to be at the station by 6.15am.

The friendly staff will give a running commentary in Spanish and English, and it is worth knowing that there is a medical service on board and oxygen supplies in case you are affected by altitude sickness during the journey. The highest point reached is 4,220m (13,842ft) above sea level.

The train chugs along at an average speed of 35kph (28mph), heading out of the northwestern suburbs of Salta. You will soon find yourself out in the countryside of the green Valle de Lerma and reach the first main station, Alvarado, a few minutes later.

Beyond Campo Quijano, the tracks run alongside the RN-51 and the majestic Quebrada del Toro (▷ 238–239).

The route gets steep through the gorge and the train travels quite fast as you go through two zigzags in close succession, before reaching Ingeniero Maury.

The station at Ingeniero Maury was named after the American engineer Richard Fontaine Maury, who oversaw the construction of the track in the 1920s and 1930s. The line to the mines in Chile was eventually completed in 1948.

The beguilingly multi-hued rocks take over from the lush valley as the train continues its climb. After Tacuara station you are spun through the itinerary's two loops, which heave the train up to the 3,000m (9,840ft) mark. By the time you get to Diego de Almagro station, you are at 3,503m (11,490ft) above sea level and your ears might well be popping.

Lovers of statistics might like to know that you worm through 21 tunnels, cross 13 viaducts and 29 bridges along the route taken by the Tren a las Nubes.

Much of the time the train and the RN-51 part ways but they come close again to clamber over the Abra de Muñano.

After the Abra, at 4,008m (13,146ft), you are officially in the altiplano (high plains) and reach San Antonio de los Cobres at around 2pm. At this point, you will have crossed a dozen viaducts and there is one more to negotiate, the magical Polvorilla viaduct, which is 63m (207ft) high and 224m (735ft) long. This curved wonder of metal is a superb sight.

The train now doubles back and you get into San Antonio de los Cobres for a second time at 16.22, according to the schedule.

The train stops for half an hour at San Antonio de los Cobres, so you can stretch your legs and, perhaps, buy a souvenir from the vendors selling woollens and other crafts. Alternatively, you might prefer to leave the train at this point and explore Salinas Grandes (▷ 244) and Purmamarca (▷ 236) with one of the tour operators in Salta. Staying on the train, most of the journey downwards is in darkness but is usually rendered more entertaining by musicians and vendors that board the train at San Antonio.

WHEN TO GO
The train runs only in the dry season, from April to November. High season is Holy Week and the latter half of July, when ticket prices rise and seats get booked in advance.

WHERE TO EAT
There is a buffet service on the train serving snacks, such as pasta and sandwiches, and drinks but you might prefer to take your own food.

TIP
▸▸ Organize an onward trip with a tour operator in Salta (▷ 240–243), who can pick you up at San Antonio de los Cobres and take you off to explore some of the fabulous sights of the northwest, rather than taking the train back down to Salta in the dark. An onward tour means losing half the ticket price but is generally a worthwhile option.

Opposite *The train passes through some spectacular landscapes*
Right *The famous Viaducto de la Polvorilla, a superb metal structure*

ANTOFAGASTA DE LA SIERRA

SOCOMPA TOURS

www.socompa.com

This highly professional outfit specializes in tours of the *puna* or altiplano of the great Andean high plains. A tour is really the only viable way of getting to see the fabulous sights of the Catamarca Province, such as the flamingo lagoons and pumice fields. You can also ask them about accommodation possibilities and other destinations in the whole region.

✉ Balcarca 998, Salta ☎ 0387/416-9130 ◷ Mon–Sat 9–1, 5–8 ✋ Varies

BELÉN

PONCHOS

Belén calls itself the 'national capital of the poncho', which may be a slight exaggeration but you should still check out the many woollen workshops dotted around the village. The local sheep's and llama wool is often mixed with walnut bark, giving the material a rough texture. In addition to ponchos, you can also buy some fabulous blankets and shawls.

CAFAYATE

HELADERÍA MIRANDA

This ice-cream parlour close to the main square serves all the usual flavours but has gained nationwide fame for its wine sorbet (sherbert). Savour a scoop of cabernet sauvignon or torrontés, transformed magically into refreshing sorbet, in a cone or a tub. Heavenly.

✉ Avenida General Guemes s/n ◷ Daily 10–10 ✋ From $10

MERCADO ARTESANAL

Just off the main square, this jumble of varied stalls is a good place to explore if you are looking for traditional arts and crafts to take home as a souvenir or a gift. The quality varies but there is usually something for most tastes.

✉ Plaza 20 de Febrero ◷ Daily 9am–11pm

PUNA TURISMO

www.punaturismo.com.ar

Puna Turismo is one of the region's most reliable tour operators, offering tours all around the valleys, taking in the *bodegas* and other attractions around Cafayate. The company also organizes more demanding trips involving mountain climbing, safaris, horse treks and mountain biking.

✉ San Martín 82 ☎ 03868/421808 ◷ Mon–Sat 10–6 ✋ Day trip $200

FIAMBALÁ

FINCA DON DIEGO

www.fincadondiego.com

Catamarca Province has finally joined the ranks of the northern wine-producing provinces and this impressive boutique winery produces some extremely palatable reds and whites that you might like to taste here and purchase.

✉ Fiambalá ☎ 011/4954-6835 ◷ Mon–Sat 10–12.30, 4–7

SALTA

BOLICHE DE BALDERRAMA

www.boliche-balderrama.com.ar

This famed *peña* (folk music club) was a den of rebelliousness during Argentina's years of dictatorship in the 1970s and '80s but is now more of a tourist attraction than anything. The menu is fairly basic and the premises are a bit run down, but the music is usually good.

✉ Avenida San Martín 1126 ☎ 0387/421-1542 ◷ Daily 8.30pm–2am

Opposite Bodegas *in the northern provinces produce some fine wines*

CASA DE LA CULTURA

Complementing the Teatro Provincial (▷ 258), it is worth taking a peek at the billings at the modern Casa de la Cultura, which hosts a range of activities, such as tango classes and folk music lessons, in addition to art exhibitions and a gamut of concerts and other spectacles.

✉ Casero 460 ☎ 0387/421-6285
🕐 Mon–Sat 10–7 ✋ Exhibitions free; other events vary

LA CASONA DEL MOLINO

This is the best of the traditional *peñas* in Salta, the type of place where locals gather to chew coca leaves and serenade each other with harmonious *zambas* and other regional songs. Housed in a beautiful neo-colonial house, this is an excellent place to try northwestern specialities such as *empanadas* (small pasties) and *humitas* (creamed corn steamed in maize husks). It is some way from the city centre, so it's advisable to take a taxi to get there.

✉ Caseros 2500 ☎ 0387/434-2835
🕐 Daily 9pm–3am

CLARK EXPEDICIONES

www.clarkexpediciones.com
Ricardo Clark, a leading ornithologist, and his associates pride themselves on running an eco-conscious outfit, based in Salta and San Lorenzo. The company runs birdwatching tours and safaris in the north, in particular to Parque Nacional Calilegua. Clark also arranges tours to other parts of Argentina, as well as neighbouring Brazil, Chile and Paraguay. Choose from a range of two- to six-day expeditions with the possibility of tailoring a tour to your requirements.

✉ Mariano Moreno 1950, San Lorenzo
☎ 0387/497-1024 🕐 Mon–Fri 10–1, 4–7
✋ Varies

MARINA TURISMO

www.marina-semisa.com.ar
In addition to running excursions and organizing tours in the region, this reliable and experienced team

can arrange vehicle rental, including 4WD. One of the best ways of seeing places like Cachi and Cafayate, or somewhere off the beaten track like Colomé or Yavi, without the stress of driving or organizing your own tour.

✉ Caseros 489 ☎ 0387/431-2097
🕐 Mon–Sat 10–1, 5–8
✋ Half-day tour $90

MERCADO ARTESANAL

Salta is an excellent place for picking up fine arts and crafts, with a large number of shops and stalls along calles Caseros and Buenos Aires, not far from the intersection at the Plaza 9 de Julio. Another possibility is the Mercado Artesanal, which is run by the provincial authorities and housed a short way from the city centre. In addition to the distinctive red and black ponchos, you can find some interesting ceramics and basket ware.

✉ Avenida San Martín 2555
☎ 0387/434-2808 🕐 Daily 9–9

NEW TIME CAFÉ

One of the most popular cafés on bustling Plaza 9 de Julio, this modern *confitería* is where locals gather for a drink and to watch the world go by.

✉ Caseros 602 ☎ 0387/431-7567
🕐 Daily 8am–2am

SALTA RAFTING

www.saltarafting.com
Salta Rafting not only offers exciting rafting trips on the nearby Río Juramento, but can arrange mountain biking in the hill country, canopy trips, treks and 4WD safaris.

✉ Buenos Aires 88 ☎ 0387/401-0301
🕐 Mon–Sat 9–1, 5–8 ✋ Rafting plus canopy $250

Below *A cable car whisks visitors to the top of Cerro San Bernardo for panoramic views of Salta*

TEATRO PROVINCIAL

www.teatroprovincial.gob.ar

On the Plaza 9 de Julio, Salta's sumptuous provincial theatre hosts a wide variety of shows, from musicals and cabaret to classical concerts. The city's prestigious symphonic orchestra has its permanent home here, too.

✉ Zuviría 70, Plaza 9 de Julio
☎ 0387/422-4515 🕓 Mon–Fri 9–1.30, 4.30–9 ✋ Varies

TELEFÉRICO

▷ 243.

VIEJA ESTACIÓN

By contrast with the more traditional *peñas* in the city, the Vieja Estación, in the trendy Balcarce district, has tourist-oriented northwestern folk music evenings, with impressive displays of *gaucho* dancing. Many of the bands are very entertaining and the crowds (which do include locals) are allowed to make requests.

✉ Balcarce 885 ☎ 0387/421-7727
🕓 Daily 8pm–3am ✋ There is no cover charge but you are expected to eat and drink

SAN LORENZO

RESERVA DEL HUAICO

www.reservadelhuaico.org.ar

Salta's genteel suburb isn't all about eating cake and admiring the

Below *Vieja Estación in Salta stages entertaining displays of* gaucho *dancing*

ceibo trees. There are wonderful panoramas of San Lorenzo and Salta from this admirable nature reserve, Reserva del Huaico, and it is a great place to get close to nature and watch for birdlife. Contact the helpful owners and arrange for an ornithological tour.

✉ Mariano Moreno s/n ☎ 0387/497-1024
🕓 Daily 8–6 ✋ Four-hour tour $25

TURISMO SAN LORENZO

www.turismo-sanlorenzo.com.ar

For more outdoor activities in and around San Lorenzo's green belt, contact this dedicated tour operator that can arrange horse riding, four-wheel buggy rides as well as cycling and trekking.

✉ Juan Carlos Dávalos 960
☎ 0387/492-1757 🕓 Mon–Sat 10–1, 4–7
✋ Three-hour horse ride $135

SAN MIGUEL DE TUCUMÁN

EL ALTO DE LA LECHUZA

This is one of the northwest's most famous *peñas* and was carefully renovated in 2009. Tucumán has a strong musical tradition so you should not miss an opportunity to attend a show here. Whether you see a major folk artist or an improvised jamming session, you are usually guaranteed a good night out. The hearty traditional food is excellent and the house wine flows in liberal quantities.

✉ 24 de Septiembre and Marco Avellaneda
☎ 0381/15-477-9527
🕓 Thu–Sun 8pm–2am

MONTAÑAS TUCUMANAS

www.montanastucumanas.com

One of the leading tour operators in the province, Montañas Tucumanas organizes trekking expeditions and more adventurous activities, including canyonning and rappelling, and even paragliding.

✉ Laprida 196 ☎ 0381/467-1860
🕓 Mon–Sat 10–1, 4–7 ✋ Half-day $120

SAN SALVADOR DE JUJUY

MERCADO DEL SUR

For a taste of the Andean culture that makes Jujuy so special, wander around the lively market opposite the

main bus station. In addition to all kinds of regional goods, you will see locals buying bags of coca leaves, which are chewed as a cure for altitude sickness, or made into coca-leaf tea. There are a number of food vendors here, selling peanut soup, fried pork with corn and *mazamorra* (corn broth).

✉ Dorrego and Alem
🕓 Daily 7am–midnight

EL TANTANAKUY

www.tantanakuy.org.ar

This is a wonderful arts centre, where you stop for refreshments or share a *mate*. Folk concerts, literary events and art shows, plus regular screenings of art-house films are all staged here.

✉ Salta 370 ☎ 03887/421538
🕓 Open most days of the week, afternoon (for tea) and evening

TAFÍ DEL VALLE

YUNGAS (LA CUMBRE HOSTEL)

Yungas is a friendly tour operator, based at the remarkable La Cumbre Hostel on the main drag, and can organize trekking tours across the mountains that encircle Tafí.

✉ Avenida Presidente Juan Domingo Perón 120 ☎ 03867/421768 ✋ $80 for a short trek

TILCARA

CARAVANA DE LLAMAS

www.caravanadellamas.com

Argentina's indigenous people have used llamas as pack animals for thousands of years, so why shouldn't you? This super-friendly outfit organizes caravan tours to fabulous out-of-the-way spots around the northwest, mostly in the Humahuaca and Tilcara region, allowing you to trek while your llama takes the strain of your luggage.

✉ Pasaje Eduardo Cabana 345
☎ 0388/495-5326 ✋ Varies

TILCARA MOUNTAIN BIKE

This extremely helpful little enterprise rents out high-quality mountain bikes so you can explore the valley at your own pace.

✉ Belgrano s/n 🕓 Daily 10–1, 5–8

FESTIVALS AND EVENTS

JANUARY
VIRGEN DE BELÉN
The village of Belén (▷ 233) hosts a major pilgrimage on 6 January each year, including a *Via Crucis* (Way of the Cross) procession up the mountainside.

ENERO TILCAREÑO
During the last two weeks of January, Tilcara (▷ 249) hosts a festival of folk culture, which includes music, folk dancing, and arts and crafts.

JANUARY/FEBRUARY
CARNAVAL
This carnival is celebrated with great enthusiasm throughout the region. Quebrada de Humahuaca probably has the most colourful festivities, with many of the celebrants parading through the streets wearing multicoloured feather headdresses.

FEBRUARY
VIRGEN DE CANDELARIA
The main annual festival in the town of Humahuaca (▷ 235) is celebrated with much fanfare and religious processions on 2 February.

FIESTA DE LA PACHAMAMA
The celebrations to commemorate Mother Earth, pre-Columbian-style, are held across the North, but the star fiestas are in Purmamarca (▷ 236) and Amaicha (▷ 233). The date varies from year to year.

FIESTA NACIONAL DEL QUESO
Tafí del Valle (▷ 248) hosts Argentina's national cheese festival in early February. In addition to sampling some of the best local cheeses, there is folk dancing, music and displays of arts and crafts.

FIESTA NACIONAL DE LA NUEZ
Londres's (▷ 236) national walnut feast is held in early February. Even if you miss the festivities be sure to taste the luscious candied walnuts.

SERENATA CAFAYATEÑA
www.serenata-cafayate.com.ar
Cafayate hosts a major folk festival on the first weekend after Shrove Tuesday. It is worth noting the date, as accommodation within 50km (31 miles) is reserved well in advance.

FESTIVAL DEL CAMINO HACIA EL NUEVO SOL
In the middle of February, a major indigenous festival takes over Fiambalá (▷ 235), with Andean music, dancing and festivities that show elements of both pre-European and Christian culture.

MARCH
FIESTA DE SAN JOSÉ
Cachi (▷ 233) celebrates its patron saint with plenty of family fun and saintly corteges on 19 March.

FERIA ARTESANAL Y GANADERA DE LA PUNA
Craftspeople and herdsmen from all over the province attend Antofagasta de la Sierra's (▷ 233) annual fair. Expect plenty of arts and crafts as well as displays of animal husbandry.

APRIL
SEMANA SANTA
Holy week is celebrated throughout the region. The Maundy Thursday festivities in Yavi (▷ 244), centred on the church, are worth seeking out.

JULY
FIESTA NACIONAL DEL PONCHO
In addition to fabulous textiles, Catamarca's annual celebration of the poncho offers the chance to listen to folk stars from across the country and try a variety of traditional dishes.

AUGUST
TOREO DE LA VINCHA
Festivities for the feast of the Assumption (15 August) at the remote village of Casabindo have distinctly pre-Columbian overtones, with a procession of mask-wearing revellers and a bloodless *corrida*. Ritual items are buried as an offering to Pachamama. This unique event is definitely worth attending.

SEMANA DE JUJUY
A week-long festival recalls how the city of San Salvador de Jujuy was saved by General Belgrano's forced evacuation in the early 19th century. Expect dancing and revelry in the streets of San Salvador.

SEPTEMBER
FIESTA DEL MILAGRO
Salta's major annual event starts on 6 September and lasts nine days. Religious images are paraded through the city in commemoration of a similar procession to save the city from destruction by earthquake. The same procession takes place several times but there is also much revelry, too, with plenty of singing, dancing and selling of arts and crafts.

OCTOBER
FIESTA DE LA VIRGEN DEL ROSARIO
www.iruyaonline.com/iruya-rosario.html
On the first Sunday in October, the Mudéjar Iglesia de Nuestra Señora del Rosario y San Roque in Iruya (▷ 235) is the scene of a mysterious feast with a solemn procession of masked figures.

NOVEMBER
TODOS LOS SANTOS
The villagers of Antofagasta de la Sierra (▷ 233) remember their dead every 1 and 2 November with age-old ritual ceremonies. Todos Los Santos (Day of the Dead) and All Saints are also widely marked along the Quebrada de Humahuaca.

DECEMBER
From 8–10 December, Cerro de la Cruz is the destination of processions held to honour St. Joseph and the Virgin of Loreto, patron saints of Antofagasta de la Sierra.

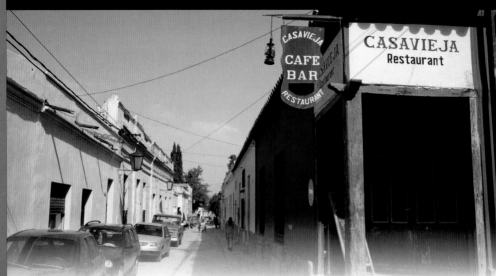

PRICES AND SYMBOLS

The restaurants are listed alphabetically (excluding El, La and Los). The prices given are the average for a two-course lunch (L) and a three-course dinner (D) for one person, without drinks. The wine price is for the least expensive bottle. All the restaurants listed accept credit cards unless otherwise stated. Prices are given in Argentine pesos ($) unless otherwise noted.

For a key to the symbols, ▷ 2.

BELÉN
1900

This is by far the best place to eat for miles around and is popular with locals and tourists alike—it's a good idea to reserve a table. Expect brisk, friendly service, jugs of house wine and large portions of traditional fare. The *bife de chorizo* is particularly good and the cheese and potato *tortilla* (omelette) is a meal in itself.
✉ Belgrano 390 ☎ 03835/461100
🕐 Daily 12–4, 8–12 ✋ L $40, D $58, Wine $17

CACHI
OLIVER

Overlooking the main square, Oliver holds pride of place, with its pavement tables and a small terrace on the plaza. This is the place to

head if you want an espresso or an ice-cold beer, but the pizzas and meat-based Andean dishes are also excellent. Upstairs is an intimate bar serving some of the best wines in the region, from the Colomé *bodega*.
✉ Ruiz de los Llanos 160 ☎ 03868/491903
🕐 Daily 8am–midnight ✋ L $27, D $38, Wine $15

CAFAYATE
EL RANCHO

www.elranchocafayate.com.ar
There are a number of good places to eat around the main plaza but El Rancho stands out for its pleasing decor and comfortable seating. The varied menu includes dishes based on rabbit, llama and trout. There is an open fire beneath a traditional cane ceiling and the tables are covered in fine linen. The *locro* (maize and bean stew) and the roast goat are both excellent. Wines from the Bodega Río Colorado are served in jugs.
✉ Vicario Toscano 4 ☎ 03868/421256
🕐 Daily 12–3.30, 8.30–1 ✋ L $32, D $47, Wine $17

HUMAHUACA
CASA VIEJA

This delightful cornerhouse is more authentic and less touristy than most of the popular restaurants in town.

The mainstay on the menu is a range of llama-based dishes and the house wine is excellent. Another attraction is the regular live folk concerts, which are held several evenings a week.
✉ Buenos Aires and Salta
☎ 03887/421181 🕐 Daily 12–3, 8–1am
✋ L $38, D $54, Wine $17

PURMAMARCA
LOS MORTEROS

Apart from the restaurant at the Comarca hotel, this is definitely the best place for dining in Purmamarca. The sumptuous traditional building is beautiful, decorated with framed Andean textiles on the walls.
The refined cuisine is based on indigenous food, with emphasis on local produce such as goat's cheese, beans, quinoa and llama, which are transformed into delicious *empanadas*, stews and casseroles.
✉ Salta s/n ☎ 0388/490-8063 🕐 Daily Mon–Sat 12–3, 8–12 ✋ L $45, D $60, Wine $19

SALTA
EL CORREDOR DE LAS EMPANADAS

The airy patio of this rambling restaurant is the best place in Salta to taste *empanadas* (pasties). These are popular throughout Argentina but particularly so in the northwest, where they probably originated. The *empanadas* here are high in the rankings for the title of best.

✉ Caseros 117 ☎ 0387/422-0345
🕐 Daily 12–12 ✋ L and D $25, Wine $15

JOSÉ BALCARCE

For a special occasion it is difficult to beat the refined decor, service and cuisine at this fabulous restaurant, which is well established on the gourmet circuit. Perhaps try a simple but superbly cooked dish of steak with oven-baked potatoes or, if you're feeling more adventurous, try the llama carpaccio with capers, lamb ravioli or llama steak. There is an excellent wine list, too.

✉ Necochea 590 ☎ 0387/421-1628
🕐 Mon–Sat 8.30pm–1am
✋ D $70, Wine $22

PLAZA DE ALMAS

www.plazadealmas.com

This fun, down-to-earth place has live music inside and outside on the attractive patio. The food is simple but delicious, with huge crispy salads or kebabs, which are large enough to share, and wok-based stir-fries.

✉ Pueyrredón 6 ☎ 0387/422-8933
🕐 Mon–Sat 9pm–2am ✋ D $32, Wine $17

EL SOLAR DEL CONVENTO

This superb restaurant, close to the central plaza, takes a neo-colonial theme, from the masks adorning the walls to the polite service and *criollo* furniture. It specializes in trout and beef, both of which are served with style and in a variety of ways. Diners are welcomed with a complimentary glass of sparkling wine.

✉ Caseros 444 ☎ 0387/421-5124
🕐 Daily 11–3, 8–midnight
✋ L $40, D $55, Wine $21

SAN LORENZO
EL DUENDE DE LA QUEBRADA

www.restaurantelduende.todowebsalta.com.ar

Sitting literally over the stream that gushes down through Quebrada de San Lorenzo, this rustic pub-cum-restaurant is nearly always crowded. Enjoy delicious pizzas, sandwiches, grilled meat and salads at one of the wooden benches, perched around terraces with breathtaking views overlooking the rapids.

✉ Juan Carlos Dávalos 2309 ☎ 0387/492-2053 🕐 Daily 12.30–4, 8–12 ✋ L $38, D $55, Wine $17

SAN MIGUEL DE TUCUMÁN
SETIMIO VINOTECA Y WINE BAR

This is the perfect place to dine if you want to combine a tour of a *bodega* with dinner. The helpful owners will take you round the excellent selection of syrahs and malbecs produced up in the high mountain valleys around Amaicha. Stay for dinner and the stylish surroundings lend themselves to an elegant dining experience. Try the perfectly braised lamb or order a *picada*—a platter of cheese, cold cuts and olives, to accompany a glass of perfectly kept ruby red.

✉ Santa Fe 512 ☎ 0381/431-2792
🕐 Mon–Sat 7.30pm–12 ✋ D $60, Wine $25

SAN SALVADOR DE JUJUY
MADRE TIERRA

www.casadebarro.com.ar

The lunchtime menu at this outstanding vegetarian and organic restaurant includes hearty soups, pancakes, quiches, *empanadas* and delicious desserts, accompanied by fresh fruit juice. If you are lucky, a local guitarist may serenade you while you eat. The breads baked on site are delicious and this is a great place to stock up for a picnic.

✉ Belgrano 619 ☎ 0388/422-9578
🕐 Mon–Sat 11–4, 8–11 ✋ L $42, D $53, Wine $16

MANOS JUJEÑAS

If you would like to try authentic northwestern food, look no further than this old favourite. The warm atmosphere, often enhanced by live folk music, complements the delicious, down-to-earth fare served in traditional earthenware vessels. The freshly made *empanadas* are filled with chopped (not minced) beef. The excellent house wine is also served in earthenware jugs.

✉ Pérez 222 ☎ 0388/422-2366 🕐 Daily 12–3, 8.30–2am ✋ L $28, D $35, Wine $14

ZORBA

The varied menu at this bright modern establishment on the main drag includes plenty of Argentine dishes, pizzas and sandwiches as well as Greek favourites such as *pastitsio* (macaroni bake), moussaka, Greek salad and *dolmades* (stuffed vine leaves). It's a good place to relax with a cup of coffee, too.

✉ Belgrano 802 and Necochea
☎ 0388/424-3048 🕐 Daily 11.30–4, 8–2am ✋ L $40, D $55, Wine $17

TILCARA
LOS PUESTOS

Los Puestos, at the entrance to the village, is a winner for its friendly service and handsome design. Sit on the airy terrace or inside and admire the photographs of the region and a wonderful mural of the Quebrada. Expect succulent meats cooked *parrilla*-style as well as a few more sophisticated dishes, such as llama or goat. You might want to finish your meal with a regional dessert of fresh cheese with candied fruit.

✉ Belgrano and Padilla ☎ 0388/495-5100
🕐 Daily 12–3, 8–1 ✋ L $42, D $55, Wine $19

Q'OMER

In a small shopping arcade off one of the main streets leading up to the central plaza, this excellent little restaurant has a faultless wine list and serves a wide range of Andean dishes. Meat-free dishes include marinated broad beans, succulent quinoa omelette, pumpkin purée and a flavoursome salad of mini-potatoes, chickpeas, goat's cheese, quinoa and sun-dried tomatoes. Meat eaters may enjoy the succulent llama and chicken specialities. The only distraction from the excellent food is a DVD playing in the background.

✉ Pasaje Kusiqa, Belgrano 417
☎ 0388/495-5439 🕐 Daily 12–3, 8.30–12
✋ L $42, D $56, Wine $18

Above *Stylish Castillo de Piedra, Tafí del Valle*

PRICES AND SYMBOLS

Prices are the lowest and highest for a double room for one night. Breakfast is included unless noted otherwise. All the hotels listed accept credit cards unless otherwise stated. Note that rates vary widely throughout the year. Prices are given in US dollars (US$) unless otherwise stated.

For a key to the symbols, ▷ 2.

ANTOFAGASTA DE LA SIERRA
HOSTERÍA DE ANTOFAGASTA

The municipal *hostería,* the only place to stay in Antofagasta, is clean and comfortable, with heating for those bitterly cold winter nights. All rooms are double—albeit a little cramped— and come with rudimentary but functional bathrooms. The *hostería* can put you in touch with local guides to help you get out to the marvellous volcanic scenery.
✉ Antofagasta de la Sierra
☎ 03835/471001 ✋ $80–$100 ⓘ 12

BELÉN
HOTEL BELÉN

www.belencat.com.ar
This modern hotel offers the best accommodation in the vicinity. It is also part of an interesting tourist complex that is harnessing increasing interest in travel to the area. Choose between the smaller Sullka rooms or the larger Suma mini-suites, decorated with white walls, sombre wood furnishings and ethnic-style bathrooms decorated with pre-Columbian designs. The hotel also offers an excellent youth hostel alternative with impeccable dorms.
✉ Belgrano and Cubas ☎ 03835/461501 ✋ $200–$300 ⓘ 28

CACHI
EL CORTIJO

www.elcortijohotel.com
Reminiscent of a neo-colonial roadside inn, with a wooden gallery overlooking an inner patio, El Cortijo is a real winner. The comfortable rooms are handsomely decorated. Some rooms are a little cramped, so ask to see the room you have been allotted before accepting. The lovingly prepared breakfasts will set you up for the day. Parking is limited.
✉ Avenida del ACA s/n ☎ 03868/491034 ✋ $240–$270 ⓘ 12

LA MERCED DEL ALTO

www.lamerceddelalto.com
La Merced, in a wonderful neo-colonial building occupying a former convent, has 13 rooms and one suite. The rooms are simply decorated in white, with beautiful furnishings and plenty of attention to detail. The fabulous grounds slope towards a swimming pool and spa complex, with breathtaking views across the valley to the Andean peaks. Inside a well-stocked bar adjoins a handsome restaurant where you can try a range of traditional dishes. The breakfasts are excellent.
✉ Fuerte Alto, Cachi ☎ 03868/490030 ✋ $500–$600 ⓘ 14 ☀ Outdoor

EL MOLINO DE CACHI

www.bodegaelmolino.com.ar
El Molino de Cachi enjoys a stunning location overlooking the Cachi valley, with amazing views of the surrounding peaks. Beautifully restored, this neo-colonial house plus the new purpose-built lodgings are furnished and decorated to a high standard. The hotel now functions as a *bodega,* too; so you can taste the Durand family's prize vintages at your convenience. Expect excellent home-cooked food in the restaurant and, of course, superb wines to accompany your meal.
✉ Cachi Adentro, Cachi ☎ 03868/491094 ✋ US$210–US$260 ⓘ 5 ☀ Outdoor 🍷

CAFAYATE
KILLA
www.killacafayate.com.ar
Only a couple of blocks away from
the central plaza, this exceedingly
welcoming little hotel offers a
range of spacious rooms, where
comfort and hospitality are the buzz
words. The rambling patio has a
swimming pool and sun deck. The
construction is a felicitous melange
of contemporary fun and neo-colonial
tradition. During your stay, you will be
treated like an honoured houseguest
and all the produce on offer at
breakfast is home-made.
✉ Colón 47 ☎ 03868/422254
✋ $280–$420 ⓘ 16 ⛱ Outdoor

PATIOS DE CAFAYATE
www.patiosdecafayate.com
Part of an international chain
(Sheraton), but with the feel of
an independent boutique hotel,
Los Patios is the most luxurious
accommodation for miles around.
Occupying one of Cafayate's most
historic wineries, the rooms are along
a neo-colonial gallery, complete with
jasmine-filled patios and open views
across the extensive grounds. At the
enticing outdoor swimming pool,
you can smell the rich bouquet of
the wine press and can follow up
with a grape wellness treatment at
the stunning Winespa. The rooms
and the public spaces are exquisitely
decorated with a judicious blend of
neo-colonial and modern decor.
The food and service are of the same
high standard.
✉ RN-40 and RN-68 ☎ 03868/422229
✋ US$255–US$430 ⓘ 29 ⛱ Outdoor
and spa pool

HUMAHUACA
SOLAR DE LA QUEBRADA
www.solardelaquebrada.com.ar
This new *hostería* is very well located,
a stone's throw from the main plaza
with easy access and parking. The
rooms (mostly doubles) are smart
and bright with en-suite bathrooms
and comfortable beds. Breakfast is
the only meal available, though the
helpful staff will point you in the right
direction for lunch and dinner and

even arrange transport if need be.
✉ Santa Fe 450 ☎ 03887/421986
✋ $240–$270 ⓘ 10

IRUYA
HOSTERÍA DE IRUYA
www.hosteriadeiruya.com.ar
With its 15 attractively decorated
double bedrooms, this well-run
hostería is the best accommodation
available in remote Iruya. The trip
here can be quite gruelling so you
will be relieved to be welcomed at
this excellent lodging. The *hostería's*
lofty location affords incredible views
of the Andean valley and you can eat
breakfast on the balcony, weather
permitting. The restaurant is passably
good, but there isn't much else on
offer in this remote place.
✉ Avenida San Martín s/n
☎ 03887/482002 ✋ $400–$430 ⓘ 15

MOLINOS
ESTANCIA COLOMÉ
www.bodegacolome.com
Swiss-owned Colomé is building
itself a reputation as one of the best
places to stay in South America. It
certainly lacks nothing: It is located
20km (12.5 miles) from Molinos via
a well-maintained gravel track that
heads deep into the Andes. The
neo-colonial building encircles a
handsome patio and fountain, and
each beautifully decorated room has
a spacious bathroom and an open
fire, which a butler will light for you if
required. The restaurant is excellent
and there is a museum dedicated to
the renowned artist James Turrell,
who plays with light and perspective
to intriguing effect. The cherry on
the cake is the on-site winery, which
you can tour and sample the sun-rich
wines.
✉ RP-53 km20 Molinos ☎ 03868/494044
✋ US$350–US$500 ⓘ 9 ⛱ Outdoor

HACIENDA DE MOLINOS
www.haciendademolinos.com
This fabulous *hacienda* was the
residence of the last royalist governor
of Salta in the 18th century but the
18 rooms have been renovated to
make it fit for 21st-century travellers.
The atmospheric building is arranged

around two enticing patios, one of
them shaded by an ancient pepper
tree. The high-ceilinged rooms give
a feeling of space, while the four-
poster beds add a touch of style.
There is also a swimming pool in the
back garden and a restaurant serving
delicious regional dishes.
✉ Abraham Cornejo s/n ☎ 03868/494094
✋ $250–$280 ⓘ 18 ⛱ Outdoor

PURMAMARCA
AMAUTA
www.hosteriadelamauta.com
Mercedes runs a tight ship at this
appealingly intimate *hostería* in
the heart of Purmamarca. The nine
capacious rooms are exquisitely
decorated in a restrained rustic
style and all have king-size beds
and modern bathrooms. There is a
handsome tea room that doubles
up as a breakfast room and a small
deck with a Jacuzzi. Much attention
is paid to detail, such as the quirky
furnishings.
✉ Salta 3 ☎ 0388/490-8043
✋ $315–$400 ⓘ 9

LA COMARCA
www.lacomarcahotel.com.ar
Outside Purmamarca on the road up
to the Salinas Grandes, luxurious La
Comarca is a jumble of appealing
terracotta-coloured buildings strewn
around a landscaped garden.
Accommodation ranges from
standard rooms to roomy *cabañas*
sleeping up to four people. The
immense suites are particularly
good value, with a Jacuzzi and two
balconies. The restaurant combines
innovative flair with traditional
produce and recipes, while the wine
cellar, alone, is worth a visit.
✉ Ruta 52 km3.8 ☎ 0388/490-8001
✋ $420–$530 ⓘ 17 ⛱ Outdoor heated

SALTA
BLOOMER'S
www.bloomers-salta.com.ar
Bloomer's, in central Salta, prefers
to call itself a bed-and-brunch rather
than bed-and-breakfast, which
speaks volumes about its laid-back
approach to looking after visitors. It
has only five suites, all decked out in

warm colours and bright traditional fabrics. The friendly owners will do all they can to make your stay memorable.

✉ Vicente López 131 ☎ 0387/422-7449 🖐 $240–$280 🚪 5

DESIGN SUITES

www.designsuites.com

The Salta branch of this deluxe chain occupies a rather functional looking modern tower adjoining a restored patrician palace, which overlooks one of the handsomest squares in the city. The rooms are minimalist and comfortable. Rooms in the older building are cosier but offer the same high-quality accommodation. The big attraction is the restaurant, which is also housed in the renovated mansion, where the chef is local star gastronome Gonzalo Doxandabarat.

✉ Avenida Belgrano 770 ☎ 011/5199-7465 (Buenos Aires); 0387/422-4466 (Salta) 🖐 US$150–US$270 🚪 51 🈳 🏊 Outdoor 🍴

FINCA VALENTINA

www.finca-valentina.com.ar

Conveniently located near Salta airport, this rural retreat is effectively a family home owned, designed and run by a dynamic couple from northern Italy. The two exquisite rooms in the main house and two further rooms in the independent smaller house are delightful beyond belief, as is the enthusiastic welcome reserved for guests. The food combines Italian *dolce vita* with local ingredients. There is a swimming pool and horse rides or walks in the surrounding countryside.

✉ Ruta 51 km11, La Merced Chica ☎ 0387/452-3490 🖐 $560–$650 🚪 4 🏊 Outdoor

KKALA

hotelkkala.com.ar

Located in the exclusive residential *barrio* of Tres Cerritos, Kkala has all the peace and quiet of suburbia without being that far from the city centre and its attractions. The architecture is both handsome and practical, with every room enjoying breathtaking views of the Cerro San

Bernardo. The six sumptuous rooms fall into three price categories but all are lovingly decorated and furnished. There is a swimming pool and inviting sun deck.

✉ Las Higueras 104, Tres Cerritos, Salta ☎ 0387/439-6490 🖐 US$150–US$200 🚪 6 🏊 Outdoor

LEGADO MÍTICO

www.legadomitico.com

This cleverly themed hotel outshines even its sister hotel in Buenos Aires. The eleven sumptuous rooms are arranged around a converted town house. Part of this magic is the stylish decor and clever use of space, while the themes themselves are witty and stimulating rather than contrived. One of the more sober rooms is named for a local heroine known as the Capitana, while the beautiful El Calchaquí suite has a superb carpet and a print depicting a pre-Columbian ceramic.

✉ Mitre 647 ☎ 0387/422-8786 🖐 US$170–US$210 🚪 11

SOLAR DE LA PLAZA

www.solardelaplaza.com.ar

With its entrance on one of Salta's most charming plazas, the park-like Plaza Guemes has the atmosphere of a colonial town house. Stylishly decorated throughout, the rooms are classy and comfortable, while the suites have king-size four-poster beds. The hotel's Terraza restaurant is a favourite lunchtime meeting place for locals, including those on business at the nearby provincial legislature.

✉ Leguizamón 669 ☎ 0387/431-5111 🖐 US$200–US$240 🚪 30 🈳 🏊 Outdoor

SAN LORENZO

CERROS DE SAN LORENZO

www.cerrosdesanlorenzo.com.ar

A lovely new hotel located in the tranquil heights of San Lorenzo, the Cerros has 11 charming rooms in a neo-colonial building, complete with whitewashed walls and *criollo* ceilings made of cane bound with leather. The staff can organize horse rides up into the hills, bicycle rides

and treks or fix you up with a round of golf at the local course. A stylish restaurant and swimming pool mean you hardly need to leave the hotel for a day or two.

✉ Joaquín V. González s/n, Loteo Los Berros ☎ 0387/492-2500 🖐 US$160–US$190 🚪 11 🏊 Outdoor

EATON PLACE

www.eatonplace.com.ar

Your host Eugenio is a gentleman and an aesthete, as is reflected in his refined house. An imperial avenue of palms leads up to the elegant brick mansion, fronted by a white rose garden. Inside, the French decor and museum-piece furniture are almost intimidating but the kind welcome and warm hospitality will soon put you at ease. The small number of rooms, both in the main house and in an extension, means that you are guaranteed quiet and discretion. In the well-kept garden is a fine swimming pool where you can watch hummingbirds sipping at nectar.

✉ Avenida San Martín 2457 ☎ 0387/492-1347 🖐 $300–$350 🚪 8 🏊 Outdoor

POSADA DON NUMAS

www.donnumas.com.ar

Don Numas is a family-run *posada* firmly imprinted with the exuberant hospitality of its principal hostess, the larger-than-life Josefina. The spacious rooms are decorated in pastels and have charming wood and wicker furniture. The breakfasts are memorable and plentiful. There are two heated outdoor pools; one for families and the other part of the excellent spa complex within the *posada's* extensive grounds.

✉ Pompilio Guzman 1470 ☎ 0387/492-1296 🖐 $340–$370 🚪 24 🏊 Two outdoor 🍴

SAN MIGUEL DE TUCUMÁN

POSADA ARCADIA

www.posadaarcadia.com.ar

The first advice for any visitor to Tucumán is to try to spend as much time as possible in leafy Yerba Buena. The next advice would be to book a room at this charming *posada*. There is a small but perfectly formed swimming pool amid the clipped lawns in the back garden.

✉ Güemes 480 ☎ 0381/425-2214
✋ $200–$340 🛏 4 ▨ Outdoor

TUCUMÁN HOSTEL

www.tucumanhostel.com

One of the best youth hostels in the region, the Tucumán has several double rooms plus small dorms. The delightful patio is shaded by avocado trees, under which hammocks are regularly slung for restful siestas. Things liven up at the Mala Mala bar, the hostel's hub of social life.

✉ Buenos Aires 669 ☎ 0381/420-1584
✋ $40 dorm; $100–$120 double 🛏 16

SAN SALVADOR DE JUJUY
EL ARRIBO

www.elarribo.com

El Arribo's motto is 'making you feel at home' and they certainly succeed. This late 19th-century family house has been successfully converted into one of the city's best places to stay. There is a pleasant common room plus a small garden with a plunge pool. The rooms are simply decorated, with beautifully polished floors and discreet pictures on the plain walls, all in keeping with the neo-colonial theme.

✉ Belgrano 1263 ☎ 0388/422-2539
✋ $255–$280 🛏 13 ▨ Plunge

TERRAZA BALCARCE

www.terrazabalcarce.com.ar

This handsome three-star hotel in the heart of Jujuy is far better value than the tower-block hotels that earn more stars. The 12 appealing rooms are well equipped with heating and air-conditioning. There is free parking and 24-hour room service. Breakfasts are complete and ample, and you also have free use of the hotel's computer and WiFi access if you have a laptop.

✉ Balcarce 354 ☎ 0388/431-0030
✋ $210–$240 🛏 12 🔧

TAFÍ DEL VALLE
CASTILLO DE PIEDRA

www.castillodepiedra.com.ar

Styled like a fairy-tale castle, the Castillo de Piedra is a model of how a hotel should be run—from the heart. Each room is decorated with personal taste and impeccable style. The views of the valley are truly breathtaking, while the grounds are perfect for gentle rambles. Part of the garden is given over to an ambitious organic kitchen garden and walnut orchard. There is an attractive outdoor swimming pool and colourful flowers in the garden attract beautiful hummingbirds. Soraya, the owner, is a fabulous cook and you will be treated to her special culinary skills during your stay.

✉ Avenida de los Jesuitas
☎ 03867/421199 ✋ $730–$800 🛏 8
▨ Outdoor 🔔 In Tafí follow signs to the Estancia Las Carreras and watch out for a signpost on the right, up the hill

ESTANCIA LAS CARRERAS

www.estancialascarreras.com

Some 12km (7.5 miles) out of Tafí del Valle, this 18th-century Jesuit *estancia* reeks of tradition. There is the occasional whiff of cheese, too, as the *estancia* produces some of the best manchego-style cheese in the country. Built around 1712, during the Jesuits' heyday in the Spanish colonies, the main building is decorated to reflect three periods in Tafí's history: pre-Incan, Incan and Hispanic. The ten delightful rooms are extremely comfortable and the whole place is run with true professionalism.

✉ Tafí del Valle ☎ 03867/421800
✋ US$130–US$160 🛏 10

TILCARA
DON JUAN

www.posadadonjuan.com.ar

There are plenty of excellent places to stay in Tilcara, but Don Juan is one of the best. Officially a three-star *hostería*, this place deserves a higher rating. The traditionally decorated rooms are light, comfortable and well appointed. Built in an appealing beige-ochre adobe, the building overlooks a well-tended garden. The buffet breakfast is very appetizing, too.

✉ Lavalle 1064 ☎ 0388/495-5422
✋ $250–$280 🛏 12

POSADA DE LUZ

www.posadadeluz.com.ar

Posada de Luz is now a reference for how to run a hotel in the northwest of Argentina. The owner, Luz, designed the hotel, and she and her family run it with admirable passion, making everyone feel at home. The lush gardens, with a fine swimming pool, are regularly visited by shimmering hummingbirds, which can be seen from the mini-patios fronting each room. The six rooms are utterly enchanting, but get booked up well in advance. The *posada* seems organically integrated into the majestic landscape of the Quebrada de Humahuaca.

✉ Ambrosetti and Alverro ☎ 0388/495-5017 ✋ $240–$320 🛏 6 ▨ Outdoor

YAVI
PACHAMÁ

www.pachamahosteria.net

At the entrance to the village, the Pachamá is a splendid traditional altiplano house, with adobe walls and straw thatching. Inside, the restaurant serves delicious but simple indigenous fare. The rooms are a little cramped but functional and very clean. The alternatives for miles around simply do not compare, so this is as good as it gets.

✉ Avenida Senador Pérez s/n
☎ 03885/423235 ✋ $100–$120 🛏 6

Below *The popular Posada de Luz, Tilcara*

IGUAZÚ FALLS AND THE LITORAL

Jointly shared with Brazil, the Iguazú Falls is one of the world's most powerful sights. Standing by the storm-like Garganta del Diablo (Devil's Throat) amid a dense fog of vapour, you are left in no doubt about the potency of nature. The rest of Misiones Province, with its blood-red soil and green vegetation, attracts far fewer tourists but has a number of minor sights to explore, such as the curious longitudinal falls of Saltos del Mocona along the Brazilian border. Over towards Paraguay, separated from Argentina by the Río Paraná, the sandstone ruins of San Ignacio Miní once formed one of the region's largest Jesuit *estancias*.

Four fertile provinces, Misiones, Corrientes, Entre Ríos and Santa Fe, form the Litoral and their respective capitals—Posadas, Corrientes, Paraná and Santa Fe—are pleasing backwaters. The region's biggest city, Rosario de Santa Fe, has some stunning architecture and beaches along a curve in the Río Paraná. Other towns worth visiting include two more riverside resorts, languid Colón on the Río Uruguay and up-and-coming Victoria, which can be reached from Rosario via a fabulous road-bridge. Gualeguaychú is best known for its carnival while Oberá gives access to the soothing green corridor in Misiones.

Getting to Iguazú is easiest by air and there are several airports, while the RN-9, RN-12 and RN-14 will get you to the region's other sights. You will definitely need a vehicle to get the most out of the Litoral, centred on the *gaucho* town of Mercedes. This is the entry point for the Esteros del Iberá, where caiman and capybaras splash around in the massive lagoons. These boundless marshes are home to dozens of species of birds, too. Chaco, to the northwest, is also blessed with a wealth of flora and fauna but its poor infrastructure and harsh climate make it a greater challenge to visit.

CHACO

The remote Gran Chaco region comprises Chaco and Formosa, two of the poorest yet most fascinating provinces in the country. A tropical wilderness, the Chaco is inhabited by intrepid groups of indigenous peoples, such as the Toba and Wichí, famed for their crafts, and an amazing wildlife. Few visitors ever make it here, as most are discouraged by the extreme climate with its blistering summer temperatures and storm-induced floods. But if you are willing to brave the tough conditions, you will be rewarded with some of the best concentrations of flora and fauna in the country. If you are patient and in luck you might even catch sight of a jaguar or a giant armadillo, a maned wolf or *mirikiná* (nocturnal monkey).

To get the most out of the challenging Chaco, it is a good idea to visit the national parks with a tour operator based in either Resistencia or Formosa. The cities' tourist information offices will be able to provide you with a list of reputable tour operators and guides.

RESISTENCIA AND FORMOSA

Resistencia is known for its statues, which are dotted all over town. The central Plaza 25 de Mayo, shaded by indigenous trees, hosts a small crafts market. A trio of good museums take you through the region's human history, ethnology and wildlife: Museo del Hombre Chaqueño (Juan B. Justo 280; tel 03722/453005; Mon–Fri 8–12, 3.30–8.30, Sat 9–1; free); the Museo de Antropología (Avenida Las Heras 750; tel 03732/446958; Mon–Fri 8.30–12.30, 2–7.30, Sat 5–8; free); and the Museo de Ciencias Naturales (Pellegrini 802; Mon–Fri 8.30–12.30, 2–7.30, Sat 5–8; free). The main attraction, however, is the Fogón de los Arrieros (▷ 294), a nationally famous arts foundation and folk centre.

Formosa squats by a loop in the Río Paraguay. This sleepy backwater brightens up in September when the *lapacho* trees bloom. The main sight in the town is the pink Museo Histórico (25 de Mayo and Belgrano; tel 03717/425000; Mon–Fri 8–12.30, 5–7.30; free), in a late-19th-century house, with an eclectic collection that ranges from a stuffed Swiss bear to indigenous crafts.

You probably won't linger long in Resistencia or Formosa, but either city makes a convenient base for seeking out the region's mesmerizing flora and fauna. It is best to base yourself in Resistencia if you want to visit Parque Nacional Chaco or Formosa if you intend to explore Parque Nacional Río Pilcomayo.

PARQUE NACIONAL CHACO

The small Parque Nacional Chaco (Capitán Solari, Provincia de Cacho; tel 03725/496166; daily 9–6; $10) is within relatively easy reach of Resistencia. The park conserves the endangered Chaco habitat around the banks of the Río Negro, including the dense forest, palm-dotted savannah and extensive wetlands. The 150sq km (58sq miles) of land, much of it inaccessible, swarms with small mammals and a huge variety of birds, including the fetching red-crested cardinal and the turquoise-fronted Amazon parrot.

PARQUE NACIONAL RÍO PILCOMAYO

The other major nature reserve is the Parque Nacional Río Pilcomayo (Laguna Blanca; tel 03718/470045; Mon–Fri 7–4; free), which is squeezed up against the Paraguayan border to the north of Formosa. Its 519sq km (202sq miles) of tropical wetlands often flood in the rainy season and are best visited by boat with one of the tour operators based in Formosa (▷ 293). In addition to comical howler monkeys, you are likely to come across large numbers of birds. Look out for the monk parakeets that build monastery-like nests in the palm fronds. The swamps and lagoons are carpeted with the beautiful *camalote*, a water lily-like plant that produces masses of delicate lilac flowers.

INFORMATION

www.granchacoturismo.net
www.resistencia.gov.ar/turismo/turismo.htm
www.formosa.gov.ar/turismo.html

🗺 337 H4 ✉ Provincia de Chaco and Provincia de Formosa 🛈 Resistencia Turismo, Provincia de Chaco ✉ Julio A. Roca 20 ☎ 03722/458289 🕐 Mon–Fri 8–8, Sat 8–1 🛈 Formosa Turismo ✉ Uruburu 820, Plaza San Martin, Provincia de Formosa ☎ 03717/420442 🕐 Mon–Fri 8–12, 4–8 🚌 Buses from Corrientes to Resistencia; buses from Resistencia to Formosa ✈ Resistencia international airport is 5km (3 miles) west of the city. Formosa's airport (El Pucú) lies 6km (4 miles) southwest of the city. Each has regular flights from Buenos Aires. Alternatively, there are regular flights to Corrientes airport 25km (15.5 miles) from Resistencia 🚤 Tour operators in Formosa organize boat trips to Parque Nacional Río Pilcomayo 🚗 To reach Resistencia from Corrientes, take the RN-16 northwest. To get to the Parque Nacional Chaco from Resistencia keep along the RN-16 for 56km (35 miles) then turn in a northerly direction along RP-9, continuing 40km (25 miles) to Capitán Solari; the park entrance is 6km (4 miles) away (well signposted). Formosa is 168km (104 miles) from Resistencia by the RN-11 🚗 Tours from Resistencia (▷ 294) and Formosa (▷ 293)

TIP

›› Winters can be dull and dreary while summers may see temperatures well over 40°C (104°F). Visit in the spring when the weather is warm and balmy, the flora is blooming and the fauna is most active.

Opposite *Lilac-flowered* camalote *grow in the swamps and lagoons of the Parque Nacional Río Pilcomayo*

INFORMATION

www.colonentrerios.net

✚ 347 K9 ✉ Colón, Entre Rios

ℹ Avenida Costanera and Gouchon

☎ 03447/421233 🕐 Mon–Fri
6am–10pm, Sat 7am–10pm, Sun
8am–10pm 🚌 Buses from Buenos Aires
🚗 From Buenos Aires take the RN-9
Panamericana in the direction of Rosario.
Turn onto RN-12 at Zárate (bridges over
Paraná) before taking the RN-14 branch at
El Empalme. Colón is a total of 321km (199
miles) from Buenos Aires 🚢 Tours from
Colón (▷ 292)

TIPS

» The best place hereabouts for a relaxing
soak is the spacious, state-of-the-art
Termas Villa Elisa (▷ 292) thermal
complex. There is also a thermal spa
complex in the centre of town.

» Take a tour around the abandoned
Liebig meat-processing plant (ask at the
tourist office about guided tours), which
is all that remains of the region's formerly
great beef export industry. Anyone who
likes industrial architecture will be in their
element and vegetarians can rest assured
that there is no blood and gore in sight.

Above *Colón makes a good base for
visiting nearby Parque Nacional El Palmar*

COLÓN

Friendly Colón spreads languorously along the Río Uruguay, the great river
that forms Argentina's border with Uruguay. Thanks to its superb location and
well-preserved buildings, Colón is easily the most attractive of all the Entre
Ríos resorts. The town makes an excellent base for visiting the Parque Nacional
El Palmar (▷ 278), 50km (31 miles) to the north, and the Palacio San José
(▷ 278), about 40km (25 miles) to the southwest.

A sandy beach runs for several kilometres alongside its promenade, the
Costanera Gobernador Quirós. The central square, Plaza Washington, is home to
the historic *municipalidad* but far more elegant is the smaller Plaza San Martín,
a leafy square east of Plaza Washington along Colón's busy shopping street
Avenida 12 de Abril.

A short way to the north of Plaza San Martín, around the port, is where you
will find the best places to stay and eat. This is a small but charming quarter with
cobbled streets, lined with handsome colonial-style buildings, which gently slope
down to the river.

WHAT TO SEE

A short boat ride from Colón takes you out to the middle of the Río Uruguay
and a series of sandy islands, partly carpeted with dense vegetation and pristine
dunes. The islands are great places for observing the abundant birdlife and
indigenous flora and fauna. The best way to get to the islands is in a motorized
dinghy with a local tour operator (▷ 292).

If you prefer dry land, an excellent tour visits the petrified tree trunks in the
nearby quarries. Here, you can also see a display of semi-precious stones, some
of which are real works of art. These sites can be visited under your own steam
(ask at the tourist office) but a guided tour brings them to life.

Closer to town is the Reservorio de Piedras Semipreciosas (Barrio Troncos
Petrificados, RP-26 km3.5; tel 03447/15-625263; daily 9–6; free). The owner
Selva, known locally as the queen of the agates, is always delighted to show
visitors her remarkable collection of semi-precious gems and sells beautiful
jewellery made from the rocks.

CORRIENTES

www.corrientes.com.ar

The beautiful subtropical city of Corrientes curls around a bulge in the Río Paraná, known for its treacherous currents. Founded in the late 16th century, the city has preserved many of its elegant colonial houses, most of them clustered around the leafy Plaza 25 de Mayo. Check out the rosy Casa de Gobierno, on the eastern side of the square, built in late 19th-century Italianate style.

One of the city's highlights is the Museo de Artesanías Correntinas (Fray José de la Quintana 905; Mon–Fri 8–8, Sat–Sun 9–1; free), on the plaza and housed in a low, whitewashed building around a galleried patio. Inside are exhibits of the province's indigenous crafts, including the fascinating carvings of San La Muerte (Saint Death): little wooden, metal or bone skeletons worn as talismans to ensure a painless death. Modern versions are sold at the museum's shop.

On the southern side of the square, the 19th-century Iglesia de Nuestra Señora de la Merced (daily 7–12, 4–8; free) has a beautiful carved wooden retable with spiralled wooden pillars and rich inlay work. For an authentic flavour of the city, amble along the riverfront promenade, which is lined with pink-flowered *lapacho* trees. From here, you can look across to the flat coast of the Chaco.

338 K5 ✉ Corrientes, Provincia de Corrientes ℹ 25 de Mayo 1330 ☎ 03783/427200 🕔 Daily 7–1, 3–8 🚌 Buses from Rosario and Buenos Aires ✈ Aeropuerto Fernando Piragine Niveyro, 10km (6 miles) northeast 🚍 20km (12.5 miles) to the east, via the suspension bridge, from Resistencia

ESTEROS DEL IBERÁ
▷ 272.

GUALEGUAYCHÚ

www.gualeguaychuturismo.com

Gualeguaychú is famous for its great Carnaval (▷ 295), otherwise, it is a quiet place with a handful of old buildings and a luxuriant riverfront.

Around the main square, Plaza San Martín, you will find most of the town's hotels and shops and the late 18th-century Solar de los Haedo, housing the Museo de la Ciudad (Congreso 593; tel 03436/421063; Wed–Sun 9–12, Wed–Sat 6–9; free). Behind the simple limewashed house is a lush garden full of vines and orchids. The museum contains original furniture and other objects belonging to the Haedos, the city's most aristocratic colonial family. Along with Hispanic religious art and French porcelain is a collection of the 19th-century satirical magazine *Caras y Caretas*, whose founder José 'Fray Mocho' Álvarez was born in the city. Italian hero Giuseppe Garibaldi stayed in the house in 1845 when he was fighting on the Liberal side in the Uruguayan Civil War.

347 K10 ✉ Provincia de Entre Ríos ℹ Plazoleta de los Artesanos, Paseo del Puerto ☎ 03446/423668 🕔 Dec–Mar daily 8am–10pm; Apr–Nov 8am–8pm 🚌 Buses from Buenos Aires 🚍 217km (135 miles) from Buenos Aires; take the RN-9, cross the Paraná at Zárate, and then continue on the RN-14 at El Empalme

IGUAZÚ
▷ 274–277.

MERCEDES

www.corrientes.com.ar/mercedes

Mercedes, the main gateway town to the Esteros del Iberá (▷ 272), is a traditional settlement of adobe buildings with some elegant 19th-century mansions and villas. Horses are often seen in town, especially on Saturdays when traditionally garbed *gauchos* come to the market.

The main square, Plaza 25 de Mayo, is dotted with small fountains and flanked to the south by the 19th-century Iglesia Nuestra Señora de las Mercedes, whose towers are topped with Moorish domes. One of the main attractions of the town is the opportunity to buy traditional crafts, including *gaucho* wear.

Some 9km (5.5 miles) west of town, along the RN-123, is the principal roadside shrine to the popular local hero 'Gauchito' Gil

(▷ 23). Every year on 8 January (▷ 295) the area turns into a huge campsite, as thousands of pilgrims flock to pay homage to their hero.

343 L7 ✉ Provincia de Corrientes ℹ Acceso oeste ☎ 03778/420100 🕔 Daily 8–12, 4–8 🚌 Buses from Buenos Aires 🚍 From Buenos Aires, take the RN-9 and RN-14 to the fork with the RN-119

OBERÁ

www.fiestadelinmigrante.com.ar

Oberá, the second-largest town in Misiones Province, is a tidy modern place sitting amid the province's gentle central sierras. First settled in the early 20th century by Swedish and Swiss immigrants, the town now hosts more than a dozen different communities, including French, German, Japanese, Russian and Ukrainian. There are a couple of Russian and Ukrainian churches as well as the only Swedish cemetery in Latin America.

The second week in September sees the annual Fiesta Nacional del Inmigrante, which is held in the large Parque de las Naciones to the east of town. The celebration lasts a week and consists of dancing, music and gastronomy from each ethnic group. The leafy park contains a collection of houses built in the style of each community. If you miss the festival, you can still visit the houses at the weekend and taste each country's national cuisine. For more information on opening times visit the tourist information office.

339 N5 ✉ Provincia de Misiones ℹ Avenida Libertad 90 ☎ 03755/421808 🕔 Mon–Sat 8–9 🚌 Buses from Posadas 🚍 125km (77.5 miles) from Posadas; take RP-105 to San José and then RN-14

Below *A roadside shrine to folk hero 'Gauchito' Gil, outside Mercedes*

INFORMATION

www.ibera.gov.ar

🔢 343 L6 ✉ Provincia de Corrientes
🕐 Daily dawn–dusk ℹ By the bridge
across the lagoon ☎ 03773/1562-9656
🕐 Daily dawn–dusk 💵 Reserve free;
visitor centre free 🚌 Buses to Mercedes
(▷ 271), then onward transfer with
one of the agencies at the bus station
🚖 Pellegrini is best reached via
Mercedes; take the RP-40 (dirt road) from
Mercedes (allow two hours) 📖 The best
guide to the birdlife is *Birds of Southern
South America and Antarctica* by Martin
R. de la Pena and Maurice Rumboll
(Princeton) 🎫 Tours from Posadas
(▷ 293)

INTRODUCTION

The Esteros del Iberá is a fabulous self-contained landscape of wetlands where you can observe myriad birds and other wildlife. The wetlands extend over almost 13,000sq km (5,070sq miles). The Reserva Natural del Iberá protects the central core of the wetlands, where herons and capybaras, caiman and howler monkeys seem oblivious to the camera-sprouting humans. The *esteros* (marshes) are dotted with lakes, ponds, streams and an archipelago of floating islands. Since the creation of the reserve in the 1980s, hunting has been banned and many local people work as nature guides and park rangers, helping to preserve this unique environment.

WHAT TO SEE
CARLOS PELLEGRINI

Along the banks of the 53sq km (21sq-mile) Laguna del Iberá is the sprawling hamlet of Carlos Pellegrini. Access to the village is over a rickety bridge made of soil, rock and planks of wood; it is safer than it seems. It is worth investigating the short trail on the right-hand side of the road just before the bridge. The path leads through a grove of dense palms, jacarandas and rose-blossomed *lapachos*, and is a perfect place to see and hear howler monkeys. There are also lots of birds, such as the plush-crested jay with a velvety pom-pom on its head. You don't have to go far to see capybaras as they often graze on the lawns in front of the visitors' centre. These huge guinea-pig-like rodents are elegant swimmers and you will see dozens around the lagoon. In the mating season you will often see males fighting.

The village is a compact grid of sandy streets, centred on the grassy Plaza San Martín, and has basic amenities. Everything you need, however, you will find in the village's handful of sumptuous eco-lodges. Wildlife safaris are run by each *posada* and guests can go out several times a day in small motor launches or kayaks. The motor boats go out to the centre of the lake, dip under the bridge, call in at the visitors' centre to register and then drift silently through the brooks and channels that form a labyrinth of isles on the other side of the lagoon. It is worth going out in the early morning, working up an appetite for breakfast, and then going out again in the late afternoon to see the sunset and observe a different set of wildlife.

Above *Black caiman are among the wildlife regularly spotted in the Reserva Natural del Iberá*

BIRDLIFE

The marshes are home to 300 bird species and one that you will hear frequently is the *chajá* (also called a southern screamer), a large grey bird with red around the eyes and a coy disposition. *Chajáes* mostly perch on branches chanting 'aha-aha' but from time to time let out a blood-curdling screech. Look out, too, for the sleek cormorants, the black and white plumage of *maguari* storks, and striated herons with their distinctive black crowns. In the spring, hundreds of herons gather together to nest—a fabulous sight. If you are lucky you might see a jabiru, a long-legged stork with a white body, red neck and black head, grazing on the marshy meadows. In addition to several varieties of kingfisher, you will be treated to frequent sightings of the curious jacanas that use the water lilies as stepping stones rather than flying.

A number of small field birds can be spotted around the lake. Look out for scarlet-headed blackbirds, and white *monjitas* (little nuns), which can be seen perching almost motionless on reeds and tiny twigs. Three local kinds of flycatcher, known as 'tyrants' because of their aggressive behaviour, can often be spotted, as can the forked-tailed flycatcher. And everyone loves the red-crested cardinals, which are curious little white and grey birds with vivid scarlet plumage on their heads.

REPTILES AND MAMMALS

Another favourite sight is the black caimans, prehistoric-looking reptiles that are now reared for their meat and leather, which are indigenous to the Esteros del Iberá. By torchlight, after nightfall, their transparent eyes shine like red cats' eyes along the lagoon's edge. Far prettier is the rare marsh deer, the largest in South America, often seen gently grazing on the plant rafts. Its Bambi-like face is one of the most sought-after sights for avid photographers.

Below *A boat trip on the Laguna del Iberá is a great way to explore the region*

TIPS

›› At the visitors' centre, to the left just before you cross the bridge, you can see a small display of photos of the Esteros and their wildlife.

›› Do not try to drive towards Posadas from Pellegrini (or vice versa) without first getting advice about the state of the road; it is at best sandy and at worst a muddy bog in parts, especially after heavy rain. The best route is via Mercedes.

›› It is worth splashing out on one of the lagoon-side lodgings in Carlos Pellegrini (▷ 298). Many of the hotels run their own nature-watching trips and you can usually spot plenty of local wildlife while lounging by the swimming pool.

›› On wildlife trips run by the *posadas*, the boatmen act as guides and often carry English-speaking field guides, too. Check with the tour operator in advance.

›› There are no banks or exchanges in Pellegrini and the lodgings do not accept credit cards, so make sure you bring enough cash for the duration of your stay.

›› Take a good pair of binoculars and a field guide plus sunscreen and insect repellent.

INTRODUCTION

The Iguazú Falls (the Cataratas del Iguazú) is a stunning set of more than 250 cascades shared between Argentina and Brazil. Not only is the roaring mass of water hurtling over rocky cliffs impressive but you are also treated to an idyllic setting amid luxuriant subtropical forests, protected by two national parks. The falls, some narrow spurts and others great curtains of white water, gush from the upper Río Iguazú to the lower Río Iguazú. The main feature is the Garganta del Diablo (Devil's Throat), a deafening maelstrom of water foaming over a giant horseshoe of rock and down a ravine over 70m (230ft) below.

Another asset of the falls is the rich wildlife, which includes dozens of butterflies (members of the Morphidae family have hand-sized wings of a dazzling shiny blue) and large numbers of raccoon-like coatis, which will pester you for food. Friar-like capuchin monkeys are frequently seen and the sound of howler monkeys often disturbs the quiet. Minute corzuela deer, pumas, jaguars and tapirs are here, too, but are mostly too shy to show themselves in public. Of the birds, several species of toucans are some of the easiest to see, but there is also the black cacique, many different woodpeckers and crested *yacutingas*. Near the waterfalls, look out for the swallow-like *vencejo*, which builds its nest behind the torrents, and swirls up towards you when you look down into the Garganto del Diablo.

WHAT TO SEE

PARQUE NACIONAL IGUAZÚ (ARGENTINA)

www.iguazuargentina.com

From the visitors' centre, you can choose between the Sendero Verde (Green Path) and the Tren de la Selva (Jungle Train) to reach the Estación Cataratas, from where two routes formed of catwalks and paths take you past the waterfalls. First follow signs for the Paseo Superior along a short wooded trail that takes you above the first cascades. Then take the Paseo Inferior down through the forest that takes you right up close to the minor Salto Ramírez and Salto Bossetti.

INFORMATION

www.iguazuargentina.com

✚ 339 N4 ✉ Provincia de Misiones 🚌 Frequent buses from Buenos Aires via Posadas ✈ Airport 20km (12.5 miles) southeast of town. Direct flights from Salta and Córdoba 🚗 Take the RN-12 for 300km (186 miles) from Posadas 🚐 Tours from Parque Nacional Iguazú (▷ 293), Parque Nacional do Igaçu (Brazil) and Posadas (▷ 293)

Above *The Garganta del Diablo (Devil's Throat) waterfall, Parque Nacional Iguazú*
Opposite *Salto Bossetti on the Paseo Inferior (Lower Trail), Parque Nacional Iguazú*

›› The cooler season between Easter and late October is regarded as the best time to visit Iguazú. The falls are at their most amazing after heavy rains (April to July), but the water may have a less photogenic rusty hue from the red soil. Avoid Easter and early July, the peak holiday seasons, while the falls can also be packed in January and February.

›› The water debit varies a lot and the falls dried up completely in 1978 and 2006. It shouldn't happen again for some time.

›› Whenever you choose to visit, allow a day or two extra in case of bad weather. It is better to laze around your hotel for a day or so rather than be disappointed and the rain doesn't usually last too long.

›› The best places to stay are within the parks. The Sheraton (▷ 299) on the Argentine side is a featureless hulk but has a fabulous location. Far more atmospheric is the Hotel das Cataratas (▷ 299) overlooking the falls on the Brazilian side.

›› Inside the Parque Nacional Iguazú there are shops and cafés plus a visitors' centre with lots of maps and information leaflets. Don't miss the small museum full of photographs and stuffed birds and other creatures.

Below *An aerial view shows the sheer number and power of the falls at Iguazú*

Another trail takes you down to the jetty from where (conditions permitting) a free boat service takes you over to the Isla San Martín, a rocky island in the middle of the Río Iguazú. There's a small beach at the northern end of the island, where you can bathe in the summer. Again conditions permitting, short boat trips speed you right up to the curtain of water, where you will get a thorough soaking.

To reach the Garganta del Diablo, the throbbing heart of the Cataratas, climb back up to the Estación Cataratas and take the free train to the Estación Garganta del Diablo, 3km (2 miles) away (the last train departs at 4.30pm). A 10-minute walk along a new catwalk leads to a small viewing platform overlooking this giant plughole, where the plunging water forms a great foaming white mass.

Leave some time, too, for the Sendero Macuco, a less-visited 4km (2.5-mile) nature trail through the jungle where you are bound to see toucans and possibly capuchin monkeys. Heading west from the visitors' centre, a signposted path leads to the start of the Sendero, which wends down past the Salto Arrechea, another cascade, to the riverbanks and a secluded bathing spot.

✚ 339 P4 🛈 Visitor Centre ☎ 0800 266 4482 or 03757/491469 🕐 Daily 6–6 ✋ $85 🚌 Every hour from the town centre terminal in Puerto Iguazú, from 7.30am; last bus from the park 8pm 🚗 Around 20km (12.5 miles) southeast of Puerto Iguazú, along the RN-12 🚢 Tours from Posadas (▷ 293); boat rides cost $100–$200 per person, depending on length 🎁 ☕ Cafés and snack bars (daily 6–6) and a restaurant near the visitor centre

PARQUE NACIONAL DO IGUAÇU (BRAZIL)

www.cataratasdoiguacu.com.br/index_en.asp

The Brazilian side can be seen more quickly than the Argentine, but a visit to the Parque Nacional do Iguaçu is rewarding for the amazing panoramic views you get of the falls. First cross to Brazil via the Ponte Presidente Tancredo Neves, and pass through customs, which can be time-consuming.

The entrance to the Parque Nacional do Iguaçu is around 20km (12.5 miles) southeast of Foz. From here, a special bus takes you to the stop opposite the Hotel das Cataratas (▷ 299) where there are fabulous views of the falls. Cliff-top walks take you closer to the cascades and a series of viewing platforms offer subtly changing vistas of the falls, the river and the Isla San Martín. The 1.5km (1-mile) path descends to a walkway that takes you up to the lower end of the Garganta del Diablo (wear waterproofs and protect cameras). You can take the elevator back up to the cliff top or walk and enjoy more good views.

✚ 339 P4 🛈 Centro de Visitação 🕐 Daily 12–4 ☎ (+55) 45/3521-4400 🕐 Parque: daily 9–5 ✋ Adult R$37, child (under 11) R$6, child (under 2) free 🚗 20km (12.5 miles) southeast of Foz 🚢 Macuco Safari (▷ 293) offers one of the best excursions in the park 🎁 🍴 Restaurant (daily 12–4) ☕ Cafés (daily 9–5)

MORE TO SEE

PUERTO IGUAZÚ

www.welcomeargentina.com/puertoiguazu/index_i.html

Little Puerto Iguazú is the nearest Argentine town to the great falls and, though it has no major sights of its own, makes a great base from which to explore the area. There are a handful of varied lodgings and places to eat dotted around the town's tree-lined streets. The most convenient lodgings are located on the main road leading to the park entrances and have swimming pools, restaurants and large gardens where you can laze and wallow in the tropical languor. There are shops and tour agencies around the intersection of Avenida Aguirre, Calle Brasil and Calle Ingeniero Gustavo Eppens. Avenida Tres Fronteras runs west for 1.5km (1 mile) or so to the Hito Argentino de las Tres Fronteras, where there are views across the Río Iguazú to Brazil and the far mightier Paraná to Paraguay. Each country has erected a small obelisk overlooking the water painted in the colours of their national flag.

✚ 339 N4 ✉ Provincia de Misiones ℹ Avenida Aguirre 311 ☎ 03757/420800 🕐 Daily 8–8 🚌 Frequent buses from Buenos Aires via Posadas ✈ Airport 20km (12.5 miles) southeast of town 🚗 20km (12.5 miles) northwest of the Argentine park entrance; from Posadas take the RN-12 north

FOZ DO IGUAÇU (BRAZIL)

www.fozdoiguacu.pr.gov.br/portal2/home_turismo

Modern Foz do Iguaçu in Brazil lies across the Río Iguazú from Puerto Iguazú, its population swollen since the construction of the massive Itaipú dam complex (www.turismoitaipu.com.br; daily 8–4; 90-minute tours every hour; US$20). The main commercial street is Avenida Brasil, parallel to the major thoroughfare Avenida Juscelino Kubitschek. There are not many sights but a plethora of excellent shops, restaurants and lodgings makes the town an excellent base for visiting the Brazilian side of the falls. The most convenient lodgings are located along the main road leading to the national park.

✚ 339 N4 ✉ Brazil ℹ Avenida Jorge Schimmelpfeng and Rua Benjamin Constant ☎ (+55) 45/574-2196 🕐 Daily 7–11 ✈ Foz do Iguaçu Airport 🚗 20km (12.5 miles) to the Brazilian park entrance; follow the signs to Cataratas/Parque Nacional

LA ARIPUCA

www.aripuca.com.ar

On the outskirts of Puerto Iguazú, heading towards the national park, La Aripuca is a huge replica of the wooden traps (*aripucas*) used by indigenous peoples to catch birds. Over 10m (33ft) high, it is built out of 29 species of native trees, which died naturally or were felled as part of forest management. The friendly English-speaking owners want to draw visitors' attention to ecological issues and organize interesting eco-tours in the region. You can have a *mate* ice cream or other snacks and buy a range of locally made crafts.

✉ RN-12 km4.5 ☎ 03757/423488 🕐 Daily 9–6 ✋ Adult $10, child (under 12) $5 🚗 Take the main road towards the airport/national park and look for signs to the right after 4.5km (3 miles)

PARQUE DAS AVES

www.parquedasaves.com.br

The best way of seeing the region's birdlife is in the well-organized Parque das Aves, near the park entrance on the Brazilian side. A series of cages and walk-through aviaries allow you to get up very close to a variety of parrots and other brightly plumed birds, including some of the toucans that you might see in the parks. There are also indigenous snakes and reptiles and a butterfly house.

✉ Avenida das Cataratas km17.1 ☎ (+55) 45/3529-8282 🕐 Daily 8.30–5.30 ✋ Adult and child US$12 🚗 The entrance to the Parque das Aves is clearly marked opposite the entrance to the national park

Above *Green macaw, Parque das Aves*

TIPS

›› Operators in the parks will try to sell you their range of trips and tours, by truck, boat or on foot. Take your time to decide how much you are willing to spend. The tours are expensive but the boat rides ($100–$200) take you right up to the falls.

›› The best time to see wildlife is either late afternoon or early evening, when there are fewer visitors and the birds and mammals are at their most active. Keep as silent as possible and wear camouflage.

›› There are many handsome trees to admire. Look out for the lofty *palo rosa*, with its pallid straight trunk that divides into twisting branches, and the *pindó* and *palmito*, two of several species of palm that grow here. Lianas and ferns also thrive in this humid environment.

›› New catwalks have provided wheelchair access to all of the Paseo Superior and much of the Paseo Inferior (on the Argentine side), but turning room is often limited.

›› On the Argentine side you should keep your ticket and its stamp, as it will entitle you to a half-price entry if you return the following day.

›› Bear in mind that Brazil is one hour ahead of Argentina between November and February. The rest of the year the time is the same, though it's worth checking, just in case there has been a change, especially if you have a plane to catch.

to Santa Fe and then the RN-168 (under the river via the Raúl Uranga–Carlos Sylvestre Begnis tunnel) to Paraná

PARQUE NACIONAL EL PALMAR

www.turismoentrerios.com/colon/parqueelpalmar.htm

The fabulous Parque Nacional El Palmar is an 85sq km (33sq mile) reserve created in the 1960s to protect the *yatay* palm from extinction due to excessive felling and farming. Huge numbers of the noble *yatays*, some of which are several hundred years old and up to 20m (66ft) tall, form a splendid jungle-like landscape that falls away to the banks of the Río Uruguay. The park is an excellent example of a gallery forest and pockets of subtropical vegetation have formed from seeds and soil from Brazil. There are *guardaparques* (rangers) at the entrance to the park where you can get a map and information brochure. Continue for another 10km (6 miles) to the visitors' centre and restaurant.

The best time to visit the park is in the late afternoon, when the majestic silhouettes of the palms stand out against the sky. A number of well-signposted paths take you around the park, along streams and through the forest, while longer tracks are meant to be driven. One of these tracks leads to the La Glorieta, a hill overlooking an ocean of *yatays*. You may spot *ñandús* (rheas), armadillos and foxes plus chinchilla-like *vizcachas* and monitor lizards. Ask about the guided walks organized by Jorge Díaz.

✚ 347 K9 ✉ RN-14, 50km (31 miles) north of Colón ❓ *Guardaparques* at park entrance; information centre ☎ 03447/493053 ⏱ Daily 8–7 💵 $20 🚌 Buses from Colón to Posadas drop passengers at the entrance ⓘ Park entrance is about 50km (31 miles) north from Colón along the RN-14 ⛴ Tours from Colón (▷ 292); ask at the information centre for details of the many walks and tours available

POSADAS

▷ 279.

PALACIO SAN JOSÉ

www.palaciosanjose.com.ar

When General Justo José de Urquiza had the Palacio San José built in the 19th century, it was the most modern and luxurious private residence in the land. Italian architect Fosatti lent the palace an unmistakeably Tuscan appearance with its elegant arches and fine decoration but, owing to the insecurity of Urquiza's times, he placed the entrance at the back. The chapel is lined with fabulous frescos and a majestic baptismal font made of Carrara marble. The palace's 30 or so rooms are laid out around two vast courtyards around which Urquiza and his family lived.

The Sala de la Tragedia was Urquiza's bedroom, where he was murdered on 11 April 1870 by followers of rival *caudillo* (warlord) López Jordán. Turned into a shrine by Urquiza's widow, it retains traces of blood on the door and bullets stuck in the wall. Take a walk out into the French-style garden, for fantastic views back to the palace.

✚ 347 K9 ✉ RP-39 km128, Provincia de Entre Ríos ☎ 03442/432620 ⏱ Mon–Fri 8–7, Sat–Sun 9–6; guided visits Mon–Fri 10, 11, 3, 4 (plus 12 and 2 on Sat and Sun); Jan, Feb also open Fri 9pm–midnight with guided tours 9–10pm 💵 $5 (Fri evening tours, Jan and Feb $12) 🚌 From Buenos Aires, take the RN-9 and RN-14 towards Colón. At the turn-off to Concepción del Uruguay (to the right) take the RP-39 to the left (westwards); the Palacio is 23km (14 miles) away ⛴ Tours from Colón

PARANÁ

www.turismoparana.gov.ar

Paraná, the capital of Entre Ríos Province since 1822, is a bustling city set among the hills overlooking the river. The dramatic neoclassical cathedral, with its deep-blue brick-tiled central dome and Byzantine-style campaniles, dominates the city's main square. Paraná's best museum is the Museo Histórico Provincial Martiniano Leguizamón (tel 0343/431-2735; Tue–Fri 8–12.30, 3–8, Sat 9–12, 5–7, Sun 9–12; $1), whose upper floor is a jumble of items recording provincial history back to pre-Columbian times. The highlight is the dazzling assortment of *gaucho* silverware on the ground floor. Paraná is also worth visiting for its enticing sandy beaches and Parque Urquiza. The dense vegetation of the park is a favourite resting spot for locals in the hot summer and there are lovely views of the city. At the western end of the riverside is the Puerto Viejo (Old Port), which is distinguished by its attractive cobbled streets and appealing old houses. Far more vibrant, especially on summer evenings, is the *costanera* (waterside promenade), where you will find bars, restaurants and the public beaches.

✚ 346 J9 ✉ Provincia de Entre Ríos ❓ Buenos Aires 132 ☎ 0343/423-0183 ⏱ Daily 8–8 🚌 Buses from Buenos Aires ✈ Aeropuerto General Justo José de Urquiza, 5km (3 miles) southeast of city; regular flights from Buenos Aires 🚗 490km (304 miles) from Buenos Aires; take the RN-9

POSADAS

The capital of Misiones Province, Posadas is a prosperous, lively town on the banks of the broad river Paraná, joined to Paraguay's second city, Encarnación, by a grand road bridge. The first recorded settlement in these parts was the Jesuit Mission of Nuestra Señora de Itapuá, founded in 1615.

On Posadas's central Plaza 9 de Julio you will find the rather austere early 20th-century Iglesia Catedral (daily 9–12, 4–7; free), by Alejandro Bustillo, who designed buildings in Buenos Aires and Patagonia also. The superior Casa de Gobierno, a rosy-hued rococo mansion, dominates the square with its grove of *pindó* palms and pink-bloomed *lapacho*.

MUSEUMS

A short walk to the southwest of the plaza is the interesting Museo de Ciencias Naturales e Históricas (San Luis 384; Tue–Fri 8–12, 3–7, Sat–Sun 9–12; free), which covers the city's history from the Jesuits and the indigenous Guaraní, to settlement at the turn of the 20th century. There are also wildlife displays of endangered species, such as the jaguar. On the patio, there are some live monkeys and a serpent house, housing several species of snakes, including the aggressive *yarará* plus some pickled specimens and a section on bite antidotes.

The Museo Regional Aníbal Cambas (Mon–Fri 8–12, 3–8, Sat 9–12, 5–8, Sun 5–8; $2, child $1, free Wed) is housed in an attractive century-old brick building to the northwest of the plaza. There are some interesting and well-labelled exhibits in the historical and ethnographical collections, including vestiges of the ruins of Jesuit missions. There are also artefacts, including urns and musical instruments made by the Guayaquí, the Chiripá, the Mbyá and the Guaraní.

INFORMATION

www.misionesturismo.com.ar/posadas/index.html

🔢 339 M5 ✉ Provincia de Misiones
ℹ Colón 1985 ☎ 03752/447539
🕐 Daily 7–1, 2–8 ✈ Frequent flights from Buenos Aires; airport 7km (4 miles) west of city 🚌 From Buenos Aires, take the RN-9, then RN-12 and then RN-14 to Posadas

TIPS

›› Look out for the bright red and yellow flowers of the *chivato*, a tree native to Madagascar. There are also large numbers of great rubber trees and their glossy leaves can provide welcome shade from the blazing sun in the summer.

›› From the *costanera* (riverside promenade) there are great views across to Paraguay. Stop at one of the lively bars and restaurants here and admire the view.

Above *Posadas, capital of Misiones Province, on the banks of the Paraná river*

INFORMATION

www.rosario.com.ar/turismo.htm

✚ 346 J10 ✉ Provincia de Santa Fe
ℹ️ ETUR, Avenida Belgrano and Buenos
Aires ☎ 0341/480-2230 🕐 Daily 9–7
🚌 Frequent buses from Buenos Aires
✈ Frequent flights from Buenos Aires.
Islas Malvinas International Airport is
13km (8 miles) northwest of the city; take
a taxi from the airport to the city 🚲 Bike,
kayak and boat trips available locally
(▷ 294–295)

INTRODUCTION

Argentina's third-biggest city, Rosario is one of the great urban destinations in the country, with its old-fashioned downtown, cobbled streets and majestic municipal buildings, vibrant arts scene and subtropical beaches. Having built its wealth on the farm produce of its fertile hinterland in the 19th century, Rosario went into decline in the 20th century but has been enjoying a renaissance since the beginning of the 21st, thanks to a dynamic city government and a huge rise in exports of farm goods.

Rosario is, in many ways, like a mini-Buenos Aires, with its grand apartment blocks and monumental architecture, atmospheric cafés and lively tango joints. But it is also a river port and the great Paraná looms large on its cityscape with its 20km (12.5-mile) long esplanade, a string of parks and popular beaches.

Some of Argentina's finest turn-of-the-century architecture can be seen in Rosario, while a number of compelling contemporary projects make the city sights feel fresh and modern. These include the Museo de Arte Contemporáneo, housed in a former cereal silo on the banks of the river and within sight of the fabulous road bridge across to Victoria (▷ 284) in Entre Ríos Province. Other highlights in the city are the historic downtown area around Plaza 25 de Mayo and the nearby Monumento a la Bandera, dedicated to the national blue and white flag. Some interesting museums focus on art from different periods, while children are served by a couple of museums of their own.

Parque Independencia is well worth a visit, as are the islands in the middle of the Río Paraná. In the evening there is always something going on. Rosarinos love going out and there are some excellent restaurants, good nightclubs and plenty of places to hear music or watch tango.

PLAZA 25 DE MAYO

Built on the site of a chapel to the Virgen del Rosario, Plaza 25 de Mayo is located just a couple of blocks away from the riverfront. In the centre of the square is the Monumento a la Independencia, a marble monument commemorating national independence, which is flanked by some majestic buildings, including the post office, the city hall and the late 19th-century cathedral. Peek inside the cathedral to see the Italianate altar, sculpted in Carrara marble and, down in the crypt, the colonial wood carving of the Virgin of Rosario herself, brought from Spain in the late 18th century.

Above *People in an outdoor bar in Paraná river beach, Rosario*

MUSEO MUNICIPAL DE ARTE DECORATIVO (MUSEO ESTEVEZ)

www.museoestevez.gov.ar

Rosario's wonderful decorative arts museum is housed in a gorgeous early 20th-century mansion on the plaza. The house was the residence of the Estevez family, Galician immigrants who were *mate* magnates, and the mansion and contents were donated to the municipality in 1966. Inside, you can easily spend an hour or so admiring the Egyptian glassware and Greek sculptures, Flemish tapestries and Limoges porcelain, plus an interesting set of pre-Columbian ceramics and Spanish ivory figures. Among the splendid paintings are *A Portrait of a Gentleman* by Jacques Louis David (1748–1825) and a Goya portrait of *Doña Maria Teresa Ruiz de Apodaca de Sesma* (1787).

✉ Santa Fe 748, Plaza 25 de Mayo ☎ 0341/480-2547 🕐 Wed–Fri 3–8, Sat–Sun 10–8 ✋ Free

MONUMENTO A LA BANDERA

www.monumentoalabandera.gov.ar

Many Argentines make the pilgrimage to Rosario—known popularly as the Cradle of the Flag—to see the famed monument to the national flag, familiar to many from its depiction on the back of 10 peso notes. The monument was built in the 1950s to a design by Ángel Guido. General Belgrano is said to have designed the flag when he was staying in the city in 1812, soon after Independence. The President and other dignitaries attend national Flag Day celebrations at the monument on 20 June every year.

The enormous sculpture, which covers two blocks of the city between Plaza 25 de Mayo and the river, depicts Argentina as a great stone vessel sailing towards glory. Between the cathedral and the Palacio de los Leones, in the Pasaje Juramento, there is a set of fine marble classical sculptures by Lola Mora (1866–1936), which lead to the monument itself. Below the Propileo, a shrine-like structure has an eternal flame to honour the nation's heroes. Formed out of steps, the Patio Cívico leads down to the riverside avenue and above looms a 70m-high (230ft) tower of rough marble. You can take the elevator to the top for fabulous views of the city and the river beyond.

✉ Santa Fe 581 ☎ 0341/480-2238 🕐 Elevator: Mon 2–7, Tue–Sun 9–7; last trip to viewing platform 5.30pm ✋ Elevator: $2

PARQUE DE LA INDEPENDENCIA

The huge, graceful Parque de la Independencia, opened in 1902, is a great place for gentle strolling or jogging and contains several museums, a football stadium and a racetrack. Much of the park is beautifully landscaped and there is a formal Jardín Francés (French Garden), near the entrance on Bulevar Oroño, plus a large lake with dancing water fountains, which are lit up every evening to great effect.

On Avenida Pellegrini is the outstanding Museo Municipal de Bellas Artes Juan B. Castagnino (tel 0341/480-2542; www.museocastagnino.org.ar; Apr–Nov Wed–Mon 2–8; Dec–Mar Wed–Mon 3–9; $5), which has two permanent collections. One collection comprises European painting from the 15th century to the present day, including works by Goya, Sisley and Daubigny. The other collection features Argentine painting by major artists such as Spilimbergo, Quinquela Martín, Antonio Berni and Lucio Fontana. Arranged over two floors in spacious well-lit rooms, the museum also stages very good temporary exhibitions, often of local artists.

To the west of the lake is the well-organized Museo Histórico Provincial Dr. Julio Marc (tel 0341/472-1427; Tue–Fri 9–5, Sat–Sun 12–6; free), with a vast collection of exhibits representing Latin America but focusing on religious art. The collection includes a fabulous 18th-century silver altar from Bolivia and beautiful polychrome works in wood, wax and bone from Ecuador. There is a room dedicated to General San Martín, plus an exhibit of indigenous South American ceramics and some wonderful textiles.

TIPS

❱❱ You won't need a car while in Rosario, so don't rent one for the duration of your stay. The best way to explore the city is on foot; see the walk on ▷ 286–287.

❱❱ Rosario is a big metropolis but is generally safe as long as you take the usual precautions in a large city (▷ 310).

❱❱ The city is not geared to tourism and there are very few good hotels, so book ahead and avoid 20 June, National Flag Day.

❱❱ Rosario is a great place to learn tango or Spanish; there are fewer visitors than in Buenos Aires and lessons are much cheaper.

Below *The Monumento a la Bandera, a symbol of Argentine Independence*

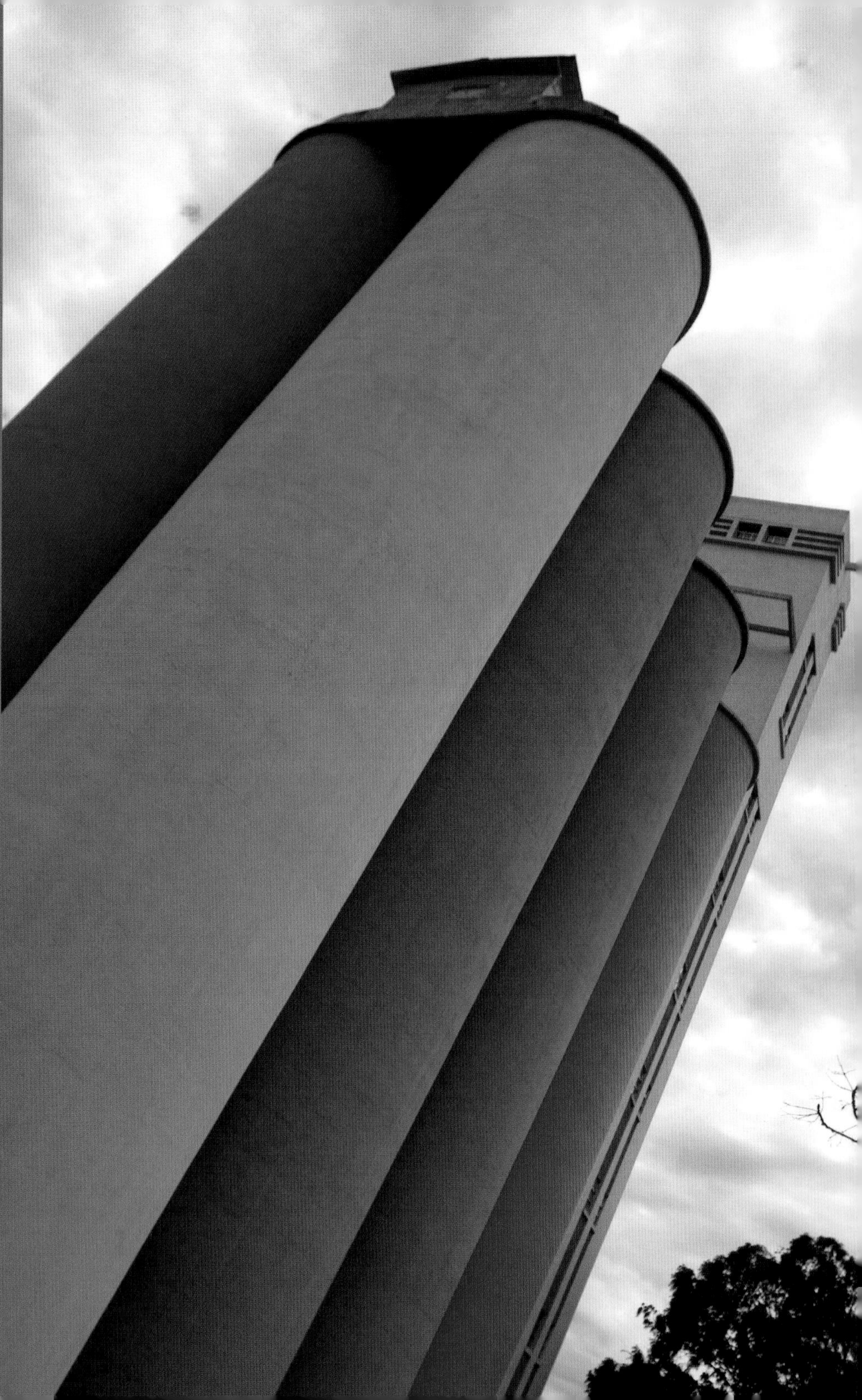

MUSEO DE ARTE CONTEMPORÁNEO DE ROSARIO (MACRO)

www.macromuseo.org.ar

At the northern end of the beguiling Bulevar Oroño, with its lush palms and equally exuberant sphinx benches, is the former red-light district Pichincha, which now hosts funky bars and antique shops. Overlooking the riverside Parque Sunchales is the Museo de Arte Contemporáneo de Rosario, known by its initials MACRo. Housed in a former grain silo belonging to the wealthy Anglo-Argentine Davis family, the exterior cylindrical parts of the silo are now painted in garish pinks and violets, while inside you can view small art shows dedicated to promising local and national artists. But the main reason to visit MACRo is to ride in the elevator to the top-floor viewpoint and enjoy the magnificent views of the Paraná, the city and the skein of railway tracks leading north. The gallery's Davis Restaurant on the riverfront is also worth a visit.

✉ Boulevard Oroño s/n ☎ 0341/480-4981 ◷ Apr–Nov Thu–Tue 2–8; Dec–Mar 4–10
✋ Adult $5, child (under 12) $2.50 🍴

THE COSTANERA AND ALTO DELTA

Over 20km (12.5 miles) from north to south, the *costanera* (waterside promenade) is one of the city's major assets, with extensive parkland and inspiring views over the Río Paraná. Around 8km (5 miles) north of the centre is Rosario's most popular mainland beach, the Balneario La Florida, with bars, restaurants and shower facilities. At the southern end of the beach are the Rambla Catalunya and Avenida Carrasco, which are lined with stalls, trendy bars, smart restaurants and some of the city's best nightclubs.

At the southern end of the Parque Nacional de la Bandera, opposite the Monumento a la Bandera, is the riverside La Fluvial complex (▷ 294), from where boats can take you across the river to a string of islands with beaches. Known as the Alto Delta, the low-lying islands off Rosario's river coast are a mass of subtropical vegetation fed by soil and seed from the Upper Paraná River in Misiones and Brazil.

On the remote island of Charigüé is a small village with a handful of restaurants but most of the islands are uninhabited except for sunbathers and holidaymakers in the summer months. The best way of seeing the Alto Delta is to take an excursion (ask at the tourist office for details of the best tour operators) but you could also explore by taking the regular passenger services from La Fluvial. Local operators offer canoeing trips and guided walks around and on the islands, too.

MORE TO SEE

ISLA DE LOS INVENTOS

www.rosario.gov.ar

Rosario's former main rail station now functions as the wonderful Isla de los Inventos (Island of Inventions). Inside the marvellous old hangars, children of all ages will enjoy the hands-on and interactive exhibits and workshops where visitors can help make their own toys. A highlight is an eerily dark chamber that tells the history of the universe since the Big Bang. Locomotive fans can explore a train engine on one of the old platforms.

✉ Guillermo Wheelwright 1402 ☎ 0341/480-2571 ◷ Feb–Dec Fri–Sun 2–7
✋ Adult/child $3

JARDÍN DE LOS NIÑOS

www.rosario.gov.ar

In the beautiful Parque de la Independencia, the city's former zoo has become the Jardín de los Niños, aimed at visitors aged four or more. This amusing theme park teaches children about everyday phenomena such as sound, flight and equilibrium.

✉ Avenida del Lago s/n ☎ 0341/480-2421 ◷ Fri–Sun 1–6 ✋ Adult/child $3

Opposite *The brightly painted Museo de Arte Contemporáneo de Rosario (MACRo)*
Below *Church spire, Rosario*

SALTOS DEL MOCONÁ

www.saltos-del-mocona.com.ar

The Saltos del Moconá waterfalls form part of the international border between Argentina and Brazil. For almost 3km (2 miles) immensely powerful waterfalls spill down the middle of the Río Uruguay from a higher riverbed in Argentina into a deep canyon on the Brazilian side. These split-level waterfalls are the longest in the world and are formed where the Uruguay and Pepirí-Guazú rivers meet. The collision of the rivers forces one river to flow along the western side of the gorge and the other to plunge down into it. When the water levels are right, water from the higher level cascades down into the gorge creating a wall of foaming water up to 13m (43ft) high.

The falls lie 80km (50 miles) northeast of El Soberbio, via a partly paved road, and can be seen from both Argentina and Brazil. El Soberbio sits on the banks of the Río Uruguay, 170km (105.5 miles) east of Oberá, in a gorgeous riverside setting amid lush undulating sierras. If you are taking a boat trip, your guide will drive you down to the river and you will complete the journey by water. Having surveyed the waterfalls from the spectacular Brazilian side, you will be transferred to land on the Argentine side, where you can look across the river from the shore, swim in the shallows and admire the butterflies and, perhaps, wade over to view the waterfalls from above. While you are there, you may spot capuchin monkeys, tapirs, toucans and others birds (over 200 species of birds inhabit the area).

✉ El Soberbio, Provincia de Misiones
➥ Tours from Oberá (▷ 271), Posadas (▷ 279) and El Soberbio

SAN IGNACIO MINÍ ▷ 285.

SANTA FÉ

www.turismosantafe.com.ar

One of Argentina's oldest cities, Santa Fé is an important commercial centre. Lying along the banks of a tributary of the mighty Río Paraná, Santa Fe has a quiet *centro histórico*, where you will find the late 17th-century Iglesia de Nuestra Señora de los Milagros (San Martín 1588; www.nsdelosmilagros.com. ar; Mon–Fri 6.30–12, 6.30–8.30, Sat 6.30pm–8.30pm, Sun 10–12, 6.30–8.30; free). The church has a fine colonial facade and inside there are carvings produced by Guaraní craftsmen in the Jesuit Missions.

Another late 17th-century church, the Iglesia de San Francisco at Amenábar 2557 (Mar–Nov Mon–Sat 8–12, 3–6.30, Sun 3.30–6; Dec–Feb Mon–Sat 8–12, 4–7, Sun 9.30–12, 4.30–7; free) is notable for its fabulous ceiling, constructed using native timbers held together with wooden pegs. On the left, when you face the altar, is an ornate baroque pulpit laminated in gold.

The nearby Museo Histórico Provincial (tel 0342/457-3529, www. museohistorico-sfe.gov.ar; Dec–Feb Tue–Fri 9–12, 5–8, Sat–Sun 5.30–8.30; Mar–Nov Tue–Fri 8.30–12, 3–7, Sat–Sun 4–7; free), in a late-colonial family house, contains interesting religious and secular artefacts from the 17th century.

In the Museo Etnográfico y Colonial (25 de Mayo 1470; tel 0342/459-5857; Jan–Feb Tue–Fri 8.30–12, 5–8, Sat–Sun 5–8; Mar–Dec Tue–Fri 8.30–12, Sat–Sun 3.30–6.30; free) is an impressive array of indigenous ceramics, well-preserved *tinajas* (large ceramic urns) and delicate amulets in the shape of shells or the *higa*, a clenched fist symbol used to ward off the evil eye.

✚ 342 J9 ✉ Provincia de Santa Fe
ℹ San Martín 1389 ☎ 0342/457-4824
◷ Daily 7–1, 3–9 🚌 Frequent buses from Rosario and Buenos Aires ✈ Aeropuerto de Sauce Viejo, 7km (4 miles) south of city; frequent flights from Buenos Aires 🚗 From Rosario take the RN-9 northwards

VICTORIA

www.turismoentrerios.com/victoria

Immigrants from northern Italy and the Basque country founded attractive Victoria, a typical Litoral riverside town, in the 19th century. It is relatively close to Rosario, thanks to the magnificent state-of-the-art suspension bridge over the Río Paraná, which opened in 2003. The town's streets, most of which are unpaved, are lined with fine neo-colonial buildings adorned with highly ornate wrought-iron grilles *(rejas)*.

On the lively main square, you'll find stalls selling handicrafts and an Italianate 19th-century church with a fine interior and delicate frescos. The Avenida Costanera Dr. Pedro Radío skirts the town's southern flank, following the contours of the Paraná's grassy riverbanks, where people gather to bathe along the sandy beaches.

Victoria's main attraction is the 1899 Abadía del Niño Dios (tel 03436/421082, www. abadiadelniniodios.org.ar; daily 8–12, 3–6.30), 3km (1.8 miles) outside town, which is home to Latin America's oldest Benedictine foundation. The modern monastery and church are worth a visit, particularly on Sundays, when the monks sing Mass. There is also an excellent shop selling jams, bee products, liqueurs and cheeses.

✚ 346 J9 ✉ Provincia de Entre Ríos
ℹ 25 de Mayo and Boulevard Sarmiento
☎ 03436/421885 ◷ Daily 9–7 🚌 Buses from Rosario and Paraná 🚗 58km (36 miles) northeast of Rosario; take the toll bridge over the river Paraná from Rosario and the airport

Below *Colegio de la Inmaculada Concepcion, Santa Fé*

SAN IGNACIO MINÍ

San Ignacio Miní, located in the modern riverside settlement of San Ignacio, is the largest and best preserved of all the Jesuit missions, also known as *reducciones* (reductions), in northern Argentina. The romantic ruins of the dark red sandstone church, standing in a lush green setting of vast lawns and subtropical vegetation, bring the tragic story of the Jesuit settlements to life. Other magnificent ruins, many of them tangled in the prolific jungle, can be seen nearby and further sites lie across the border in Paraguay and Brazil.

REDUCCIÓN DE SAN IGNACIO MINÍ

The highlight of the ruins is the ornate facade of San Ignacio's church, designed by Italian architect Brazanelli and executed around 1700 by Guaraní masons and sculptors. Look out for the handsome pair of angels carved in the deep red sandstone. At the entrance are the melancholic remains of the small basalt houses where the Guaraní lived and the grander cloisters and priests' quarters. Don't miss the ornate doorway between the cloisters and the baptistry, which has an elegant triangular pediment. The entrance to the ruins is in the centre of the village; follow signs to Reducción.

CASA DE HORACIO QUIROGA

Uruguayan writer Horacio Quiroga (1878–1937) lived in San Ignacio from 1910 onwards and wrote many of his magical stories while living here. You can visit a replica of his wooden house and the stone bungalow that he built himself, which is filled with his possessions. The lush jungle-like setting inspired his tropical tales of preternatural horror. The museum is about 1km (0.5 miles) south of the village centre on Avenida Horacio Quiroga (tel 03752/470130; daily 8–7; $10).

PARQUE PROVINCIAL TEYÚ CUARÉ

If you have time, visit the Parque Provincial Teyú Cuaré, about 10km (6 miles) south of San Ignacio—another patch of subtropical forest draped over sandy rocks overlooking the glorious Río Paraná (*guardaparques* are there 24 hours a day; free). Contact local operator Misiones Excursiones (tel 03752/15-653456) for kayak trips, 4WD drives and bike excursions in the park. Before the park, there is a private reserve, Osununú, located 5km (3 miles) south of San Ignacio, where you can go horseback riding or just admire the views of the river and Teyú Cuaré (tel 03752/15-644937; daily 9–6; $1).

INFORMATION

www.argentinaturismo.com.ar/sanignacio

339 M5 Provincia de Misiones

03752/470186 Daily 7–7; sound-and-light show Apr–Oct 7pm, Nov–Mar 8.15pm $30 Buses from Posadas

The nearest airports are Posadas, 60km (37 miles) on RN-12, and Iguazú, 245km (152 miles) to the north There are organized tours from Posadas (293).

TIPS

» If you have time, try to visit the other Jesuit missions, the wild ruins of Loreto and Santa Ana, too. The ticket for San Ignacio is also valid for visiting the other ruins (daily 7–7). Santa Ana is the nearest to Posadas, just 40km (25 miles) north on the RN-12. Loreto lies just off the RN-12, 12km (7.5 miles) to the north of Santa Ana.

» The early morning and late afternoon light makes it easier to see the fine detailing on the ruins and makes the red sandstone glow.

» There are multilingual audio-guide stands dotted around the site; just press the appropriate button to find out about different aspects of the Mission.

» The sound-and-light shows at the ruins are well worth attending; ask at the ticket-office for details.

Above Entrance to the ruins of the Jesuit church of San Ignacio Miní

ESSENTIAL ROSARIO

Rosario, Argentina's third-largest city, is a great place to explore on foot. The terrain is totally flat apart from a slight slope down to the riverside, where strolling along the *costanera* (waterside promenade) is a real pleasure. Along the way you will visit all the city's major sights.

THE WALK

Distance: 4.5km (3 miles)
Time: 6 hours
Start at: Museo Municipal de Bellas Artes
End at: Plaza 25 de Mayo

★ Start at the Museo Municipal de Bellas Artes, on the corner of Avenida Carlos Pellegrini and Boulevard Oroño. You could visit the splendid Parque de la Independencia (▷ 281) before starting out, but bear in mind this walk takes a day if you want to visit all the sights along the way. With your back to the park, head up the boulevard.

❶ Boulevard Oroño is a beautiful wide avenue and perfect for strolling, thanks to the spacious central walkway that runs straight to the Río Paraná. Two rows of majestic palm trees create shade and a sense of tropical luxuriance. Look out for the white benches decorated with gryphons, which provide resting

places along the way. This central pavement is popular with walkers and inline skaters, so watch out for the latter. There are handsome villas and mansions on either side of the avenue. Most of these function as clinics and offices but have retained their early 20th-century grace, recalling the city's wealthy heyday.

After 20 blocks, a little over 2km (1.25 miles), cross the *costanera* (watch out, the traffic is busy) to reach the MACRo, Rosario's groundbreaking contemporary art museum.

❷ The MACRo (▷ 283) is housed in a striking multicoloured former grain silo. You might want to stop for refreshments at the Davis café/restaurant on the riverfront. The museum is set in green parkland that is a favourite picnic site. Here, you have great views of the Río Paraná, the modern road bridge across the

river to Victoria and the busy shipping traffic. Look out for the surprisingly large clumps of grass and vegetation bobbing along, on their way down river to form the islands of the delta around El Tigre.

From here, back towards the city, keep the river on your left as you stroll along the *costanera*. There are plenty of opportunities to stop for a drink or a meal. One of the first you come across is Aux Deux Magots (Entre Ríos 2; daily 11am–1am), a laid-back café with great views of the river. Just before this spot, you will pass the former railway station, now a cultural complex (1km/0.5 miles from MACRo).

❸ Rosario's disused main train station now functions as a cultural complex, part of which is a wonderful hands-on museum for kids, the Isla de los Inventos (▷ 283). Some 300m (327 yards) from the Isla de los Inventos is the Casa del Tango (▷ 294), a tango centre, which you might like to check out for evening events.

Back in the fresh air, head along the *costanera* again. You pass the Complejo Cultural de España. This is a Spanish arts complex inaugurated by the Infanta Cristina in 1992 but sadly it fell into disrepair and has since been cordoned off. It is quite safe to walk past it, though.

Another 1km (0.5 mile) or so and you reach the city's main tourist information office. If you have time, pop in and find out more about Rosario and its surroundings. On weekend evenings the stretch of promenade beyond the office is given over to the Mercado de Pulgas del Bajo, with stalls selling everything from bric-à-brac to arts and crafts.

You now have a full view of the Monumento a la Bandera, which is the next stop on this tour. Cross the avenue and climb on to this great landmark.

❹ The Monumento a la Bandera (▷ 281) is the most famous sight in the city, a great hulk of sculptured stone that dominates the cityscape at this point along the *costanera*.

Walk up past the monument to the right, go alongside the city's cathedral and you reach your final destination, the Plaza 25 de Mayo.

❺ Centred on the Monumento a la Independencia, a marble monument to freedom, Plaza 25 de Mayo is the historic heart of Rosario. Here, you will find the cathedral, along with the majestic post office building (Palacio del Correo) at the southeast corner. To the right, as you enter, is the imposing Palacio de los Leones, the brick-hued city hall, with a pair of sculptured lions guarding its entrance. The highlight is opposite, the Museo Municipal de Arte Decorativo (▷ 281), which is open until well into the evening, so you

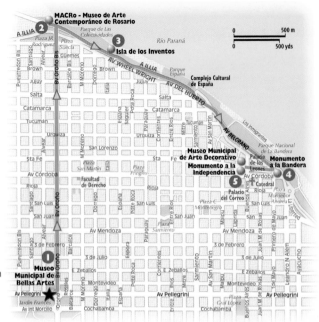

should get in before closing time. The collection of paintings and furniture is really outstanding.

WHEN TO GO

Bear in mind that most museums are shut in the mornings and some are closed on Mondays or Tuesdays. Try to time your walk so that you can enjoy the late afternoon light on the river. Also note that Rosario can be unbearably humid in summer.

WHERE TO EAT
DAVIS
▷ 297.

Opposite *An eternal flame commemorates the nation's heroes at the Monumento a la Bandera*

Below *Mercado de Pulgas del Bajo, which takes place on weekend evenings*

ACROSS ENTRE RÍOS PROVINCE

Hilly and verdant Entre Ríos, the southernmost province in Argentina's Mesopotamia region, is squeezed between the Paraná and Uruguay rivers. On this away-from-the-crowds drive starting in the regional hub of Rosario, you cross the Paraná over a stunning road bridge and explore some of the province's highlights. You might like to stop over in Colón, the province's most alluring resort, on the banks of the Uruguay, before heading back.

THE DRIVE

Distance: 290km (174 miles)
Time: 4 hours
Start at: Rosario
End at: Colón

★ From the centre of Rosario (▷ 280–283) follow signs to Victoria. A few kilometres north of the city, along the riverside, is the slip road that will take you up on to one of the most impressive road bridges on the continent, the Puente Nuestra Señora del Rosario.

❶ The Puente Nuestra Señora del Rosario is a magnificent work of civil engineering, opened in 2003 after six years of construction. Although the main section of the crossing over the principal course of the Río Paraná is only 610m (665 yards) long, the whole structure is almost 60km (37 miles) of raised causeway and smaller bridges, flying you over the vast green marshlands that line the river. The taut wires of its main pylons resemble the rigging of a giant ship. You must pay a $9 toll for a car. The bridge and causeways bring you to

Victoria, Entre Ríos, via the RN-174. A right turn takes you into the town itself.

❷ Victoria (▷ 284) is a typical sleepy Entre Ríos town, with some fine neo-colonial architecture and a lovely riverside setting.

From Victoria take the RP-26 to Nogoyá, in the heart of the province's farm country, 43km (25 miles) away. Then take the RP-39 all the way to Gobernador Basavilbaso, 83km (50 miles) from Nogoyá. On the way

you cross the typical scenery of Entre Ríos, a series of rolling hills known locally as *cuchillos* (little knives), formed by deep valleys carved out by rivers such as the Río Gualeguay and Río Gualeguaychú. Just 4km (2.4 miles) along the RP-39 in the direction of Concepción del Uruguay you will see the turn-off to the Palacio San José.

❸ Palacio San José (▷ 278), built for General Justo José de Urquiza, is one of the country's great 19th-century mansions, symbolizing the power of the *caudillos* before the modern state of Argentina finally gelled. Allow at least an hour to do it justice, plus more time to wander through its handsome grounds.

Then resume your journey eastwards along the RP-39, reaching the RN-14 trunk road after only 25km (15 miles). Turn left and head up the highway for another 30km (19 miles), when you reach the slip road leading to Colón. Make sure you don't keep going as you will reach the international border, a bridge over the River Uruguay—instead turn left to reach your destination, Colón.

❹ Colón (▷ 270) is the most appealing of all the towns along the Río Uruguay and is worth a stopover (preferably two nights) to visit its island beaches, taste some wines at Bodega Vulliez Sermet (▷ 292), the only *bodega* in the Litoral, and wallow in thermal baths.

WHEN TO GO
This drive can be done at any time of year.

WHERE TO EAT
As always, a picnic is a good option and there are various towns along the way with plenty of restaurants.

WHERE TO STAY
HOSTERÍA DEL PUERTO
▷ 298.

Opposite *Elegant 19th-century Palacio San José, southwest of Concepción del Uruguay*
Below *Capybara in the Río Uruguay*

AROUND MISIONES PROVINCE

Most visitors to the northeastern province of Misiones visit the Iguazú Falls and possibly make a side trip to the Jesuit ruins at San Ignacio. This circuit will enable you to see more of this beautiful province. The drive links some of the major sites, such as Posadas and Oberá, and gives you the chance to discover some of the lesser-known attractions in the province.

THE DRIVE

Distance: 570km (342 miles)
Time: 7 hours (see When to Go, ▷ 291)
Start at: Posadas
End at: Posadas

★ From the centre of Posadas (▷ 279) follow signs to Puerto Iguazú and Jardín América along the RN-12. About 43km (27 miles) from the city take the right turn to Oberá, 55km (33 miles) to the east.

❶ Set in the foothills of the Sierra del Imán, Oberá (▷ 271) is the second-biggest town in Misiones Province and the starting point for the Corredor Verde (Green Corridor), the central swathe of the province where patches of the once huge tropical jungle have managed to survive.

Now take the RN-14 to Aristóbulo del Valle, 65km (40 miles) northeast from Oberá.

❷ Aristóbulo del Valle is a typical central Misiones town, its neat bungalows with luxuriant gardens strung along the main avenue, dotted with odd sculptures and strange avant-garde monuments. The main sight nearby is the wonderful Salto Encantado. This 60m (197ft) waterfall is set among exuberant vegetation, fed by the Arroyo Caña Pirú, one of the many brooks that crisscross the Misiones jungle. The entrance to the provincial park is 6km (4 miles) to the north of town via the RN-14 (there are facilities and a cafeteria).

Beyond the entrance to the falls, the RN-14 meanders along the Sierra de Misiones, the province's backbone, cloaked in dense jungle interspersed with plantations and neat fields, continuing to the agricultural town of San Pedro, a quiet place nestling among a grove of Paraná pines, endemic trees related to the monkey-puzzle tree. The nearby Parque Provincial Cruce Caballero protects large numbers of remaining specimens. Continue to Pozo Azul, turn left on to the RP-17 and you will reach the RN-12 at Eldorado, where you could stay at the welcoming Las Mercedes *estancia* (▷ 299).

❸ Eldorado is a busy junction town, located close to the Río Paraná and known for its excellent cattle-ranching country. Stay at Las Mercedes *estancia* for a taste of the rural life. You could make a major detour up the scenic RN-12 to Iguazú (▷ 274–277) and visit the world's greatest waterfalls.

Otherwise, head southwards along the main road (in the direction of Posadas and Buenos Aires), taking in the rolling landscapes of western Misiones, with its sweeping views and rollercoaster ups and downs.

Opposite A mate plantation at Oberá
Right The cemetery at San Ignacio Miní

Some 150km (93 miles) or so and you reach San Ignacio.

❹ Quiet San Ignacio is home to the most famous of all the Jesuit missions in Argentina, San Ignacio Miní (▷ 285). There are a couple of other places worth visiting and it is a good place to taste the delicious river fish that are a local speciality.

The ticket for visiting San Ignacio Miní also entitles you to visit three other missions. One of them, little-visited Santa María La Mayor, is tucked away by the Brazilian border near Concepción de la Sierra, but the other two are located just off the RN-12, farther south from San Ignacio, and are far easier to visit.

Just 8km (5 miles) down the road is the turn-off to Loreto.

❺ The Nuestra Señora de Loreto mission is truly in ruins and little remains apart from the 17th-century chapel, subsumed in the voracious jungle. Here and at Santa Ana it is well worth going on a guided visit (ask at the entrance), which will help breathe life back into the site.

Santa Ana is another 12km (7.5 miles) along the road towards Posadas. The ruins are far larger than Loreto, and its main plaza is huge. Built around 1660, the massive walls of the ruined church are prevented from collapsing under the weight of snake-like ficus branches by makeshift scaffolding. Equally atmospheric is the ruined graveyard next to the church.

Posadas is 43km (27 miles) from the Santa Ana turn-off. The road makes a huge sweep to the right as it follows the river and you are treated to panoramic views of the Misiones capital and the Paraguayan city of Encarnación, the two linked by a dramatic road bridge.

WHEN TO GO

This route is feasible all year round. The drive is best spread over two days (though it is feasible in one long day), and it's a good idea to set out early in the morning to leave time for visits along the way and avoid the afternoon tropical showers.

WHERE TO EAT

Oberá's Engüete restaurant (▷ 297) would be a great place for lunch on the first day, while you might want to eat river fish in San Ignacio on the second—the best place there is Carpa Azul (▷ 297).

WHERE TO STAY

Estancia Las Mercedes (▷ 299) would be an ideal stopover.

PLACES TO VISIT
IGUAZÚ
▷ 274–277.

SALTO ENCANTADO
✉ Parque Provincial Salto Encantado, 6km (3.5 miles) to the north of Aristóbulo del Valle by the RN-14. ☎ 03752/490995 🕐 Daily 9–6 👋 Free

SAN IGNACIO MINÍ
▷ 285.

TIP
›› The advantage of starting and finishing at Posadas is that you can easily rent a car there (book ahead). Flights to and from Posadas are cheaper than those to Iguazú, so you could easily tag on a side trip to the great falls; the RN-12 from Eldorado runs another 70km (43.5 miles) before reaching Puerto Iguazú.
›› If you have more time at your disposal and wish to explore the area in more depth, the Saltos del Moconá waterfalls (▷ 284) on the Río Uruguay are around 220km (150 miles) northeast of Oberá.

COLÓN

BODEGA VULLIEZ SERMET

www.bodegavulliezsermet.com.ar

Just 10 minutes outside Colón, Bodega Vulliez Sermet is the only commercial winery in Entre Ríos province. The French Swiss began making wine here in the 19th century but the government banned viniculture outside the Cuyo region for decades and this *bodega* only sprang back to life a few years ago. Jesús Vulliez produces delicious wines on 3ha (8 acres) of vineyard that would not look out of place in northern Italy—especially when the tastings take place in an appealing pink house. Enquire about the luxurious *cabaña* lodgings within the handsome grounds with a swimming pool and an excellent restaurant—a great place to sample some of the wines.

✉ RP-135 km8 ☎ 03447/15-645925

🕐 Call ahead

LA CASONA

www.artesanoslacasona.com.ar

La Casona, meaning 'the big house', is a lovely neo-colonial house on the Plaza San Martín, where you can find a huge range of local arts and crafts, particularly finely made ceramics turned out by students and teachers at the municipal pottery school.

✉ 12 de Abril 106 ☎ 03447/425097

🕐 Mon–Sat 9–7

ITA I CORÁ

www.itaicora.com

Charlie Adamson is a highly professional tour guide with in-depth knowledge about Colón and its fascinating hinterland. With his endless supply of jokes, he makes any trip a memorable experience. Don't miss his informative and exciting boat trips on the Río Uruguay or his jeep tours of the precious stones, Liebig ruins and other natural and human wonders of the region.

Charlie and his friendly partners are also interested in ecology.

✉ San Martín 97 ☎ 03447/423360

🕐 Daily 9–6 🖐 Varies

TERMAS VILLA ELISA

www.termasvillaelisa.com

One of the best spa complexes in the country, Termas Villa Elisa is a great place to unwind. You could easily spend a day soaking in the various pools and baths, pampering yourself with massages and beauty treatments, gently working out in the gym or playing a round of golf. The natural hot spring water is used to treat a number of ailments including rheumatism and all manner of skin diseases. Refreshments are available, too.

✉ RN-130 km20 ☎ 03447/480687

🕐 Daily 9–7 🖐 Day pass $45

🚌 30km (18.5 miles) northwest of Colón (15km/9 miles off the fork of the RN-14 and RN-130)

Opposite *A safari tour in the forest of the Parque Nacional do Iguaçu (Brazil)*
Below right *Garganta del Diablo, Iguazú*

FORMOSA
AVENTURA FORMOSA
www.formosa.gov.ar/turismo.semanasanta.aventuraformosa

Fredy Izardo is an ultra-friendly, professional guide based in Formosa, who runs a range of trips into the Chaco's national parks. One of the most popular trips (best done in spring) is a four-day tour that includes boat trips, camping in the wilds, a day-long canoe ride into the deepest swamps to see the fauna, and a catch-your-own fish lunch.

✉ Paraguay 520, Formosa
☎ 03717/433713 ⊙ Mon–Sat 9–6
✋ Half-day $130

CASA DE LA ARTESANÍA
www.welcomeargentina.com/paseos/casa_dela_artesania

This non-profit organization is the best place to buy indigenous crafts from across Formosa Province. You can find a wide variety of delicately hued Wichí bags made of *yica* (a resistant natural fibre), Pilagá woollen carpets, tightly woven Komlek *carandillo* and *tortora* basketwork, plus *palo santo* carvings and *algarrobo* (indigenous carob) seed necklaces and bracelets.

✉ San Martin 802 ☎ 03727/424010
⊙ Mon–Sat 8–12, 4–8

IGUAZÚ
CAMPO DE DESAFIOS
www.campodedesafios.com.br

This enterprise is three outfits rolled into one: Cânion Iguaçu, Brazil Discovery and 4 Elementos, which between them offer exciting but safe climbing, rafting and rappel activities in and around Iguazú falls.

✉ Rodavia das Cataratas, Brazil
☎ (+55) 45/3529-9175 ✋ From US$40 for a half-day outing

IGUAZÚ JUNGLE EXPLORER
www.iguazujungle.com

This highly professional company based inside the Argentina national park offers a range of exciting

trips around the park and into the waterfalls. Their 'Great Adventure' starts with an 8km (5-mile) ride in a jeep through the jungle followed by a boat ride along the Río Iguazú gorge over rapids to the lower falls.

✉ Inside Parque Nacional Iguazú, close to entrance ☎ 03757/421696 ⊙ Daily 6–6
✋ Boat trips cost between $100–$200

MACUCO SAFARI
www.macucosafari.com.br

This dynamic operator offers excellent tours around the Brazilian national park. Their 1.5-hour safari combines a jeep trip through the forest, followed by a short walk and boat trip on the rapids of the lower river. Alternatively, you can try one of their fishing trips, go on a half-hour rafting adventure or opt for the more sedate Iguaçu Explorer excursion in a large river boat.

✉ On the main road to Parque Nacional do Iguaçu (clearly signposted) ☎ (55) 45/3529-7976 ⊙ Daily (see website for details of different tours) ✋ Safari R$250 (Brazilian reais) all inclusive

TRILHA DO POCO PRETO
www.macucoecoaventura.com.br

This ecologically minded outfit based in the Brazilian national park specializes in safaris in the forest and along the river. The Banana Tree Trail combines a 1.5km (1-mile) walking or bike tour with a boat trip along the upper Río Iguazú and a visit to a high observation tower to watch wildlife. The company also offers silent boat trips (floatings) following the currents and getting right up close to flora and fauna.

✉ Avenida das Cataratas km22 ☎ (+55) 45/529-9627 ⊙ Daily 7–11

MERCEDES
CALLES SAN MARTÍN AND JUAN PUJOL
Mercedes is the main gateway to the Esteros del Iberá and the town bristles with craft shops and places selling *gaucho* gear including belts, knives and *bombachas* (traditional *gaucho* trousers), but the best hunting ground is along calles San Martín and Juan Pujol.

FUNDACIÓN MANOS CORRENTINAS
www.corrientes.com.ar/manoscorrentinas

Housed in a colonial building, this non-profit enterprise sells an admirable range of locally produced goods, including basketwork, *mates*, rustic woollen ponchos, berets and sweaters, plus handmade bone and horn buttons.

✉ San Martin 487 ☎ 03773/422671
⊙ Mon–Sat 9–7

PARANÁ
BAQUEANOS DEL RÍO
www.proteger.org.ar

This laudable eco-tourism foundation offers fabulous river trips along the Río Paraná in small boats. Many of the guides are fishermen and are able to share their incredible knowledge about the waterway with visitors.

☎ 0342/455-8520 ✋ Varies

POSADAS
GUAYRA
www.guayra.com.ar

Guayra offers a wide range of excellent excursions from Posadas, with tours to the Jesuit ruins at San Ignacio Miní, the waterfalls at Iguazú or the Saltos del Moconá, and wonderful visits to the Esteros del Iberá. You can also tour some of the region's *estancias*, while a three-day journey takes you in the footsteps of the jaguar. Specific birdwatching tours are also on their agenda.

✉ San Lorenzo 2208 ☎ 03752/433415
⊙ Mon–Sat 9–7 ✋ Full-day $120

RESISTENCIA

CHAC...CUEROS

www.chaccueros.com.ar

This outlet specializes in capybara leather, prized by indigenous populations and *gauchos* for its softness. Choose from leather items such as gloves, slippers, moccasins and jackets, plus a variety of bags, wallets and purses.

✉ Guemes 165 ☎ 03722/433604 ⏰ Mon–Sat 9–2, 5–8

CHACO TUR

www.chacotur.com.ar

This excellent outfit leads a variety of excursions into the Chaco, to see the wildlife and scenery, as well as tours to visit indigenous communities. It also organizes *pirogue* trips through the lagoons and marshes, horseback rides through the forest and trips to *estancias* to watch *gaucho* displays.

✉ Juan B. Justo 147, Resistencia ☎ 03722/422058 ⏰ Mon–Sat 9–6 ✋ Half day $120

FOGÓN DE LOS ARRIEROS

This famous arts foundation thrives on the quality of its cultural programme and its friendly, laid-back ambience. Visit during the day to see the collection of paintings and sculptures. In the evening, enjoy a drink and some succulent *criollo* fare, then attend a folk music concert

Below *Dancing the tango*

inside or on the wonderful patio. Saturday evenings are the best bet.

✉ Brown 350, Resistencia ☎ 03722/426418 ⏰ Daily 9–midnight

FUNDACIÓN CHACO ARTESANAL

This excellent non-profit-making outlet sells a surprisingly good range of arts and crafts including shiny earthenware Mocoví nativity figures, rougher Wichí pottery, Komlek basketware and *palo santo* crucifixes.

✉ Pellegrini 272 ☎ 03722/422649 ⏰ Mon–Sat 9–12, 6–9

ROSARIO

ALTO ROSARIO SHOPPING

www.alto-rosario.com.ar

Rosario's main shopping centre has a wide range of chain shops and boutiques as well as a cinema and a food patio. There is a duty-free booth for foreign visitors.

✉ Junin 501 ☎ 0341/410-6400 ⏰ Daily 10–10

BIKE ROSARIO

www.bikerosario.com.ar

Sebastián Clérico offers excellent bike and kayak tours around Rosario and motorboat tours along the river.

✉ Zeballos 327 ☎ 0341/15-571-3812 ✋ Varies

CASA DEL TANGO

www.lacasadeltangorosario.com

Casa del Tango, next to the old railway station, combines a space where you can watch slick nightly shows with an excellent *parrilla*. There is a bar, too, where you can sip cocktails and listen to tango.

✉ Avenida Arturo Illia ☎ 0341/449-4666 ⏰ Daily 9–midnight, tango show every night ✋ Dinner and show $150

CENTRO ASTURIANO

One of the best places to dance the tango, this traditional Spanish club acts as a popular *milonga* (tango dance hall) on Saturdays, with tango and salsa classes before the dance floor is opened to the public.

✉ San Luis 650 ☎ 0341/424-2317 ⏰ Classes from 9pm, *milonga* 11pm ✋ Lessons $40

CENTRO CULTURAL BERNARDINO RIVADAVIA

www.ccbr.gov.ar

The CCBR's action-packed programme ranges from art and photography exhibitions to seminars and recitals, plus an excellent series of cinema screenings and concerts (tango, folk and classical guitar).

✉ San Martin 1080 ☎ 0341/480-2401 ⏰ Most events at 6, 7 or 8pm; consult website or call ahead

LAS CHIRUSAS

www.milongalaschirusas.com.ar

This tango outfit offers an excellent programme of dance classes at venues around the city on different days of the week, and holds *milongas* at two different locations, Quintana Roo and Café de la Flor. Definitely worth checking out.

✉ Mendoza 862 ☎ 0341/15-583-2255 ⏰ Wed, Sun evening ✋ Classes $50

EXTREME BIKE

www.extremebike.com.ar

If you want to join the Rosarinos and cycle along the marvellous 20km-long (12.5-mile) *costanera* (waterside promenade), this is a good place to rent a bicycle.

✉ San Lorenzo 981 ☎ 0341/421-5952 ⏰ Mon–Fri 9–1, 3.30–7.30, Sat 10–1 ✋ $20 an hour

LA FLUVIAL

www.lafluvialrosario.com.ar

This marvellous complex on the riverbank offers a range of services including a beautiful beach, bars and restaurants, and boat trips on the Paraná and to the islands. There is even a museum with exhibits on the river and the islands, and the original Chaná-Tambú inhabitants.

✉ Los Inmigrantes 410 ☎ 0341/447-3838 ⏰ Daily 9–8

GOTIKA

www.gotikacityclub.com.ar

One of Rosario's main nightclubs beats to the sound of drum 'n' base and house at weekends. There are occasional gay nights, too.

✉ Mitre 1539 ☎ 0341/421-7162 ⏰ Thu–Sun from 11pm

GRANJA DE LA INFANCIA

This is a wonderful farm, where children can interact with animals and learn about the various tasks of a farmer, as well as take part in activities such as watering, weeding and feeding animals.

✉ Avenida Pte Peron to 8100 – alongside Canal 3 de Rosario ☎ 0341/480-7848 🕐 Tue–Fri 9–4, Sat–Sun 10–6 ✋ $3

NEWELL'S OLD BOYS

www.newellsoldboys.com.ar

Named for English immigrant Isaac Newell, who arrived in Rosario in the 1960s, Newell's Old Boys is one of Rosario's main soccer teams (alongside rivals Rosario Central) and has its stadium inside the Parque de la Independencia (▷ 281). This is one of the country's top teams and watching a match is an experience worth having. Tickets can be bought from the box office in the park.

✉ Parque Independencia
☎ 0341/411-7725

PEÑA LA AMISTAD

Chamamé is the great dance form of the Litoral and this folk centre is one of the best places in the city to see it being performed. Traditional criollo fare such as empanadas (meat pasties), tamales (maize and meat balls) and lomitos (steak sandwiches) are on offer to stave off hunger while you soak up the wonderful atmosphere.

✉ Maipu 1121 ☎ 0341/411-0339
🕐 Daily 9pm–3am

LA SEDE

This is a literary café housed in a fine art nouveau building where you can browse through books, while you sample delicious quiches, pies, tarts and cakes. At weekends there are recitals and jazz sessions.

✉ San Lorenzo and Entre Ríos
☎ 0341/425-4071 🕐 Daily 8–midnight

SPANISH IN ROSARIO

www.spanishinrosario.com

Choose from a range of packages designed for people who want to learn or improve their Spanish. There is an immersion course and tailored classes to enable you to get the most out of your stay. Some packages combine learning with travel and one popular tour includes stopovers in Rosario and Buenos Aires plus two days of kayaking and camping on the river islands.

☎ 0341/437-2860

TEATRO EL CÍRCULO

www.teatro-elcirculo.com.ar

Rosario's symphony orchestra is based at this sublime early 20th-century theatre, a real vestige of Rosario's heyday as one of the richest cities in South America. Inaugurated as the city's opera house in 1904, it still stages opera and ballet, plus a wide range of music and theatre, including cabaret and top-notch tango concerts. If you cannot make it to a performance, go on a guided tour to see its beautifully restored splendours.

✉ Laprida 1223 ☎ 0341/424-5349
🕐 Guided visits Mon, Wed and Fri 10.30 and 5.30, Sat 10.30 ✋ Guided visits free; concerts vary

FESTIVALS AND EVENTS

JANUARY
FIESTA DEL GAUCHITO GIL

The major shrine to folk hero 'Gauchito' Gil (▷ 23) just outside Mercedes becomes a nationwide pilgrimage site. Expect lots of folk music and revelry.

FEBRUARY
CARNAVAL

www.carnavaldelpais.com.ar

Colón, Corrientes and other towns in the Litoral hold Brazilian-style carnivals, but the region's biggest and most famous takes place on weekends in February and early March in Gualeguaychú (▷ 325). The town's Corsódromo sees exuberant parades with different comparsas (carnival schools) competing for prizes for the best costumes, music and artistic merit.

FIESTA NACIONAL DE LA ARTESANÍA

www.fiestadelaartesania.com.ar

In the second week of February, Colón hosts this important craft fair attended by exhibitors from all over Latin America and Europe. There are also lively musical events and a festival queen is elected.

JUNE
SEMANA DE LA BANDERA

Rosario is the home of the national flag, celebrated by a public holiday on 20 June. The whole week around that date sees thousands of patriots flock to the city for celebrations at the Monumento a la Bandera. There are displays of gaucho skills and demonstrations of horsemanship, plus food and crafts stalls. There is even a national championship of the card game truco.

JULY
BIENAL DE ESCULTURA

www.bienaldelchaco.com

Every even-numbered year Resistencia, capital of the Chaco province, hosts a remarkable event dedicated to sculpture. At the Bienal dozens of sculptors from all over the world come together to compete for a prestigious prize.

OCTOBER/NOVEMBER
FESTIVAL DE JAZZ

Rosario's annual jazz festival takes place from late October to early November and attracts some of the best acts in Argentina and South America, with occasional guests from farther afield.

NOVEMBER
FIESTA NACIONAL DEL RÍO

The area by Formosa's port comes alive for three days in mid-November when there are lively chamamé folk-music concerts, displays of water sports and parades.

PRICES AND SYMBOLS

The restaurants are listed alphabetically (excluding El, La and Los). The prices given are the average for a two-course lunch (L) and a three-course dinner (D) for one person, without drinks. The wine price is for the least expensive bottle. All the restaurants listed accept credit cards unless otherwise stated. Prices are given in Argentine pesos ($) unless otherwise noted.

For a key to the symbols, ▷ 2.

COLÓN

CHIVA CHIVA

www.chivachiva.com.ar
This tropical-looking restaurant doubles as an art gallery, showcasing local potters, painters and other artisans. Try the river fish, succulently prepared and beautifully decorated—after all, their motto is 'art on a plate'. The service is ultra-friendly, the cocktails are dangerously moreish and there is an excellent wine list. As a bonus there are frequent live music shows at weekends.
✉ Urquiza and Almirante Brown
☎ 03447/424815 ◷ Dec–Mar Thu–Tue 12–4, 8–1; Apr–Nov Thu–Sun 12–4, 8–1
✋ L $75, D $100, Wine $25

VIEJO ALMACÉN

Brick walls and ranks of wooden tables and chairs are part of the no-nonsense decoration at this 'old store', which is now one of the most popular restaurants in town. An added bonus is the evocative collection of old photographs of Colón hung on the walls. The tasty food is a real treat and the house special is grilled river fish—the *pacú* and *surubí* both melt in the mouth. There is also a range of pasta dishes and well-prepared meats.
✉ General Urquiza and J.J.Paso
☎ 03447/422216 ◷ Mon–Sun 12–4, 8–12
✋ L $45, D $65, Wine $21

CORRIENTES

LAS BRASAS

Here, succulent meats and freshly caught river fish are grilled on hot coals (*brasas*). Try the *pacú*, *surubí* or the *dorado*. Las Brasas is one of several cavernous *parrillas* at the southern end of the city's wonderful *costanera* (waterside promenade) heading towards the bridge over the Paraná to Resistencia. Portions are huge, the service is brisk and the entertainment is excellent.
✉ Costanera and San Martín
☎ 03783/435106 ◷ Daily 12.30pm–1am
✋ L $55, D $70, Wine $35

ENÓFILOS

A wine bar and shop, Enófilos also happens to serve the most sophisticated cuisine in the province. The place may look rustic but the gastronomy is definitely worthy of any great city. Another plus is the emphasis on regional cooking, with specials such as *chipá* (cassava bread) and a pie made with beef and *mandioc* (cassava). Try the *surubí* (freshwater fish) in a sauvignon blanc sauce. The perfect accompaniment to a glass or two of wine is the *tabla ywy mará ey*, a mixed platter of Corrientes specialities.
✉ Junín 172 ☎ 03783/439271
◷ Mon–Sat 12–3.30, 8–12 ✋ L $55, D $80, Wine $30

FOZ DE IGUAÇU (BRAZIL)

TEMPERO DA BAHÍA

www.restaurantetemperodabahia.com
Even if you don't stay on the Brazilian side of the Iguazú falls it might be worth crossing the border for dinner at a typical Brazilian restaurant. Tempero de Bahía specializes in the exotic food of the northeast region around Salvador de Bahía. Try the *acarajé* (black-eyed pea fritters), *vatapá* (bread-based dip) or *moqueca de camarão* (seafood stew), based on the emblematic ingredients of shrimp, coconut milk and palm oil. Live samba adds to the ambience.
✉ Rua Marechal Deodoro 1228, Foz do Iguaçu, Brazil ☎ (+55) 45/3025-1144
◷ Daily 11.30–2, 6–11 ✋ L US$15, D US$20, Wine US$8

Opposite A platter of cheese and salami
Below right Beef assado

OBERÁ
ENGÜETE
This suburban restaurant is by far the best place to eat in Oberá. Try one of the local specialities, such as *yacaré* (caiman), which are bred in farms in the northeast for their leather and meat—marinated *yacaré* with a pepper sauce is delicious. There are some good wines to accompany the food. The service and ambience are decidedly laid-back.
✉ Alvar Núñez Cabeza de Vaca 340 ☎ 03755/421965 ⏱ Daily 12–3, 8–midnight ✋ L $48, D $60, Wine $22

POSADAS
LA QUERENCIA
In a great location on Plaza 9 de Julio, La Querencia is known as the best restaurant in the city. Surprisingly formal on the inside, with flags of every South American country decorating the walls, this place is nevertheless relaxed and you can savour all manner of typical dishes along with classics such as *milanesas* (schnitzel). The house special is the *galeto*, a Brazilian dish introduced by Italian immigrants—juicy chicken brought to the table on a spit.
✉ Bolívar 1849 ☎ 03752/437117 ⏱ Daily 12.30–3, 8–12 ✋ L $35, D $60, Wine $19

PUERTO IGUAZÚ
LA RUEDA
www.larueda1975.com
If you want to get a taste of Puerto Iguazú, La Rueda is the place to go. Years of experience show in the professional, friendly service, the mellow atmosphere and the fine cuisine twinned with an outstanding wine list. Whatever you choose you won't go wrong, whether you plump for the luscious pasta (such as beef ravioli with Roquefort), the perfectly grilled steaks or one of the array of dishes using freshwater fish, such as *pacú* and *boga*.
✉ Avenida Córdoba 28 ☎ 03757/422531 ⏱ Daily 12–4, 8pm–1am ✋ L $42, D $55, Wine $22

ROSARIO
CAFÉ DE LA OPERA
The café-bar at the beautiful early 20th-century Teatro El Círculo (▷ 295) often provides musical entertainment, while the simple food includes pasta, salads, omelettes and delicious chicken in a herb sauce. This is also a good place for just a glass of wine, a cold beer or coffee and cake.
✉ Mendoza and Laprida ☎ 0341/421-9402 ⏱ Mon–Sat 12.30–3, 8–midnight ✋ L $45, D $60, Wine $21

DAVIS
www.complejodavis.com
Although the Davis restaurant conjures up some interesting full-blown lunches and dinners, this place is all about location. Adjoining the state-of-the-art MACRo (▷ 283), Davis has a modern indoor dining room and a wonderful riverside terrace where you can watch yachts and container ships sail past on the mighty Río Paraná and admire the road bridge to Victoria. This is also a great place for a beer and a sandwich.
✉ Avenida de la Costa Brigadier Estanislao López 2550 ☎ 0341/435-7142 ⏱ Daily 11am–midnight ✋ L $38, D $52, Wine $23

POBLA DEL MERCAT
Pobla del Mercat is a sumptuous restaurant (with a wine and food shop attached) in a neo-classical mansion that has been converted into an elegant dining room, with crisp white linens and sparkling glassware. The wine list is impressively long, with something for all budgets. The chef offers up tempting dishes like salmon *tartare* and fillet steak in a wine sauce. Desserts are particularly good—the crème brûlée and raspberry charlotte are both memorable.
✉ Salta 1424 ☎ 0341/447-1240 ⏱ Mon–Sat 12.30–3.30, 8–midnight ✋ L $65, D $80, Wine $25

RICH
www.rosario.com.ar/richrestaurant
Ignore the unassuming exterior because this is one of the best restaurants in Rosario. Located in the heart of downtown and established in the 1930s, it has a stylish, understated interior. The food in the main restaurant strikes a balance between *criollo* favourites, such as steak and *puchero* (a rustic stew), and more sophisticated dishes influenced by French, Italian and Spanish cuisines, such as steak *chasseur*, pasta with pesto and paella. There is a budget rotisserie next door, where you can try fabulous grilled chicken and a variety of other meats.
✉ San Juan 1031 ☎ 0341/411-5151 ⏱ Mon–Sat 12–3, 8–12, Sun 12–3 ✋ L $48, D $60, Wine $19

SAN IGNACIO MINÍ
CARPA AZUL
If exploring the Jesuit ruins has given you an appetite, look no further than the distinctive Carpa Azul, right by the entrance to San Ignacio Miní. The dining room is a huge sky-blue marquee with cavernous dimensions and able to accommodate coach loads of visitors. Come a little before or after the lunchtime rush and you won't have to battle for a seat to taste the perfectly grilled *surubí*. A house speciality is *milanesas* (breaded fried fish). Choose from a succulent fillet of *pacú* or *dorado*. The accompanying chips (French fries) are delicious.
✉ Rivadavia 1295 ☎ 03752/470096 ⏱ Daily 12–4, 8–12 ✋ L $42, D $55, Wine $17

PRICES AND SYMBOLS

Prices are the lowest and highest for a double room for one night. Breakfast is included unless noted otherwise. All the hotels listed accept credit cards unless otherwise stated. Note that rates vary widely throughout the year. Prices are given in US dollars (US$) unless otherwise stated.

For a key to the symbols, ▷ 2.

CARLOS PELLEGRINI
ESTANCIA RINCÓN DEL SOCORRO

www.rincondelsocorro.com
A few kilometres south of Carlos Pellegrini and set in 120sq km (47sq miles) of former cattle ranch, Rincón del Socorro is a luxurious eco-hotel. The beautiful main *casco* (historic house) contains six fabulous individually decorated rooms with exquisite furniture, stunning black-and-white photographs of the region and its wildlife, and gorgeous retro bathrooms. Activities include horse riding and birdwatching trips.
✉ Esteros del Iberá ☎ 03782/497172
🖐 US$300–US$500 ⓘ 6 rooms, 3 bungalows

POSADA AGUAPÉ

www.iberaesteros.com.ar
Aguapé is a marvellous lagoon-side lodge with 12 double rooms in galleried longhouses overlooking immaculate lawns. The chef Laura Perez Bourbón cooks up some fabulous meals and regular barbecues feature black-faced Scottish lamb. In addition to the launch trips, you can try canoeing through the marshland's channels or go on a trek across the drier parts of the Esteros.
✉ Carlos Pellegrini ☎ 03773/499412
🖐 $400–$480 per person including all meals ⓘ 12 🏊 Outdoor

POSADA DE LA LAGUNA

www.posadadelalaguna.com
On the banks of the Laguna de la Luna, the main lagoon within the Esteros del Iberá, this outstanding place leads the way in terms of eco-tourism in the reserve. The owner Elsa Güiraldes—related to the famous novelist Ricardo Güiraldes (1886–1927)—runs a professional ship. The understated elegance of the main house is reflected in the galleried building where the simple but comfortable rooms are located. The food is faultless and there is a bar if you want to relax with a drink after dinner. Thanks to the location you can spot birds while in the swimming pool or on your verandah and there are morning and evening launch trips on the lagoon to see the wildlife.
✉ Carlos Pellegrini ☎ 03773/499413
🖐 $600–$750 per person including all meals ⓘ 6 🏊 Outdoor

COLÓN
HOSTERÍA DEL PUERTO

www.hosteriadecolon.com.ar
A beautiful deep-pink neo-colonial cornerhouse standing by the portside, this fine *hostería* dates from 1880 and has large rooms with handsome wooden floors and furniture. All the rooms have private bathrooms and some have their own balcony as well. There is a garden and swimming pool as well as a delightful colonial-style patio with an old well. Credit cards are not accepted.
✉ Alejo Peyret 158 ☎ 03447/422698
🖐 $160–$240 ⓘ 17 🏊 Outdoor

FORMOSA
ASTERIÓN

www.asterionhotel.com.ar
Formosa doesn't have a particularly good choice of hotels but the Asterión, next to the roundabout (traffic circle) at the gateway to the city, is an exception. The pleasantly decorated rooms are comfortable, with modern bathrooms. In the public areas you can see displays of indigenous crafts made by the local Wichí ethnic group. There is

Opposite Stylish hostería accommodation

also a large, attractive garden with a swimming pool.

✉ RN-11 km1170 ☎ 03717/452999 ✋ $280–$310 🛏 20 🏊 Outdoor

GUALEGUAYCHÚ
PUERTO SOL
www.hotelpuertosol.com.ar
By far the best hotel in Gualeguaychú, the Puerto Sol is located on the banks of the river. In addition to 20 well-appointed rooms there are also some self-catering apartments. Breakfasts are generous. One of the hotel's advantages is that you can cross the river in the hotel launch to reach a secluded spot on the other side—great for lazing and sunbathing.

✉ San Lorenzo 477 ☎ 03446/434017 ✋ $320–$350 🛏 20

IGUAZÚ
LA ALDEA DE LA SELVA
www.laaldeadelaselva.com
Jungle Village sums up this eco-lodge and spa close to the town centre very well. In a precious patch of tropical jungle, the Aldea has a number of timber buildings scattered among the vegetation, which can be explored by a series of plank walkways. The rooms are spacious and pleasingly simple, with balconies where you can swing in a hammock and watch the birds. A climbing wall, rope bridge and rappel (abseiling) await those who want to play at Tarzan.

✉ Selva Iriapú, Puerto Iguazú ☎ 03757/425777 ✋ US$140–US$180 🛏 16 🏊 Outdoor

ESTANCIA LAS MERCEDES
www.estancialasmercedes.com
Dating from 1923, this working *estancia*, which is located a short way outside Eldorado (south of Iguazú), is enchanting. The friendly owners will tell you all about the *estancia's* fascinating past, and will keep you busy with activities, such as horse riding, canoeing, biking through the jungle and trekking along the nearby trails. Hearty food is all made from farm produce.

✉ Eldorado ☎ 03751/1541-8224 or 03751/1540-1910 ✋ $800–$1,000 including all meals 🛏 5 🏊 Outdoor 🚗 Eldorado is 100km (62 miles) to the south of Iguazú. There are local buses that take around 2 hours. In Eldorado turn left along Avenida San Martín, then right onto Avenida Córdoba at the corner where the Banco Nación stands

HOTEL DAS CATARATAS
www.hoteldascataratas.com
More aesthetically pleasing than the Sheraton on the Argentine side, the luxury Hotel das Cataratas, located within the Brazilian national park, is the best place to stay if you want to have the waterfalls on your doorstep. The 192 rooms and suites are decorated and furnished to a high standard. You can choose to eat in the Ipê Grill or the Itaipú Restaurant and the Bar Tarobá serves wonderful caipirinhas. The sumptuous buffet breakfast is served at the Grill. There is a fine swimming pool and an excellent spa. The hotel arranges transport from the airports on either side of the border.

✉ Rodovia Br 485km (opposite Falls) ☎ (+55) 45/2102-7000 ✋ US$340–US$450 🛏 192 🏊 Outdoor

PANAMBÍ LODGE
www.panambilodge.com.ar
Some 50km (31 miles) east of Iguazú, the Panambí Lodge is a wonderful eco-lodge located on the Río Iguazú. Surrounded by fascinating flora and fauna, which can be observed from a panoramic watchtower, the lodge's buildings are constructed of eco-friendly timber. The hotel organizes trips to the falls, to a nearby *palmetto* (indigenous palm) reservation and to *yerba mate* plantations, where you can see how the plant is grown and processed. You'll need to arrange a transfer from the airport to the hotel.

✉ Iguazú ☎ 03757/497418 ✋ $800 including all meals 🛏 5

POSADA PUERTO BEMBERG
www.puertobemberg.com
Each of the sumptuous rooms has a small library of books by Latin American authors, restored bed-heads from Buenos Aires tenements,

a small patio and views of the river or jungle. The restaurant serves traditional Misiones cuisine based on *mandioc*, freshwater fish and tropical fruit. There is even a 1930s chapel built by Alejandro Bustillo, Argentina's answer to Le Corbusier.

✉ Fundadores Bemberg s/n, Puerto Libertad ☎ 03757/496500 ✋ US$280–US$350 🛏 14 🏊 Outdoor 🚗 From Iguazú, drive south along the RN-12 to Puerto Libertad at km1598. Turn left onto Avenida Juan Domingo Perón and along Avenida Fundadores Bemberg for 2.5km (1.5 miles); the entrance is to the left

SHERATON IGUAZÚ
www.starwoodhotels.com
This concrete hulk in the midst of the national park, built in 1978 in violation of planning rules during the last dictatorship, is nonetheless one of the best lodgings in the region, not least for the views from its rooms, overlooking the Falls themselves. Restored in 2003, the hotel features an excellent spa and the Lobby Bar, with unbeatable vistas of the Cataratas. The rooms are spacious and comfortable, but note you must pay the park entrance fee every day to get back, if you leave the park territory.

✉ Parque Nacional Iguazú ☎ 03757/491800 ✋ US$300–US$450 🛏 180 🏊 Outdoor

Below *The luxury Hotel das Cataratas, on the Brazilian side of the Iguazú falls*

YACUTINGA

www.yacutinga.com

Four of the 570ha (1,408 acres) of virgin jungle on the banks of the Río Iguazú have been used to build this amazing eco-friendly lodge. The striking timber construction avoids the need for air-conditioning even in the hot summer months. You need to stay at least two nights (minimum allowed) to get the most out of its exciting programmes, which include night walks in the *selva* to see nocturnal wildlife. Longer four-night packages are available.

✉ Near Andresito. The address is kept secret; contact the lodge by email (see website) 🖐 US$800 for two nights including all meals ⬤ 21

PARQUE NACIONAL EL PALMAR
AURORA DEL PALMAR

www.auroradelpalmar.com.ar

Far enough from the RN-14 main road to be tranquil, this eco-complex lies opposite the entrance to the Parque Nacional El Palmar. It comprises a neo-colonial main building, a scattering of *cabañas* and, quirkily, a set of converted train carriages. Activities include safaris and treks in the national park, canoe trips and camping in the forest.

✉ RN-14 km202, Ubajay, Provincia de Entre Ríos ☎ 03447/15-431689 🖐 $200–$240 ⬤ 12 ⬛ Outdoor

POSADAS
ESTANCIA SANTA CECILIA

www.santa-cecilia.com.ar

Built in 1908, Estancia Santa Cecilia, a short way north of Posadas, occupies a commanding position overlooking the Río Paraná. In the main building are four modern en-suite bedrooms on two floors, plus a comfortable living room. There are horse rides in the grounds and you can play polo at the local club.

✉ RN-12 km1366, Posadas, Provincia de Misiones ☎ 03752/493018 🖐 US$230–$270 ⬤ 4 ⬛

ESTANCIA SANTA INÉS

www.estancia-santaines.com.ar

Nanny and her brother, Ricardo,

descendants of the original owners, run this enchanting *estancia* a short distance outside Posadas. Built in 1906, the English-style house is set among luxuriant forest. Ricardo looks after the food, producing delicious local dishes. Nanny will lead you off on horseback through the extensive *mate* plantations, on which the *estancia's* wealth was founded, to a stone pool amid a bamboo thicket.

✉ RN-105 km8.5, Posadas, Provincia de Misiones ☎ 03752/15-639670 🖐 US$120–US$140 ⬤ 6 ⬛ Outdoor

PUERTO VALLE

www.hotelpuertovalle.com

The idyllic Puerto Valle overlooks a stretch of the mighty Río Paraná where a nearby dam has turned it into a lake and springy grass leads down from the galleried rooms to the river. There is also a large swimming pool and an enticing outdoor living room shaded by canopies. Boating, horse riding and other activities are available and there are launch trips into the Esteros del Iberá (▷ 272). The restaurant is truly remarkable and a great place to try *yacaré* (caiman), from the *estancia's* farm. Stay at least two nights to get the most from the marvellous facilities.

✉ RN-12 km1282, near Ituzaingó, Provincia de Corrientes ☎ 03786/425700 🖐 US$230–US$300 ⬤ 5 ⬛ Outdoor
🚗 Take RN-12 from Posadas and turn right at signpost to Puerto Valle at km1282

RESISTENCIA
CASINO GALA

www.hotelcasinogala.com.ar

Accommodation tends to be unappealing in Resistencia, so you might like to splash out on this rather glitzy but very efficiently run casino hotel in the middle of town. The rooms are stylishly decorated and most offer dramatic views of the city and the Río Paraná. In a city where gastronomy is as rare as a cool day, you could do worse than dine at the hotel's smart Valentino restaurant.

✉ Juan D. Perón 330 ☎ 03722/452400 🖐 $260–$320 ⬤ 145 ⬛ Outdoor

ROSARIO
SAVOY

www.esplendorsavoyrosario.com

The landmark Savoy hotel symbolizes Rosario's recent revival. A refined palace in the city's 1920s and '30s heyday, the building eventually fell into decay. Lavish restoration in the early 2000s has resulted in an opulent modern boutique hotel, with all the art nouveau splendour of the original and plenty of modern amenities. Everything from the designer lobby to the impeccably restored cupola on the roof suggests finesse.

✉ San Lorenzo 1022 ☎ 0341/429-6007 🖐 US$100–US$150 ⬤ 84 ⬛ Indoor

EL SOBERBIO
DON ENRIQUE LODGE

www.donenriquelodge.com.ar

Don Enrique is an ideal base for visiting the Saltos de Moconá, and the hotel organizes a transfer from El Soberbio. The main house is an alluring wooden building on the waterfront with a huge deck where you can dine, weather permitting. The kitchen offers plenty of gluten-free and vegetarian options, using organic produce from the garden. Rooms have wood stoves for hot water and heating and you are provided with a full set of ecological toiletries. Consult the lodge for transport arrangements.

✉ El Soberbio ☎ 011/4743-2070 🖐 US$200–US$220 including all meals ⬤ 3

POSADA LA MISIÓN

www.lodgelamision.com.ar

La Misión is one of the best eco-lodges in the Moconá region. The cedar timber and bare stone building has a wooden deck overlooking the river and there is a waterfall in the grounds. On guided visits you can see a variety of wildlife, including toucans, capybaras and butterflies. Each cabin has its own balcony, so you can admire the views from the privacy of your own lodgings.

✉ Puerto Paraíso, El Soberbio ☎ 011/5199-0185 🖐 US$180–US$195 ⬤ 6

PRACTICALITIES

Practicalities gives you all the important practical information you will need during your visit, from money matters to emergency phone numbers.

WEATHER

CLIMATE

Argentina stretches from the Tropic of Capricorn down to the southernmost point of the continent, and from the Atlantic beaches to the sky-scraping peaks of the Andes. Not surprisingly then, there is a mosaic of climates across the country.

» The verdant pampas, which is abundant from Buenos Aires to Córdoba, owes its fertility to a mild, wet climate throughout the year. Thunderstorms can be violent in midsummer, with hailstones the size of walnuts. Similar storms are experienced in the northwest, where the summers are warm and wet and the winters are bone-dry and permanently sunny.

» The Andean Patagonia steppe and the sandy Cuyo, including Mendoza, San Juan and La Rioja, are irrigated by the snowmelt from the Andean *cordillera* and register more than 300 days of sunshine every year.

» Tierra del Fuego and the far South feel the frigid influence of their proximity to the Antarctic—even summers are chilly, with snow possible in December. Winters are usually harsh, with frequent blizzards and bitter winds that last well into spring. Atlantic Patagonia and the Lake District have a similar climate, albeit less extreme.

» In the Litoral, summers are hot and sticky, while winters are cool and temperate. Certain localities in neighbouring Chaco register the country's highest temperatures, reaching upwards of 50°C (122°F) in December and January.

» Cyclones and hurricanes are extremely rare but torrential rain can lead to flash floods, so pay attention to weather reports and listen out for alerts.

WHEN TO GO

Spring and autumn, reversed when compared to the northern hemisphere, are ideal times for travelling.

» The peak season is summer, with a preference for January, while droves of Chileans cross the border into Argentina in February, their favourite holiday month. Resorts and accommodation fill up, roads are relatively busy and prices go up. Big cities, such as Buenos Aires and Córdoba, pretty much close down in the summer, although this can make seeing the sights more

Opposite *Canal de los Témpanos, Parque Nacional los Glaciares*

pleasurable. You are restricted to December and January if you want to climb the highest mountains, such as Aconcagua, or go trekking in southern Patagonia.

➤➤ The austral winter corresponds to the northern summer and the South is largely out of bounds during the coldest months, when the days are short, temperatures plummet, snowfalls can be dramatic and many hotels close. In the cities, cultural events are often in full swing, as are the ski resorts. In the North, the crisp air and mild daytime temperatures make winter a prime time to travel and leafless trees are great for seeing wildlife. Many Argentines take a winter break around 9 July, a national holiday (➤ 311).

➤➤ Spring (October and November) sees colourful flowers in town and country alike, but is a bit late for watching whales off the Atlantic coasts of Patagonia (best between July and September). The Tierra del Fuego and the far South can remain windy well into the summer.

➤➤ Depending on the region, autumn is March to May and invariably pleasant. City life is reactivated after the summer holidays, Patagonian gales abate and the deciduous trees in the Tierra del Fuego and Lake District blaze with fiery colours. Holy Week is a major holiday period, so plan ahead if you want to travel around Easter. March is the wine harvest month across Argentina and you might like to attend the festivities and even take part in the picking.

WEATHER REPORTS
BBC World News and CNN International broadcast regular weather bulletins but South America often gets short shrift. It is better to consult national and regional newspapers or www.accuweather.com. Forecasting is particularly unreliable in mountainous and maritime areas, where microclimates abound.

TIME ZONES
Argentina is 3 hours behind Greenwich Mean Time (GMT). There is no daylight saving time. Compared to noon in Buenos Aires, the time differences in other major cities are as follows:

CITY	TIME DIFFERENCE*	NOON IN BUENOS AIRES
Amsterdam	+4	4pm
Auckland	+15	3am**
Bangkok	+10	10pm
Berlin	+4	4pm
Brussels	+4	4pm
Chicago	-3	9am
Dublin	+3	3pm
Johannesburg	+5	5pm
London	+3	3pm
Madrid	+4	4pm
Montréal	-2	10am
New York	-2	10am
Paris	+4	4pm
Perth, Australia	+11	11pm
Rome	+4	4pm
San Francisco	-4	8am
Sydney	+13	1am**
Tokyo	+12	midnight

* In the northern winter
** The following day

BUENOS AIRES
TEMPERATURE

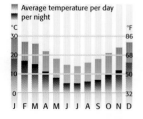

RAINFALL

CORDOBA
TEMPERATURE

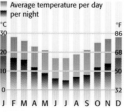

RAINFALL

USHUAIA
TEMPERATURE

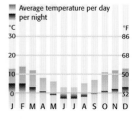

RAINFALL

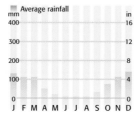

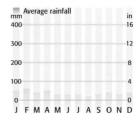

DOCUMENTS

PASSPORTS AND VISAS

›› All visitors must have a passport valid for 6 months from date of entry.

›› EU nationals and citizens from the US, Canada, Australia, New Zealand and South Africa do not need a visa to enter Argentina.

›› Citizens of the US, Canada and Australia, entering the country at Ezeiza International Airport in Buenos Aires (▷ 46–47), however, have to pay a reciprocity fee of US$140, US$70 and US$100 respectively. It can be paid in local currency or US dollars, by credit card or with traveller's cheques. More information can be obtained at www.argentina. gov.ar or tel 011/5480-9514. Visitors from the US, Canada and Australia will need to fill in a special form (valid for 10 years) and queue at a different window. This does not apply at any other point of entry.

›› A landing form (*tarjeta de entrada*) must be filled in, signed and presented with your passport at border controls upon entry to Argentina. Cabin crew will provide forms before landing. Another form has to be completed when you depart; you will be given one when you check in for departure. There is no exit fee unless you have stayed longer than the statutory 90 days.

›› Your passport will be stamped on entry (and departure) and visitors are allowed to stay for 90 days. If required, you can extend your stay once at the immigration department of the Dirección de Migraciones (Avenida Antártida 1350, Buenos Aires; tel 011/4317-0237 or 011/4317-0238; Mon–Fri 8am–1pm; $100). The best way to avoid this fee is to leave the country, if only for a few hours, and then re-enter. Many people visit Colonia (▷ 73) in Uruguay, a three-hour round trip from Buenos Aires.

›› If you want to work in Argentina you must obtain a valid visa in your home country before departure.

›› All visitors must carry a valid passport or ID at all times. It is wise to make a photocopy and the original in a safety deposit box at your hotel.

›› For more information visit the Argentine government site at www. argentina.gov.ar.

TRAVEL INSURANCE

›› There is no reciprocal health agreement between Argentina and most other countries, so it is vital to take out comprehensive travel insurance before departure. The policy should, as a minimum, cover medical emergencies, evacuation by air ambulance and repatriation, as well as personal effects.

›› Check that your policy covers all activities that you may do, including trekking, climbing, skiing or diving.

›› Report theft to the police as soon as possible and obtain an official signed and dated report (*parte*) for your insurer.

CUSTOMS ALLOWANCES

Travellers over 18 years of age arriving from Bolivia, Brazil, Chile, Paraguay or Uruguay may import the following goods to a value of US$100:

›› 200 cigarettes

›› 25 cigars

›› 1 litre of alcohol

›› 2kg of foodstuffs

Travellers over 18 years of age arriving from elsewhere may import the following goods to a value of US$300:

›› 400 cigarettes

›› 50 cigars

›› 2 litres of alcohol

›› 5kg of foodstuffs

More information about customs and importing/exporting goods can be obtained at www.afip.gov.ar/english or tel 0810/999-2347 (Mon–Fri 8–8).

ARGENTINE EMBASSIES AND CONSULATES ABROAD

COUNTRY	ADDRESS	WEBSITE
Australia	7 National Circuit, Floor 2, Barton, Capital Territory 2600 tel 02/6273-9111	www.argentina.org.au
Canada	81 Metcalfe, 7th floor, Ottawa K1P6K7 tel 613/236-2351	www.argentina-canada.net
Republic of Ireland	14 Ailesbury Drive, Ballsbridge, Dublin 44 tel 01/269-1546	
New Zealand	142 Lambton Quay, Level 14, Wellington tel 04/472-8330	www.arg.org.nz
South Africa	200 Standard Plaza, 440 Hilda Street, Pretoria 0083 tel 012/430-3516	www.embassyofargentina.co.za
UK	65 Brook Street, London W1K 4AH tel 020/7318-1300	www.argentine-embassy-uk.org
US	1600 New Hampshire Avenue, Washington DC 20009 tel 202/238-6400	www.embassyofargentina.us

MONEY

BEFORE YOU GO

How you carry your money largely comes down to personal preference, but in Argentina cash (US dollars and pesos) and credit cards are the best option. Outside the major cities, traveller's cheques can be difficult to change and, particularly in rural areas, working ATMs might be hard to find. Keep a note of your credit card details in case of loss or theft.

When budgeting for your trip, take into account that inflation in Argentina is currently running at around 25 per cent per annum.

LOCAL CURRENCY

» The currency in Argentina is the peso—sometimes referred to as *peso argentino* to distinguish it from the peso used in other countries, including neighbouring Uruguay and Chile. The symbol most used for the peso is $. This can be confusing, especially since the US dollar is often quoted for hotel rates and large transactions. Generally, it is clear if the price quoted is in US dollars (US$, USD or *dólar EEUU*) or pesos ($), but it is worth double-checking before paying any money.

» The peso is divided into centavos (¢). There are 5, 10, 25 and 50 centavo coins, but small change is often in short supply, especially in the countryside, so you might be offered a sweet instead of change. Notes are available in denominations of $2, $5, $10, $20, $50 and $100. You cannot purchase pesos before you travel or exchange them once you leave.

» For the latest exchange rate consult www.xe.com/ucc.

PRICES OF EVERYDAY ITEMS

50cl bottle of mineral water	$2
Takeaway sandwich	$10
Cup of coffee/tea	$5
Bottle of beer	$10
Glass of wine	$15
Foreign newspaper	$10
Ice cream	$10
A litre of petrol (gas)	$4.50
Bus ticket	$1.10
20 cigarettes	$3

BANKS

There are banks in most towns and many belong to international chains. When changing money, bureaux de change are usually the best choice as commission is lower, but in some places banks will be your only option. Banking hours are usually Monday to Friday 10–4.

BUREAUX DE CHANGE

There are bureaux de change *(cámbios)* in all cities, resorts and airports and their opening hours are much longer than for banks. You will need to show your passport to change money.

ATMS

» ATMs *(cajeros automáticos)* are plentiful in towns and cities but few in more remote rural areas.

» Most international debit and credit cards are accepted, although it is best to check before travelling.

» You can choose English over Spanish when using the machines.

» Most ATMs allow you to take out a maximum of $700 (pesos) per transaction, so you may have to make several withdrawals, in succession, until you reach your bank limit or the amount you require.

CREDIT CARDS

» Credit cards *(tarjetas de crédito)* are widely accepted in towns and cities, but not in rural areas or in small shops.

» Check with your hotel or *estancia* beforehand to establish whether they accept credit cards.

TIPPING

Bars and cafés	round up to the nearest peso
Restaurants	5–10 per cent, unless a service charge is included (rare)
Taxis	round up to the nearest $0.50 or peso
Porters	$5
Hairdressers	$2–$5
Luggage/cloak-room attendants	$0.50–$1 (may be compulsory)
Petrol station attendants	$1

» Most transactions will not require you to enter your PIN number but you might be asked for ID to check your signature.

VAT REFUNDS

» VAT *(IVA)* is included in prices for most items and might be added on to hotel bills. The current rate is 21 per cent for most goods and services.

» You can claim back VAT (minus an administration fee) at the airport before checking in for departure on certain purchases, provided the shop takes part in a special duty-free scheme (participants are listed at www.globalrefund.com). The minimum purchase value is $70. You must obtain a form when making a purchase, which will be filled in and stamped either by the sales assistant or, in the case of shopping malls, at the designated Tax Free booth.

» To get a VAT refund at the airport, you will have to present the receipt and the goods you have purchased at the Tax Free desk in departures and have the form stamped by a customs official. Take the form to the Tax Free booth in the departures lounge area to get the refund. If the booth in unmanned, you will need to fill in your credit card details and place the form in a box. Refunds to your credit account are carried out quite quickly.

WIRING MONEY

» The main company handling money transfers is Western Union (www.westernunion.com.ar), which has offices or agencies in post offices in many towns and cities.

» Commission rates can be high but you receive the funds immediately.

» Large sums of $500 or more may have to be retrieved at the central office in Buenos Aires rather than at local post offices.

TIPPING

Leaving a tip *(propina)* is common but not compulsory. It is customary to leave a small gratuity for waiters/waitresses, hairdressers, luggage attendants and taxi drivers. See the tipping box (left) for a guide to amounts to leave.

HEALTH

HEALTH SERVICES

» Health services are excellent in most of the country and there are good clinics or health centres (*clínicas* or *centros médicos*) in most towns. Remote rural areas are often poorly served with clinics and hospitals.

» Medical tourism is big business in Argentina with many people travelling here to take advantage of the excellent and affordable dental and ophthalmological treatments, as well as cosmetic surgery. Discuss any treatment or surgery with your health professional at home and check that the clinic in Argentina has an international certification before undergoing any treatments or operations.

BEFORE YOU GO

» See your doctor or travel clinic at least six weeks before your departure in case you need any vaccinations or anti-malaria tablets. Your doctor or health professional can also give advice on the travel risks.

» Make sure you have comprehensive travel insurance (▷ 304).

» Have a dental check-up, especially if you will be away for more than a month.

» Get a repeat prescription for vital medicines before you leave and make a note of the pharmaceutical name of your drugs in case you need to obtain them while you're away, as the local brand name might be different.

HEALTH HAZARDS

» The most common health hazards facing visitors are mosquito bites, diarrhoea, sunstroke and sunburn.

» Be aware that high altitudes or extreme temperatures can present more of a hazard for anyone with health problems, such as heart ailments.

» Mosquito-born malaria fever is rare, although your health professional may prescribe anti-malarials if travelling to the rural areas of Salta and Jujuy provinces (along the border with Bolivia) and Misiones and Corrientes provinces (along the

border with Paraguay) or Iguazú Falls. There have also been outbreaks of mosquito-dengue fever (malaria is transmitted at night and dengue fever in the day), so insect repellant should be worn at all times. 'Off!' is a good local brand or any repellant containing DEET. In addition, wear long-sleeved shirts and trousers during the day and stay in screened, air-conditioned accommodation. It is a good idea to use a coil or other method of repelling mosquitoes in your room at night.

» There are few poisonous snakes or spiders in Argentina—mainly confined to the North of the country—but get medical attention as soon as possible if you are bitten by a snake, spider or any animal that might be carrying rabies, or if you are stung by jellyfish (a rare occurrence).

WHAT TO TAKE

» Any prescription medicines that you require.

» A spare pair of spectacles or contact lenses, although it might

be worth getting these made in Argentina as prices can be attractive.

» A small first-aid kit, also compulsory when driving.

» High-factor sunscreen and insect repellent, although these items are widely available in Argentina.

SUMMER HAZARDS

» Wear loose-fitting, lightweight clothing, preferably with long sleeves, cover your head with a brimmed or peaked hat and wear sunglasses.

» Wear a high-factor sunscreen at all times during the day as the sun can be very strong, especially in the far South, where the cool air can be deceptive.

» Drink plenty of water, even if you feel you don't need to, and make sure you carry a spare bottle of water when driving.

» Keep out of the sun between 11am and 3pm, when it is at its strongest.

WATER

» The tap water in Argentina varies across the country. It is safe to drink in theory, but you might prefer to drink mineral water, especially in Buenos Aires, where it often tastes of chlorine.

›› Bottled water is fairly expensive compared to other everyday items and it is more cost-effective to buy a multi-litre bottle.

›› Drink plenty of water when you are in hot places or doing a lot of physical exercise.

›› It is safe to swim in most rivers and lakes but water for consumption should be boiled or treated with water-treatment tablets.

EMERGENCIES

›› Dial 107 for an ambulance in the case of an emergency. Otherwise, ask someone to drive you to the emergency department of the nearest hospital. It is usual to pay your medical expenses yourself and claim the cost back later from your insurer, so make sure you get a proper invoice from the hospital or clinic.

FINDING A HOSPITAL, DOCTOR OR DENTIST

›› For non-emergencies, the best source of finding a medical practitioner is the local Yellow Pages, listed under *servicios médicos*, (medical practitioners) or online at www.paginasamarillas.com.ar. Alternatively, contact your consulate for a list of recommended physicians.

›› Local pharmacies have a list of doctors and dentists. It's also worth asking at your hotel.

›› If you need medical assistance, ask your hotel to call for a doctor *(médico)*; most will speak some English, and staff at pharmacies *(farmacias)* can usually give advice for minor health issues.

›› You can find a list of clinics in Argentina at www.todoar.com.ar/d/ Salud/Hospitales or try Swiss Medical (www.swissmedical.com.ar) for English-speaking staff. This website also has a list of hospitals.

PHARMACIES

›› The sign for pharmacies *(farmacias)* is a green cross, sometimes on a white background.

›› You can find a nationwide list of pharmacies at www.enfarmacias. com.ar. This website includes addresses, contact numbers, opening times and whether or not credit cards are accepted.

›› Each pharmacy displays a notice giving the location of the nearest pharmacy on 24-hour or late-opening duty.

›› Drugstore chains such as Farmacity are ubiquitous and sell basics such as painkillers and health products, as well as having a pharmacy counter for prescription medicines.

EMERGENCY DEPARTMENTS

Buenos Aires	Hospital de Clínicas, Avenida Córdoba 2351	011/5950-8000
Córdoba	Hospital Italiano, Roma 550	0351/410-6500
Mendoza	Hospital Español San Rafael, Avenida Libertador	02627/423960
Salta	Hospital San Bernardo, Dr. M Boedo s/n	0387/431-8320
Ushuaia	Hospital Regional, Avenida 12 de Octubre and Maipú	02901/423200

GUIDE TO VACCINATIONS

All vaccinations should be organized at least 6 weeks before departure	
Hepatitis A	Recommended; the disease can be caught easily from food and water
Polio	Required, if last vaccination was at least 10 years ago
Tetanus	Required, if last vaccination was at least 10 years ago (but after 5 doses you are protected for life)
Typhoid	Required, if last vaccination was at least 3 years ago
Yellow fever	Recommended; mosquitoes carrying the disease are prevalent in the Iguazú Falls and Litoral region and along the border area between Argentina and Bolivia, Paraguay and Uruguay

BASICS

CLOTHING

>> The clothes you need will depend on where and when you intend to travel. For most of the country, basic summer wear will be shorts and T-shirts. Waterproofs and bathing costumes will be useful, too, as rainfall is highest in the summer and you will have plenty of opportunities for sunbathing or swimming. In the South, it can be cold and windy even in the height of summer, especially near the glaciers, so you should take the full panoply of windcheaters, hats and gloves. The onion method of layering is often useful, as temperatures may suddenly change if the sun comes out or the wind changes direction. In the winter, warmer clothing will be vital throughout the country, although, it only snows once a century in Buenos Aires.

>> You'll need waterproofs and hiking gear for trips to Andean Patagonia and the North during the wet season (December to February).

>> Don't overestimate the effect of altitude on the temperature. It can get very cold even in the relatively low sierras around Córdoba, let alone the high Andean peaks and the windswept *puna* (high plains). Take warm pullovers, a scarf and hat if you go above 1,000m (3,280ft), even in summer.

>> Footwear can often be flip-flops or sandals but comfortable shoes are vital for city sightseeing while proper boots are advisable for trekking. You can buy good-value shoes in Argentina.

>> Dress codes tend to be casual even in chic venues but scruffiness or scanty clothing is frowned upon in most establishments (especially religious buildings) while nudity is never tolerated. Fashion and elegance are highly regarded and a smart appearance will be appreciated in good hotels and restaurants. Jackets and ties are hardly ever a requisite.

REMEMBER TO PACK

>> Photocopies of all your important documents in case of loss or theft and note the details of your travel insurance in a safe place.

>> Your driver's licence.

>> Enough medication to last the whole trip and a little longer, although you should be able to buy any over-the-counter medicines at the local pharmacy but they might have a different name or be of lesser quality than you are used to.

>> A bag or backpack for daily use.

>> A torch (flashlight) and binoculars.

>> Sunscreen (high factor) and insect repellent.

>> A first-aid kit, including antiseptic and antihistamine creams, plasters (Band Aids) and painkillers.

>> A Spanish phrasebook or pocket Spanish dictionary.

>> You can buy most things you need in Argentina and often they will be cheaper than at home, so don't worry too much if you forget to pack important items.

ELECTRICITY

>> The current is 220 volts at 50 hertz throughout Argentina.

>> There are two types of plugs: two-pin, with a slightly thicker pin than the European two-pin plugs, and three-pin, with flat pins in a

Above *Boca del Diablo, Lago Argentino*

triangular format. Sockets usually take European two-pin plugs but don't accept any other type of plugs, so you will need an adaptor. These can be bought in most big towns and cities.

>> US visitors will need a transformer, to cope with the different voltage, which can be bought in Argentina, but it might be wiser to get one before travelling.

LAUNDRY

>> Most hotels and other lodgings offer a fast and reliable laundry service, although the more stars the higher the price.

>> There are always plenty of laundries *(lavaderos* or *lavanderías)*, even in small villages, which charge very little for a good service and return your laundry the next day. Some laundries offer a valet service. Some laundries charge per item, especially if you want clothes ironed *(planchado)*, but often the price is per bag or by weight.

>> Drycleaners *(tintorerías)* are harder to find and tend to be not as good as in many other countries.

PUBLIC TOILETS

>> There are few public toilets in Argentina and they are not usually of a very high standard. Shopping malls and museums have the best

CONVERSION CHART

FROM	TO	MULTIPLY BY
Inches	Centimetres	2.54
Centimetres	Inches	0.3937
Feet	Metres	0.3048
Metres	Feet	3.2810
Yards	Metres	0.9144
Metres	Yards	1.0940
Miles	Kilometres	1.6090
Kilometres	Miles	0.6214
Acres	Hectares	0.4047
Hectares	Acres	2.4710
Gallons	Litres	4.5460
Litres	Gallons	0.2200
Ounces	Grams	28.35
Grams	Ounces	0.0353
Pounds	Grams	453.6
Grams	Pounds	0.0022
Pounds	Kilograms	0.4536
Kilograms	Pounds	2.205
Tons	Tonnes	1.0160
Tonnes	Tons	0.9842

toilets and these are free of charge. Alternatively, find a fast-food outlet or café and ask to use the *baño* (toilet), although you might be expected to buy a coffee or a drink.

›› In addition to a variety of icons and symbols, male and female facilities are distinguished by the words *hombres/caballeros/señores/varones* and *damas/mujeres/señoras,* respectively. The letters 'H' *(hombres)* for men and 'M' *(mujeres)* for women are also used.

SMOKING

›› Smoking is banned in many public places, such as airport buildings and aeroplanes, all over Argentina.
›› Smoking is usually also prohibited in museums and on public transport.
›› In some cities and provinces, such as Buenos Aires and Tucumán, there is a total ban on smoking in restaurants, cafés, taxis and public buildings.
›› Tobacco is grown in Argentina and is relatively cheap, with most international and domestic brands widely available.

VISITING WITH CHILDREN

›› Argentines love children so expect to have yours fussed over, thoroughly spoiled and, even, petted. This is socially acceptable in Argentina but if you, or your child, are uncomfortable with the attention politely remove your child from the situation.
›› Facilities for changing nappies, high chairs and children's menus are increasingly available.
›› Argentines go out late at night and often take young children. Hotels will nevertheless arrange for babysitting services if you prefer.
›› Keep children out of the sun and heat, especially in the North in summer, and use a high factor (50+) sunscreen to protect them, as well as a hat and long-sleeved shirt or T-shirt.
›› Health and safety standards in hotels and public buildings are lower than in many other countries, so keep a watchful eye on children at all times.
›› Most hotels can provide a cot or an extra bed in your room and

neighbouring rooms can be joined together by unlocking doors or closing an outer door. Triple and quadruple rooms are common, too. Accommodation is family-oriented and no-child policies are rare.
›› Disposable nappies/diapers *(pañales)* and other baby products are widely available in supermarkets, drugstores and pharmacies but you might prefer to bring your own brand.
›› Discreet breastfeeding is accepted indoors, perhaps less so in the open air.

VISITORS WITH DISABILITIES

›› Facilities for people with disabilities *(discapacitados)* are slowly improving. Hotels are required to cater for people with wheelchairs or mobility difficulties but, otherwise, access can be limited.
›› Poorly surfaced pavements and narrow streets, despite the introduction of corner ramps, in some cities can make getting around more difficult.
›› Argentines are usually helpful, however, and will often offer to help people in wheelchairs or elderly people with mobility difficulties.

›› There are several reputable travel companies and charities that can assist people with disabilities travel to Argentina (▷ 58).

PLACES OF WORSHIP

›› The majority of Argentina's population is Catholic and there are churches and chapels in all major cities, resorts and most villages. There are a string of religious festivities, pilgrimages and other events held all over the country at any give time. Check the local tourist information office for details, as well as the service times of places of worship.
›› The influence of the Anglo-Argentine community is such that there are several Anglican churches around the country. Non-conformist churches are also represented and Mormons and Jehovah's Witness have a strong presence.
›› Buenos Aires and some other cities have large Jewish populations and Buenos Aires has the only kosher McDonalds outside the US and Israel.
›› There is a small Muslim community in Argentina.

NON-CATHOLIC PLACES OF WORSHIP IN BUENOS AIRES		
Anglican	Catedral Anglicana, 25 de Mayo 282	www.catedralanglicana.org
Baptist	Iglesia Evangélica Bautista del Once, Ecuador 370	www.ibonce.org.ar
Islamic	Centro Islámico Rey Fahd, Avenida Bullrich 45	www.ccislamicoreyfahd.org.ar
Jewish	Templo Libertad, Libertad 769	www.judaica.org.ar

Below *A bustling weekend craft market at Plaza Independencia, Mendoza*

FINDING HELP

PERSONAL SECURITY

Argentina has far lower levels of crime than the media suggests and it is rarely directed at tourists. Although some wise precautions should be taken, particularly if you are visiting Buenos Aires or other large cities.

›› Hold on to your belongings at all times when travelling on public transport and places such as stations, airports and bus terminals. Keep a look out for pickpockets and bag-snatchers, too, when in high-density tourist areas.

›› Be aware of tricks used by thieves to steal bags or watches, such as invading your personal space or distracting your attention.

›› Keep valuables, documents and money in the hotel safe or the safety deposit box in your room.

›› In big cities, be discreet and avoid showing off expensive jewellery, camera or electronic equipment.

›› When travelling by bus at night,

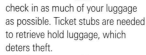

check in as much of your luggage as possible. Ticket stubs are needed to retrieve hold luggage, which deters theft.

›› Lock your car and keep any belongings out of sight when leaving it parked.

›› Carry the minimum amount of cash necessary and leave at least one credit or debit card at your hotel.

›› Take your mobile (cellular) phone with you or rent one at the airport; it can be useful in an emergency but keep it out of sight.

›› Violent attacks on tourists are rare and mostly confined to big cities but if you are unfortunate enough to be a victim of mugging or bag snatching, put your personal safety first and do not resist, especially if weapons are involved.

LOST PROPERTY

›› Always keep a separate note of your passport number and a photocopy of the page that carries your photo. Keep the copy separate from your passport and leave another copy with someone at home.

›› Report the loss or theft of a passport to the police and then contact your embassy or consulate (▷ panel below for details).

›› If you lose valuables, inform your travel insurance company as soon as possible.

›› If you lose your debit or credit card report it missing or stolen to the issuing bank as soon as possible.

›› In the event of theft, you will need a police report *(parte)* in order to make a claim on your travel insurance. Given the amount of time

it takes to process a complaint, it is usually not worth the trouble for inexpensive items.

POLICE

›› Apart from the Policía Federal (PFA), who wear dark-blue uniforms with berets or peaked caps, there are some provincial police forces and the capital's Policía Metropolitana. There is also the military police force, known as the Gendarmería Nacional Argentina (GNA), who wear green military-style uniforms and are in charge of border controls and other matters of national interest.

›› Police officers in Argentina are mostly polite and helpful, although many do not speak English. Unless you are driving or behaving suspiciously, you are unlikely to be stopped and asked for your ID.

›› Police checks along main roads and at some city junctions are frequent. These inspections are usually carried out courteously and you will be asked to show various documents, including the car papers, your driver's licence and possibly your ID and car rental contract. Don't be surprised to be asked about your journey or nationality, these are usually just conversation starters.

›› There are tourist police stations in all big cities (tel 0800/999-5000 in Buenos Aires).

›› In an emergency, call 101.

EMERGENCY NUMBERS	
Police	101
Fire	100
Ambulance	107

EMBASSIES AND CONSULATES		
COUNTRY	**ADDRESS**	**WEBSITE**
Australian Embassy	Villanueva 1400, Buenos Aires 1426, tel 011/4779-3500	www.argentina.embassy.gov.au
Canadian Embassy	Tagle 2828, Buenos Aires 1425, tel 011/4808-1000	www.buenosaires.gc.ca
Irish Embassy	Avenida del Libertador 1068, Piso 6, Buenos Aires 1112, tel 011/5787-0801	www.embassyofireland.org.ar
New Zealand Embassy	Carlos Pellegrini 1427, 5th Floor Buenos Aires 1011, tel 011/4328-0747	www.nzembassy.com/argentina
South African Embassy	Marcelo T. De Alvear 590, Piso 7-8, Buenos Aires 1058, tel 011/4317-2900	www.sudafrica.org.ar
UK Embassy	Dr. Luis Agote 2412, Buenos Aires 1425, tel 011/4808-2200	www.ukinargentina.fco.gov.uk
US Embassy	Avenida Colombia 4300, Buenos Aires 1425, tel 011/5777-4533	argentina.usembassy.gov

OPENING TIMES AND TICKETS

Opening hours are usually 9am to 7 or 8pm, closing earlier on Saturdays and all day on Sundays. The siesta, often from 1pm to 4 or 5pm, is respected in some rural areas, especially in the North in the summer. In tourist areas, opening hours, including weekends, are often longer.

BANKS
Banking hours are usually Mon–Fri 10–4.

BARS
Hours vary according to location and season, but bars seldom close before midnight and are often open until the early hours.

CAFÉS
Most cafés open around 7 or 8am and stay open until late evening.

PLACES OF WORSHIP
Many places of worship stay open all day, though some open for Mass only. Cathedrals and churches will often request tourists not to visit during services.

MUSEUMS AND GALLERIES
Museums and galleries are usually open from 10 or 11am to 6 or 7pm but opening times vary, so check before setting out. Most museums close at least one day a week (usually Mondays) and might be closed for part of the year, for example January in Buenos Aires and the winter in the South. Some museums have late-night opening, often on Wednesdays.

OFFICES
Businesses usually open Mon–Fri 9–5 but there are wide seasonal and geographical variations.

POST OFFICES
Post offices are usually open Mon–Fri 9–6, Sat 9–1 but there are seasonal and geographical variations.

SHOPS
The standard opening hours for shops are Mon–Sat 9–7, closing earlier on Saturdays and closed on Sundays. Supermarkets and malls often have longer hours and stay open until 9 or 10pm. Souvenir shops often open seven days a week in the summer and close for the winter.

PHARMACIES
Pharmacies have the same opening hours as shops (usually Mon–Sat 9–7) but some have longer opening hours, particularly in towns, cities and popular tourist resorts. Most towns have a pharmacy open 24 hours, according to a rota (information is posted in each pharmacy).

RESTAURANTS
In Argentina mealtimes are later than in other countries. Lunch is usually between 12 and 3pm, and dinner is from 8pm until the early hours, especially during high season. Some restaurants close one day a week, usually Sunday or Monday or possibly both. Many restaurants and confiterías in cities and popular tourist destinations are open all day (horario corrido).

ENTRANCE FEES
Most museums and sights charge admission fees and these vary enormously, from a token $1 to $20 or more, while national parks charge tourists as much as $80. Don't be surprised if ticket prices are lower for Argentines than overseas visitors.

COMBINED TICKETS
There are currently no official combined ticket schemes but discount booklets, available from tourist information offices, exist in a few destinations.

DISCOUNTS
Many attractions have reductions for children under the age of 12, students and pensioners, and often have free entry one day a week.

NATIONAL HOLIDAYS
Many shops, restaurants, museums and places of interest close on national holidays but transport is mostly unaffected. Note that when certain national holidays fall on a Tuesday or Thursday, a 'bridge' holiday may be added to link it with the weekend. Holidays that fall on a Wednesday may be moved to the previous Monday. See the chart below for a list of national holidays and dates.

NATIONAL HOLIDAYS	
1 Jan	New Year's Day
Shrove Tuesday (dates vary)	Carnaval
Friday before Easter Sunday	Good Friday
24 Mar	National Truth and Justice Day
2 Apr	Malvinas Veterans' Day
1 May	Labour Day
25 May	Anniversary of the first national government
20 Jun	National Flag Day
9 Jul	Independence Day
17 Aug	Anniversary of death of General San Martín
12 Oct	Day of Respect and Cultural Diversity
20 Nov	Day of National Sovereignty
8 Dec	Immaculate Conception
25 December	Christmas Day

Opposite Members of the Policía Federal

TOURIST OFFICES

Only a handful of countries have official Argentine tourist offices. In the US, there are Argentine tourist offices in California (5505 Wilshire Blvd., Suite 210, Los Angeles CA 90036; tel 323/954-9155), Florida (2655 Le Jeune Road P I Suite F Coral Gables, Miami 33134; tel 305/442-1366) and New York (12 West 56th Street, NY 100; tel 212/603-0443). Otherwise, the best way to obtain up-to-date tourist information is to consult www.turismo.gov.ar.

Argentina has a number of national, regional, provincial and local tourist offices. There are several offices in the capital (▷ 313) and almost every town has its own office. Services and opening hours vary but tourist offices tend to stay open later during high season. Most of the provinces have a tourist board in the capital (▷ 313), which can be a very useful port of call before touring the region. Many tourist offices have displays of local arts and crafts, too, some of which may be on sale.

REGIONAL TOURISM WEBSITES

www.buenosairesquerible.gob.ar
Provides useful information about visiting the capital and Buenos Aires province.

www.patagonia-argentina.com
Tourist information, which covers the entire region of Patagonia.

www.tierradelfuego.org.ar
The official website for visitors to Argentine Tierra del Fuego.

www.ripioturismo.com.ar
An excellent website for information about some of the more remote sights in southern Argentina.

www.cordobaturismo.gov.ar
Tourist information and accommodation listings for the Córdoba Province.

www.cuyoargentina.gov.ar
Tourist information for the Cuyo (mid-western Argentina), including Mendoza, San Juan and La Rioja provinces.

www.regionnortegrande.com.ar
Information about the northwest, the Norte Grande.

www.trenalasnubes.com.ar
Everything you wanted to know, including booking tickets and timetables for the Tren a las Nubes (▷ 254–255).

www.visit-uruguay.com
Tourist information about neighbouring Uruguay (Colonia and farther afield).

USEFUL WEBSITES
TOURISM

www.turismo.gov.ar
Argentina's main tourist information website, which covers every aspect of travel in Argentina.

www.ruta0.com
Find route suggestions, distances, tolls, plus other useful information about driving in Argentina.

www.welcomeargentina.com
This general tourist information website covers the main sights, resorts and accommodation in Argentina with links and descriptions in English and Spanish.

TOURIST INFORMATION IN ARGENTINA

TOWN/CITY	LOCATION	TELEPHONE
Bariloche	Centro Cívico	02944/426784
Cachi	Gral Güemes s/n	03868/491902
Cafayate	Nuestra Señora del Rosario 9	03868/422442
El Calafate	Rosales 53	02902/491090
Catamarca	República 446	03833/437791
El Chaltén	M. M. Guemes 21	02962/493011
Colón	Avenida Costanera and Gouchón	03447/421233
Colonia del Sacramento	Flores and Rivera	+598 052/26141
Córdoba	Cabildo, Plaza San Martín	0351/434-1200
Esquel	Alvear and Sarmiento	02945/451927
Formosa	Uriburu 820	03717/420442
Gualeguaychú	Plazoleta de los Artesanos	03446/423668
Jujuy	C. Ignacio Gorriti 295	0388/422-1325
Junín de los Andes	Padre Milanesio and Coronel Suárez	02972/491160
La Rioja	Avenida Gobernador Gordillo	03822/434-1227
Malargüe	RN-40 s/n	02627/471659
Mar del Plata	Boulevard Marítimo P. Peralto Ramos 2270	0223/495-1777
Mendoza	San Martín 1143	0261/420-2656
Oberá	Avenida Libertad and Entre Ríos	03755/421808
Posadas	Colón 1985	03752/447539
Puerto Iguazú	Avenida Aguirre 311	03757/422722
Puerto Madryn	Julio Roca 223	02965/453504
Resistencia	Plaza 25 de Mayo	03722/458289
Río Gallegos	Roca 863	02966/438725
Rosario	Avenida Belgrano and Buenos Aires	0341/480-2230
Salta	Buenos Aires 93	0387/431-0950
San Antonio de Areco	Arellano and Zerboni	02326/453165
San Isidro	Plaza Mitre	011/4512-3209
San Juan	Sarmiento 24	0264/421-0004
San Martín de los Andes	Plaza San Martín	02972/427347
San Rafael	Avenida Hipólito Yrigoyen and Balloffet	02627/424217
Sarmiento	Regimiento de Infantería 25	0297/489-8220
Tandil	Avenida Espora 1120	02293/432073
Trelew	San Martín and Mitre	02965/426819
Tucumán	24 de Septiembre 484	0381/430-3644
Ushuaia	Avenida San Martín 674	02901/432000

www.argentinaturistica.com
An independent website with details about tourist services and activities.

www.visitingargentina.com
This website gives good-quality information about what to see and where to stay in Argentina.

www.parquesnacionales.gov.ar
The official website for Argentina's national parks (Spanish only).

ACCOMMODATION
www.destinationargentina.com
This independent website has details and links to accommodation in Argentina.

www.nativacollection.com
Excellent hotel network website, featuring a selection of accommodation around the country.

www.hoteleriaargentina.com
A useful website for finding and booking hotel accommodation.

www.hostels.org.ar
This is one of the best websites for tracking down youth hostels.

www.hostelsofargentina.com
This unofficial website has plenty of information about youth hostels.

www.estanciasargentinas.com
Information and booking for *estancias* throughout Argentina.

www.estanciasdesantacruz.com
Information and booking for *estancias* in Patagonia.

www.estanciasdebsas.com.ar
Information and booking for *estancias* in Buenos Aires.

SPECIAL INTEREST
www.argentinatango.com
This website gives advice about where to see tango and specialist information for enthusiasts.

www.argentinasanglers.com
This is the best website for finding out where to go angling in Argentina.

www.golfinargentina.com
Golfers will want to consult this website to find out where they can tee off.

www.termasdeargentina.com.ar
This website lists all of the spas and wellness centres in Argentina.

www.vinosdeargentina.com
Details about Argentine wines, *bodegas* and wine tours.

www.cha.org.ar
Tourist information for gay travellers.

DOCUMENTATION
www.fco.gov.uk
Travel advice from the UK Foreign and Commonwealth office.

www.travel.state.gov.uk
US Department of State travel advice.

PROVINCIAL TOURIST OFFICES IN BUENOS AIRES

TOWN/CITY	ADDRESS	TELEPHONE
Buenos Aires	Avenida Callao 237	011/4373-2636
Catamarca	Avenida Córdoba 2080	011/4374-6891
Chaco	Avenida Callao 322 Piso 1	011/4372-0961
Chubut	Sarmiento 1172	011/4382-8126
Córdoba	Avenida Callao 332	011/4372-8859
Corrientes	San Martín 333, Piso 4	011/4394-7390
Entre Ríos	Suipacha 844	011/4328-2284
Formosa	Hipólito Yrigoyen 1429	011/4381-2037
Jujuy	Avenida Santa Fé 967	011/4393-6096
La Rioja	Avenida Callao 745	011/4813-3417
Mendoza	Avenida Callao 445	011/4371-0835
Misiones	Avenida Santa Fé 989	011/4393-1812
Neuquén	Tte. Gral. Juan D. Perón 687	011/4311-9440
Río Negro	Tucumán 1916	011/4375-5489
Salta	Avenida Pte. Roque Sáenz Peña 933	011/4326-0501
San Juan	Sarmiento 1251	011/4382-5580
San Luis	Azcuénaga 1083/87	011/4822-0426
Santa Cruz	25 de Mayo 277, Piso 1	011/4334-8327
Santa Fé	Montevideo 373, Piso 2	011/4375-4570
Tierra del Fuego	Sarmiento 745, Piso 4	011/4325-5539
Tucumán	Suipacha 140	011/4322-0299

BUENOS AIRES TOURIST OFFICES

LOCATION	CONTACT DETAILS	OPENING TIMES
National Tourism Secretariat, Information Centre	Av. Santa Fé 883, tel. 011/4312-2232 or 0800/555-0016 (free calls)	
La Boca (Caminito)	Vapor de la Carrera, Pedro de Mendoza 1851	Fri–Sun 10–6
Puerto Madero	Avenida Alicia Moreau de Justo 200, tel 011/4313-0187	Mon–Fri 11–8, Sat–Sun 10–8
Microcentro	Florida and Diagonal Roque Sáenz Peña	Mon–Sat 9–6
Microcentro	Sarmiento 1551, tel 011/4372-3612	Mon–Fri 10–5
Microcentro	Carlos Pellegrini between Perón and Sarmiento	Mon–Fri 10–6
Micocentro: Café Tortoni	Av. de Mayo 829, tel 011/4342-4328	Mon–Fri 2–6
Retiro: Galerías Pacífico	Av. Córdoba and Florida, First level	Mon–Fri 10–7, Sat 11–7
Retiro bus terminal	Av. Antártida Argentina and Calle 10, Local 83	Mon–Sat 7.30am–1pm

COMMUNICATION

Argentina has a reasonably good telephone system but rates, especially for inter-regional and international calls, are high. The postal system is expensive and has a reputation for being unreliable but you'll find internet cafés and *locutorios* (public telephones and internet kiosks) everywhere in Argentina so it's fairly easy to stay in touch.

INTERNATIONAL DIALLING CODES

To call home from Argentina, dial 00, then the country's access code (see below). To call Argentina from your home country, dial 00 54 before the number.

Australia	61
Canada	1
New Zealand	64
Ireland	353
UK	44
US	1

USEFUL TELEPHONE NUMBERS

Police	101
Ambulance	107
Fire	100
Speaking clock	113
Directory enquiries	110
National operator	19
International dialling code	00
International operator	000

AREA CODES FOR MAJOR CITIES

Bariloche	02944
Buenos Aires	011
Córdoba	0351
Jujuy	0388
Mar del Plata	0223
Mendoza	0261
Neuquén	0299
Paraná	0343
Posadas	03752
Puerto Iguazú	03757
Río Gallegos	02966
Rosario	0341
Salta	0387
San Juan	0264
San Martín de los Andes	02972
Trelew	02965
Tucumán	0381
Ushuaia	02901

TELEPHONES

» Rates for calls from hotels are very high so avoid using the telephone in your room.

» You will spot a few public telephones (credit cards only) but most people use the public call centres *(locutorios)*, which are located at train stations, bus terminals, airports and most street corners.

» *Locutorios* often double up as internet centres, where you can send emails, make photocopies and buy drinks, snacks and sweets, too. Make sure you have change to pay for calls because large notes will not be appreciated or even accepted.

» Ask the employee at the *locutorio* for a phone booth *(cabina)* or a computer *(máquina)* if you need internet access. You will be assigned a number and there is a meter in each booth or cubicle, so you can keep track of your expenditure on calls or the internet.

» It is not always possible to call international or mobile phone numbers from *locutorios* or there might be a specific booth for making these calls.

» Kiosks, *locutorios* and Farmacity drugstores sell pre-paid phonecards called *Hablemás* and *Colibrí*, which cost $3.50 and are easy to use. Dial the telephone number on the card, scratch off the silver section and enter the number on the card. Using these cards reduces the cost of calling abroad but they are less advantageous if you are calling from outside Buenos Aires.

MOBILE PHONES

» You need a Triband phone for use in Argentina. Many phones in North America are not, so check with your mobile-phone provider before you leave to see if it will work in Argentina.

» Using your mobile is expensive in Argentina—even for text messages— so it is more economical to replace your SIM card with a local one for the duration of your stay. Sim cards are widely available and can be purchased at the airport on arrival.

» 3G coverage in Buenos Aires is very good.

Opposite *A post office (correo)*
Below *A public telephone*

counter. Envelopes should be clearly addressed as follows:
LAST NAME first name
Lista de Correos
Correo Argentino
Full address of post office including postcode
ARGENTINA

INTERNET ACCESS AND LOCUTORIOS

›› Argentina is well served by the internet and most companies, tourist offices, hotels and *estancias* have email addresses and websites.

›› There are *locutorios* all over Argentina but the quality of the computers and internet connections is highly variable.

›› Usually, you are assigned a computer by the receptionist and pay the amount displayed on the screen when you leave. Make sure you have change to pay.

›› If the keyboard is worn and you can't see the letters, ask for another computer because Spanish keyboards differ slightly from English-language ones.

›› Rates are relatively low (often as little as $1 an hour) but higher in tourist resorts or places where there is little competition (as much as $10 an hour).

WIFI AND LAPTOPS

›› WiFi is widespread in Argentina, especially in hotels. Some hotels will charge extra for the service, while others will make a desktop computer or their business centre available to guests for free.

›› Many hotels offer WiFi in rooms, while the service is also offered in many cafés.

›› If you intend to bring your laptop to Argentina, remember to bring a power converter to recharge it and a plug socket adaptor.

›› If you use an international internet service provider, such as AOL or Compuserve, it's cheaper to dial up a local node rather than the number you use at home.

›› Dial-tone frequencies vary from country to country, so set your modem to ignore dial tones.

SENDING A LETTER

›› Stamps *(estampillas)* are sold at post offices *(correos)* and, occasionally, at hotels and shops selling postcards. The rates for international mail are very high by world standards (see the chart below for postage rates).

›› The postal service in Argentina is fairly slow and unreliable, so it is always worthwhile sending important correspondence by a courier company, despite the extra cost. Postcards should arrive at their destination but may take a week or two at least to reach Europe and North America.

›› It is worth paying the extra for registered and express, though this can greatly increase the rate.

›› It is safer to hand in mail to the post office for dispatch rather than use the postal boxes.

POST OFFICES

›› The postal service is called Correo Argentino. Post offices and staff can be recognized by the company's dark blue and gold livery and logo.

›› Post offices are usually open Mon–Fri 9–6, Sat 9–1.

›› You can receive mail *poste restante* (general delivery) at any post office in Argentina. Make sure you have the full name and address of the post office before asking for mail to be sent there. Most post offices have a *Poste Restante* or *Lista de Correos*

POSTAGE RATES

Postage rates for a standard letter (maximum 50g) or postcard

Within Argentina	$1.50
To neighbouring countries	$25.00
To the rest of the Americas	$25.50
To the rest of the world	$26.00

COURIERS

DHL	Avenida Corrientes 315	www.dhl.com.ar
Federal Express	25 de Mayo 386	fedex.com/ar
UPS	Pte. Luis Saenz Peña 1351	www.ups.com

MEDIA

NEWSPAPERS

Argentina's press is very good, both at a national and regional level. The country's biggest-selling national newspapers are *La Nación*, *Clarín* and *Página 12*.

La Nación (www.lanacion.com) gives extensive political and financial coverage and an excellent weekend arts supplement with listings. *Clarín* (www.clarin.com) is the most serious and traditionally conservative broadsheet, renowned for the quality of its writing and doorstep-sized Sunday editions with travel and arts supplements. *Página 12* (www. pagina12.com.ar) has left-of-centre politics with pithy front pages and plenty of anti-establishment articles — no one escapes their sarcasm. Other publications you might find useful if you want to practise your Spanish include *Los Andes*, Mendoza's local newspaper (www.losandes.com.ar), *La Voz del Interior*, published in Córdoba (www.lavozdelinterior.com.ar) and *La Capital*, Rosario's newspaper, which is known for its top-notch journalism (www.lacapital.com.ar).

ENGLISH-LANGUAGE NEWSPAPERS

The Buenos Aires Herald (www. buenosairesherald.com) was first published in 1876, making it one of the oldest English-language newspapers in Latin America. The paper has changed hands frequently over the years and now belongs to an Argentine media mogul. The style is patchy but the standard is generally high. It is a great place to find out what the Anglo-Argentine community is up to, follow national and international news and find arts listings in English. It is widely available around the country, in large cities and tourist destinations.

MAGAZINES

It is usually possible to get *Newsweek* and *The Economist* at pavement news kiosks but if you want to practise your Spanish there is plenty of choice, too. *Lugares* (www.lugaresdeviaje.com) is a glossy travel magazine with English translations and practical information about resorts, hotels and restaurants. *Gente* and *Caras* are two of the most popular gossip magazines, although you might not be familiar with the TV presenters, polo players and *vedettes* (show girls) they feature in their pages.

TELEVISION

If you have a TV in your hotel room or apartment, you will probably have multi-channel cable. Coverage is inconsistent but usually includes a number of foreign-language channels, such as BBC World and CNN International, plus the CNN en Español. Domestic channels include *Clarín*-owned Todo Noticias (TN), which has rather repetitive round-the-clock news plus some interesting programmes on politics, sport and music, and good political analysis. Most of the other channels feature wall-to-wall sport, soaps or raucous chat shows.

RADIO

Argentina's many national and local radio stations broadcast a wide range of music, including tango and folk, as well as sport and chat shows, all in Spanish. Cadena 100 (99.9FM) has a good mix of Latin pop and provides easy listening for long road trips.

BOOKS, MAPS AND FILMS

BOOKS

Argentina has produced a number of internationally recognized novelists, such as Jorge Luis Borges. Equally, plenty of books have been written about Argentina, which provide valuable and entertaining insights into its culture and history.

FICTION

» *The Honorary Consul* by Graham Greene is a typical Greene thriller set in northern Argentina, near the porous Paraguayan border, with a line-up of radical priests, dissolute diplomats and misplaced expats.

» *Facundo*, or *Civilization and Barbarism* (*Facundo: Civilisación y Barbarie*) was written by Domingo F. Sarmiento, who became Argentina's seventh president. Sarmiento wrote this classic of national literature in 1845 and it tells the tale of a *gaucho* who terrorized provincial Argentina in the days shortly after independence.

» *Labyrinths* by Jorge Luis Borges, who is widely regarded as Argentina's best writer, is a collection of short stories and an excellent introduction to his work.

» *Hopscotch* (*Rayuela*) by Argentine author Julio Cortázar is a classic 1960s stream-of-consciousness novel written in Paris and offers the reader an alternative order in which to read the chapters.

» *The Story of the Night* by Colm Tóibín is the tale of a young Anglo-Argentine protagonist, who struggles with his national and sexual identity against a background of conflict and post-junta political turmoil.

NON-FICTION

» *In Patagonia* by Bruce Chatwin remains the most influential book about Patagonia and has a strong cult following even today, with larger-than-life characters that seem based more on imagination than real experiences.

» *The Old Patagonian Express* by Paul Theroux traces his train journey from New England to northern Patagonia where he ends up on the Esquel-based locomotive (▷ 160) that is now a tourist attraction.

» *The Uttermost Part of the Earth* by Lucas Bridges is a fascinating chronicle of the Bridges's family, who were missionaries that settled in Tierra del Fuego in the 1870s.

» *The Whispering Land* and *The Drunken Forest* by Gerald Durrell, the British naturalist and writer of *My Family and Other Animals*, are set in northwestern Argentina and Patagonia, respectively.

» *Wine Routes of Argentina* by Alan Young, published by the International Wine Academy, is an erudite publication that steers the reader around the vineyards of Argentina with competence and *savoir-faire*.

MAPS

The maps in this book should be enough to get you around Argentina. The national, regional and local tourist boards distribute fairly good maps of the country, regions, towns and cities and they are usually free of charge. You can also buy maps in shops and at fuel stations. The ACA provincial maps are usually worth buying but their regional editions are more difficult to read. YPF produces an excellent road atlas, the *Atlas Vial*, which is extremely detailed.

There are also some useful maps of the national parks, although you should get local advice about trails before setting out alone. If you require maps, you can obtain colour satellite maps at a scale of 1:100,000 from the Instituto Geográfico Nacional, Avenida Cabildo 381, Buenos Aires.

FILMS

Argentine cinema covers a range of genres, from deep philosophical movies manifestly influenced by French cinema to hilarious comedies. There have been waves of international success over the years, culminating in the 2010 Oscar win for the political drama *El secreto de sus ojos* (*The Secret in their Eyes*), directed by Juan José Campanella. The film starred Ricardo Darín, one of the country's most popular actors, who also starred in the hits *Nueve reinas* (*Nine Queens*, 2000), *El hijo de la novia* (*Son of the Bride*, 2001) and *XXY* (2007).

The only other Argentine film to have won the Oscar for Best Foreign Language Film (Argentina has been nominated six times) was Luis Puenzo's 1985 drama *La historia oficial* (*The Official Story*). The film stars two of Argentina's greatest actors, Héctor Alterio and Norma Leandro, and tells the story of an upper-class woman who discovers that her adopted child was the daughter of a disappeared couple.

Other directors to watch out for are Carlos Sorín, who directed *Historias mínimas* (*Minimal Stories*, 2002), and Lucrecia Martel, who won acclaim for *La ciénaga* (*The Swamp*) in 2001 and *La mujer sin cabeza* (*The Headless Woman*) in 2007.

Above *Browsing for books in the capital*
Opposite *A news-stand on Avenida 9 de Julio, Buenos Aires*

SHOPPING

The quality of leather goods, arts and crafts and many other products in Argentina is excellent, and it is worth leaving room in your suitcase to bring back a few must-have souvenirs. Argentines adore their shopping malls but, equally, you can find a plethora of small boutiques and specialized shops in every town. Food and wine are great buys, but always check first that you can import them to your country, especially in the case of meat. Wine, sold at prices noticeably lower than in North America, Europe and Australasia, is a particularly good buy—though difficult to transport home.

DEPARTMENT STORES AND SHOPPING MALLS

Shopping malls (shoppings) are very popular in Argentina, for their multitude of shops, late-night food patios, bars and cinemas. Most big towns have a shopping mall and there are several worth visiting in Buenos Aires. Most contain a range of Argentine chain stores as well as independent boutiques. International and designer brands are usually found in the larger, more exclusive malls in cities such as Buenos Aires.

There are a few department stores left in Argentina, although many have lost out to shopping malls—as is evident from the derelict Harrods building in Buenos Aires. Although there are still a couple of useful national department stores such as Falabella, which sells household goods, and Musimundo where you can buy a range of goods including CDs, books and electrical items.

CLOTHES

You can find some excellent clothing for sale in Argentina, including tango and gaucho wear, plus trendy outfits in designs you won't find anywhere else. Good-quality outdoor wear can be expensive in Argentina, so if you intend to go trekking or if adventure sports are on the agenda, ensure that you bring the appropriate clothes with you. Ponchos and other Andean woollens can be found in the North.

Garments made from precious alpaca and llama (vicuña) wool can be quite expensive but last for years.

HANDICRAFTS, CERAMICS AND TEXTILES

Mate paraphernalia and other crafts are sold at specialist shops and market stalls all over the country, often at festivals and fairs. Even if you don't drink mate, the receptacles make good souvenirs. Many objects such as masks and bowls are made of native woods, such as balsa-like palo borracho and warm-hued lapacho.

Some very fine ceramics and pottery are made in various parts of Argentina. In the North, it may be decorated with pre-Columbian designs, while the distinctive coal-black pots and vases sold around Nono in Córdoba province have a shiny glaze made with cow dung.

Rugs, blankets, ponchos and tablecloths of the highest quality make wonderful gifts. A wide range of designs and colours can be found across the country. In the North, you will find some of the finest textiles, made of llama and alpaca wool, while the beautiful merino sheep reared in Patagonia yield a soft fleece used to produce the finest woollen clothing and other items.

LEATHER AND JEWELLERY

Grazing cattle in the fertile pampas provide first-class leather as well as meat, which is made into some outstanding jackets, bags and footwear. Saddles and other riding equipment, including polo gear *(talabartería)*, are of the highest standard.

The national stone, rhodochrosite, a type of pretty pink onyx, is used for brooches and earrings. You can also find some fine silver, pewter and gold, plus endless amounts of excitingly original costume jewellery fashioned by skilled designers.

FOOD AND WINE

The main nationwide supermarket chains are low-priced Coto and the mid-range stores Disco or Jumbo, while the French-owned hypermarket chain Carrefour has megastores on the outskirts of nearly every city. Markets are usually a good place to pick up local produce for a picnic.

Many people become addicted to *dulce de leche* while they are in Argentina and you might like to take a jar or two with you when you go home. Alternatively, boxes of *alfajores* (biscuits sandwiched with *dulce de leche*) make good gifts. Bottles of wine are an excellent buy though

do think about how to get them home. The airport duty-free shops sell a bewildering range of wines and pack bottles safely for transporting. Vacuum-packed prime cuts of beef are also sold at Ezeiza. You will be given an import certificate for your destination but some countries limit amounts or have a total ban on the import of meat products.

PAYMENT, TAX REFUNDS AND SALES

Credit cards are widely accepted but you might get a discount if you pay cash. You might also need to show photo ID, such as your passport, when paying with plastic.

On departure, visitors from overseas can get the VAT refunded for purchases made at establishments displaying the TAX FREE shopping logo (▷ 305). Participants in the scheme are listed at www.globalrefund.com. These stores are mostly found in shopping malls, airports and tourist resorts.

Above *Tienda Diversia in San Telmo, BA*
Left *Plaza Independencia, Mendoza*

Argentines love going out and having a good time, whether it's a night at the theatre or an evening in a jazz joint, a rock concert or a few hours at a *milonga* or tango hall. Of course, the bigger the city, the more entertainment there will be on offer. Buenos Aires barely sleeps at the weekend, with a huge selection of events and nightlife venues on offer. Other major cities also have their fair share of opportunities but even small towns and villages will usually have at least one lively bar and a disco. In destinations like El Calafate, where many people like to get an early night in readiness for a long day's trekking, the casino often doubles up as the focus of nocturnal fun and games.

CINEMA

Argentines are avid moviegoers and are rightly proud of their film industry. Multiplex movie-houses, often located in shopping malls, have invaded just about every town and city in Argentina but there are still many independent cinemas and arts centres. Since subtitling is preferred to dubbing for all but the biggest blockbusters or some children's films, few films will pose a problem for non-Spanish speakers. Tickets are cheaper (around $25) than in Europe and North America, even more so on Wednesdays (discount day) or if you book online. Check national and regional press for listings.

CLASSICAL MUSIC, BALLET AND DANCE

Classical music is easiest to find in the capital, where the renovated Teatro Colón (▷ 100) attracts big names such as Yo-Yo Ma and András Schiff to show off its top-rate acoustics. But most towns and cities have an opera house and concert hall. Outstanding, in particular, are the bijou theatres in Jujuy (▷ 258) and Córdoba (▷ 221) and Salta's fabulous Teatro Provincial (▷ 258), which is home to one of the country's finest orchestras.

Although ballet star Julio Bocca has officially retired, his Ballet Argentino lives on, maintaining a strong tradition. The Teatro Colón has always enjoyed a solid reputation for classical dance, while Argentina's latest gift to ballet, Iñaki Urlezaga, started out at the prestigious Teatro Argentino de La Plata and now performs and choreographs around the world. If he is dancing in Buenos Aires, go and see him.

Naturally tango supersedes all other dance forms in Argentina, but salsa and folk dancing are also on offer at nightclubs and *peñas* all over the country. The annual Buenos Aires Danza Contemporanea festival is held in a number of locations around the city (www.buenosairesdanza.gob.ar).

TANGO

Born in the lowly docklands of Buenos Aires at the end of the 19th century, Argentina's emblematic dance, tango, now has millions of fans all around the world. In the midst of a major revival in its home city, the popularity of tango has spread around the country and become a lucrative tourist attraction. Many visitors to the country build their stay around tango classes—of which there are plenty to choose from—or an international event, such as the Festival y Mundial del Tango (▷ 115), held annually in August in the capital.

The moody music that accompanies the sensuous sliding and acrobatic footwork of tango is

an art form in its own right—and ageism is not allowed, with many of the top-name bands and orchestras having an average age of between 70 and 80 years. There are several historic venues in the capital and tango music is often heard in the streets, too.

CONTEMPORARY LIVE MUSIC

Rock nacional, as Argentine rock is known, is very popular but bands and solo artists from English-speaking countries also have huge followings. After a few lean years following the 2001 crisis, the country's stadiums and big venues (mainly in the capital) have been pulling in crowds to concerts by all of the top stars, including Madonna and Oasis. The line-up at the Buenos Aires Creamfields, held in either November or December, invariably includes local lad Hernán Cattaneo, one of the world's leading house DJs. Keep a lookout for flyers, posters and advertisements in the national and local press.

FOLK AND JAZZ

There is a vibrant folk tradition in Argentina, especially in the Litoral, where polka-flavoured chamamé livens up every festivity and is often shown off to tourists. The North is the home of folklore and you should try to save at least one evening for a visit to a peña, the folk clubs that abound in cities like Salta (▷ 240–243, 256) and Tucumán (▷ 246, 258).

Jazz is more of a minority interest but there are a few excellent jazz lounges around the country, the best being the Thelonious Club in Palermo (▷ 113), although all the big cities have a place where jazz can be heard. Any performances by pianist Adrián laies are worth checking out.

THEATRE

Argentine theatre, both classical and avant-garde, is truly excellent but unless your Spanish is up to it you might find the drama hard to follow. Buenos Aires's answer to Broadway, Avenida Corrientes, is the country's theatrical epicentre.

LISTINGS

You can find full listings in the two main national newspapers, La Nación (www.lanacion.com.ar) and Clarín (www.clarin.com), plus a more limited selection in the Buenos Aires Herald, though the latter obviously targets English-speakers. The regional and local press are fertile sources of information while tourist offices will usually have a list of events, sometimes published in a booklet or free magazine.

To save visiting the venue itself, you could take advantage of the various ticket services available. Two reliable ticket agents are Cartelera Baires (Avenida Corrientes 1382, local 24 Buenos Aires; tel 011/4372-5058; www.cartelerabaires.com) and Ticketek (Viamonte 560 Buenos Aires; tel 011/5237-7200; www.ticketek.com.ar).

BARS AND NIGHTCLUBS

Argentines pride themselves on being able to stay out all night and there are plenty of chances to follow suit. Friday and Saturday nights are 24-hour events in most towns and cities, with late-night dining, discos and a host of after-hours venues that keep going past breakfast. Bars and pubs are extremely popular, with something to suit every taste in all urban centres, ranging from old-fashioned confiterías (a kind of brasserie), where regulars sip a coffee or knock back a couple of beers, to designer bars with baristas concocting elaborate cocktails. In rural areas you might still find a traditional pulpería, the haunt of gauchos, with plenty of Fernet (a herby liqueur) and Coca-Cola on tap. Although drunkenness is not unheard of, Argentines tend to eat whenever they drink and public displays of alcohol-induced loss of control are still frowned upon.

The downtown district (microcentro) of most towns and cities is usually where you'll find bars and Irish pubs, often formica-and-neon dives where the name of the game is a quick drink. In Buenos Aires, trendy Puerto

Madero (▷ 91) is the place to be seen, with a number of fashionable establishments, and Palermo (▷ 84–87) overflows with bars and small clubs. The Palermo riverfront, away from residential areas, has plenty of discos, which range from hangar-like giants to more select clubs with strict dress codes (smart casual or slinky) and rigorous door controls. Other cities each have their trendy districts—Pichincha in Rosario, Chateau Carreras in Córdoba and the Balcarce in Salta—while larger nightclubs are often on the outskirts. There will usually be someone at the tourist office that can tell you where to go, to suit your taste.

GAY AND LESBIAN NIGHTLIFE

There has been a change in attitudes towards homosexuality in Argentina, especially in the cities. Under the 1976–1983 dictatorship gays were persecuted but Buenos Aires now promotes itself as the leading pink destination in Latin America. Discrimination is illegal and marriage between members of the same sex, with full adoption rights, was passed into legislation in July 2010.

Away from the capital, the number of gay bars and nightclubs is fairly low. Mendoza elects a gay wine harvest queen every autumn and Córdoba has one or two good discos. While there are only a handful of specifically gay and lesbian hotels and restaurants, mainly in the capital, increasing numbers make a point of being gay-friendly. For self-catering apartments for gay and lesbian visitors, visit www.ba4uapartments.com.ar.

In Buenos Aires, there are several gay and lesbian venues, listed together with events in the main gay publication, La Otra Guía, distributed free. Information can also be obtained from the useful Gmap (www.Gmaps360.com), given away at shops and restaurants all over the city.

Opposite An evening to remember—a tango display at Esquina Homero Manzi, a Buenos Aires institution

SPORTS AND ACTIVITIES

Anyone interested in animal rights will be pleased to know that bullfighting was banned in Argentina in the early 20th century but there are plenty of sports and other activities to watch and take part in. Soccer is an obsession in Argentina, while golf, polo and tennis are also popular. Keeping fit is something many Argentines take seriously, so there are plenty of gyms plus opportunities for riding, swimming and hiking across the country. The country's great rivers, mountain streams and lakes make angling a huge attraction.

FISHING
You must get a permit to have a go at landing that record-weight brown trout or delicious *pacú* for your dinner. All along the river Paraná in Corrientes Province, the rivers and lakes of Patagonia and Tierra del Fuego are the prime locations. Permits are available from tourist offices and some petrol stations.

FOOTBALL
Football is omnipresent in Argentine life and everyone is expected to support a club and have favourite players. The capital's two biggest clubs, River Plate, based in the affluent northern *barrio*, and Boca Juniors, with its famed La Bombonera (▷ 72) stadium in the working-class south of Buenos Aires, divide the city and the country. Other Porteño teams, plus the squads representing just about every city,

have mass followings, too. The 20 teams in the top-flight premier division play two tournaments, the Clausura from February to June and the Apertura from August to December. Travel agencies can organize match tickets and it is wise to go with knowledgeable guides, although violence is less frequent than the media like to claim.

GOLF
Since Ángel Cabrera won the US Open in 2007, golf has enjoyed greater popularity in his home country. Argentina has some superb courses, including in Buenos Aires, Córdoba Province and Salta.

GYMS AND FITNESS
Keeping fit is important for most Argentines and you will see many joggers in the parks, gardens and streets, or even way out in the

country. Gyms are plentiful and reasonably priced, even for a day pass, and opening hours are often long, usually 8am to 10pm, six or seven days a week. Pilates classes are widespread and hiring a personal trainer is within the financial reach of most overseas visitors. Ask for information at the gym.

HORSEBACK RIDING
Horses are perhaps more numerous than bicycles and there is little of the elitism associated with horseback riding to be found in many other countries. Equestrian holidays are easy to arrange, while *cabalgatas* (tours on horseback)—from an hour or two to several days—are an excellent way of seeing the countryside. The technique (one rein only) and some of the equipment (such as the saddles) may differ from what you are used to, but most

Opposite Fans celebrate at La Bombonera, home of the legendary Boca Juniors

stables take safety very seriously and Argentina is an excellent place to learn to ride. The *gaucho* culture means there are plenty of opportunities to watch horsemanship at its most impressive, particularly in the *estancias* of Buenos Aires and the mountains of Salta, Córdoba and Nuequén provinces.

POLO AND *PATO*

Polo and the related *gaucho* sport of *pato*, originally played with a live duck but long since exchanged for a ball with handles, are widespread in Argentina. Experienced riders might like to try their hand at polo, and many *estancias* lay on classes. If you prefer to watch rather than take part, the Palermo ground stages a year-end tournament or you might like to watch a match at the Hurlingham polo club (www.hurlinghamclub.org. ar), just outside the city, where the season is longer.

SPAS

Wellness is big business in Argentina and many hotels vaunt their spas and beauty treatments, which tend to be far more affordable than in other countries. Natural springs feed thermal baths at various locations around the country, such as Colón in Entre Ríos (▷ 270) and Fiambalá (▷ 235) in Catamarca. You might have to consult a physician first, although the examination is usually a formality. The cure resort of Termas de Río Hondo is a somewhat depressing place and best avoided.

SWIMMING AND DIVING

Argentina's beaches do not equal those in Brazil, but some of the country's river and lakeside *balnearios* (bathing resorts) have refreshing waters, excellent amenities and attract large crowds. Many hotels and apartments have swimming pools and most towns have a municipal or privately run swimming pool, although these vary in quality and price, and get very busy in warm

weather. Puerto Madryn (▷ 134) is the country's diving capital and it is very well organized.

TENNIS

Many hotels and *estancias* have tennis courts, nearly always clay. The Buenos Aires Lawn Tennis Club hosts the national open championship, the Abierto de Buenos Aires or Copa Claro, every February and local hero Guillermo Vilas has won a record eight times.

WALKING AND HIKING

Walking and hiking are the principal attractions in the national parks, not least the Parque Nacional Los Glaciares (▷ 166–168), in the Fitz Roy sector around El Chaltén. Trekking with an experienced guide or group is recommended as trails are not always well marked and the terrain and climate can be testing. A number of highly professional outfits organize treks to the various national parks (see regional listings for details).

Below *Seeing Argentina's marine fauna from underwater is an unforgettable experience*

FOR CHILDREN

Children are worshipped in Argentina, which has a higher-than-average birth rate for an industrialized country. The second Sunday in August is El Día del Nino (Children's Day), when little ones get spoiled rotten and there are events, such as puppet shows or toy fairs, around the country. Travelling with children is seldom problematic as tolerance of children is high and it is usually easy to find a reliable babysitter. Most hotels are happy to add a cot or small bed to your room. Children's menus in restaurants are very common and most children will love the delicious cakes and ice creams, which are available across the country. There are some child-specific attractions, while the wonderful opportunities to see wildlife will fascinate travellers of all ages.

FAMILY-FRIENDLY DESTINATIONS

There is not much point in coming to Argentina for a beach holiday because you will find warmer water and silkier sand in Brazil and the Caribbean. But if your children are demanding sea and sand, you will find that most of the *balnearios* along the Atlantic cater for young and old alike.

Each region has elements that children will find fun. Special tourist trains are one example: the Tren de la Costa in Buenos Aires (▷ 106–107); the Tren del Fin del Mundo in Tierra del Fuego (▷ 147); the Tren a las Nubes in Salta (▷ 254–255); and the Old Patagonian Express (also known as La Trochita) in Esquel (▷ 160).

White-water rafting and cycling, horseback riding and trekking appeal to older children and teenagers. Spectator sports, such as football and polo, may also appeal to families. If you go to a soccer match get advice

about the best place for children in the stadium when buying your tickets and book through an agency or your hotel.

Many museums around the country have special facilities for children, such as guided visits, safe playgrounds or specific areas with interactive exhibits. Zoos, gardens and parks are usually winning choices for children but they might enjoy shopping, too. There are plenty of clothes boutiques, bookstores and toyshops that will delight youngsters from tots to adolescents.

THEME PARKS

The two best theme parks for children lie within a short radius of Buenos Aires. Parque de la Costa (▷ 114), at the end of the Tren de la Costa in the sultry suburb of Tigre, offers a dazzling array of rides and other fun stuff. The other is a wildlife park, Temaikèn (▷ 114), 50km (31 miles) northwest of the capital,

where pumas and tapirs are housed in roomy enclosures.

CITIES

Buenos Aires, with its parks, is an enjoyable place for children but the Argentine city that does most to entertain little travellers is Rosario. In addition to the city's riverside beaches and a fabulous urban park, the Parque de la Independencia (▷ 281), children have three specific attractions of the highest calibre at their disposal. The Isla de los Inventos (▷ 283) is an excellent didactic museum housed in the old train station. The Granja de la Infancia (▷ 294) is a farm where little ones can get up close to goats and capybaras. The third one is the Jardín de los Niños (▷ 283), a fabulous playground that teaches the young about everyday phenomena such as gravity and balance.

Below *Taking time out for a kick-about*

FESTIVALS AND EVENTS

Wherever you happen to be in Argentina, regardless of the time of year, you are bound to stumble across a festival. Many of these are related to a locally revered saint or image of the Virgin Mary, and will involve colourful processions of the kind most people associate freely with Latin America. Others are more secular in nature and might revolve around typical produce—cherries, walnuts or tobacco, for example. Music is often central to celebrations or some kind of craftsmanship might be the main theme, as in the national poncho festival in Catamarca.

RELIGIOUS

Holy Week is celebrated with more gusto than Christmas and religious festivals are extremely important in this Catholic country. Often it is syncretism with pre-Columbian beliefs that produces the most interesting rituals. For example, in the North, *Carnaval*, Easter and saints' days are excuses for noisy celebrations, with much banging of drums and dressing up in elaborate costumes and feather headdresses.

TRADITIONAL

A number of traditional red-letter days punctuate the year and most are related to agricultural products, such as grapes or watermelons, or celebrate *gaucho* customs or *criollo* culture, such as horse riding or *mate*. The best fiestas are held in the pampas of Buenos Aires Province, in the North and in Córdoba Province.

ARTS

The main arts and tango events are held in Buenos Aires, though a good many music festivals take place in the provinces.

THE BIGGEST AND BEST
Carnaval de Gualeguaychú
(▷ 295)
Weekends from February to early March see the sleepy Litoral town of Gualeguaychú come alive as music and dance schools compete for a prestigious prize in the Corsódromo .
Fiesta Nacional de la Vendimia
(▷ 223)
This mega Wine Harvest Festival takes over the city of Mendoza every autumn, on the first weekend of March, with every hotel bed occupied for the week-long event that culminates in the election of a harvest queen in the amphitheatre in the city's Parque General San Martín.
Buenos Aires Festival Internacional de Cine Independiente (▷ 115)
One of the major independent film festivals in Latin America attracts movie fans and hordes of actors, directors and wannabes to Buenos Aires in early April.
ArteBA (▷ 115)
Held in late June, ArteBA is a week-long celebration of contemporary art from Argentina and around the world in Palermo, Buenos Aires.
Fiesta Nacional e Internacional del Poncho (▷ 259)
For more than four decades poncho makers from all over Argentina have flocked to Catamarca for the last two weeks in July to enjoy folk music, traditional food and drink and lots of family fun.
Fiesta del Milagro (▷ 259)
Every year in early September, Salta celebrates the miracle of 1692, when religious icons were paraded in the streets following a series of strong earthquakes, and the city was saved. The same images of the Virgin and Christ are the centrepiece of colourful processions.
Día de la Tradición (▷ 115)
On 10 November, the birthday of José Hernández, author of *Martín Fierro*, the *gaucho* epic poem that every Argentine studies at school, is feted countrywide. In San Antonio de Areco, the festivities last a whole week, with *asados* and displays of *gaucho* horsemanship.

Above *Bicentennial celebrations*

EATING

Argentina is famous for its wonderful, locally reared beef and the standard of fare, whether you are eating in a humble *parilla* or a gourmet restaurant, is usually very high. The foundation of Argentina's cuisine is, of course, Spanish and paella and tortillas are very popular. Equally, Italian cuisine has also influenced national tastes and excellent pasta dishes and pizza are available everywhere. As you explore Argentina, there are a few regional differences. In the North, for example, menus feature more Andean specialities using products such as quinoa, corn, llama and goat's cheese, while in Atlantic Patagonia expect to see plenty of fresh seafood on the menu. Argentine wines, especially the rich malbecs, marry perfectly with the country's delicious beef.

MEALTIMES

Desayuno (breakfast) for most Argentines is a *café con leche* and a *medialuna* (milky coffee and a croissant), but most good hotels usually put on an impressive (US-style) buffet, which may include *tocino* (bacon) and eggs. *Almuerzo* (lunch) is quite late and eating anytime between noon and 3pm is quite usual. The lunchtime set menu *(menú del día)* usually represents good value for money.

Merienda (afternoon tea) is a popular custom, partly because dinner is served so late. Sandwiches, scones and cakes are often served between 4 and 5pm at upper-end establishments and *estancias*. *Cena* (dinner) is often very late in Argentina. In big cities and holiday resorts, don't be surprised to see families turning up to eat as late as midnight. Restaurants usually start serving around 8pm but most Argentines dine much later.

WHERE TO EAT AND WHAT TO EXPECT

Confiterías fall somewhere between a café and a modest restaurant, serving hot and cold drinks, breakfasts and plain wholesome food, such as pasta or *lomitos* (beef sandwiches), all day. *Bodegones* and *cantinas* are down-to-earth neighbourhood taverns specializing in *tapas* or Italian cuisine, such as pasta and tiramisu. *Restaurantes* vary enormously from unpretentious hole-in-the-wall establishments to gourmet extravaganzas with famous chefs, exciting menus and prices to go with their reputations. There are thousands of *pizzerías* across the country and Argentine pizzas are extremely good. If you are especially hungry, try a *tenedor libre*, where you can eat as much as you want, though you might have to order and pay for some dishes, such as steaks, separately. *Parrillas* are temples to the cow and every part of the beast is served. If you prefer, however, you can cut straight to the best steaks and leave out the sweetbreads and blood sausage. Remember to ask for your meat *jugoso* (rare) if you don't want it overcooked. Portions can be huge so don't be shy about asking for a doggy bag *(¿Lo puedo llevar?)*.

CAFÉS AND TEA ROOMS

Cafés and *confiterías* are open all day, mostly seven days a week, making them ideal places to have breakfast or grab a snack outside normal mealtimes. Argentines rarely drink without eating and a glass of beer or wine will usually come with some peanuts, potato crisps or other nibbles.

Salas de té (tea rooms) are mostly to be found in chic neighbourhoods such as Recoleta (▷ 92–93) in Buenos Aires or in the Welsh tea rooms of Gaiman (▷ 129). The quality of scones and tortas (cakes and pies) is usually exceptional and will keep you satisfied until dinner.

REGIONAL VARIATIONS

In the Lake District, in particular, game is often on the menu, while native animals such as nandú (rhea), yacaré (caiman) and vicuña (llama) are increasingly found on restaurant menus around the country. River fish are much appreciated, ranging from salmon and trout to the less familiar surubí (South American catfish) and pacú (related to the piranha). A vegetable on many restaurant menus is acelga (chard), a tough-stemmed spinach-like leaf often made into tartas (quiches). Most fruits will be instantly recognizable but the calafate shrub, native to southern Patagonia, produces delicious purple berries, which are often made into jams, jellies and ice cream.

The northwest of the country has perhaps the most distinctive cuisine of any region and locally grown maize, quinoa, ancient potato varieties and llama meat form the basis of hearty fare, which is welcome on cold evenings up in the altiplano (high plains).

INTERNATIONAL CUISINE

Outside Buenos Aires and some of the big cities, the nearest to international cuisine that you'll find will be a pizza or American-style hamburger. In the capital, however, the restaurants are highly sophisticated with Indian food and sushi increasingly available. Other countries whose culinary specialities are represented in the city include France, Poland, Brazil, Mexico, Lebanon and Germany.

Although beef is synonymous with Argentine food, it is becoming easier to find good vegetarian fare, notably in Buenos Aires. The quality of fruit and vegetables, cheese and eggs makes for a delicious meatless diet.

LOCAL CUSTOMS

Smoking is not allowed in restaurants and cafés in Buenos Aires and some of the provinces. Elsewhere, you may find a full or partial (voluntary) ban in restaurants but not in cafés.

It is quite common for the television to be on in confiterías and other modest establishments.

The better the restaurant the smarter the dress code but you will seldom be required to wear a jacket and tie. If you are invited to someone's house, a box of facturas will be appreciated as well as flowers or wine. You can buy these popular sweet pastries at any good confitería.

The Spanish for bill (check) is cuenta, though the waiter or waitress may ask '¿Le cobro?' ('May I charge you?'). Service is seldom included and it is usual to leave a (5–10 per cent) tip. Note that modest and rural restaurants might only accept cash, not credit cards. Any extras, such as service or a cover charge, must be indicated on the menu.

WHAT TO DRINK

Coffee (café) is excellent in Argentina and is served in bars, confiterías and cafés. If you ask for a coffee, expect to get an espresso, sometimes called a cafecito (small coffee), often served with a glass of water, a small glass of orange juice and biscuits. Otherwise, ask for café con leche (milky coffee) or café cortado (coffee with a little milk). Tea (té) is also quite popular, although it is usually served as a cup or glass of hot water with a teabag. Some tea is grown in Argentina and can be quite aromatic. Herbal infusions such as manzanilla (camomile) and boldo (a bay-like native tree) are frequently available. Mate is the national drink, a hot stimulating infusion made from the leaves of a holly-related tree, served in special cups (matecitos) and sucked through a straw (bombilla) that strains out the yerba (leaves). Fruit juices are very popular—orange, apple and grapefruit are the most common—and frescamente exprimido means freshly squeezed. Gaseosas (fizzy drinks) are drunk in

large quantities and cerveza (beer) is found everywhere. Much of it is industrially brewed lager, with Quilmes taking three-quarters of the market and Heineken a distant second. Salta has its own brand, called Salta. You can also find excellent real ale (cerveza artesanal) at various locations around the country. A standard glass of draft beer is known as a chopp or, in some areas, a liso.

Wine (vino) ranges from vino patero, inexpensive table wine, to fine vintages that sell for several hundred pesos a bottle. It is increasingly possible to have a glass (copa) but few bodegas sell half-bottles. The grape-growing areas of the North also produce a very drinkable spirit, aguardiente, which tastes somewhere between brandy and grappa. The favourite liqueur is Fernet (Branca), a dark herby concoction originating in Italy and usually mixed with Coca-Cola. Although cocktails (cocteles) are much appreciated, there is no typical Argentine concoction but Mexican margarita, Chilean pisco sour and Brazilian caipirinha are found in bars around the country.

Opposite Freshly baked bread for sale at Masamadre es con M café in Buenos Aires
Below A platter of cold meats and cheese

MENU READER

Above *Küar bar and restaurant, Ushuaia*

Although the menu *(carta)* in tourist resorts will often be in English, you cannot rely on it being in any language but Spanish. Even if you do speak Spanish you may find that a number of the words are unfamiliar, especially as culinary vocabulary tends to vary a lot from one Hispanic country to another. For example, *papa* is used for potato not *patata*. It is worth noting also that the word *menú* means fixed meal, as in *menú del día* (day's menu) or *menú ejecutivo* (business lunch).

COURSES AND HEADINGS
aperitivo appetizer
aves y caza poultry and game
carta de vinos wine list
cubierto cover charge
dulces y postres desserts and puddings
ensalada salad
entrada starter

pan bread
plato del día dish of the day
plato principal main dish
sopa soup

FOOD PREPARATION
ahumado smoked
a la casa in the house style
asado roasted
cocido boiled
frito fried
grillé, a la plancha grilled

CARNES (MEAT)
bife steak
bife de chorizo rump steak
cabrito goat
carne (de vaca) beef
cerdo pork
ciervo venison
conejo rabbit
fiambres cold cuts
jamón (crudo) (raw) ham
lomo tenderloin beef
nandú rhea or ostrich
pato duck
pavo turkey
pollo chicken
rana frog
vicuña llama
yacaré caiman

PESCADOS (FISH)
abadejo cod
anchoa anchovy
atún tuna

corvina sea bass
dorado golden dorado (river fish)
lenguado sole
merluza hake
pacú delicious fish related to piranha
pejerrey a soft-fleshed freshwater fish
salmon (ahumado) (smoked) salmon
surubí South American catfish
trucha trout

MARISCOS (SEAFOOD)
camarones shrimp/prawns
cangrejo crab
centolla king crab
langosta lobster
mejillones mussels
ostras oysters
vieiras scallops

PRODUCTOS LÁCTEOS Y HUEVOS (DAIRY PRODUCTS AND EGGS)
manteca butter
crema cream
huevos eggs
leche milk
queso cheese
yogur yogurt

VERDURAS (VEGETABLES)
aceituna olive
acelga chard
alcauciles artichokes
Apio celery
arvejas peas
berenjena aubergine
cebolla onion
champiñón, hongo mushroom
chaucha green bean
choclo maize/sweetcorn
coliflor cauliflower
espinaca spinach
garbanzo chickpea
hinojo fennel
lechuga lettuce
lentejas lentils
morrón sweet pepper
palmito palm heart
palta avocado
papa (frita) potato
(chips/French fries)
poroto bean
puerro leek
remolacha beetroot
rúcula rocket
tomate tomato
zanahoria carrot
zapallo pumpkin
zapallito gem squash

PLATOS TRADICIONALES (TRADITIONAL DISHES)
carbonara/guiso/charqui
wind-dried meat (usually llama)
choripán grilled sausage sandwich
chorizo meat sausage, grilled
and served hot
empanadas hot pasties filled
with meat or cheese
estofado/locro different types
of hearty stew
humita creamed sweetcorn
and cheese steamed in corn husks
lomito beef sandwich served
with chips
milanesa schnitzel
morcilla black (blood) pudding
parrillada selection of grilled offal
and meat
provoleta provolone cheese grilled
on a barbecue
puchero meat stew like French
pot-au-feu

tamales corn balls stuffed
with chopped meat and cooked
in corn husks
vittel tonné slices of cooked
veal served in a tuna mayonnaise
with capers

CONDIMENTOS (CONDIMENTS)
aceite (de oliva) (olive) oil
ají chilli
ajo garlic
albahaca basil
alcaparras capers
azúcar sugar
chimichurri parsley and garlic sauce
for barbecues
mostaza mustard
perejil parsley
pimienta pepper
pimentón paprika
sal salt
salsa (criolla) sauce (tomato-based
for barbecue)
tomillo thyme
vinagre vinegar

FRUTAS (FRUIT)
almendra almond
ananá pineapple
arándano cranberry/blueberry
avellana hazelnut
banana banana
batata sweet potato
castaña chestnut
cereza cherry
ciruela plum
dátiles dates
damasco apricot
dulce de cayote
candied spaghetti squash
durazno peach
frambuesa raspberry
frutilla strawberry
higo fig
lima lime
limón lemon
maní peanuts
manzana apple
melón melon
membrillo quince
naranja orange
nuez walnut
pasa de uva raisin
pera pear
pomelo grapefruit

quinoto kumquat
sandía watermelon
uva grape

DULCES Y POSTRES (SWEETS AND PUDDINGS)
alfajores chocolate- or sugar-coated
biscuit sandwiches filled with jam or
dulce de leche
arroz con leche rice pudding
budín de pan bread pudding
crema custard
dulce de leche milk jam
(caramel in a jar)
dulce vigilante fresh cheese
with candied fruit
ensalada de fruta fruit salad
facturas sweet pastries
flan creme caramel
helado ice cream
medialuna (dulce/salado) sweet/
plain croissant
mermelada jam
miel honey
panqueque pancake
sambayón zabaglione (often ice
cream flavour)
torta tart or cake

BEBIDAS (DRINKS)
agua mineral con/sin gas
sparkling/still mineral water
aguardiente grappa- or
brandy-like spirit
café coffee
café con leche coffee with milk
café cortado coffee with little milk
(macchiato)
café descafeinado
decaffeinated coffee
cerveza beer
clericó sangría made with
white wine
hielo ice
gaseosa fizzy drink
jugo de naranja orange juice
jugo de manzana apple juice
leche milk
licuado milkshake or liquidized juice
té tea
submarino hot milk with
chocolate bar
vino blanco white wine
vino tinto red wine

The quality and range of accommodation in Argentina has improved beyond recognition in recent years. At the budget end, you can stay in lively youth hostels and simple *residenciales* (self-catering apartments) in towns and *cabañas* or bungalows in more rural areas. Luxurious *estancias* (traditional ranches also known as *fincas*) and five-star hotels are at the top end of the price range and yet can be extremely good value for money by international standards. Special to Argentina, *estancias* tend to offer home-from-home accommodation with gourmet food, polo classes and all manner of activities in beautiful grounds. *Estancias* in Patagonia, however, tend to be more authentic and rustic and many are still working ranches.

ACCOMMODATION

Hotels in Argentina have star ratings (one to five), but there are provincial differences and, as always, the system can seem arbitrary. Most hotels offer single and double rooms, plus triples and quadruples or the possibility of joining two bedrooms for families—it is usually possible to have an extra bed or cot added to your room. The term boutique hotel applies to small establishments (no more than a dozen rooms), usually in towns, where the decor and comfort are extra special and the service is personalized.

Posadas and *hosterías* are small or medium-sized upper-end options, generally family-run with lots of character and a good *posada* is usually more appealing than a low-end hotel. *Hospedajes*, *hostales* and *residenciales* are different names for more modest places to stay and are classified A, B or C,

Opposite Hostería Rincón del Socorro, *Esteros del Iberá*
Below Küar bar and restaurant, Ushuaia

though again these grades can be misleading. Services vary, too, and some rooms may not have their own bath, so it is always worth checking with the hotel before making a booking. Good websites that list accommodation in Argentina are www.destinationargentina.com, www.nativacollection.com and www.welcomeargentina.com. For *estancias* consult: www. estanciasargentinas.com, www. estanciasdesantacruz.com or www.estanciasdebsas.com.ar.

SELF-CATERING

Self-catering apartments are often an excellent idea if you are staying for any length of time in a big city, especially Buenos Aires. There are also *aparthotels*, a hybrid between a hotel and an apartment because the rooms have kitchenettes. *Cabañas* are bungalows or villas, which often have plenty of space but vary enormously in terms of quality, service and price. Try www.4rentargentina.com, www. luxuryba.com, www.ba4uapartments. com.ar or www.bytargentina.com.

CAMPSITES

Camping is very popular in Argentina and might prove the only viable option on long treks, but site quality is extremely unreliable. Some campsites *(campings)* are owned by the municipality and often offer very basic facilities, while others are on private property with swimming pools and showers. Most sites get very crowded in the summer months, so call ahead or arrive early to be sure of a place. If you are planning to

camp you can get information at www.voydecamping.com.ar, www.solocampings.com.ar and www.acampante.com.

YOUTH HOSTELS

Known as *albergues de juventud* or hostels, this budget-style accommodation is plentiful in Argentina. Just about every town has at least one hostel and in larger destinations you can usually choose between a number of establishments. Many hostels offer simple single or double rooms, sometimes with en-suite bathrooms, in addition to dorms. Members of Hostelling International normally get a small discount but membership is seldom compulsory. For useful information on hostels in Argentina visit www.hostels.org.ar and www. hostelsofargentina.com.

PRICING

There is usually a high season and low season, which varies from destination to destination but Christmas, Easter and July tend to be high season. Note that more expensive hotels, especially in southern Argentina, quote their prices in US dollars. As always, clarify whether the $ sign means US dollars or pesos and whether value-added tax (IVA) is included in the quoted rate. You will often get a discount by paying cash, equally many hotels ask for a deposit for reservations, which may involve cumbersome bank transactions but they may make an exception if you explain that you are an overseas visitor.

PRACTICALITIES STAYING

Once you have mastered a few basic rules, Spanish is an easy language to speak. It is a phonetic language and, unlike English, particular combinations of letters are always pronounced the same way. When a word ends in a vowel, 'n' or 's', the stress is usually on the penultimate syllable; otherwise, it falls on the last syllable. If a word has an accent, this is where the stress falls. There are a few differences between the Spanish spoken in Argentina (always referred to as *castellano*) and the version you may know from Spain. In addition to some noticeable pronunciation changes (above all, 'll' and 'y' sounding like the 's' in treasure, and no lisping 'z' or 'c'), the main differences are in everyday vocabulary (especially food, drink and clothing) plus a major grammatical peculiarity, the use of *vos* instead of *tú*, the informal word for you.

a	as in	**pat**
e	as in	**set**
i	as e in	**be**
o	as in	**hot**
u	as in	**flute**
ai, ay	as i in	**side**
au	as ou in	**out**
ei, ey	as ey in	**they**
oi, oy	as oy in	**boy**

Consonants as in English except:
g before i or e as h in **hello** (slightly more guttural)
gü as w in **well**
h is silent
j as **h** in **hello** (slightly more guttural)
ll as **s** in **treasure**
ñ as **ny** in **canyon**
qu is hard like a **k**
r is rolled—more so at the beginning of a word or when double
v is a **b** (though softens to v in some words)
y as **s** in **treasure** at the beginning or between vowels
z is an **s**

COLOURS

black	negro
blue	azul
brown	marrón
gold	dorado
green	verde
orange	naranja
pink	rosa
purple	morado
red	colorado
silver	plateado
white	blanco
yellow	amarillo

CONVERSATION

What is the time?
¿Qué hora es?
I don't speak Spanish
No hablo castellano
Do you speak English?
¿Habla inglés?
I don't understand
No entiendo
Please repeat that
Por favor repita eso
Please speak more slowly
Por favor hable más despacio
What does this mean?
¿Qué significa esto?
Can you write that for me?
¿Me lo puede escribir?
Good morning/afternoon
Buen día/buenas tardes
Good evening/night
Buenas noches
Goodbye
Adiós/chau
That's all right
Está bien
I don't know
No lo sé
Don't mention it
De nada

USEFUL WORDS

yes	sí
no	no
please	por favor
thank you	gracias
fine	bien
there	allí
where	dónde
here	acá
when	cuándo
who	quien
how	cómo
free (no charge)......	gratis
I'm sorry	Lo siento
excuse me	permiso
large	grande
small	chico
good	bueno
bad	malo

TIMES AND DAYS

morning	la mañana
afternoon	la tarde
evening	la tarde/noche
day	el día
night	la noche
today	hoy (en día)
yesterday	ayer
tomorrow	mañana
now	ahora
later	más tarde
Monday	lunes
Tuesday	martes
Wednesday	miércoles
Thursday	jueves
Friday	viernes
Saturday	sábado
Sunday	domingo

MONEY

Is there a bank/bureau de change nearby?
¿Hay un banco/una oficina de cambio cerca?
Can I cash this here?
¿Puedo cobrar esto aquí?
I'd like to change sterling/dollars into euros
Quisiera cambiar libras/dólares a euros
Can I use my credit card to withdraw cash?
¿Puedo usar mi tarjeta de crédito para sacar dinero?
What is the exchange rate?
¿Cómo está el cambio?

GETTING AROUND

Where is the information desk?
¿Dónde está el mostrador de información?

Does this train/bus go to...?
¿Va este tren/colectivo a...?
Does this train/bus stop at...?
¿Para este tren/colectivo en...?
Can I have a one-way/return ticket to...?
¿Me da un billete sencillo/de ida y vuelta para...?
Where are we?
¿Dónde estamos?
I'm lost
Estoy perdido
Is this the way to...?
¿Es éste el camino para ir a...?
Where can I find a taxi?
¿Dónde puedo encontrar un taxi?
Please take me to...
A..., por favor
Can you turn on the meter?
¿Baje la bandera, por favor?
How much is the journey?
¿Cuánto cuesta esta carrera?

SHOPPING

Could you help me please?
¿Me atiende por favor?
How much is this?
¿Cuánto vale esto?
I'm looking for...
Busco...
Do you accept credit cards?
¿Aceptan tarjetas de crédito??

bakery	la panadería
pharmacy	la farmacia
supermarket	el supermercado
market	el mercado
sale	las rebajas

NUMBERS

1	uno
2	dos
3	tres
4	cuatro
5	cinco
6	seis
7	siete
8	ocho
9	nueve
10	diez
11	once
12	doce
13	trece
14	catorce
15	quince
16	dieciséis
17	diecisiete
18	dieciocho
19	diecinueve
20	veinte
21	veintiuno
30	treinta
40	cuarenta
50	cincuenta
60	sesenta
70	setente
80	ochenta
90	noventa
100	cien
1,000	mil

HOTELS

Do you have a room?
¿Tiene una habitación?
I have a reservation for ... nights
Tengo una reserva para ... noches
How much per night?
¿Cuánto por noche?
double room with double bed
habitación doble con cama matrimonial
single room
habitación single
twin room
habitación twin
with bath/shower
con bañera/ducha
air-conditioning
aire acondicionado
non-smoking
no fumador
Is breakfast included?
¿Está el desayuno incluido?
When is breakfast served?
¿A qué hora se sirve el desayuno?
Is there a lift (elevator)?
¿Hay ascensor?
I'll take this room
Me quedo con la habitación
The bill (check), please?
¿La cuenta, por favor?

RESTAURANTS

See also ▷ 328–329.
I'd like to reserve a table for ... people at...
Quisiera reservar una mesa para ... personas para las...
A table for ...
Una mesa para ... por favor
Could we sit here?
¿Nos podemos sentar acá?
waiter/waitress
el mozo/la moza

Where are the toilets?
¿Dónde están los baños?
Could we see the menu/wine list?
¿Podemos ver la carta/carta de vinos?
I can't eat wheat/sugar/salt/pork/ beef/dairy/nuts
No puedo comer trigo/azúcar/cerdo/ carne/productos lácteos/frutos secos
I ordered...
Yo pedí...
I'd like...
Quisiera...
May I have the bill, please?
¿La cuenta, por favor?
Is service included?
¿Está incluido el servicio?
The bill (check) is not right
La cuenta no está correcta
I'd like to speak to the manager
Quiero hablar con el encargado
knife/fork/spoon
el cuchillo/el tenedor/la cuchara

ILLNESS AND EMERGENCIES

I don't feel well
No me encuentro bien
Could you call a doctor?
¿Puede llamar a un médico?
I am allergic to...
Soy alérgico/a a...
I am on medication
Estoy con medicación
I am diabetic
Soy diabético/a
I am pregnant
Estoy embarazada
I have asthma
Soy asmático/a
hospital
el hospital
I need to see a doctor/dentist
Necesito un médico/dentista
Help!
Socorro
Stop thief!
Al ladrón
I have lost my passport/wallet/ purse/bag
Perdí el pasaporte/la billetera/el monedero/la cartera
I have had an accident
Tuve un incidente
I have been robbed
Me han robado
Where is the police station?
¿Dónde está la comisaría?

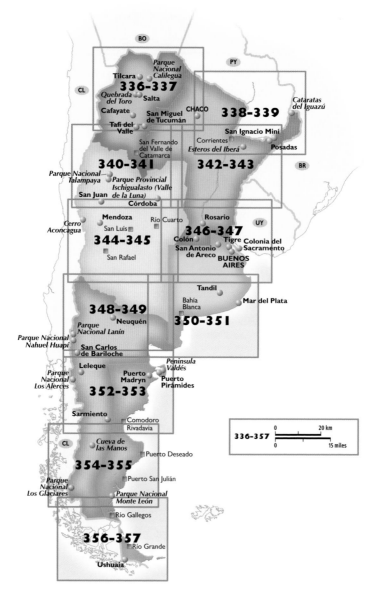

BO

PY

CL

336-337

Tilcara
Parque Nacional Calilegua
Quebrada del Toro
Salta
Cafayate
Tafi del Valle
San Miguel de Tucumán

CHACO

338-339

Cataratas del Iguazú

San Ignacio Miní

San Fernando del Valle de Catamarca

Corrientes
Esteros del Iberá
Posadas

BR

Parque Nacional Talampaya
Parque Provincial Ischigualasto (Valle de la Luna)
San Juan

340-341

Córdoba

342-343

Cerro Aconcagua
Mendoza
San Luis
Rio Cuarto

Rosario

UY

344-345

San Rafael

Colón
San Antonio de Areco
Tigre
Colonia del Sacramento
BUENOS AIRES

346-347

Tandil

Bahía Blanca
Mar del Plata

348-349

Neuquén
Parque Nacional Lanín

350-351

Parque Nacional Nahuel Huapí
San Carlos de Bariloche

Península Valdés

Leleque

Puerto Madryn
Puerto Pirámides

Parque Nacional Los Alerces

352-353

Sarmiento
Comodoro Rivadavia

CL
Cueva de las Manos
Puerto Deseado

354-355

Parque Nacional Los Glaciares
Puerto San Julián
Parque Nacional Monte León

Río Gallegos

356-357

Río Grande
Ushuaia

| 336-357 | 0 — 20 km |
| | 0 — 15 miles |

MAPS | ARGENTINA

Motorway

National road

Regional road

Local road

Minor road

Railway

International boundary

Regional boundary

Featured place of interest

City / Town

National park

Swamp

Glacier

Airport

621 ▲ **Height in metres**

⛴ **Port / Ferry route**

MAPS

Map references for the sights refer to the atlas pages within this section or to the individual town plans within the regions. For example, Rosario has the reference ✚ 346 J10, indicating the page on which the map is found (346) and the grid square in which Rosario sits (J10).

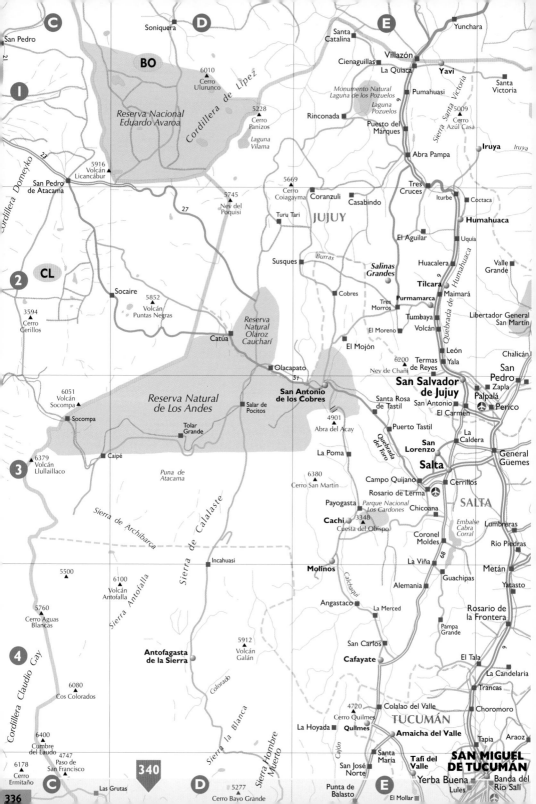

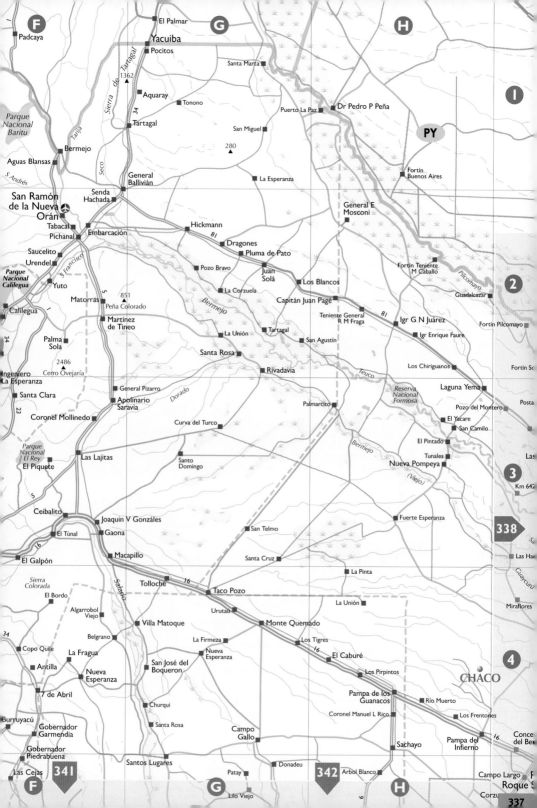

Padcaya

El Palmar

Yacuiba

Pocitos

Santa Marta

Sierra de Tartagal

1362

Aquaray

Tonono

Puerto La Paz

Dr Pedro P Peña

Parque Nacional Baritu

34

Tártagal

San Miguel

PY

Bermejo

280

Aguas Blansas

La Esperanza

Fortín Buenos Aires

S Andrés

General Ballivián

San Ramón de la Nueva Orán

Senda Hachada

General E Mosconi

Tabacal

Hickmann

Pichanal

Embarcación

81

Dragones

Saucelito

Pluma de Pato

Urendel

S Francisco

Pozo Bravo

Juan Solá

Fortín Teniente M Caballo

Pilcomayo

Parque Nacional Calilegua

Yuto

851

La Corzuela

Los Blancos

Guadalcazar

Calilegua

Matorras

Peña Colorado

Bermejo

Capitán Juan Pagé

Teniente General R M Fraga

81

Igr G N Juárez

Fortín Pilcomayo

34

Martínez de Tineo

La Unión

Tártagal

San Agustín

Igr Enrique Faure

Palma Sola

Santa Rosa

Rivadavia

Teuco

Los Chiriguanos

Fortín S

2486

Cerro Ovejaría

Reserva Nacional Formosa

Laguna Yema

Ingeniero La Esperanza

General Pizarro

Dorado

Palmarcito

Pozo del Montero

Posta

23

Santa Clara

Apolinario Saravia

El Yacare

San Camilo

Coronel Mollinedo

Curva del Turco

Bermejo

El Pintado

Las

Parque Nacional El Rey

Las Lajitas

Santo Domingo

Tunales

El Piquete

Nueva Pompeya

3

5

(Viejo)

Km 647

Ceibalito

Joaquin V Gonzáles

Fuerte Esperanza

338

El Túnal

Gaona

San Telmo

16

Macapillo

Santa Cruz

Las Had

El Galpón

La Pinta

Guaycurú

Sierra Colorada

Salado

Tolloche

16

Taco Pozo

La Unión

Miraflores

El Bordo

34

Algarrobol Viejo

Urutaú

Monte Quemado

16

Copo Quile

Villa Matoque

La Firmeza

Los Tigres

El Caburé

4

La Fragua

Belgrano

Nueva Esperanza

CHACO

Antilla

San José del Boqueron

Los Pirpintos

Nueva Esperanza

Churqui

Pampa de los Guanacos

Río Muerto

Los Frentones

7 de Abril

Burruyacú

Gobernador Garmendia

Santa Rosa

Campo Gallo

Coronel Manuel L Rico

Pampa del Infierno

16

Conce del Be

Gobernador Piedrabuena

Sachayo

Las Cejas

341

Santos Lugares

Patay

Donadeu

342

Arbol Blanco

Campo Largo

Roque S

Lilo Viejo

Corzu

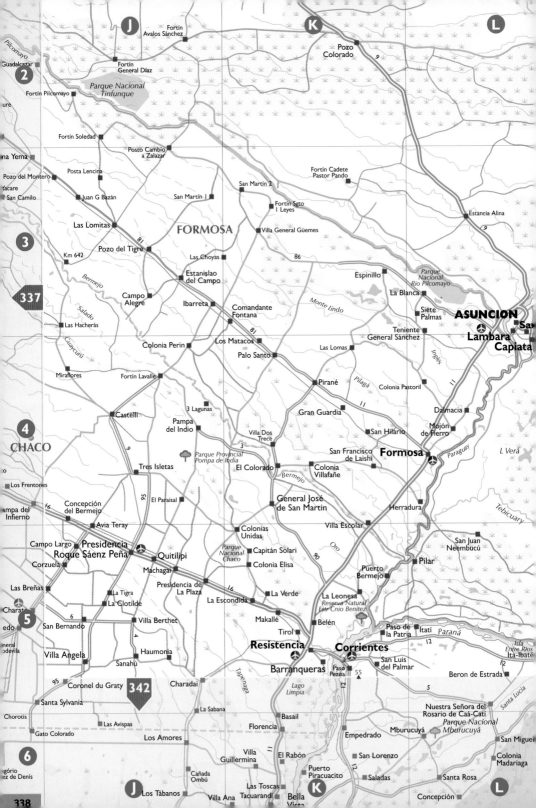

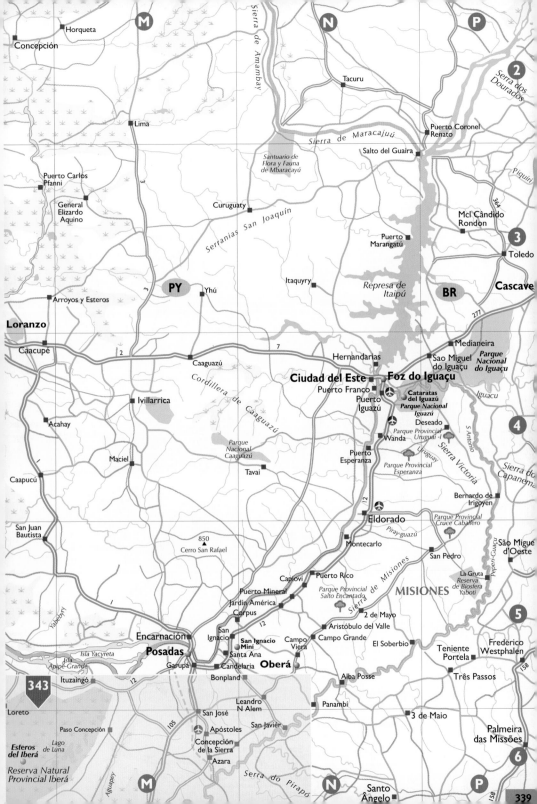

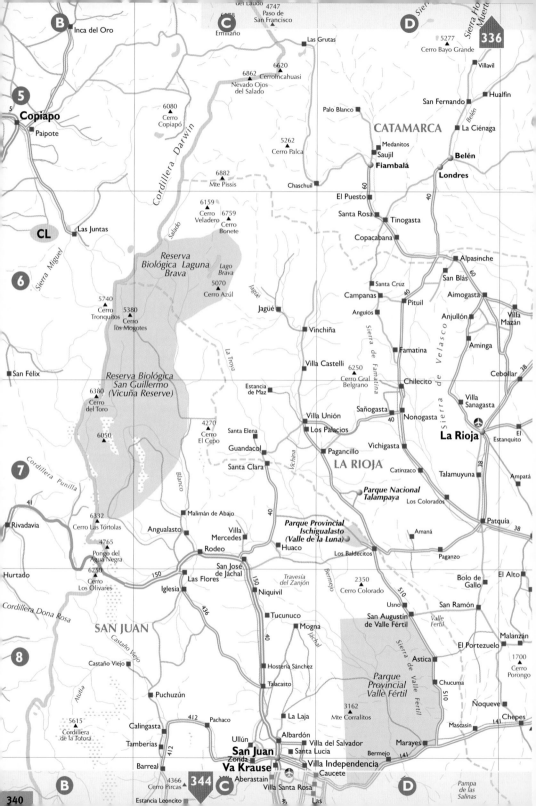

Inca del Oro

del Laudo
4747
Paso de
San Francisco

4558

Ermitaño

Las Grutas

5277
Cerro Bayo Grande

Villavil

5

Copiapo

Paipote

6862
Cerro Incahuasi

6620

Nevado Ojos
del Salado

6080
Cerro
Copiapó

Palo Blanco

San Fernando

Hualfin

CATAMARCA

Belén

La Ciénaga

5262
Cerro Palca

Medanitos

Saujil

Fiambalá

Belén

Londres

CL

Las Juntas

Mte Pissis
6882

Chaschuil

El Puesto

Santa Rosa

Tinogasta

Copacabana

40

Alpasinche

6159
Cerro
Veladero

6759
Cerro
Bonete

Reserva
Biológica Laguna
Brava

Lago
Brava

5070
Cerro Azúl

Santa Cruz

San Blás

Aimogasta

Anjullón

Villa
Mazán

Sierra Miguel

6

5740
Cerro
Tronquitos

5380
Cerro
los Mogotes

Jagüé

Campanas

Pituil

Anguios

Vinchiña

Famatina

Aminga

Chilecito

Villa
Sanagasta

Cebollar

38

San Félix

Reserva Biológica
San Guillermo
(Vicuña Reserve)

6380
Cerro
del Toro

6050

Estancia
de Maz

Villa Castelli

6250
Cerro Gral.
Belgrano

Sierra de Famatina

Sañogasta

Nonogasta

40

La Rioja

El
Estanquito

4270
Cerro
El Cepo

Santa Elena

Villa Unión

Los Palacios

Sierra de Velasco

Villa
Sanagasta

7

Cordillera Punilla

41

Guandacol

Santa Clara

Pagancillo

Vichigasta

Catinzaco

LA RIOJA

Talamuyuna

Ampatá

Rivadavia

6332
Cerro Las Tórtolas

Malimán de Abajo

Parque Nacional
Talampaya

Los Colorados

Patquía

38

4765
Pongo del
Agua Negra

Angualasto

Villa
Mercedes

Rodeo

Parque Provincial
Ischigualasto
(Valle de la Luna)

Amaná

Paganzo

Hurtado

6250
Cerro
Los Olivares

Las Flores

150

San José
de Jáchal

Huaco

Los Baldecitos

Bolo de
Gallo

El Alto

Cordillera Doña Rosa

Iglesia

Niquivil

Travesía
del Zanjón

Bermejo

2350
Cerro Colorado

Usno

San Ramón

Malanzán

8

SAN JUAN

436

Tucunuco

Mogna

40

San Augustín
de Valle Fértil

Valle
Fértil

El Portezuelo

1700
Cerro
Porongo

Castaño Viejo

Castaño Viejo

Puchuzún

Hostería Sánchez

Talacasto

Astica

Sierra de Valle Fértil

Chucuma

Parque
Provincial
Valle Fértil

510

Ñoqueve

5615
Cordillera
de la Totora

412

Pachaco

La Laja

3162
Mte Corralitos

Chepes

Maseasin

141

Calingasta

Tamberías

412

Ullún

Albardón

Villa del Salvador

Marayes

Barreal

4366
Cerro Pircas

344

San Juan

Zonda

Va Krause

Villa Aberastain

Santa Lucia

Villa Independencia

Caucete

Bermejo

141

Estancia Leoncito

Villa Santa Rosa

Las

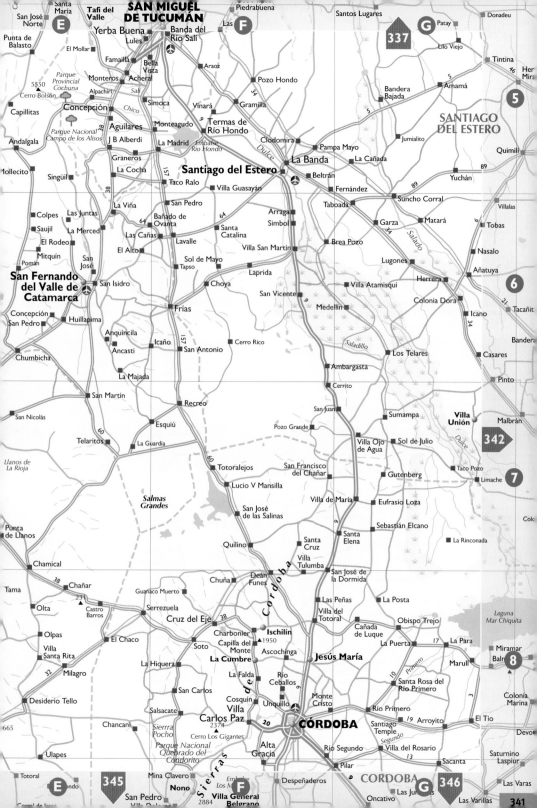

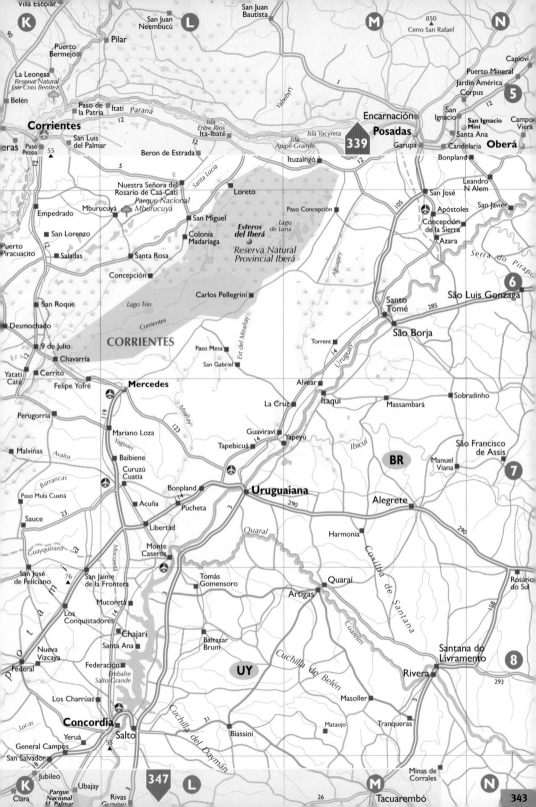

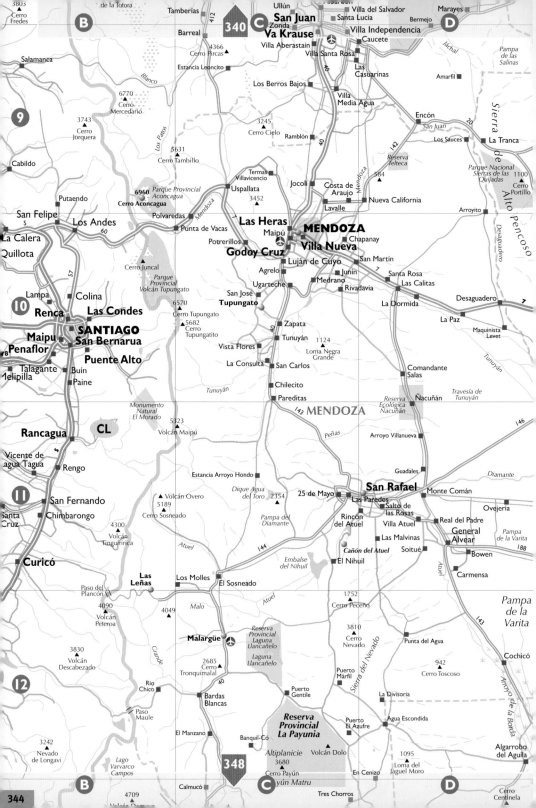

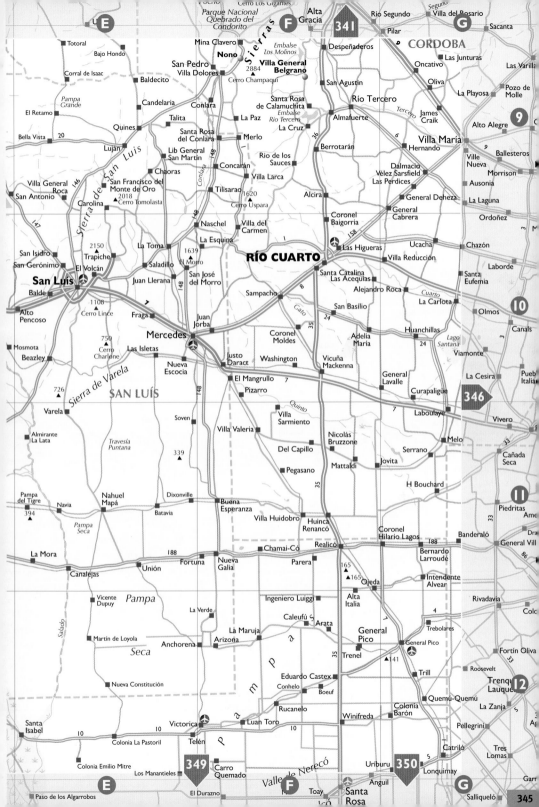

Top row markers: E · F · 341 · G

Parque Nacional Quebrado del Condorito · Cerro Los Gigantes · Alta Gracia · Río Segundo · Segundo · Villa del Rosario · Sacanta

Totoral · Mina Clavero · Nono · Despeñaderos · Pilar · CORDOBA · Las Junturas · Las Varillas

Bajo Hondo · Sierras · Embalse Los Molinos · Oncativo · Oliva · Pozo de Molle

Corral de Isaac · San Pedro · Villa General Belgrano · San Agustín · La Playosa · 9

Baldecito · Villa Dolores · 2884 Cerro Champaquí · Río Tercero · Alto Alegre

Pampa Grande · Candelaria · Conlara · Santa Rosa de Calamuchita · Almafuerte · James Craik · Ville Nueva

El Retamo · Talita · La Paz · Embalse Río Tercero · Tercero · Villa María · Ballesteros

Bella Vista · 20 · Quines · Santa Rosa del Conlara · Merlo · La Cruz · Hernando · Morrison

Luján · Lib General San Martín · Río de los Sauces · Berrotarán · Dalmacio Vélez Sarsfield · Ausonia

Villa General Roca · San Francisco del Monte de Oro · Chaoras · Concarán · Las Perdices · La Laguna

San Antonio · 2018 Cerro Tomolasta · Villa Larca · General Deheza · Ordoñez

Carolina · Tilisarao · 1620 Cerro Uspara · Alcira · General Cabrera

147 · Naschel · Villa del Carmen · Coronel Baigorria · Santa Eufemia

San Isidro · 2150 Trapiche · La Toma · La Esquina · 1639 El Morro · RÍO CUARTO · Las Higueras · Ucacha · Chazón · Laborde

San Gerónimo · El Volcán · Saladillo · Villa Reducción · Santa

San Luís · Juan Llerana · San José del Morro · Santa Catalina Las Acequias · Alejandro Roca · La Carlota · Olmos · 10

Balde · 1108 Cerro Lince · Sampacho · San Basílio · Canals

Alto Pencoso · Fraga · Cato · San Basílio · Huanchillas · Lago Santana · Viamonte · Pueblo Italia

Mosmota · 750 Cerro Charlone · Juan Jorba · Mercedes · Coronel Moldes · Adelia María · Viamonte · La Cesira · 346

Beazley · Las Isletas · Justo Daract · Washington · Vicuña Mackenna · General Lavalle · Curapaligue · Vivero

Nueva Escocia · El Mangrullo · Pizarro · Laboulaye · Melo

Varela · Sierra de Varela · SAN LUÍS · Soven · Villa Valeria · Villa Sarmiento · Serrano · Cañada Seca

Almirante La Lata · 339 · Del Capillo · Nicolás Bruzzone · Jovita · Mattaldi · H Bouchard · Piedritas · 11

Pampa del Tigre · Nahuel Mapá · Dixonville · Buena Esperanza · Quinto · Serrano · General Vill

Navia · 394 · Batavia · Villa Huidobro · Huinca Renancó · Coronel Hilario Lagos · Banderaló

Pampa Seca · Pegasano · Bernardo Larroudé · Intendente Alvear · Rivadavia

La Mora · Canalejas · Unión · Fortuna · Nueva Galia · Parera · Chamai-Có · Realicó · 188 · Col

Pampa · Vicente Dupuy · La Verde · Ingeniero Luiggi · 165 · Ojeda · Alta Italia · Trebolares · Fortín Oliva

Martín de Loyola · Arizona · La Maruja · Caleufú · Arata · General Pico · Roosevelt · Trenque Lauque · 12

Seca · Anchorena · Eduardo Castex · Trenel · Trill · Quemú-Quemú · La Zanja

Nueva Constitución · Conhelo · Boeuf · Colonia Barón · Pellegrini

Santa Isabel · Victorica · Rucanelo · Luan Toro · Winifreda · Catriló · Tres Lomas

Colonia La Pastoril · Telén · 349 · Carro Quemado · Uriburu · 350 · Lonquimay · Salliqueló · 345

Colonia Emilio Mitre · Los Manantieles · El Durazno · Valle de Nerecó · Anguil · Toay · Santa Rosa · Garr

Paso de los Algarrobos · E · F · G

Numbers/roads visible: 146 · 147 · 148 · 20 · 188 · 339 · 10 · 726 · 394 · 165 · 165 · 41 · 8 · 35 · 36 · 158 · 24 · 7 · 33 · 86 · 4 · 5 · 3

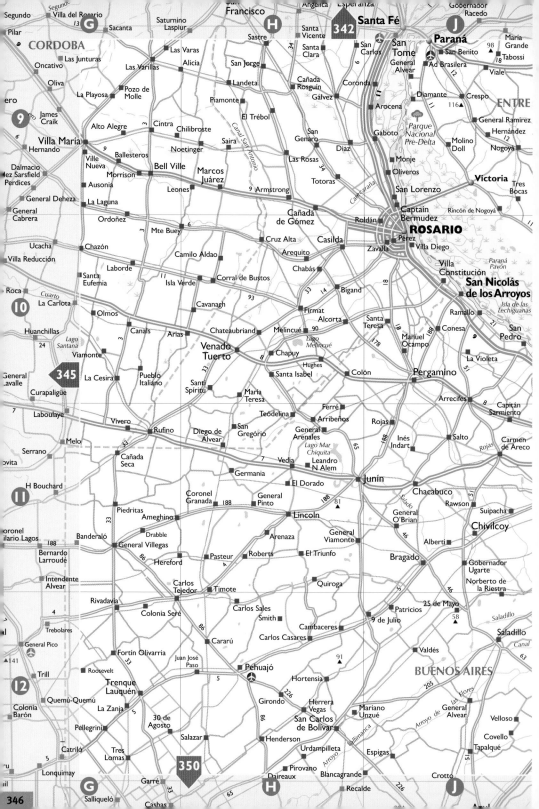

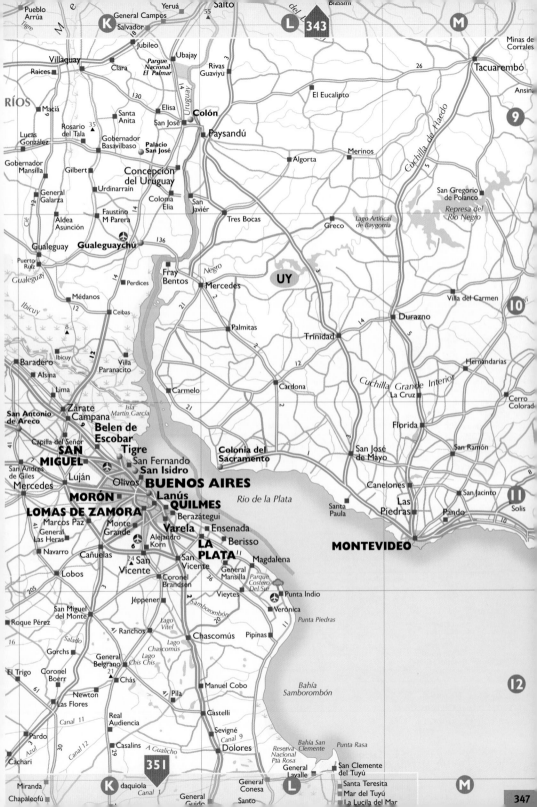

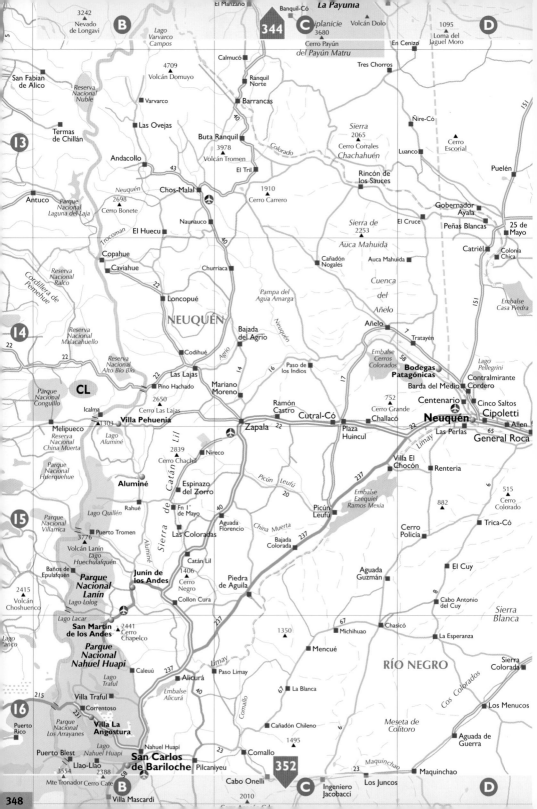

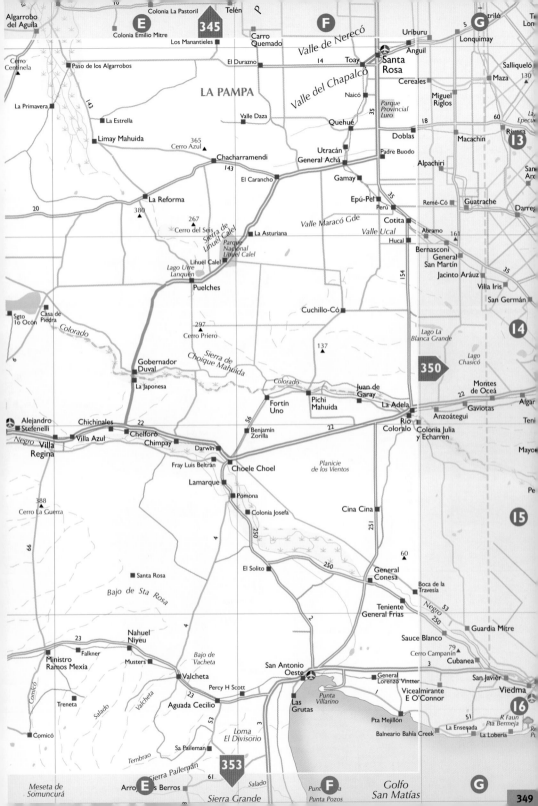

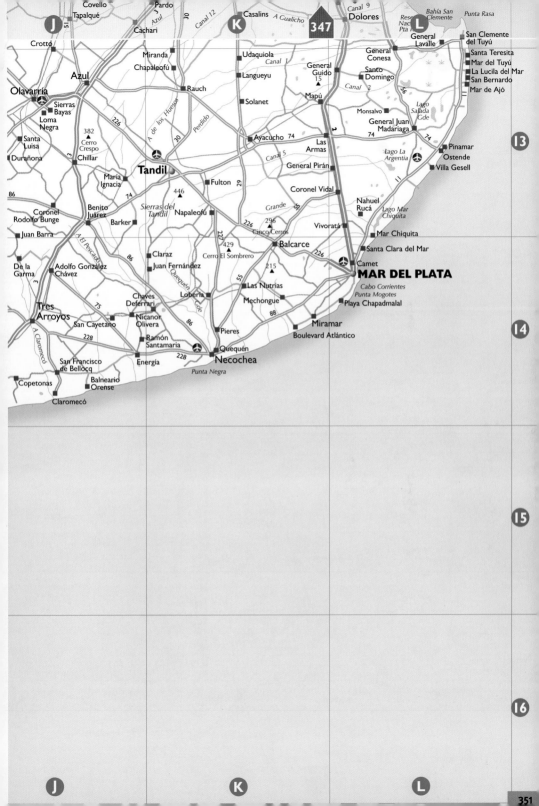

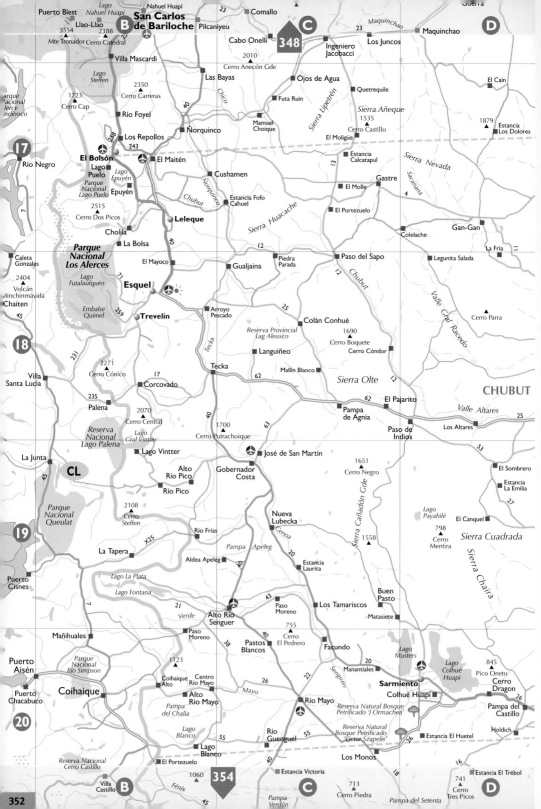

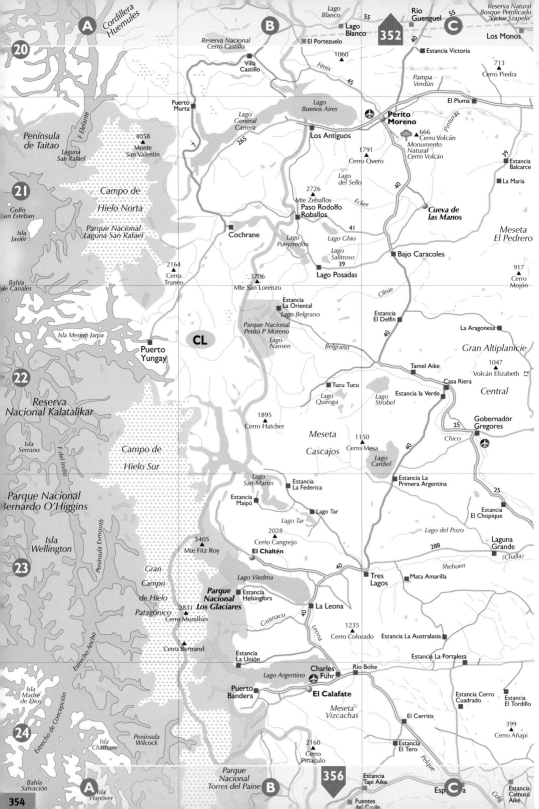

MAPS INDEX

MAPS INDEX

PICTURES

The Automobile Association would like to thank the following photographers, companies and picture libraries for their assistance in the preparation of this book.

Abbreviations for the picture credits are as follows: (t) top ;(b) bottom;(l) left; (r) right; (c) centre ;(AA) AA World Travel Library.

144 AA/J Tims
146 AA/J Tims
148 AA/J Tims
150 AA/J Tims
154 AA/J Tims
156 AA/J Tims
157 Per Karlsson - BKWine.com/Alamy
158 Marka/Alamy
159 Javier Etcheverry/Alamy
160 AA/J Tims
161 AA/J Tims
162 AA/J Tims
163 AA/J Tims
164 AA/J Tims
165 AA/J Tims
166 AA/J Tims
167l AA/J Tims
167r AA/J Tims
168 AA/J Tims
169 AA/J Tims
170l AA/J Tims
170r AA/J Tims
171 AA/J Tims
172 AA/J Tims
173 Javier Etcheverry/Alamy
174 AA/J Tims
175 AA/J Tims
176 AA/J Tims
177 AA/J Tims
178 AA/J Tims
179 AA/J Tims
180 AA/J Tims
182 AA/J Tims
186 AA/J Tims
187 AA/J Tims
188 AA/J Tims
189 AA/J Tims
190 AA/J Tims
192 AA/J Tims
194 AA/J Tims
195 AA/J Tims
196 AA/J Tims
197 AA/J Tims
198 AA/J Tims
199 AA/J Tims
200 AA/J Tims
201 AA/J Tims
203 AA/J Tims
204 AA/J Tims
205l AA/J Tims
205r AA/J Tims
206 AA/J Tims
207 AA/J Tims

208 AA/J Tims
209 AA/J Tims
210 AA/J Tims
211 AA/J Tims
212 AA/J Tims
214 AA/J Tims
216 AA/J Tims
217 AA/J Tims
218 AA/J Tims
219 AA/J Tims
220 AA/J Tims
222 AA/J Tims
224 AA/J Tims
226 AA/J Tims
229 AA/J Tims
230 AA/J Tims
232 AA/J Tims
234 AA/J Tims
235l AA/J Tims
235r AA/J Tims
236 AA/J Tims
237l AA/J Tims
237r AA/J Tims
238 AA/J Tims
239 AA/J Tims
240 AA/J Tims
241l AA/J Tims
241r AA/J Tims
242 AA/J Tims
243l AA/J Tims
243r
245 AA/J Tims
246l AA/J Tims
246r AA/J Tims
247 AA/J Tims
248 AA/J Tims
249 AA/J Tims
250 AA/J Tims
252 AA/J Tims
254 AA/J Tims
255 AA/J Tims
256 AA/J Tims
257 AA/J Tims
258 AA/J Tims
260 AA/J Tims
262 AA/J Tims
265 AA/J Tims
266 AA/J Tims
268 AA/J Tims
270 imagebroker/Alamy
271 AA/J Tims
272 AA/J Tims
273 AA/J Tims
274 AA/J Tims

275 AA/J Tims
276 AA/J Tims
277 AA/J Tims
278 AA/Y Levy
279 Richard Wareham Fotografie/Alamy
280 Francisco Bononato/Alamy
281 Richard Wareham Fotografie/Alamy
282 Harriet Cummings/Alamy
283 Harriet Cummings/Alamy
284 AA/Y Levy
285 AA/J Tims
286 Richard Wareham Fotografie/Alamy
287 AA/J Tims
288 Design Pics Inc.—RM Content/Alamy
289 AA/J Tims
290 AA/J Tims
291 AA/J Tims
292 AA/J Tims
293 AA/J Tims
294 AA/Y Levy
296 AA/Y Levy
297 AA/J Tims
298 AA/J Tims
299 AA/J Tims
301 AA/J Tims
302 AA/J Tims
304 AA/Y Levy
307 AA/Y Levy
308 AA/J Tims
309 AA/J Tims
310 AA/J Tims
314 AA/J Tims
315 AA/Y Levy
316 AA/Y Levy
317 AA/Y Levy
318 AA/Y Levy
319l AA/J Tims
319r AA/Y Levy
320 AA/Y Levy
322 AA/Y Levy
323 AA/J Tims
324 AA/Y Levy
325 AA/Y Levy
326 AA/Y Levy
327 AA/Y Levy
328 AA/J Tims
330 AA/J Tims
331 AA/J Tims
334 AA/J Tims

Every effort has been made to trace the copyright holders, and we apologise in advance for any unintentional omissions or errors. We would be pleased to apply any corrections in a following edition of this publication.

CREDITS

Series editor
Sheila Hawkins

Project editor
Laura Linder

Copy editor
Sandy Draper

Design
Tracey Butler

Picture research
Lesley Grayson

Image retouching and repro
Jacqueline Street

Mapping
Maps produced by the Mapping Services
Department of AA Publishing

Author
Andrew Benson

Verifier
Matt Chesterton

Indexer
Marie Lorimer

Production
Lorraine Taylor

Published by AA Publishing, a trading name of AA Media Limited, whose registered office is
Fanum House, Basing View, Basingstoke, RG21 4EA. Registered number 06112600.
A CIP catalogue record for this book is available from the British Library.

ISBN   978-07495-7067-5

KeyGuide is a registered trademark in Australia and is used under licence.
Colour separation by AA Digital Department.
Printed and bound by Leo Paper Products, China.

The content of this book is believed to be accurate at the time of printing. Due to its nature the content is likely to vary or change and the
publisher is not responsible for such change and accordingly is not responsible for the consequences of any reliance by the reader on
information that has changed. Any rights that are given to consumers under applicable law are not affected. Opinions expressed are for
guidance only and are those of the assessor based on their experience at the time of review and may differ from the reader's opinions based
on their subsequent experience.

We have tried to ensure accuracy in this guide, but things do change, so please let us know if you have any comments at
travelguides@theAA.com.

A03997
Mapping in this title produced from map data supplied by Global Mapping, Brackley, UK.
Copyright © Global Mapping/ITMB
Additional data from Mountain High Maps® Copyright © 1993 Digital Wisdom, Inc.
Transport maps © Communicarta Ltd, UK
Weather chart statistics supplied by Weatherbase © Copyright 2011 Canty and Associates, LLC.

Find out more about AA Publishing and the wide range of travel publications and services the AA provides by visiting our website at
theAA.com/shop